American Reference Books Annual

Volume 49

2018 Edition

American Reference Books Annual
Advisory Board

2018
EDITION

AMERICAN
REFERENCE
BOOKS
ANNUAL

Volume 49

 LIBRARIES
UNLIMITED™
An Imprint of ABC-CLIO, LLC
Santa Barbara, California • Denver, Colorado

LIBRARIES UNLIMITED
An Imprint of ABC-CLIO, LLC
130 Cremona Drive
P.O. Box 1911
Santa Barbara, California 93116-1911
www.abc-clio.com

Library of Congress Cataloging-in-Publication Data
American reference books annual, 1970-
Santa Barbara, CA, Libraries Unlimited.
v. 19x26 cm.
Indexes:
1970-74. 1v.
1975-79. 1v.
1980-84. 1v.
1985-89. 1v.
1990-94. 1v.
1995-99. 1v.
2000-04. lv.
2005-09. lv.
2010-14. 1v.
I. Reference books--Bibliography--Periodicals.
Z1035.1.A55 011'.02
ISBN 978-1-4408-6256-4 (2018 edition)
ISSN 0065-9959

Contents

Preface

Here is the interesting and challenging landscape for reference resources today. On the one hand, we clearly see the reference book diminished in the work of students, and the priorities of libraries. Going or gone are the vast collections of bound volumes in designated reference reading rooms. The disruptive element of course is technology: instantaneous access to online information. And reference seems to be the loser.

On the other hand, technology makes reference activity a winner too, but so seamlessly that the connection to old-fashioned reference work can be overlooked. All of us enjoy and use online tools to find airline ticket prices and flight schedules, weather forecasts and current conditions, currency exchange rates, stock prices, hotel and restaurant reviews, street maps, and foreign language translators. In the past we turned to print tools to meet these needs, with less convenience and less currency. Thanks to technology, we now have alternatives that match, and often surpass, yesterday's print reference works: timetables, weather almanacs, financial reports, tourist guidebooks, atlases, and bilingual dictionaries. So if reference is alive and well, but living under another name, where is the crisis? Which is to say, where is the change taking place?

Scholars have defined reference works in administrative, descriptive, and functional terms. The administration definition was something like this: "a reference book is a book located in a non-circulating reference collection." Today, we no longer focus on printed books (though we may work with their e-book descendants), and resource access is no longer confined to a specific place. The descriptive definition has been more durable: a reference work incorporates elements of organization and presentation that reflect and promote its intended use … consultation as quickly and easily as possible. Hence subject indexes, alphabetical order for entries, or numerical coding, as well as newer features like cross-reference hot links. The functional definition perhaps has held up the best: while many sources can conceivably be used to answer a "reference question," a reference work is created for that purpose, and its form (those elements in the descriptive definition) follows that function. As long as readers seek information, that function has value.

Nor have the characteristics of "good" reference tools changed: when we want information, we want information that is accurate, objective, authoritative, current, and complete, as well as reliably accessible, clearly presented, and easily understood. Online reference sources meet these requirements just as thoroughly as do print-format classics like the OED, the World Book, the National Geographic World Atlas, or the Statistical Abstract of the United States (all of which have expanded to online versions).

One final element makes modern life tough for reference: the general discounting of authority. Reference tools rely on the notion that important information is stable and therefore can be discovered, described, and evaluated. Behind the pursuit of "facts" to answer a reference query is an assumption that "facts" exist, that one answer is true and "best," that the "right" answer is available to us, and that reasonable people will agree about the "correct" answer when they see it. We may expect to argue about the best 10 American novels, but we expect to agree about the melting temperature of copper. In a world of relativism, conspiracy theories, and Heisenberg's uncertainty principle, not only are authorities in doubt, but even the facts themselves. And without the concept of correct facts, reference has no leg to stand on.

It is encouraging to see this aphorism widely quoted: "Everyone is entitled to his own opinion, but not to his own facts." When most of us can agree about facts, reference can thrive. Incidentally, this quotation itself illustrates the reference value of truth-seeking and fact-checking. Generally attributed to Daniel Patrick Moynihan, the *Dictionary of Modern Proverbs* (Yale, 2012) also documents similar statements extending back to Bernard Baruch in 1946.

If there are four participants in the ecology of reference–readers, authors, publishers, and librarians–then perhaps it is fair to say that two are leading and two are catching up. Readers still have plenty of questions to answer, and authors still eagerly turn out resources to meet that need. The challenges seem greatest for publishers and librarians, as value-added contributions shift from presentation in print to presentation in online form.—**Steven W. Sowards, Michigan State University Libraries**

Introduction

We are pleased to provide you with volume 49 of *American Reference Books Annual* (ARBA), a far-reaching review service for reference books and electronic resources. As Steven Sowards points out in the preface, the reference landscape has changed considerably since the publication of ARBA's first volume in 1970. Reference users no longer need to spend hours in a library consulting bound volumes, microfiche, or microfilm when much sought-after information is available online. As the preface also highlights, this easy accessibility does not eliminate the need for well-curated, professionally produced reference material and the guidance of trained librarians.

ARBA strives to provide comprehensive coverage of English-language reference resources, both digital and print, published in the United States and Canada during a single year. We review both subscription-based and free websites, as well as dictionaries, encyclopedias, indexes, directories, bibliographies, guides, concordances, atlases, gazetteers, and other types of ready-reference tools. Generally, encyclopedias that are updated annually, yearbooks, almanacs, indexing and abstracting services, and other annuals or serials are reviewed at editorially determined intervals. Reviews of updated publications attempt to point out changes in scope or editorial policy and comparisons to older editions.

Certain categories of reference sources are usually not reviewed in ARBA: foreign-language titles, books of fewer than 48 pages that are not part of a larger set, those produced by vanity presses or by the author as publisher, and those generated by library staff for internal use. Highly specialized reference works printed in a limited number of copies and that do not appeal to the general library audience ARBA serves may also be omitted.

For nearly two decades, ARBA has also been a go-to source for reviews of new literature written specifically for the library professional; this year's ARBA features approximately 100 reviews of professional development titles. These include monographs and handbooks that address the concerns of library and information specialists and can be found in chapter 11, titled "Library and Information Science and Publishing and Bookselling."

In 2002, Libraries Unlimited launched ARBAonline, an authoritative database designed to provide access to all reviews published in the print version of ARBA since 1997. The editorial staff updates ARBAonline monthly, giving librarians evaluations of the most up-to-date materials along with depth of coverage as they make purchasing decisions.

Reviewing Policy

To ensure well-written, balanced reviews of high quality, the ARBA staff maintains a roster of more than 400 scholars, practitioners, and library educators in all subject specialties at libraries and universities throughout the United States and Canada. Because ARBA seeks to be a comprehensive reviewing source, the reviews are generally longer and more critical than other review publications to detail the strengths and weaknesses of important reference works. Reviewers are asked to examine books and electronic resources and provide well-documented critical comments, both positive and negative. Coverage usually includes the usefulness of a given work; organization, execution, and pertinence of contents; prose style; format; availability of supplementary materials (e.g., indexes, appendixes); and similarity to other works and previous editions. Reviewers are encouraged to address the intended audience but not necessarily to give specific recommendations for purchase.

Arrangement

This year's ARBA consists of 36 chapters, an author/title index, and a subject index. It is divided into four alphabetically arranged parts: "General Reference Works," "Social Sciences," "Humanities," and "Science and Technology." "General Reference Works" is subdivided by form: almanacs, bibliography, biography, and so on. Within the remaining three parts, chapters are organized by topic. Thus, under "Social Sciences" the reader will find chapters titled "Economics and Business," "Education," "History," "Law," "Sociology," and so on.

Each chapter is subdivided to reflect the arrangement strategy of the entire volume. There is a section on general works followed by a topical breakdown. For example, in the chapter titled "Literature," "General Works" is followed by "National Literature." Subsections are based on the amount of material available on a given topic and vary from year to year.

Users should keep in mind that many materials may fall under several different chapter topics. The comprehensive author/title and subject indexes found at the end of the volume will assist users in finding specific works that could fall under several different chapters. Additionally, readers seeking out reviews of digital resources can find these quickly using the Website and Database Review Locator (p. xxiii).

Acknowledgments

In closing, we wish to express our gratitude to the many talented contributors without whose support this volume of ARBA could not have been compiled. Many thanks also go out to our distinguished Advisory Board members whose contributions greatly enhance ARBA and ARBAonline. We would also like to thank the members of our staff who were instrumental in its preparation.

Contributors

Alicia Abdul, Librarian, Albany High School, Albany, N.Y.

Anthony J. Adam, Senior Training Consultant, Strategic Planning Online, Brenham, Tex.

Kathy Adams, Professor Emerita, Wright State Univ.

Maria Agee, Indiana Univ. Bloomington, Hays, Kans.

James W. Agee, Library Director, Hays Public Library, Hays, Kans.

Elizabeth Andersen, Librarian, Westbrook (Maine) High School.

Adrienne Antink, Medical Group Management Association, Lakewood, Colo.

Thomas E. Baker, Assoc. Professor, Department of Criminal Justice, Univ. of Scranton, Pa.

Augie E. Beasley, Retired Media Specialist, Charlotte, N.C.

Joshua Becker, Information Literacy and Assessment Librarian, Assistant Professor, Southern New Hampshire Univ.

Michael Francis Bemis, Asst. Librarian, Washington County Library, Woodbury, Minn.

Barbara M. Bibel, Reference Librarian, Science/Business/Sociology Dept., Main Library, Oakland Public Library, Calif.

Daniel K. Blewett, Reference Librarian, College of DuPage Library, College of DuPage, Glen Ellyn, Ill.

Alicia Brillon, Head of Technical Services and Acquisitions, James E. Faust Law Library, Univ. of Utah.

Kim Brown, Library Media Specialist, North Reading High School, North Reading, Mass.

Patricia Brown, Educational Reviewer, Tipp City, Tipp City, Ohio.

John R. Burch Jr., Library Director, Univ. of Tennessee at Martin, Ky.

Frederic F. Burchsted, Reference Librarian, Widener Library, Harvard Univ., Cambridge, Mass.

Joanna M. Burkhardt, Head Librarian, College of Continuing Education Library, Univ. of Rhode Island, Providence.

Lisa Castellano, Library Media Specialist, Larkspur Middle School, Virginia Beach, Virginia, Virginia Beach, Va.

Bert Chapman, Government Publications Coordinator, Purdue Univ., West Lafayette, Ind.

Boyd Childress, Reference Librarian, Ralph B. Draughon Library, Auburn Univ., Ala.

Rosanne M. Cordell, (formerly) Head of Reference Services, Franklin D. Schurz Library, Indiana Univ., South Bend, Ind.

Gregory A. Crawford, Head of Public Services, Penn State Harrisburg, Middletown, Pa.

Norman Desmarais, Professor Emeritus, Providence (Rhode Island) College.

Scott R. DiMarco, Director of Library Services and Information Resources, Mansfield Univ., Mansfield, Pa.

Laura Dooley-Taylor, Librarian, Lake Zurich Middle School North, Hawthorn Woods, Ill.

Lucy Duhon, Scholarly Communications Librarian, Univ. of Toledo, Ohio.

Joe P. Dunn, Charles A. Dana Professor of History and Politics, Converse College, Spartanburg, S.C.

Bradford Lee Eden, Dean of Library Services, Valparaiso Univ., Valparaiso, Ind.

Sheri Edwards, Assistant Univ. Librarian, Florida Atlantic Univ.

Susan Elkins, Digital Resources Librarian, Sam Houston State Univ., Huntsville, Tex.

Autumn Faulkner, Asst Head of Cataloging and Metadata Services, Michigan State Univ. Libraries, East Lansing.

Josh Eugene Finnell, Reference Librarian, Ohio.

Kristin Fletcher-Spear, Administrative Librarian, Foothills Branch Library, Glendale, Ariz.

Zev Garber, Professor and Chair, Jewish Studies, Los Angeles Valley College, Calif.

Denise A. Garofalo, Systems and Catalog Services Librarian, Curtin Memorial Library, Mount Saint Mary College, Newburgh, N.Y.

Kasey Garrison, Lecturer & Children's Specialization Coordinator, Charles Sturt Univ., Sydney, NSW, Australia.

John T. Gillespie, College Professor and Writer, New York.

Caroline L. Gilson, Coordinator, Prevo Science Library, DePauw Univ., Greencastle, Ind.

Michelle Glatt, Librarian, Chiddix and Evans Junior High Schools, Bloomington-Normal, Ill.

Cynthia Goode, Thesis Clerk, Sam Houston State Univ., Huntsville, Tex.

Anitra Gordon, Educational Reviewer, Ann Arbor, Mich.

Carin Graves, Social Science Librarian, Michigan State Univ. Libraries, East Lansing.

Deb Grove, Retired Library Media Specialist, Omaha, Neb.

Michael W. Handis, Assoc. Librarian for Collection Management, CUNY Graduate Center, New York.

Ralph Hartsock, Senior Music Catalog Librarian, Univ. of North Texas, Denton.

Muhammed Hassanali, Independent Consultant, Shaker Heights, Ohio.

Alexandra Hauser, Business Librarian, Michigan State Univ. Library, East Lansing.

Lucy Heckman, Reference Librarian (Business-Economics), St. John's Univ. Library, Jamaica, N.Y.

Mark Y. Herring, Dean of Library Services, Winthrop Univ., Dacus Library, Rock Hill, S.C.

Ladyjane Hickey, Reference Librarian, Austin College, Tex.

Jennifer Brooks Huffman, Serials/ILL Librarian, Univ. of Wisconsin - Stevens Point.

Jonathan F. Husband, Program Chair of the Library/Reader Services Librarian, Henry Whittemore Library, Framingham State College, Mass.

Amanda Izenstark, Asst. Professor, Reference and Instructional Design Librarian, Univ. of Rhode Island, Kingston, R.I.

Jeffrey A. Jensen, Lead Librarian, Independence Univ., Salt Lake City, Utah.

Melissa M. Johnson, Reference Services, NOVA Southeastern Univ., Alvin Sherman Library, Ft. Lauderdale, Fla.

Elizabeth Kahn, Librarian, Patrick F. Taylor Sci Tech Academy, Jefferson, La.

Donna J. Kearns, Professor, Psychology Department, Univ. of Central Oklahoma-Box 193, Edmond, Okla.

Craig Mury Keeney, Cataloging Librarian, South Caroliniana Library, Univ. of South Carolina.

Andrea C. Kepsel, Health Sciences Educational Technology Librarian, Michigan State Univ. Libraries, East Lansing.

Dianna L. Kim, Assistant Professor/Research and Instruction Librarian, Newton Gresham Library/Sam Houston State Univ., Huntsville, Tex.

Ian King, Librarian, Independence Univ., Salt Lake City, Utah.

Cynthia Knight, (retired reference librarian), retired.

Amy Koehler, Distance Learning Librarian, Univ. of Chicago, Chicago, Ill.

Robert V. Labaree, Reference/Public Services Librarian, Von KleinSmid Library, Univ. of Southern California, Los Angeles.

Martha Lawler, Assoc. Librarian, Louisiana State Univ., Shreveport.

Shelly Lee, National Board Certified Library Media Specialist, Central Junior High, Moore, Okla.

Richard Nathan Leigh, Metadata & Digital Resources Developer, Ball State Univ. Libraries, Muncie, Ind.

Karen Leon, Librarian, Roslyn High School, Roslyn Heights, N.Y.

Suzanne Libra, Teacher Librarian, Silver Hills and Alternative Campus, Westminster, Colo.

Robert M. Lindsey, Instruction and Reference Librarian, Pittsburg State Univ., Pittsburg, Kans.

Megan W. Lowe, Reference/Instruction Librarian, Univ. of Louisiana at Monroe.

Janet Luch, Educational Reviewer, Adjunct Instructor, SUNY New Paltz, Touro College, Visiting Professor DeVry Univ.

Tyler Manolovitz, Digital Resources Coordinator, Sam Houston State Univ., Newton Gresham Library, Huntsville, Tex.

Peter H. McCracken, Library Technical Services, Cornell Univ.

Kevin McDonough, Reference and Electronic Resources Librarian, Northern Michigan Univ.—Olson Library, Marquette.

Jessica Crossfield McIntosh, Reference Services Coordinator, Asst. Professor, Otterbein Univ., Westerville, Ohio.

Lawrence Joseph Mello, Asst. Reference and Instruction Librarian, Florida Atlantic Univ., Boca Raton.

Rachel Meredith Minkin, Head of Reference Services, Michigan State Univ. Libraries, East Lansing.

Janis Minshull, Library Consultant, Phippsburg, Maine.

Sara Mofford, Youth Services Librarian, Catawba County Library System, Newton, N.C.

Emily Lauren Mross, Business and Public Administration Librarian, Penn State Univ., University Park, Pa.

Theresa Muraski, Associate Professor, Univ. of Wisconsin-Stevens Point, Stevens Point, Wis.

Paul M. Murphy III, Director of Marketing, PMX Medical, Denver, Colo.

Madeleine Nash, Reference/Instruction Librarian, Molloy College, Rockville Center, N.Y.

Elizabeth Nebeker, School Librarian, Jersey Village High School, Houston, Tex.

Thomas O'Brien, Librarian, Florida Atlantic Univ., Boca Raton.

Cynthia Ortiz, School Librarian, Hackensack (New Jersey) High School, Hackensack.

Amy B Parsons, Catalog Librarian/Assistant Professor, Columbus State Univ., Columbus, Ga.

Alexandra Quay, Librarian, Sinai Akiba Academy, Los Angeles, Calif.

Jack Ray, Asst. Director, Loyola/Notre Dame Library, Baltimore, Md.

Kali A. Rippel, Librarian, Las Positas College Library, Livermore, Calif.

Emily Rozmus, Integration Librarian, INFOhio, Ohios PreK-12 Digital Library.

Richard Salvucci, Professor, Economics, Trinity Univ., San Antonio, Tex.

Michaela Schied, Librarian, Indian River Middle School, Philadelphia, N.Y.

Lisa Schultz, Instructional Services Research Librarian, Univ. of Colorado School of Law, Boulder.

Cynthia Schulz, Retired Teacher Librarian, Lacey, Wash.

Mark Schumacher, Art and Humanities Librarian, Univ. of North Carolina, Greensboro.

Ralph Lee Scott, Professor, Assistant Head of Special Collections for Public Services, and Curator of Printed Books and Maps, East Carolina Univ. Library, Greenville, N.C.

Colleen Seale, Humanities and Social Sciences Services, George A. Smathers Libraries, Univ. of Florida, Gainesville.

Shanna Shadoan, Librarian, Metropolitan Library System, Choctaw, Okla.

Stephen J. Shaw, Library Director, Antioch Univ. Midwest, Yellow Springs, Ohio.

Kay Shelton, Instructor, Kishwaukee College, Malta, Ill.

Trent Shotwell, Special Collections Librarian, Sam Houston State Univ., Huntsville, Tex.

Darshell Silva, Librarian and Technology Integration Specialist, Rocky Hill School, East Greenwich, R.I.

Breezy Silver, Collection Coordinator and Business Reference Librarian, Michigan State Univ. Libraries, East Lansing.

Todd Simpson, Assistant Professor/Catalog Librarian, York College, CUNY, Jamaica, New York.

Kay Stebbins Slattery, Coordinator Librarian, Louisiana State Univ., Shreveport.

Steven W. Sowards, Asst. Director for Collections, Michigan State Univ. Libraries, East Lansing.

John P. Stierman, Reference Librarian, Western Illinois Univ., Macomb.

Martha E. Stone, Coordinator for Reference Services, Treadwell Library, Massachusetts General Hospital, Boston.

Eric Tans, Environmental Sciences Librarian, Michigan State Univ. Libraries, East Lansing.

Melissa Thom, Teacher Librarian, Bristow Middle School, West Hartford, Conn.

Linda M. Turney, E-Resources Cataloging Librarian, Walker Library, Middle Tennessee State Univ., Murfreesboro.

Elizabeth Webster, Teaching & Learning Librarian, Michigan State Univ. Libraries, East Lansing.

Marney Welmers, Retired Middle School Librarian, Marana USD, Tucson, Ariz.

C. Ellen Wickham, Library Media Specialist, Raytown South High School, Raytown, Mo.

W. Cole Williamson, Instruction Librarian, Univ. of Arkansas, Little Rock.

Angela Wojtecki, District Library Media Specialist, Nordonia Hills City Schools, Macedonia, Ohio.

Julienne L. Wood, Head, Research Services, Noel Memorial Library, Louisiana State Univ., Shreveport.

Mary Rebecca Yantis, Assistant Professor/General Reference Librarian, Univ. of Louisiana at Monroe.

Laura Younkin, Librarian, Ballard High School, Louisville, Ky.

Susan Yutzey, School Library Media Specialist, Upper Arlington High School, Columbus, Ohio.

Website and Database Review Locator

Reference is to entry number.

Part I
GENERAL
REFERENCE
WORKS

1 General Reference Works

Almanacs

1. **World Almanac and Book of Facts 2018.** New York, Infobase Publishing, 2018. 1010p. illus. maps. index. $36.95. ISBN 13: 978-1-60057-211-1.

The World Almanac and Book of Facts 2018 chronicles historical anniversaries of global achievements that provide pathways to timely information and factual explanations. The all-inclusive 1,010-page almanac addresses the economy, business, energy, health, and vital statistics. In addition, this book focuses on personalities, science, technology, consumer information, U.S. history, government, population, sports, world history, culture, and nations, etc. The almanac includes timeline events, bullet formatting, and questions in bold font followed by succinct descriptions. Statistical highlights emphasize prevalent stories of the year. The "World at a Glance" feature delivers interesting facts that describe a world in transition. Superior formatting, organization, graphics, images, tables, fonts, line spacing, and charts offer navigational signposts for piloting through copious data. The volume includes a substantial index system.

The anniversary edition celebrates a long history of reader satisfaction and tradition. Contemporary consumers will find the 150th edition worth celebrating. Infobase Publishing hits a home run—all library acquisition decision-makers will consider this contribution an essential resource.—**Thomas E. Baker**

Biography

2. **The Britannica Guide to the World's Most Influential People.** New York, Britannica Educational Publishing, 2017. 3v. illus. index. $54.00/vol. ISBN 13: 978-1-6804-8223-2.

This series includes three titles: *The 100 Most Influential Religious Leaders of All Time; The 100 Most Influential Medical Pioneers of All Time;* and *The 100 Most Influential Military Leaders of All Time.* Each book provides an introduction to people in the fields covered. Worldwide in scope and arranged in chronological order starting in the earliest of recorded times, the books discuss individuals and their impact. The encyclopedia-type articles are brief in nature and the text is rather dense, with few illustrations or photos included. These titles will be very useful to students writing reports, who need solid introductory material with a global focus. Each book includes resources for further reading and an index. Recommended.—**C. Ellen Wickham**

3.   **Current Biography Yearbook 2016.** Bronx, N.Y., H. W. Wilson, 2016. 666p. illus. $199.00. ISBN 13: 978-1-61925-731-3.

First published in 1940, *Current Biography* continues to be a key source of biographical information of notable people representing a variety of fields including politics and government, arts and entertainment, journalism, sports, business people, literature, and the sciences. Among those profiled in the 2016 edition are: Megyn Kelly, David Muir, Daisy Ridley, Adam Driver, Sadiq Khan, Rob Delaney, Eddie Redmayne, Justin Trudeau, Michael Daniel Higgins, Amy Hood, Katie Ledecky, and Helen MacDonald. Each entry lists year born, occupation, entry about life and career, and suggested readings; a photograph is included with most of the entries. Obituaries are also included for those who passed away in 2015/16—among notables profiled are Edward Albee, Muhammad Ali, David Bowie, Umberto Eco, Merle Haggard, Anne Jackson, Harper Lee, Patrice Munsel, Arnold Palmer, Maureen O'Hara, Simon Peres, Prince, Nancy Reagan, Morley Safer, Anthony Scalia, Elie Wiesel, and Gene Wilder. In addition to the obituary a cross-reference is provided to the year the individual was profiled in *Current Biography. Current Biography Yearbook* is a must have for libraries—it is a staple as a source for biographical information. Very highly recommended.—**Lucy Heckman**

Dictionaries & Encyclopedias

4.   **Oxford Research Encyclopedias. http://oxfordre.com/.** [Website] New York, Oxford University Press, 2017. Price negotiated by site. Date reviewed: 2017.

Oxford Research Encyclopedias (ORE) is a body of journal articles and reference entries from Oxford's encyclopedias collected in a single database. Articles are peer reviewed and updated regularly.

ORE contains more than 10,000 articles, with more being added over time; more than 2,000 of those articles can be accessed without a subscription. The site has articles on a wide variety of topics, divided into sections for a number of subjects in the humanities, social sciences, and sciences, which can be selected from the homepage. A separate page for each section includes a menu of subsections. For example, the Criminology and Criminal Justice section includes such subsections as Crime, Media, and Popular Culture; Criminological Theory; Prevention/Public Policy; and Women, Crime, and Justice. ORE's journal articles—"long-form overview articles written, peer-reviewed, and edited by leading scholars"—include an online publication date (but no source; encyclopedia entries do list the source) as well as a summary and list of keywords; each keyword links to a list of other articles containing the same keyword. The summaries are, of course, very handy in giving users an overview of what the article covers. Articles are accompanied by a sidebar with a linked table of contents and, in many cases, a list of related articles. Journal authors' professional affiliations are noted, but no additional biographical material is included. Some articles include images, maps, charts, tables, or graphs.

The site is fairly easy to navigate, with several options to refine search results (including an option to search only for articles that are accessible without a subscription). Options to print, save, cite, or email articles, or to view them as a PDF, are convenient. APA, MLA, and Chicago citations are provided, with options to export the citation using ProCite, RefWorks, Reference Manager, BibTeX, Zotero, and EndNote.—**ARBA Staff Reviewer**

Directories

5.   **Associations Canada, 2017.** Toronto, Grey House Publishing Canada, 2017. 1600p. index. $459.00pa. ISBN 13: 978-1-68217-473-9; 978-1-68217-474-6 (e-book).

Associations Canada covers over 20,000 associations including those "headquartered in Canada, as well as those headquartered elsewhere with branches in Canada." In addition, the book contains a section on foreign associations of special interest to Canadians. The organizations and international groups "represent industry, commercial and professional organizations, registered charities, and special and common interest organizations." The text is in English and French. As a bonus, this title also includes the following articles: "Associations," which describes the historical background of associations in general, their origins and growth, types, organization and operation, and contribution to society; "Building a Government Relations Program"; and "Is Your Organization Ready for a Cyberattack." Each individual association entry includes name, address, telephone numbers, email, website address, social media addresses, previous name, and an organization overview. Activities, finances, membership fees, staff, meetings/conferences, and publications are also provided. The volume covers a wide range of associations, including housing, farming and agriculture, home schooling, museums, parks and recreation, chambers of commerce, law, the performing arts, ecology, travel and tourism, human rights, and other areas. Several indexes complete the work: Acronym Index, Budget Index, Conferences and Convention Index, Executive Name Index, Geographic Index, Mailing List Index, and Registered Charitable Organizations Index. *Associations Canada* fills a need for locating specific agencies and organizations in Canada; it is recommended to larger public and research libraries and to academic libraries. It can serve as a "quick" reference resource or as a research starting point. It also is of value for businesspeople and tourists traveling to Canada.—**Lucy Heckman**

6.   **Awards, Honors & Prizes.** 38th ed. Farmington Hills, Mich., Gale/Cengage Learning, 2017. 2v. index. $635.00/set. ISBN 13: 978-1-4103-1824-4.

These two volumes present almost 15,000 awards given out by over 4,300 organizations in the United States and Canada. Arranged alphabetically by the group giving the award, the entries provide both information about the group (officers and contact details, including Facebook, LinkedIn, and Twitter, when applicable) and a description of the criteria for each of the recognitions. The number of awards ranges from a single honor for many of the groups to 41 for the Saskatchewan Music Festival Association (most being scholarships). At first, the choice of awards included seemed curious. There is a listing for several awards from the Oberhasli Breeders of America [goat breeders], but no mention at all of the Heisman Trophy, probably the best-known sports award in the United States. I have learned that this volume, which in fact will be the last edition of this title, focuses on monetary awards, which explains this situation. Each of the award listings designates the criteria for receiving the award, while some of the entries also indicate the current amount of the prize. The edition reflects the evolution of such awards, as a number of associations present in earlier editions (e.g., 27th, 2008), no longer appear here.

Detailed indexes provide access to 400 subjects, past and current names of groups giving the awards, and the names of the thousands of individual awards. Although potentially of interest to large public and academic libraries, the cost may be a barrier for some libraries. (If one adds the third volume, which covers the awards from 134 other countries, the price is $1,192.00.)—**Mark Schumacher**

7.   **The DiRT Directory. https://dirtdirectory.org.** [Website] Free. Date reviewed: 2018.

"The DiRT Directory aggregates information about digital research tools for scholarly use," making the online researcher's job much easier. The directory is supported by the Andrew W. Mellon Foundation; content is overseen by an editorial board and a steering/curatorial board (*see* the About link for individual members and credentials). Users can find analytical, organizational, communicative, and other systems to employ across a variety of projects. Simply structured, users can select from a directory of 40 processes such as Visualize Data, Store Data, Disseminate Data, Model Data, and much more. The directory also includes processes related to other aspects of research, including Collaboration, Design, and Writing. These processes can then be aligned with roughly 150 research categories such as Sheet Music, Raw Text, Geospatial Data, Animation, Blogs, Artwork, and Dissertations (although it is important to note that every process does not necessarily align with every category). After establishing the precise need, the site presents a listing of relevant tools, programs, applications, platforms, and more. For example, affiliating the Writing process with the Articles category lists Google Docs, Scalar, Paperpile, Annotum, and many other tools. The listing generally includes a brief description of the tool, its website, code license, and last update. Above the listing, users can continue to refine their search with cost, license, research object, and other parameters. Users can also select the Tools tab from the top of the homepage to organize the directory by recent additions/updates, category, or tags.—**ARBA Staff Reviewer**

Websites and Databases

8.   **BBC Archive. www.bbc.co.uk/archive.** [Website] Free. Date reviewed: 2017.

Extracted from the storied collections of the British Broadcasting Corporation, this archive offers access to a significant amount of programming via video and audio recordings, still photographs, documents, and more. Users will find information relating to a wide range of subjects spanning the social sciences, humanities, and science and technology. Much of the site's content (but not all) is organized into collections, which are easy to browse. The diverse collections are thoughtfully designed and are grouped under Art and Artists, Books and Writers, Broadcasting and Performing Arts, Business, Finance and Industry, Cultural Heritage, Events, Family and Lifestyle, Health and Wellbeing, Locations-UK, Nature and Environment, Politics and Government, Politics and Government-non-UK, Science and Technology, Society and Welfare, Sports, Transport and Travel, and War and Conflict. Within each collection, users can peruse such things as relevant performer interviews, musical recordings, photo galleries, letters, and documentary films. Some of the notable figures and institutions profiled in these archive collections include sculptor Henry Moore, writer George Orwell, the Duke of Edinburgh, the James Bond character, and the National Health Service. Other, more globally minded collections include "Cuba and the Cold War," "Hollywood Voices," and "Apartheid in South Africa." Users can alternatively browse via alphabetical listings under the Subjects,

People, or Programmes tabs, and can learn about the creation and maintenance of the BBC Archive by clicking on the Meet the Experts tab. It is important to note that, as of this review, the site is "archived and no longer updated." Nonetheless, the wealth of material tells a good portion of the rich BBC story and would be a clever resource for research on a number of subjects.—**ARBA Staff Reviewer**

9.   **Explora for Schools and Libraries. https://www.ebsco.com/products/explora.** [Website] Birmingham, Ala., EBSCO Publishing, Inc., 2017. Price negotiated by site.

This site offers a database of thousands of documents suitable for student research on myriad topics. Simply structured, the homepage offers users a generous display of broad categories and affiliated topics from which to explore the greater database. Researchers can conduct a basic or advanced search from the bar at the top of the page, or can browse from the homepage display of eight umbrella categories: Arts & Literature, Biography, Business & Government, Current Issues, Geography, Health, History, and Science & Math. Each category contains its own A-Z listing of topics with which to search the database. For example, within the Science & Math category, users can find information on Algebra, Biometrics, Chlorine, Erosion, Information Theory, Real Numbers, Speed of Light, and much more. Users can alternatively scroll through the homepage slide show of selected topics for inspiration. Search results will begin with a Topic Overview consisting of a brief foundational essay (or audio file). Students can then select from a varied collection, including periodicals, journal articles, reviews, encyclopedia entries, videos, and other materials. Text materials may generally be viewed or downloaded as html, pdf, or audio files. Users also have access to a variety of tools regarding citations, email, and more for use in managing their research. The wide range of topics and aligned materials offer an excellent resource to high school students across many types of research.—**ARBA Staff Reviewer**

10.   **Global Issues In Context. http://solutions.cengage.com/InContext/Global-Issues/.** [Website] Farmington Hills, Mich., Gale/Cengage Learning, 2017. Price negotiated by site. Date reviewed: 2017.

This database covers an awesome gamut of social studies and science topics and resources from Euroskepticism to South China Sea disputes to female circumcision. The information is kept very up-to-date and features global news providers, giving the topics a huge breadth of international coverage and perspectives. A wide array of resources and media are included with each topic like magazine articles, academic journals, images, videos, audio, websites, and more. Features allow for saving articles to a folder, compiling highlights and notes from within the articles, and saving a user's search history. Curriculum standard searches make connections to international standards from the United States, Canada, and other English-speaking countries. The United States is broken into State and National Standards, even mapping to the AASL Standards for the 21st Century Learner. The database as a whole is comprehensive and advanced, making it good research practice for upper secondary students graduating to higher education. This database offers opportunities to scaffold novice researchers and develop their information-seeking skills and understanding of these unique global issues. This is a good option for large schools spanning these grade levels. Recommended.—**Kasey Garrison**

11.   **Points of View Reference Center. https://www.ebsco.com/products/research-databases/points-of-view-reference-center.** [Website] Birmingham, Ala., EBSCO Publishing, Inc., 2017. Price negotiated by site. Date reviewed: 2018.

The EBSCO Points of View Reference Center offers access to a range of information relative to numerous topics in the current national conversation. The site offers a selection of summary essays, affiliated materials, and tools ideal for basic research purposes. Users can scroll through a display of selected topics (e.g., Globalization, Police Brutality, Voter ID Laws, etc.), can conduct a basic or advanced search via the bar at the top of the page, or can Browse by Category through an alphabetical display of thirty-four umbrella categories presented with related topic links underneath. For example, under the larger category of Immigration, users can click on specific links for Border Walls, Federal Identification Cards, Immigration Restrictions, and more. Clicking a link provides access to a summary overview essay. Users can alternatively listen to an audio file of the essay. The essay may be accompanied by other materials such as infographics, links to other articles or publications, photographs and more. An Understanding the Discussion section within the essay defines terms particular to the topic. Some topics may include a Related Items section which shares links to further essays conveying point/counterpoint opinions. There mayarly stages of a research project, as they can find good foundational material on an array of timely issues.—**ARBA Staff Reviewer**

12.   **The Worlds of David Darling. http://www.daviddarling.info/.** [Website] Free. Date reviewed: 2018.

British author and scientist David Darling has encapsulated his passion for learning into this Web page featuring five encyclopedias targeting a range of learning levels. The encyclopedias, accessible by scrolling down the page, broach four main topics: History, Modern Music, Science, and Alternative Energy. A fifth encyclopedia—the *Children's Encyclopedia of Science*—extracts materials from a lengthy and diverse list of Darling's own science books aimed at younger students (ages 8-16), such as "Could You Ever Build a Time Machine?" or "Climate Change for Kids." The four remaining encyclopedias offer a simple A-Z bar from which users can select a letter for a listing of places, people, objects, phenomena, and other terms related to the broader subject category. The lengthy Science listing also includes subcategory headings with their own listings (e.g., Biochemistry, Biologists, etc.), indicated in bold, uppercase type. Entries vary in length and may include links to related entries, color photographs, maps, and more. For some entries, users will find a link on the right side of the page for Related Categories as well. Science entries cover much in between "abacus" and "zygote," while History explores topics ranging from "Achilles" to "ziggurat" and Modern Music describes terms like "a capella" and "zydeco." Speaking to the expertise of the website author, the Science and Alternative Energy encyclopedias are particularly generous and informative. Alternative Energy is a unique and timely collection full of terms related to the newest discoveries and methods related to sustainability and new technologies (e.g., heat engine, landscape windbreaks, reaction turbine). The Web page is a commercial endeavor and contains advertisements, which may interfere slightly with the overall browsing experience. Nonetheless, the expansive, broadly appealing information, interesting subject categories, and straightforward presentation makes this database highly useful to researchers across the learning spectrum.—**ARBA Staff Reviewer**

Part II
SOCIAL SCIENCES

2 Social Sciences in General

General Works

Dictionaries and Encyclopedias

13. **Immigration and Migration: In Context.** Thomas Riggs, ed. Farmington Hills, Mich., Gale/Cengage Learning, 2018. 2v. illus. index. (In Context series). $361.00/set. ISBN 13: 978-1-4103-3894-5; 978-1-4103-3895-2 (e-book).

This new volume in the Gale/Cengage Learning In Context series addresses topics related to immigration and migration in an authoritative and engaging manner. Front matter in both volumes includes an introduction, comments on the In Context series, notes about the book, a guide to using primary sources, a glossary, and a chronology that extends from prehistoric times to the present. In two volumes comprised of 158 signed entries, the title covers topics from acculturation to Anti-Semitism to chain migration to forced migration to human trafficking and human smuggling to populist backlash to Syrian refuges to sanctuary cities and beyond. The entries are structured to facilitate use. Each entry includes an introduction, a shaded sidebar of words to know, a historical background, and a discussion of impacts and issues. The "Words-to-Know" sidebars include words and terms like cost of living that are familiar and some words and terms that are not so well known, like boutique multiculturalism. Bibliographies are divided into three sections: books, periodicals, and websites. The text includes fifty primary sources, such as the account of a Syrian woman who emigrated from her home country to Germany as part of a family group. Moreover, the book makes generous use of hundreds of color photographs which serve to enforce the subject matter and rivet reader attention. In volume 2, readers will find a general index, a list of selected organizations and advocacy groups, and a compilation of sources consulted. The book is intended for general users and students in high schools, community colleges, and four-year colleges. This reliable set is highly recommended to public, school, and academic libraries.—**ARBA Staff Reviewer**

14. Kenny, Erin, and Elizabeth Gackstetter Nichols. **Beauty around the World: A Cultural Encyclopedia.** Santa Barbara, Calif., ABC-CLIO, 2017. 416p. index. $94.00. ISBN 13: 978-1-61069-944-0; 978-1-61069-945-7 (e-book).

In *Beauty around the World: A Cultural Encyclopedia* Erin Kenny and Elizabeth Gackstetter Nichols tackle the daunting task of unraveling the relevant themes and topics that have formed our cultural fascination with beauty. As noted in the introduction, Kenny and Gackstetter Nichols aimed to create an encyclopedia that was informed by intersectional feminist scholarship that would be accessible to many readers. Kenny's background is in anthropology, and the encyclopedia reads very much in that line of scholarship, particularly in its efforts to avoid ethnocentrism and the "othering" of non-Western forms of beauty. In fact, "The 'Other'" is its own encyclopedic entry.

Beauty around the World is broken up into two parts. The first part is the traditional collection of encyclopedic entries, 166 in all. Entries from Hair, Body Positivity, and Eating Disorders to Manscaping and Moko Tattoos highlight and investigate the various ways that beauty is shaped around the world, often in conflicting ways. The entries are edifying and engaging, but it is unclear how the decisions were made to include certain entries and exclude others. To cover every topic on "beauty" in cultures across the world is certainly too harsh a litmus test, but I would have appreciated more discussion in the introduction on the process, particularly regarding the inclusion of select countries and regions as entries. The index is especially helpful in finding relevant entries on a topic of interest given the breadth of material needed to be covered. The second part of the encyclopedia is an Opposing Viewpoints section: a set of five questions on different topics relevant to the interrogation of beauty. Each of the five questions is answered by two essays, written by various contributors. These essays largely provide a nice complement to the more straightforward encyclopedic entries by digging deeper into the issues. The contributors come from a wide variety of backgrounds, not all of them experts on the topic chosen. This approach certainly has its advantages by bringing in a diversity of viewpoints, but it leads to some problematic assertions and wordings, specifically in the set of essays on transgender beauty pageants. This is doubly unfortunate given the lack of substantive representation of trans issues in the encyclopedic portion of the text aside from an entry on transpageants.

Overall, I would recommend this work for its relevance as a beginner's guide to the subject, and its potential usefulness for starting conversations among students regarding the powerful hold "beauty" has over our culture and cultures across the globe.—**Carin Graves**

Handbooks and Yearbooks

15.   **Gale Researcher Master Collection.** [Website] Farmington Hills, Mich., Gale/ Cengage Learning, 2017. Price negotiated by site. Date reviewed: 2017.

College students taking introductory courses will welcome the Gale Researcher database and its support for 11 popular areas of study: American Literature, British Literature, Criminal Justice, Economics, Philosophy, Political Science, Psychology, U.S. History, Western Civilization, World History, and Sociology. Subject-area specialists curated the scholarly entries in all sections, and materials follow the sequence of a typical college course. Within each section, students will find articles (typically 4,000-5,000 words), bibliographies, images, and videos, all of which are fully citable. The database is especially accessible to students as it contains some of the same functionality found in popular sites like YouTube and Wikipedia in addition to easy navigation and impressive graphic quality. Individual lessons are downloadable to personal devices, including smartphones. There are hyperlinks throughout, even within videos, and Gale Researcher connects to a purchasing library's holdings. Librarians can also create customized links. Professors will benefit as database materials can be used in lectures or as out-of-classroom supplements.

A collection of this sort takes some of the fear out of starting a research topic on an unfamiliar subject because it provides accurate contextualizing information and the ability for students to find further, applicable resources.

This is a highly recommended purchase for academic libraries.—**ARBA Staff Reviewer**

16.   **The International Year Book and Statesmen's Who's Who 2018.** 65th ed. London, Global Reach Publishing Ltd., 2017. 1590p. illus. maps. $985.00pa. ISBN 13: 978-0-9954972-1-4.

This is the 65th edition of a title that covers international organizations, states of the world, and biographies. This edition includes information about more than five hundred international organizations ordered by subject matter; political, economic, and social information about all the countries in the world in alphabetic order; and biographies of more than two hundred leaders worldwide—politicians, diplomats, heads of state, etc. The first section on organizations covers international groups, large and small. These include the UN, the Southern African Development Community, the Sierra Club, and the World Council of Churches, among hundreds of others. Users will find a generous amount of information on countries worldwide. Included in most entries is data on area & population; employment; banking & finance; manufacturing, mining & services; communications & transport; health; education; religion; communications & media; and the environment. The biographies list names in bold face and include basic information about a person's job or position, reason for inclusion, life dates, political affiliation, education, and address. Libraries can buy the print version, the ebook, or both. The online version contains more information and is updated regularly. For those who buy the print, the purchase comes with complimentary electronic access until the end of 2018.—**ARBA Staff Reviewer**

17.   **metaBUS. www.metabus.org.** [Website] Free. Date reviewed: 2017.

This site offers access to a vast, carefully curated collection of social science data. It stands out from other academic search engines as it collects and curates its research findings before employing platforms with which to use them. The site consolidates over one million findings sourced from over 11,000 academic articles, and is an excellent example of innovative and collaborative cloud-based information management. It is important to note that users must register with MetaBUS in order to access the data, and access is password protected. There is a helpful video tutorial explaining how to navigate the site and how to best make use of its information. Registered users may then access the site via three distinct interfaces: Classic (only 200,000 findings), Premier (most up-to-date and accessible) and Shiny (for "tech savvy" users). The Features tab at the top of the page provides good background on the site; pointing to its flexible and evolving database analytics, easily searchable topics, and fluid database structure which allow for both targeted searches and general browsing. With its state-of-the-art approach to information management and dissemination, metaBUS would greatly appeal to researchers and professionals.—**ARBA Staff Reviewer**

18.   **The SAGE Handbook of Social Media Research Methods.** Luke Sloan and Anabel Quan-Haase, eds. Thousand Oaks, Calif., Sage, 2017. 679p. illus. index. $175.00. ISBN 13: 978-1-4739-1632-6.

The SAGE Handbook of Social Media Research Methods offers a systematic guide to help researchers overcome challenges in conducting projects that deal with the vast data that social media creates, from the formulation of research questions through to the interpretation of findings. The handbook includes chapters on specific social media platforms, as well as a series of critical chapters that address designing social media research, collecting and storing data, and diverse approaches to accomplish this type of research. This handbook includes chapters on specific social media platforms such as Twitter, Sina Weibo, and Instagram, as well as a series of critical chapters. With coverage of the entire research process in social media, data collection and analysis on specific platforms, and innovative developments in the field, this handbook is the ultimate resource for those looking to tackle the challenges that come with doing research in this sphere.

The editors organized the handbook into the following sections: Conceptualizing & Designing Social Media Research; Collection & Storage; Qualitative Approaches to Social Media Data; Quantitative Approaches to Social Media Data; Diverse Approaches to Social Media Data; Analytical Tools; and Social Media Platforms. The use of current resources; diagrams, charts, graphs, and figures; and case studies enhances the content. An index rounds out the work.

The SAGE Handbook of Social Media Research Methods is the single-most comprehensive resource for any scholar or graduate student embarking on a social media project, with contributions from over 40 international experts from diverse disciplines. Recommended for academic libraries.—**Thomas E. Baker**

19.   **The Statesman's Yearbook 2017: The Politics, Cultures and Economies of the World.** 153d ed. New York, Palgrave Macmillan, 2016. 1529p. illus. maps. $375.00. ISBN 13: 978-1-137-44008-2.

In this volume, the 153rd edition, users will find political, social, and cultural information about all countries in the world, including dependencies and territories. The front matter includes an essay on the current state of democracy, quick facts about democracy, a page on world population developments, key world facts, recommendations for further reading, and a week-by-week chronology of happenings between April 2015 and March 2016. The volume is organized in two parts, with the first focusing on organizations. This section is further subdivided into: international, Europe, Africa, Americas, Asia/ Pacific, Middle East, Environmental Organizations, Treaties, and Leading Think Tanks. This is followed by the country analyses, arranged in an A to Z format. For countries, users will find information on key historic events; territory & population; climate; constitution & government; economy; energy & natural resources; industry; communications; social institutions; religion; culture; international trade; and social institutions (justice, education, health , and welfare). This edition introduces data on a country's civil and criminal justice world rankings. Libraries can purchase the print copy alone or consider the online version, which receives monthly updates and helpful search and browse tools along with access to *The Statesman's Yearbook* archive going back to the first 1864 edition. This trustworthy reference is recommended to academic and public libraries.—**ARBA Staff Reviewer**

20.   **The Twentieth Mental Measurements Yearbook.** Janet F. Carlson, Kurt F.

Geisinger, and Jessica L. Jonson, eds. Lincoln, New Bruns., The Buros Center for Testing, University of Nebraska, 2017. 1012p. index. $210.00. ISBN 13: 978-0-910674-66-9.

The latest volume of this legendary guide "to the complex task of test evaluation, selection, and use (p. xi)," first published in 1938, offers readers 215 entries, of which 191 have reviews. The entries, which are arranged alphabetically in the volume, provide detailed information about the test: cost, levels and categories of scoring, population for the test, publisher, and other useful information. Each entry receives two reviews, done by academics (including doctoral students) or medical/psychological professionals, depending on the content of the instrument. Those reviews usually include references the authors provide. The tests selected for inclusion are either new or substantially revised since their appearance in earlier editions of this work. Among the 15 categories (or "classifications") into which the tests are grouped are vocations, behavior assessment, personality, developmental, and reading. A classified subject index, name index, publisher directory, and score, title, and acronym indexes enhance reader access to this large volume.

Academic libraries, and possibly some practitioners, will want to consider this resource, whether in print format, particularly if they have the earlier volumes, or in the online versions provided by EBSCO or Ovid.—**Mark Schumacher**

3 Area Studies

General Works

Dictionaries and Encyclopedias

21. **Etiquette and Taboos around the World: A Geographic Encyclopedia of Social and Cultural Customs.** Ken Taylor and Victoria Williams, eds. Santa Barbara, Calif., Greenwood Press/ABC-CLIO, 2017. 374p. illus. index. $100.00. ISBN 13: 978-1-4408-3820-0; 978-1-4408-3821-7 (e-book).

Written for the American student, this encyclopedia contains descriptions of social conventions and behavior, including etiquette, taboos, body language, cultural customs, and dress codes for many countries of the world. Each entry is several pages long covering people groups, countries, minorities, and regions in addition to bits of history, folklore, politics, religion, and sociology. However, not every country or people group is included. The structure of the encyclopedia comprises a table of contents, an introduction giving the details of the definition and historical background of etiquette, ninety-three entries, a selected bibliography, and an index. Bibliographic references are included at the end of every entry for further reading. This reviewer would like to see a map indicating the countries and regions included in the book. For example, in a careful search of the articles, this reviewer did not find entries for Syria or Jordan, although there were entries for Iran, Saudi Arabia, and the de facto state of Palestine. The inclusion of a labeled map could have quickly identified the absence or presence of an encyclopedia entry.—**Linda M. Turney**

Handbooks and Yearbooks

22. **CultureGrams. https://online.culturegrams.com/.** [Website] North Salt Lake, Utah, ProQuest HeritageQuest, 2017. Price negotiated by site. Date reviewed: 2017.

CultureGrams was established in 1974 as a cultural content provider and acquired by ProQuest in 2004. The site was previously reviewed in ARBA (see ARBA 2009, entry 67) but has been significantly updated. The product includes four cultural sites: the World Edition, States Edition, Provinces Edition (Canada), and a Kids Edition. The sites are easily navigable via graphics or words. The home page of each site features a map from which users can navigate to the country, state, or province they want to view. Alternatively users can select their choice from a list as well.

Each country, state, or province has its own homepage with fun "Did you know?" facts, as well as statistics, related flag, and links to additional articles about that place that include geography, history, people, and culture. The information on the sites are generally bite-sized, many of the articles are only a few paragraphs long, making them approachable to students. The Kids Edition, which focuses on world cultural content, features articles that are even easier to read than the other three sites.

One truly unique feature of CultureGrams is its collection of interviews of people around the world. Users can read about what it's like to be a scientist in Antarctica, or a student in Brazil. Each place has a photo gallery, a slideshow, and recipes, and many places also have accompanying video. The sites offer a world time clock and currency converter, in addition to definitions and build-your-own graphs and tables. Teachers will appreciate the variety of maps available from a simple outline map that students can fill in, to detailed maps provided by National Geographic. In addition, nearly the entirety of information for each place can be printed in a neat packet and pages can be saved to Google Drive and/or added to Google Classroom. The sites lack a translator, but do provide audio capability, allowing users to hear, rather than read, the material.

The sites themselves do not contain integrated activities or exercises, but there is one 213-page downloadable packet of 79 classroom activities that pertain to all four sites. The activities are sorted by age group (K-12, with most activities for the K-5 group) and type of activity such as game, research, discussion, or presentation. A guide on how to use the sites to meet Common Core standards is also included.

Overall, the CultureGrams sites are easy to read and easy to navigate. They provide quality cultural content, approachable to K-12 students.—**ARBA Staff Reviewer**

23.   **Nations of the World: 2017: A Political, Economic, and Business Handbook.** Amenia, N.Y., Grey House Publishing, 2017. 2298p. maps. index. $180.00pa. ISBN 13: 978-1-61925-937-9.

Nations of the World: A Political, Economic, and Business Handbook "profiles every national and self governing territory around the world." Each entry among the 235 profiles includes political, economic, and business information and includes maps, charts, and tables. This resource is arranged alphabetically by country name. Each profile contains a side bar of key facts: official name, head of state, head of government, area (in square kilometers), population, capital, official language, currency, exchange rate, GDP per capita, GDP real grown, GDP, inflation rate, labor force, unemployment, and balance of trade. Each country includes a map and a review of the political and economic developments during the previous year, a profile with a timeline of key events during the country's history, the political structure which features recent election results, legal system, population, education, main cities with their populations, languages spoken, media, geography, working hours, hotels, and transportation. A business directory is also provided with area codes, useful telephone numbers, chambers of commerce, travel information, ministries, and other useful addresses (news services, major trade associations, and key Internet sites). In addition to the individual country studies there is an essay "The World in 2016," featuring a look at leading economic and political developments and essays on specific regions: The Americas (which contains the essay "American Turns Again on Cuba, or Does It?"); Asia; Europe (featuring the essay "Brexiteers, Refugees, and Immigrants"); and the Middle East. For each region there are statistics presented from

January 2012-January 2016 on currencies; key indicators (population, area, etc.); and a regional map (e.g., United States and Canada; Central America, and the Caribbean for the Americas). *Nations of the World* is a resource for quick reference for those researching economic indicators for specific countries, what major air carriers provide transportation, government officials, and other data. It can be used by students and faculty and by those planning business and vacations in specific countries. Highly recommended.—**Lucy Heckman**

24.   **Nations Online Project. www.nationsonline.org.** [Website] Free. Date reviewed: 2017.

This site was launched in 1998 and is regularly updated. It offers basic characteristic profiles of the many countries of the world, and acts as a gateway to further external research on aspects about them. From the homepage, users can click on a country's name and corresponding photograph to access its profile. Each profile contains a number of color landscape photographs, brief topical essays, national flag, and assorted quick facts and figures covering a range of national particulars, such as capital city, geography, nationalities, populations, and industries. Each profile also includes a great number of external links to sites with further and likely more detailed information, from the general (e.g., Google Maps or Wikipedia) to the very specific. In the case of Iceland, for example, users can follow links to sites for a museum, an airline, the stock exchange, a tourist agency, and pop culture icon Bjork. Users can alternatively select to examine Continents, Cities (profiling the largest or most prominent regional cities) or Landmarks (e.g., the Taj Mahal or Statue of Liberty). Languages provides general statistical data in list and table form (e.g., List of Languages of Asia by Country). The Maps tab leads to a generous selection of maps (administrative, satellite, physical, etc.) of specific countries and regions. It is important to note that the site, though freely accessible, uses cookies and advertisements (generally nonobtrusive). Its straightforward organization of national facts, in concert with the lovely photographs, would appeal to a range of casual users including younger students or armchair travelers. However, the overall content merely skims the surface of a locale's character, and would greatly benefit by fleshing out the narrative of a nation's story. Still, the site would serve as a good launching point for further research.—**ARBA Staff Reviewer**

United States

25.   **Arkansas   Extension   Circulars.   http://digitalcollections.uark.edu/cdm/landingpage.** [Website] Free. Date reviewed: 2018.

This special collection from the University of Arkansas gathers Extension Service Circulars which for years provided basic educational information on agricultural and domestic topics to rural working and farming families. The site offers access to over four hundred circulars spanning the years between 1914 and 1945 (more recent circulars will be digitized as part of another project). Users will note the sample display of circulars on the homepage, including Recent Additions, for good examples of the range of topics they present, such as "Removing Stains from Fabrics," "4-H Beef Cattle," or "Money Talk for Young People." Users can then either Search the Collection from the bar on the right corner or select the Browse This Collection tab underneath. From here, users can scroll through a display to browse thumbnail photographs alongside titles, creator(s), and subject categories. Clicking the thumbnail or the title connects users to the pdf file for examination or downloading. The file is accompanied by ample metadata regarding formatting, identification, and more. The abundant topics are quite fascinating and speak to the skills and know-how demanded of a rural community, from pest control to farm irrigation, or from canning to interior design. Users can trace the presentation of information through the years, noting the evolution of circular cover art and technology, among other things. Ease of navigation in addition to the large and engaging collection would greatly interest researchers studying Arkansas historical, sociological, agricultural, or other topics.— **ARBA Staff Reviewer**

26.   Barsanti, Chris. **The Handy New York City Answer Book.** Canton, Mich., Visible Ink Press, 2017. 444p. illus. maps. index. $21.95pa. ISBN 13: 978-1-57859-586-0; 978-1-57859-655-3 (e-book).

The Handy New York City Answer Book is an outstanding historical overview of the largest city in the United States that makes a valuable contribution to overall understanding of the city's urban environment. The book traces the city's history back to precolonial times and focuses on individual boroughs. It also addresses the arts, sports, and night life. The front matter includes a timeline (1300-2015), photo credits, and a substantial introduction that includes discussion of immigration, population, religion, politics and government, schools, and much more. The clarity of the author's writing style encourages active rather than passive learning. The question-and-answer format helps readers retain essential content and increases motivation to continue reading. Appendixes offer opportunities for further research, a list of mayors, and an explanation of idioms, slang, and expressions particular to the city. A substantial index rounds out the work. This title is recommended for public, school, and academic libraries. Moreover, it would serve as an excellent book for anyone who identifies with New York City and its long history.—**Thomas E. Baker**

27.   **Baylor University Institute for Oral History. http://digitalcollections.baylor. edu/cdm/landingpage/collection/buio.** [Website] Free. Date reviewed: 2018.

This site allows access to roughly four thousand transcript pdfs and many of the accompanying audio recordings conducted at Baylor University in Waco, Texas. Interviews capture the lives and experiences of many Baylor alumni and affiliates as well as residents of the surrounding community. Users can conduct a basic or advanced search at the top of the page, or watch a ten-minute tutorial video for information on how to explore the archive. The small link here directly beneath the tutorial lists general subject categories— with some subtopics—of the collected oral histories, including Arts & Culture (Church Music, Modern Texas Artists, etc.); Baylor University, Education (Charter Schools, Civil Rights in Texas Prisons, etc.); Historic Preservation, Religion & Culture (Jerry Falwell & The Moral Majority, Branch Davidians, etc.); Texas Judicial, War & Society; and more. Choosing a category displays the applicable portion of the oral history database sorted by name of interview subject. Items within the database are listed by Title (generally including subject name), Interviewee, Interviewer, and brief Interview Details. Users can view, download, or print a selected interview transcript pdf, which carries further identification information (e.g., number of interviews, interview date, collection, summary, etc.). If available, links to accompanying audio and any associated material will be found on the right-hand column of the page. Longer interviews may contain indexes noting places or names for ease of reference. The project is notable for capturing the impressions of Texans as they experienced national or global events like the Great Depression or the Vietnam War in addition to local events.—**ARBA Staff Reviewer**

28. **Encyclopedia   of   Chicago.**   **http://www.encyclopedia.chicagohistory.org.** [Website] Free. Date reviewed: 2017.

In conjunction with the Chicago History Museum, this site offers an excellent immersion into the history of the city of Chicago. Users can select from one of three main links to explore the site. The Entries link offers a generous alphabetical listing of general topics, places, organizations, events, and people. Users can simply click on a subject link to access essays of varying lengths, some which may include photographs and other digital artifacts which users can examine in full. Alternatively, users can access the primary source directly via the Historical Sources link. Maps are culled from Historical Sources for ease of reference and include a good collection of early city layouts. Entries describe Garfield Park, the Fire of 1871, Pizza, the Great Migration, Wrigley Field, Chicago Tribune, Abbott Laboratories, Polka, and much more. There are anecdotal pieces as well ("Saul Bellow on Chicago," "Royko: What Clout Is," etc.) to align personal impressions alongside objective history. The Special Features link is further subdivided into the following: Interpretive Digital Essays (e.g., "Water in Chicago"), Galleries, which use primary sources to tell a larger story (e.g., "The Public Faces of Religion"), Indices, two timelines, and Tables (e.g., "Chicago's Tallest Buildings Since 1854"). Under the Indices link, users will find an extensive biographical dictionary and a dictionary of Chicago business, 1820-2000. This site is now more than ten years old, but the wealth of material curated by subject-area specialists and the creative presentation make this a place where students and others can find reliable and comprehensive information about a great American city.—**ARBA Staff Reviewer**

29. **Madison Historical Society. https://madison-historical.siue.edu/encyclopedia.** [Website] Free. Date reviewed: 2018.

The Madison County Historical Society has created a thorough and easy-to-use resource for users interested in information about this particular corner of southwestern Illinois. The Steering Committee and Editorial Committee are comprised of academics and other professionals. Users can choose to explore an Encyclopedia of cited articles covering a range of Madison County topics or browse an Archive of historical materials. Within the Encyclopedia, users can find articles on both contemporary and historical subjects organized into several themes: Government, Industry, Education, Law, and Culture. Users click on an article title to access the concise but informative entry which may also include photographs, author, publication date, genealogies, items from the Archive, and more. Articles run the gamut of topics, providing information on Madison County school districts, the Mill Fires of Bethalto, the World's Largest Catsup Bottle, and William Bolin Whiteside, a Madison County pioneer who farmed, fought, and served as sheriff in the area's early years. Articles may appear under more than one theme. The Archive organizes its nearly five hundred items thematically as in the Encyclopedia, and users can browse by theme or tag. Items include a good selection of Oral History interviews, local industry catalogs, high school newspapers, an 1820 census, photographs, and other items. Users can further explore by era or community map, which accesses individual municipality materials. Archive items are generally accompanied by tags, collection, and other identifying information. The site's contemporary visual style and engaging, easy-to-navigate material offer a prime example of how even regional resources can up their game when it comes to providing educational and historical material. The site would appeal to students and educators of Connecticut history.—**ARBA Staff Reviewer**

30.   **The Mississippi Encyclopedia.** Ted Ownby and Charles Reagan, eds. Oxford, Miss., Center for the Study of Southern Culture/University Press of Mississippi, 2017. 1451p. $70.00. ISBN 13: 978-1-4968-1161-5.

Years in the making, this is the first encyclopedia in over a century to cover the entire state of Mississippi. Under the direction of Ted Ownby, Director of the Center for the Study of Southern Culture, and Charles Reagan, Professor Emeritus of History and Southern Studies, this title has 1,600 entries written by more than 700 scholars. Entries vary in length, with more lengthy ones on such important topics as agriculture, the Civil War, music, and religion. Entries are signed and conclude with suggestions for further reading. The index indicates main entries with bold-faced numbers and indicates images and tables with italics. Users will find information on musicians, battles, government, literature, and much more. Recommended for public, school, and academic libraries looking for a reliable and curated reference.—**ARBA Staff Reviewer**

31.   **Profiles of Florida.** 5th ed. Amenia, N.Y., Grey House Publishing, 2017. 734p. illus. maps. index. $149.00pa. ISBN 13: 978-1-68217-342-8; 978-1-68217-343-5 (e-book).

Grey House Publishing just released the 5th edition of their *Profiles of Florida—Facts, Figures & Statistics for 990 Populated Places.* Like the other state profiles, Grey House Publishing built on the content from the older edition. The researcher is provided data on all populated communities and counties in the State of Florida, data which is taken from the U.S. Census. This newer edition includes profiles of 73 unincorporated places derived from U.S. Census data based on local zip codes. The book is broken down to the following parts: About Florida, Profiles, Comparative Statistics, Community Rankings, Education, Ancestry and Ethnicity, and Climate. About Florida is a four-color section that gives the researcher a true sense of the state and its history through the use of such things as a photo gallery, subsections on history and government, and demographic maps. It serves as a great launching point to the rest of the book. The Profiles section includes 990 places and 67 counties based on 2010 Census data along with 2011-2015 American Community Survey data. Besides the information from the older profiles on geography, housing, education, religion, ancestry, transportation, population, climate, economy, industry, and health, this edition adds new profiles: public and private health insurance, dentists per capita, language spoken at home, disabilities, and veterans. Comparative Statistics, the third section, includes tables that compare Florida's 100 largest incorporated communities by dozens of data points. Section four, Community Rankings, includes tables that rank the top 150 and bottom 150 incorporated communities with a population over 2,500 in dozens of categories. Next, the Education section begins with an Educational State Profile, summarizing number of schools, students, diplomas granted, and educational dollars spent. Following the state profiles are school district rankings on 16 topics ranging from student/teacher ratios to current expenditures per student. Following these rankings are statewide National Assessment of Educational Progress (NAEP) results and data from the Florida Standards Assessments (FSA)—an overview of student performance by subject, including easy-to-read charts and graphs. Section six, Ancestry and Ethnicity, details the ancestral, Hispanic, and racial makeup of Florida's 200-plus ethnic categories. Profiles are included for the state, for all 67 counties, and for all places with 50,000 or more residents. The final section, Climate, includes a state summary, three colorful maps, and profiles of both national and cooperative weather stations. This well-laid-out work makes it easy to locate and understand material. It is thoroughly cited, and this allows the user to trace the data they are using from this work to the original source. The *Profiles of Florida* is a source worth adding to any reference collection.—**Lawrence Joseph Mello**

32.   **Profiles of Texas.** 5th ed. Amenia, N.Y., Grey House Publishing, 2017. 1169p. illus. maps. index. $149.00. ISBN 13: 978-1-68217-348-0; 978-1-68217-349-7 (e-mail).

This title is included in Grey House Publishing's State Profiles series; it also includes content from *Profiles of America.* The demographic data has been updated. Key facts, a photo gallery, a brief history of Texas, a timeline of Texas history, an introduction to Texas government, land, and natural resources, several color maps, a Texas energy profile, household energy use in Texas, and demographic maps are all included in this new section. Details were added so it is more granular.

The profiles are organized alphabetically by county, then by place. Although the listings for each place are easy for patrons to use and understand, other portions, such as the Comparative Statistics and the Community Rankings, require more expertise to properly interpret and analyze the data. In this book, Community Rankings includes places with a population of 2,500 or more. *Profiles of America* includes populations of 10,000 or more in their Regional Rankings. Two new statistics, "median selected monthly owner costs," were calculated with and without mortgage. The Texas Public School Educational Profile includes school district rankings and summaries from the state tests.

For libraries who own *Profiles of America,* this may not be worth buying unless you have a substantial collection of Texas materials. For libraries in Texas, you'll want this updated data. Highly recommended for all academic and public libraries.—**Ladyjane Hickey**

33.   **Recollection Wisconsin. http://recollectionwisconsin.org.** [Website] Free. Date reviewed: 2017.

Recollection Wisconsin allows access to over 250,000 digital artifacts for users interested in the history of the Badger State. Compiled from historical societies, museums, and libraries throughout the state, items include maps, photographs, newspaper clippings, books, audio recordings, letters, and much more. Users can examine individual artifacts, the broader collections from which the artifacts originate, or a sampling of inspired projects. Selecting the Explore tab will present a number of search or browse options. Users can conduct a basic or guided search, browse by category, or choose a pinned museum via Google maps. Users who browse by category will access 236 individual collections viewable either by alphabetical list (title, subject, description, and source) or gallery (title and thumbnail). Collection topics include, among other things, politics, architecture, recipes, Native Americans, and music. Users can also scroll through the appealing Stories from Wisconsin feature, displaying projects that have effectively drawn from the extensive digital archives. "McDonalds in Wisconsin," for example, uses photographs, newspaper clippings, and other materials to tell the story of the fast-food giant's existence in the state. The Teach tab offers resources for K-12 educators such as lesson plans, guidelines, and activities. The Participate link encourages new artifact contributions to the site and its collections. The Latest News blog shares news on research partnerships, funding, and more. With so much to offer, the site is an easy-to-use resource.—**ARBA Staff Reviewer**

Africa

34.   Shoup, John A. **The Nile: An Encyclopedia of Geography, History, and Culture.** Santa Barbara, Calif., ABC-CLIO, 2017. 420p. illus. maps. index. $89.00. ISBN 13: 978-1-4408-4040-1; 978-1-4408-4041-8 (e-book).

This book discusses the Nile River, from its beginnings in Lake Victoria and Lake Tana in Ethiopia. The book is supposed to be the history of the river, which includes the partial history of the five countries the Nile flows through, although only the histories of three of the countries (Egypt, Southern Sudan, and Sudan) have their own voluminous entries included in the encyclopedia. There are three parts of the book: thematic essays; the topical entries; and the primary documents. The thematic essays cover several topics: environment; geography; culture; religions, to name a few. The essays are meant to be a guide to the entries in the encyclopedia, but the names appearing in the encyclopedia do not have a different font or have any way to indicate that the topic has an entry. Some primary documents seemed to be indexed while others are not. The entry for Ra does not mention the Hymn to Ra in the primary documents; the goddess Nut is not even indexed even though a hymn is included in the primary documents. There is no collective bibliography but each entry does have its own. Two maps, one of Egypt and the other of the Nile and its tributaries, are included along with illustrations. Recommended.—**Michael W. Handis**

35.   Wiafe-Amoako, Francis. **Africa: The World Today Series 2017-2018.** 52d ed. Lanham, Md., Rowman & Littlefield, 2017. 358p. illus. maps. (The World Today Series). $23.00pa; $21.00 (e-book). ISBN 13: 978-1-4758-3524-3; 978-1-4758-3525-0 (e-book).

This is a "complementary analysis" of the countries in Africa. Africa is a politically, economically, and socially diverse continent made up of fifty-four countries with over one billion people. The author uses a statistical analysis to measure the cultural, economic, and political changes that have occurred over the last year. Some of these countries have unstable governments, while others like Ghana, Senegal, Sierra Leone, and Benin have successful democratic governments. The troubled countries of Somalia, Libya, and Eritrea have made slow and steady positive changes which are important to the quality of life in Africa. These country studies are the kind of information you will find in this World Today series volume.

You will encounter black-and-white photos and maps. The country entries are alphabetically arranged, and the volume includes an extensive bibliography. I would recommend this analytical report on Africa to public and academic libraries, as well as businesses and corporations interested in doing business on the African continent.—**Kay Stebbins Slattery**

Asia

36.   Leibo, Steven A. **East and Southeast Asia: The World Today Series 2017-2018.** 50th ed. Lanham, Md., Rowman & Littlefield, 2017. 324p. illus. maps. (The World Today

Series). $23.00pa.; $21.00 (e-book). ISBN 13: 978-1-4758-3522-9; 978-1-4758-3523-6 (e-book).

China is the country to watch as it emerges as one of the world powers of the 21st century. Though China is the largest country, Australia, Japan, North and South Korea, Myanmar, Indonesia, the Philippines, and Micronesia also comprise the region, which contains various ethnic and linguistic groups. In order to promote further understanding of events in this part of the world, the book describes each country's geography and demographics, history, government and politics, foreign policy, peoples and cultures, energy, and environment, as well as how each country is effected by the actions of other nations. Black-and-white photos, maps, and a bibliography enhance the work.

I would recommend this series, with its in-depth and succinct discussions of each country, for the current events collections at public libraries and academic libraries.—**Kay Stebbins Slattery**

37.   Ooi, Keat Gin. **Historical Dictionary of Malaysia.** 2d ed. Lanham, Md., Rowman & Littlefield, 2018. 592p. illus. (Historical Dictionaries of Asia, Oceania, and the Middle East). $145.00; $137.50 (e-book). ISBN 13: 978-1-5381-0884-0; 978-1-5381-0885-7 (e-book).

This second edition (see ARBA 2010, entry 81), by a well-known scholar and professor, addresses politics, the economy, and sociocultural topics in Malaysia, a democratic country that celebrated its 60th year of independence from Great Britain in 2017. The book begins with acronyms and abbreviations followed by maps and a chronology (fifty pages). The informative introduction covers the land and people, climate and vegetation, sociocultural fabric, economy, and history of this diverse nation. This second edition contains more than five hundred entries. For this second edition, the author gave the book a complete overhaul: some entries were deleted, some were combined under an umbrella topic, some were revised, all were evaluated, and some were completely rewritten. In sum, this title provides users with up-to-date information. Guide words, *see,* and *see also* references facilitate navigation, and the content is enhanced by black-and-white photographs. Three appendixes follow on the kings of Malaysia since 1957, prime ministers since 1955, and statistical data (area, population, ethnic groups, etc.). The book is intended for the interested individual as well as students and scholars. The book's users will especially appreciate the extensive bibliography with more than one hundred pages of citations covering many broad topics, such as history, politics, economy, culture, and the environment, science, and technology. Highly recommended for public and academic libraries.—**ARBA Staff Reviewer**

38.   Seekins, Donald M. **Historical Dictionary of Burma (Myanmar).** 2d ed. Lanham, Md., Rowman & Littlefield, 2017. 648p. $130.00; $123.00 (e-book). ISBN 13: 978-1-5381-0182-7; 978-1-5381-0183-4 (e-book).

This comprehensive volume, an update of the 2006 edition (see ARBA 2007, entry 93) with over 100 more pages, explores the social, political, religious, and cultural dimensions of 1,000 years of Burmese history. An excellent 48-page introduction guides the reader through the numerous regimes the country has known: a series of kingdoms, British rule beginning in the 19th century, Japanese occupation, independence in 1948, and various forms of unrest since. The 700 plus entries range from broad subjects (women in Burmese society, foreign investment, Buddhism) to narrow topics such as individual events of importance (elections for instance), locations (towns, rivers, etc.), and individuals of importance throughout Burmese history. The subject of Rohingyas, a frequent topic in today's news, is also examined. Maps, a chronology, excellent cross-references within the text, and an extensive subject bibliography enhance the usability and add to the value of this source.

This book will serve well any library population with an interest in world history or Southeast Asia. Academic libraries will be most likely to add it to their collections, but public and high school libraries should consider it as well.—**Mark Schumacher**

39.   Shrestha, Nanda R., and Keshav Bhattarai. **Historical Dictionary of Nepal.** 2d ed. Lanham, Md., Rowman & Littlefield, 2017. 530p. (Historical Dictionaries of Asia, Oceania, and the Middle East). $125.00; $125.99 (e-book). ISBN 13: 978-1-4422-7769-4; 978-1-4422-7770-0 (e-book).

This recent addition to the Historical Dictionaries series by Rowman & Littlefield provides second edition insights into mysterious Nepal (see ARBA 2004, entry 467). During this time of Google and Wikipedia, such a print resource is a treasure for searchers because of the well-arranged, in-depth, and well-researched compilation of precise and legitimate information by experts who provide this support for scholarly research projects. Content includes both historical and contemporary depth. In several aspects, the historical (beliefs, traditions) collides with contemporary practices (Internet, wireless communities) that are a result of the shift from an agrarian to an information society (largely skipping an industrial era). The dictionary begins with a list of abbreviations, informative maps, a chronological history, and an insightful introductory comment of nearly 40 pages prior to the bulk of the text which is about 350 pages of traditional alphabetical entries. There are apparent gaps, perhaps because of the ignorance of the reader. But in the easy-to-search alphabetical arrangement, there are no entries for crime, law, legal, or other such terms. If a student seeks information about crime in Nepal, it would not be as easily or readily available as one might hope. Although there is mention of hooligans who foment frequent chaos and disorder, this is in an entry about education.

Entries consider Nepali people and places across many centuries of time. Geography, religion, economics, and other topics give good balance to the scope of entries. The great depth of information provided makes this a very good source for historical perspective, as well as contemporary insights. An almost thematic note permeates the book—that Nepal is a nation of chaos; one that has evolved quickly and by stepping over entire eras to arrive as children in a modern time with parents firmly rooted in the traditions and beliefs of the past.

Good appendixes and tables follow the main entries, supplemented by a glossary and an extensive bibliography that is packed with many further resources. This is highly recommended as an addition to academic and research libraries, or any that serve users who seek international, political, mountain culture, religious, or south-central Asian information.—**James W. Agee**

40.   Sidhu, Jatswan S. **Historical Dictionary of Brunei Darussalam.** 3d ed. Lanham, Md., Rowman & Littlefield, 2017. 402p. illus. maps. (Historical Dictionaries of Asia, Oceania, and the Middle East). $100.00; $99.99 (e-book). ISBN 13: 978-1-4422-6458-8; 978-1-4422-6459-5 (e-book)

This recent addition to the Historical Dictionaries series by Rowman & Littlefield continues to provide excellent insights into largely unknown Brunei Darussalam. During this time of Google and Wikipedia it is wonderful for searchers to find an extensive and genuinely expert compilation of factual information that can support research projects. Content is well-focused on the country with restricted mentions of the region, and only as they relate to the "Abode of Peace." As perhaps the oldest Muslim nation in Southeast Asia, and with a people who have seen centuries of change that continues with the 29th sultan of an uninterrupted line, this nation is resilient and filled with contrasts. The dictionary begins with a list of abbreviations, too few maps, a chronology, and introductory comments prior to bulk of the text which is nearly 300 pages of traditional alphabetical entries.

Entries are well-focused on Brunei Darussalam people and places across many centuries of time. There is great depth of information that makes this a very good source for historical perspective, as well as for contemporary insights. The ultra-wealth of the nation, especially the ruling class, is explained with many entries about the modern era discovery of oil and even more recent development of natural gas as a huge export and source of income.

About 60 pages follow the entries with appendixes A-E, a glossary, and an extensive bibliography that is packed with many further resources in 15 subcategories. This is a highly recommended addition to academic and research libraries, or any that serve users who seek international, political, ASEAN, South China Sea, or Southeast Asian information.—**James W. Agee**

Canada

41. **British Columbia Historical Photographs Online. http://aabc.ca/resources/ historical-photographs/.** [Website] Free. Date reviewed: 2018.

Presents a listing of Online Photograph Databases and Online Photograph Galleries that link to individual digital collections reflecting the Canadian province of British Columbia in photographs and other media. The page lists twenty databases, large and small, created by institutions such as the West Vancouver Archives, University of British Columbia Library, City of Surrey Archives, and others. The archives contain a range of media such as photography, drawings, maps, correspondence, and audio recordings—all working toward preserving and sharing the rich history of the region. In addition, the page lists twenty-three Online Photograph Galleries specific to photography but also focused on the history of many of the cities and towns within British Columbia. Some of the galleries listed include Prince Rupert City and Regional Archives, Enderby & District Museum and Archives, Salt Spring Island Archives, and Chiliwack Museum and Archives. Each database or photo gallery may be arranged differently as conceived by the host institution, yet taken together offer comprehensive insight into the people, landscapes, activities, industries, and more that populate the large Canadian province. The singular focus of this page makes it an excellent launching point for research on British Columbia as a whole or on individual areas within the province.—**ARBA Staff Reviewer**

Developing Countries

42. **Eldis. http://www.eldis.org/.** [Website] Free. Date reviewed: 2017.

From the United Kingdom-based Institute of Development Studies, this website shares research covering a host of global development issues. It is home to over 50,000 policy or research summaries carefully selected by the Eldis editorial board with links to complete work (full-text documents) as well. Submitted research is balanced between established global entities and smaller organizations representing the concerns of developing nations. Some of the most recently published work concerns nutrition education and agricultural policy in developing nations. The site is well-organized for easy access. Key Issues gives a broader reading of topics relevant today, such as climate change or gender inequality. Latest Documents presents the most recently acquired research and the Blog shares editorial opinion and commentary. From the menu bar, users can access research summaries via a basic or advanced search, or can choose via Topics (such as Aid and Debt, Health Systems, Food Security, etc.) or Countries. Each summary includes publishing notes (e.g., author, etc.), a listing of related summaries, and a link to the full report. With its emphasis on free and open access, this site promotes a collaborative and progressive approach to the international market of ideas, a mission appealing to policy-makers, students, community activists, and others.—**ARBA Staff Reviewer**

Europe

43.   Gasimov, Zaur. **Historical Dictionary of Azerbaijan.** Lanham, Md., Rowman & Littlefield, 2018. 276p. maps. $90.00; $85.50 (e-book). ISBN 13: 978-1-5381-1041-6; 978-1-5381-1042-3 (e-book).

This reference gives quick access to the key people, places, events, and cultural happenings in Azerbaijan history with an emphasis on the modern period, from 1920 when it became a Soviet Republic to 1991 when it became the independent Republic of Azerbaijan to the present. Through the thumbnail entries, we learn that this small Caucasian state, about the size of Austria and sharing borders with Iran, Armenia, Georgia, and Russia, is predominately Shiite Muslim; yet, in 1918 it was the first nation in the Muslim world to give women voting rights. During World War II (known as the Soviet-German War in Azerbaijan), this Soviet Republic was the main provider of oil for the Soviet war effort. Oil is still the main driver of the economy. Heydar Aliyev became president in 1993, establishing an autocratic regime that has continued with his son, Ilham Aliyev, who took over the presidency from his father in 2003. The Aliyev regime, under both father and son, is marked by ongoing human rights abuses. With an eye to keeping power within the family, Ilham's wife serves as vice president. In 2016 Ilham put in place constitutional changes to reduce the eligible age for the presidency to 18, setting the stage for the regime to continue under his son. In order to contextualize the information, the dictionary includes an extensive chronology; a helpful introductory essay describing the land, people, and history; lists of Communist Party leaders and presidents since 1920; and historical population and ethnic statistics. Given the large number of political activists listed in this resource and the volatility of the region, it would not be surprising if Azerbaijan is soon prominent in the news.—**Adrienne Antink**

44.   Hierman, Brent. **Russia and Eurasia: The World Today Series 2017-2018.** 48th ed. Lanham, Md., Rowman & Littlefield, 2017. 336p. illus. maps. $23.00pa.; $21.50 (e-book). ISBN 13: 978-1-4758-3516-8; 978-1-4758-3517-5 (e-book).

This 48th edition begins with introductory comments followed by an analysis of the Russian Federation; it includes information on the land and people, the Communist era, the Putin presidency, the culture, the changing economy, and much more. This is the largest section of the book, at 137 pages. This section is followed by a discussion of the Commonwealth of Independent States. Although shorter in length, the sections on Belarus, Ukraine, Moldova, Armenia, Azerbaijan, Georgia, Kazakhstan, Kyrgyzstan, Tajikistan, Turkmenistan, and Uzbekistan contain plentiful information about such things as the land, people, culture, history, and economy of each country. Country sections also begin with handy facts on the size of the country and population, cities, the climate, neighboring states, languages spoken, ethnic composition, principal religions, chief commercial products, currency, per capita annual income, recent political status, chief of state, head of government, national flag, and national day. The addition of easy-to-read black-and-white maps enhances the work, as does the use of black-and-white photos. Authored by Brent Hierman, assistant professor in the Department of International Studies at the Virginia Military Institute, this reference work provides quick and authoritative answers. Recommended to public and academic libraries.—**ARBA Staff Reviewer**

45.   Payerhin, Marek. **Nordic, Central, and Southeastern Europe: The World Today Series 2017-2018.** Lanham, Md., Rowman & Littlefield, 2017. 612p. illus. maps. $23.00; $21.50 (e-book). ISBN 13: 978-1-4758-3512-0; 978-1-4758-3513-7 (e-book).

This is the seventeenth edition of this tome, part of the nine-volume World Today Series 2017-2018 from Rowman & Littlefield Publishers. It focuses on the historic, social, economic, political, and cultural history of the twenty-five countries that comprise the Nordic, Central, and southeastern areas of Europe. They include: Iceland, Norway, Sweden, Finland, Estonia, Latvia, Lithuania, Kaliningrad, Denmark, Poland, Germany, the Czech Republic, the Slovak Republic, Austria, Hungary, Slovenia, Croatia, Bosnia and Herzegovina, Montenegro, Kosovo, Albania, Macedonia, Bulgaria, Serbia, and Romania. The volume includes many black-and-white photographs and extensive maps of these countries at various times throughout history. Updated annually, an extensive bibliography and listing of websites is included. This reference book and its companion volumes provide up-to-date research on all of the countries in the world, and are a trustworthy and valuable addition to any academic library's reference section.—**Bradford Lee Eden**

46.   Purs, Aldis, and Andrejs Plakans. **Historical Dictionary of Latvia.** 3d ed. Lanham, Md., Rowman & Littlefield, 2017. 410p. (Historical Dictionaries of Europe). $100.00; $95.00 (e-book). ISBN 13: 978-1-5381-0220-6; 978-1-5381-0221-3 (e-book).

Latvia has become an international player after achieving independence in 1991 following years of domination by power-hungry states. The *Historical Dictionary of Latvia,* third edition (see ARBA 2009, entry 114), covers an extensive period of the country's history in a broad range of over 500 entries that include historical and political perspectives. Other entries consider Latvia's economy, society, religion, and culture. In addition, topics include personalities, peripheral conflicts, lethal weapons systems, and political and military strategies. Entries that focus on Latvian women, cultural, and social figures enhance reader interest. Moreover, the book includes a list of acronyms and abbreviations, a chronology, and an extensive bibliography. Extensive cross-references in the dictionary section facilitate use.

The volume offers current information that supports student curiosity and academic inquiry. All high school, public, and university libraries should retain a copy in their research section. The dictionary also serves the needs of history buffs and enthusiasts—**Thomas E. Baker**

47.   Smith, Angel. **Historical Dictionary of Spain.** 3d ed. Lanham, Md., Rowman & Littlefield, 2018. 790p. maps. (Historical Dictionaries of Europe). $170.00; $161.50 (e-book). ISBN 13: 978-1-5381-0882-6; 978-1-5381-0883-3 (e-book).

Like other titles in the various historical dictionary series, this one begins with a chronology (1469-2017), a list of abbreviations and acronyms, and a general introduction that covers the land and people, the period of Spanish empire (1479-1898), the Spanish Civil War, the period of democracy building, and globalization, among many other things. As expected, the entries (approximately seven hundred) are listed in an A to Z format; they may contain bold-face cross-references and *see* references. Entries vary in length from a short paragraph to many pages—the Franco Regime entry comprises nearly ten pages, for example. For those wanting to do further reading and research, there is a nearly eighty-page bibliography divided by topic so users can jump, for example, to works on Basque nationalism. The last edition of this book (see ARBA 2010, entry 97) was published nearly a decade ago. This updated version incorporates vital political, economic, and other changes in Spain over the last ten years and is recommended for public and academic libraries.—**ARBA Staff Reviewer**

Latin America and the Caribbean

48.   Bizzarro, Salvatore. **Historical Dictionary of Chile.** 4th ed. Lanham, Md., Rowman & Littlefield, 2017. 2v. illus. maps. (Historical Dictionaries of the Americas). $225.00/set. ISBN 13: 978-1-4422-7634-5; 978-1-4422-7635-2 (e-book).

This fourth edition of the *Historical Dictionary of Chile* incorporates Chilean history, economics, politics, geography and environment, and constitutions and political parties since the last 2005 edition. The purpose of this book is to provide biographies of major figures, as well as descriptions of basic institutions, religion, economic policies, literature, art, and culture, giving the reader an overview of Chile, ancient to modern. The chronology begins in the year 6500 BCE, the date of hieroglyphics found in Patagonia and the Tierra del Fuego, and ends with the November 8, 2016, U.S. elections. Spanish names and terms are translated for better understanding. The entries are in alphabetical order and accompanied by black-and-white photos, tables, and maps. There is an extensive bibliography of books, articles, pamphlets, and Internet sites. The bibliography is arranged by subject in chronological order.

I would recommend this handbook to academic college and university libraries because it is a tool for the students and faculty who are interested in South American research.—**Kay Stebbins Slattery**

49.   Huck, James D., Jr. **Modern Mexico.** Santa Barbara, Calif., ABC-CLIO, 2018. illus. maps. index. (Understanding Modern Nations). $97.00. ISBN 13: 978-1-4408-5090-5; 978-1-4408-5091-2 (e-book).

If there is a better one-volume reference to Mexico than this, it would be hard to find. James Huck has done the nearly impossible: provide a comprehensive historical and cultural reference, nuanced, and, for the most part, up to date. The bibliographical and scholarly foundations are mostly impeccable. There is very little with which to disagree, and I warmly recommend this to anyone in need of a single-volume reference to Mexico. There are chapters, subdivided topically, that deal with politics, government, history, culture, and language. They are uniformly well informed and of very high quality. Even instructors in college courses would find this a useful volume, because there are such features as timelines, glossaries of key terms, facts and figures, and a select, but helpful, bibliography in English. Each chapter is subdivided into relevant articles, and each article has its own bibliography. It is hard not to be impressed with the timeliness of virtually every entry, so that anyone seeking an introduction to the current state of the economy (at least as of 2014) or the political system would find the volume quite helpful. There are very few errors, most of the trivial typographical variety, and they should stop no one (or any library) from investing in the volume. It is more than worth its price.

I had very few disagreements with what I read. The author may be somewhat optimistic about the transparency and honesty of elections in Mexico, but time will tell. Overall, I found the volume useful, relevant, and quite instructive.—**Richard Salvucci**

50.   Klarén, Peter F. **Historical Dictionary of Peru.** Lanham, Md., Rowman & Littlefield, 2017. 462p. maps. (Historical Dictionaries of the Americas). $110.00; $104.50. ISBN 13: 978-1-5381-0667-9; 978-1-5381-0668-6 (e-book).

This work is part of the Historical Dictionaries of the Americas series. It describes the people, land, resources, economy, history, and politics of Peru from 13,000 B.C. E. to the inauguration of the current president in 2016. There is a brief introduction to the series written by the series editor, Jon Woronoff. The author, Peter F. Klarén, is a Peruvian expert and scholar. He is professor emeritus in History and International Affairs at George Washington University in Washington, D.C. He has written numerous books and journal articles about Peru and Latin America and was awarded the Orden del Sol del Peru by the Peruvian government.

A brief section called "Reader's Notes" provides information about the abbreviations used for political parties, the naming conventions for Spanish names, and the use of real names cross-referenced to aliases. Five pages of acronyms and abbreviations are followed by a map of Peru. The map is too small to be really useful but it shows the borders, the departmental divisions, and significant cities and regions. A twelve-page chronology of prehistoric and historic periods follows. Major events in each period are briefly outlined. The introduction provides an excellent twenty-one-page overview of Peru that includes descriptions of the country, its people, resources and infrastructure, economy, history, international relations and defense, and politics since 2000.

A-Z entries cover all aspects of the country. Entries run from one paragraph to three pages long. Entry topics are listed in bold. Listings for people include birth and death dates. Within each entry other topics that have their own listings are given in bold. Cross-references include *see also* listings that direct readers to more information directly related to the original topic, and *see* listings directing readers to more information that informs the entry. An appendix, "Profile of Peru," provides statistics of all kinds about the country.

The thirty-page bibliography has its own two-page introduction. It is divided into sections by historic time period followed by major subject categories. It includes categories for historiographies, websites, government sources, foundations and nongovernmental organizations, and newspapers and magazines at the end of the list. Information about the author completes the volume.

This work provides a useful introduction to all things Peruvian. Information is brief and clearly written. The number of prehistoric, historic, and modern entries are well balanced. Beginning researchers can easily browse this volume or go directly to specific entries of interest. This historical dictionary will be useful in high school and academic libraries. It is available in paperback and as an e-book at a relatively affordable price.— **Joanna M. Burkhardt**

51.   Straka, Tomás, Guillermo Guzmán Mirabal, and Alejandro E. Cáceres. **Historical Dictionary of Venezuela.** Lanham, Md., Rowman & Littlefield, 2018. 418p. (Historical Dictionaries of the Americas). $105.00; $99.50 (e-book). ISBN 13: 978-1-5381-0949-6; 978-1-5381-0950-2 (e-book).

A list of abbreviations and acronyms, a map, and a chronology covering the period from 1498 to 2017 begin this third edition authored by three professors at the Universidad Católica Andrés Bello, Caracas. An introduction, which discusses the historiography, history, pre-Hispanic period, discovery and conquest, the colonial period and independence, and the republican period, comes next. The introduction is followed by more than seven hundred entries, which contain *see* and *see also* references. The entries vary in length from a short paragraph to nearly ten pages on the economy. A series of appendixes provides users with more information. Appendix A, "Venezuela at a Glance," provides basic facts on area, climate, life expectancy, the flag, the unemployment rate, external debt as percentage of GDP, and more. "Presidents of Venezuela," appendix B, starts with Cristóbal Mendoza (1811-1812) and ends with Hugo Chávez (2007-2013). For each, there is supplemental information: position, origin of mandate, and end of mandate. The next appendix, "Population," gives the total number as well as percent growth, starting in 1920 and running through 2016. Further population data is provided in appendix D, "Population Pyramid (2011 Census)." Statistics on racial structure are covered in appendix E, while real GDP and percent growth numbers from 1920 to 2016 are given in appendix F. The last appendix, "Inflation," provides users with year-by-year statistics since 1920. A bibliography rounds out the work. The information in this work will help readers make sense of a country currently in turmoil. Recommended for academic and public libraries.— **ARBA Staff Reviewer**

52.   Turner, Blair. **Latin America: The World Today Series 2017-2018.** 51st ed. Lanham, Md., Rowman & Littlefield, 2017. 454p. illus. maps. (The World Today Series). $23.00pa; $21.00 (e-book). ISBN 13: 978-1-4758-3514-4; 978-1-4758-3515-1 (e-book).

Political, economic, technological, and cultural change is accelerating as the twenty-first century progresses in Latin America. The Latin American countries have had the reputation of being "third world banana republics" for most of the twentieth century. The last twenty years have seen the transformation from a dictatorship form of rule to a democratic form of government in these countries. Along with the new forms of government, cultural growth, technological transformations, new infrastructure, and economic diversification with job expansion has improved in 38 percent of these Latin American countries.

The country studies are alphabetically arranged; black-and-white photos and maps accompany the text. There is an extensive bibliography of sources. This series updates current affairs in four regions of the world. I would recommend this series to public, academic, business, and corporate libraries to get the latest updates of SWOT (strengths, weaknesses, opportunities, and threats) information for these countries.—**Kay Stebbins**

Slattery

Middle East

53.   Cantey, Seth. **The Middle East and South Asia: The World Today Series 2017-2018**. 51st ed. Lanham, Md., Rowman & Littlefield, 2017. 296p. illus. maps. $23.00pa; $21.00 (e-book). ISBN 13: 978-1-4758-3518-2; 978-1-4758-3519-9 (e-book).

This volume covers an area of the world facing many difficult challenges, including the Islamic State and Syria; the continuing war between Saudi Arabia and Iran; the Sunnis vs. the Shiite Muslims; the Afghan War and U.S. involvement in it; and the ISIS expansion of its terrorist activities into Europe and the United States. The question for this region is whether the United States and Russia, as well as other Middle Eastern countries, continue to fund the conflict in Syria and Iraq to oust ISIS or not? That is a question that has to be considered by the Middle Eastern countries in the near future.

The Middle East and South Asia provides a "state of the state" analysis of the current history and the conflicts occurring in this region of the world. The text is accompanied by black-and-white photographs, maps, and an extensive bibliography of key English-language sources. I would recommend this to public and academic libraries' current issues collections.—**Kay Stebbins Slattery**

54.   **Qatar Digital Library. https://www.qdl.qa/en.** [Website] Free. Date reviewed: 2018.

The many artifacts in the Qatar Digital Library help tell the story of the intersection between ancient cultural traditions of the area and the modern colonial era. The site has digitized thousands of items stored within the vast British Library and the Qatar National Library that open a large window onto the history and culture of the Persian Gulf region. Simply structured, the site allows users to select from two options. Explore the Archive accesses a database of over one million items, some dating as far back as the tenth century C.E. Users can search among manuscripts, letters, maps, photographs, illustrations, and much more. Additional search filters include date, place, people/organizations, and subjects such as trade, Arab nationalism, military operations, astronomy, tribes, agriculture, and religious conflicts. The database includes helpful tools with its timeline filter visualization, allowing users to note the item chronology, and an A-Z glossary of relevant terms and concepts. Items come to the archive from general and specific locations all around the gulf region, including Bahrain, Saudi Arabia, Persia/Iran, Qatar, Dubai, Yemen, Zanzibar, and Egypt. Items are accompanied by a description of the content, format, physical characteristics, language, archival information, and other details. Users can zoom in on items for a close examination; images are also downloadable. Items of note include early scientific manuscripts covering mathematics, astronomy, and more, and J.G. Lorimer's *Gazetteer of the Persian Gulf, Oman and Central Arabia,* which offered the first encyclopedic overview of the area's geography and history. Users can alternatively select the Articles from Our Experts tab, which features a generous catalog of scholarly essays addressing topics such as "The Coming of the Wireless Telegraph to Bahrain," "Muscat and the Monsoon," "The Brutal End of Persia's Zand Dynasty," individual country profiles, and much more. Articles may incorporate such things as sound recordings, videos, and further resources. The homepage guides users to particular articles and artifacts via its

See, Watch, Listen banner, its Featured Articles, and listing of Popular Searches.—**ARBA Staff Reviewer**

55.   Schmitz, Charles, and Robert D. Burrowes. **Historical Dictionary of Yemen.** 3d ed. Lanham, Md., Rowman & Littlefield, 2018. 572p. maps. (Historical Dictionaries of Asia, Oceania, and the Middle East). $145.00; $137.50 (e-book). ISBN 13: 978-1-5381-0232-9; 978-1-5381-0233-6 (e-book).

This updated edition, coauthored by two country experts, begins with a chronology (1200 B.C.E.-2017), a list of acronyms and abbreviations, and an introduction that discusses the history; land and people; social and political developments since the 1970s; the civil war, 2015-2017; and so much more. There are approximately one thousand cross-referenced entries that use *see* references when necessary. Entries range in length from a short paragraph to several pages for a topic like religion. The bibliography, arranged by topic, is a valuable resource for users. This is an essential reference for users wanting to understand the current situation in Yemen, as the previous edition published in 2010 (see ARBA 2011, entry 123). Recommended for academic and public libraries.—**ARBA Staff Reviewer**

4 Economics and Business

General Works

Dictionaries and Encyclopedias

56. **The American Middle Class: An Economic Encyclopedia of Progress and Poverty.** Robert S. Rycroft, ed. Santa Barbara, Calif., Greenwood Press/ABC-CLIO, 2017. 2v. index. $198.00/set. ISBN 13: 978-1-61069-757-6; 978-1-61069-758-3 (e-book).

This is an ambitious two-volume set that aims to define what "Middle Class" is, who is in the "Middle Class," and what issues concern these individuals. The text consists of seven parts. Each part includes an introductory essay or essays and entries dealing with issues discussed in the introduction. The parts include: Economic Uncertainty; Politics, Public Policy; Education, Housing, Labor; Health; Crime; Norms; and Culture, Media. The essays were typically several pages long and in an atypical fashion some were coauthored by undergraduates. The entries were from one page to several pages. Overall the first volume provides a strong sociological look at the concept of being middle class. Parts of the second volume seem forced and sections became shorter and shorter as the text progressed. The fourth part dealing with health issues was surprisingly short. The section dealing with crime was uneven; for example, there was no entry for domestic violence, but there was one for organized crime. It seems the entire section on crime provided very general information that had little to do with the middle class. The set concludes with the list of contributors, containing brief biographical information and a good index. The books are hardback with sturdy binding and thick pages; the typeface is clear and a good size. Overall this is an optional purchase for academic and large public libraries.—**Melissa M. Johnson**

57. **Economics: The Definitive Encyclopedia from Theory to Practice.** David A. Dieterle, ed. Santa Barbara, Calif., Greenwood Press/ABC-CLIO, 2017. 4v. index. $399.00/set. ISBN 13: 978-0-313-39707-3; 978-0-313-39708-0 (e-book).

Since economics is a broad, interdisciplinary subject area, it is helpful to students and researchers to have access to a resource to learn the basics on topics within the field. This four-volume encyclopedia set covers the foundations of economics, macroeconomics, microeconomics, and global economics. The editor is a professor of economics and the contributors are independent scholars or are associated with academia including secondary schools, a company, or institute. It would have been nice to have more information on the independent scholars.

This title includes a table of contents with each volume represented, introductory content, and entries for each of the topics followed by information about the editor and a list of contributors. Finally, a concluding index includes listings for all four volumes. Volume four also includes a list and overview of 27 primary documents like acts or agreements in economic history, a list of Nobel laureates in economics, a timeline of economic events from 1776 to 2016, and a glossary of approximately 1,000 entries. The table of contents and indexes make it is easy to find any related topics or items. Since the subject area is so broad, it is difficult to know what topics are included or how they are arranged without the table of contents. The preface does help to explain the organization a little bit, but the table of contents and index are definitely needed for users. In addition, it is difficult to understand the inclusion or placement of some entries. For example, there is an entry on Steve Jobs, which is not a topic readily identified with economics. There is a listing for "Reasons" which is quite a vague label. There is also an entry for "United Nations System" in the economics' foundation volume rather than the global economics volume.

The encyclopedia covers all areas of economics, which is useful for anyone trying to understand the many parts of economics. Entries are succinct and easy to understand. A couple of nice additions to the entries are *see also* references and citations for further reading. Overall, this encyclopedia would be beneficial to researchers or general users looking for basic information about economics. Undergraduate students looking for topics related to economics and further readings would probably benefit the most.—**Breezy Silver**

58.   **Encyclopedia of African American Business.** 2d ed. Jessie Carney Smith, ed. Santa Barbara, Calif., Greenwood Press/ABC-CLIO, 2018. 2v. index. $198.00/set. ISBN 13: 978-1-4408-5027-1; 978-1-4408-5028-8 (e-book).

Given the changes in the business world and new historical scholarship, updating Carney Smith's first edition (2006) was essential. The two-hundred-plus signed entries run two to four pages, with cross-references and short secondary bibliographies. Black-and-white illustrations are scattered throughout. Three tables ("Entries," "Topics," and "Leaders by Occupation") preceding the entries simplify locating individuals and similar entries, and the enhanced font and layout improve readability. Twenty-seven tables, a final index, and a secondary bibliography conclude the set. Although Carney Smith notes that the entries draw upon "the expertise of users and business professionals," contributors were overwhelmingly librarians and humanities faculty. However, these well-written entries exhibit solid research by the writers. Obviously given space limitations, individuals and topics are missing—no entries exist, for example, on banker William Madison McDonald (1866-1950, Texas' first African American millionaire), the Colored Farmers' Alliance, or the southern miners' strikes between 1890 and 1915. But the attention to contemporary business more than makes up for that. An excellent recommended companion volume for all academic and public libraries to Kranz' *African-American Business Leaders and Entrepreneurs* (see ARBA 2005, entry 140) and Walker's *Encyclopedia of African American Business History* (Greenwood, 1999).—**Anthony J. Adam**

59.   **The SAGE Encyclopedia of Corporate Reputation.** Craig E. Carroll, ed. Thousand Oaks, Calif., Sage, 2016. 2v. index. $375.00/set. ISBN 13: 978-1-4833-7651-6.

These days announcements of corporate scandal, consumer fraud, and celebrity bad behavior are quickly and widely broadcast via social media outlets and newsfeeds and may justifiably wreak havoc on the reputations of those companies and individuals involved. *The SAGE Encyclopedia of Corporate Reputation* edited by Craig E. Carroll (Ph.D., University of Texas at Austin) is both a timely and authoritative reference work. This two-volume encyclopedia covers all theoretical aspects of the field of corporate reputation studies. Articles are signed by the contributors (mainly from prestigious academic institutions) and include additional readings. An alphabetical list of entries is provided and the entries follow in alphabetical arrangement, A-N and O-Z. A reader's guide brings terms together under broader headings such as Global and International Aspects of Corporate Reputation; Legal, Moral, Ethical and Social Issues; Reputation and the Environment; and Reputation Contents and Dimensions. Specific companies and individuals do not have separate article entries but are covered in the context of the relevant issues such as reputation gap or reputation crisis and are listed in the index. Appendixes provide: "A History of Corporate Reputation" with a chronology; a "Resource Guide" covering books, edited collections, key journals, research centers, degree programs, and associations; "Most Cited Articles on Corporate Reputation by Academic Discipline"; "Mapping the Phenomenon of Reputation"; and "Key References." Highly recommended for academic as well as other large research and corporate libraries.—**Colleen Seale**

Directories

60. **The Directory of Business Information Resources, 2017.** 24th ed. Amenia, N.Y., Grey House Publishing, 2017. 1876p. index. $195.00pa. ISBN 13: 978-1-68217-341-1.

The Directory of Business Information Resources, now in its 24th edition, covers over 102 industries with resource listings for each including associations, directories, databases, and trade shows. This new edition has added a chapter covering national security and international affairs with updates across all chapters. Among the wide range of industries covered are: Environment and Conservation; Motor Vehicles; Pharmaceutical Drugs and Devices; Telecommunications; Healthcare; Engineering; Financial Services; Computers and Data Processing; Aviation and Aerospace; and Motion Pictures. The guide includes the directory information plus indexes for entry names and publishers. A Content Summary of Chapter Listings shows subjects covered in each industry chapter; for example, the chapter on public relations includes the following subjects: career skills press, consumer affairs, and public affairs. Included also are cross-reference tables for NAICS and SIC codes. Each entry contains: record number, title, address, phone number, toll-free number, fax number, e-mail, website, key executives, description, members, year founded, frequency, subscription price, circulation (if listing is a publication), schedules special issues (if listing is a magazine), attendees (if listing is a trade show), and month (if listing is a trade show). Listings for many associations, in addition to providing the URL, include coverage on social media (Facebook, Twitter, Google+, LinkedIn, etc.). *The Directory of Business Information Resources* is a highly recommended guide to locating industry information resources and can be used as a starting point to research, as a place to obtain data and information, and for librarians building a collection on specific industries and/or preparing subject guides. This resource is highly recommended to academic, public, and special libraries.—**Lucy Heckman**

Handbooks and Yearbooks

61.   **Business Rankings Annual, 2018: Lists of Companies, Products, Services, and Activities.** Farmington Hills, Mich., Gale/Cengage Learning, 2017. 4v. index. (Business Rankings Annual Series). $710.00/set. ISBN 13: 978-1-4103-2616-4.

Business Rankings Annual provides approximately 5,000 rankings for companies, products, services, and activities and lists the top 10 in each of the rankings categories. The data is compiled from print and online sources and the 2018 edition "draws most of its entries from serials and periodicals published between July 2016 and June 2017." The bibliography lists the approximately 400 original sources used to compile the data found in *Business Rankings Annual.* Each entry in the citation includes: publication name; publisher; address, telephone, fax number and URL; frequency of publication; price; and ISSN, if applicable. The lists of top 10 rankings are grouped by subject and arranged alphabetically. Subject headings are from the Library of Congress Subject Heading list; if no appropriate or up-to-date heading was available from the Library of Congress, headings were taken from *Wilson Business Periodicals Index* and ABI/INFORM, a CD-ROM index from UMI. A wide variety of subjects are covered including: leading actuaries; highest paid MLS Soccer players; world's most admired beverage companies; top pretzel brands; and top U.S. companies for executive women. Each entry includes sequential entry number; ranking title (e.g., Largest Global Insurance Brokers); ranked by (describes criteria that establishes the hierarchy—e.g., number of paid admissions, revenue, etc); remarks (additional details); number listed (number of listees from source of data); top 10 items on list; and source, with complete bibliographic details. Also included in *Business Rankings Annual* are an outline of contents (with cross-references) and the index of companies, people, and products that appear on the lists with their entry numbers. In addition to the 2018 listings, the resource comes with a three-volume cumulative index covering the years 1989-2018. The index is by name of companies, products, and people and each entry contains the years covered and entry numbers within each year. *Business Rankings Annual* should be a staple publication for libraries supporting undergraduates and advanced degree programs in business schools. It also is a starting point for further research in company and industry information. Its ranking of companies in specific fields also should prove helpful to job seekers. And it can give "quick reference" data for those who wish to find, for example, the 10 highest paid celebrities. A highly recommended resource for academic, public, and research libraries.—**Lucy Heckman**

62.   **Business Statistics of the United States 2017: Patterns of Economic Change.** 22d ed. Susan Ockert, ed. Lanham, Md., Bernan Press, 2018. 496p. index. $175.00. ISBN 13: 978-1-59888-948-2; 978-1-59888-949-9 (e-book).

Business Statistics of the United States is "a basic desk reference for anyone requiring statistics on the U.S. economy. It contains more than 3000 economic time series portraying the period from World War II to December 2016 in industry, product and demographic detail." Also there are some statistical series that have been compiled back to 1919 for industrial production and going back to 1913 for consumer and producer prices. Data was compiled from federal government resources. The preface describes the arrangement of the resource, the history of the publication, and how data was compiled. Also in the preface are essays on "Cycle and Growth Perspectives," "The U.S. Economy 1929-1948," "The

Great Recession 2007-2009 and Recovery 2010-2016," and "General Notes" describing the major divisions of the book and including a list of data sources (e.g., Bureau of Labor Statistics and Census Bureau). Part A., The U.S. Economy, is about the economy "as a whole" and is arranged by chapter containing primarily tables of data for National Income and Product; Industrial Production and Capacity Utilization; Income Distribution and Poverty; Consumer Income and Spending; Government; U.S. Foreign Trade and Finance; Prices; Employment, Hours and Earnings; Energy; Money, Interest, Assets, Liabilities, and Asset Prices; and International Comparisons. Part B., Industry Profiles, contains chapters on Product and Income by Industry; Employment, Hours, and Earnings by NAICS Industry; and Key Sector Statistics (e.g., Housing Starts, Retail and Food Services Sales, and Manufacturers' Inventories). "Notes and Definitions," included throughout the book, explain and define terms and include references to sources. An index by subject rounds out the book. *Business Statistics* is highly recommended to larger public libraries and academic libraries supporting business programs as a "quick reference source" and for extensive research projects.—**Lucy Heckman**

63. **Corporate Research Project. www.corp-research.org.** [Website] Free. Date reviewed: 2017.

This project aims to support the greater movement toward corporate accountability. While affiliated with Good Jobs First, which examines and upholds accountability standards within the companies that receive government subsidies, the aim of this site is to educate and support community, environmental, and labor organizations with broader research and helpful tools. Several features are accessible via the menu and along the right sidebar. The Guide to Corporate Research provides a detailed four-part outline for site users/organizations with which to begin their corporate research project. Selecting an outline item (e.g., media coverage) expands on how to approach the particular source of research. The outline informs users about "the Key Sources of Company Information," "Exploring a Company's Essential Relationships," and "Analyzing a Company's Accountability Record" and provides a generous listing of "Industry-Specific Sources." The Violation Tracker offers the "first national search engine on corporate misconduct." Users can conduct advance searches incorporating information such as violation type, year, regulatory agency, penalty, industry, and more. Corporate Rap Sheets include detailed reports on dozens of companies including Dow Chemical, Chevron, Volkswagen, Walmart, and Bank of America. The Dirt Diggers Digest shares blog posts on a number of topical issues such as creating jobs at the risk of environmental protection, or the current administration's deregulatory approach towards for-profit education. The site seems particularly attuned to the times, and its use of straightforward information and focus on education will be of genuine interest to its target audience.—**ARBA Staff Reviewer**

64. **Digital Entrepreneurship and Global Innovation.** Ioan Hosu and Ioana Iancu, eds. Hershey, Pa., Business Science Reference/IGI Global, 2017. 301p. index. (Advances in Business Strategy and Competitive Advantage (ABSCA)). $195.00. ISBN 13: 978-1-52250-953-0; 978-1-52250-954-7 (e-book).

This volume in the Advances in Business Strategy and Competitive Advantage (ABSCA) book series emphasizes the importance of digital technologies in helping to advance goals of innovative global business.

With backgrounds in economics, management, entrepreneurship, computer science, and more, the volume's diverse contributors show how the integration of entrepreneurial business strategies with digital innovation can work to enhance opportunities in the global market.

A preface and a detailed table of contents help lay out the volume's organization and explain its highly specialized focus. Twelve chapters then examine traditional business practices (collaboration, pitching, etc.), business education (institutional, e-learning, etc.), and more through the lens of innovation and digitization. Chapters discuss such concepts as cloud computing, competitive intelligence, and neuromarketing and relate them to the development of the family business ("Entrepreneurship and Innovation in Latin American Family Firms: The Case of Mexico"), global change ("Digital Entrepreneurial Charity and Solidarity for Social Change: KIVA and the 'Social-on-linezation' of Poverty"), the development of youth entrepreneurship ("Pitching and the Other International Practices of Innovation Competitions: Channel for Youth Entrepreneurship"), and more.

Each chapter opens with an abstract to establish the impetus and methodology of the research that follows. Chapters may be organized into well-defined sections and make generous use of headers, subheaders, bullet points, illustrations, key terms and definitions, and other tools. References are listed at the end of each chapter and compiled again at the end of the book, alongside brief contributor biographies and an index.

Readers of this volume may also be interested in the *Case Studies as a Teaching Tool in Management Education*—another volume in the ABSCA series The material in this volume would likely appeal to educators and students in the business, marketing, and entrepreneurship fields.—**ARBA Staff Reviewer**

65.   **Economic Indicators. https://www.census.gov/economic-indicators/.** [Website] Free. Date reviewed: 2017.

This page from the larger U.S. Census site provides a listing of 15 economic indicators tracked by the census. Indicators include Advance Monthly Sales for Retail and Food Services; Advance Report on Durable Goods, Manufacturers' Shipments, Inventories and Orders; Advance U.S. International Trade in Goods; Homeownership Rate; Manufacturers' Shipments, Inventories and Orders, Manufacturing and Trade Inventories and Sales; Monthly Wholesale Trade; New Residential Construction; New Residential Sales; Quarterly Financial Report—Manufacturing, Mining, Wholesale Trade and Selected Service Industries; Quarterly Financial Report—Retail Trade; Quarterly Services Survey; Rental Vacancy Rate; U.S. International Trade in Goods and Services; and the Value of Construction Put in Place/Construction Spending.

Each indicator is marked by an icon and listed with a general description, available viewing/downloading formats, release dates, and monthly comparisons. Clicking on an indicator will generally display an overview, links to the full report, tables, FAQs, related indicators, related information (such as historical data), and additional census resources, such as definitions. While the presentation of each indicator's information is different, users will generally find similar coverage. The green menu bar offers users the option to select the 2017 or 2016 Economic Indicator Calendar showing a listing (or calendar view) of release dates and times for all indicators.

Business professionals, educators, and students of the American economy will appreciate the direct presentation and generous information on this focused site. Highly recommended for public, school, and academic libraries.—**ARBA Staff Reviewer**

66. **The Economics of Standards.** Albert N. Link, ed. Northampton, Mass., Edward Elgar, 2016. 738p. (The International Library of Critical Writings in Economics). $390.00. ISBN 13: 978-1-78471-731-5.

This volume, no. 312 in Elgar's International Library of Critical Writings in Economics series, examines the nature, importance, and multitudinous effect of standards on not only the production and pricing of manufactured products but also the linkages that make our interlocking electronic systems work. Editor Albert N. Link of the University of North Carolina at Greensboro, a leading scholar in the field, has assembled 34 articles from scholarly journals on standards: how they are set, their economic implications, the relationship of standards to computer sciences and technology diffusion, governmental and public involvement in setting standards, and more. Link's introduction makes the point that at a high level, there are two categories of standards—product-element standards and non-product-element standards. The former relate to only one element of a product, such as the structure of a computer's operating system, while the latter refers to such things as the standards and test methods used to measure the operating system's performance. The chapters in part one, An Overview of Standards, discuss the history and processes of standard setting, comparability standards, and the social benefits and costs of the application of standards. Part two, Competition and Standards, looks at standards from an industrial organization perspective. The chapters in part three, Standards and Technology Diffusion, cover standards in relation to advanced technologies, with an emphasis on communications. Part four deals with Standards and Computer-Related Technologies, part five offers Case Studies on Standards, and the chapters in part six investigate Public Involvement in Standards Development. The articles are reprinted from the journals in which they were originally published, and thus vary in style and the presentation of reference material. All have notes and references, and many chapters include graphs and tables, some extremely complex. This book is not for the layman or the beginning student of economics. As Link notes in his introduction, "the set of scholars who have advanced intellectual thought about the economics of standards is relatively small." However, as the world becomes more integrated, standards assume an ever more important role in the global economy and in the policies that govern it. Recommended for academic libraries.—**ARBA Staff Reviewer**

67. **FRED. https://fred.stlouisfed.org/.** [Website] Free. Date reviewed: 2017.

This site from the Federal Reserve of St. Louis (eighth district of the United States Federal Reserve system), offers a wealth of economic data within the general areas of Money & Banking, Macroeconomics, and International & Regional Economics. Users can study over 500,000 U.S. and international series from 87 diverse sources (such as Bank of England, Bank of America Merrill Lynch, U.S. Council of Economic Advisors, etc.) in addition to a vast research archive of working papers, essays, and more.

For data, users can conduct a basic search from the prominent search bar, or browse data by Tag, Category, Release, Source, etc. Users can also select featured data from the At a Glance, Popular Series, and Latest Releases tabs near the bottom of the page.

Selecting a data series will display the particular chart/graph identified with observation date, units, frequency, and source. Users can edit the graphic to display different time ranges. The graphic is accompanied by Notes (which may offer a narrative description, suggested Citation, etc.) and a listing of Related Content which can be quite extensive and include such items as charts, blog posts, journal articles, and podcasts. Data series are downloadable, constantly updated, and include Consumer Price Index, Civilian Unemployment Rate, Personal Consumption Expenditures, Real Median Household Income U.S., Corporate Profits After Tax, Lightweight Vehicle Sales, Existing Home Sales, GDP for Japan, and much, much more.

A number of tools can help users manage their preferred data, including the Microsoft Excel Add-In and My Data Lists (with free site registration). Users can also access further research materials such as Regional Reports, and Research Journals by clicking on the searchable Publications or Working Papers tabs on the menu bar.

Highly recommended for public and academic libraries.—**ARBA Staff Reviewer**

68.   **World Wealth and Income Database. www.wid.world/wid-world/.** [Website] Free. Date reviewed: 2017.

Available in several languages, this website tracks the development of global wealth distribution via a vast database examining a number of economic factors. The material is produced by an international team of scholars (details can be found in the FAQ link at the bottom of the home page). Users can examine a variety of charts and graphs pertaining to national and regional data, gathered primarily since the turn of the current century, across a number of indicators, including average income, average wealth, income inequality, and wealth inequality. Selecting the Data tab allows users access to singular information by indicator, county/region, and years. Users can also download a full data set or series. The Methodology tab offers an essay pointing to the varied data sources, systematic processes, and globally sourced research behind the current database, in addition to a library of technical notes, working papers, presentation slides, articles, and more, most downloadable as a PDF. The News tab features blog posts related to data updates and new research. Students of and practitioners within the global economy, policy-makers, educators, and others will appreciate the singular focus of this website, its sharp graphics, and commitment to the acquisition of the latest data.—**ARBA Staff Reviewer**

Consumer Guides

Handbooks and Yearbooks

69.   **Consumer Financial Protection Bureau. https://www.consumerfinance.gov/.** [Website] Free. Date reviewed: 2017.

Created as a result of the 2008 financial collapse, this government agency website offers consumer support and education regarding a host of financial practices and issues. Primarily, users can directly submit claims against companies they feel have not treated them fairly. Users also have access to a variety of tools and resources to enhance their own financial education. The site is simply structured. Users who have a specific complaint can click the Submit your Complaint button to access the generally straightforward process. Other users can select from a variety of drop-down topics focused around Consumer Tools, Educational Resources, Data & Research, and Policy & Compliance. Under the Consumer Tools tab, users will find information about particular financial situations, such as Getting an Auto Loan, Prepaid Cards, and Paying for College. Education Resources offers both site-based and external resources (libraries, industry professionals, etc.) for further financial education, such as worksheets, websites and brochures. The Data & Research tab consolidates and publishes complaint data and research on a variety of topics including mortgages, credit cards, and more. This section allows access to a monthly complaint report pointing to trends and other data. The site also publishes a blog covering a number of topical issues (e.g., debt collection) as well as the latest news from the agency. The generous and clear information on this site would be helpful to general users as well as specific consumer groups, such as students, veterans, retirees, and homeowners.—**ARBA Staff Reviewer**

70.   **Consumer Product Safety Commission. https://www.cpsc.gov/.** [Website] Free. Date reviewed: 2018.

In addition to offering a straightforward listing of recalled consumer products, the Recalls page of the Consumer Product Safety Commission (CPSC) connects users with additional resources regarding consumer safety. The recalls are the prominent feature, however, and users can conduct a basic product search to find recall information or can scroll down through the page display. Users will see the recall date, a photograph of the product, and basic information such as product flaw description, remedy, units sold, and consumer contact information. Clicking on the product link provides further information about the product importer, distributor, recall number, retailer, incident description, related recalls, and more. Other resources can be accessed through the Menu icon in the top right corner of the page, or through links at the bottom of the page. Users can link to international recall information via the Global Recall Portal tab, and can search extensive Product Safety Reports via its hyperlink. There is also a Research & Statistics link which displays a range of Injury Statistics and Technical Reports by Product Category (chemicals, kitchen & dining, public facilities & products, etc.) or Hazard Category (carbon monoxide, fire, pediatric poisoning, etc.) Users can also Search for Injury Estimates from the CPSC's National Electronic Injury Surveillance System database going back to 2009, and can find generous Safety Education Resources, Toy Recall Statistics, and a Violations database going back to 2013. The generous information on this site would appeal to consumers, product manufacturers and designers, policy makers, and others.—**ARBA Staff Reviewer**

71.   **Edmunds.com. https://www.edmunds.com/.** [Website] Free. Date reviewed: 2017.

Edmunds.com is a free to use and trusted source of used and new car information intended to serve those in the automotive industry, consumers, and journalists. Once a print publication, Edmunds.com launched online in 1995 (print publication ceased in 2006). Edmunds maintains a staff of PhDs, statisticians, and other experts tasked with analyzing the data behind Edmunds' True Market Value and True Cost to Own Projections and other services. Data is largely derived from automakers, dealers, and auto industry companies. The site updates some information daily; Edmunds updates other data monthly. Edmunds' funding comes from advertising and referral fees from insurance companies and dealers recommended by the site, among other sources. For those who want to know more about the company, there is a link under the FAQs at the bottom of the main page. The home page offers a variety of links under five main headings: New Cars, Used Cars, Car Types, Cars for Sale, and Research. There is also a place to create an account, which allows users to save and share research, get price alerts, and access buying experts. Links at the bottom of the page feature such things as calculators, car comparisons, selling tips, and more.—

ARBA Staff Reviewer

Finance and Banking

Directories

72.   **The Directory of Venture Capital & Private Equity Firms, 2017.** Amenia, N.Y., Grey House Publishing, 2017. 1442p. index. $395.00pa. ISBN 13: 978-4-68217-345-9.

The directory provides profiles of "more than 3,000 of the most active venture capital and private equity firms operating today. The directory is organized into four sections: Domestic Firms, Canadian Firms, International Firms, and National and State Associations; in each section, firms are arranged alphabetically. Five indexes are included: College/ University Index, an alphabetical list of 1,200 colleges and universities worldwide and the venture capitalist who attended them; the Executive Index of names of key partners and the listing number of their firm; the Geographic Index, of firms by state for domestic listings and by country for international listings; the Industry Preference Index, listing over 700 industry segment and names of firms investing in them; and the Portfolio Companies Index, listing more than 40,000 companies that received venture capital from a listed firm. Each entry in the directory sections contains: name of company, address, phone, fax, website, mission statement, geographic preference, fund size, year founded, average investment, investment criteria, industry group preference, portfolio companies, other components, and key executives (with email address, education, and background). Also included is an introduction which contains a user guide, user key to directory information, and statistical charts and graphs among which are: "Venture Fundraising Increases During 4Q 2016"; Largest Venture Capital Funds Raised in 4Q 2016"; "U.S. Venture Investment in 4Q 2016 Decreases"; and "Equity Financings Into U.S.-Based, Venture Capital-Backed Companies by Round Class (Quarter over Quarter, 2013-2016)." In addition is KPMG Enterprise's Global Analysis of Global Funding. *The Directory of Venture Capital & Private Equity Firms* is a comprehensive guide and directory and is an excellent guide to those seeking the best firm to suit their needs. Especially helpful is the index that arranges the firms by industry group preference making it easier for entrepreneurs and business owners to readily locate relevant venture capital and private equity firms. It is recommended to academic libraries that support a business school or program; larger public libraries should consider purchasing this title.—**Lucy Heckman**

Handbooks and Yearbooks

73.   **Cash and Credit Information for Teens.** 3d ed. Keith Jones, ed. Detroit, Omnigraphics, 2017. 350p. index. (Teen Finance Series). $62.00. ISBN 13: 978-0-7808-1551-3.

Cash and Credit Information for Teens delivers an outstanding message on financial issues and provides guidance for avoiding financial pitfalls. Advertisements serve as lures and incentives to make purchases on impulse. Many teens find it difficult to resist temptations motivated by enticing advertisement campaigns. Bad decisions are further enabled by handheld devices, laptops, and credit cards that make financial transactions simple, quick, and convenient. The result—overextended budgets and substantial debt. To make matters worse, the preface states that one in six American teenagers do not reach baseline level regarding financial literacy; a majority of parents, moreover, are reluctant to discuss financial issues with their teens.

This book provides an excellent format that attracts young readers. There are six basic parts: Earning Money, Managing Your Money, Managing Debt and Credit, Smart Spending, Avoiding Financial Pitfalls, and If You Need More Information; all information is presented in a reader-friendly format. Every high school, community college, and university should consider adding this book to resource collections. Library acquisition decision makers will also consider this contribution appropriate for their teen resource center.—**Thomas E. Baker**

74.   Leo, David, and Craig Cmiel. **The Financial Advisor's Success Manual: How to Structure and Grow Your Financial Services Practice.** New York, AMACOM/ American Management Association, 2018. 276p. index. $30.00. ISBN 13: 978-0-8144-3913-5; 978-0-8144-3914-2 (e-book).

The Financial Advisor's Success Manual is "designed for financial advisors (FAs) who want to grow their business by bringing organization and structure to their practices." The authors' goal is to "help advisors define and implement a set of processes that will save them time and energy while 'ensuring' their clients are well serviced, so little if anything falls through the cracks throughout the life of the client-adviser relationship." Additionally, the intent of the book "is to describe how to create both value and differentiation that is better than your competition." The authors draw on their expertise to offer practical advice: David Leo is a business coach and strategic consultant to financial advisors and his financial industry experience includes over seven years in Paine Webber's private client group. Craig Cmiel is cofounder and managing partner of Great Lakes and Atlantic Wealth Management and Advisory Partners. The book's chapters are: "Develop Your Differentiation Strategy"; "Formal Book Segmentation"; "The Client Loyalty Process"; "But What's the Cost of Loyalty?"; "Your Intake Process"; "Your Client Planning and Review Process"; "Your Business Plan"; "Metrics: Daily Game Plan"; "Business Development"; and the "Benefits of Implementation." These chapters cover such topics as how to attract and retain clients, how to develop a business plan, and much more. The book also includes bibliographical notes, tables, worksheets, and an index. *The Financial Advisor's Success Manual* presents practical advice and guidance for practitioners, potential business owners, and students of business. Recommended especially to public library collections.—**Lucy Heckman**

75.   **Principles of Business: Finance.** Richard Wilson, ed. Hackensack, N.J., Salem Press, 2017. 330p. index. $165.00. ISBN 13: 978-1-68217-328-2; 978-1-68217-329-9 (e-book).

This title is the first of six volumes planned for a new series Principles of Business from Salem Press. The resource is meant to be an introduction to fundamentals of finance in an easy-to-understand format. The editor is Richard Wilson from the University of Tennessee at Chattanooga. There are several contributors from scholars to experts in business according to the publisher. However, that is not exactly true as you will find an anthropologist and others from various backgrounds, but the editor explains the reasoning for that in the introduction. There are short biographies for each of the contributors except for the editor.

The book has a standard format—table of contents, introduction, and entries followed by a glossary and an index. The table of contents makes it is easy to navigate the book. Since the subject area is so broad, it is difficult to know what topics are included or how they are arranged without it. The introductory content does a good job of explaining the layout. Compared to other finance titles, this book is comparable in the subjects covered. Unfortunately, the index does not include all the times that a topic is covered or it leaves things out entirely. For example, the entry for Financial Incentives includes a picture of Abraham Maslow. He must be important enough to warrant a picture, but he is not listed in the index.

The title gives a nice overview of finance. The entries are formatted similarly with an abstract, overview, application, and conclusion with some entries varying in format. They also have sections for a bibliography and suggested readings. There are a few pictures and diagrams. It might be nice if there were more visuals, as this book is very text heavy, but it does not take away from the content. Overall, this title would be useful to researchers or general users looking for basic information about finance. Undergraduate students would probably benefit the most.—**Breezy Silver**

76. **Savings and Investment Information for Teens.** 3d ed. Keith Jones, ed. Detroit, Omnigraphics, 2017. 362p. index. (Teen Finance Series). $69.00. ISBN 13: 978-0-7808-1553-7.

While teens can be hard to reach, the teenage years are the perfect time to teach young people about saving, spending, earning, and investing habits. This book, broken into five parts, offers a format that attracts young readers. The parts are: How the Economy Works, Keys to Wealth Development, Banks and Bonds, Stocks and Mutual Funds, and If You Need More Information. The language used is age appropriate and information is presented in a logical progression of nonthreatening concepts and clearly explained terminology. Meaningful observations and question/answer formats that convey teen money management practices may result in rewarding financial futures. This hardbound book also offers a directory of saving and investment organizations and additional resources for saving and investing. This book may serve as the basis for an important conversation with teenagers and may help them avoid financial disasters from which it would take years to recover, especially now that technology has accelerated the pace at which financial decisions must be made. Recommended for high school, public, and academic libraries.—**Thomas E. Baker**

77. **Weiss Ratings Financial Literacy Basics.** Amenia, N.Y., Grey House Publishing, 2017. 8v. index. $359.00/set. ISBN 13: 978-1-68217-614-6.

Financial Literacy Basics is a new series from Grey House Publishing and Weiss Ratings; each volume "provides readers with easy-to-understand guidance on how to manage their finances." The eight titles in the series are: *Guide to Understanding Health Insurance Plans; How to Make and Stick to a Budget; How to Manage Debt; Starting a 401 (k); Tips for Paying Back Student Loans; Understanding Renters Insurance; What to Know about Auto Insurance;* and *What to Know about Checking Accounts.* Each brief and to-the-point title uses a step-by-step approach and includes graphs to emphasize the various steps, as well as worksheets. A listing of Weiss' ratings and recommendations is included as a helpful guide. For instance in the publication *What to Know about Auto Insurance,* the volume lists Weiss' Ratings Recommended Auto Insurers by State; these insurers receive a Weiss Safety Rating of A+, A, A-, or B+. For each recommended company the name, address, and telephone number are listed. Appendixes include resources for further information, an explanation of the Weiss ratings system, and a glossary of terms. Specifics for each topic are covered and explained clearly and concisely in all the volumes. For example, *What to Know About Checking Accounts* defines what a checking account is, the benefits, how to choose a bank, types of checking accounts, overdraft fees, how to open a checking account, how to balance the account, electronic transfers, and how to use the check register. This is a highly recommended source for consumers and it can be used for young people or for anybody who needs guidance in the area of financial literacy. Public libraries should consider keeping this series in their reference departments and those teaching financial literacy classes should definitely consult this series.—**Lucy Heckman**

78.   **Weiss Ratings Guide to Banks, Spring 2017.** Amenia, N.Y., Grey House Publishing, 2017. 312p. index. $249.00pa. (single edition); $449.00pa. (4 quarterly editions). ISBN 13: 978-1-68217-407-4.

The stated purpose of the *Weiss Ratings Guide to Banks* is "to provide consumers, businesses, financial institutions, and municipalities with a reliable source of banking industry ratings and analysis on a timely basis." For instance those contemplating dealing with a specific bank can obtain assistance by consulting Weiss ratings and analysis. Weiss ratings are "calculated based on a complex analysis of hundreds of factors that are synthesized into five indexes": Capitalization, Asset Quality, Profitability, Liquidity, and Stability. The Capitalization Index "gauges the institution's capital adequacy in terms of its cushion to absorb future operating losses under adverse business and economic scenarios"; the Asset Quality Index is a measure of the company's past underwriting and investment practices "based on the estimated liquidation value of the company's loan and securities portfolios"; the Profitability Index "measures the soundness of the company's operations and the contribution of profits to the company's financial strength"; the Liquidity Index "evaluates a company's ability to raise the necessary cash to satisfy creditors and honor depositor withdrawals"; and the Stability Index examines some "subfactors" that affect consistency maintaining financial strength over time and the factors include risk diversification in terms of company size and loan diversification, number of years in operation, and relationships with holding companies and affiliates. Weiss ratings of banks are A. Excellent; B. Good; C. Fair; D. Weak; E. Very Weak; F. Failed; and U. Unrated. A plus sign indicates it is in the upper third of the letter grade and the minus sign indicates it is in the lower third. Section one of the guide contains an alphabetical list of banks and each contains the bank's institution name, city where main office is located, state, safety rating, prior year safety rating, safety rating two years prior, total assets, asset growth, commercial loans/total assets, consumer loans/total assets; home mortgage loans/total assets, capitalization index, leverage ratio, risk-based capital ratio, asset quality index, adjusted nonperforming loans/total loans, adjusted nonperforming loans/ capital, net charge-offs/average loans, profitability index, net income, return on assets, return on equity, net interest spread, overhead efficiency ratio, liquidity ratio, hot money ratio, and stability index. In the introductory notes, each data category is explained by the editors. Section two contains Weiss Recommended Banks by State: A Compilation of U.S. Commercial Banks and Savings Banks receiving a Weiss safety rating of A+, A, A-, or

B+. Banks are listed by state with the city, name, and telephone numbers included. Section three contains a list of Rating Upgrades and Downgrades: A List of all U.S. Commercial Banks and Savings Banks receiving a rating upgrade or downgrade during the current quarter. The appendix includes a list of recent bank failures by year, a description on how banks and credit unions differ; and a glossary. The *Weiss Ratings Guide to Banks* is a thorough, excellent source of performances of banks and their ratings by Weiss. It is highly recommended to practitioners and consumers as well as to faculty and students of business schools. Recommended to public and academic libraries.—**Lucy Heckman**

79.   **Weiss Ratings Guide to Credit Unions, Spring 2017.** Amenia, N.Y., Grey House Publishing, 2017. 310p. index. $249.00pa. (single edition); $449.00pa. (4 quarterly editions). ISBN 13: 978-1-68217-445-6.

The stated purpose of the *Guide to Credit Unions* is "to provide consumers, businesses, financial institutions, and municipalities with a reliable source of industry ratings and analysis on a timely basis." Each credit union is given a Weiss rating which consists of: A. Excellent; B. Good; C. Fair; D. Weak; E. Very Weak; F. Failed; and U. Unrated. A plus sign indicates the credit union is in the upper third of the letter grade and the minus sign that it is in the lower third. Weiss ratings are calculated based on indexes for capitalization asset quality, liquidity, and stability. The guide is arranged within three sections: Index of Credit Unions, listed in alphabetical order; Weiss Recommended Credit Unions by State that receive ratings of A+, A, A -, or B+; and Rating Upgrades and Downgrades. Each section includes explanatory information including how indexes are calculated. Each entry in the first section contains: institution name, city, state, safety rating, prior year safety rating, safety rating two years prior, total assets, one year asset growth, commercial loans/ total assets, consumer loans/total assets, home mortgage loans/total assets, securities/total assets, capitalization index, net worth ratio, asset quality index, nonperforming loans/ total loans, nonperforming loans/capital, net charge-offs/average loans, profitability index, net income, return on assets, return on equity, net interest spread, overhead efficiency ratio, liquidity index, liquidity ratio, hot money ratio, and stability index. Section two includes entries for "best rated" credit unions, with entries arranged by state and city with name of organization and telephone number. Section three lists all credit agencies (name of organization, state, and exact date of ratings change) receiving a rating upgrade or downgrade during the current quarter. The appendix includes tables of recent credit union failures, an explanation on how banks and credit unions differ, and a glossary of terms. The guide contains a wide range of data on credit unions and ratings to assist consumers. Faculty and students in business degree programs should also benefit. Recommended to academic and public libraries.—**Lucy Heckman**

Industry and Manufacturing

Dictionaries and Encyclopedias

80.   **Encyclopedia of Tourism.** Jafar Jafari and Honggen Xiao, eds. New York, Springer Publishing, 2016. 1054p. maps. $729.00. ISBN 13: 978-3-319-01384-8.

More than 700 contributions by 766 international experts from 113 countries comprise this edition which covers tourism, hospitality, recreation, and related fields. Routledge published the first edition of this title in 2000, under the editorship of Jafar Jafari (see ARBA 2001, entry 146). In light of copyright concerns, all entries in this edition are new. In addition to the new entries, the encyclopedia boasts other changes. For instance, the latest UN member states appear as country entries. Not included are geographic territories under dispute or territories without UN recognition. The encyclopedia is international, and the editorial policy of limiting authors to one entry (in most cases) furthers this goal. Ninety-five percent of the entries are written by academics.

The purpose of the book is "to act as a guide and updated source of reference to a wide range of basic definitions, theories and concepts, disciplines and fields of studies, themes and issues, methods and approaches, products and sectors, organizations and associations, media and publications, as well as countries and world regions contributing to, or embraced by, tourism in its disparate manifestations" (vii-viii). In achieving this end, the editorial team adhered to two guiding principles: to make this reference as comprehensive and updated as possible and to gather a more international and culturally diverse team of authors.

The entries are arranged in a traditional A to Z format and are either 500 (+/-), 1,000 (+/-), or 2,000 (+/-) words in length. The shorter entries have 3 to 5 cross-references. One-thousand-word entries include 5 to 7 references, and 2,000-word entries end with 7 to 10 references. The longer entries have in-text subdivisions. All entries have a headword title, brief definitional introduction, discussion, and prospective closure. There are 9 types of entries: concept/theory, discipline/field of study, country/region, issue-based, method/methodology, product, sector, organization/association, and journal/publication/media.

Tourism is a fast-growing academic discipline. This encyclopedia answers the need for a foundational text. It is intended for a variety of users from students to instructional staff to research scholars along with policy makers, consultants, practitioners, and anyone involved in the world's largest industry. As such, it is highly recommended for all academic libraries.—**ARBA Staff Reviewer**

Handbooks and Yearbooks

81.   **Fashion and Textiles: Breakthroughs in Research and Practice.** Edited by Information Resources Management Association. Hershey, Pa., IGI Global, 2018. 540p. index. $345.00. ISBN 13: 978-1-52253-432-7; 978-1-52253-433-4 (e-book).

This book documents the challenging landscape that surrounds the current fashion and textile industry, and provides a review of the critical issues on cutting-edge theories and developments. It is divided into four major sections containing 23 chapters: Consumer Engagement and CRM; Digital Innovation; Education, Ethics, and Management; and Manufacturing and Logistics. Issues discussed include sustainable fashion consumption, virtual reality in fashion retail, managing and influencing customer behavior, fashion retail innovation, brand personality and social status, marketing and design, supply chain and logistical processes, green strategies, electrotextiles, and globalization and diversification, to name just a few. This book is a wealth of information on breakthroughs in research and practice for this industry, and I highly recommend to those libraries which have specialized collections or researchers in this area.—**Bradford Lee Eden**

Insurance

Handbooks and Yearbooks

82.   **Weiss Ratings Guide to Health Insurers, Spring 2017.** Amenia, N.Y., Grey House Publishing, 2017. 516p. index. $249.00pa. (single edition); $499.00pa. (4 quarterly editions). ISBN 13: 978-1-68217-419-7.

This guide provides "policyholders and prospective policy purchasers with a reliable source of insurance company ratings and analyses on a timely basis." The guide is designed to assist in evaluation of medical reimbursement insurance, managed health care (PPOs and HMOs), disability income, and long-term care (nursing home) insurance; ratings are included for Blue Cross Blue Shield plans and for-profit and not-for-profit insurers. Weiss safety ratings of insurers are based on indexes of: capital, investment safety, reserve adequacy, profitability, liquidity, and stability. Ratings are: A. Excellent; B. Good; C. Fair; D. Weak; E. Very Weak; F. Failed; and U. Unrated. A plus sign indicates the rating is in the upper third of the letter grade and a minus sign indicates the grade is in the lower third. An explanatory preface describes how Weiss ratings differ from those of other rating services and how to interpret data and ratings. The guide is arranged in eight sections. Section one, Index of Companies, analyzes 1,488 rated and unrated U.S. health insurers in alphabetical order. Section two, Analysis of Largest Companies, is a summary analysis of all rated U.S. health plans and Blue Cross Blue Shield Plans plus other U.S. insurers with capital in excess of $25 million and health insurance premiums equaling at least 25% of total premiums; companies are listed in alphabetic order. Section three, Weiss Recommended Companies, compiles in alphabetic order those U.S. health insurers receiving a Weiss safety rating of A+, A, A-, or B+. Section four, Weiss Recommended Companies by State, is a summary analysis of those U.S. health insurers receiving a Weiss Safety Rating of A+, A, A-, or B+; companies are ranked by safety rating in each state where they are licensed to do business; Section five, Long-Term Care Insurers, lists rated companies providing long-term care insurance, with companies listed in alphabetical order; section six, Medicare Supplement Insurance, includes answers to questions about Medigap and information about Medigap premium rates. Section seven, Analysis of Medicare Managed Care Complaints, provides an analysis of complaints filed against U.S. Medicare Managed Care Plans; companies are listed in alphabetical order. Section eight, Rating Upgrades and Downgrades, is a list of all U.S. health insurers receiving a rating upgrade or downgrade during the current quarter. An appendix includes analysis of indicators used in rating companies, a long-term care insurance planner; recent industry failures; and a glossary of terms. Each company analysis includes name, address, telephone number, rating, major rating factors, principal business, provider compensation, and where licensed. This ratings guide offers a wealth of information about health insurers and offers analysis as well as practical advice to consumers. Libraries supporting a program in insurance, risk management, and actuarial analysis need to purchase this. Recommended for academic and public libraries.—**Lucy Heckman**

83.   **Weiss Ratings Guide to Life and Annuity Insurers, Spring 2017.** Amenia, N.Y., Grey House Publishing, 2016. 300p. index. $249.00pa. (single edition); $499.00pa. (4 quarterly editions). ISBN 13: 978-1-61925-423-4.

The stated purpose of *Weiss Ratings Guide to Life and Annuity Insurers* is "to provide policyholders and prospective policy purchasers with a reliable source of insurance company ratings and analyses on a timely basis." Covered in this guide are life insurance, annuities, health insurance, guaranteed investment contracts (GICs) and other pension products; ratings for some Blue Cross Blue Shield Plans are also included. Ratings are based on indexes for: capital, investment safety, profitability, liquidity, and stability. The rating system is: A. Excellent; B. Good; C. Fair; D. Weak; E. Very Weak; F. Failed; and U. Unrated. The plus sign indicates the company is in the upper third of the letter grade and the minus sign indicates the lower third. The preface includes advice on how to use the guide and how Weiss ratings differ from those of other services. The guide is arranged in five sections. Section one, Index of Companies, is an analysis of all rated and unrated U.S. life and annuity insurers, companies listed in alphabetical order. Section two, Analysis of Largest Companies, provides a summary analysis of those U.S. life and annuity insurers with capital in excess of $25 million with companies listed in alphabetical order. Section three, Weiss Ratings Recommended Companies, is a compilation of those U.S. life and annuity insurers receiving a Weiss Safety Rating of A+, A, A, or B+, with companies listed in alphabetical order. Section four, Weiss Ratings Recommended Companies by State, is a compilation of those U.S. life and annuity insurers receiving a Weiss Safety Rating of A+, A A-, or B+, companies are ranked by safety rating in each state where they are licensed to do business. Section five, All Companies Listed by Rating, lists all rated and unrated U.S. life and annuity insurers, with companies ranked by Weiss Safety Rating and then listed alphabetically within each rating category. Section six, Rating Upgrades and Downgrades, lists all U.S. life and annuity insurers receiving a rating upgrade or downgrade during the current quarter. An appendix includes data on coverage of state guaranty funds; state commissioners' departmental phone numbers; recent industry failures; and a glossary of terms. Each analysis contains name, address, phone, domicile state, rating, major rating factors, principal business, where licensed, and group affiliation. This guide should be of use to consumers, researchers, and students and faculty of business schools. This is a "must have" for libraries supporting a program in insurance, risk management, and actuarial science.—**Lucy Heckman**

84.   **Weiss Ratings Guide to Property and Casualty Insurers.** Amenia, N.Y., Grey House Publishing, 2017. 424p. index. $249.00pa. (single edition); $499.00pa. (4 quarterly editions). ISBN 13: 978-1-68217-431-9.

This is a guide for consumers who need to choose a property and casualty insurance company for themselves, their families, their companies, or their clients. This guide provides ratings and analyses for over 2,400 property and casualty insurers. Analyzed are insurers providing coverage for homes, businesses, automobiles, workers' compensation, product liability, and medical malpractice and other professional liability insurance. Not included are companies that only provide life and health insurance or annuities. Weiss develops safety ratings based on "annual and quarterly financial statements obtained from state insurance commissioners. Ratings are based on five indexes for capital, investment safety, reserve adequacy, profitability, liquidity, and stability. Letter ratings are as follows: A. Excellent; B. Good; C. Fair; D. Weak; E. Very Weak; F. Failed; and U. Unrated. A plus sign indicates the rating is in the upper third of letter grade and a minus sign indicates the lower third. The guide is arranged in seven sections. Section one, Index of Companies, provides analysis of all rated and unrated U.S. property and casualty insurers, companies listed in alphabetical order. Section two, Analysis of Largest Companies, is a summary analysis of Weiss recommended U.S. property and casualty insurers, along with the largest companies based on capital and surplus, companies listed in alphabetical order. Section three, Weiss Recommended Companies, is a compilation of those U.S. property and casualty insurers receiving a Weiss safety rating of A+, A, A- or B+., companies listed in alphabetical order. Section four, Weiss Recommended Companies by Type of Business, compiles those U.S. property and casualty insurers receiving a Weiss safety rating of A+, A, A-, or B+, companies ranked by safety rating in each line of business where they have received more than one million in direct premiums. Section five, Weiss Recommended Companies by State, includes companies receiving a Weiss Safety Rating of A+, A, A- or B+. Section six is All Companies Listed by Rating, and section seven, Rating Upgrades and Downgrades, is a list of all property and casualty insurers receiving a rating upgrade or downgrade during the current quarter. An appendix includes state insurance commissioners' departmental contact information, recent industry failures, and a glossary of terms. Each entry in section one includes: insurance company name, domicile state, safety rating, total assets, capital and surplus, net premium, net income, capitalization index, reserve adequacy index, profitability index, liquidity index, stability index, stability factors, risk-adjusted capital ratio, premium to surplus, reserves to surplus, one-year reserve development, two-year reserve development, loss ratio, expense ratio, combined ratio, cash from underwriting, net premium growth, and investments in affiliates. *The Weiss Ratings Guide to Property and Casualty Insurers* analyzes and rates insurers enabling consumers to compare and contrast. Recommended especially to libraries supporting a program in insurance, risk management, and actuarial sciences and also to larger public library business collections.—**Lucy Heckman**

International Business

Dictionaries and Encyclopedias

85.   Sullivan, Lawrence R., and Paul Curcio. **Historical Dictionary of the Chinese Economy.** Lanham, Md., Rowman & Littlefield, 2018. 476p. (Historical Dictionaries of Asia, Oceania, and the Middle East). $115.00; $109.00 (e-book). ISBN 13: 978-1-5381-0853-6; 978-1-5381-0854-3 (e-book).

This first edition is authored by Lawrence R. Sullivan, Professor Emeritus at Adelphi University and author of several books and articles on China, and Paul Curcio, contributor to several financial news publications. The book begins with a list of abbreviations and acronyms followed by a chronology that starts in 206 B.C.E. and runs through March 2017. The introduction is significantly shorter than what readers of other titles in the various historical dictionaries series have come to expect, but this is because the more-narrow-than-usual focus is on the Chinese economy since 1949. The introduction is divided into parts that include the era of economic reform, starting in 1978, economic problems and issues, and prospects and outlook. Nearly four hundred entries comprise the heart of the book. Entries vary in length. The entry for a complex, important, and broad topic like agriculture covers approximately eleven pages while the four modernizations are covered in one paragraph. The authors make generous use of *see* and *see also* references. The book concludes with a glossary, a list of chairmen, general secretaries, premiers, and state chairmen/presidents since 1943, the U.S. ambassadors to China since 1979, and a bibliography separated into sections. China is currently the world's largest exporter and the world's second-largest economy (and growing). It has increased its economic standing in the world; consequently, China's military and political might is also on the upswing. Therefore, this book is an important resource for those wanting to learn more about the economic structure of this prominent nation. Recommended for academic and public libraries.—**ARBA Staff Reviewer**

Handbooks and Yearbooks

86. **Factors Affecting Firm Competitiveness and Performance in the Modern Business World.** Aspasia Vlachvei, Kostas Karantininis, and Nicholas Tsounis, eds. Hershey, Pa., Business Science Reference/IGI Global, 2017. 359p. index. (Advances in Business Strategy and Competitive Advantage Book Series). $195.00. ISBN 13: 978-1-52250-843-4; 978-1-52250-844-1 (e-book).

Factors Affecting Firm Competitiveness and Performance in the Modern Business World incorporates interdisciplinary perspectives through theoretical foundations and real-world case studies. Businesspersons concerned with the bottom line will conclude that this book represents entrepreneurial value. This informative book is on the cutting-edge of international business operations. Continuous re-evaluation and optimization of existing economic and business policies and practices facilitate growth and expansion. Implementing effective procedures and business activities can increase levels of competitiveness. This superior resource offers strategic pathways to accomplishing business goals and objectives. Questions regarding the key dimensions of firm competitiveness and the appropriate measures and practices to identify and achieve effective and innovative business models that lead to competitiveness are addressed. This book discusses such academic areas as competitor networks, joint ventures, and social media applications. The inclusion of graphs/charts, a glossary, and an index enhance the work. *Factors Affecting Firm Competitiveness and Performance in the Modern Business World* is perfect for professionals, practitioners, upper-level students, policy-makers, and managers interested in the optimization of business performance. Academics and others will appreciate a book that covers the most important parts and elements of firm competitiveness and combines different disciplines relevant to this topic. University libraries and business schools will value this book as an essential addition to their reference shelves.—**Thomas E. Baker**

Labor

Dictionaries and Encyclopedias

87. Encyclopedia of Careers and Vocational Guidance. New York, Infobase Publishing, 2017. 6v. $299.95/set. ISBN 13: 978-0-8160-8514-9.

The *Encyclopedia of Careers and Vocational Guidance* is a mammoth publication. In six volumes, this encyclopedia provides a treasure trove of insight that will help quiet uncertainty and offer guideposts for positive career decision transitions. The volumes embody a complete career reference center that supports individuals (reading level nine and up) seeking guidance and preparation. The first volume serves as preparation for the process of finding and applying for a job. Volumes two to six offer nearly one thousand career articles, listed from A to Z. This set represents a significant source of contemporary information in easy-to-understand language. This important resource is necessary for professionals who help youth make complex education-to-work choices and will be useful for university career centers, counseling centers, public libraries, secondary schools, guidance counselors, and job seekers. Highly recommended.—**Thomas E. Baker**

Handbooks and Yearbooks

88. American Salaries and Wages Survey. 14th ed. Joyce P. Simkin, ed. Farmington Hills, Mich., Gale/Cengage Learning, 2017. 1774p. $377.00. ISBN 13: 978-1-4103-2236-4.

American Salaries and Wages Survey (ASWS) "is a compilation of 2,226 occupational combinations (2,754 occupations) and their corresponding salaries obtained from 340 sources—federal, state, and city government, as well as various trade associations and journals." An Outline of Contents lists the primary occupational classifications covered in alphabetical order followed by a Geographical Outline of Contents that lists geographic locations down to the state level. Occupations are then presented. Entries include primary and secondary job titles, wage and geographic information, and more. There are several appendixes. "Sources" lists 340 organizations which contributed data and "Salary Conversion Tables" "translates an hourly wage into its weekly, monthly, and annual equivalents." The third appendix lists abbreviations, and the last is "Employment by Occupation."

American Salaries and Wages Survey is an excellent source for career centers and for job seekers. It is very useful to those considering relocation since it pinpoints salaries in states and cities in the United States. It is highly recommended to academic and public libraries and complements other statistical resources including the *Occupational Outlook Handbook*. The resource list is of great help to those needing to do further research.—**Lucy Heckman**

89. Bureau of Labor Statistics. https://www.bls.gov. [Website] Free. Date reviewed: 2018.

This site is a prime source for data, analysis, and general information on economic activity in the United States. The site covers a range of topics, updates relevant indicators, and presents national and regional information that would interest everyone from the beginning student of economics to the seasoned financial professional. Links at the top of the homepage help answer basic questions about the bureau, including About BLS (which includes a short video), a generous listing of FAQs, and an A-Z Index of economic terms and concepts. Throughout the rest of the homepage are myriad links that help organize the abundant information. From the menu bar, users can select from a wide range of Subjects within such broader categories as Inflation & Prices, Pay & Benefits, and Unemployment, Employment, and Productivity. Data Tools, such as Maps, Calculators, Series Reports, and Tables are available to use against individual data parameters, such as industry prices, regional employment hours and earnings, occupational projections, union affiliation, and work stoppages. There is also a good series of Publications including Research Papers, a Monthly Labor Review, and the Occupational Outlook Handbook, which covers a range of professional fields like architecture, healthcare, and the military. The Economic Releases tab presents a large amount of both historical and recent news releases regarding both broad (e.g., employment) and individual (e.g., real earnings) topics as mentioned under Subjects. Users can access Geographic Information from the Regional Homepage directory in the center of the page by choosing a State and/or Subject or selecting from one of eight regions (New England, Southeast, West, etc.). Users will be able to examine subjects and news releases particular to that region. The Students tab offers a good selection of K-12 resources—a glossary, videos, maps, games, among others—exploring careers and general economic information. Other features on the page include Spotlight on Statistics, a revolving data display currently examining African Americans in the labor force; Latest Numbers offering quick access to current data (Consumer Price Index, Average Hourly Earnings, etc.); and a calendar highlighting the news of the day and recent period. The site is well-organized, managing the scope of the information well, and would be a valuable resource within numerous avenues of professional, consumer, and student research.—**ARBA Staff Reviewer**

90.   **Education and the American Workforce.** By Mary Meghan Ryan. Deirdre A. Gaquin, ed. Lanham, Md., Bernan Press, 2018. 584p. (County and City Extra Series). $130.00. ISBN 13: 978-1-59888-951-2.

Education and the American Workforce is "a compilation of data about employment and education from federal statistical agencies" including the Bureau of Labor Statistics and the Census Bureau. This resource is organized into six parts: National; States; Counties; Metropolitan Areas; Cities; and Congressional Districts. National contains tables for: Number of Employees, Wages and Salaries, and Job Requirements for Detailed Occupations in the United States; Educational Attainment for Workers 25 Years and Older by Detailed Occupation, 2014-2015; Fastest Growing Occupations, 2014 and Projected 2024; and Fastest Declining Occupations, 2014 and Projected 2024. In addition, there is a statistical figure: "Median Annual Salary by Major Occupational Group, 2016." States contains tables on: Labor Force Participation of the Population Age 16 Years and Older; Employment and Unemployment, 2015; Employment Status and Class of Worker for the Population Age 16 Years and Older; Employment by Occupation; Employment by Industry; Educational Attainment; Homeownership, Health Insurance, and Computer Access by Educational Attainment; Field of Degree for Persons with a Bachelor's Degree or Higher; and Median Annual Earnings. States are listed alphabetically within each table and also included is a statistical figure, States with the Highest and Lowest Unemployment Rates. Counties includes a table on Labor Force, Employment, and Educational Data,

2011-2015; Metropolitan Areas includes a table on Metropolitan Statistical Area—Labor Force, Employment, and Educational Data, 2015. Cities includes a table on Labor Force, Employment and Educational Data, 2015. Congressional Districts contains a table on Labor Force, Employment, and Educational Data. Appendixes include "Geographic Concepts and Codes" and "Source Notes and Explanations." Highly recommended to business and economics collections in academic and larger public libraries. It should prove useful to Career and Job Hunting collections complementing the *Occupational Outlook Handbook*. And also to researchers in business and economics, studying data about the workforce and changing technology and cultural shifts.—**Lucy Heckman**

91.   **Employment, Hours, and Earnings 2017: States and Areas.** 12th ed. Ryan, Mary Meghan, ed. Lanham, Md., Bernan Press, 2017. 724p. $115.00pa. ISBN 13: 978-1-59888-937-6; 978-1-59888-938-3 (e-book).

This resource is a special addition to Bernan Press' *Handbook of U.S. Labor Statistics: Employment, Earnings, Prices, Productivity, and Other Labor Data*. It includes statistics on monthly and annual hours worked and earnings by industry, covering the years 2006-2016. Statistics are available for the fifty states and the District of Columbia and the seventy-five largest MSAs in the United States. Contents include: Preface; Overview; Part A. State Data; Part B. Metropolitan Statistical Area (MSA) Data; and an appendix: "Seventy-Five Largest MSAs and Components" (as defined February 2013). The Overview explains how data was obtained and defines concepts and revisions for this edition. Part A., State Data, is arranged alphabetically by state name. Each state entry includes an "At a Glance" section which provides: census date for 2010 and 2016 with the percent change in population; percent change in total nonfarm employment, 2006-2016; industry with the largest growth in employment, 2006-2016 (e.g., education and health services); industry with the largest decline or smallest growth in employment, 2006-2016; civilian labor force (2010 and 2016); unemployment rate and rank among states (highest to lowest); and over-the-year change in employment rates (2014-2015; 2015-2016). A pie chart is also included showing percentage for employment by industry. The "At a Glance" section is followed by tables for: Employment by Industry, 2006 through 2016—within each, monthly data and the annual average are included; Average Weekly Hours by Selected Industry, 2012-2016 provides average hours, by month, for total private and goods-producing and for specific industries such as financial activities and leisure and hospitality; and Average Hourly Earnings by Selected Industry, 2012-2016 provides earnings in dollars, not seasonally adjusted by month, for total private, goods producing and specific industries. Part B. Metropolitan Statistical Area (MSA) Data provides employment statistics for the seventy-five largest metropolitan statistical areas (MSAs) and New England city and town areas (NECTAs) in the United States from 2006 through 2016. A chart is provided indicating the largest growth and decline in total nonfarm employment among the seventy-five largest metropolitan statistical areas. MSAs include: New York-Newark-Jersey City, NY-NJ-PA; Atlanta-Sandy Springs-Roswell, GA; San Antonio-New Braunfels, TX; and Indianapolis-Carmel-Anderson. *Employment, Hours, and Earnings* provides a wealth of statistics for researchers about employment by industry within states and MSAs and hours and earnings. This source should be in larger public libraries and academic libraries supporting a graduate business school. Highly recommended.—**Lucy Heckman**

92.   **Technology-Driven Productivity Improvements and the Future of Work: Emerging Research and Opportunities.** Göran Roos, ed. Hershey, Pa., IGI Global,

2017. 255p. index. (Advances in Business Strategy and Competitive Advantage (ABSCA) Book Series). $265.00. ISBN 13: 978-1-52252-179-2; 978-1-52252-180-8 (e-book).

The book is an ideal place to find current information for large and small businesses, government and educational agencies, academic libraries, business students, and individuals who are particularly interested in the discussed topics. However, it is not recommended for small public libraries due to its reading and comprehension complexity. The book discusses contemporary research insights on technological developments, how these technological developments influence workplace and employee skills, and what strategies should be used to create a balanced environment between employees and technologies. It consists of eight chapters. The main advantage of the book is that each chapter has many in-text citations (in some cases, the number of in-text citations can reach about 10 after one sentence); reference lists can last a few pages. In the end of the book, a reader can find the "Related Readings" page that gives even more sources to the related book topics. Thus, it provides endless opportunities for people who want to do a research project or write a research paper. One more positive aspect of the book is that the author includes different views and opinions of one issue, so a reader has a clear understanding of an issue. The book has various figures, such as tables, bar charts, graphics, and others.

One disappointment is that the first two chapters have a summary, but there is no summary for the other six chapters. Despite that, many professionals and researchers will definitely benefit from this book.—**Maria Agee**

Management

Handbooks and Yearbooks

93. Arenofsky, Janice. **Work-Life Balance.** Santa Barbara, Calif., Greenwood Press/ABC-CLIO, 2017. 224p. (Health and Medical Issues Today). $40.00. ISBN 13: 978-1-4408-4713-4; 978-1-4408-4714-1 (e-book).

Discusses the importance of work-life balance, investigating how a positive work-life balance can help create engaged, motivated, and productive employees, as well as the serious issues imbalances produce. The book serves as a single source for information that would otherwise have to be cobbled together from numerous print and online sources. Section one, Overview and Background Information, addresses such topics as imbalances caused by home problems, self-help strategies like mindfulness, things employers can do to decrease worker stress, and government support for work-life balance. Section two, Controversies and Issues, discusses such topics as occupational inequality for women, age and ethnicity, and company culture. Particular features enhance the text: comparisons of the United States to other countries, the use of primary documents, further resources, a timeline, a glossary, and an index.

Designed for undergraduates and general nonspecialists, this exceptional book presents a current, balanced, and reliable collection of material in an easy-to-understand format and thought-provoking manner.—**Thomas E. Baker**

94. **Case Studies as a Teaching Tool in Management Education.** Dominika Latusek,

ed. Hershey, Pa., Business Science Reference/IGI Global, 2017. 326p. index. (Advances in Business Strategy and Competitive Advantage (ABSCA) Book Series). $190.00. ISBN 13: 978-1-52250-770-3; 978-1-52250-771-0 (e-book).

This volume in the Advances in Business Strategy and Competitive Advantage (ABSCA) book series focuses on the use of case studies in the advanced classroom, discussing their strengths and limitations and providing a thorough examination of the components that help make a case study effective.

A preface and a detailed table of contents help lay out the volume's organization and explain its highly specialized focus. The fifteen chapters in this volume provide straightforward information on how the case study fits in relation to management education. Early chapters juxtapose the case study with traditional teaching methods and explore the teaching possibilities within them. Other chapters analyze the direct use of case studies within management education, offering frameworks for incorporation into business practice, an analysis of the case study in marketing or entrepreneurship, and more.

The research also looks at the components of a good case study, presenting "Best Practices of Writing Case Studies," in addition to chapters on research design and the "Case Writing Canvas," an organizing tool for use in case study development. Each chapter opens with an abstract to establish the impetus and methodology of the research that follows. Chapters may be organized into well-defined sections (introduction, background, conclusion, etc.) and make good use of headers, subheaders, tables, illustrations, key terms and definitions, and other tools. References are listed at the end of each chapter and compiled again at the end of the book, alongside brief contributor biographies and an index. Readers of this volume may also be interested in *Digital Entrepreneurship and Global Innovation*—another volume in the ABSCA series. Recommended for academic libraries. Individual chapters are available for purchase in an electronic format.—**ARBA Staff Reviewer**

95. **Handbook of Employee Commitment.** John P. Meyer, ed. Northampton, Mass., Edward Elgar, 2016. 549p. index. $310.00. ISBN 13: 978-1-78471-173-3; 978-1-78471-174-0 (e-book).

Commitment has a large breadth of research and application related to the fields of organizational psychology, organizational behavior, and management. The target of this research and its applications has expanded to cover not just employees but also unions, various occupations, supervisors, customers, goals, and more. The major intent of *The Handbook of Employee Commitment* is to introduce readers to the various aspects of research and applications of employee commitment. The handbook provides contextual history and theory and identifies gaps in the understanding of commitment. It contains 36 essays, written by 60 authors, examining various aspects of employee commitment. Beginning with a section discussing the conceptualization of commitment, the volume covers related constructs of commitment, major foci, and the associated consequences and drivers of commitment as well as methodological issues within the field. Importantly, the handbook examines the impact of culture on commitment in a section of six essays that discuss commitment in both Eastern and Western cultures.

Chapters are relatively short but thoroughly referenced and most contain a section that discusses areas of future research related to that particular aspect of employee commitment. This volume is thorough in its coverage of the subject and would be most useful to graduate students and researchers looking to identify both contextual history and research gaps.—**Alexandra Hauser**

96.   **Principles of Business: Management.** Richard Wilson, ed. Hackensack, N.J., Salem Press, 2017. 463p. index. $165.00. ISBN 13: 978-1-68217-330-5; 978-1-68217-331-2 (e-book).

With a stated focus on undergraduate students and researchers, *Principles of Business: Management* aims to provide overviews of complex managerial topics and issues in an easily understandable manner. The entries in the volume are organized alphabetically; each includes an abstract, topic overview, applications of the concept, a bibliography, and additional recommended reading. End matter includes a 600-word glossary and an index. The volume can serve as a reference handbook for business management novices who seek more detailed explanations of managerial theories. Real-world examples and case studies of the principles in action can aid students in understanding theoretical content in a practical manner.

Though the entries are well-detailed and use accessible language, navigation of the volume may be slightly challenging for a business newcomer. Management is not described as an encyclopedia, but the layout creates a similar feeling with its A to Z listing format. Though the table of contents lists only 70 entries, most articles have numerous subheadings detailing additional topics which could be of interest on their own to a searcher. These subtopics are instead only discoverable by looking up specific terms in the index or by browsing each entry. Entries range from very general (Leadership & Motivation) to highly specific (Decision Process: A Core Business Activity Supported by Information Systems), giving a slightly uneven feel to coverage across the volume. The volume may be of use as a supplement to traditional business or managerial encyclopedias for libraries supporting undergraduate business programs.

Management, the second volume in a planned six-volume business reference series, follows *Finance.* The series will publish into 2018, with *Marketing, Entrepreneurship, Accounting,* and *International Business* forthcoming.—**Emily Lauren Mross**

97.   **Supply Chain Management in the Big Data Era.** Hing Kai Chan, Nachiappan Subramanian, and Muhammad Dan-Asabe Abdulrahman, eds. Hershey, Pa., IGI Global, 2017. 299p. index. (Advances in Logistics, Operations and Management Service (ALOMS) book series). $195.00. ISBN 13: 978-1-52250-956-1; 978-1-52250-957-8 (e-book).

This volume in the Advances in Logistics, Operations, and Management Service (ALOMS) book series gathers the newest research on big data applications in supply chain management as it relates to a number of industries (healthcare, transportation, etc.) and components (e.g., logistics, inventory, etc.). The book is particularly attuned to the topic as it pertains to online and emerging technologies.

The volume's preface along with its detailed table of contents lays out its organization and explains its highly specialized focus. Four sections contain twelve chapters of scholarly work which explore the subject from various angles. Early chapters define big data analytics from an academic and industry perspective; looking at research and information needs and challenges and, in the case of "Data Driven Inventory Management in the Healthcare Supply Chain" (chapter 5), its integration into demand forecasting relative to the Chinese healthcare industry. As the book progresses, chapters explore big data's effect on an evolving transport industry, its relationship with developing technology like Radio Frequency Identification (RFID), coordinating global supply chain relationships via the

Web, and more.

Like other titles in the series, each chapter begins with an abstract that summarizes the impetus and methods of the research to come. Chapters organize the material into introduction, conclusion, future research directions, and other sections, and may utilize bullet points, headers, subheaders, case studies, illustrations, and data tables. References are listed at the end of each chapter and are compiled again at the end of the book. Brief contributor biographies and an index round out the work. Educators, students, managers, and professionals throughout a number of industries would be interested in this volume.—**ARBA Staff Reviewer**

Marketing and Trade

Handbooks and Yearbooks

98.   **AdCouncil. https://www.adcouncil.org/.** [Website] Free. Date reviewed: 2017.

Taking input from a diverse range of sources—business leaders, researchers, philanthropists, public policy makers, and more—the AdCouncil creates public service advertising campaigns which address a number of pressing domestic issues to run across a variety of media. This site does an excellent job of showcasing AdCouncil campaigns, both current and historical, and providing supplementary material that could be extremely useful across the research spectrum. The Our Campaigns tab at the top of the homepage presents the AdCouncil catalog of recent work. Users can examine the entire display or focus their browsing among four umbrella themes of education, family & community, health, and safety. Users can also choose to browse a series of Classic Campaigns (The Classics) such as the "Keep America Beautiful" (a Native American weeps at rampant pollution) campaign that ran for nearly twenty years. Selecting an individual campaign allows users to Explore Campaign Media which may consist of a combination of television, outdoor, radio, Web, and other advertising. Users can read an overview of the issue, the sponsors and campaign elements, and access related campaigns here as well.—**ARBA Staff Reviewer**

99.   Fueroghne, Dean K. **Law & Advertising: A Guide to Current Legal Issues.** 4th ed. Lanham, Md., Rowman & Littlefield, 2017. 380p. index. $95.00; $90.00 (e-book). ISBN 13: 978-1-4422-4488-7; 978-1-4422-4489-4 (e-book).

In a world awash with commercial messages in an ever-increasing variety of media, there are many pitfalls that advertisers must navigate to avoid legal consequences. In this text (updated since the 2007 3d edition) Fueroghne provides a thorough treatment of the issues and the sources of legal constraints faced by advertisers. Among the latter are the Federal Trade Commission, Federal Communications Commission, federal and state statutes and court decisions, as well as industry standards and codes. The topics include comparative advertising, rights of privacy and publicity, product liability, copyright and trademark regulation, contests and lotteries, guarantees and warranties, alcohol and tobacco advertising, and political advertising. Fueroghne enlivens these discussions with accounts of specific regulatory and judicial decisions; some of these are extremely engaging, involving parties such as the Marx Brothers, Kareem Abdul-Jabbar, and the Dallas Cowboys cheerleaders. Because this is more of a treatise than a reference book, its audience is likely to be corporate and agency staff responsible for legal affairs and serious students of this area. Fueroghne himself is not an attorney, but an advertising professional who has over the years become an expert on the law. Unfortunately, this book is riddled with far too many textual errors: punctuation, misspellings, missing words, incorrect verb tenses, and some sentences that are just poorly written. Four examples from the dozens that could be cited: 1,250 for the year 1250; "the case was dismissed in its entirely"; Carry [not Carrie] A. Nation; "Similar situations may occur in almost any situation." On page 215 it is stated, "We clearly saw this in ETW Corp. v. Jireh Publishing," but this case has not been previously discussed and appears again on page 221. And there is one glaring factual error; referring to a 1928 case, Fueroghne writes that it occurred "not long after the 18th Amendment to the Constitution was adopted which repealed prohibition." In fact, the 18th Amendment instituted Prohibition in 1919; the 21st Amendment repealed it in 1933. Much later in the book he states these facts correctly, but his account of the onset of Prohibition is rather muddled. Given the inordinate number of these lapses, and despite its considerable merits, this book cannot be enthusiastically recommended.—**Jack Ray**

100. **Research Handbook on Trade in Services.** Pierre Sauvé and Martin Roy, eds. Northampton, Mass., Edward Elgar, 2016. 635p. index. (Research Handbooks on the WTO). $290.00. ISBN 13: 978-1-78347-805-7; 978-1-78347-806-4 (e-book).

The words trade, exports, and imports likely solicit reader images of tangible objects moving around the world. What is increasingly important; however, is not trade in goods, but trade in services. Services constitute the largest sector in the global economy, accounting for 70% of global GDP, 60% of global employment, and 46% of global exports measured in value-added terms. It is difficult to imagine today's businesses operating without efficient services, such as telecom, the Internet, finance, accounting, legal services, transportation, and logistics. Services are becoming increasingly "tradable," thanks to advancements in technology. International services trade is the new frontier for expanding and diversifying exports, and providing significant opportunities for developing least developed countries (LDCs).

Edited by Pierre Sauvé, University of Bern, and Martin Roy, World Trade Organization, the *Research Handbook on Trade in Services* explores the latest frontiers in services trade by drawing on insights from empirical economics, law, and global political economy. The world's foremost experts explore observations regarding services trade, address policy questions that torment analysts, and focus on a multitude of issues, old and new, that confront attentive readers in the service economy, and its intensification in cross-border exchange. The handbook's 22 chapters shed light on a subject that continues to morph by rapid evolutions in technology, data gathering, market structures, consumer preferences, approaches to regulation, and constant shifts between the market and the state. Expert contributors explore the subject using a multidisciplinary approach, offering a comprehensive overview of lessons learned over two decades of GATS (The General Agreement on Trade in Services) jurisprudence. The book further chronicles the rising stakes and involvement of developing countries in global services trade. The handbook employs diagrams, figures, tables, graphs, charts, and current references. An index rounds out the work.

The *Research Handbook on Trade in Services* is appropriate for college, university, and public libraries. Library acquisition decision-makers responsible for the selection and purchase of materials or resources will consider this book a welcome addition to research collections.—**Thomas E. Baker**

101.   **Super Bowl Ad Archive. http://adage.com/video/super-bowl-ad-archive/2.** [Website] Free. Date reviewed: 2018.

This archive from Ad Age collects television advertisements shown during the annual National Football League championship game broadcast, when advertisers pay premium prices for airtime in an event watched by millions around the world. While noncomprehensive, the archive currently holds close to one thousand ads from the humorous to the serious, promoting longstanding Super Bowl advertisers such as Budweiser, Chevrolet, and Pepsi along with current brands like Amazon, Netflix, and Airbnb. The slide show of past Super Bowl advertisement highlights (such as Coca Cola's iconic "Early Showers—Hey Kid" with Mean Joe Greene) also displays Your Archive Orientation which guides users on archive use. The homepage also features a gallery of all commercials shown during Super Bowl LI in 2017 (advertisements shown during 2018's Super Bowl LII have not yet been added to the archive as of this review). Users can search for brands, advertising agencies, or individual Super Bowls/years from the search bar on the right-hand corner of the page. Scrolling down through the gallery leads to another bar where users can select from forty particular Super Bowls going back to 1969. Ads may include contextual information such as production credits, advertising climate information, brand, advertising agency, and airing time.—**ARBA Staff Reviewer**

5 Education

General Works

Dictionaries and Encyclopedias

102. **Glossary of Education Reform. www.edglossary.org.** [Website] Free. Date reviewed: 2017.

This website from the nonprofit Great Schools Partnership shares an A-Z glossary of terms and concepts frequently used in the greater K-12 education reform conversation. Particularly targeted towards education journalists, this resource can meet a clear need as the education landscape, and the concepts around it, rapidly changes. Brief but comprehensive essays work to define over 500 particular terms or concepts and consider them against the backdrop of education reform today. Entries strive for neutrality, recognizing the differing sides of the reform debate, and are cross-referenced for greater context.

Using the site is easy and rather enjoyable, with stylized text, whimsical graphics, and an easily navigable layout. Users can search for a term/concept or select from an alphabetized menu. They can also peruse the Featured Entry of the Week or choose from a listing of entries along the right sidebar that highlight the Most Popular (curriculum), Most Recent (data masking), and Most Shared (portfolio assessment) education reform concepts. The page also shares links to affiliated sites (e.g., Education Week and the Education Writers Association) which offer more insight into particular education reform topics or help facilitate improved communication about them. With its clearly defined mission, this website provides a fresh and valuable resource for education writers, as well as administrators and community members with an eye on the future of education.—**ARBA Staff Reviewer**

Handbooks and Yearbooks

103. **The BERA/SAGE Handbook of Educational Research.** Dominic Wyse, Neil Selwyn, Emma Smith, and Larry E. Suter, eds. Thousand Oaks, Calif., Sage, 2017. 2v. index. $390.00/set. ISBN 13: 978-1-4739-1891-7; 978-1-4739-8395-3 (e-book).

This two-volume comprehensive set can serve as a useful reference or as an introduction to educational research. The book is broken down into five parts and twenty-one chapters, which follow chronologically from the theoretical conception of the idea for research all the way to the release of the research findings and how to communicate the results of the same.

While the handbook offers a structured approach to a research project, it also provides different valid theories that are equally as useful to the researcher that provide guidance for alternative approaches to research. Obviously, research is never "one size fits all" and what works in one situation may not work in another. This is not just due to the data being collected, it is also due to the form of the data being collected—for example, qualitative data is collected and analyzed differently than quantitative data. By detailing multiple approaches to similar but unique research situations, the handbook allows for multiple valid ways to frame different projects.

The handbook has also been adapted to current times. For example, one of the chapters in the book discusses social media and academic publishing. Social media has allowed academic publishing to become more open and more accessible to all people, even those outside of academia. Further, the handbook discusses how different metrics have emerged to analyze academic publishing in a way that has been unknown in the past.

The size of the handbook may be intimidating to some, which is understandable. However, the handbook is a useful resource for those beginning to explore the field of educational research in addition to those who are seasoned professionals in the field. Rare is the work that is accessible enough to serve as an introduction and in depth enough to serve as a reference source for seasoned professionals. The handbook does both, and is deserving of a place on the bookshelf of every educational research professional. This book is recommended for academic libraries.—**Sara Mofford**

104.   **Careers in Education & Training.** Michael Shally-Jensen, ed. Hackensack, N.J., Salem Press, 2017. 308p. illus. index. $125.00. ISBN 13: 978-1-68217-150-9; 978-1-68217-151-6 (e-book).

This book, comprised of 24 alphabetically arranged chapters, is a great source for high school or undergraduate students who want to learn more about different jobs in education and training. Each chapter is devoted to a particular job, and each chapter provides an overview and information on such things as occupational specialties, work environment, education, training and advancement, earnings and advancement, employment and outlook, and selected schools. Detailed descriptions of statistics, current trends, working environments, and other important topics are also included. These provide valuable insights about which schools to consider for readers who are interested in the formal education that is required for a job and what organizations can provide information about the latest current trends and changes in the field.

The most interesting book features will definitely attract the attention of the reading audience. For example, each chapter has Fun Facts, Famous Firsts, and a Conversation With. The last feature is an interview with a person who performs the selected job. The interviewee discusses interesting aspects of the profession by sharing specific details and concerns. The interviewee also advises readers on what to do to become a professional or on how they can gain knowledge and work experience to receive a certain job. The only thing that can be discouraging about the interviews in the book is that each interview has the same set of questions, which is a bit disappointing because it does not convey the sense of creativity or uniqueness of each job. Nevertheless, the book directly targets its reading audience and is easy to read and understand. The visual graphics of the book are precise, and at the same time offer different visual objects like diagrams or information boxes that catch a reader's attention. One of the most helpful tables is the table about the highest employment level and annual wage because not many print or online resources provide such information. This book is recommended for high school, public, and college libraries.—**Maria Agee**

105. **Digital Tools and Solutions for Inquiry-Based STEM Learning.** Ilya Levin and Dina Tsybulsky, eds. Hershey, Pa., IGI Global, 2017. 255p. index. (Advances in Educational Technologies and Instructional Design (AETID) Book Series). $265.00. ISBN 13: 978-1-52252-179-2; 978-1-52252-180-8 (e-book).

We all live in the digital age, and technologies have already entered many areas of our lives. Education, particularly science education, has also been influenced by using Information and Communication Technologies (ICT) in the classroom. The book represents a valuable reference source that covers a diverse range of topics. It discusses the use and application of technologies in preschool classes, the understanding of scientific concepts through mental stimulation and design-based learning, the creation of scientific argumentation and inquiry-based learning through social media, the analysis of advantages and disadvantages of ICT in STEM education, and the difficulties and opportunities of using ICT in STEM teacher education.

Like other IGI Global books, this one has great features: a detailed table of contents, a long reliable list of reference sources, and a valuable compilation of references in alphabetical order at the end. Moreover, the key terms and definitions page after each chapter highlights the important terms that were used. On the negative repetitive side, there are poor quality illustrations and tables. There are some illustrations and tables on pp. 67, 98, 99, and 183 that are especially hard to see or read. Another (and more technical drawback) is the book title. The title states *Digital Tools and Solutions for Inquiry-Based STEM Learning*; however, the table of contents is divided into two sections: Inquiry-Based Learning of STEM in Digital Era and Inquiry-Based Teaching of STEM in Digital Era. The title reflects only the learning part, but skips the teaching part. This means that because of its title the book loses a potential pool of readers who are interested in STEM teaching.

Although there are some technical shortages, the book contains a variety of articles and case studies that would be interesting for educators, instructors, teachers, and students of STEM education.—**Maria Agee**

106. **Educational Leadership and Administration: Concepts, Methodologies, Tools, and Applications.** Edited by Information Resources Management Association. Hershey, Pa., IGI Global, 2017. 4v. index. $2,925.00/set. ISBN 13: 978-1-52251-624-8; 978-1-52251-625-5 (e-book).

This impressive four-volume reference set on educational leadership and administration would be a valuable addition to education-related collections of academic libraries. This reference source reflects the complex theories and frameworks, the strategies and methods, and the future perspectives and opportunities of the educational leadership and administration field.

Each volume is divided into a few sections. In the first volume there are two main sections. Section one, Fundamental Concepts and Theories, has 12 chapters that address basic principles and concepts of the educational leadership and administration topic, and its position within the field of information science and technology. Section two, Development and Design Methodologies, has 15 chapters that describe general or specific frameworks for development and design technologies within the educational leadership and administration field. The last chapter is in the second volume. The second volume also has two sections. In section three, Tools and Technologies, 15 chapters provide information about the broad spectrum of the latest tools and technologies that can be used within the field of educational leadership and administration. The next section is section four, Utilization and Applications. The 16 chapters offer a diversity of research projects and case studies on application of technologies in the field and show the impact of research on today's society. Half of the chapters are in the third volume. The third volume also includes section five, Organizational and Social Implications, which contains 17 chapters that are aimed at providing research about the behavioral and social impact of global educational leadership and administration. The last chapter can be found in the fourth volume. The fourth volume has two sections. Section six is named Critical Issues and Challenges. The 11 chapters feature the current issues and questions within the field and promote alternative approaches and theories. The last section is section seven, Emerging Trends, which has 12 conclusive chapters that highlight the aspects of future research and applications that will help to improve and develop further the field of educational leadership and administration.

There is a five-page list of the contributors in alphabetical order, a descriptive preface, and a 14-page index. Many of the contributors are from various countries, such as Poland, Turkey, Israel, South Africa, Cyprus, Australia, Pakistan, Malta, and Croatia. Although it is challenging to keep the book consistent because of the great number of contributors and articles, this is a place that needs improvement. The final parts of the chapters do not appear to be uniform. If some chapters have a full set of additional readings, endnotes, key terms and definitions lists, then others have half a set or nothing.

Regardless of this minor drawback, this reference set can serve as an informative and convenient tool to find quick facts or information about the related topic. It is ideal for students, instructors, educators, and researchers who are involved in education.—**Maria Agee**

107. **EdWeb. https://home.edweb.net/.** [Website] Free. Date reviewed: 2017.
This site provides free professional development webinars and podcasts for educators on a broad range of topics. There more than 1,400 Professional Learning Communities to join. This is a great resource for academic as well as special subject educators working with students from grades PreK through high school. In addition to free webinars, many communities provide access to downloadable resources and discussion forums. Webinars cover popular topics such as Open Education Resources, STEAM, and Social Emotional Learning. Educational partners and sponsors include familiar names such as Common Sense Education, ISTE, Time for Kids, and Britannica Digital Learning. Educators may also earn CE Certificates by participating in live webinars or by viewing prerecorded content and successfully completing a short quiz. The site includes an interactive state map that can be used to determine if the certificates are accepted in the state where the educator is employed. Links to each state's department of education website and the State Educational Technology Directors Association (SETDA) Guide to Digital Instructional Materials are also provided. Educators who are interested in presenting a webinar can submit an application specifying the educational topic and intended audience. Users can learn about upcoming webinars via Twitter, emails, or directly on the website. Highly recommended.—**Kim Brown**

108. **Exploring the New Era of Technology-Infused Education.** Lawrence Tomei, ed. Hershey, Pa., IGI Global, 2017. 388p. index. (Advances in Educational Technologies and

Instructional Design (AETID) Book Series). $300.00. ISBN 13: 978-1-52251-709-2; 978-1-52251-710-8 (e-book).

Today the presence of technologies in every area of people's lives is ubiquitous, and education is not an exception. This book reflects different theoretical concepts, research methods, and studies of using the latest advanced technologies in educational environments. The book is divided in two big sections: Theories of Technology-Infused Education and Applications of Technology-Infused Education. There are ten chapters in the first section, and there are nine chapters in the second section. One positive aspect is that the book has a detailed table of contents which has a short description (a summary) of each chapter. Bold headings of the main ideas facilitate navigation through the case studies. Each chapter has credible reference lists, and some chapters have appendixes. Another favorable feature is that readers can find a compilation of references from all the chapters in alphabetical order at the end. In addition, the book contains articles not only from U.S. universities, but also from such countries as Canada, Ireland, China, Lebanon, and Brazil, ensuring that those educators and students who are interested in the international perspective of education will benefit from this book as well.

There are a few technical shortages that are worth mentioning. First, the structure of each article is not consistent. It is obvious that the articles have different topics and research studies, and can have a different structure. However, some articles have a conclusion, while others do not have any conclusion. Second, some tables and illustrations are not clear, especially on pages 70, 71, and 195. Despite these few negative points, this reference book is a current source of recent educational technologies, and it will be a handy tool for educators, policy-makers, instructors, students, and scholars.—**Maria Agee**

109. Lockhart, Johanna M. **Fundamentals of School Marketing.** Lanham, Md., Rowman & Littlefield, 2016. 140p. index. $25.00pa.; $23.00 (e-book). ISBN 13: 978-1-4758-2996-9; 978-1-4758-2997-6 (e-book).

In this step-by-step guide for marketing success, author Johanna M. Lockhart explains the why behind school marketing and provides concise information on how each school can develop a plan for marketing. Available in 140-page paperback or e-book format, this reference book describes real-life school promotion.

Marketing in schools? Isn't that for the business sector? This book explains that you may already be doing marketing, why marketing matters, and how marketing improves your school atmosphere. Integrated marketing is discussed in the introduction and is expanded on in later chapters as activities such as advertising, communication, media relations, and public relations demonstrate clear avenues for administrative promotion of schools.

The four chapters in *Fundamentals of School Marketing* include "Marketing: What It Is and Why It Matters"; "Getting Started"; "Marketing Research and Database Marketing"; and "Marketing Communication." *Fundamentals of School Marketing* helps to formulate what your school's strategy is for communication. Specifics such as a positioning statement, "which defines who you are, what you offer, to whom you offer it, and why you are different from other schools" (p. 30) will maximize marketing efforts. Beyond a plan, effective written and visual tactics are introduced and, finally, the critical point of creating appealing, credible, and persuasive content is reinforced. Chapters are chronological with practical information and limited black-and-white visuals. Information and process for marketing is applicable to all types of schools. Appendixes include three marketing success stories from different school systems. Internal and external stakeholders benefit from strong communications and passionate marketing of school districts; including real-life examples of successful school promotion that go beyond a newsletter portrays ways to galvanize support and achieve the end game of best educational environments for all.

A reference text for school and district administrators, boards, and staff seeking to develop and improve public relations, *Fundamentals of School Marketing* provides the means to an end. Strategies for marketing will lead to positive communication and education excellence.

Recommended.—**Janis Minshull**

110. **MOOCs Now: Everything You Need to Know to Design, Set Up, and Run a Massive Open Online Course.** Susan W. Alman and Jennifer Jumba, eds. Santa Barbara, Calif., Libraries Unlimited/ABC-CLIO, 2017. 117p. index. $65.00pa. ISBN 13: 978-1-4408-4457-7; 978-1-4408-4458-4 (e-book).

New technologies are developing very fast today. It is important to be up-to-date and to keep up with the latest technological trends and novelties. Massive Open Online Classrooms (MOOCs) have created incredible opportunities for learners to study online anytime and anywhere. The book provides great content about MOOCs, and the articles give librarians valuable practical information about how to create, develop, and implement a MOOC. However, there are a few points that may confuse readers. First, the book title does not correspond to the content of the book, potentially misleading readers. It is called: *MOOCs Now: Everything You Need to Know to Design, Set Up, and Run a Massive Open Online Course.* The title gives us the impression that the book targets a broad audience, but it is mainly aimed at librarians. The whole content of the book is based on different librarian perspectives and experiences. So, the title should include the word "librarians" to indicate the targeted audience. Second, the overall formatting of the book does not look consistent. In the first part of the book a reader sees the word "bibliography" in the end of each chapter, then in the second part and third part there is the word "references" in the end of some chapters. Third, even if the book is aimed at librarians, there may still be confusion about what type of librarians. The book consists of mixed articles from university and public librarians.

Despite these negative points, the book is an essential and necessary tool for librarians who want to be involved in creating and running a MOOC. The step-by-step instructions, the lists of resources after each chapter, and the detailed description of case studies will empower and motivate librarians.—**Maria Agee**

111. **Navigate Education in Pennsylvania.** https://nav.csats.ed.psu.edu/. [Website] Free. Date reviewed: 2017.

Penn State University's Center for Science and the Schools has created this database of all educational entities throughout Pennsylvania in order to facilitate connection and collaboration between them. The database generally defines educational agencies as public or private K-12 schools, charter schools, universities, career centers, technology training centers, and regional educational service agencies ("intermediate units"). Users can search a specific education entity or conduct a broader search using a variety of parameters such as entity type, region, and keyword. Database information for a selected entity generally includes region, web address, mailing address, phone number, and Google Map location. It might be helpful for the database to include school/entity administrator information if it is known. Demographic information is also included in some cases. The site also posts a blog which, as of this review, contains only an introductory message. While the site's singular mission might limit its general appeal, it nonetheless offers a thorough and easily navigable database for users looking for research partners or other sources of educational outreach within the state of Pennsylvania.—**ARBA Staff Reviewer**

112.   Sakai-Miller, Sharon "Sam". **Innovation Age Learning: Empowering Students by Empowering Teachers.** Eugene, Oreg., ISTE Publishing, 2016. 186p. index. 24.95pa. ISBN 13: 978-1-56484-355-5.

This book is a great source for educators, teachers, policy makers, and librarians who face challenges teaching today's students. It consists of three parts, and each part has three or four chapters. In the beginning of each part there is a short overview of each chapter that makes it easier for a reader to understand the main subtopics. In the first part, Sakai-Miller indicates that society is in the process of moving from the information age to the innovation age. This means that educators should apply innovative methods and strategies to teach students new skills. The second part describes these new skills: collaboration, communication, creativity, and critical thinking (4Cs) in great detail. The chapters about communication, creativity, and critical thinking provide examples of exercises on how to train these skills. The last part states different ways and ideas about how educators could professionally self-develop and achieve better results in their teaching. After each chapter, there is a short summary that incorporates three concepts found throughout the book "What," "So What," and "Now What." The division into these concepts promotes instructions for readers to follow to improve their teaching skills. Almost each chapter includes a table or figure that provides the bullet points of the main chapter ideas. Appendix A is the author's dissertation case study. There is a credible reference list in Appendix B that consists of reliable sources. The six-page index is consistent and well-organized.— **Maria Agee**

113.   **ViewPure. http://www.viewpure.com./.** [Website] Free. Date reviewed: 2017.

"YouTube without the bloat" is the slogan for this online video hosting resource that allows teachers to share YouTube videos with students without actually visiting YouTube. Most teachers and librarians are aware of the advertisements, unwanted related videos, and at times inappropriate comments listed with videos posted on YouTube. This can lead to awkward conversations with students or teachers choosing to not show an otherwise educational video clip to their students. This resource enables teachers to not only "export" a YouTube video URL to its safe-viewing website platform, but it also features the ability to select a certain time-stamped clip within the video. For example, if a teacher wants to only show three minutes in the middle of a six-minute video, they can enter the times they want to show and only that section of footage will appear. It is important to note that links with less than 10 views over a six-month period may be deleted according to the site's FAQ page, which may be the only drawback to this helpful resource that can remove the awkwardness and distraction that sometimes comes along with viewing online videos. Highly Recommended.—**Angela Wojtecki**

Elementary and Secondary Education

Handbooks and Yearbooks

114.   **Check123. https://www.check123.com/.** [Website] Free. Date reviewed: 2017.
This is a free database of short videos appropriate for all grade levels that address major curricular subjects, as well as the arts, popular culture, and high interest areas for young people, like pets and gaming. Professional experts have evaluated and curated these videos from across the Internet, with sources ranging from individuals on YouTube to more authoritative sources like TED-Ed, National Geographic, and the Smithsonian Museum. The videos have been assessed for content and appropriateness and given a quality rating for being informative and entertaining, making it easier to determine the best choices. Users can create their own profile to save videos or an educator profile to create lessons and organize chosen videos. Educators will find the format of short video snippets useful to support the curriculum and engage students in different topic areas. There are also options to add or suggest other videos to the database, adding a layer of social community that may be attractive to some users. Ads are included for some videos, but there are options to embed the video into other spaces which might limit the appearance of ads. This resource is a one-stop shop for educators to support different learning styles by adding some media engagement to lessons. Given the vetting of the videos by other experts and educators and the site being cost free, it is worth reviewing to determine its value to your school and teaching.—**Kasey Garrison**

115.   **Common Lit. https://www.commonlit.org/.** [Website] Free. Date reviewed: 2017.
This website provides a wealth of free resources to promote literacy for students. At the time of this writing, there were a total of 996 texts available, including poetry, nonfiction, excerpts, and short stories. Materials can be searched by lexile range, grade level, literary theme, and genre. Resources pair well with lessons in Social Studies and English Language Arts. All users can create a free account to get started. Educators are able to create classes, add assignments, assign due dates, and import classes from Google Classroom. Content can also be downloaded in PDF format to use with other learning management systems such as Edmodo or Moodle. Students join a class using a code that is generated once a class has been added. A "Featured Content" area on the home page highlights staff favorites and materials relevant to particular themes/holidays. Companion texts for books that are frequently assigned to middle and high school students are available. Students can opt to have the text read to them, use the dictionary feature to look up unfamiliar terms, translate text into Spanish, and use a highlight tool to mark-up passages. Guiding questions give students the ability to assess their understanding. According to the site FAQ, there are plans to update the site to include content for grades 3-4 and to translate content into additional languages. Highly recommended.—**Kim Brown**

116.   **EDSITEment.** [Website] Free. Date reviewed: 2017.
A partnership between the National Endowment for the Humanities and the National Trust for the Humanities, this site is a massive free database of K-12 resources and lesson plans to engage learners in humanities subjects including social studies, language arts,

arts education, science, and world languages. Organized by specific topics like "National Poetry Month," "Origins of Halloween and the Day of the Dead," and "The American Civil War," the website also allows users to search by topic, subject, level, or for state and national curriculum standards. Resources targeting both students and teachers use print and multimedia content like written articles, videos, and audio. Comprehensive, detailed lesson plans written by real teachers use supportive teaching features including vocabulary lists, read-aloud stories, extension activities, and student worksheets. Most users will find the site easy to navigate; however, novice users may experience information overload at the sheer volume of content available. Features like the "reference shelf" offer support for educators and incorporate online resources into teaching more broadly while the "after school" link is a unique area of resources created for students to explore independently. This free resource will allow educators to integrate technology into teaching and engage students in learning across levels. Recommended.—**Kasey Garrison**

117. **Share My Lesson.** [Website] Free. Date reviewed: 2017.
        Educators and paraprofessionals looking for free lessons created by fellow educators will want to check out this resource. Users can search for lessons by grade level, standards (NGSS, Common Core, and state standards), or subject and have the ability to rate and review lessons to provide helpful feedback for other members. Many of the resources fall under one of two types of Creative Commons licensing, either granting permission for modification of material for noncommercial purposes with attribution, or noncommercial use with attribution and no permissible modifications of material. One appealing section of the website, titled "Today's News, Tomorrow's Lesson," focuses on current events. Video links, background information regarding the event, and discussion questions are included. Members can sign up to receive email or text alerts for newly added lesson plans and activities. Saved lessons show up in the user profile section of the website. The site also includes free on-demand professional development webinars on a variety of timely topics. Downloadable resources including handouts, PowerPoint slides, and more accompany the Webinars. Recommended.—**Kim Brown**

118. **Workbench. https://www.workbenchplatform.com/.** [Website] Free. Date reviewed: 2017.
        Workbench is a must-have resource for those working in STEAM, STEM, or project-based classrooms and schools. Teachers will find the Projects menu on the website easy to explore based on grade levels and topics. Existing projects are great for teachers to begin working on project-based learning activities and can be edited and enhanced. The standards-aligned activities, supply lists, and detailed instructions can help save teachers and librarians time in planning for makerspace activities or blended learning rotation stations. Free accounts allow for easy sharing through Google Classroom integration of hands-on lessons that vary in length from one class period to more lengthy projects. Once students begin a project, they are able to use the Workbook feature to keep track of current projects and which tasks are completed. This helpful feature allows for easy tracking of longer projects that involve multiple steps and checklists. Teachers and districts can also opt to sign up for a paid account, which offers the ability to import class lists via Clever or other LMS tools. This resource is highly recommended for those educators looking to increase their number of project-based learning activities and those looking for an excellent resource to help accelerate student engagement.—**Angela Wojtecki**

Higher Education

Directories

119.   **Book of Majors 2018.** New York, College Board, 2017. 1391p. index. $29.99pa. ISBN 13: 978-1-4573-0923-6.

This book on college fields of study starts with a discussion of how to choose a major, when to decide on a major, and the right college for the right major. The front matter also includes a list of the college professors whose information was used to compile information about different majors, a glossary, and a usage guide. The first part provides generous descriptions of majors in many areas, from agriculture to information sciences to legal studies to public administration to visual and performing arts and hundreds more. In the second, much shorter section, the book provides brief descriptions of over 1,200 majors. This is followed by a section of college listings. Majors are listed in alphabetic order. Each major, like marketing, lists the states that offer the major. Under each state users will find the names of the community college, college, or university that offers the major; next to the college is an indicator of what degree can be earned—certificate, associate, bachelor's, master's, doctorate. As expected, the lists are quite a bit longer for majors like history, English, and physics. Following this main section are a series of lists of which schools offer special academic programs; these are also listed by state. Special programs include combined bachelor's/graduate programs in accounting, business administration, chemistry, engineering, environmental studies, law, mathematics, nursing, occupational therapy, pharmacy, psychology, and veterinary medicine. There are shorter lists for schools that offer double majors, semesters at sea, etc. The book ends with an alphabetical list of majors.—**ARBA Staff Reviewer**

Handbooks and Yearbooks

120.   **Best Grad Schools 2017: U.S. News & World Report.** Washington, DC, U.S. News & World Report, 2017. 288p. illus. $19.95pa. ISBN 13: 978-1-93146-982-1.

This is an informative, lively guide directed at undergraduates and others considering graduate school in a variety of disciplines. The book is a bit busy. There are color photographs, personal testimonies, and ads throughout, but there is also a lot of good, basic information that potential students should consider before making a commitment. The book begins with a big picture chapter that addresses why someone should go to graduate school and how to pay for the education. A textbox contains the testimony from an associate scientist who chose to pursue an advanced degree at Cornell University. Following this are chapters on graduate programs in business, engineering, law, education, and health and medicine. Within these chapters, readers will find testimonies, school rankings, discussions about job markets, and directories for the schools that offer these programs. Even though some of this information is available electronically, it is convenient to find it all in one place. At this modest cost, the book is recommended for public and academic libraries.—**ARBA Staff Reviewer**

121.   **Getting Financial Aid: Scholarships, Grants, Loans, and Jobs.** New York, College Board, 2017. 999p. $24.99pa. ISBN 13: 978-1-4573-0924-3.

This is a guide designed for students, parents, and guardians faced with the seemingly overwhelming task of financing a college education. The book provides a wealth of information on what to do and where to find money, supplying readers with worksheets, tables, and graphs and the confidence to go out and get some of the billions of dollars of monetary aid available from government and private sources. The book is reliable and as current as possible. The information in this edition comes from the College Board's most recent annual survey of colleges, which was conducted in spring 2017. That said, those applying for aid should double-check information before submitting applications. Following a usage guide, the book is divided into easily digestible parts: Financial Aid Step by Step, Tables and Worksheets, Financial Aid College by College, and Scholarship lists. The first two parts walk users through the basics, like how to fill out the (Free Application for Federal Student Aid) FAFSA form and how to ensure deadlines are met. The third part lists information about financial aid from individual colleges, alphabetically by state. Depending on the school, users will find such information as enrollment statistics, forms required, financial aid granted, and contact information for the school's financial aid representative. The scholarship lists appear alphabetically by state. Included are lists of academic, art, athletic, music/drama, and ROTC scholarships. The book concludes with a glossary and an alphabetic index of colleges.—**ARBA Staff Reviewer**

122.   **How to Get Money for College 2018.** Albany, N.Y., Peterson's, 2017. 927p. index. $29.95pa. ISBN 13: 978-0-7689-4158-6.

Students and their families often wonder how to manage the costs of a college education. This guide by Peterson's demystifies the somewhat complicated financial aid landscape, starting with a section on such basics as filling out the FAFSA form and answering commonly asked questions about whether or not parents are penalized for having a college savings account. There is also an essay by a former Director of Undergraduate Financial Aid at Princeton on how to finance a college degree. A usage guide comes next and is followed by a ready-reference guide that lists colleges and their costs by state. Here users will find tuition costs, the cost of room and board, average indebtedness on graduation, and other quick facts. The heart of the book, approximately 700 pages, profiles more than 2,400 college financial aid programs. These are in alphabetical order by college and university name. Entries vary in length from a short paragraph to approximately half a page depending on information. Private and public schools are covered. Users will find basic information about enrollment, tuition, freshman financial aid given (fall 2016 statistics), undergraduate financial aid (fall 2016 statistics), gift aid (based on need and not based on need), student loans, work study, applying for financial aid (forms and deadlines), and contact information. If available, entries provide information about ROTC scholarships and athletic award money. Some entries, however, only include contact information for the financial aid office. The book provides a generous section on state scholarship and grant programs, in alphabetic order by states. The information varies on the types of aid available. The indexes help users navigate. The first covers non-need scholarships for undergraduates, the second covers athletic grants, the third covers Co-Op Programs, and the fourth is comprised of ROTC programs. The last two cover tuition waivers and tuition payment alternatives, respectively. These indexes are subdivided, when necessary, and list the names of the schools in alphabetic order. The cost of the book is modest, particularly in comparison to paying for college. Highly recommended for public and academic libraries.—**ARBA Staff Reviewer**

123.   Tanabe, Gen, and Kelly Tanabe. **The Ultimate Scholarship Book 2018: Billions of Dollars in Scholarships, Grants and Prizes.** Belmont, Calif., SuperCollege, LLC, 2017. 800p. index. $28.99pa. ISBN 13: 978-1-61760-122-4.

Those students, parents, and guardians in search of ways to finance college have come to the right place. But this book provides much more than a guide to available funds. It starts by discussing the advantages of using a book (this book in particular) over a website. Next comes advice about everything scholarship, starting with the busting of such myths, like the one that says scholarships are only for top students or star athletes. Following this is basic, common sense guidance on where (in addition to this book) to start looking for scholarships. This includes high school counselors and websites, community organizations, and local businesses. The third chapter gives nuts-and-bolts tips on how to fill out the scholarship form, while chapter 4 focuses on how to write a winning essay. The next three chapters cover the student resume, recommendation letters, and how to ace the interview. The information is generous but not overwhelming, and the instructions are easy to follow. The directory comprises the heart of the book. Here users will find information on 2,715 scholarships, arranged in eight sections: General, Humanities/Arts, Social Sciences, Sciences, State of Residence, Membership, Ethnicity/Race/Gender/Family Situation/Sexual Orientation, and Disability/Illness. Entries typically contain the following information: name of scholarship; an address, phone number, and URL; the purpose of the scholarship; eligibility; the target applicant; the amount awarded; how to apply; and minimum GPA (if applicable). There is also a code that can be used at the book's companion website. When entered, users will find any updated information. For ease of navigation, there are a number of indexes such as general category, special circumstances, and ethnicity and race. This is a highly recommended purchase for high school, community college, academic, and public libraries.—**ARBA Staff Reviewer**

Learning Disabilities

124.   **Learning Disabilities Information for Teens. 2d ed.** Keith Jones, ed. Detroit, Omnigraphics, 2017. 351p. index. $69.00. ISBN 13: 978-0-7808-1472-1; 978-0-7808-1471-4 (e-book).

This second edition, (see ARBA 2006, entry 316) is divided into eight parts. Chapters provide definitions, causes, symptoms, information on how professionals can help, and strategies to employ at home. Additionally, other conditions that may affect learning are noted and ideas for accommodation, modification, and remediation are represented. Call-out boxes include important information, define terms, and offer summaries. White space and ease of reading is also present with bulleted lists and headlines. Additional resources will be found in one of the closing chapters and the index is resolute.

This book fills a need as "in the United States, nearly 6.5 million children and youth ages 3-21 currently receive special education services for learning disabilities, such as dyslexia, dyscalculia, and other disorders that affect language development, motor control, attention, and behavior" (p. ix). Information is timely, matter of fact, and design efforts such as short chapters make this very readable for the layman. Positive measures for adaptive equipment, study habits, and the availability of resources will enhance understanding for students, teachers, and caregivers. Tips and coping strategies make this practical, not overwhelming. "A learning disability is not an indication of a person's intelligence" (p. 1) is a resilient statement to start chapter 1. Support for those with learning disabilities includes legal information on rights and details on acts such as Section 504 of the Rehabilitation Act. Consider this an introduction with pathways to relevant additional information for deeper study.

The information presented here will be useful to middle and high school students, caregivers and parents, and educators seeking easily readable text and quick reference for support and resources. Recommended.—**Janis Minshull**

Special Education

125.   **The Praeger International Handbook of Special Education.** Michael L. Wehmeyer and James R. Patton, eds. Santa Barbara, Calif., Praeger/ABC-CLIO, 2017. 3v. $163.00/set. ISBN 13: 978-1-4408-3113-3; 978-1-4408-3114-0 (e-book).

We often like to think that we are a global society and that we have a good understanding of how education works throughout the world. In reality, we could learn a lot from compiled information about any educational topic as it exists in other countries. While visiting a South American country a few years ago, I was asked to teach some techniques that might be used to work with children with disabilities in a new school. I kept finding myself referring to legislation, mandates, and requirements we often find in the United States and realizing that they did not have the same legislation so some of my preliminary information was not applicable. What I needed before speaking to them was a review of special education in that country, and this volume of books provides just that.

The introduction in volume one provides an overview of why this information was gathered and stresses the importance of the rights of individuals with disabilities. Stressing how those rights have changed over time and the implications of those rights regarding special education as well as special needs education provides a general idea of the usefulness of the information in each volume. By viewing the needs of people—regardless of where they live—as being similar and the universal design for learning that can be utilized to help each child learn, the reader can begin to draw a cohesive picture of education across continents. With behavioral issues in schools being a major concern in many areas of the world, a brief description of Positive Behavioral Supports helps to provide suggestions of modifications that might help students learn, no matter the environment. Article 24 of the Convention of the Rights of Persons with Disabilities provides specific reasons for the need for this type of publication. Finally, the structure of the volumes enables each reader to determine the types of information presented within the description of each country. By organizing each volume according to countries within specified continents, it is easy to locate the country of interest and read information specific to special education services in that country. Overall, *The Praeger International Handbook of Special Education* is an excellent resource that can provide information for many to become more global learners and global educators.—**Donna J Kearns**

6 Ethnic Studies and Anthropology

Ethnic Studies

General Works

126. **Anti-Racism Digital Library. www.sacred.omeka.net/.** [Website] Free. Date reviewed: 2017.

Anti-Racism specifically focuses on the movement to change systems and practices which promote racist effects, emphasizing the work against racism vs. the racism itself. This site assembles a diverse array of community-based digital media that works in support of anti-racism education and promotion. It is important to note that the site and many of its features are a work in progress, as the project continues to seek out digital contributions, complete its glossary, etc. Users can conduct a basic search from the bar at the top of the page, but the site is well set up for browsing. Users can Browse Items and scroll through a listing of over 200 individual papers, videos, photography, surveys, brochures, and more which work to highlight how anti-racism manifests across the globe. Items include such things as a Kuwaiti anti-terrorism television advertisement, photographs from the 2017 Women's March, and guidelines on how to write using "inclusive and socially just language." Items are arranged by the date they were added to the project but may be sorted by title or creator as well. Selecting an item will lead to citation, collection, subject, creator, publisher, format, and date information, as well as a link to the item's original page. Users can also select the Browse Collections tab which links to 15 thematic item collections, such as "On Being White" or "American Identity." Users can also Browse Tags. The home page contains a Featured Item (currently spotlighting a research paper titled "Theology, Race and Libraries"), a Featured Collection, and a Featured Exhibit, in addition to a brief listing of Recently Added Items. Furthermore, users can also access a glossary from the About the Library tab which, when complete, will present the specialized language and concepts of the anti-racism lexicon, such as Blaxican, Colorism, and Microaggression. As it continues to develop, this site can be a vital tool in helping researchers across a number of disciplines.—**ARBA Staff Reviewer**

127.   **Race in American Film: Voices and Visions that Shaped a Nation.** Daniel Bernardi and Michael Green, eds. Santa Barbara, Calif., Greenwood Press/ABC-CLIO, 2017. 3v. illus. index. $294.00/set. ISBN 13: 978-0-313-39839-1; 978-0-313-39840-7 (e-book).

Editors Bernardi and Green have written extensively on cinema and particularly on race and representation in the genre, and this new excellent collection of essays by film scholars is a welcome addition to the growing collection of race and film references. The 337 alphabetically arranged entries cover the most important and famous U.S. films from three broad categories: those considered outright racist; those attempting to subvert racism; and those by nonwhite directors that feature nonwhite characters or racial themes. All three major film eras—silent, midcentury, and contemporary—are represented, with significant entries on individual performers and directors, feature films and series (for example, Charlie Chan), and general topics such as blackface, Civil War films, and Westerns. Signed entries vary in length depending on the topic, from one to two pages to 15 or more, and all include cross-references, films for further viewing, and secondary bibliographies. Unexpected surprises occur throughout—entries on Dracula and the sci-fi film *Them!*, for example— and this reviewer would have liked to see specific entries on "Horror Films," or "The Little Rascals," but something must always be omitted to fit publishers' requirements. Overall, however, the scope and quality of entries make for an intelligent and thought-provoking resource, coupled with more specific works such as Bogle's *Blacks in American Films and Television* (Garland, 1988) and Parish's *Encyclopedia of Ethnic Groups in Hollywood* (see ARBA 2003, entry 1178). Highly recommended for all film collections.—**Anthony J. Adam**

128.   **Race Relations in America https://www.amdigital.co.uk/primary-sources/race-relations-in-america.** [Website] Chicago, Adam Matthew Digital, 2017. Price negotiated by site.

Adam Matthew's digital collection, *Race Relations in America,* presents primary documents from 25 years of Fisk University's Race Relations Department and its annual Institute, both of which were headed by Fisk's President, Charles S. Johnson. Contents include books and booklets, posters, maps, correspondence, photos, more than 100 hours of audio (with transcripts), and much more. A lightbox provides space for users to view and store images and other content, after creating an online account. Thematic guides and series guides provide other ways of exploring the collection, along with interactive maps, chronologies, contextual essays, and other tools to maximize understanding of and discovery within the collection. Patrons can export citations, use static URLs to link directly to specific content, and download PDFs.

Potential subscribers should recognize the relatively narrow scope of this collection— both by date and by location—but balance that with its depth and the importance of the items that are included here, to say nothing of the themes it addresses. Though based primarily on the work of one institution, that institution studied race relations throughout the country. This is clearly a valuable source for any academic institution that has both a focus on US history or sociology, and the ability to acquire the collection.—**Peter H. McCracken**

129.   **Racial and Ethnic Relations in America.** 2d ed. Kibibi Mack-Shelton and Michael Shally-Jensen, eds. Amenia, N.Y., Grey House Publishing, 2017. 3v. illus. maps. index.

$295.00/set. ISBN 13: 978-1-68217-315-2; 978-1-68217-316-9 (e-book).

The first edition of this reference tool was published in 2000 (see ARBA 2001, entry 274). The second edition, coedited by Kibibi Mack-Shelton, Professor of History at Claflin University, and Michael Shally-Jensen, is comprised of three volumes containing alphabetically arranged and signed entries. There is a separate table of contents for each volume identifying only the entries contained therein. Concluding the third volume are all of the appendixes: "Time Line of Racial and Ethnic Relations"; "Categorized List of Entries"; "Pioneers of Intergroup Relations"; "Bibliography of Racial and Ethnic Relations"; and "Index." Not included is a list of the contributors and their affiliations.

While some of the entries in the second edition have been updated, there are also many new ones covering such topics as the "Charleston Church Shooting of 2015" and the "Ferguson Unrest." The quality of the content contained in the respective entries varies widely. Some of the material reflects the current scholarship in the field while other content contains very dated information. For example, in the first entry in volume one, "Ability Testing and Bias," the publication dates for the titles in the bibliography are 2003, 1984, 1980, 1984, and 1994. The coverage is very superficial and is supplemented by a chart containing data produced in 2002 by the Center for Disease Control. Even worse, the chart concerns the blood lead levels in children aged 1-5 from three different races, which has nothing to do with the article it is paired with or even the one that follows. Issues such as the one described undercut the authority and utility of the entire work.—**John R. Burch Jr.**

130. **Social Issues in Living Color.** Blume, Arthur W., ed. Santa Barbara, Calif., Praeger/ABC-CLIO, 2017. 3v. $243.00/set. ISBN 13: 978-1-4408-3336-6; 978-1-4408-3337-3 (e-book).

In *Social Issues in Living Color,* excellent scholarly contributions present racial and ethnic psychological perspectives on topics such as media, criminal justice, racism, climate change, gender bias, health, and mental health inequalities. The first volume introduces readers to the basic scientific concepts of racial and ethnic minority psychology and then examines intersections of race, ethnicity, gender, and sexual orientation. It also addresses how race and ethnicity affect communication styles, leadership styles, and media. The second volume discusses the experiences of individuals within racial and ethnic minorities, including overt racism, covert racism, and colonialism, and addresses how ethnic minority psychology plays a role in our educational system, poverty, global climate change, and sustainability. The third volume covers ethics in health and research, considers the causes of health and mental health disparities, and identifies diversity initiatives that can improve the health and well-being of all citizens. The book concludes with information about the editors and contributors and an index.

Social Issues in Living Color makes a meaningful contribution. Designed for activists, undergraduates, graduate students, and general nonspecialists, this exceptional set presents a current, balanced, and reliable collection of material. The volumes help readers understand a sensitive and mutually shared topic in an easy-to-understand format and thought-provoking manner. Private individuals, public libraries, and community college and university libraries will value this book as an essential addition to their reference shelves.—**Thomas E. Baker**

African Americans

131.   **The African American Experience: The American Mosaic. https://www.abc-clio.com/ABC-CLIOCorporate/product.aspx?pc=AFAMW.** [Website] Santa Barbara, Calif., ABC-CLIO, 2017. Price negotiated by site. Date reviewed: 2017.

This database spans from 500 C.E, to the present with a focus on African Americans throughout American history. From the main page, users may access information on one of 14 different time periods or use the search bar to type in a specific topic. On any given page there may be links that lead to additional resources within the database, primary sources, images, or video. Links within the body of an article will take you to more information. Further reading has lists of books, some of which have copyright dates that are 20 years old. Citations can be found for all articles and media in MLA, Chicago, and APA style and can be exported easily to Easybib and RefWorks. Some articles offer a tool to analyze data called CLIOview, which allows the user to select multiple categories to create graphs or charts with statistical data. Though mostly very well written and in easy-to-understand language for high school students, some typographical errors are evident. Regardless of these errors, this resource would be an excellent choice for high school libraries where students do a significant amount of history research.—**Elizabeth Kahn**

132.   **Colored Conventions. http://coloredconventions.org/.** [Website] Free. Date reviewed: 2018.

This site presents a digital archive of meeting records, newspaper articles, petitions, and other documents produced in support of "colored conventions." These meetings of free African American men assembled as far back as the 1830s. The conventions formalized the advocacy of fair employment, education, and basic civil rights. This archive helps to preserve the history of African American advocacy work as it shines a light on its origins and methods, community networks, and much more. In conventions held from Maine to California, attendees addressed such topics as temperance (e.g., 1843 Mid-Atlantic Regional Temperance Convention of Colored Citizens), veterans' rights (e.g., 1867 Report on the Colored Soldiers and Sailors Convention), opposition to national legislation (e.g., the 1850 Fugitive Slave Law Convention), and international issues (e.g., 1872 Cuban Slavery Convention). The Conventions tab on the menu bar lets users explore the archive by Year or by location (National, State, or Region). Individual materials may be identified by Subject, Description, Title, Creator, Publisher, Date, Format, etc., and may be viewed through the Document Viewer or downloaded as a pdf. Helpful transcriptions are available for some materials, and the archive hopes to include more in the future. Teaching resources include Research Guides, among other tools. In addition, archive materials have been organized into fourteen online Exhibits which put the impact of the conventions into perspective. "The Manual Labor College Initiative and the 1853 Rochester Convention" incorporates a Convention Delegate Roll Call, biographies, news coverage, and more into its essay on increasing African American women's educational opportunities. "What Did They Eat? Where Did They Stay" highlights women's work in the movement away from the convention halls, with essays, maps, and an interactive menu pointing to the role of the boardinghouse in both the literal and figurative feeding of convention-goers. The materials reflect a significant view into a foundational piece of the American civil rights movement, and would be an exceptional resource for educators and students.—**ARBA Staff Reviewer**

133.   **Great Events from History: African American History.** Mack-Shelton, Kibibi, ed. Amenia, N.Y., Grey House Publishing, 2017. 3v. illus. index. $295.00/set. ISBN 13: 978-1-68217-152-3; 978-1-68217-153-0 (e-book).

This three-volume set is part of the Great Events from History series. It is divided into two parts: Overviews and Chronology of Events. The Overviews section emphasizes essays on important topics of African American history, some of which include sports, literature, education, lynching, segregation, cowboys, agriculture, slavery, and stereotypes, to name a few. The Chronology of Events section comprises essays beginning with The Middle Passage to American Slavery (17th century) up to the present. Each essay is approximately 1,600 words in length, starting with a summary paragraph, broad discussion of the topic and its significance with focus on key figures, and *see also* references. Sprinkled throughout the volumes are sidebars which provide quotations from primary source documents. There are many black-and-white photographs and illustrations as well. Appendixes include Notable Figures in African American History, a Timeline of African American History, and a bibliography. Indexes are divided into category and subject areas. I highly recommend these volumes for high school and academic libraries.—**Bradford Lee Eden**

134.   **The HistoryMakers. http://www.thehistorymakers.org/.** [Website] Free. Date reviewed: 2017.

HistoryMakers aims to create a more complete portrait of a thriving America by profiling prominent African Americans who have achieved across a range of disciplines. The site has painstakingly gathered hundreds of oral histories of extraordinary people who have found success as civil rights activists, composers, fashion designers, aeronautical engineers, educators, artists, and more, many against all odds. These histories, in addition to the supplemental information within the site, create a good foundational source of African American historical research. All site visitors can view over two thousand brief biographical sketches about the diverse selection of individuals, from U.S. Army General Clara Adams-Ender to jazz composer Roy Ayers. Selecting the Makers tab on the bar accesses the drop down menu of fifteen Makers categories, including ArtMakers, MedicalMakers, SportsMakers, ReligionMakers, LawMakers, and BusinessMakers. Selecting a category from this menu will highlight a featured person then display an alphabetical catalog of others within the category. Clicking on a name will access a short but informative biography, photo, and listing of personal details such as specific profession, birthplace, and favorites (e.g., color, food, etc.). There is also a Timeline feature within each biography page. Users can enter a date to see a brief summary of notable events relating to general African American history or to specific Makers themselves. Users who register at one of three levels can access further, more compelling site features. The paid DigitalMaker and InstitutionalMaker subscriptions offer unlimited access to hundreds of hours of video interviews allowing users to hear each Maker's tale of success in their own voice. The free BasicMaker registration allows access to a limited number of video excerpts of the full oral history. Registered users also gain entry into the site's Special Collections, which contain exhibits on notable African American groups or organizations such as the Negro Baseball League and the National Airmen's Association of America. By amassing its large and diverse collection of biographical information in one place, the site works to preserve and share the important and underreported achievements of African Americans from all walks of life, and would be an excellent resource for educators and students.—**ARBA Staff Reviewer**

135.   Holloway, Cheryl D. **The Black Woman's Breast Cancer Survival Guide: Understanding and Healing in the Face of a Nationwide Crisis.** Santa Barbara, Calif., Praeger/ABC-CLIO, 2017. 205p. index. $37.00. ISBN 13: 978-1-4408-5608-2; 978-1-4408-5609-9 (e-book).

African American women face an increased risk of developing breast cancer. They often receive their diagnosis at a younger age, and they are more likely to receive a diagnosis of a more dangerous and more rapidly spreading variety such as triple-negative or inflammatory breast cancer. Genetics, alcohol abuse, obesity, and access to the health care system are factors that may be involved. The author, a public health researcher who has survived breast and thyroid cancers, provides accurate, accessible advice for black women facing breast cancer. She discusses the types of breast cancer, diagnosis, treatment options, and coping strategies. She also offers good advice for dealing with comments that are not welcome such as those that blame the patient for having the disease. A series of appendixes offers lists of organizations and websites that provide information and support and a glossary. A bibliography provides current clinical information. This is an excellent resource for public and consumer health libraries.—**Barbara M. Bibel**

136.   Howard, Sheena C. **Encyclopedia of Black Comics.** Golden, Colo., Fulcrum Publishing, 2017. 245p. illus. $19.95pa. ISBN 13: 978-1-68275-101-5.

This book follows the highly successful publication of *Black Comics: Politics of Race and Representation* (2013), which was an introduction to the history of black comics and black American artists across the comics medium, by the same author. It won the Eisner Award for Best Scholarly/Academic work, making the author the first woman of color to win the highest award in the comics industry. This book is an encyclopedia which focuses on people of African descent who have published significant works in the United States, and contains 100 entries on individuals both living and dead. It includes illustrators, archivists, academics, convention creators, inkers, website creators, black comic historians, artists, and self-published comic creators, along with information on their books, characters, content, and contributions to the field of black comics. Dozens of illustrations, many in full color, enhance an already lively book. A select bibliography and an index round out the work. Given that there isn't any other book like this available anywhere, I highly recommend it for high school, public, and academic libraries.—**Bradford Lee Eden**

137.   Starks, Glenn L. **African Americans by the Numbers: Understanding and Interpreting Statistics on African American Life.** Santa Barbara, Calif., Greenwood Press/ABC-CLIO, 2017. 182p. index. $45.00. ISBN 13: 978-1-4408-4504-8; 978-1-4408-4505-5 (e-book).

This volume explores the social, political, economic, demographic, and health condition of blacks in the United States, supplying critical data on various categories such as education, health, crime and criminal justice, employment, voting, family, and religion. Each chapter begins with a brief discussion on considerations for researching and using data related to that topic; different aspects of the topic are then focused upon for the remainder of the chapter, with relevant data tables and discussion along with additional statistics in discussion form. Further investigation questions are given at the end of each chapter section to stimulate debate and discussion, and the further reading sections provide additional resources. To assist the reader in using and analyzing data, the introduction provides pointers regarding primary and secondary data and how to use data correctly. Blacks currently make up 13.2 percent of the U.S. population, which is expected to increase to 14.3 percent by 2060, so this book is both timely and appropriate for research in the social sciences as well as numerous other academic disciplines.—**Bradford Lee Eden**

138.   **Umbra Search African American History. www.umbrasearch.org/pages/about.** [Website] Free. Date reviewed: 2017.

Umbra Search consolidates hundreds of thousands of digitized artifacts from libraries and archives across the nation related to the culture and history of African Americans. Users can research a wide variety of topics such as Billie Holliday, the NAACP, hip hop dance, the Harlem Renaissance, jazz, Pan-Africanism, Jim Crow, and Jesse Jackson, among many others. Users can keyword search their topic in the search bar to access a particular item or collection of interest. From here, users can browse a listing of all available items which span images, text, video, and sound recordings. Selecting an artifact allows access to descriptive information such as subject, collection, and creator. Users can also examine thumbnails of related content. Selecting the View button redirects users to the artifact's host site which may offer further information and access. Users can alternatively narrow their search via categories like creator, media type, contributing institution, and collection. The site is ideal for users with a strong idea of what they are looking for. For users looking to browse, the homepage includes several example searches and other affiliated projects for inspiration. For example, searching under "African-American Firsts" helps users connect with over 1,600 digital artifacts associated with African American achievements in education, employment, sports, and more. The simple organization of the site, in addition to the wealth of archival material, makes the site ideal for a variety of researchers, educators, and others interested in African American history and culture.—**ARBA Staff Reviewer**

139.   **Unknown No Longer: Virginia Historical Society.** [Website] Free. Date reviewed 2018.

This project has its roots in 1995 when the Virginia Historical Society (VHS) published a guide to African American manuscripts, a guide that was updated in 2002. In 2011, the VHS launched this database of the names of enslaved Virginians that appear in unpublished documents in their collections. This project began with 1,500 names; names are continuously added to this ongoing project. The site is easily navigable by tabs across the top of the homepage: Record Search, Browse by Record Type, Browse by Location, Related Resources, and About This Project. There is also a Message Board, but this is restricted to registered users. The About This Project tab hosts two videos, one on the project itself and one on how to use the database. The resources link contains the URLs of other databases/websites as well as primary and secondary sources (though these are not current). The broadest search can be conducted by clicking on Record Search. From here users can search by first or last name, gender, occupation, date range, owner's last name, record type (church records, sales book, deeds, advertisement, etc.) or location (there is a drop-down list of cities). Browse by Record takes users to thumbnails of different types of records, like wills or diaries. The Browse by Location tab links to an interactive map. Clicking on a location reveals all the documents and names in the database from this location, making it possible to do a search of slave names in and around Richmond, for example. Once a particular record is accessed, users will be able to click a thumbnail that takes them to the digitized document. There will also be a record type, record call number, record title, and document notes. The accessed page additionally provides such information as life and death dates, owner's name, slave's name, and family relationships.—**ARBA Staff Reviewer**

140.   **Working Americans 1898-2016. Volume XIV: African Americans.** Amenia, N.Y., Grey House Publishing, 2016. 381p. illus. index. (Working Americans). $150.00. ISBN 13: 978-1-68217-106-6.

This 14th volume in the Grey House Working Americans series depicts the African American working experience over nearly 12 decades. The book, based on material from the Working Americans series by Scott Derks, profiles 30 individuals from a wide range of places and occupations. They include well-known persons such as hair-care entrepreneur Madam C. J. Walker and blues singer Florence Mills and lesser-known African Americans ranging from a U.S. Army major to a baseball player, a music manager, an educator, a civil rights activist, and more. Following the format of the other volumes in this series, each individual's story is told in three parts: home life, work life, and life in the community. These parts are followed by "Historical Snapshots" for the year in question, a listing of typical prices for the year, and selected primary sources. The selected materials include a "Lynching Timeline" and newspaper accounts of actions and attitudes affecting African Americans. The chapters are copiously illustrated with photographs and each section is clearly marked and easy to follow. After the 30 stories there is an informative document from the United States Census Bureau titled "The Black Population: 2010," which offers a wealth of statistics, maps, and charts. There is also an account of Black History Month, an index, and a selection of works for further reading. Although much of the information on the African American experience is available elsewhere, the presentation of factual material linked to individual stories helps the reader to engage with it. This book should be especially helpful to teachers in conveying to their students some fundamental realities of African American life, and a boon to secondary school students doing research projects. Recommended as a useful resource for academic, school, and public libraries.—**ARBA Staff Reviewer**

Berbers

141.   Ilahiane, Hsain. **Historical Dictionary of the Berbers (Imazighen).** 2d ed. Lanham, Md., Rowman & Littlefield, 2017. 428p. (Historical Dictionaries of Peoples and Cultures). $100.00; $104.00 (e-book). ISBN 13: 978-1-4422-8181-3; 978-1-4422-8182-0 (e-book).

The social, economic, and political climate of North Africa in general, and the social, economic, and political landscape of the Berbers in particular has changed dramatically since the first edition of this work (see ARBA 2009, entry 306). The region has witnessed an increased assertion of Berber ethnicity, and the advent of the Arab Spring has dramatically changed the situation. Hence a second edition of this dictionary is appropriate.

Like the first edition (and most other dictionaries in this series), its strength lies in providing concise overviews of the entries it lists. Of course each entry can be expanded into a much larger and fuller entry, but that is not this work's intent. Instead its entries are heavily cross-referenced, and it provides an extensive thematic bibliography for readers interested in further research.

Since the previous edition, several new entries (roughly a third of the new edition) have been added, existing entries have been rewritten for clarity, and the appendix has been expanded. The chronology and list of abbreviations have been enlarged to reflect changes since the first edition. While the bibliography of the first edition was impressive, the second edition adds many more references for scholars to consult. The dictionary is still directed to the nonspecialist, with the introductory essay and appendixes helping to frame the work.—**Muhammed Hassanali**

Indians of North America

142.   **Indigenous   Digital   Archive.   https://omeka.dlcs-ida.org/s/ida/page/home.** [Website] Free. Date reviewed: 2018.

Launched in the fall of 2017 as a project of the Museum of Indian Arts & Culture in collaboration with the New Mexico State Library Tribal Libraries Program and the Indian Pueblo Cultural Center, this site presents thousands of digitized documents related to government-sponsored schools for indigenous populations in the western United States. Documents generally include annual reports of school superintendents, correspondence, student rolls, inspection reports, and other materials. Users can browse documents by Schools, Tribes, Series or Rolls, or select the Browse by Topic tab to add Place, Person, Product, and Organization categories to the choices. Users can zoom in and out on a document which may be handwritten or machine typed and will generally include a machine-generated transcription and tags. Documents may report on a host of administrative issues such as letters received, health reports, population counts, land surveys, and employment records. It is important to note that there are a number of issues with the mechanics of the site that need to be addressed. For example, many of the topic options are misspelled or contain unnecessary symbols, which could be the result of a coding or network error. Further issues include tags that do not accurately match document text, missing information, and inaccurate machine-generated transcripts. These issues are glaring and definitely interfere with browsing the site. The site could also benefit by including more historical context or identifying information about the documents and schools themselves. Nevertheless, the information provided makes this site a worthy resource.—**ARBA Staff Reviewer**

143.   McCoy, Robert R., and Steven M. Fountain. **History of American Indians: Exploring Diverse Roots.** Santa Barbara, Calif., Greenwood Press/ABC-CLIO, 2017. 258p. illus. index. $58.00. ISBN 13: 978-0-313-38682-4; 978-0-313-38683-1(e-book).

Robert R. McCoy, Associate Professor of History at Washington State University, Pullman, and Steven M. Fountain, Clinical Assistant Professor of History and Coordinator of Native American Programs at Washington State University, Vancouver, have authored a synthesis that emphasizes the continuity of the American Indian experience from first arrival in North America to the 2016 protests over the construction of the Dakota Access oil pipeline in North Dakota. Not meant to be comprehensive, the narrative nevertheless shows how American Indian peoples within the borders of the present-day United States asserted agency and sovereignty during some very challenging periods. It also shows their enduring resolve to preserve their cultures, through such efforts as the establishment of the Smithsonian's National Museum of the American Indian and the passage of the Native American Graves and Protection Act (NAGPRA).

The narrative is divided into sixteen chapters that are arranged chronologically, although there is some overlap in the time periods covered within the respective sections. Each chapter includes profiles of notable American Indians of the period, some well known and others less well known, like the Lady of Cofitachequi. The profiles are followed by suggestions for further research, which include many recent scholarly titles. That is a boon for undergraduates but may challenge high school students as their school libraries would likely not have many of the books in their collections. The influence of the scholarly literature is evident in the treatment of the subject matter, as it reflects the current thinking in the field. For instance, while identifying the Bering Land Bridge as one of the migration routes to the Americas, the book also posits other possible entryways, such as people arriving by boat from Asia and possibly Europe. It touches upon the belief held by some that there was interaction before European contact between Indians on the West Coast and Polynesians. In early chapters focused on initial contacts between American Indian groups and Europeans, the events are framed using the "shatter zone" idea posited by Robbie Ethridge in her books *Mapping the Mississippian Shatter Zone* and *From Chicaza to Chickasaw*. While these ideas are prevalent in the study of American Indian culture and history in colleges and universities today, they had not been really explored effectively in reference books designed for the high school and undergraduate patrons until the publication of this title. This volume is highly recommended for high school, public, and undergraduate libraries.—**John R. Burch Jr.**

144.   **Truth   and   Reconciliation   Commission.   http://www.trc.ca/websites/ trcinstitution/index.php?p=3.** [Website] Free. Date reviewed: 2018.

Indian Residential Schools (IRS) were set up across Canada as a partnership between the government and Christian churches with the intent of assimilating indigenous youth into the governing Euro-Canadian culture. However, forced family separation and the disenfranchisement from both native and adopted societies have led not only to a loss of native culture but to alcoholism, abuse, and other ongoing problems. This site maintains the historical record of the findings of Canada's Truth and Reconciliation Commission (TRC) which formed to address the wrongdoings of assimilation policy. While the commission's mandate has been completed, it has released a final report which users can access under the About Us tab on the homepage menu bar. The TRC Findings link presents the pdf report which users can examine by section such as The History (Origins-1939, 1939-2000); The Inuit and Northern Experience; Missing Children and Unmarked Burials; and more. Incorporated into the report are over six thousand personal statements gathered from victims, witnesses, and others affected by the IRS system. While some statements reflect gratitude for learning to read and write, many recollections tell of extreme loneliness, inadequate nutrition, punishments for speaking native languages, and an emphasis on religion and manual labor over classroom education. The report also details such issues as the legacy of poor education, loss of language and culture, and deteriorating health. The Resources tab links to supplementary information about the TRC, National Aboriginal Organizations, and The IRS Settlement Agreement in addition to broader historical resources such as the Canadian Human Rights Museum. While the final report of the TRC was submitted in 2015, statements are still being gathered and work continues along the reconciliation path. Users can explore a feed of Recent News for up-to-date information. The site is an excellent source for information on this troubling aspect of North American history and would appeal to a range of historical research. All materials from the TRC— statements, documents, etc.—will be kept in a secure database and record office by the National Centre of Truth and Reconciliation,

http://nctr.ca/about.php.—**ARBA Staff Reviewer**

145.   Webster, Laurie D., Louise I. Stiver, D.Y. Begay, and Ann Lane Pete. **Navajo Textiles: The Crane Collection at the Denver Museum of Nature & Science.** Boulder, Colo., University Press of Colorado, 2017. 230p. illus. index. $34.95pa.; $27.95 (e-book). ISBN 13: 978-1-60732-672-4; 978-1-60732-673-1 (e-book).

This book is about a unique collection of southwestern textiles and the story of their acquisition within the Crane American Indian Collection at the Denver Museum of Nature & Science. The 12,000 American Indian artifacts and objects that are the foundation of the collection arrived in 1968 from the Southeast Museum of the North American Indian in the Florida Keys, which had been closed permanently due to nonattendance of the public. There are numerous color glossy photographs of the textiles throughout, along with color photographs of many of the staff of the museum, American Indians, and the American West landscape. There are also some black-and-white historical photographs of American Indians making textiles from the late 19th century through the mid-20th century. The textiles that are featured in the book are accompanied by stories related to their acquisition, as well as stories related to the design and sometimes the making of the rug. A very well-prepared and scholarly work that would also serve as a very nice coffee table book.— **Bradford Lee Eden**

Japanese Americans

146.   **Internment Archaeology. www.internmentarchaeology.org/.** [Website] Free. Date reviewed: 2017.

The Kooskia Internment Camp Archeological Project (KICAP) focuses on research conducted at a World War II-era internment camp holding 265 Japanese between the years 1943 and 1945. This website hosts an artifact database alongside supplemental information in specific regards to this project, Users can select the Artifact Catalog tab from the menu bar to access a database of over 5,000 items recovered from the project dig (although it is important to note that some recovered items are not associated with Japanese internment). Users can conduct a keyword search or scroll through the database in which items are listed with catalog numbers, group, type, category, description, and image if available. Items are also sorted into searchable group (e.g., personal), type (e.g., jewelry) or category (e.g., accoutrements) listings on the right sidebar. Particular item data may include method of recovery, weight, condition, material, remarks, and more. Other tabs on the main page include Publications & Activities, highlighting webinars, conferences, articles, and other work related to KICAP, and Featured Artifacts (In Development) showing thematically curated collections of recovered items, such as "Health & Medicine at the Kooskia Internment Camp." Supplemental information includes a blog and links to related sites like the Kooskia Internment Camp Scrapbook. A well-organized database, clearly explained methodology, color photography, and other features make the site accessible to a range of scholars, including the novice. The site successfully adds another spoke to the wheel of research into Japanese internment, one of the understated but nonetheless essential components of America's World War II story.—**ARBA Staff Reviewer**

147.   **Japanese Americans: The History and Culture of a People.** Jonathan H.X. Lee, ed. Santa Barbara, Calif., ABC-CLIO, 2018. 495p. illus. index. $105.00. ISBN 13: 978-1-4408-4189-7; 978-1-4408-4190-3 (e-book).

This work, arranged identically to the editor's *Chinese Americans* (2016), presents a great deal of information about the lives, struggles, and triumphs of the Japanese people in the United States. Following a 24-page chronology (covering 1543 to 2017), the book is divided into four broad sections, each with a brief "Historical Overview" introduction: 1) Context of Japanese Emigration, 2) Political Activity and Economic Life, 3) Cultural and Religious Life, and 4) Literature, the Arts, Popular Culture, and Sports. Within each section, articles are arranged alphabetically. Of the 149 entries, 59 are devoted to individuals, such as Senator Daniel Inouye, weightlifter Tommy Kono, and artist and architect Isamu Noguchi. Each of the entries is signed by one of the 76 contributors to this volume (from the United States and several other countries). The entries, ranging from one to eight pages, are clearly written, explaining Japanese terms used in the text, and continually providing the broader context in which the topic should be understood. One strength of this volume is the detailed discussion, throughout the volume, of the situation of Japanese Americans following the 1941 attack on Pearl Harbor. Another is the inclusion of the texts of 15 primary documents, dating from 1854 to 1976, including President Roosevelt's executive order establishing the War Relocation Authority in 1942.

Any library with an interest in American history and/or multiculturalism will find this book a useful addition to their collection.—**Mark Schumacher**

Latin Americans

148.   **The Latino Student's Guide to STEM Careers.** Laura I. Rendón and Vijay Kanagala, eds. Santa Barbara, Calif., Greenwood Press/ABC-CLIO, 2017. 275p. $58.00. ISBN 13: 978-1-61069-791-0; 978-1-61069-792-7 (e-book).

The purpose of *The Latino Student's Guide to STEM Careers* is clearly stated in the text—to inspire and educate the Latino/a community about educational and career opportunities in STEM fields. The book is well written using easy-to-understand language, and includes explanations for specialized terms. It provides information and guidance to young Latino/a students and their parents who want to better understand STEM requirements, including information about choosing schools, financial aid and scholarships, career paths, and tips for success.

The guide is organized into six parts, starting with steps guiding pre-high school students through early learning requirements, personal testimonials, lists of college and university programs, plus a chapter on other resources for students, parents, and teachers to explore. Emphasis is placed on choosing the best learning environment for Latino/a students, especially those schools containing staff and organizations that can best support this group of students.

Setting this text apart from others are the personal testimonials from successful Latino/a scientists. These stories provide real insight into how people from a variety of backgrounds can overcome difficult odds to achieve their goals. Another useful tool is the list of institutions and their STEM programs. This list is organized alphabetically by state, followed by institutional name, and contains information about the type of college, percentage of Hispanic students, name of the STEM program, plus links to each program's website. Every effort is made throughout this text to link readers to relevant information, and it is certainly a useful tool for anyone interested in working in the sciences.—**Cynthia Goode**

149.   Martinez, Sara E. **The Chicano Movement: A Historical Exploration of Literature.** Santa Barbara, Calif., Greenwood Press/ABC-CLIO, 2017. 179p. index. (Historical Explorations of Literature). $63.00. ISBN 13: 978-1-61069-707-1; 978-1-61069-708-8 (e-book).

This book examines four literary works in depth—*Bless Me Última* by Rudolfo Anaya (1972), *This Migrant Earth* by Tomás Rivera (1970), *The Revolt of the Cockroach People* by Oscar Z. Acosta (1973), and *The House on Mango Street* by Sandra Cisneros (1984)—documented with numerous primary sources in order to explore the origin and evolution of the Chicano movement. Each of the books is prefaced by a synopsis and includes historical background, related documents that provide pertinent verifiable information, a biography of each featured author, political events, and essays which depict the struggles of influential individuals who impacted Chicano society and culture. The consequences of each featured literary work, notes, and suggested readings are also included. Martinez deliberately selects noteworthy documents which convey the significance of each literary work. This reference is a wonderful resource for students and teachers curious about the birth and importance of the Chicano movement. The book includes a bibliography and an index. Recommended.—**Cynthia Schulz**

150.   Mitchell, Pablo R. **Understanding Latino History: Excavating the Past, Examining the Present.** Santa Barbara, Calif., Greenwood Press/ABC-CLIO, 2018. 304p. illus. maps. index. $37.00pa. ISBN 13: 978-1-4408-4168-2; 978-1-4408-4169-9 (e-book).

This book presents over five hundred years of history, from early Spanish exploration of the Americas to the present day. Unlike most other such histories, this work does not study the different communities—Cubans, Dominicans, Puerto Ricans, etc.—separately. Instead, a broader view is taken, while touching on the interaction between these groups. A ten-page chronology, from 1493 to 2016, begins the book, and is followed by ten chapters which divide the story into chronological slices, from "Spanish Beginnings, 1500-1800," to "Latina/os in a New Century, 1986-Present." There is also a section of thirty-seven profiles of important Latina/o figures, from explorer Cabeza de Vaca (ca. 1490-1559) to jurist Sonia Sotomayor (b. 1954), and then a group of twenty primary documents ranging from the 1530s to 2011. The 1819 Adams-Onís Treaty, ceding Florida to the United States, and the 1848 Treaty of Guadalupe Hidalgo, which ended the Mexican-American War, are the key items in the documents collection. A nine-page bibliography of English-language books and a glossary of Spanish terms complete the work.

Readers of all types—high school and college students, interested adults, and possibly academics—will this find this a work of value, at a quite reasonable price. Libraries serving all these constituencies should certainly consider adding this volume to their collections. It should be noted, however, that this title appears to be very similar to Mitchell's 2014 somewhat shorter volume *History of Latinos,* (2014, also published by Greenwood Press. The chapter titles are identical; the additions appear to be the profiles and the primary documents.—**Mark Schumacher**

151. **The Routledge Companion to Latina/o Media.** María Elena Cepeda and Dolores Inés Casillas, eds. New York, Routledge/Taylor & Francis Group, 2017. 442p. index. (Routledge Companions). $250.00. ISBN 13: 978-0-415-71779-3; 978-1-315-85800-5 (e-book).

This volume provides an overview of the current status and future directions of Latina/o media and communication studies. It has elements of other recent books (*Latina/os and the Media* (2010), *Contemporary Latina/o Media: Production, Circulation, Politics* (2014), and *Reinventing the Latino Television Viewer: Language, Ideology, and Practice* (2017), including addressing an essential question: why, when their five-hundred-year history here predates the existence of our nation by centuries, are Latinos still considered foreigners and continuously misrepresented and misunderstood? Similarities in coverage, especially on issues like images and representation, political economy, and Latino media consumption, suggests this book be recommended especially for academic libraries with Latina/o studies and/or media studies programs but may not be necessary for many other libraries.

The editors are both professors of Latina/o studies and authors of books on the subject. Contributors are professors and graduate students in departments of Latina/o studies, media studies, communication, and culture. The book lacks, and would have benefited from, an overall introduction. It is divided into four parts that examine different aspects of Latina/o media, respectively: understanding contemporary Latina/o media; access, policy, and production in Latina/o media; representations of Latinas/os in the media; and engendering new practices and meanings behind Latina/o media consumption. Each part contains an unsigned introduction with a list of references and five to eight relevant articles by contributors. The contributions vary widely, from specialized scholarly essays to original systematic research to business and professionally oriented articles on emerging trends. All contain notes and extensive references. Figures, tables, and an index are included.—**Madeleine Nash**

152. Urioste, Donaldo W., Francisco A. Lomelí, and María Joaquina Villaseñor. **Historical Dictionary of U.S. Latino Literature.** Lanham, Md., Rowman & Littlefield, 2017. 460p. (Historical Dictionaries of Literature and the Arts). $140.00; $139.99 (e-book). ISBN 13: 978-1-4422-7548-5; 978-1-4422-7549-2 (e-book).

Until recently, U.S. Latino/a literature was not considered a viable and historic literature, which resulted in little effort at organization and categorization. Now, however, as Latinos have become the fastest growing minority in the country and more authors write in English, numerous reference books on Latino/a literature are being published—*Latino and Latina Writers* (see ARBA 2004, entry 1068); *Encyclopedia of Hispanic-American Literature* (2008); *Greenwood Encyclopedia of Latino Literature* (see ARBA 2009, entry 982); *Historical Dictionary of Latin American Literature and Theater* (see ARBA 2012, entry 891); and *Norton Anthology of Latino Literature* (2011). The present volume joins these works in recovering, preserving, and showcasing the literary record of Latino people in the United States and also makes a successful case that this literature is an integral part of the American literary experience.

It is the newest addition to the Historical Dictionaries of Literature and the Arts series by Rowman & Littlefield and follows a design that is well organized and user friendly. In 460 pages, it also provides surprisingly comprehensive, well-researched information, especially in its dictionary of thoughtful essays, each signed by one of the three authors. Urioste, the lead author, and Villaseñor are professor and associate professor, respectively, at California State University, Monterey Bay, and Lomeli is professor at the University of California at Santa Barbara. Starting with a list of acronyms and abbreviations, the book includes a 40-page chronology beginning in the 14th century when the Aztecs established their capital in what is today Mexico City, through 2016. The information is rich and wide ranging, and is complemented by the introduction, which focuses on defining U.S. Latino/a literature, the colonial era, U.S. expansion and imperialism, immigration, protest and liberation movements, and the current internationalization of Latino literature. Details are provided in the dictionary section, with 110 entries on significant famous and lesser-known authors and 60 entries on important concepts, terminologies, trends, and issues. Entries are alphabetical and range from 100 to several pages, with cross-references to full entries in boldface and related entries shown through *see also.* The volume concludes with an outstanding 125-page bibliography of scholarly writing on Latino/a literature in general and on specific authors included in the dictionary section.

The overall work was so fascinating that this reviewer was moved to read it from cover to cover. The only weakness is a lack of illustrations. It is highly recommended for academic and public libraries.—**Madeleine Nash**

7   Genealogy and Heraldry

Genealogy

153.   Bowen, Jeff, transcriber **Choctaw by Blood Enrollment Cards, 1898-1914, Volume XI.** Baltimore, Md., Genealogical Publishing, 2016. 330p. index. $35.00pa. ISBN 13: 978-0-8063-5803-1.

154.   Bowen, Jeff, transcriber **Choctaw by Blood Enrollment Cards, 1898-1914, Volume XII.** Baltimore, Md., Genealogical Publishing, 2016. 332p. index. $25.00pa. ISBN 13: 978-0-8063-5810-9.

155.   Bowen, Jeff, transcriber **Choctaw by Blood Enrollment Cards, 1898-1914, Volume XIII.** Baltimore, Md., Genealogical Publishing, 2016. 332p. index. $35.00pa. ISBN 13: 978-0-8063-5819-2.

156.   Bowen, Jeff, transcriber **Choctaw by Blood Enrollment Cards, 1898-1914, Volume XIV.** Baltimore, Md., Genealogical Publishing, 2016. 330p. index. $35.00pa. ISBN 13: 978-0-8063-5825-3.

The Dawes Commission, enacted under an act of Congress in the late 19th century, served the purpose of redistributing communal Indian tribal lands into individual allotments assigned throughout the membership of the "Five Civilized Tribes" (Cherokee, Choctaw, Creek, Chickasaw, and Seminole). Over 6,100 enrollment cards were registered for members of the Choctaw tribe alone (although it is to be noted that under the law members were only allowed to register under one tribe, even if they claimed relation to others). These volumes, 11-14, include Choctaw enrollment cards 8796 through 11782 transcribed by Jeff Bowen from microfilm in the National Archives.

Each card reports the age, sex, and degree of Choctaw blood applicable to each registrant, as well as the date of enrollment. Additional information may include parents' names, spousal information, and other miscellaneous notes. An alphabetical index helps readers find particular names with ease.

These volumes would be highly useful to students in many fields or anyone interested in pursuing genealogical histories.—**ARBA Staff Reviewer**

157.   Boyle, Joseph Lee. **"much addicted to strong drink and swearing": White**

Pennsylvania Runaways, 1769-1772. Baltimore, Md., Genealogical Publishing, 2016. 452p. index. $39.95pa. ISBN 13: 978-0-8063-5815-4.

This book transcribes newspaper advertisements for runaway white indentured servants from 1769 to 1772. Compiler Joseph Boyle has published other volumes on white Pennsylvania runaways, and, like the other volumes, this one provides a wealth of information on the age, sex, height, place of origin, clothing occupation, traits, and much more about a population that sometimes gets overlooked. The introduction briefly relays the history of white indenture and provides a list of the newspapers consulted by Boyle. The advertisements vary in length; Boyle did not change spelling, capitalization, or punctuation; he put brackets around illegible words. Entries conclude with a citation of the newspaper(s) in which the advertisement appeared. These are a delight to read. For example, the person to whom the title of the book refers is Alexander Cunningham, approximately 5' 8", 25 years old, a weaver wearing a grey coat, and "much addicted to strong drink and swearing." These and other details appeared in a series of ads that appeared after Cunningham ran away in December 1771. This is a valuable source, conveniently transcribed and packaged, that suggests research possibilities for genealogists, historians, and others. Recommended for public and academic libraries.—**ARBA Staff Reviewer**

158.   Dobson, David. **The Scottish Jacobites of 1715 and the Jacobite Diaspora.** Baltimore, Md., Genealogical Publishing, 2017. 196p. $25.00pa. ISBN 13: 978-1-8063-5856-7.

Some of the Jacobite leaders from the 1715 uprising are well known—Mar, Derwentwater, Forster, and McIntosh. This does not hold true for the rank-and-file participants. This book, based on a variety of manuscript and printed primary sources, does a great deal to rectify this situation. In an A to Z format, the author presents hundreds of names that include soldiers, carters, farmers, grooms, writers, bursars, merchants, bakers, and others. Entries are typically a few lines long and contain various amounts of information based on what the author could find in the records. This information can include family connections, birth and death dates, occupation, place of capture, and sentence. While many were imprisoned, others went to Italy, Spain, France, and colonies in North America. Each entry indicates the printed primary source or manuscript consulted. Recommended for libraries with genealogy sections.—**ARBA Staff Reviewer**

159.   Goodson, Noreen J., and Donna Tyler Hollie. **Through the Tax Assessor's Eyes: Enslaved People, Free Blacks and Slaveholders in Early Nineteenth Century Baltimore.** Baltimore, Md., Genealogical Publishing, 2017. 264p. illus. index. $37.95pa. ISBN 13: 978-0-8063-5858-1.

This book transcribes and indexes property tax lists for free blacks, slaves, and slaveowners in Baltimore in 1813 and 1818, respectively. The assessments were done in response to economic growth and an increasing demand for city services. During this time, the free black population was on the rise in Baltimore while the slave population was decreasing. In the transcription, users will find ward-by-ward information that can include: name, race/status, residence, real property, occupation, enslaved property (name, age, value), and comments. What emerges is a portrait of free blacks, slaves, and slaveholders. The book serves as more than a treasure trove for genealogists as it contextualizes the information in the tax rolls in a very informative introduction that includes 18 biographical profiles of free blacks (men and women), slaves, emancipated slaves, abolitionists, and slaveowners. The book concludes with a glossary, a list of the streets and alleys where blacks were taxed for lots and improvements, a list of surnames that have become street names, suggestions for further reading, and a name index. The authors have done genealogists, historians, and other researchers a major service in transcribing the old records and making them easily available. Recommended for college and public libraries.—**ARBA Staff Reviewer**

160. Greenwood, Val D. **The Researcher's Guide to American Genealogy.** 4th ed. Baltimore, Md., Genealogical Publishing, 2017. 780p. index. $49.95pa. ISBN 13: 978-0-8063-2066-3.

The fourth edition of *The Researcher's Guide to American Genealogy* by Val D. Greenwood adds two chapters on technology and genealogical research and adds technology information to the other chapters. The third edition was printed in 2000 so these were much needed updates. The book is divided into two parts. The first part contains background to research information and the second part records information. The first chapter addresses understanding genealogical research; further chapters in the first part of the book cover language, terminology, evidence, reference works, the technology chapters, organizing, and correspondence. The second part discusses newspapers, vital records, wills, probate, census, land, court records, church records, military records, burial records, and more. It also contains an especially interesting chapter on the property rights of women. The book contains some uncommon illustrations, such as BLM land patent records, and more common records like the census records and birth certificates. The book ends with a very thorough index.

The book is written in an easy-to-read style but is not easy on the eyes if you are over 40. The print is small with a hard-to-read font. Colored sections would make it easier to find parts while researching. In addition, a spiral format for the book binding would be even better. Unfortunately I bent pages and almost tore them just reviewing the book. The next edition may be able to alleviate size issues by consolidating information.

The price of the book is a steal with all the useful information and with the current price of textbooks. I recommend this book for every high school to adult library and for anyone doing genealogical research.—**Kathy Adams**

161. Kemp, Thomas Jay. **International Vital Records Handbook.** 7th ed. Baltimore, Md., Genealogical Publishing, 2017. 756p. $84.95pa. ISBN 13: 978-0-8063-2061-8.

Vital personal records including birth, marriage, divorce, and death records are important sources for historical and genealogical research and also serve as critically important legal documents. It is important for individuals and organizations needing such records for personal or other reasons to know where and how to find these records, how much to pay for reproductions of them, and how long government agencies are required to store them.

This work provides this information in exhaustive detail for all U.S. states, relevant U.S. government agencies, U.S. trust territories and commonwealths such as Puerto Rico, and for multiple foreign countries ranging from Afghanistan to Zimbabwe. Sections for obtaining vital records from entities such as the State of Indiana list the physical address, phone number, and website URL for the Indiana State Department of Health's Vital Records Department, the years it possesses birth and death records, a citation to the statutory authority in Indiana state law giving this agency the authority to set up requirements for the release of these records, the cost of obtaining and searching for certified vital personal records, information on obtaining vital records, and information for sources on obtaining additional personal genealogical information including the Indiana State Library's Genealogy collection and the Allen County Public Library in Fort Wayne which has the U.S.' second-largest genealogy collection. Printouts of sample application forms for requesting vital records are provided and requestors of vital records are also instructed to contact county government offices to request marriage and divorce certificates.

Information for requesting these records from foreign governments includes the name of the relevant national government vital records agency and contact information for that country's U.S. embassy if they maintain diplomatic relations with the United States. English-speaking countries such as Australia, Canada, and the United Kingdom feature detailed documentation and forms on obtaining vital records from provincial and state governmental jurisdictions.

This handbook is an extremely valuable resource for individuals seeking information on obtaining vital personal records. Providing global coverage especially enhances its value in a globalized society where international migration is increasingly common. It provides exhaustive detail on relevant procedures and fees as well as forms. Highly recommended for genealogy, family studies, and comparative international collections.— **Bert Chapman**

162.   McCartney, Martha W., and Helen C. Rountree. **Powhatan Indian Place Names in Tidewater, Virginia.** Baltimore, Md., Genealogical Publishing, 2017. 130p. index. $20.00pa. ISBN 13: 978-0-8063-2062-5.

The book begins with a brief introduction and an extensive list of the sources consulted, which include manuscripts and miscellaneous published primary sources and cartographic works. The place-names, listed in alphabetic order, follow. As the introduction explains, the spelling of place-names varied (sometimes widely). In this book, readers will see a main heading for Quantico, for example, that uses the most common name spelling or modern equivalent of the name. This is followed by the earliest dated spelling of the name by a cartographer. Variations of place-name spellings are listed in chronological order. Again using the example of Quantico, this spelling is followed by six variations dating from 1654 to 1677. The name was spelled Quantico on a 1751 map by Joshua Fry and Peter Jefferson, and this is the one included in the book. An index to Indian place-names rounds out the work.—**ARBA Staff Reviewer**

163.   Mills, Elizabeth Shown, and Ruth Brossette Lennon. **Tips & Quips for the Family Historian.** Baltimore, Md., Genealogical Publishing, 2017. 174p. index. $14.95. ISBN 13: 978-0-8063-2041-0.

Elizabeth Shown Mills, internationally recognized professional genealogist and historian and author of numerous books and standard genealogical research guides, here has collaborated with her granddaughter, Ruth Brossette Lennon, designer and typesetter, to produce an attractive, deceptively slim, volume of brief, but precise and useful, quotations. Readers likely will not choose to read the entire book at once, but rather selectively choose among the many categories of quotations or "Tips and Quips" ranging from Accuracy and Brick Walls to Document Analysis, Luck, Plagiarism, Tax Records, and Truth. Some quotations appear in multiple categories. Individuals quoted vary widely, some are popular figures or authors such as Jennifer Anniston and Studs Terkel and many others are outstanding genealogists directing their advice to gatherings of professional researchers. The quotations supply advice and counsel for users as diverse as beginning genealogists, aspiring family historians, dinner speakers, professional historians, and serious family history researchers, quite an accomplishment for a book small enough to fit easily into a purse or briefcase.

Mills and Lennon provide three excellent appendixes permitting direct access to specific "References" for each quotation as well as an "Index to Individuals Quoted" and an "Index to Keywords" for each quotation. Mills' typical precision and accuracy in the appendixes permit readers to discover or rediscover bibliographic information about many important genealogical research sources and guides together with works by noted genealogists including those specializing in Native American and African American family history. The over 300 sources cited include print reference books, genealogical seminar and conference materials, print journals, and various online source materials.

Given its size, format, and price this book will appeal to a popular audience, but both the author's sterling reputation and the "References" together justify its inclusion in public and academic library genealogical collections.—**Julienne L. Wood**

164.   Ports, Michael A. **Baldwin County Georgia Lottery Drawers for 1820 and 1821.** Baltimore, Md., Genealogical Publishing, 2016. 234p. index. $24.95pa. ISBN 13: 978-0-8063-5812-3.

This book contains transcribed records kept on two separate land lotteries held in Baldwin County, Georgia. Conducted in 1820 and 1821, these lotteries grouped eligible citizens by district of current residence (generally named after the commanding officer of the militia who protected it). The lotteries would then distribute parcels to draw winners. The transcriptions in this book list lottery registrants who had confirmed their eligibility against a set of requirements. In addition, the volume includes a transcription of lottery winners or "Fortunate Drawers" for the 1820 lottery.

Transcriptions for the 1820 lottery cover 10 militia districts within Baldwin County. Records are presented in a tabular format, with registrants listed alphabetically by family name. Although no headings are listed for the seven following columns, they indicate number of draws per category such as widows, orphans, Revolutionary Officers and Soldiers, etc. An eighth column represents the total number of draws per registrant. Two copies, representing both state and country records, are transcribed for some militia districts, with differences noted. A table of "Fortunate Drawers" is also transcribed, and conveys the winner name (also alphabetical), current militia district, newly awarded lot number, district number, and county. Transcriptions for the 1821 lottery include records for 10 militia districts. While some are structured similarly as in the 1820 draw (names and draws per category), some tables list applicant name, district, and number of draws. Remarks noting family status or occupation may accompany name. Supplementary information includes generous background on the Georgia state laws which authorized the draw, a description of militia district formation and a map of Baldwin County militia districts.

The book is indexed by registrant's family name for ease of reference. These records could be of great interest to those tracing family histories in the southern states and/or studying the early mechanisms of American state government.—**ARBA Staff Reviewer**

165.   Ports, Michael A. **Indian Wars of the American South 1610-1858: A Guide for Genealogists & Historians.** Baltimore, Md., Genealogical Publishing, 2017. 398p. illus. index. $39.95pa. ISBN 13: 978-0-8063-5849-9.

Written for lay historians and genealogists, this work documents conflicts between Euroamericans and American Indian groups in the present-day states of Alabama, Florida, Georgia, Kentucky, Louisiana, Mississippi, North Carolina, South Carolina, Tennessee, Virginia, and West Virginia. Its coverage ranges from the First Anglo-Powhatan War of 1609-1614 to the Third Seminole War, which concluded in 1858.

The book is presented in two parts. In part one, each of the respective wars is presented with one to three sections. All include an overview of the events that precipitated the fighting along with a description of the military campaigns undertaken by the combatants. Some of the entries include a list of places that can be visited that relate to the respective wars along with pictures of historical markers. Many of the entries also provide suggestions for further research. The second half of the book is a goldmine for researchers as it identifies where the major research collections on the respective wars can be found. The list includes federal repositories, state archives, the capitols of American Indian nations, libraries, organizations, and historical societies. Contact information for each of the repositories is included along with descriptions of the collections that they house. For some of the federal and state archives, it details the finding aids that are available along with warnings about restrictions and quirks that may be unique to a particular institution. This work is recommended for libraries in the South supporting genealogical research.—**John R. Burch Jr.**

166.   Ports, Michael A. **Jefferson County Georgia Lottery Drawers for 1827 and 1832.** Baltimore, Md., Genealogical Publishing, 2016. 126p. index. $18.50pa. ISBN 13: 978-0-8063-5818-5.

This book contains transcribed records kept on two separate land lotteries held in Jefferson Country, Georgia. Eligible citizens were grouped by district of current residence, generally named after the commanding officer of the militia who protected it. The transcriptions in this book list lottery registrants (not necessarily winners) who had confirmed their eligibility against a set of requirements, for the draws to be held in 1827 and 1832.

The first half of the book covers the 1827 lottery taking place in nine militia districts, while the second half includes records for five districts. Records appear district by district in table format, and generally include registrant name (family and given), number of draws allowed, and remarks reflecting age or family status (e.g., "single man" or "widow"). Registrants are listed alphabetically by family name. Each district roll is preceded by a brief contextual paragraph. Auxiliary information includes parcel size, background on the Georgia state laws which authorized the draw, a description of militia district formation, and a map of Jefferson County militia districts. There is also a table describing draw participation parameters. For example, a widow living three years in Georgia would be eligible for one draw, while a widow whose husband died in service to the United States and living three years in Georgia would be eligible for two draws.

The book is indexed by registrant's family name for ease of reference. These records could be of great interest to those tracing family histories in the southern states and/or studying the early mechanisms of American state government.—**ARBA Staff Reviewer**

167.   Thode, Ernest. **Swiss Pioneers of Southeastern Ohio.** Baltimore, Md., Genealogical Publishing, 2017. 124p. index. $20.00pa. ISBN 13: 978-0-8063-5847-5.

This book shares a narrative account of Swiss emigration to the Unites States via the stories of four individuals: Ludwig Gall, Jacob Tischer, Johann von Steiger, and Jean Labarthe. Each man had different reasons for leaving their homeland, and the record left behind helps illuminate those reasons alongside how (or if) they established a foundation in the United States, in particular the state of Ohio in the developing Northwest territories. Brief but detail-packed chapters follow a condensed telling of how the men and their charges came to sail across the ocean—establishing their unique circumstances of homeland dissatisfaction (e.g., strict marriage laws, warfare, etc.) alongside their success (or not) at creating a stateside foundation. Information includes supply itemizations, vessel descriptions, and cameos from interesting figures, like U.S. Secretary of State John Quincy Adams or a young Cornelius Vanderbilt. Readers compelled by their genealogical interest will enjoy pouring over the many names, lineages, dates, and places in both the United States and Switzerland.. Anecdotal tidbits help readers learn about Swiss tradition (e.g., washing their clothes only twice a year), bureaucratic frustrations of emigration, and the U.S. government approach towards it. Supplemental material enhances the narrative and includes black-and-white illustrations and photographs as well as the original and transcribed versions of passenger lists from the ships that carried the Swiss to American lands. The index is thorough and exceptionally helpful in regards to the amount of detail in the book, (although the addition of a timeline would further clarify the story). This well-sourced and concise book provides an engaging and easily digestible look at what would only be the beginning of European emigration stateside.—**ARBA Staff Reviewer**

168.   Watson, Marston. **Royal Families: Americans of Royal and Noble Ancestry.** Baltimore, Md., Genealogical Publishing, 2017. 902p. index. $75.00pa. ISBN 13: 978-0-8063-2063-2.

In his detailed introduction to this massive book, Gary Boyd Roberts, Senior Research Scholar Emeritus, New England Historic Genealogical Society, points out the unique characteristics of this most recent title in author Marston Watson's now four-volume set. Per Boyd, volume four deals with the Pelham-Avery-West cluster of "royally descended, near-kin immigrants to the American colonies," treats persons in Massachusetts, Connecticut, New York, and Virginia, includes immigrants to the South and, hence, Confederates, covers nine generations of American descendants of Thomas West (b. 1556) and Anne Knollys (b. 1555), possible granddaughter of England's King Henry VIII, and reveals other possible American descendants of Henry and his mistress Mary Boleyn, sister of Henry's later wife, Anne Boleyn. Roberts also identifies related genealogical studies and points out prominent individuals in each geographical area. Boyd credits Marston Watson, distinguished genealogist, researcher, author, and public speaker, with extensive research in both print and online sources.

The book's page numbering begins with Generation One and persons are numbered within each generation. The more than 700 pages of text contain thousands of names and family connections. The casual family historian will find the text daunting, but will appreciate the comprehensive Person Index (with page numbers), itself some 170 pages. The bibliography confirms Watson's diligent research. Also useful are three appendixes: Royal Family Charts and two separate lists of persons with possible royal connections who belong to the "Original Members of the Society of the Cincinnati" and the "General

Society of Mayflower Descendants," respectively.

This volume belongs in specialized genealogical libraries as well as in public, academic, and state libraries with large genealogical collections, especially those libraries owning the previous three volumes in the set. Serious individuals determined to prove a family connection to English royalty will need to peruse this intimidating set. Users should heed Watson's caution in his acknowledgments that "hundreds of proposed birth, marriage and death dates in this book are estimates and should not be considered proof of these events …" sufficient for applications to lineage societies.—**Julienne L. Wood**

8 Geography and Travel Guides

Geography

General Works

Atlases

169. **AAA Road Atlas.** Heathrow, Fla., American Automobile Association, 2017. 144p. maps. $12.95pa. ISBN 13: 978-1-59508-585-6.

The atlas begins with a map legend, a mileage table, a distance chart, and a two-page map of the United States. State and city maps follow and comprise the bulk of the 145-page book. These are alphabetic by state and include places and map coordinates, inset maps of cities, and local mileage charts. The maps show the location of some national parks (these are also listed in the table of contents); points of interest like colleges and universities, ski areas, and monuments and memorials; all types of roads and highways; certain boundaries (time zones, state, etc.); and areas of interest like Indian reservations, forests, and grasslands. The atlas includes basic maps of each of the Canadian provinces. These include driving distances between selected cities, an alphabetical list of places with map coordinates, and inset maps. Inset maps are included for most of the major cities. The atlas includes only a country map for Mexico, with inset maps for Mexico City, Cancun, Monterrey, Guadalajara, and Acapulco. The atlas provides driving distance information, an alphabetic list of places and map coordinates, and a paragraph on the documents needed at border crossings. The maps are in color, which enhances readability, though the font is necessarily small.—**ARBA Staff Reviewer**

170. **ArcGIS Online for the National Park Service. https://nps.maps.arcgis.com.** [Website] Free. Date reviewed: 2018.

Mapping platform ArcGis Online has worked in concert with the U.S. National Park Service to create an excellent online resource that helps tell the rich and varied stories of some parks. The project currently focuses on a small portion of the fifty-nine official national parks; however, the maps created nonetheless demonstrate a good range of research possibilities. From the homepage, users can scroll through the display of Featured Maps or go directly to the Gallery via the link in the upper left corner of the page. The Gallery currently presents eight maps in either a list or visual grid.

Two maps track bear movement through the Great Smokey Mountains National Park and coastal resilience research through several parks damaged by 2012's Hurricane Sandy. The other six maps reflect themes related to the 1804-06 Lewis and Clark Expedition across the northwestern territories. These maps are used to trace the explorers' specific water routes, track expedition encounters with volcanoes as well as "new" flora and fauna, and mark the major expedition stops now listed in the National Register of Historic Places. Another map affiliated with Lewis and Clark focuses exclusively on the Alice Creek Historic District in Montana, detailing its long history as a travel route for many Native American tribes. Users can open a map directly from the thumbnail or select the Details tab for each map which provides a brief description, tags, and other information. In concert with their distinct subjects, each map may organize and present their data in different ways. Some include additional resources, such as videos, photographs, and charts. It would be great to see the maps expand into other national parks. The site would appeal to a variety of educators, Lewis and Clark scholars, environmentalists, historians, etc.—**ARBA Staff Reviewer**

171.   **Atlas of the Historical Geography of the United States. www.dsl.richmond. edu/historicalatlas/.** [Website] Free. Date reviewed: 2017.

Based upon the eponymous print publication of 1932, this site brings a remarkable work of the past into the digital age. Users can access over 700 maps of the United States reflecting numerous topics of historical and geographical interest. The site employs a variety of digital tools to enhance the visually striking and compelling maps. The process of "Georectification" bends the original map to shape it over a digitally constructed counterpart. Additionally, some maps are animated to reflect changes over time, and many maps contain clickable data points relative to particular topics such as crop production and population demographics. Like the original atlas, the digital version uses the same table of contents for ease of navigation. Some of the general subjects include Indians 1567-1930; Military History 1689-1919; Colleges, Universities and Churches 1775-1890; and The Natural Environment. Each of these broader categories may then encapsulate a larger variety of individually mapped topics. When viewing the maps, users may select from a number of options, such as adding corresponding text, enlarging the map legend, or comparing the default georectified visual with the original plate. The Farther Afield blog elaborates on map data. A map will display an icon if it connects to a particular blog post. This site does an excellent job of staying true to the authentic intent and feel of the original work while stretching its impact via modern technology.—**ARBA Staff Reviewer**

172.   **Google Maps. https://www.google.com/maps.** [Website] Free. Date reviewed: 2017.

Google Maps, the go-to site for those in search of directions from point A to point B, has many useful tools that make navigation a snap. By simply typing in an address or the name of a place, Google Maps will produce directions for driving, walking, or using public transportation. Users can choose to view the maps in satellite or terrain mode. For some places, street views are available. As an online tool, Google Maps can be continuously updated (even showing current levels of road traffic for some places). Users can adjust the scale of coverage by zooming in and out. Drivers can get turn-by-turn instructions via cell phone or can print out maps prior to a trip. Google provides previews for some routes.

Google Maps can also serve as an interactive online travel guide. Tourist attractions, restaurants, and other places of business may include links to handy information such as hours of operation, photographs, and reviews. Users can make their location publicly available, submit reviews and photographs, save a route or place in a personalized list, and more.—**ARBA Staff Reviewer**

173.   **Historical Topographical Map Digitization Project. https://ocul.on.ca/ topomaps/.** [Website] Free. Date reviewed: 2018.

This website displays the results of a project to digitize older topographic maps of Ontario, Canada. The project has digitized over one thousand maps originally printed throughout the first half of the twentieth century. Users can scan the selected maps presented on the homepage, or can click on the Full Collection tab on the left sidebar. From here, users can search maps by sheet name or Canada's National Topographic System (NTS) sheet number or scroll through an alphabetized listing of place-names, from Aberfoyle to Wyoming. Clicking on a place-name may bring up more than one map depending on if the map was re-created over time. Maps can be downloaded or viewed offsite in Scholar GeoPortal, which can layer the historical map over a current base map so users can observe the geographical evolution of the area. Maps can also be viewed in two different scales. Each map includes a brief "abstract" providing additional information regarding publishing, map features, and more. Other tabs offer further information on the project and the maps themselves. About the Maps uses an excellent chronology and other resources to share a history of topographical mapping in Canada. FAQs may help with technical aspects of the site. Collection Highlights show interesting examples of the ways in which these maps can be used, such as mapping "Urban Growth in the Ottawa area." Using the Maps explains some of the more technical details behind the Scholar GeoPortal mapping site in regards to finding, exploring, downloading, and searching.—**ARBA Staff Reviewer**

174.   **Mapquest. https://www.mapquest.com/.** [Website] Free. Date reviewed: 2017.

This multifunctional website offers users an enhanced mapping experience for locations throughout the United States. Employing the open source OpenStreetMap platform as a foundation, MapQuest contains information on thousands of U.S. locations from the smallest park to the largest metropolis and provides a number of tools for use in studying routes, geography, local resources, etc.

Users can select from a number of options on the drop down menu on the left tool bar, or work directly from the large U.S. map graphic. The Map tab offers a search bar where users can enter their desired location. It is important to enter precise information (e.g., name, address, city, state, etc.) due to the commonality of many place-names throughout the country. The graphic will then show the pinned location alongside a number of details and options, such as street address, phone number, website link, and directions. The Get Directions tab on the main menu allows users to map routes as well. Users simply enter the location from which they are starting the trip with any potential stops, in addition to the location they have mapped. The site will display any available routes, estimate fuel costs, and more. The Route Planner tool allows users to incorporate up to 26 separate locations within a trip and estimate time and distance.

The map graphic can be layered with a good variety of local services and attractions relating to things like food, gas, hotels, shopping, coffee, airports, hospitals, and parks. Users can manipulate the map by zooming in or out, expanding the view to fit the entire page, incorporating traffic information and/or employing a satellite view. Registered users may incorporate new locations into the map, and can Create a Custom My Map (printable and shareable) from the menu as well.

The site also provides local travel tips and national park guides, and allows users to directly book hotels, flights and rental cars with a partner business. It is important to note that MapQuest will highlight partner businesses (e.g., Hampton Hotels) in its search fields or layering function, and that a number of advertising banners will appear throughout the browsing experience. Nonetheless, MapQuest is an excellent, easy-to-use site.—**ARBA Staff Reviewer**

175.   **Osher Map Library. http://www.oshermaps.org/.** [Website] Free. Date reviewed: 2018.

The Osher Map Library based out of the University of Southern Maine has brought together a significant collection of maps, navigational charts, atlases, and more, many of which are now available for viewing online. Specifically, this site allows digital access to over six thousand items culled from sixteen prominent collections and primarily (but not exclusively) focused on the geography of North America. Users can access the materials in several ways but it is likely best to click through the tabs on the menu bar. Browse Maps is actually more of a search engine, where users can conduct a basic, advanced, or imagery search. This browse/search function is ideally suited for users who know what they are looking for (they can only "browse" after they "search"). General users may simply choose to search by region in addition to the time frame parameter. The search page includes a brief listing of Popular Topics for each search alternative (e.g., Holy Land, New England, Propaganda, Mermaids, Colonial America, etc.). Data accompanying each map can be quite generous and may include title, creator, publisher, region depicted, date produced, date published, language, dimensions, printing technique, and historical context. Users can zoom in on maps and download them as a low-resolution image (high-resolutions images must be officially requested). The Learn tab allows users to explore curated Exhibitions, such as "To Conquer or Submit? America Views the Great War," which includes tactical atlases, propaganda maps, and Map Commentaries, which align selected maps with scholarly essays. Online Exhibits are exclusive to the website and include such offerings as "20th Century Maps of the Soviet Union" and "Civil War Monuments in Maine." Under the About tab, users can select the Collections Lists to view a general description of the contents of each of the sixteen separate collections which comprise the greater corpus. It is important to note that all items in the collections are not currently included in the digital library. Educators may find information under the Teacher Resources tab useful, as it includes a generous series of downloadable activities, games, lesson plans, and other resources aimed at a range of grade levels. While the site would benefit from improved browsing capabilities, it is nonetheless home to a fascinating digital collection which, when combined with the site's other resources, truly shows how maps help shape the stories of civilization and the lands it occupies.—**ARBA Staff Reviewer**

176.   **Oxford Atlas of the World.** 24th ed. New York, Oxford University Press, 2017. 450p. maps. index. $89.95. ISBN 13: 978-0-19-084362-5.

This atlas, now in its 24th edition, begins with a user guide and detailed table of contents followed by a section on world statistics for countries (population, capital, annual income in U.S. dollars, area) and cities with more than nine hundred thousand inhabitants.

Next comes a short section on land and maritime boundaries. After this, the section Images of Earth presents satellite photos of urban areas like Paris, Bangkok, and Boston. The Gazetteer of Nations lists countries A to Z and includes pertinent details about geography, politics and economy, population, languages, currency, religion, government, and more. Each of these short profiles (some are a short paragraph, some are several paragraphs) includes a country flag and small map that shows where a nation is located within the continent. World Geography, which follows, has forty-two maps, charts, graphs, and diagrams. Here users will find information on the solar system, seasons, geology, climate change and global warming, population, trade, and health, among other topics. World Cities maps seventy urban areas and is followed by urban maps, the main part of the atlas. As is immediately apparent, the maps are of the highest quality. More can be learned about the production of the maps in the User Guide. Maps start with Europe followed by Asia, Africa, Australia and Oceania, North America, and South America. A glossary of geographical terms and a one-hundred-page-plus index to world maps round out the work. The latter includes a key to abbreviations and a pronunciation guide. This is a highly recommended purchase for libraries of all sorts.—**ARBA Staff Reviewer**

177.   **Rand McNally Road Atlas 2018.** Skokie, Ill., Rand McNally, 2017. 137p. illus. maps. index. $14.95pa. ISBN 13: 978-0-528-01731-4.

The *Rand McNally Road Atlas* packs a large amount of information into a compact and affordable guide. The inside front cover contains a map legend, followed by a nice bonus, six suggested "best of" road trips to northern New England, the Blue Ridge Parkway, Miami and the Florida Keys, Lake Michigan, Canyon Country, and San Francisco and the California central coast. Following is the handy mileage chart that covers ninety North American cities and U.S. national parks. Readers can find more mileages at randmcnally.com/MC. Front matter also provides quick map references for states and provinces as well selected cities and national parks, which allows readers to jump quickly to their desired location. Following is a two-page map of the United States. State maps appear in alphabetic order, with map insets of cities. The atlas concludes with maps of individual Canadian provinces and a map of Mexico. An index rounds out the work. Readers can also visit RandMcNally.com/index for an even more complete map index.

The accuracy, reliability, detail, and affordability of the road atlas make this a highly recommended suggestion for public and academic libraries.—**ARBA Staff Reviewer**

Dictionaries and Encyclopedias

178.   **Online around the World: A Geographic Encyclopedia of the Internet, Social Media, and Social Apps.** Laura M. Steckman and Marilyn J. Andrews, eds. Santa Barbara, Calif., ABC-CLIO, 2017. 400p. illus. index. $94.00. ISBN 13: 978-1-61069-775-0; 978-1-61069-776-7 (e-book).

This book attempts to record and document the use of the Internet, social media, and social apps in countries around the world, hence a geographical encyclopedia. Many people assume that the entire world has access to the same websites and apps, as well as Internet access, which is available in the United States; obviously, this is not so. The editors and contributors provide a snapshot of what "online" means in over 75 countries. Each essay describes the size, population, per capita, and percentage of Internet access in that country, and then details various political and social challenges, major telecommunications and telephony entities, and which social media and social apps are most prevalent, active, and available. Some would be surprised that Facebook and other popular websites are not the most favored or used by various worldwide populations. The introduction provides the parameters for the content, and includes an overview of popular international social media sites, along with a chronology of significant events in cyber history. This volume is an excellent reference work which documents online usage and activity around the world.—**Bradford Lee Eden**

Handbooks and Yearbooks

179.   Sechrist, Robert. **Planet of the Grapes: A Geography of Wine.** Santa Barbara, Calif., Praeger/ABC-CLIO, 2017. 326p. maps. index. $48.00. ISBN 13: 978-1-4408-5438-5; 978-1-4408-5439-2 (e-book).

The author of this volume broadly explores both the geography and history of wine—its production, its consumption, and its place within a country's culture and society. (The earliest discussions [briefly] involve Pangaea 65 million years ago, as continents formed!) The author traces numerous aspects of the evolution of wine production: for example, archaeological evidence of wine dates back thousands of years, when the development of pottery allowed storage of the fermented juice. In often wildly different ecosystems, wine production has developed across the globe. In some regions, the grapes grown, and thus the wines made, have evolved considerably over the past century.

Major chapters explore the wines of Europe, of South America, and the United States, examining the various grapes used for the scores of wines currently being made, the climates they grow in, and even the chemical processes in fermentation. Tables of production by region or by grape appear frequently as well. This volume provides a fine introduction to the world of wine on a global scale. Libraries with readers interested in this topic would do well to add this tome to their collection.—**Mark Schumacher**

Travel Guides

180.   **DK Eyewitness Travel Berlin.** Rev ed. New York, DK Publishing, 2017. 352p. illus. maps. index. $25.00pa. ISBN 13: 978-1-4654-6040-0.

This revised edition begins with a handy user guide before moving into an introduction of Berlin that includes suggested itineraries, a brief history of the city, and sights to see, among other things. The next section breaks Berlin down by area and provides travelers with color maps, photos, and diagrams of such distinct places as Museum Island, Tiergarten, and Unter den Linden. Here readers will find a list of sights at a glance, a general description, entry fees, operating hours, and much more. An entire section is devoted to where to stay, where to shop, where to eat and drink, and where to find entertainment. The descriptions are generous and appeal to travelers whose budgets are small, large, or anywhere in between. The last section, Survival Guide, provides information on tours, visas and customs, culture and language, consulates and embassies, banking and currency, and health and safety. It also discusses how to travel around Berlin. There is a street finder index, a general index, a transit map, and a pull-out map of the city. The photographs, maps, and diagrams are of the highest quality as is the information provided. This most recent edition is highly recommended to public libraries.—**ARBA Staff Reviewer**

181.   **DK Eyewitness Travel Prague.** Rev ed. New York, DK Publishing, 2018. 272p. illus. maps. index. $25.00pa. ISBN 13: 978-1-4654-5507-9.

Following a usage guide, the book begins with an introduction to the city that provides sample itineraries; a short, but very useful, history of Prague, including timelines; information on Prague's "best of" sights; and suggestions for viewing Prague from the Vltava River. All of this information is supplemented by color photographs, maps, and illustrations. The second portion of the book, Prague Area by Area, walks readers through the city's distinct regions: Old Town, Jewish Quarter, Prague Castle and Hardcany, Little Town, and New Castle. A portion of this section is devoted to day trips around Prague. The entire section is beautifully illustrated with color photographs, building diagrams, and maps and concludes with four guided walks. The third part of the book is devoted to helping travelers find dining, lodging, shopping, and entertainment. Within this portion, DK recommends its top picks. The final section is a survival guide with basic information: how to get to Prague as well as how to get around Prague; the addresses and phone numbers of embassies and consulates; customs information; police and security services, and much more. The book concludes with two indexes, a street finder index and a general index, a phrase book, and a two-page Prague transit map. A pull-out map is an added bonus. The book is light enough to carry and detailed enough to satisfy most travelers. Highly recommended.—**ARBA Staff Reviewer**

182.   **DK Eyewitness Travel Rome.** Rev ed. New York, DK Publishing, 2017. 442p. illus. maps. index. $25.00pa. ISBN 13: 978-1-4654-6046-2.

This revised and updated guidebook to Rome begins with a Rome by area color map, a table of contents, a user guide, suggestions for two-day, three-day, and five-day stays, and color maps of Italy and of central Rome. This is followed by a brief, but very helpful, history of Rome that includes a timeline and color photos. Within this history, the book provides two pages of explanation on understanding Roman architecture. For those who like to make sure to see the top sights a city has to offer, the Rome at a Glance section lists the top attractions—churches and temples, museums and galleries, fountains and obelisks. This is followed by the heart of the book—Rome by Area. The section covers such areas as the capitol, the Campo de'Fiori, and Trastevere, and ends with nine guided walks. The book provides an abundance of color maps in this section. No guide book would be complete without basic information on where to stay, where to eat and drink, where to shop, and where to find entertainment. This book covers all of the above and includes a section on what to do with children in Rome. Additionally, there is a survival guide section that provides practical information as well as advice on how to travel to Rome and within Rome. A street finder index and ten pages of detailed (in color) city maps follow. A general index rounds out the work. It is important to note that the maps and color photographs are of exceptionally high quality and enhance the value of this guidebook, which is recommended highly to public libraries.—**ARBA Staff Reviewer**

183.   **Fodor's Essential Israel.** Linda Cabasin, ed. New York, Fodor's Travel Publications/ Random House, 2017. 552p. illus. maps. index. $24.99pa. ISBN 13: 978-0-14-754676-0.

If planning a trip to Israel, this guide from Fodor's Travel is definitely a good choice. The beginning of the book includes a wealth of information on what travelers need to know about the country's people, religion, major holidays, and more. Here readers will also find ideas for what to do if traveling with kids and suggested itineraries. Tucked into this section is a helpful timeline of Israel through the ages starting in prehistoric times. Cities and regions are covered in the following chapters: "Jerusalem," "Around Jerusalem and the Dead Sea," "Tel Aviv," "Haifa and the Northern Coast," "Lower Galilee," "Upper Galilee and the Golan," "Eilat and the Negev," and "Petra." These chapters give readers suggestions for lodging, restaurants, sights, shopping, sports and entertainment, and more. All of this information is highlighted with beautiful color photographs and highly readable maps. The table of contents also includes a list of maps for quick reference. At the end of the book, users will find a Hebrew vocabulary and a Palestinian Arabic vocabulary, followed by transportation and other travel tips and an index. This guide will be useful to a variety of travelers to Israel. The historical and cultural context is generous, and Christian, Muslim, and Jewish sights get equal treatment. Highly recommended to public libraries.—**ARBA Staff Reviewer**

184.   Jewers, Jack. **Frommer's Ireland.** New York, Frommer Media LLC, 2018. 595p. illus. maps. index. $26.95pa. ISBN 13: 978-1-62887-342-9; 978-1-62887-343-6 (e-book).

The handy, travel-sized book begins with a table of contents, list of maps, country map (in color), and several lists of the bests: the best authentic experiences, the best driving tours, the best castles and stately homes, the best prehistoric sites, the best early Christian ruins, the best museums, the best for lovers of literature, the best family activities, the best hotels, the best restaurants, the best shopping, and Ireland's most overrated. This information is followed by several suggested itineraries, which include advice for golfers, lovers of ancient history, those traveling with family or on a budget, and more. Chapter 3, "Ireland in Context," discusses history and culture as well such topics as eating, drinking, accommodations, and tips on when to travel. Next are chapters on thirteen areas, starting with Dublin, and including the southeast, County Cork, Donegal and the Atlantic Highlands, Belfast, and other locations. Within each of these chapters, users will find various pieces of information on transportation, attractions (museums, castles, churches, etc.), lodging, eating, shopping, and entertainment, and other activities. Color photographs and maps enhance the usability of the information. The book concludes with an index, and users will find a fold-out map of Ireland tucked inside the back cover. The author, an Englishman who has been writing about Ireland since 2006, conveys his enthusiasm for the country in these pages. This book is recommended for public libraries.—**ARBA Staff Reviewer**

185.   Lesbros, Dominique. Simon Beaver. **Curiosities of Paris: An Idiosyncratic Guide to Overlooked Delights…Hidden in Plain Sight.** New York, The Little Bookroom, 2017. 238p. illus. maps. index. $22.95pa. ISBN 13: 978-1-68137-110-8.

Those tourists looking for a travel guide with detailed street maps, transportation information, contact numbers for embassies and consulates, packing lists, suggestions on where to shop, eat, and stay, operating times for museums, lists of sights that must be seen, or other typical information should move on from this book. What this guide provides instead is a look at what it calls the curiosities of Paris—structures and objects that relay the character of the city but are hiding in plain sight. These curiosities cover a broad time span, from Roman times to the present. The book begins with a chapter on equine-related sights that include, for example, images and locations of the city's many corner guards, which protected the corners of buildings from horse-drawn vehicles. There are also chapters on unusual trees, signs, interesting tombs, particular ceramics & mosaics, antique wall engravings, and much more. Three chapters read like traditional walking tours: "On the Trail of the City Walls," "The Quasimodo Tour," and "Revolutionary Paris." In all the chapters, users will find a generous number of color photographs of the sights discussed, as well as the addresses associated with those sights. There are more than eight hundred color photographs in total. An historic water pump, for example, is located in the 6th arrondissement at 47, Rue Saint-André. The book concludes with a street index organized by city district.

The book is small enough to carry around Paris's neighborhoods, but users may have a hard time deciphering some of the smaller print. Nevertheless, this fun look at some of Paris's more unusual sights will appeal to many readers, including armchair travelers.— **ARBA Staff Reviewer**

186.   **Let's Go Europe 2018.** Cambridge, Mass., Let's Go, 2018. 672p. illus. maps. index. $19.99pa. ISBN 13: 978-1-61237-052-1.

Let's Go Europe 2018: The Student's Travel Guide lives up to its name. Written by Harvard University students and geared to fellow young adult travelers, the book's language and suggestions for lodging (hostels), food, activities, and transportation target those on a budget. That said, the descriptions of cities and sights, along with basic information on passports, visas, currencies, embassy locations, international calling, and more will likely have a broad appeal. Like many travel guides, this one covers the necessaries in the introduction: when to go, what to do, suggested itineraries, how to use the book, and what to do before departure. It then goes through the countries in alphabetic order: Austria, Belgium, Croatia, Czech Republic, Denmark, France, Germany, Great Britain, Greece, Hungary, Iceland, Ireland, Italy, The Netherlands, Norway, Poland Portugal, Slovakia, Spain, Sweden, and Switzerland. The authors focus on the cities within each of these countries. Entries start with a short introduction and provide information on how to get there, orienting yourself geographically, emergency numbers, accommodations, sights, food, outdoor activities, nightlife, and city-specific information like drinking age or speed limits. This is a great pick for a young person planning a European vacation. The information is current and accurate. Even though most users will likely rely on Google Maps for navigation, this reviewer wishes there were maps included within country sections. The only map in the book is a two-page spread depicting all of Europe (with no detailing). Overall, however, this is not just useful but fun to read and is highly recommended for public libraries.—**ARBA Staff Reviewer**

187.   Steves, Rick, and Gene Openshaw. **Rick Steves London 2018.** Berkeley, Calif., Avalon Travel, 2017. 614p. illus. maps. index. $21.99pa. ISBN 13: 978-1-63121-672-5.

This guidebook by well-known travel guru Rick Steves and Gene Openshaw makes accessible a popular tourist destination. Starting with a few color maps, the book next gives readers an orientation to London that includes suggested itineraries and tours, in-city transportation tips, and more. Next comes a chapter on London sights, divided by region: Central London, North London, The City, East London, the South Bank, and West London and greater London. For some of the sights, there is also an audio tour available via the Rick Steves Audio Europe app. The self-guided walks and tours include such popular destinations as Westminster Abbey, the National Gallery, Historic London, the Tower of London, Greenwich, South Kensington, and more. Following are suggestions on where to eat, what to do when traveling with children, lodging, and entertainment. As an added bonus, the book also covers day trips to Windsor, Cambridge, and Stonehenge. The "Britain: Past & Present" chapter near the end of the book helps readers put what they are seeing into a historical and cultural context. Like any good guidebook, this one includes travel basics—what to know before you go, what to do if you are robbed or need medical help, the exchange rate, tipping policies, what to expect at hotels, good chain restaurants, mobile phone use, taxis and ubers, etc. An appendix contains useful contacts, a list of holidays and festivals, a list of books and films about London, conversions and climate, units of measurement, clothing sizes, a packing checklist, and a "British-Yankee Vocabulary." An index rounds out the work. Black-and-white photographs and maps throughout enhance the book's usefulness, as does the included fold-out map of London. Highly recommended for public libraries.—**ARBA Staff Reviewer**

188.   Steves, Rick. **Rick Steves Spain 2017.** Berkeley, Calif., Avalon Travel, 2016. 1,000p. illus. maps. index. $25.00pa. ISBN 13: 978-1-63121-451-6.

For those planning a trip to Spain and looking for common-sense advice on what to see, how to travel within country, where to stay, and more, this Rick Steves travel guide is a good place to start. The book begins with a brief overview of contemporary Spain prior to an introduction that provides basic information: a map legend, trip costs, suggested tours, and other basics. Next follow thirteen sections: Barcelona, Near Barcelona, Basque Country, The Camino de Santiago, Santiago de Compostela, Salamanca, Madrid, Northwest of Madrid, Toledo, Sevilla, Córdoba, and Andalucia's White Hill Towns. Steves does not attempt to cover every town in each region; instead, he showcases selective cities and towns in order to give a good representation of the country. For each area, readers will find suggestions for restaurants and lodging, for museums and tours, and much else. Additional information is provided, such as maps, black-and-white photographs of churches and other destinations, and historical snippets. The writing style is casual and engaging, and the advice is quite sound. Those traveling to just one of the regions might consider taking Steves' suggestion and (literally) ripping out that portion of this book. An added bonus is the inclusion of a pull-out map of Spain, which has detailed city maps. Highly recommended for public libraries.—**ARBA Staff Reviewer**

189.   Williams, Nicola, and Virginia Maxwell. **Florence & Tuscany.** London, Lonely Planet, 2018. 352p. illus. maps. index. $21.99pa. ISBN 13: 978-1-78657-261-5.

This 10th edition guidebook to one of the world's most popular regions begins with a chapter of general information on things from what to pack to where to stay to where/what to eat and drink to what to do if traveling with children. This is followed by detailed sections on each microregion, beginning with Florence. This generous section includes a short history, city maps, details about notable sites, a diagram of The Uffizi, and color photographs, as well as information on tours, food and drink, shopping, and more. There are even suggestions for what to do if you are lucky enough to have leisure time—a garden stroll, a long lunch, a coffee. The next section covers similar information for Siena and Central Tuscany. The guidebook devotes less space to Southern Tuscany, the Central Coast and Elba, Northwestern Tuscany, and Eastern Tuscany, but each section gives ample information to the traveler. These sections also have their own tables of contents, making it easy to navigate directly to the spot of interest. The second-to-last chapter "Florence & Tuscany Today" aims to help readers understand the area, and, to this end, details the region's history, way of life, The Tuscan table, Tuscany on page and screen, and Tuscan art and architecture. The last chapter is a survival guide with information on embassies and consulates, maps, money, legal matters, visas, language, people with disabilities, and other topics. The work includes an index and a pull-out map of Florence & Tuscany. This book, by two experienced travelers and authors, is recommended to public libraries.—**ARBA Staff Reviewer**

9 History

American History

Dictionaries and Encyclopedias

190.   Holloran, Peter C. **Historical Dictionary of New England.** 2d ed. Lanham, Md., Rowman & Littlefield, 2017. 622p. (Historical Dictionaries of Cities, States, and Regions). $145.00; $137.00 (e-book). ISBN 13: 978-1-5381-0218-3; 978-1-5381-0219-0 (e-book).

In straightforward alphabetic order, with over 1,690 entries (persons, places, institutions, and events), this is a nonscholarly compendium for a general audience of adults and young people, written by Worcester State University professor of history Peter C. Holloran, who also wrote the original (2003) edition (see ARBA 2005, entry 78). It is about 100 pages longer, with about 200 more individual entries, and expanded topic entries. It appears that few, if any, entries have been deleted from the previous (2003) edition. The broad topic of African Americans has been greatly expanded since the original edition and is divided into sections, including Higher Education where one learns that the first black man to graduate from Yale was Edward Bouchet (1852-1918). The straightforward alphabetical listing of entries means that Myles Standish, artist Frank Stella, Stockbridge Indians, and Stone Walls (vernacular architecture) are all within a few pages of each other, as are Indian Pudding, the Irish Famine Memorial (in Boston), and the Isles of Shoals (off the Maine-New Hampshire border).

It is always difficult to decide who and what to include and exclude in books of this sort, but certainly one could argue that New Hampshire poet, Pulitzer winner, and Poet Laureate Maxine Kumin (1925-2014) deserves inclusion. The famed tragedy of 1942, Boston's Cocoanut Grove Fire, has its own entry, but the 2003 Station Nightclub Fire in Warwick, Rhode Island, which killed 100, has no entry. A new entry for this edition is America's first trained nurse, Linda Richards (1841-1930). However, it states that her husband died from his Civil War wounds. Richards was, in fact, never married; it was her fiancé who had died. Also, in 1878 she established a training school for nurses at Boston City Hospital, not, as was erroneously stated in the entry, Boston College Hospital. In 2005, widely disseminated scholarly research showed that the middle name of Massachusetts artist Fitz Hugh Lane (1804-1865) was actually Henry. The dictionary does not include this correct information but rather repeats the same entry from the 2003 edition. Photographer and publisher Fred Holland Day (1864-1933) makes his first appearance in this new edition, and there is a *see* reference to the entry for his now little-remembered but important friend, the poet and Boston personality Louise Imogen Guiney (1861-1920).

The dictionary's bibliography, greatly expanded since the previous edition, consists of a gratifyingly wide variety of secondary sources. Large public libraries, especially those in New England, will probably want to purchase this new edition.—**Martha E. Stone**

191.   **Opposition to War: An Encyclopedia of U.S. Peace and Antiwar Movements.** Mitchell K. Hall, ed. Santa Barbara, Calif., ABC-CLIO, 2018. 2v. illus. index. $198.00/set. ISBN 13: 978-1-4408-4518-5; 978-1-4408-4519-2 (e-book).

For as long as there has been war there have been those willing to fight for peace. The history of the United States is no different in this regard. Many alive today still remember the charged and sometimes bloody protests of the 1960s where passionate and courageous students, academics, and veterans challenged the validity of the Vietnam War against seemingly insurmountable odds. In *Opposition to War: An Encyclopedia of U.S. Peace and Antiwar Movements* contributors list these and a multitude of other less-well-known movements for peace as well as calls for social reform that often coincided with these movements.

This encyclopedia contains 375 entries from over 130 academic contributors. Each entry is followed by the author's name, a list of related entries as well as a list of references for the entry itself. Many entries are also accompanied by black-and-white illustrations or photographs of their subject. An introduction to the work provides the reader with a brief historical overview of peace movements conveniently divided into chronological eras. The encyclopedia also contains a chronology of events, contents, bibliography, and an index. The work includes a guide to related topics for those who want to expand their research beyond individual entries. Such topics listed include artist and musicians such as Bob Dylan, social reforms including the abolition movement, religious groups like the Quakers, important events in the peace process such as the Geneva Convention, and tactics used by protesters like civil disobedience.

This compact two-volume set would be an excellent addition to an academic library without requiring vast amounts of shelf space. The overall emphasis of the work as well as the topics covered provides an excellent beginning to an often-overlooked section of U.S. history. Students of American wars will also find this information invaluable as it provides a glimpse of the context and conversations in which these events occurred, how they began, and how they were ultimately brought to a close. Individual entries are very well written, each with ample references to other topics facilitating a deeper dive into lesser-known historical topics. This work would also be useful for those studying the arts or social sciences because many of its entries detail artist and cultural movements and the events that inspired them.—**W. Cole Williamson**

192.   **Reforming America: A Thematic Encyclopedia and Document Collection.** Jeffrey A. Johnson, ed. Santa Barbara, Calif., ABC-CLIO, 2017. 2v. index. $189.00/set. ISBN 13: 978-1-4408-3720-3; 978-1-4408-3721-0 (e-book).

For those who daydreamed during sessions of American History 101—the words of their professor's lectures going in one era and out the other, so to speak—a refresher may be in order. Briefly, the Progressive Movement was a reaction against the evils of the Industrial Revolution. Slums, sweat shops, dangerous working conditions, patent medicines that killed more than cured; all these and more were targets of reformers from about the turn of the last century until 1917, when America's entry into World War I directed the public's attention overseas. The work under review here takes a somewhat expanded scope, examining people, places, and events during the period lasting from 1893 until 1920.

Contents are presented in five sections: Social and Political Life; Work and Economic Life; Cultural and Religious Life; Science, Literature, and the Arts; and Sports and Popular Culture. Each section opens with an introductory essay, followed by entries listed in alphabetical order (200+ total). As might be expected, crusaders figure prominently within these pages. To cite just two examples, articles cover Jane Addams, who more or less single-handedly created the profession of social work and founded Chicago's famous Hull House, and President Theodore Roosevelt, the so-called "trust buster," who was the sworn enemy of monopolies. Ditto for landmark legislation, such as the Pure Food and Drug Act of 1906 and precedent setting court cases, such as *Muller v. Oregon,* which upheld a State of Oregon law setting a limit on the number of hours women could work in commercial laundries (ten, the eight-hour work day would only come about with the Adamson Act of 1916). Other entries cover a wide range of topics, such as social issues ("Birth Control"), labor unrest ("Anthracite Coal Mine Strike"), and media hysteria ("Yellow Journalism"). Entries are signed and contain short bibliographies for further reading. Each section concludes with a selection of primary document excerpts. Special features include a chronology and a bibliographical essay. Writing style is clear and concise, perfectly appropriate for the intended audience of senior high school and undergraduate college students.

Editor Johnson is a professor of history and Director of American Studies at Providence College in Rhode Island. He holds a Ph.D. from Washington State University and has been widely published in his field. Contributors to these volumes are a mix of academics (many holding doctoral degrees) and independent scholars and researchers.

While the Progressive Era has not attracted as much scholarly attention as other periods of American history, it should be noted that other reference print titles have been published in the recent past that compete with the work under review here. *Historical Dictionary of the Progressive Era* (see ARBA 2010, entry 377) is a straight A-Z compilation of short, informative articles in one volume of 697 pages and has received good reviews in *Choice* and *Booklist.* Another possibility is *Encyclopedia of the Gilded Age and Progressive Era* (see ARBA 2006, entry 440). As the title attests, a broader span of time is encompassed, from the end of the Civil War onwards, which accounts for its length, three volumes in 1,256 pages. Unfortunately, a copy was not available at the time of this writing to make a comparison.

All told, *Reforming America* is a solid work attractively packaged in two compact volumes. It is recommended for purchase by all public and academic libraries, especially those of the latter that support a curriculum in American history.—**Michael Francis Bemis**

Handbooks and Yearbooks

193.   **American Panorama. http://dsl.richmond.edu/panorama/.** [Website] Free. Date reviewed: 2017.

A project from the Digital Scholarship Lab at the University of Richmond, this site offers a unique perspective on the history of the United States as it employs a series of interactive maps and auxiliary tools that examine compelling topics of American progress.

Currently, the site hosts six topics with more in development. Users simply select one of the six featured maps, each of which conveys basic instructions particular to the topic. Each topic has a distinct visual style and uses different data formats to tell its story.

The Executive Abroad 1905-2016 maps the development of our government's international travel by pointing to changes in technology and politics. Users may note details of state visits or examine by region or administration, among other things. Mapping Inequality: Redlining in New Deal America focuses on the legacy of inequity created by New Deal housing policies. It shares a series of maps and reports originated by the Home Owners Loan Corporation (HOLC) during the Great Depression from which users can glean a good range of sociological and economic data. A separate, more detailed review of this particular URL is available at Mapping Inequality (www.dsl.richmond.edu/panorama/redlining) as the scope of this particular topic is significant. The Forced Migration of Enslaved People 1810-1860 conveys the story of the spread of slavery and includes a series of graphs accompanied by personal narrative excerpts. Users can visualize migration patterns, incorporate crop data, and more. The Overland Trails 1840-1860 illustrates the great western migration using a timeline, personal narratives, and flow maps. Users can compare migrant numbers over twenty years as they moved along the Oregon, California, and Mormon trails west from Missouri. Foreign-Born Population 1850-2010 points to the diverse origins of the American population, using census data to track the ebb and flow of regional migration. Users can track migrants by country and by year, and note changes over time. Canals 1820-1860 discusses a less obvious aspect of American history—the impact of canals on regional trade and identity. Users can examine such things as trade volume and individual commodities.

For each topic, users can click or hover on a number of data points, titles, regions, and more to access further detail. With its solid (and growing) range of topics, state-of-the-art graphics, and well-sourced data, this site can be a powerful research tool with a broad appeal across many areas of study.—**ARBA Staff Reviewer**

194. **Brooklyn Historical Society Oral History Foundation. http://www. brooklynhistory.org/library/oralhistory/.** [Website] Free. Date reviewed: 2018.

This page is home to over 1,200 interviews conducted with residents of Brooklyn, New York. The interviews capture the myriad cultural, historical, religious, and political flavors of the diverse community over many years. Organized into18 distinct collections, the histories encompass interviews recorded since 1973 and feature interviewees born as far back as the 1880s. Users can scroll down to view the gallery of collections focused on such themes as Veterans and Wartime, West Indian Carnival, AIDS, Hispanic Communities, Civic Leaders, Community Activists, and Business & Industry. Selecting a collection displays a brief introduction alongside a listing of the contributors and recording date. Users can listen to the recording which is indexed for ease of reference and includes a brief interview description including a listing of interview topics, people, and places mentioned. Some recordings are accompanied by a transcript. Users can listen to Madeline Castellano, who describes living with a disability during the Great Depression and World War II. Seth Edwards talks about the changes in the Brooklyn-Stuyvesant neighborhood via the Brooklyn-Stuyvesant Restoration Corporation. And an anonymous subject discusses, in her native Mandarin, the challenges of living as a Chinese immigrant and small business owner in the Sunset Park neighborhood. The project offers valuable first-hand information on a range of topics from crime to cooking, offering a compelling portion of the American story told with a strong Brooklyn accent.—**ARBA Staff Reviewer**

195.   **Chicago History Museum Online. http://digitalcollection.chicagohistory.org/.** [Website] Free. Date reviewed: 2018.

This website functions as a digital gallery of artifacts connected with the history of the great Midwestern city of Chicago, Illinois, although it additionally presents items representative of the greater American story as well. Users can conduct a basic or advanced search from the top of the homepage, can browse select items in a slideshow, or can examine recent additions to the digital collection. Users can also browse from a list of thirteen suggested topics including Costume/Fashion, Civil War, Great Chicago Fire, Eastland Disaster 1915, and specific era (starting in the eighteenth century). Alternatively, the Browse Collections tab will access over one thousand digitized artifacts arranged by title, artist/maker, or date. Items can be displayed in several formats, all including a thumbnail image. There is quite a range of items to examine, including nineteenth century jewelry and corsets, sports equipment (Basketball Shoes "Air Jordans"), political buttons, and more. A forty-five item collection of such things as campaign banners, paintings, and personal effects honors Abraham Lincoln (his top hat is particularly evocative), while Marbles Melted by The Great Chicago Fire serves both as a relic of one of the greatest disasters in American history and as an item of significant visual interest. Users can download or print the item page, and can find identifying information alongside the digital image, such as type, date, physical description, materials, object history, curatorial statement, and related terms.—**ARBA Staff Reviewer**

196.   **Columbia Oral History Archives. http://library.columbia.edu/locations/ccoh/ digital.html.** [Website] Free. Date reviewed: 2018.

This site gathers five distinct oral history collections into one accessible location. The collections are all structured differently, and will generally include varying supplemental content, such as videos or narrator biographies. Most oral histories contain transcripts. From this page, users can scroll through the listing of oral history selections. The Carnegie Corporation of New York Oral History Project was conducted in several phases, and contains interviews with various people, from general staff to grantees, within one of the largest American benefactors of education. The interviews offer a wealth of information that covers the breadth of the organization's impact on the social sciences (e.g., adult education, library science, music, and teacher education), its expansion into global concerns, and more. Supplemental material includes information on Andrew Carnegie and the Oral History Process. The oral histories may consist of both video and audio content, and feature interviews with U.S. President James E. Carter, Bishop Desmond Tutu, and others. Notable New Yorkers presents interviews with ten individuals who have made their mark on New York City, including Mayor Ed Koch, cabinet secretary Frances Perkins, publisher Bennett Cerf, and philanthropist Mary Lasker. Interviews may be supplemented by a photo gallery and summary biography, and may also include a table of contents, transcription, and an index of names mentioned throughout the interviews. The Institute for Research on Women, Gender, and Sexuality (IRWGS) Oral History Project focuses on the twenty-five-year-plus history of the institute as interviews discuss phases of its existence at Columbia. The project includes curated selections from over ninety hours of interviews conducted between 2014 and 2015. Site users can also examine digital Ephemera, such as meeting flyers and lecture announcements. The Rule of Law Oral History Project is a two-tiered project initially exploring the topic of capital punishment within the broader issue of human and civil rights post 9/11. Later interviews discuss issues revolving around the use of the Guantánamo Bay detention facilities. Users can scroll through a gallery of select video interviews with government officials, activists, journalists, lawyers, and other legal experts. Interviews with former Guantánamo detainees are particularly compelling. Robert Rauschenberg Oral History Project contains accounts from the late American artist's friends, family, and collaborators. Users can examine a brief biography of the narrator, transcripts of interview excerpts, video content, and photographs. The project does an excellent job of following the arc of the artist's career. Archibald Cox Oral History represents a singular but extensive interview with Archibald Cox, famous for his role in the Watergate scandal. The interview emphasizes Cox's years as solicitor general from 1961 to 1965 when he argued civil rights cases before the U.S. Supreme Court. The project includes a brief biography of Cox as well as a description of the interviewer's experience with the man.—**ARBA Staff Reviewer**

197.   **Defining Documents in American History: Dissent & Protest.** Aaron Gulyas, ed. Hackensack, N.J., Salem Press, 2017. 2v. illus. index. $175.00/set. ISBN 13: 978-1-68217-289-6; 978-1-68217-290-2 (e-book).

This two-volume series is part of the Defining Documents in American History series. The 93 primary source documents with their essays are divided into eight sections: From Colonies to Nation; Slavery and Abolition; Sectional Conflict, Civil War, and Reconstruction; Native American Dissent; African American Civil Rights; Women's Rights; Political and Social Protest; and Anti-War Activism. Each essay that accompanies the primary source document includes a summary overview, defining moment, author biography, document analysis, and essential themes, followed by a bibliography and further reading section. The book examines a broad range of dissent and protest movements from 1635 to 2017, with a diversity of texts including government reports, laws, treaties, trial notes, letters, political and religious sermons, pamphlets, speeches, and diplomatic communications. The appendixes include a chronological list that arranges all the documents discussed by year, a Web resources section for various supplemental resources, and an overall bibliography. I highly recommend this book for high school and academic libraries, given that it covers a broad range of protest and dissent movements in the United States along with their primary source documents.—**Bradford Lee Eden**

198.   **Defining Documents in American History: Immigration & Immigrant Communities (1650-2016).** James S. Pula, ed. Hackensack, N.J., Salem Press, 2017. 270p. index. $175.00. ISBN 13: 978-1-68217-285-8; 978-1-68217-857-0 (e-book).

Due to the impact of immigration on the political discourse of the United States today, this is a timely resource. Editor James S. Pula, Professor of History at Purdue University, Northwest, and 29 other scholars have combined their talents to produce this latest volume in Salem Press' Defining Documents in American History series (see ARBA 2015, entries 234-241). It features 31 documents organized into four categories: In Their Own Words: Immigrant Descriptions; Anti-Immigrant Rhetoric; Federal Legislation; and Executive and Judicial Actions. Among the writings included are the Chinese Exclusion Act of 1862, an excerpt from Jacob Riis' *How the Other Half Lives,* and the U.S. Supreme Court's affirmation of the decision made by Justice Jerry E. Smith of the U.S. Court of Appeals for the Fifth Circuit in the 2016 case *State of Texas v. United States.* Each of the primary sources is accompanied by analyses, biographical information about the author of the document, and bibliographical information for further research. The work concludes with a chronology that lists the documents in sequential order by year of publication, a list of web resources that only includes four URLs, a six-page bibliography, and an index.

While the analysis of the respective documents is generally excellent, the appendixes add very little to the main body of the work. Overall, this would be a useful resource for public and undergraduate libraries. The one caveat is that the cost of this title is exorbitant.—**John R. Burch Jr.**

199. **Defining Documents in American History: The 1910s (1910-1919).** Michael Shally-Jensen, ed. Hackensack, N.J., Salem Press, 2016. 400p. index. $175.00. ISBN 13: 978-1-68217-187-5; 978-1-68217-188-2 (e-book).

Editor Michael Shally-Jensen and 29 scholars produced this volume in Salem Press' Defining Documents in American History series. It contains 38 documents divided into six categories: Domestic Developments; The War Front; International Affairs; Labor and Immigration; Women's Rights; and African American Affairs. Among the documents are the "Progressive Party Platform," which was drafted for Teddy Roosevelt's 1912 presidential campaign, "Emiliano Zapata: Plan of Ayala," and "NAACP: Thirty Years of Lynching in the United States." The supplementary materials accompanying the respective documents are organized according to the template utilized by the entire series. One benefit of this work is that access to an online edition is provided with the purchase of a print copy. Public and academic libraries serving high school and undergraduate clientele would find this to be a useful reference tool.—**John R. Burch Jr.**

200. **Geography of Slavery.** **http://www2.vcdh.virginia.edu/gos/index.html.** [Website] Free. Date reviewed: 2017.

Honing in from the broader aspects and larger storylines within the era of slavery, this project turns its eye on the personal as it examines contemporary advertisements for missing or captured slaves in the State of Virginia. Simply structured, users can select from a number of listed options on the homepage. Advertisements allows access to over 4,000 newspaper advertisement transcriptions spanning the years 1736-1803. Users can conduct basic text and advanced searches or can browse via publication date or location. Contextual information precedes the advertisements, and includes newspaper name, advertisement type, names of captured/runaway slave(s), geographical location, subscriber name, and associated documents. The ad transcripts can be rich with detail: the captured John Bostock is described as "an Englishman, about twenty one years old…and has lost the second joint of the little finger of his right hand." The Maps and Timelines feature within this section is particularly useful in visualizing locations and times of individual slave activity. The Documents tab links to supplemental historical papers, such as court records, correspondence, diary entries, etc., which can help to illustrate the slave stories. Explanatory Essays provides additional academic context. The Profiles section (still in development) will consist of brief narrative accounts of both slaves and slave owners as gleaned from the advertisements and auxiliary documents gathered on this site. The Resources tab offers a good selection of materials to aid in the study of the advertisements. In particular, the A-Z glossary clarifies the language of the era, defining terms such as calamanco, duffill, pistole, and pettiauger. The site is a work in progress, with some features still in development, but certainly has the potential to be a vital resource as the echoes of slavery continue to reverberate.—**ARBA Staff Reviewer**

201.   **George   Washington   Papers.**   https://www.loc.gov/collections/george-washington-papers. [Website] Free. Date reviewed: 2017.

This archive from the Library of Congress focuses on the collected papers of George Washington. At over thirty-five thousand items, the prized collection includes farm reports, speeches (such as his first inaugural address), military orders, account books, business and military correspondence, and much, much more. Users can navigate via three tabs. About this Collection explains how the documents are organized into nine "series," (quite helpful in regards to its overall size) and provides a general overview on series content. The series are generally thematic as they group documents according to Washington's long career. Series 1 shares schoolwork, diary entries, and survey work, Series 3 contains correspondence from his ten years as Commander of the Continental Army, Series 5 is home to financial papers, and so on. Later series contain document duplicates as well as more recently acquired or extraneous papers. Users will also find information about transcriptions (available for only some items in the collection) and a display of featured content. Articles and Essays provides a number of excellent contextual essays including the "Introduction to the Diaries of George Washington," which explicates the importance of the journals in illuminating the first president's character. There is also a timeline of significant events in Washington's life, a spotlight on the collection's maps, and an article providing further detail on series content. Collection Items lists all documents and auxiliary items held in the digital library. Users can scroll through the items as listed, or can conduct a basic or advanced search via date, online or original format, contributor, subject, and other qualifiers. Selecting an item presents its digital image with descriptive information (e.g., title, repository, genre, creation date, etc.) beneath. The site also includes a good number of teaching and expert resources.—**ARBA Staff Reviewer**

202.   Gilbert, David T. **Civil War Battlefields: Walking the Trails of History.** New York, Rizzoli, 2017. 336p. illus. maps. $50.00. ISBN 13: 978-0-8478-5912-2.

This book covers 32 Civil War battlefields at 25 sites in 12 different states. Part history, part guidebook, readers will find 124 different battlefield hikes ranging from .2 miles to 14 miles. The introduction provides historical context for both the war and the creation of the battlefield memorials. It also has a chronology of battles that includes the date and the name of the site where the battle took place. The 1862 Battle of Malvern Hill, for example, is part of the Richmond National Battlefield Park. The presentation is geographical, not chronological. Geographical sections covered are as follows: Eastern Virginia; West Virginia, Maryland, and Pennsylvania; West Tennessee, Mississippi, and Louisiana; Kentucky, East Tennessee, and Georgia; and Other Regions. Entries vary in length from roughly 6 pages to roughly 15 pages. Each entry discusses the battle history and includes a map of battlefield hikes and hike descriptions. The book uses black-and-white and color photographs throughout. A list of suggested readings rounds out the book. For those planning to tour a Civil War site, this may prove to be a valuable planning tool. Recommended for public libraries.—**ARBA Staff Reviewer**

203.   Goss, K. David. **Documents of the Salem Witch Trials.** Santa Barbara, Calif., ABC-CLIO, 2018. 181p. index. $94.00. ISBN 13: 978-1-4408-5320-3; 978-1-4408-5321-

0 (e-book).

The Salem, Massachusetts, witch trials of the late seventeenth century have captivated academics and general audiences for centuries. This tale of childhood antics turned mass hysteria and the tragic executions that resulted from it have served as a cautionary tale for religious fervor run rampant. *Documents of the Salem Witch Trials* provides a wealth of primary resources to the researcher and helps to establish a historical context for these fascinating events.

This work includes many tools to aid the researcher beginning with an introduction to the history of witchcraft as well as to the contemporary events that set the stage for the documents that follow. The book also contains a table of contents, a brief guide to reading and evaluating primary resources, and a chronology of events. Individual entries are divided into chronological chapters and listed with exact dates and headings. Entries consist of a variety of documents including letters, examinations, and depositions. Some of the themes that may be found are the role played by spectral evidence in the trial, the character of William Stoughton who contributed to the massive scope of the trials, and the contrasting characters of Thomas Brattle and Robert Calef who helped bring these events to a close. Finally the book speaks to a historical context on the perceived reality of witchcraft by the populace and the sincere desire, even among the accused, to see it expelled from their society. The entries are followed by a historical conclusion that discusses the effects of the witch trials on the inhabitants of Massachusetts. A bibliography and index round out the work.

Documents of the Salem Witch Trials would be an excellent addition to the United States history collections of any academic or research-based library. Students will find this slim volume an easily accessible source of primary resources for their searches and thus it serves well for lower-level undergraduates. The extent and depth of the documents also make this work valuable to upper-division students focusing on colonial American history.—**W. Cole Williamson**

204. **The Historian's Narrative of Frederick Douglass: Reading Douglass's Autobiography as Social and Cultural History.** Robert Felgar, ed. Santa Barbara, Calif., Praeger/ABC-CLIO, 2017. 146p. index. (The Historian's Annotated Classics Series). $37.00. ISBN 13: 978-1-4408-4686-1; 978-1-4408-4309-9 (e-book).

Published in 2018 in conjunction with the 200th anniversary of Douglass's birth, this annotated edition of *Narrative of the Life of Frederick Douglass* offers an enriched reading experience for a foundational American text. As part of The Historian's Annotated Classics Series, which positions works of literature within their historical and cultural contexts, the accompanying essays and annotations reveal added angles for analysis and exploration, either from a literary or a historical standpoint. A chronology table outlining key points in American history alongside the events of Douglass's life is provided first. This chronology is followed by one essay giving a summary of Douglass's life, and one essay giving a historical overview of slavery in America. Next, the text of *Narrative of the Life of Frederick Douglass, an American Slave* is presented with extensive annotations by the editor. These provide a rich contextual background to support the reading of the text: the sources of Douglass's many literary allusions; further information about people or places or events mentioned; and historical details on topics like slave marriage, cultural attitudes regarding manhood, views of black women and sexuality, and the racialization of Christianity. This enhanced experience permits the reader to enter into a deeper, more nuanced understanding of the manifold depravities of slavery, of Douglass's significant position in American history, and of the enormity of his achievements. In all, this rigorously compiled work could serve as both an excellent jumping off point for further in-depth research or a helpful reference copy of the text for already expert scholars.—**Autumn Faulkner**

205.   **The History Engine.www.historyengine.richmond.edu/.** [Website] Free, Date reviewed: 2017.

This site uses the vehicle of American history to detail the processes of historians and encourage a more active relationship with the subject itself. Home to thousands of historical "episodes," the site encourages input from users, primarily university students and educators, as it builds a chronological database of historical moments which may otherwise be lost. Properly sourced and vetted, these "episodes" expand the timeline of American history. Users can navigate along the timeline which can be measured in several ways: year/decade, month/year, etc. Episode titles are marked accordingly along it, but it is important to note that as more episodes are recorded, the timeline becomes visually cluttered and somewhat difficult to read. While the timeline approach is a good choice for this data, it may be helpful to streamline the proliferation of episode titles for improved navigation. Users simply click on a title to access a brief summary and analysis of the historical episode as well as auxiliary information such as episode date, location, tag, and other details. Episodes reference such topics as emancipation, the Great Chicago Fire of 1871, victory gardens, internment camps, Native American education, women's suffrage and much, much more. Some of the more compelling titles include "A Chapter for Young Husbands," "Going Once, Going Twice, Resold into Slavery," and "Fun Times During the 1918 Spanish Influenza Epidemic." Below the timeline, a Google map pins locations for the episodes. Users can click on the pins to access the episode summaries as well. A basic search from the home page will bring up a listing of all relevant episodes. With the inclusion of foundational information (goals, guides, and other resources), the site would be an excellent resource for students and educators.—**ARBA Staff Reviewer**

206.   Johnson, Claudia Durst. **Daily Life in Colonial New England.** 2d ed. Santa Barbara, Calif., Greenwood Press/ABC-CLIO, 2017. 372p. illus. index. (Greenwood Press Daily Life Through History Series). $61.00. ISBN 13: 978-1-4408-5465-1; 978-1-4408-5466-8 (e-book).

This book, by accomplished scholar Claudia Johnson, is crafted to provide readers an open window from which to view the culture that actually had an extensive impact on the populace. The author uses the introduction as a prequel to the central story that looks at colonial life in New England. It illuminates the political, cultural, and religious affairs that engulfed the English landscape, which compelled individuals and whole families to board ships like the *Mayflower* and brave not only the high seas but a new world. The individual chapters in the book serve like acts in a play, each thematically unique, yet when viewed in their totality offer readers and researchers a complete story that is life in colonial New England. Claudia Johnson offers acts like: domestic life, economic life, intellectual life, material life, political life, recreational life, and religious life. It is within those individual acts that the story comes to life, and a good play relies on good actors to present the story so that the audience may fully enjoy and understand its message. The chapters are the actors in her book and serve in a similar fashion. Some of the actors that grace her stage include but are not limited to "The Lives of Children," "Marriage and Sex," "Education," "Crime and Punishment," and "Witchcraft." Each of their performances offers a distinct characteristic of New England colonial culture, which onto itself is suitable exposition. The author writes in such a manner that allows each section and chapter to build on the next and provides the reader a larger and more complete picture of the daily life of colonial New England.

The primary material that Claudia Johnson has selected and used in her book is substantial and of high value. If it were not for those primary materials like well selected props, ranging from legal documents to sermons, letters, diaries, and even recipes, the play would falter and close after the opening night. It would become yet another source left on the shelf to collect dust. Instead, the story of this particular time period in American history and the people who lived and made it their own comes alive. For example, readers will find an authentic cranberry tart recipe, a recipe of a Thanksgiving food that was actually eaten by the Puritans, as recorded by John Josselyn of Maine in the 1670s. Other materials will help readers grasp various realities, such as marriage as a contract that most often favored husbands; shorter life expectancy, especially for infants; the lives of underclass citizens (indentured servants, African slaves, debtors, and criminals); the integral role of pirates in business and employment; and the horrors of being an accused witch.

Johnson's Further Reading sections in each chapter provide the reader with sources that will allow them to become even more immersed in the life and times of colonial New England. Near the back of the book is a useful chronology that has important dates that pertain to New England and its place in world history. The last important section of the work is the index, and it is well indexed, always an important facet for the researcher. The overall construction of the book will stand up to heavy use, but if one's library is short on space, there is an electronic version.

Life in colonial New England may not have been as pleasant as a Norman Rockwell painting or a Hallmark card depicting Thanksgiving. It was in many cases a life-and-death struggle especially in the early days and years of the colonial region's history. Thanks to Claudia Johnson's talents readers today are able to relive and feel daily life during this period.—**Lawrence Joseph Mello**

207. **Mark Twain's Mississippi.http://twain.lib.niu.edu/.** [Website] Free. Date reviewed: 2017.

This website collects a variety of materials dedicated to painting a vibrant portrait of the Mississippi Valley of the 19th century. Among its top sources is the author Mark Twain, aka Samuel Clemens, who famously captured the spirit of the valley via his seminal characters of Tom Sawyer and Huckleberry Finn. Users can conduct a basic or advanced search or browse through the nearly 2,500 items in the digital collection. Users can also select materials from the specific tabs on the homepage. Items include evocative musical recordings, maps, advertisements, sheet music, letters, books, illustrations, photographs, and much more. In addition, the site includes numerous interpretive tools such as academic essays and video interviews with Twain scholars. Descriptive information accompanies each listed item, and will generally incorporate publishing date, title, genre, category (tag), and source. The site has also created 10 lesson plans—accessible by tab—which serve to inspire educators with themes from migration to steamboats and beyond. It is important to note that as of this review the site appears to be under construction and all referenced materials may not be available for viewing. Nonetheless, the singular and engaging focus, solid scholarship, and diverse selection of artifacts mark an important resource for many researchers and educators.—**ARBA Staff Reviewer**

208. **Milestone Documents of American Leaders: Exploring the Primary Sources of Notable American Leaders.** 2d ed. Paul Finkelman, James A. Percoco, and David Simonelli, eds. Dallas, Tex., Schlager Group, and Grey House Publishing, 2017. 4v. illus. index. $395.00/set. ISBN 13: 978-1-68217-165-3; 978-1-68217-166-0 (e-book).

The second edition of this four-volume set contains 133 entries with over 250 illustrations and photographs. The entries follow a standardized set of headings: Overview (summary of the leader's life and place in American history), Time Line (key events both in the life of the leader and events in American history during that leader's lifetime), Explanation and Analysis of Documents (a detailed examination of each featured document text), Impact and Legacy (the historical influence and legacy of the leader, as well as the lasting impact of the documents), Essential Quotes (a selection of key quotes from the documents), Questions for Further Study (a study guide for students/teachers for use of these volumes in the classroom), Further Reading (articles, websites, and books for more information), and Document Text (the actual text of each primary document, along with a glossary). Some of the entries in the Document Text area are abridged, given that many are extremely lengthy (for example, Supreme Court decisions). Since the focus of these volumes is reprinting primary source documents, any typographical errors and unusual spellings have not been corrected. There are also eight distinct teachers' activity guides which are based on the National History Standards provided in volume one, as well as a list of documents by category and a cumulative subject index at the end of volume four. This set provides a one-stop reference work of primary documents related to American history and its leaders.—**Bradford Lee Eden**

209. **North Carolina Runaway Slave Advertisements. http://libcdm1.uncg.edu/ cdm/landingpage/collection/RAS.** [Website] Free. Date reviewed: 2017.

Similar to the University of Virginia's Geography of Slavery project, this website allows access to an extensive digitized collection of advertisements for runaway slaves in North Carolina. Currently numbering close to 2,500, the ads were published in a variety of newspapers from the mid-eighteenth century well into the 1860's. Users can browse all advertisements, which are listed by date of publication, or conduct a basic or advanced search. Listings include a thumbnail of the original advertisement, ad headline, ad date, publishing newspaper, and transcript. Users who click on the thumbnail can access further information such as subscriber/slaveholder name, county of residence, date of slave departure, presumed destination, and more, including ad metadata and an enlarged copy of the ad (which can be downloaded and printed). While generally simple in structure, the ads can certainly convey a good amount of historical detail in describing the clothing, skills, and other features of the runaways, in addition to shedding light on the particular laws, values, and vernacular of the times. Additional features of the website include an annotated bibliography and several excellent essays summarizing the history of North Carolina slavery and noting trends running through the breadth of the ads. This website is a fine tool in the pocket of anyone studying the American slavery era.—**ARBA Staff Reviewer**

210.   Olson, James S., and Mariah Gumpert. **The Great Depression and the New Deal: Key Themes and Documents.** Santa Barbara, Calif., ABC-CLIO, 2017. 296p. illus. index. $48.00. ISBN 13: 978-1-4408-3462-2; 978-1-4408-3463-9 (e-book).

High school students who are planning to take the AP American history exam may want to use the ABC-CLIO Unlocking American History series, which now includes *The Great Depression and the New Deal* (June 2017) by James S. Olson with Mariah Gumpert. The series was launched in June 2014 with the publication of *The Industrial Revolution: Key Themes and Documents* by the same author. Another title, *The New Era of the 1920s,* also by Professor Olson, came out in October, 2017.

The title under review is set up like the other titles in the series. The handbook opens with a description of each theme. For this volume they are agriculture, arts/culture, banking/economics, business/industry, communication/media, environment, government programs, organized labor/protest, politics, race relations, and work. A list of entries by theme follows.

The bulk of this study aid is an A to Z collection of one-two page entries on one or more of the key themes mentioned above. Each entry is tagged with the themes that relate to it. For example, the entry "Federal Dance Project" has tags for arts/culture, work, and government programs. *See also* references and sources for "Further Reading" complete the entry. Primary documents related to the topic, including significant presidential speeches, government acts, and images, make up the last fifty pages.

While the focus of this book is on the content entries and primary documents, it also includes a few exam preparation-specific pages, such as a sample documents-based essay question, a list of "Top Tips" for answering documents-based essay questions, and period-specific learning objectives that are in alignment with the fall 2014 AP U.S. history curriculum framework.

The Great Depression and the New Deal: Key Themes and Documents will serve well-advanced high school and lower-level undergraduates who can use it to test their knowledge of these crucial events in twentieth-century U.S. history.—**John P. Stierman**

211.   Olson, James S., and Mariah Gumpert. **The New Era of the 1920s: Key Themes and Documents.** Santa Barbara, Calif., ABC-CLIO, 2017. 334p. illus. index. (Unlocking American History series). $61.00. ISBN 13: 978-1-4408-6024-9; 978-1-4408-6025-6 (e-book).

This book is a partial update of a previous title: *Historical Dictionary of the 1920's: From World War I to the New Deal, 1919-1933* by James S. Olson (New York: Greenwood Press, 1988). This "new" work contains only about half the entries and half the pages of the original volume. The only apparent revisions are updated end-of-article bibliographies and a mere 10 primary documents concerning the decade in question. In this reviewer's opinion, the volume under consideration is a poor substitute for the original, which, while a solid work itself, is now 30 years old. Therefore, *New Era* it is not recommended for purchase by any library. Rather, what is recommended are 2 noteworthy and relatively current titles on the market. For basic factual information concerning this period of United States history, there is the 3-volume work *The Twenties in America* edited by Carl Rollyson (see ARBA 2013, entry 372). The set's more than 670 alphabetically arranged articles cover "...the most significant people, institutions, events and developments spanning both the United States and Canada" (p. ix). This set is one in a series examining each decade of the twentieth century. As for relevant primary sources, any serious reader or researcher would do well to consult *Defining Documents in American History, The 1920's (1920-1929)* (see ARBA 2015, entry 238). This single-volume reference work contains 45 representative full-text examples/excerpts of journals, letters, speeches, laws, government reports, and court cases (among other formats), giving the reader a very good sense of issues of importance to the body politic at the time. In addition to the text of the historical document in question, each chapter includes clearly written explanatory paragraphs with headings such as "Summary Overview," "Defining Moment," "Author Biography," "Document Analysis," and "Essential Themes." These titles in combination will give researchers an excellent introduction to the "Roaring Twenties" here in the United States of America.—**Michael Francis Bemis**

212.   **Salem Witch Museum. www.salemwitchmuseum.com.** [Website] Free. Date reviewed: 2017.

The Salem Witch Museum in Salem, Massachusetts, houses an interpretive experience and guided exhibits about the scandalous time when area residents were accused of witchcraft. Designed primarily to promote the museum, this site nonetheless offers some historical reference which may be helpful to students and casual visitors. Of the nine menu tabs, several lead to noteworthy information. The Trials provides a brief and basic summary of the events of 1692 accompanied by a few photos from museum galleries. Videos offers a series of visual answers to common questions posed by younger students (e.g., How did the Salem Witch Trials end?", "What type of people were accused of witchcraft?", etc.). The thematic videos of "Witch Trials Weekly" focus on individual topics of the era, such as Church Control or Sarah Good's Mistake. There are also supplemental videos about broader witchcraft topics (e.g., Wiccan holidays) and the Salem Witch Museum restoration project. Users can also employ the Sites Tour tab to explore locations relevant to the witch trial era, with maps, brief narrative descriptions, and photographs of buildings, cemeteries, and headstones. The Blog is notable for its transcript of Elie Wiesel's Salem Witch Trial Memorial dedication speech from 1992.—**ARBA Staff Reviewer**

213.   **Salem Witch Trials Documentary Guide. http://salem.lib.virginia.edu/home. html.** [Website] Free. Date reviewed: 2017.

This straightforward site offers access to a rich trove of primary source materials connected to the Salem witch trial era of the late seventeenth century. Simply structured, the site lists a series of links that open to a generous array of maps, letters, court documents, sermons, literature, and more which help paint a vivid portrait of this notorious episode of American history. Documents & Transcriptions collects links to court transcripts, records, and miscellaneous files from a variety of regional archives. Users can access such items as digital transcripts of individual case files (depositions, interrogations, indictments, etc.), petitions, expense accounts, and bills. Historical Maps lists links to contemporary maps of Salem Village and neighboring areas afflicted by accusations of witchcraft. Archival Collections organizes documents by sources such as the Massachusetts Historical Society and the Boston Public Library. Contemporary Books links to selected literature of the trials and witchcraft in general, such as "Cases of Conscience Concerning Evil Spirits" by Minister Increase Mather. The right sidebar offers helpful contextual information and tools, such as an overview of the trials, related images, a notable name index, and media reviews. Particularly helpful is the name index which can sort the figures of this historical period in a variety of ways (e.g., trial critics, "afflicted" girls, executed, etc.). Much of the same material is accessible in different ways within the site which may create a bit of confusion in terms of what is actually offered. Nonetheless, this site would be an excellent launching point for students and educators.—**ARBA Staff Reviewer**

214.   **The Salem Witchcraft Site. http://www.tulane.edu/~salem/.** [Website] Free. Date reviewed: 2017.

The Salem Witchcraft Site provides data covering a range of factors circling around the Salem witch episode of 1692. Sixteen downloadable data sets examine three distinct areas of late-seventeenth-century New England information: chronology, geography, and socioeconomic demographics. Users can click through each menu tab sequentially to access background information, the data sets, and conclusions, or they can navigate via the Site Map link at the bottom of the page or underneath the Home tab. Data is available in an array of forms, including pie charts, scatter plots, maps, and more, and is accompanied by specific download and analysis instructions. Data commentary is generally limited to encouraging objective analysis and new interpretations. The Setting tab from the menu leads to brief but well-detailed background of the Salem witch era, touching on principal players, the church dynamic, and a description of the areas of Salem Town and Salem Village. Chronology presents data related to patterns of accusations and executions, including an Accused Witches Scatter Plot Data Set and an Execution Scatter Plot Data Set. The Geography section points to the locations of the witch accusation outbreak and includes tables and maps showing such things as the impact of accusations on communities around the Salem area and how accusations spread. Salem Village provides data related to social, economic, and political factors using tax information, petitions, and more. Data is summarized under the Conclusions tab, where users can also find the notes, bibliography, and credits. This well-organized site provides an excellent tool to encourage further scholarship into this most intriguing era.—**ARBA Staff Reviewer**

215.   Spar, Ira. **Civil War Newspapers: Histories and Excerpts of Nine Union Newspapers.** Jefferson, N.C., McFarland, 2017. 246p. index. $39.95pa. ISBN 13: 978-1-4766-6560-3; 978-1-4766-2529-4 (e-book).

This volume is a fascinating compilation and discussion of nine Civil War newspapers, all on the Union side, describing their founding and history, content, and audiences, as well as providing numerous excerpts from each. The nine newspapers are: *Hospital Register, Armory Square Hospital Gazette, The Soldiers' Journal, The Cripple, The Crutch, Hammond Gazette, The Cartridge Box, Knight Hospital Record, and Voice of the Soldier.* There are numerous illustrations, black-and-white photographs, pictures of documents and newspaper articles, and many stories related to the conditions of hospitals, medicine, medical care, and medical equipment during the time of the Civil War. Six appendixes provide more detailed information related to hospital districts and conglomerates, including medical officers in charge, number of beds, and number of occupied beds at certain time periods during the Civil War. This book would be of interest to libraries with special collections and/or holdings related to aspects of the Civil War.—**Bradford Lee Eden**

216.   **State Historical Society of Iowa. https://iowaculture.gov/history.** [Website] Free. Date reviewed: 2017.

The State Historical Society of Iowa has creatively compiled Iowa History Standards information onto this smart Web page. Part of the larger state cultural website, the page showcases 12 themed sets of primary source materials encompassing a range of broader historical subjects and revealing their impact on the lives of Iowans. Users can search via subject, time period, or grade-level filters in order to find the most appropriate set. Alternatively, users can scroll through a listing of available tagged sets, which include Agriculture in a Global World, America's Involvement in World War I, Geography with Iowa Connections (two parts), Immigration, Underground Railroad, The Civil War, The Cold War, and more. Each set contains a topical overview of its subject (e.g., The Cold War), including any connections relative to Iowa history (e.g., "In the 1948 election, Iowa's Henry A. Wallace ran for president on a platform that sought to reduce (Cold War) tensions and find ways to cooperate with the Soviet Union"). A series of Supporting Questions (e.g., "What role, if any, should the military play in a war of ideals?") follows, each accompanied by links to affiliated primary source items, such as photographs, letters, and audio recordings. The items are presented alongside a brief description, transcript (if necessary), Text-dependent Questions, and citation information. Users can also download individual images and a pdf set of all resources. In addition, The Primary Source Toolkit is a 54-page pdf guide to teaching with primary sources with particular insight into grade-level activities.—**ARBA Staff Reviewer**

217.   **Statue of Liberty—Ellis Island Foundation. https://www.libertyellisfoundation. org/.** [Website] Free. Date reviewed: 2018.

While primarily devoted to the foundation which supports Ellis Island and the Statue of Liberty, this website also offers historical information about the landmarks and the people who passed through them that could connect with a variety of research needs. Most of the information is available to all site users, while some information requires free registration. The Statue of Liberty tab on the bar at the top of the page lists a series of informative links. Users can access detail about the building and preservation of the statue and the history of the small island it sits upon. A Statue Gallery offers a small selection of photographs and video content. The Statue Timeline includes more photographs and a capsule chronology of events directly beginning with the 1667 issuance of the first land grant on the island which would eventually anchor the statue.

Users can also find historical information on the Stamps & Coins using statue imagery, Emma Lazarus' poem "The New Colossus," and Statue Facts about the torch, crown, face, steps, and other components. The Ellis Island tab offers a bit more comprehensive material, including an Ellis Island Timeline spanning over three hundred years, an Immigration Timeline focused on the changing motivations for new world immigration, and an Ellis Island History section with nine brief chronological essays such as "The Origin of the Island," "Journeying by Ship to the Land of Liberty," and "Arrival at the Island & Initial Inspection." Users can additionally view information on Famous Passengers and other basic passenger information such as arrival year, birthplace, and ship name, via the Passenger Search link. Users who register for free can potentially access more detailed information such as Passenger Record, Ship Image, and Ship Manifest. These users also have access to a library of nearly two thousand Oral Histories (either text transcript or audio recording) collected from immigrants and employees of the landmarks.—**ARBA Staff Reviewer**

218.   **This Is Who We Were: In the 1900s.** Amenia, N.Y., Grey House Publishing, 2017. 566p. illus. index. $160.00. ISBN 13: 978-1-68217-351-0; 978-1-68217-352-7. (e-book).

Like the other titles in Grey House Publishing's This is Who We Were series (see ARBA 2016, entry 253) or (see ARBA 2017, entry 264), this volume draws material from the same publisher's Working Americans series. It begins with the profile of 27 people organized into three categories: "Life at Home"; "Life at Work"; and "Life in the Community." There are no citations provided so the sources of the information in the respective profiles is unknown. Section two is comprised of three bulleted lists that function as both a chronology and a source for "can you believe it" factoids. Section three provides economic data from the period, including what everyday items like milk cost and the standard wages provided to different categories of workers in the years 1900, 1903, and 1908. The following section proffers 28 primary sources drawn from popular newspapers and magazines. They focus on issues related to such topics as education, music, and politics. The final section, which comprises more than half of the volume, contains census data from 1900, 1910, and 2010. Also included is the U.S. Census Bureau's 2002 report "Demographic Trends in the 20th Century" which utilizes demographic data from 1900, 1950, and 2000. Concluding the work is a two-page bibliography and a four-page index. It should be noted that the text is accompanied by numerous black-and-white illustrations.

As a reference tool this volume cannot be viewed as authoritative. Much of its content is presented without context or citations identifying the source material. It is also difficult to ascertain the target audience. Sections one to four are written in language accessible to a high school student. Suddenly in section five the user is tasked with interpreting hundreds of pages of census data without any guidance as to how to use the information presented therein. The bibliography only provides 36 suggestions for further research and the index is woefully inadequate. Considering the cost of the volume, libraries would be better served putting their money to use elsewhere.—**John R. Burch Jr.**

219.   Vile, John R. **The Civil War and Reconstruction Eras.** Santa Barbara, Calif., ABC-CLIO, 2017. 296p. index. (Documents Decoded series). $81.00. ISBN 13: 978-1-4408-5428-6; 978-1-4408-5429-3 (e-book).

Historical documents are rich resources for students and scholars, a contemporary portrait or reflection of the past—often rare but always rewarding. The same can be said for the now 13th volume in the Documents Decoded series, ABC-CLIO's edited volumes of original documents. This volume on the Civil War and Reconstruction presents some sixty-five documents ranging from the Emancipation Proclamation to the Civil Rights Act (1866) to the words to "Dixie." Following a brief introduction, the documents are divided into three sections representing historical periods. Some are rather lengthy (the Confederate Constitution) while others far less so (Lincoln's second inaugural address) but all include an introductory description, explanatory notes, document source, and, in select cases, a conclusion. A timeline, reading suggestions, and index conclude the volume; all of these features are brief. Aimed at school and public libraries, the Documents Decoded series serves a very useful purpose. Although most if not all of these documents can be found through an Internet search (I located fifteen of fifteen as a sample search), the introduction, notes, and, where included, the conclusion, should prove valuable especially in school libraries.—**Boyd Childress**

220.   **Visualizing Emancipation. www.dsl.richmond.edu/historicalatlas/.** [Website] Free. Date reviewed: 2017.

A selection from the fine mapping repertoire of the University of Richmond's Digital Scholarship Lab, Visualizing Emancipation consolidates elements that point to the demise of slavery throughout the course of the U.S. Civil War. The interactive map gathers diverse threads of the same story—military, political, and individual. Recording primary source documents as "events" along the timeline of emancipation, the project helps users visualize the complexities behind the huge social upheaval. General users may select the Get Started button from the home page, which will guide them to the main map. Users can track the data points of Emancipation Events and Union Army Locations, and may additionally select to view an Emancipation Event Heatmap and a Legality of Slavery Overlay. A timeline bar at the bottom of the page allows users to note the Emancipation Events and Union Army Locations at monthly increments between January 1861 and January 1866. They may also choose to animate the timeline to reflect all event/location changes throughout those years. Further detail is accessed via the List function of the map, which chronologically notes the date, event type, location, and source of the data point. The list also includes a brief transcribed excerpt of the sourced event. Events are marked by an icon on the list and may range from examples of slaves helping the Union soldiers to reports of fugitive slaves, and beyond. The site encourages a collaborative approach to its content, conveying a desire for additional "event" submissions with which to improve the map. A Learn More button offers helpful information about such collaboration (e.g., evidence collection methods) and offers valuable perspective on the data collected so far. A For Teachers button encourages a range of educators to use the site with suggestions for lesson plans and other material.—**ARBA Staff Reviewer**

221.   **Woodrow Wilson Presidential Library & Museum. http://www.woodrowwilson. org/campus/library.** [Website] Free. Date reviewed: 2018.

This page from the Woodrow Wilson Presidential Library allows access to materials which help tell the story of the 28th president of the United States and the era in which he governed. The good-sized archive contains letters, documents, photographs, and more that touch on significant events like World War I or women's suffrage, and shine a revealing light on the character of early-twentieth-century America. Users can scroll down to the bottom of the page and select from a list of links that will take them to particular parts of the digital archive which has been arranged into thirty-four distinct collections. The Cary T. Grayson Papers, for example, contain thousands of letters, notes, telegrams, and more connected to Wilson's friend and personal physician which provide an inside look at White House activity in addition to common observances of the era's concerns. Other collections include the Woodrow Wilson Political Cartoon Collection, The Race & Segregation Collection, The Wilson Family Genealogy Records, and The U.S. Signal Corps Photographs. The Images link focuses on the collections which emphasize photographs. The Items link presents the total archive of over 7,500 items, which users can search (keyword or advanced) or browse by subject or tag. The site displays an A-Z listing of nearly 700 subject headings of people and events for ease of navigation. Users can find information on the 1919 Paris Peace Conference, Automobiles, International Relations, Influenza Epidemic, Alice Wilson, the Roosevelts, and much more. Users can also access two digital exhibits. "The Trotter Incident" gathers artifacts related to a confrontation about segregation in the federal government, and "A World War I Soldier's Trunk" is an excellent examination of America's path into the Great War. Capturing both the daunting obstacles and enormous progress for Americans of the early twentieth century, in addition to the legacy of the man who led them through it, this archive would appeal to historians, educators, students, and others.—**ARBA Staff Reviewer**

222.   **Zoom In! http://zoomin.edc.org.** [Website] Free. Date reviewed: 2017.

Created by educators and historians from the Educational Development Center and the American Social History Project, this free online blended learning platform engages secondary students to think critically about important events and issues in US history while developing writing skills. The site offers 18 full inquiry units covering six time periods in U.S. history, from the Revolution to contemporary times, aligned to the Common Core. Each unit presents five to eight lessons incorporating content, various teaching strategies, and scaffolds for educators to customize the experience for their students. The units have a strong emphasis on building understanding of historical context by engaging with primary sources and using those to support writing argumentative essays. According to the site, the focus on writing stems from trends in national assessments asking more complex writing tasks of students. In a one-to-one device format, students access the lessons, record notes, and complete their essays within the platform itself, allowing educators to easily monitor student progress and grade final products. Supportive features provide educators with instructional tutorial videos and detailed guides offering suggestions for utilizing the units while also allowing flexibility for teachers to tailor to their own style and individual needs. While the content focus is quite limited, the comprehensive inquiry-based units, focus on critical thinking and writing, and free cost make this a very worthwhile resource for secondary educators.

Highly recommended.—**Kasey Garrison**

African History

223.   **African Kingdoms: An Encyclopedia of Empires and Civilizations.** Saheed Aderinto, ed. Santa Barbara, Calif., ABC-CLIO, 2017. 364p. illus. index. $89.00. ISBN 13: 978-1-61069-579-4; 978-1-61069-580-0 (e-book).

This reference explores the diversity and sophistication of the civilizations of Africa before the 1880s when European colonization of the continent began. The entries introduce the reader to the political, social, religious, and cultural institutions of empires and kingdoms long gone, like Ancient Egypt, as well as those that were thriving when the Europeans arrived, like the Asante. This rich precolonial history was largely unappreciated by Western scholars until the second half of the twentieth century. As an example of the content, the reader learns that the Borno empire lasted from the ninth century to 1893. It dominated the Lake Chad region, was a hub of trans-Saharan commercial links, and was the first sub-Saharan polity to adopt Islam, (in the eleventh century), going on to become a respected center of Islamic culture. At the end of the nineteenth century it was split up and colonized by Germany and Britain. Postcolonial Borno is now part of Nigeria. The city state of Nri flourished from the eleventh century to the seventeenth century, declining in the nineteenth century. It is an example of an ancient kingdom that continues to exist within the modern state of Nigeria with His Highness Eze Nri Enweleana II Obidiegwu

Onyeso as ruling monarch. Features include a timeline of African history from 100,000 B.C.E. to the postcolonial present, a small selection of primary documents primarily from European writers but with some African voices, and extensive references for further reading. This encyclopedia provides an insightful introduction to the continent's history and demonstrates how its rich past continues to influence Africa today.—**Adrienne Antink**

224.   **A Liberian Journey: History, Memory, and the Making of a Nation. http:// chnm.gmu.edu/news/a-liberian-journey/.** [Website] Free. Date reviewed: 2017.

This fine digital exhibit showcases the work of a 1926 Harvard expedition to the coastal African nation of Liberia. Sent in advance of a Firestone Plantations Company business venture, the researchers amassed a compelling record, via photographs, video, oral histories, documents, and other items which shines a light on Liberia's obscure history and Western interest in the region. The menu bar contains several straightforward options. Users can click a pin on the interactive Map to access artifacts connected to that location. The map is also helpful in establishing the scope of the Harvard expedition. Exhibits currently features "Chief Suah Koko: Warrior and Peacemaker," which relates the story of the female chief who defied cultural norms to unify and strengthen her country. Collections accesses the artifacts, and users can search by themes (e.g., ants, camp, rubber trees, snakes, rafts, etc.) unique to the project. Users can also browse artifacts grouped by medium, and can examine nearly 600 images of Liberian people, flora, fauna, and more; film footage of Liberian life; diary entries of two Harvard researchers; and a selection of maps, letters, and sketches. In addition, users can watch video of current Liberians who reflect on a variety of topics regarding the legacy of the Harvard expedition and Liberia's future. This well-defined site certainly draws attention to the skew of Western attitudes, but nonetheless does an excellent job of injecting Liberian history into the global discussion.—**ARBA Staff Reviewer**

Ancient History

225.   **The Ancient World: Extraordinary People in Extraordinary Societies.** Michael Shally-Jensen, ed. Hackensack, N.J., Salem Press, 2017. 4v. illus. maps. index. $395.00/ set. ISBN 13: 978-1-68217-189-9; 978-1-68217-190-5 (e-book).

The set is a revised version of *Encyclopedia of the Ancient World* (see ARBA 2002, entry 503) with hundreds of new essays (making a total of 1,440) offering a cross-cultural view of the ancient world, which is defined as covering prehistory to 700 C.E. in most cases. Eleven regions are covered: Greece, Rome, Near East, India, Far East, Africa, Central Asia, Oceania, Europe and the British Isles, Americas, and Egypt and Alexandria. Each section has an overview introducing the major themes of life in that region, followed by A to Z entries of people and places specific to that region. There are dozens of black-and-white illustrations and two dozen black-and-white maps. There are circa 375 contributors, mostly American academics. Bibliographies accompany each subsection and there is an extensive bibliography, a glossary, detailed chronologies, a subject index, and a detailed table of contents.

Given the coverage and the scholarly detail, most libraries (secondary school, academic, public) will want this set. Few libraries will have extensive coverage of all the areas delineated. However, there are caveats: the illustrations and the maps are inadequate, most of the biographies can be found in standard sources, and the set is intimidating to the average user. Not for ready reference, but for browsers and term paper creators.—**Jonathan F. Husband**

226.   **The Atlas of Ancient Rome: Biography and Portraits of the City.** Andrea Carandini, ed. Princeton, N.J., Princeton University Press, 2017. 2v. illus. maps. index. $199.50/set. ISBN 13: 978-0-691-16347-5.

Every generation publishes a ground-breaking work on ancient Rome and this is such a work for the current generation. Although there are many other excellent atlases of ancient Rome, none provides the detail, the scholarship, or the comprehensiveness of this source. Meant for scholars as well as the wider public interested in ancient Rome, this work updates and expands Rodolfo Lanciani's *Forma Urbis Romae* which was published from 1893 to 1901. The current authors and editors base this new work on recent topographical research, archaeological finds, and modern stratigraphic and architectural analysis. Covering the period from the pre-urban foundations of Rome in the ninth and tenth centuries B.C.E. to the late period of antiquity (mid-sixth century C.E.), the work seeks to be comprehensive. Volume one examines the city both as a whole and as a sum of its 14 regions and provides textual descriptions and analysis as well as wonderful illustrations of archaeological sites, reconstructions, artifacts, paintings, photographs, etc. Volume two contains the actual maps and plans of buildings, labeled as "tables," as well as serviceable indexes divided into several sections: ancient names of monuments and places, conventional and modern names of monuments, topographical units (based on the regions of Rome), and types of monuments. Taken as a whole, *The Atlas of Ancient Rome* represents a monumental undertaking that will prove its use for decades to come. The main deficiency of the set is the mixing together of items labeled "illustrations" with those called "figures," making it difficult to find the referenced images quickly. For those academic libraries that support programs in ancient history, ancient cultures, classics, Italian studies, or even cartography, this is a required purchase.—**Gregory A. Crawford**

227.   McIntosh, Jane R. **Mesopotamia and the Rise of Civilization: History, Documents, and Key Questions.** Santa Barbara, Calif., ABC-CLIO, 2017. 256p. index. (Crossroads in World History series). $61.00. ISBN 13: 978-1-4408-3546-9; 978-1-4408-3547- (e-book).

Part of the Crossroads in World History series, this book focuses on the emergence of civilization in ancient Mesopotamia. A timeline identifies the essential elements of the event and a brief historical overview provides the historical context. A little more than half the book consists of brief entries about the people, places, themes, movements, institutions, and other topics of Mesopotamian civilization. Some look at aspects of its technology, knowledge, and culture, such as its works of art and architecture. Others provoke interesting questions about the working of society and its political and economic systems, such as currency, finance, slavery, and the responsibilities of rulers. The twenty primary source documents included have an introductory paragraph followed by source information. These documents are usually studied at the college level and will give students a good preparation for advanced study. This section is followed by original essays responding to key questions, each offering a different perspective on a particular topic. Books in this series intend to help students understand the causes and effects associated with historical events and this one achieves its goal. Additional resources, a bibliography, and an index are included. Recommended.—**Norman Desmarais**

228.   Mendoza, Barbara. **Artifacts from Ancient Egypt.** Santa Barbara, Calif., Greenwood Press/ABC-CLIO, 2017. 340p. illus. index. $100.00. ISBN 13: 978-1-4408-4400-3; 978-1-4408-4401-0 (e-book).

This book showcases forty-five artifacts from ancient Egypt, specifically from the late fourth millennium B.C.E. to just before the first century C.E. Most were produced during the Pharaonic Period of Egypt between the First and Thirty-first Dynasty. These primary source objects are typical examples studied in ancient Egyptian archaeology and introductory Egyptology courses, and are divided into seven major sections: Beauty, Adornment, and Clothing; Death and Funerary Equipment; Food and Drink; Household Items, Furniture, and Games; Literacy and Writing; Religion, Ritual, and Magic, and Tools and Weapons. The introduction provides a chronology and discusses periodization and artifact evaluation. Each object is then introduced (with place and dating information) with description, significance, and a further information section. Black-and-white photographs of the objects are included, along with sidebars focused upon definitions, primary source documentation, and other crucial information. This book would be most useful for academic and research programs in archaeology and/or Egyptology; it would also be nice as a coffee table book.—**Bradford Lee Eden**

Asian History

229.   **Samurai Archives. http://www.samurai-archives.com/.** [Website] Free. Date reviewed: 2017.

Deeply devoted to all things samurai, this archive offers a vast array of information and resources covering the long history of the regaled Japanese warriors. Simply structured but with plenty to offer, the site will engage users whether they are looking for general or specific information. From the homepage, users can simply select one of the many links correlating to an aspect of the samurai story. The umbrella Historical Research category encompasses either individual articles, databases of entries, or other reference materials. For example, selecting Famous Samurai links to an alphabetized database of over 1,500 unique entries on individual samurai. Other article databases include Famous Women, Samurai Battles, and more. Entries are of varying length and it should be noted that some may only be placeholders with information yet to be added. Other links under the Historical Research umbrella may be more focused, such as Famous Generals, Samurai Culture (with articles on clothing, food, death, etc.), or Military Rulers of Japan which allows users to select from one of three families in order to chronologically chart their rule. And still other links offer excellent visual or interactive features, such as Samurai Banners, Samurai Family Crests, and the Japanese Castle Explorer, whereby users can click on a location within a map of Japan for photographs and descriptions of historical sites. Users can additionally find Genealogies, a good series of Maps, and Selected Translations regarding historical figures, fiction, and battles. Further reference material runs the length of the right sidebar. Here users can find Interviews, an A-Z Glossary, several blogs, forums, and two chronologies examining both broader historical periods and more clan-specific events.

Articles, in the center of the Web page, presents a categorized listing of scholarly essays on topics such as Weapons & Armor or Military History, in addition to fictional excerpts and fan fiction. The size and scope of the contents make this a valuable and engaging choice for historians, educators, and others.—**ARBA Staff Reviewer**

230.   Xiong, Victor. **Historical Dictionary of Medieval China.** 2d ed. Lanham, Md., Rowman & Littlefield, 2017. 2v. maps. (Historical Dictionaries of Ancient Civilizations and Historical Eras). $200.00/set; $190.00 (e-book). ISBN 13: 978-1-4422-7615-4; 978-1-4422-7616-1 (e-book).

This two-volume book is now in its second edition, and is perhaps the most comprehensive dictionary on medieval China available. Over 1,500 new entries have been added and errors from the first edition have been corrected. More coverage of county and local governments has been included, more historical figures added, substantial thematic content on a number of topics has been expanded, homonymic place-names have been separated, extensive cross-references with *see* and *see also* related terms are now available, the chronology and the bibliography have been lengthened, and a pronunciation guide for difficult Chinese characters is now available. Eleven maps are included in the front of the book, along with an extensive index to locate important cities, towns, etc. in medieval China from 262 C.E. to the mid-10th century. An appendix includes the various reigns from the late second century to the 10th century, listed alphabetically rather than chronologically. Overall, this is an essential reference guide to medieval China, and would be appropriate in any college and university library.—**Bradford Lee Eden**

Archaeology

231.   Adovasio, J. M., and David Pedler. **Strangers in a New Land: What Archaeology Reveals about the First Americans.** New York, Firefly Books, 2016. 348p. illus. maps. index. $49.95. ISBN 13: 978-1-77085-363-8.

For much of the twentieth century, it was essentially canon that the first human inhabitants of the Americas arrived over the Bering Land Bridge from Asia. The time of their arrival had been determined by the presence of the Clovis stone points at numerous sites in North America. The theory received a strong challenge in 1997 after a group of scientists confirmed that Thomas Dillehay's Monte Verde site in Chile had in fact been inhabited at least 200,000 years, which meant humans had arrived before the land bridge existed. Monte Verde had not been the only archaeological site threatening the prevailing wisdom as the Meadowcroft Rockshelter site in Pennsylvania had also yielded artifacts that did not fit into the established chronology. The work at Meadowcroft was led by J. M. Adovasio, Research Associate of the Senator John Heinz History Center and Director of Research and Services of the Harbor Branch Oceanographic Institute, Florida Atlantic University, who co-authored this reference tool with David Pedler, Research Associate of the Senator John Heinz History Center who also works at the Rensselaer Polytechnic Institute's Lighting Research Center. Their book explores the major archaeological sites in the Americas and details their place in the ongoing debate as to who colonized the Americas and how.

The book is divided into two parts. Part one is entitled "Questions and Answers" and addresses the who, how, when, and why conundrum. Part two, "The Evidence," examines 24 archaeological sites organized into four categories: "Clovis and Folsom Age Sites"; "Disputed Pre-Clovis Sites"; "Legitimate Pre-Clovis Sites"; and "Controversial Pre-Clovis Sites." For each site, a narrative is provided that describes the history of the archaeological work undertaken and a description of the most important artifacts discovered along with an explanation of their context within the debate over the peopling of the Americas. Also included are copious illustrations, maps, and photographs, many in full color and some the size of an entire page. Appendixes include a glossary and a nine-page explanation of carbon dating that includes the carbon dates for the artifacts discussed in the main body of the work. Concluding the book is a bibliography and index.

This work is highly recommended to all libraries as it details a scientific debate that continues to roil the archeological community in language that is easily understandable by lay readers.—**John R. Burch Jr.**

232.   **EAMEANA: Endangered Archaeology: Middle East and Africa.** https://eameana.arch.ox.ac.uk/. [Website] Free. Date reviewed: 2018.

EAMEANA was launched in 2015 to respond to threats to archaeological sites in turbulent areas of the Middle East and Africa. The project is based at three universities: Oxford, Leicester, and Durham, and has outside support. The project uses aerial data gathered from annual aircraft expeditions over the Middle East and Northern Africa (MENA), satellite imagery, and other resources. The site's primary resource is its Database which offers both a broad view of the MENA landscape and the ancient sites within as well as detailed information on the sites themselves. Users can search the Public Database or browse site types (e.g., fortified farms), disturbances (e.g., destroyed sites), or specific site locations (e.g., Petra in Jordan). Selecting a site location allows access to a satellite image and record detailing site name (e.g., toponym, designation), site functions (e.g., domestic, religious), cultural periods (e.g., iron age, Hellenistic), feature forms (e.g., wall, structure), feature interpretations (e.g., bath house, chapel), condition, disturbance extent percentage, disturbance type, and more. Related Resources of reports, books, and other materials may be available at the bottom of each site page. Users can alternatively access information via a satellite Map View of the MENA area with pinned site locations. This approach gives an excellent overview of the MENA landscape and the sites within. Other general materials are available from the homepage. Case Studies presents three reports borne out of EAMENA work: "Endangered Architecture in the al-Jufra, Libya," "Roman Military Sites in the Eastern Desert of Egypt," and "The Madaba Ring Road, Jordan." Threats offers essays and photographs to describe Agriculture, Construction, Natural Erosion, Looting, and Conflict disturbances (with the Great Mosque in Aleppo, Syria, as a recent example of the latter). Other Resources include a Blog, along with links to posters, podcasts, and affiliated projects.—**ARBA Staff Reviewer**

233.   **Encyclopedia of Geoarchaeology.** Allan S. Gilbert and others. New York, Springer Publishing, 2017. 1046p. illus. index. (Encyclopedia of Earth Sciences Series). $549.00. ISBN 13: 978-94-007-4827-9; 978-1-4020-4409-0 (e-book).

This encyclopedia begins with a table of contents, a list of authors and affiliations, and a preface that traces the development of this relatively new discipline. Geoarchaeology, put simply, strives to use methods and concepts from both geology and archaeology to further knowledge about interactions between humans and their environment. In this book, designed to be accessible to students and nonspecialists, users will find terms defined, concepts explained, and geoarchaeological sites showcased. Entries vary in length, but all are signed and all contain a basic definition or description and a bibliography. Basics like dendochronology, radiocarbon dating, the history of geoarchaeology, and microstratigraphy are discussed as are such general types of sites as petroglyphs, pastoral sites, coastal settings, privies/latrines, and dumps/landfills. Particularly important geoarchaeological sites are highlighted in this volume. The international sites include, among others, Zhoukoudian near Beijing; York in northern England; Atapuerca in north-central Spain; Ain Ghazal in Jordan; Cactus Hill, Virginia; and Monte Verde, Chile. Entries conclude with bibliographies and cross-references, where necessary. The inclusion of figures (black-and-white diagrams, color photos, etc.) reinforce information about the concept or site under discussion. An author index and subject index round out the work. Highly recommended for academic libraries.—**ARBA Staff Reviewer**

European History

General Works

234.   **Brill's Encyclopedia of the Middle Ages.** Gert Melville and Martial Staub, eds. Boston, Brill Academic, 2017. 2v. $420.00/set. ISBN 13: 978-90-04-29315-1.

This two-volume encyclopedia is a translation from the original German, a process that involved both a team of translators and a translation oversight team. The content is directed at an academic audience. The editors structured the book thematically into eight parts: Society, Faith and Knowledge, Literature, Fine Arts and Music, Economy, Technology, Living Environments and Conditions, and Constitutive Historical Events and Regions. Within these sections users will find essays of varying length on a slew of medieval topics, including, but certainly not limited to: kingship, feudalism, guilds and confraternities, religious life, men's and women's clothing, women in society, law, sexuality, languages, mysticism, sermons, books and libraries, literature, art, architecture, agriculture, climate, urban areas, and the Crusades. In sum, this encyclopedia provides a very fleshed-out picture of life in medieval Europe. The articles are signed; there is a list of contributors at the end of volume 2. Entries are also cross-referenced. The encyclopedia includes an extensive bibliography, over two hundred pages long. Granted, many of the sources are in German or another non-English language, but there are enough English-language sources to make perusal quite worthwhile. This book is highly readable despite it being a translation. Highly recommended for public and academic libraries.—**ARBA Staff Reviewer**

Great Britain

235.   **Digital Panopticon. https://www.digitalpanopticon.org/.** [Website] Free. Date reviewed: 2018.

This site allows users to search millions of historical records gathered from nearly fifty sources regarding the criminally convicted in Great Britain. It specifically hosts records on the lives of ninety thousand individuals convicted at the Old Bailey between the years 1780 and 1913. The site contains scholarly articles, data visualizations, and an immense collection of records which work together to provide interesting perspectives on criminal justice history and numerous avenues for research. Although rich in offerings, the site is easy to navigate. Users can conduct a search from the bar, employing names, crimes, locations, and more. The more specific the search, the better, as the records are immense. Any search can be made into a visualization such as the sample on the homepage illustrating "what actually happened to defendants sentenced to death." Users can alternatively select from a series of tabs on the menu bar. Records provides excellent background information on the different types of records held in the archive, such as Trial Records, Post-Trial and Sentencing Records, Transportation Records, Imprisonment Records, and Civil Records. These broader categories are further broken down by record type, e.g., capital convictions, judges' reports on criminals, and petitions for pardons. Selecting a specific record type presents well-organized, cross-referenced explanations, including illustrations and links to an original dataset. Convict Lives examines the lives of selected convicts whose stories have been pieced together by the information in the databases. Users can browse a list of over fifty individuals, categorized by offense (juvenile, property, violent, etc.) and punishment (transported, imprisoned, and other). A further category lists recidivists—or repeat offenders. Selecting an individual presents a good biographical essay as pertains particularly to their crime and punishment. Essay sections may include Early Life; Crimes and Trials; Punishment and Outcomes; Personal Details and Life Events; Wider Context; and other information. There may also be a photograph. Historical Background offers a drop-down menu of numerous topics that provide insight on Stages of Justice (policing, sentencing etc.) and more. There are also excellent overviews on the general subjects of crime, punishment, London, and Australia (the main destination of criminal transportation). Research and Teaching offers a selection of tools for educators and others, such as Thematic Research and Teaching Guides. Digital Panopticon shares an important and fascinating history—it is easy for even casual users to become happily lost in its rich content.—**ARBA Staff Reviewer**

236.   **Foreign Office Files for Japan, 1919-1952. https://www.amdigital.co.uk/ primary-sources/foreign-office-files-for-japan-1919-1952.** [Website] Chicago, Adam Matthew Digital, 2017. Price negotiated by site. Date reviewed: 2017.

In 1919, following the Treaty of Versailles that concluded World War I, Great Britain and Japan were close allies, though their relationship was fraying. By 1952, the two countries had fought each other during World War II, and then reunited as allies. This collection of original documents from the United Kingdom's National Archives, will, when complete, provide a British-based overview of that period, through correspondence, diplomatic dispatches, maps, contracts, summaries of events, and more. At present, documents from the period of 1931 to 1945 are available, and the subsequent and prior periods will be added in 2018 and 2019, respectively.

Searching through the collection uses the familiar Adam Matthew interface, and the digitization quality is quite remarkable. Tools for viewing, saving, and storing documents are excellent. Handwriting has not yet been converted to searchable text, though extensive subject tags—for countries, places, people, topics, etc., have been assigned throughout the collection. The set reflects the British Foreign Office's primary documents associated with Japan in these time periods, and the content includes many typed dispatches sent to London, as well as newspaper clippings, hand-drawn maps, reports, correspondence, and more. Documents are organized by the series and folder structure of the Foreign Office's originals. The "Chronology" tab, which combines relevant events from across collections, is a particularly nice feature for understanding how a collection's subject interacts with the rest of the world. The "Interactive World Map" is somewhat less impressive, as it references resources from collections that one cannot access; some might see this as useful, while others might just find it frustrating.

Overall, when complete, this collection should be a valuable tool for exploring the British Government's fraught relationship with its Japanese counterpart.—**Peter H. McCracken**

237.	**Literary Print Culture: The Stationers' Company Archive, London. https:// www.amdigital.co.uk/primary-sources/literary-print-culture.** [Website] Chicago, Adam Matthew Digital, 2017. Price negotiated by site. Date reviewed: 2017.

This new database from Adam Matthew presents numerous types of documents from The Worshipful Company of Stationers & Newspaper Makers, which was first established in 1403 and incorporated in 1557. Among other items, there are trade records, court records, financial records, charities and property records, membership records, photographs, and a collection of recent oral histories. These items trace the history of the book and of publishing in England, as well as the development of copyright there. Seven introductory essays dealing with the materials provide users with the history of the organization and the different sorts of documents included in this rich database. Topics of the essays include plays, ballads, printed music, "Liber A," and membership of the Company from 1550 to 1700.

This resource is clearly aimed at a particular group of scholars/researchers, who are familiar with the various roles of the Stationers' Company, who can navigate the diverse categories of documents presented here, and perhaps most importantly, decipher English penmanship (for some documents). The visual quality of the documents is excellent; readers can zoom in to examine the minute details of a particular page, an ability most helpful for the handwritten texts. There is a possibility that handwritten text recognition software will be available in the future, as a couple Adam Matthew databases now have. (A minor note—once in a while, document titles can be a bit misleading: "Clerk's letters concerning accounts, 1797-1888" actually only has documents from 1797-1802, 1873, and 1888.)

Clearly aimed at research institutions, this resource will be best utilized by academic libraries anywhere that have patrons researching the areas of history mentioned above. Having this treasure trove of information literally at their fingertips, rather than many miles away, will serve them well indeed.—**Mark Schumacher**

238.	Olsen, Kirstin. **Daily Life in 18th-Century England.** 2d ed. Santa Barbara, Calif., Greenwood Press/ABC-CLIO, 2017. 459p. illus. index. (The Greenwood Press Daily Life Through History Series). $40.00. ISBN 13: 978-1-4408-5503-0; 978-1-4408-5504-7 (e-book).

Like our own time, England in the eighteenth century was a time of wrenching economic change, disruptive new technology, and political upheaval. In this second edition (see ARBA 2000, entry 471), the author brings alive what it was like to live in England during that time with chapters on family, gender, and sexuality; health care, hygiene, and death; class and race; work and the economy; life in London; education; science; clothing and fashion; food and drink; housing and furnishings; transportation and communication; the government; sports, arts and entertainment; and religion. For example, in the entertainment chapter we learn London's Bethlehem Hospital (Bedlam) was one of the city's top tourist attractions where for a fee you could tour the asylum and torment inmates. Cricket became popular in the eighteenth century and was played by the upper class as well as laborers with teams for men as well as women. Cricket even affected the royal succession when the heir to the throne Prince Frederick was hit in the head while playing the game in 1751 and died, making way for his son to become King George III. The high level of literacy at this time resulted in an unprecedented consumption of reading material, such as newspapers, tracts, periodicals, pamphlets, and books. The novel found a mass market in the eighteenth century with authors such as Henry Fielding and Daniel Defoe. In the religion chapter, we discover in this century civil and financial penalties were still being imposed on Catholics, Jews, Moravians, Quakers, Methodists, and anyone else who was not an Anglican. Each chapter ends with extensive suggestions for further reading and a primary source document related to the topic. There is also a detailed chronology.— **Adrienne Antink**

Ireland

239.   Gillespie, Gordon. **Historical Dictionary of the Northern Ireland Conflict.** 2d ed. Lanham, Md., Rowman & Littlefield, 2017. 368p. maps. index. (Historical Dictionaries of War, Revolution, and Civil Unrest). $100.00; $95.00 (e-book). ISBN 13: 978-1-4422-6304-8; 978-1-4422-6305-5 (e-book).

The first edition of this work authored by Dr. Gordon Gillespie was published in 2008 (see ARBA 2008, entry 437). He builds on the previous version through the inclusion of new entries, the updating of some of the original entries, and expanding coverage of events to 2016. Like all volumes in Rowman & Littlefield's Historical Dictionaries of War, Revolution, and Civil Unrest, the entries are preceded by "Acronyms and Abbreviations"; "Maps"; "Chronology"; and "Introduction." Notable is the chronology, which is comprised of 36 information-packed pages. The dictionary follows with approximately 300 chronologically arranged entries. Concluding the text is a bibliography. The volume lacks an index, which severely hampers the reference utility of the book. Despite its limitations, this work does provide in-depth information on the Northern Ireland conflict, or "The Troubles," and the impacts it has had, and continues to have, since the 1998 Good Friday Agreement. It is recommended for academic libraries that do not own the earlier edition.—**John R. Burch Jr.**

240.   **Mapping Death. http://www.mappingdeathdb.ie/.** [Website] Free. Date reviewed: 2017.

Mapping Death offers an informative inventory of the burial grounds of early medieval Ireland, maintaining a database of discovered burial sites accompanied by descriptive reference. Users can select the Query tab to focus a search using particular parameters (location, grave structure, trauma, etc.). Selecting the Browse tab allows access to either a Table View or a Map View of the database, which holds information on nearly two hundred sites spanning close to nine hundred years of early medieval (the first century through the eighth century) burials. The database lists sites alphabetically and includes information on townland, county, number of inhumations, number of cremations, and more. The Map View allows a more illustrative perspective on burial site location. Clicking on the arrow next to the site name displays further detail (identification and location) related to site excavation, such as precise geographical location or discovery details. Users can also select from a number of tabs for further, often absorbing detail. Description notes topography, chronology, burial era, description of burial cemetery, and other details. Cremations & Inhumations describe remains with information such as grave goods, position of body(ies), gender, wrapping, trauma, etc. Publications offer a listing of relevant resources and the Additional tab provides information on radiocarbon testing if applicable.—**ARBA Staff Reviewer**

Italy

241.　Byrne, Joseph P. **The World of Renaissance Italy.** Santa Barbara, Calif., Greenwood Press/ABC-CLIO, 2017. 2v. illus. index. (Daily Life Encyclopedias). $198.00/set. ISBN 13: 988-1-4408-2959-8; 978-1-4408-2960-4 (e-book).

Part of the Daily Life Encyclopedias series, this two-volume set focuses on the Renaissance in Italy, specifically from 1300 to 1600. The editor makes clear that this set is not an introduction to the Renaissance but to life as it was lived during the Renaissance period in Italy. Major figures and monuments are not provided entries, so that the broader trends and issues are highlighted. The over three hundred entries are divided into ten topical sections: Arts, Economics and Work, Family and Gender, Fashion and Appearance, Food and Drink, Housing and Community, Politics and Warfare, Recreation and Social Customs, Religion and Beliefs, and Science and Technology. In addition, a Primary Documents section provides a number of sources for each of the ten topical sections. Each entry has a *see also* references section, along with further readings. A historical chronology is provided in the first volume, while an appendix listing popes and European rulers from 1350 to 1600 is provided at the end of the second volume. This work is intended for upper-level high school and nonspecialist college students, as well as nonspecialist public library patrons. Recommended.—**Bradford Lee Eden**

Poland

242.　**Institute of National Remembrance. https://ipn.gov.pl/en.** [Website] Free. Date reviewed: 2017.

This project from the Polish Institute of National Remembrance aims to dispel the historical inaccuracies of Poland's role in World War II, particularly in relation to the concentration camps and death camps within its borders. A series of essays in addition to a fascinating database would likely appeal to researchers interested in recent European history or criminal justice (among other disciplines). Most of the information is available in English translation from the original Polish. Users can access the topical essays via tabs on the menu bar. It Began in The Third Reich explains how German Nazis established the concentration camps and their systems within their own country and then transplanted the concepts to occupied territories, including Poland. Other essays discuss Poles Under German Occupation, Repressions Against Poles and German Camps, with the final text, Holocaust, focusing on the Nazis' ultimate plan of extermination. Each essay works to describe in brief but specific detail the German takeover of Poland and administration of camps there, and to clarify the impossible situation of the Polish people. A final tab, SS KL Auschwitz Garrison, links to an A-Z database of known Auschwitz prison guards (directly available at the www.pamiec.pl/pa/form/60,Zaloga-SS-KL-Auschwitz.html URL). Users can search over 8,000 records via family or given names (original German and Polish translation) and date of birth. Records can include military service information, photographs, judicial information, and other details. Contextual information relates the difficult yet ongoing efforts to prosecute crimes of the Holocaust and German occupation. A map of concentration and death camps (unfortunately noninteractive) illustrates the German extension into occupied territories, while a generous use of graphic photos reflecting life and death within camp and ghetto perimeters works to devastating effect.— **ARBA Staff Reviewer**

243.   **The Lodz Ghetto Photos of Henryk Ross. http://agolodzghetto.com/.** [Website] Free. Date reviewed: 2017.

The true story of the Lodz ghetto—a Nazi established "corral" for Jews in World War II Poland—may have been buried in its rubble without the foresight and bravery of Henryk Ross. As the official photographer of the ghetto's Department of Statistics, Ross created identification cards and propaganda for his captors' use. They did not know that he also captured images of reality—reflecting both the surprising normalcy and devastating horrors of ghetto life. This collection showcases nearly three thousand of the surviving images taken by Ross during his four years in the ghetto. It additionally provides a wealth of further resources, contextual information, and research opportunities for a range of scholars and educators.

From the menu bar, users can select the Learn about Lodz tab to find essays about the history of Lodz and the Ross photographs, a map, and a timeline. Explore the Collection allows access to the photographs, which are organized thematically into The Artist, The Chronicle, and The Legacy. Users can conduct a basic or advanced search, and can curate and save their own collections with free site registration. Photographs depict personal ephemera, posted announcements, family life, ghetto work, landscapes, deportations, death, and more. It can be quite affecting to observe an image of a seemingly happy "Child with a Rocking Horse" next to the image of a "Boy Fallen on Street from Hunger." For Teachers and Students offers a variety of lesson plans and other resources, with Contemporary Connections, in particular, examining parallels between the simple cameraman of 1940s Europe and the explosion of multimedia documentation today. Reflect and Respond shares visitors' personal thoughts on viewing the collection. The impact of the photographs is huge, as they individually and collectively testify to the valuable lives of Lodz's residents and the tragedy of the war, while at the same time exemplifying the power of one determined individual to educate. This site is well designed for teachers and students (high school +) across a number of disciplines.—**ARBA Staff Reviewer**

Latin America and the Caribbean

244.   **Haiti: An Island Luminous. http://islandluminous.fiu.edu/.** [Website] Free. Date reviewed: 2017.

Home to a digital library of maps, letters, books, manuscripts, photographs, and more, this simply structured website shares the history of the island nation of Haiti. Over one hundred internationally based contributors provide commentary alongside a diverse collection of primary sources. The homepage is quite bare and slightly mysterious (contributor names encircle a sketched conch shell). Users must first choose their preferred language (English, Creole, or French) before proceeding. From here the options remain simple: About, Learn, or Support. The simplicity of the site design and dearth of user options suggests a rather secretive journey of discovery, which is quite appealing. It is ultimately the Learn button which allows access to the summary history of Haiti. This narrative extends back to the prehistory of the island of Hispaniola and culminates with the aftermath of the massive 2010 earthquake. Within this narrative are numerous text links focused on particulars of Haiti's history which, when clicked, point to primary sources and affiliated scholarly essays. Sources may include books, illustrations, letters, and maps. Text link terms can be conceptual (sugar, free people of color, etc.) or represent specific people or places (Tainos, Jean-Baptiste Riche, etc.). Artifacts and contributor analysis will appear along the right hand side of the page opposing the narrative, creating the effect of examining an open book. This straightforward structure suits the material well and enhances the site's appeal to educators and students.—**ARBA Staff Reviewer**

Middle Eastern History

245.   Kia, Mehrdad. **The Ottoman Empire: A Historical Encyclopedia.** Santa Barbara, Calif., Greenwood Press/ABC-CLIO, 2017. 2v. illus. maps. index. (Empires of the World). $198.00/set. ISBN 13: 978-1-61069-388-2; 978-1-61069-389-9 (e-book).

As part of the Empires of the World series, this 2-volume reference work focuses on the Ottoman Empire, from its establishment in the late thirteenth century to its fall after World War I. The 160 entries are divided into 8 topical categories: Battles and Treaties; Beys and Pashas; Empire and Administration; Historians, Writers, Poets, and Scholars; Peoples and Cultures; Popular Culture; Rebels, Reformers, and Revolutionaries; and Sultans of the Ottoman Empire. Each essay is concise, with *see also* references listed along with a Further Reading section. In addition, there is a Primary Documents section containing 22 various historical documents. There are numerous black-and-white pictures and photographs throughout, along with a historical chronology, an appendix listing various rulers, and a glossary and selected bibliography. This work is intended for high school and university students looking for general and basic information related to the Ottoman Empire. Recommended.—**Bradford Lee Eden**

World History

Biography

246.   **A Database of Crusaders to the Holy Land: 1095-1149. https://www.dhi.ac.uk/ crusaders/.** [Website] Free. Date reviewed: 2018.

This database focuses on cataloging the intrepid individuals participating in the crusades to the Holy Land. While not fully developed and cataloged, the site has nonetheless amassed information on hundreds of individual crusaders involved in either the first campaign (1096-99) or the second (1145-49). Users can conduct an advanced search via the tab at the top of the homepage, using filters such as crusade, leader, country of origin, forename, gender, title, and role. There are also several browsing options available (crusader, crusade, country of origin, etc.), allowing users to approach the information in various ways. Browsing by role, for example, gives users a look at the types of people making up the crusaders' party, such as abbots, barons, clerks, nuns, pilgrims, servants, tradesmen and, of course, knights. Entries for individual crusaders provide basic biographical detail, some more generous than others. Users may learn family information, region of origin, expedition, consequences of expedition, actions, and financial arrangement (particularly interesting). Entries include source information as well. Entries range from describing the illustrious Frederick Barbarossa of Hohenstaufen, partaking in two crusades, to the lowly servant Eberhard, who perished while attending Conrad III of Germany. A bibliography— also accessible by homepage tab—notes abbreviations used throughout individual entries. This site offers engaging foundational material about the Crusades that can only improve upon continued development.—**ARBA Staff Reviewer**

247.   Paldiel, Mordecai. **Saving One's Own: Jewish Rescuers during the Holocaust.** Philadelphia, Jewish Publication Society, 2017. 586p. illus. index. $70.00. ISBN 13: 978-0-8276-1261-7; 978-0-8276-1295-2 (e-book).

This powerful volume dismantles the belief that Jews did little to try and save their fellow Jews from the annihilation of the Holocaust, perpetrated by the Nazis and their allies. The author presents heroes from fifteen countries, including France, Croatia, Italy, Slovakia, England, and the United States. Chapters are by country, and following a description of the general situation of Jews there, the reader is then given biographies of the men and women (as well as some organizations) who, by diverse methods, saved the lives of Jewish men, women, and often children. Other aspects of this struggle presented here include 1) the role of Palestine as a safe haven for Jewish people, particularly children, who got there through a variety of means, and 2) the heroism of certain persons within the concentration and extermination camps, such as Sobibór and Auschwitz.

Although this book is a scholarly work, with close to two thousand footnotes and a ffiteen-page bibliography, it reads quite easily, despite its somber topic, and is accessible to a wide range of readers. High school, public, and academic libraries should consider adding *Saving One's Own* to their collections, especially given its modest cost and its broad coverage of an important topic.—**Mark Schumacher**

Dictionaries and Encyclopedias

248.   **The Encyclopedia of Empire.** John MacKenzie, ed. Hoboken, N.J., Wiley-Blackwell, 2016. 4v. illus. maps. $795.00. ISBN 13: 978-1-11844-064-3.

This four-volume encyclopedia under the direction of professor emeritus John MacKenzie provides reliable and broad coverage of empires worldwide throughout history. The set includes more than four hundred signed, peer-reviewed entries by an international cast of scholars. The set is comprehensive; it includes articles from the ancient, medieval, and modern periods along with European and non-European perspectives. Entries appear in alphabetic order, but all include *see also* references for ease of navigation to related topics. There are entries for specific empires—Assyria, Egypt, Inca, Nazi, Spanish, Russian, Mixtec, Dutch, British, and American. Some empires have more than one entry. The British Empire, for example, has twelve. Topics like Wars of Independence, Architecture, Imperial, Administration and Bureaucracy, Revolution and Social Change, and Diplomacy and Empire also have entries as do events like the Boer War and World War II. Entry lengths vary. All start with an abstract, while entries for complex subjects like World War II and Empire are subdivided. Entries include suggestions for further reading—these include books with recent publication dates—that provide users with several options for further research. Entries can also contain references. The writing is accessible, but is definitely geared toward college-age students.

This encyclopedia is highly recommended for academic libraries.—**ARBA Staff Reviewer**

249.   **The Encyclopedia of the Atlantic World, 1400–1900: Europe, Africa, and the Americas in an Age of Exploration, Trade, and Empires.** David Head, ed. Santa Barbara, Calif., ABC-CLIO, 2018. 2v. $198.00/set. ISBN 13: 978-1-61069-255-7; 978-1-61069-256-4 (e-book).

This 2-volume set provides a great deal of information on the history of the lands bordering the Atlantic Ocean, following their discovery by Europeans. From the Norse explorations of North America and the Portuguese exploration of Africa in search of a route to Asia, to the end of slavery throughout the nineteenth century, it examines the social, political, agricultural, and cultural dimensions of the diverse interactions among many players. For example, 9 articles address various aspects of slavery. Other categories include indigenous populations in the Americas, such as the Arawaks and the Choctaws, various wars fought during this period, and 44 pieces on individuals, from Queen Elizabeth I and Napoleon to Pocahontas, Phillis Wheatley, and Thomas Jefferson. The range of topics is quite broad and diverse; for instance, there are entries on Ghana, Islam, the Mali Empire, wine, witchcraft, the Industrial Revolution, and London. Each of the 220 entries includes cross-references to related topics and useful further reading suggestions, nearly all of which are books. There are several maps and images included.

Libraries of all kinds will find this a useful set, if they can afford it. For libraries at several levels, this will provide "student and interested nonspecialist readers" (p. xiv) an introduction to this fascinating and important world. The book is available both in print and as an e-book and is quite readable. (A minor note: careful copy editing was overlooked at times, leading to a few misspellings and confusing sentences—**Mark Schumacher**

250.   **The Holocaust: An Encyclopedia and Document Collection.** Paul R. Bartrop and Michael Dickerman, eds. Santa Barbara, Calif., ABC-CLIO, 2017. 4v. illus. maps. index. $435.00/set. ISBN 13: 978-1-4408-4083-8; 978-1-4408-4084-5 (e-book).

The Holocaust is one of the defining events of twentieth-century world history. Much has been written about it, but there is still a great deal to discover. This new encyclopedia from ABC-CLIO combines historical information with primary source documents and survivor testimonies. The contributors are scholars from universities in the United States, Canada, and Europe. The signed articles include resource lists and volume four has a chronology, a glossary, and a bibliography of English-language resources. Volume one contains a historical introduction, overview essays, and maps. Volumes one and two cover significant people, places, events, and doctrines in alphabetical entries. Volume three has testimonies of survivors and resistors and volume four contains documents about Nazi doctrines and policies, the invasion of Europe, genocide, and response to the events. The testimonies included here have not appeared elsewhere.

This is a good starting point for anyone interested in learning about the Holocaust.— **Barbara M. Bibel**

251.   **The Palgrave Macmillan Encyclopedia of Imperialism and Anti-Imperialism.** Immanuel Ness and Zak Cope, eds. New York, Palgrave Macmillan, 2016. 2v. $480.00/set. ISBN 13: 978-1-349-57691-3.

This two-volume set covers imperialism and anti-imperialism worldwide, focusing largely on the period since the eighteenth century. The editors divided the two volumes into seven sections: Biographies, Country Analysis, Culture and the Arts, History, Movements and Ideologies, Political Economy, and Themes and Concepts. There are guide words at the top of pages, but the index will be most helpful for those looking for a particular topic since the table of contents is quite sparse. All entries are signed; author interests and affiliations appear in the front matter. Entries of varying length comprise the main part of the book. Users will find less information on such subjects as Hugo Chávez, the Truman Doctrine, Henry Kissinger, the Greenlandic Inuit, paternalistic capitalism, and the Communist Party of Indonesia than they will on such topics as class, capitalism, revolution, abolition, money, nationalism, U.S. imperialism, socialism, and the Cold War. The book concludes with an extensive index. The print is small, and there is nothing to break up the walls of text. These minor considerations aside, this book on important subject matter is highly recommended for academic and public libraries.—**ARBA Staff Reviewer**

Handbooks and Yearbooks

252.   **BBC   History.   http://www.bbc.co.uk/history/ancient/british_prehistory/.** [Website] Free. Date reviewed: 2018.

Users can examine a number of featured topics displayed throughout the page or select from broader subject category links at the bottom of the page such as Ancient History, British History, World Wars, and Historic Figures. Within the broader categories, the material is well organized into topical links listed chronologically so users can easily find what they are looking for in the context of time. Material may consist of timelines, scholarly essays, video clips, interactive games, photographs, individual profiles, and much more. Many of the topics within the Ancient History, British History, and World Wars categories are virtual rabbit holes of information with one topic leading to another. For example, in examining the Victorian era within the broader category of British History, users will learn about clothing, women's roles, the Industrial Revolution, the royal family, sport, crime, technology, and other topics. Historic Figures presents an A-Z listing of significant individuals from all over the world (with an emphasis on Britons) who have left their mark on history. Users can gather information in the form of essays, chronologies, videos, and other material on Napoleon Bonaparte, Florence Nightingale, William Shakespeare, and other notable individuals. The Family History tab links to a public records search for genealogical purposes. On This Day lets users find historical detail for a selected date. Aside from these main category links the BBC History homepage features highlights from the IWonder archive for users to browse via an interrogative display (e.g., "Were Scots Responsible for the Ku Klux Klan?" or "Why Should I Care About 1066"). It is important to note that the page has been archived as of some time with no further updating. In addition, some video content may no longer be available for viewing. However, the abundance of information, range of topics, engaging multimedia presentation, and reliability of the data makes this an excellent resource.—**ARBA Staff Reviewer**

253.   **Defining Documents in World History: Nationalism & Populism (320 BCE-2017 CE).** David Simonelli, ed. Hackensack, N.J., Salem Press, 2017. 2v. illus. index. $295.00/set. ISBN 13: 978-1-68217-293-3; 978-1-68217-294-0 (e-book).

If, as Tacitus once said, "money is the sinew of war," then documents are its muscle, either to commence a war, or to end one. The current volumes nicely undergird this assumption. Contained in these volumes are facsimiles of the documents from the beginning of the common era of states, with Aristotle and the Athenian Constitution, to the present day.

However, it isn't just reproductions of those documents. Each section begins with an evaluative essay about the era. Each chapter in that section explains the historical document in its context; stressing so-called tipping points that may well have been the defining moment for the defining document, as well as a brief overview of the author or authors of the document. Following the document itself is a careful, studied but highly readable analysis of it, why it is important, and what it may have led to: prosperity or impoverishment. Short bibliographies follow each chapter.

Volume one contains documents in relation to nationalism and populism, beginning with the ancient and medieval eras and including the American and French Revolutions, the nineteenth century, and the First World War. The second volume follows a similar pattern, beginning with the Second World War followed by Cold War documents and other documents from the twentieth and twenty-first centuries. While it may well be in the eye of the beholder, it's hard to imagine anyone finding the announcement of the Trump candidacy equivalent to Magna Carta and the Declaration of Independence, but all three are here.

The Renaissance and early modern era volume (roughly 1380-1600) follows a very similar pattern, collecting documents that define those years. Included are documents referring to the Black Death, Joan of Arc's letter to Henry VI, a brief snippet of the *Divine Comedy,* Columbus's letter about the discovery of America, the Dutch declaration of independence, and much more.

These volumes are indispensable aids in an age that relies more and more on second hand or even tertiary reported information rather than the ipsissima verba, the very words themselves. While most, if not all such documents are on the ubiquitous web, not many still look at them, or read them in context. These volumes go a long way to act as an anodyne to our penchant for responding first and thinking, if at all, much later.—**Mark Y. Herring**

254.   **Defining Documents in World History: 17th Century (1601-1700).** David Simonelli, ed. Hackensack, N.J., Salem Press, 2017. 2v. illus. maps. index. $295.00/set. ISBN 13: 978-1-68217-301-5; 978-1-68217-302-2 (e-book).

This collection uses a broad range of primary source documents from the seventeenth century to illustrate the key themes of that eventful era—scientific discovery and exploration; religious wars; flowering of political theory; and the expansion of the mercantile economy and global trade. The editor draws documents from Europe, with a separate section on England's Civil War and the Restoration; Asia; the Muslim world; and the European colonies in the Americas. Each of the 49 articles starts with the historical context for the document, a brief biography of the document's author, the historical document itself, an analysis of the key points of the document, and a summary of essential themes and the document's historical significance. The types of documents range from religious tracts and sermons to speeches, essays, laws, edicts, and letters written by scholars, scientists, philosophers, clerics, kings, and revolutionaries. As an example, the editor has included Galileo's *Starry Messenger* in which the astronomer asserts the earth revolves around the sun, raising questions as to man's place in the universe and illustrating a key debate of this century—science versus religion. Tokugawa Ieyasu's *Laws of Military Households,* which led to the demise of the samurai class and thus indirectly to the urbanization of Japan, shows us that this century was also a turning point in the East as well as in the West. Reading these primary sources with their accompanying explanatory notes brings alive this pivotal time when the world shifted from the medieval period to the modern age—a historical period that has relevance to us today as we go through our own disruptive transition from the scientific to technological age.

Recommended.—**Adrienne Antink**

255.   **George C. Marshall Foundation. https://marshallfoundation.org.** [Website] Free. Date reviewed: 2018.

This website works to honor the legacy of George C. Marshall, the man instrumental in shaping post-World War II European recovery. Serving in prestigious military and diplomatic roles throughout several twentieth century conflicts, Marshall is recognized for the eponymous plan to help Europe rebuild after years of war. This website allows access to a wealth of materials which not only fill in the portrait of this notable American, but also tell the story of American postwar leadership and dedication to the democratic ideal. Users can access materials via two main tabs on the homepage. The George C. Marshall (or the About Marshall) tab links to generous foundational information including many photographs on the man's long career as well as his signature achievement, the European Recovery Program—ultimately referred to as the Marshall Plan. Users can examine a Timeline and Chronology of Marshall's life and career, explore Essays and Interviews from A. J. Liebling, Dean Acheson, Dwight D. Eisenhower, and numerous others, view a significant collection of Films & Videos, read Marshall's most memorable Quotes, and much more. Additionally, The Marshall Plan link holds a vast array of essays, primary documents, and other materials including a chronology, posters and films, congressional testimonies, speeches, and a section called The History of the Marshall Plan which leads to memos, committee reports, funding statistics, studies, and articles on the plan's relevance today, including Susan Stern's "Marshall Plan 1947-1997: A German View" and Henry A. Kissinger's "Reflections on the Marshall Plan." Users can also access the 3,700-page Marshall Plan Volume, containing the laws, reports, appropriations, and more which established the plan before Congress. Back on the homepage, the Research Library tab offers links to broader holdings organized by categories including Digital Documents (such as Marshall's personal papers), Posters, Maps, Audio/Video, Photographs, and Oral Histories. Many of the items have been incorporated throughout the main site as previously noted but there are additional resources here (although only some are available online).—**ARBA Staff Reviewer**

256.   **Global Medieval Sourcebook: A Digital Repository of Medieval Texts. https:// sourcebook.stanford.edu/.** [Website] Free. Date reviewed: 2018.

The Global Medieval Sourcebook is a straightforward, easy-to-use database offering a diverse collection of medieval texts in conjunction with their modern translations. The database has digitized and transcribed nineteen texts, spanning the years 600-1600 and originating from Europe, North Africa, the Middle East, and Asia and created for a variety of purposes. The diversity of the site's curated collection speaks to a desire to provide a broad overview, rather than an exhaustive catalog of medieval culture. Users can scan the two-page gallery of available texts, or view them in list format. They can also employ author, keyword, language, period, or genre filters in a search. Selecting a text will lead users to a title page which includes basic source and transcription material, although some texts are accompanied by a more detailed introduction. The text display includes the original version on the left of the page with its corresponding English translation on the right. As users move the cursor over the text, the lines will be highlighted in yellow. Users can employ a number of tools as they read through the text. They have the option to use line numbers, and can view each version of the text separately as well. In addition, selecting Source Information allows the material from the title page to also be displayed next to the text/translation, while selecting Notes allows critical notes to appear alongside corresponding lines. Texts represent an array of languages—Literary Chinese, Old French, Middle High German, Tuscan, and more. They further encompass a good sampling of style (narrative verse, lyric verse, history, etc.) and content, with references to love, drinking, sex, ghosts, and even the weather. The planned addition of more texts to the collection will further enhance the site's profile.—**ARBA Staff Reviewer**

257.   **Great Events from History: The 21st Century.** Thomas Tandy Lewis, ed. Hackensack, N.J., Salem Press, 2017. 3v. illus. index. $295.00/set. ISBN 13: 978-1-68217-305-3; 978-1-68217-306-0 (e-book).

For many expensive reference works, a reviewer has to ask the question, just why is this source needed? Who will actually consult it? Seldom have I asked the question more plaintively than with this 3-volume set. Clearly the entries are interesting, but 400 eclectic essays on events of a mere 16 years at the beginning of the century is a problematic enterprise. Three hundred of them, albeit updated, were published previously in five Great Events from History reference works, including *The 2000s in America* (2013), *African-*

American History (2005), and *Gay, Lesbian, Bisexual, Transgender Events* (2006) to cite a few. The essays, with average length of 1,500-2,000 words, cover a wide span of topics. They follow a common format of summary of event, significance, author, further reading, and *see also* for related essays.

The editor's introduction attempts to justify why the volume in recent and contemporary history is necessary. While he makes his case for contemporary history, the question remains, why this wide-ranging and totally unrelated set of essays. The appendixes, which comprise most of volume three, include a lengthy list of significant persons in the essays, a massive topical bibliography, Web resources, a chronological list of the most important events, and a category and a subject index. The category index is the most important because it can be employed to find articles on common subjects.

In sum, it is an interesting work, but one whose necessity I question.—**Joe P. Dunn**

258.   **Journey: An Illustrated History of Travel.** New York, DK Smithsonian, 2017. 440p. illus. maps. index. $50.00. ISBN 13: 978-1-4654-6414-9.

This book traces the history of human travel from ancient times to the present. The book itself is large (10 x 12), and it contains hundreds of color illustrations. Seven chapters are followed by biographies, journeys, and an index. The first chapter "The Ancient World, 3000 B.C.E.-400 C.E." has information on travel in Persia, Africa, Greece, Europe, and beyond. This chapter contains special pieces on the travels of Odysseus, the geographer Strabo, and Ptolemy's *Geographia,* among other things. All information is supplemented by color maps and photographs. "Trade and Conquest, 400 to 1400" comes next and contains information on the such things as the Viking voyages, the spread of Islam and Christianity, and medieval pilgrimages. There is also information on medieval maps, the evolution of wheels, and more. The third chapter, "The Age of Discovery, 1400-1600," includes discussions of Cortés, Pizarro, Columbus, Champlain, the Northwest Passage, and other important explorers and episodes. The following chapters follow the same format and are as follows: "The Age of Empires, 1600-1800," "The Age of Steam, 1800-1900," "The Golden Age of Travel, 1880-1939," and "The Age of Flight, 1939-Present." Users will find information about the spice trade, coffee, settling the Americas, The Gold Rush, early alpinists, mapping the oceans, travels in Arabia, the Model T, Route 66, and airplane travel, among many other things. Topics within these main chapters receive roughly two to four pages of coverage. There are approximately one hundred biographies of such travelers as Amelia Earhart, Hernán Cortés, Mark Twain, Daniel Boone, Ptolemy, and Sacagawea. Like the rest of the book, these are enhanced by generous use of color photographs. The book also includes descriptions of iconic journeys, replete with maps and color photographs. This section includes information about a Nile cruise, visiting the Great Wall of China, travel to Petra and Wadi Rum, the Silk Road, and other destinations. An index rounds out this work that is recommended for school and public libraries.—**ARBA Staff Reviewer**

259.   **Migration to New Worlds. Modules I and II. https://www.amdigital.co.uk/ primary-sources/migration-to-new-worlds.** [Website] Chicago, Adam Matthew Digital, 2017. Price negotiated by site. Date reviewed: 2017.

This resource is organized into two modules—"The Century of Migration," focused on the period from 1800 to 1924, with supplemental materials from earlier years, and

"The Modern Era," which comes further into the twentieth century. It focuses primarily on people from Great Britain, Ireland, Europe, and Asia heading to the "New World" and Australasia.

As with all Adam Matthew resources, the collections digitized are rich and often complex, drawn from "26 archives, libraries and museums." The collections are incredibly diverse, from nineteenth-century government documents, collections of letters, and other items from organizations such as the New Zealand Company and various shipping companies, to family photos, convict records from New South Wales (covering almost forty years), and oral histories (both audio and video) collected in the last forty years. Searching is powerful, with numerous ways to refine a search, either by using the advanced search page or by limiting options after obtaining results: by date range, by document type, and by individual library/archive. It appears that every word in the scanned documents will show up in a search! The visual clarity of print pages, photos, and maps is excellent; one can zoom in to view very small parts of an image.

This is a resource for serious scholars and researchers in fields such as history, human geography, demography, and American Studies. Academic libraries, in several countries in fact, will find the material here of use to their patrons.—**Mark Schumacher**

260. **Persuasive Maps. https://persuasivemaps.library.cornell.edu/.** [Website] Free. Date reviewed: 2018.

This collection gathers over eight hundred historical maps that share the unique and not entirely geographical purpose of persuasion. Sourced from around the world and dating as far back as the fifteenth century, the maps creatively call upon both familiar and fictional landforms, waterways, and place-names as a means to influence the public regarding a number of subjects, from war to religion and more. The blue Browse Collection tab lets users browse the entire collection or Browse by Subject or Date Posted to the site. The subject categories are quite diverse and include Alcohol, Imperialism, New York City, Suffrage, Railroads, Communism, and a number of international and regional conflicts. The site also groups maps according to style and device; that is, whether they employ such tools as satire, allegory, deception, and unusual graphics/text. Users can additionally browse maps by era. The collection is presented in either a list or gallery view, with a map thumbnail alongside identifying information such as title and date. Clicking on a title allows a larger view from which users can zoom in/out and download. Additional information accompanies the digital image, including subject tags, creator, extent, identification number, and edifying collector's notes. Highlights include the early Sanctification of the Seventh Day or Chamber of Hell maps, which attempt to explain the origin of the cosmos; Mark Twain's farcical Map of Paris complete with personal commentary; and the allegorical Map of Matrimony depicting fanciful locations such as the "Lake of Presents," "Electorate of Bridesmaids," and "Settlement Bay."—**ARBA Staff Reviewer**

261. **The Sea in World History: Exploration, Travel, and Trade.** Stephen K. Stein, ed. Santa Barbara, Calif., ABC-CLIO, 2017. 2v. illus. index. $189.00/set. ISBN 13: 978-1-4408-3550-6; 978-1-4408-3551-3 (e-book).

Maritime history does not get much respect, and it is always good to see new publications that try to bring it to the fore. This two-volume set does that in a somewhat strange manner; it is mostly laid out like a textbook, but its size and price certainly preclude that use. The two volumes contain eight chapters based on chronology, which are then divided by geography. An essay provides overview and analysis of a region's maritime activity in the chapter's time frame, followed by additional subsections on related topics. Primary source documents, chronologies, bibliographies, maps, and images supplement each section. Since the book is not organized alphabetically by subject, using it as a reference resource requires that one refer to the index. Alas, unlike other multivolume sets from this publisher, the extensive index is unfortunately not at the back of both volumes.

The writing is interesting, and the collection is valuable, but it is hard to determine exactly what to make of this title, and how best to use it. For an encyclopedia, the four-volume, decade-old *Oxford Encyclopedia of Maritime History* (see ARBA 2008, entry 600) remains unbeatable. For a comprehensive overview, Lincoln Paine's *The Sea & Civilization* (2013) will likely serve better. This title's greatest value is perhaps in providing an overview of a particular region's maritime history over time. Given this, it might be most useful at institutions with a particular interest in regional area studies. For those with interest, it will be useful in large high school, undergraduate, and public reference collections.—**Peter H. McCracken**

262.   **Slave Voyages. http://www.slavevoyages.org/.** [Website] Free. Date reviewed: 2018.

This excellent site curated by an international team of scholars brings the scope of the African slave trade into focus via its database of information on over thirty-five thousand ship voyages that transported Africans across the Atlantic Ocean to the Americas. The site uses this foundational database in conjunction with other resources to examine locations, logistics, and the sheer numbers involved in nearly three centuries of the trade. Users can explore five locations (Brazil, North America, Caribbean, Europe, Africa) on the homepage map image for general background information about slave origins and destinations. The Voyages Database itself lists Vessel Names, Captain's Name, Year Arrived with Slaves, Principal Region of Slave Purchase, Principal Region of Slave Landing, and more. Selecting a particular ship accesses available information about Flag, Tonnage, Guns Mounted, Vessel Owners, Crew Numbers, Slave Mortality Rate, and many other variables about slaves, crew, and the voyage itself. Generous contextual information regarding each variable is available in the Understanding the Voyages Database link under the main database tab. From the database, users can also access a Map, Summary Statistics, and Table view by year, and can customize Graphs, Timelines, and Animations with selected variables. Assessing the Slave Trade provides examples of data scholarship with essays on topics derived from data, a series of maps (e.g., "Old World Slave Trade Routes in the Atlantic before 1759"), and a Table of Estimates which helps quantify slave numbers by location and timeframe. Resources and Educational Materials are extensive and, alongside Lesson Plans and a good listing of Web Resources, include a searchable gallery of nearly two hundred images of manuscripts, places, slaves, and vessels. Users can click on a thumbnail image to enlarge it and to access descriptive and source information. The African Name Database contains over ninety thousand entries with information such as age, height, gender, and arrival date.—**ARBA Staff Reviewer**

10 Law

General Works

Dictionaries and Encyclopedias

263.   **First Amendment Encyclopedia. http://mtsu.edu/first-amendment/.** [Website] Free. Date reviewed: 2018.

Focusing on the right to free expression of speech, the press, and religion, the First Amendment to the United States Constitution has been tested on the street and in the courtroom. This site from Middle Tennessee State University offers a good examination of the amendment via its presentation of over 1,500 entries covering court cases, people, events, laws, and more. The Encyclopedia tab at the top of the homepage offers access to the entries in addition to helpful contextual materials. Users can read an introductory overview, an essay ("The First 45 Words") on the creation of the amendment, and a chronology of important dates. They can also employ the table of contents in order to browse by Articles (which list all entries alphabetically), Court Cases by Category, Court Cases by Date, and roughly 30 topics and subtopics such as Controversial Works, Groups & Organizations, Laws & Proposed Laws, and People (e.g., Journalists, Presidents, Reformers, Scholars). Articles provide general coverage of events like the civil rights movement, or focus on specific entities like 2 Live Crew or the Chicago Seven Trial. The large variety of court cases, which argue that anonymous speech, book banning, academic freedom, campaign finance, incitement, hate speech, and much more, attest to the impact of the First Amendment on American lives. The entries generally include a substantial but straightforward essay, photograph, references, and a list of further resources. Other site features include news and columns which provide media coverage and commentary related to the First Amendment in current events. The 1 For All link offers teacher and student resources. In combination with these site features, the encyclopedia is adept at providing both historical perspective and contemporary relevance on the issue of free speech—**ARBA Staff Reviewer**

264.   **Grossman, Mark. Constitutional Amendments: An Encyclopedia of the People, Procedures, Politics, Primary Documents Relating to the 27 Amendments of the U.S. Constitution. 2d ed.** Amenia, N.Y., Grey House Publishing, 2017. 2v. illus. index. $245.00/set. ISBN 13: 978-1-68217-176-9; 978-1-68217-177-6 (e-book).

This two-volume encyclopedia is an excellent reference tool for a high school or undergraduate library. For each amendment, there is a brief summary, a timeline of the ratification process, and a discussion of the historical context in which the amendment was proposed, debated, and ratified. In addition, the encyclopedia includes excerpts from Congressional debates and other relevant historical documents such as first drafts of the amendments, newspaper articles, and political speeches. Finally, each amendment includes selected Supreme Court cases which have interpreted the language of the amendment. These additional materials are by no means comprehensive, but would be a very useful starting place for a researcher who is relatively unfamiliar with the amendments, their history, or their current legal application.—**Lisa Schultz**

265.   **The U.S. Supreme Court, Second Edition.** Thomas Tandy Lewis, ed. Hackensack, N.J., Salem Press, 2016. 3v. illus. index. $295.00/set. ISBN 13: 978-1-68217-180-6; 978-1-68217-180-6 (e-book).

This encyclopedia of the Supreme Court is considerably updated from the 2007 edition (see ARBA 2008, entry 469), with more than 100 new entries (567 in all, according to the introduction). The articles, from Abington School District v. Schempp to Zoning, are all signed by an army of 147 contributing scholars. As might be expected, they vary considerably in length from a few paragraphs to several pages. Specific court decisions, biographies of justices, and legal subjects treated by the court are all included. Each article has a precis at the beginning that summarizes the salient facts in the article (e.g., for court decisions, the citation, when announced, the issues it addressed, and its significance). Many of the articles have references for "further reading"; the reference lists for major topics are often annotated. Many articles also have *see also* references to other articles. Appendixes include "Categories of Cases and Topics" (a rough subject grouping), glossary, timeline of Supreme Court events, annotated bibliography, a list of justices ranked by years of service (William O. Douglas is the champ at 36 years), notable rulings (many of which are not the subject of articles), the U.S. Constitution and its amendments, and a detailed subject index. The illustrations are primarily portraits of the justices that appear with their biographies. This source is current enough to include the controversy over President Obama's nomination of Merrick Garland to replace the late Justice Scalia, but just missed the nomination and confirmation of Neil Gorsuch. The writing is clear and aimed at a general audience. This is a superb reference source that is appropriate for high school, college/university, and public libraries.—**Jack Ray**

266.   Utter, Glenn H., and Robert J. Spitzer. **The Gun Debate: An Encyclopedia of Gun Rights & Gun Control in the United States.** 3d ed. Amenia, N.Y., Grey House Publishing, 2016. 490p. index. $165.00. ISBN 13: 978-1-68217-102-8; 978-1-68217-103-5 (e-book).

The Gun Debate: An Encyclopedia of Gun Rights & Gun Control in the United States, serves the needs of anyone who is interested in gun debate and its contentious bearing on today's society. This encyclopedia offers opportunities to approach related issues with a balanced perspective. It combines history and current events that continue to confront and confound the American people; case studies offer concrete examples and explanations. This third edition (see ARBA 2012, entry 545) considers the needs of nonspecialist readers, and emphasizes a clear representation of facts by inserting tables, charts, graphics, photographs, and illustrations. The more than 370 entries range in length from 500 to 3,000 words and are cross-referenced to related topics within the encyclopedia. Moreover, entries include further reading lists for additional study. The Guide to Selected Topics arranges entries into categories that include court cases, gun control issues, historical individuals and groups, legislation and constitutional amendments, and more. The encyclopedia also features an expanded primary documents section, three appendixes, an updated chronology through 2016, a bibliography, and two indexes. Combining the history of important issues with current events and groundbreaking viewpoints, this encyclopedia serves as an important addition to public, university, and high school libraries. Library acquisition decision-makers responsible for the selection and purchase of materials or resources will consider this book a welcome addition to their collection.—**Thomas E. Baker**

Handbooks and Yearbooks

267. Carter, Gregg Lee. **Gun Control in the United States: A Reference Handbook.** Santa Barbara, Calif., ABC-CLIO, 2017. 401p. illus. index. (Contemporary World Issues). $60.00. ISBN 13: 978-1-4408-3566-7; 978-1-4408-3567-4 (e-book).

This is a balanced, well-researched, and formidable book in the Contemporary World Issues series. Carter, always careful to present multiple viewpoints, uses recent, vetted research on gun control, including current statistics and up-to-date studies, articles, and books. The opening section provides information about the prevalence of guns, the nature of gun violence, causality, the Second Amendment, public opinion, and the role of politics. Carter then highlights what he identifies as the Public Health Approach, the Law Enforcement Approach, and the Lawsuit Approach. Subsequently, three different views are presented in essays that argue for stricter gun laws, fewer laws, and for a flexible approach depending on the type of law invoked. The book also profiles key individuals and organizations for both sides of the issue and collects extensive data and documents relevant to the topic. This book would be a valuable resource for public and academic libraries, and perhaps might be useful in and appropriate for high school libraries which have extensive collections and a strong research focus. The book includes a timeline, glossary, and index.—**Marney Welmers**

268. **Court Listener. https://www.courtlistener.com/.** [Website] Free. Date reviewed: 2017.

Court Listener, created by the nonprofit Free Law Project, primarily functions as a search engine offering free access to millions of federal and state court opinions. Users can conduct a basic search from the home page or run an advanced search through three key categories presented on the menu bar. Opinions runs a search through applicable parameters, such as case name, judge, filing date, citation, and docket number. The Judges tab allows users to search through a pool of over 8,000 judges, using name, jurisdiction, place of birth, school, political affiliation, and options. Oral Arguments offers a vast collection of oral argument audio and can also be searched via jurisdictions, judge, docket number, etc. The RECAP Archive allows a search of a unique archive devoted to PACER documents, i.e., documents from U.S. Federal and Bankruptcy courts that are ostensibly available to the public, yet cost-prohibitive and difficult to access. The RECAP Archive makes it easier and more affordable to access and utilize PACER documents. The Visualizations tab links to an interactive tool to help users (with registration) create citation networks which graphically depict the connections between select case content and precedent. These networks provide quick access to associated Supreme Court case data and opinions. Users can examine a gallery of submitted citation network scatterplots or create, edit, or share their own. From the homepage, users can also note the latest downloaded opinions and oral arguments, and see a snapshot data profile—The Numbers—of Court Listener's work, showing the number of opinions and queries made in the last 10 days, etc. Users can additionally access a generous variety of supplemental information. Coverage links to charts which map an annual count of cases in the database in addition to a large listing (links) of courts for which the site provides real time coverage and alerts. There is also a Citation Lookup Tool and a Blog/Newsletter.—**ARBA Staff Reviewer**

269.   **Federal Judicial Center. https://www.fjc.gov/.** [Website] Free. Date reviewed: 2017.
        The Federal Judicial Center offers research and educational material related to the work of the judicial branch of the U.S. government with the primary goal of enhancing the administration of the branch. This website offers access to such materials as reports, studies, a Federal Court case database, topical research projects, educational guides, and much more. Navigation through these resources is straightforward. Users select from one of several tabs on the page. Research About the Courts connects users with generous options, including nearly three hundred topical Reports and Studies (e.g., "Survey of Harm to Cooperators," etc.), a listing of research projects in progress (e.g., "Guide for Judges on Litigation Financing"), and nearly two hundred documents described as Federal Rules of Procedure. Users can also access the Integrated Database (IDB) of information concerning Civil, Criminal, Appeals, and Bankruptcy cases relating to filing, termination, and other issues (users can download or view datasets), and a good selection of Special Topics Research such as Technology in Litigation, National Security Cases, and more. Education for the Courts offers materials and programs aimed at judges, staff, lawyers, officers, and others affiliated with the judiciary, including Videos; Manuals, Monographs & Guides on numerous topics; and podcasts. Some of the topics include "Navigating Chapter 9 of the Bankruptcy Code" and "The Elements of Case Management." For most resources, users can simply scroll through a list of offerings. Alternatively, Civic Education About the Courts is aimed at students, educators, the media, and anyone less familiar with the judiciary. It offers foundational materials about the courts, famous trials (such as the U.S. vs. Susan B. Anthony), and general judicial history. History of the Federal Judiciary compiles historical data on the courts, biographies of federal judges reaching back to 1789, publications on federal judicial history, and much more. The section includes timelines, graphs, maps, and other easy-to-use resources. International Judicial Relations offers materials and programs to facilitate understanding of U.S. law for foreign officials and to assist with the administration of justice abroad. Users will find the U.S. Constitution translated into a number of languages, Briefing Materials for international advocates dealing with U.S. courts, and other resources. The Publications Catalog link allows users to search for materials covering topics such as Election Litigation and Managing Capital Cases. While primarily aimed at users familiar with the judiciary, the generous material would additionally appeal to educators, students, historians, and others.—**ARBA Staff Reviewer**

270.   **Fordham Law Archive of Scholarship & History. Twenty-Fifth Amendment Archive. http://ir.lawnet.fordham.edu/twentyfifth_amendment_archive/.** [Website] Free. Date reviewed: 2018.

The Twenty-fifth Amendment Archive is one of the more compelling exhibits found on the Fordham Law Archive of Scholarship and History (FLASH) website. Under the Special Collections link on the FLASH homepage, users will discover a trove of materials related to the amendment and Fordham Law's connection to it. The introductory page explains this connection—from the prescient 1963 *Fordham Law Review* article titled "The Problem of Presidential Inability—Will Congress Ever Solve It?" (published just before President Kennedy's assassination) to Fordham's Presidential Succession Clinic convened just this year. Items in this significant collection are generous and not only shine a light on the challenges of the past which led to the ratification of the amendment but offer an excellent foundation for the management of succession issues arising in the future. The 25th Amendment page is highlighted by a timeline reaching back to the initial drafting of the U.S. Constitution's Succession Clause in 1787. Users can select from a number of timeline events, including Lincoln's Assassination, the Presidential Succession Act of 1886, FDR Dies Amid World War II, Agnew Resignation & First Use of the 25th Amendment, and more. Each timeline item is accompanied by a brief paragraph and an illustration or photo. Users can then browse through a series of links pointing to particular media: Books, Congressional Materials, Correspondence, Executive Branch Materials, Photos & Video, Reports, and 25th Amendment Articles. Each link contains a brief description of category contents. Highlights include transcripts of congressional subcommittee hearings regarding succession reform, an executive branch memo regarding succession and delegation of powers written shortly after President Reagan's attempted assassination, video of the recent Fordham Law School clinic on Presidential Succession, Senator Birch Bayh's 1968 book—*One Heartbeat Away: Presidential Disability and Succession*—describing his role in moving the 25th Amendment through Congress, and much more. Scholars of constitutional law or history, and perhaps casual users interested in current events, would find this Web page richly informative.—**ARBA Staff Reviewer**

271.   **Free Law Project. https://free.law/.** [Website] Free. Date reviewed: 2018.

This site serves as a starting point for basic legal research. It has initiated several projects (e.g., Court Listener, RECAP) which facilitate public access to United States Federal, District, and Bankruptcy Court documents, and offers foundational information that can assist site visitors in their acquisition and use of the documents and other research. Visitors to this site can link directly to Court Listener or RECAP from the right sidebar. There are some resources of note on this homepage, as well. The Archives tab in the upper right corner lists Free Law Project blog entries which offer good instructional information regarding Court Listener/RECAP contents, access, and usage. Under the About tab, the site lists seven research projects which exemplify the work the Free Law Project pursues. These include a "Supreme Court Mapping Project" and an "Exploring the U.S. Judicial System" Web visualization. Aside from the links to Court Listener and RECAP users can access database information under Projects and Initiatives on judicial seals, judges and appointees, miscellaneous Supreme Court data, and more. Users interested in matters of the American court system would find the Free Law Project to be a vital gateway to research.—**ARBA Staff Reviewer**

272.   Hudson, David L., Jr. **Freedom of Speech: Documents Decoded.** Santa Barbara, Calif., ABC-CLIO, 2017. 208p. index. (Documents Decoded). $81.00. ISBN 13: 978-1-4408-4250-4; 978-1-4408-4251-1 (e-book).

Freedom of Speech is an accessible volume which focuses on four aspects of the First Amendment right to free speech: categorization, content, context, and principles. Each of the four areas includes excerpts from landmark Supreme Court cases and other influential materials, namely speeches, but also including such items as presidential statements and House of Representatives documents.

Some unique features of the book include an introduction before each specific case, speech, etc. which explains the material to follow, as well as a brief conclusion. Highlighted text with accompanying footnotes in the margin is another helpful feature. A timeline, 1787 to 2011, a further reading section, and an index complete the volume.

Freedom of Speech is a useful reference for those who are just beginning to study the free speech aspect of the First Amendment and as such would be a welcome addition to any high school or undergraduate library.—**Alicia Brillon**

273.   **Legal Information Institute. https://www.law.cornell.edu/.** [Website] Free. Date reviewed: 2017.

This site from Cornell Law School's Legal Information Institute (LII) offers free access to two collections of U.S. Supreme Court decisions: nearly three hundred decisions rendered 1990-present and over six hundred historic decisions focused on landmark cases going back to the early years of the court.

The page is structured as a listing of Recent Decisions, followed by simple presentation of search or browse options relating to both collections. The Current Awareness category allows users to access current court Decisions, Orders, Case Updates, Cases Granted Certification, Cases Pending, Oral Arguments, Cases Argued this Term, and Oral Argument Calendars. Information within these categories varies between basic listings and substantial detail. Users can browse the Archive of Decisions for both 1990-Present and Historic Collections via a listing of alphabetized topics (e.g., antitrust law, capital punishment, Fifth Amendment, obstruction, etc.), author, or party. Depending on the case, users can access a syllabus, written decision, concurrence, notes, and dissent. Recent cases are generally downloadable in one or more formats. A Cites tab will link to a listing of relevant cases if the chosen case has been cited in later decisions. Supplementary information under LII Resources is generous, and includes the excellent LII Bulletin, offering objective previews of each case on the docket, biographical information on seven of the nine current justices, current court rules, a glossary of legalese, and more. The Other Resources tab offers links to sites hosting oral argument recordings, briefs, and transcripts.

Advertisements within the page may affect the browsing experience. In addition, some of the links may not be complete or functional (e.g., links to the biographies of past justices). Nonetheless, the site carries sufficient material that would appeal to students, educators, and other researchers interested in the U.S. Supreme Court.—**ARBA Staff Reviewer**

274.   **Neil Gorsuch Project. http://library.law.virginia.edu/gorsuchproject/.** [Website] Free. Date reviewed: 2017.

This site allows for a glimpse into the legal mind of the newest U.S. Supreme Court justice, Neil Gorsuch. Consolidating his work on the 10th Circuit Court of Appeals, the simply structured site allows access to his majority opinions, concurrences, and dissents in addition to published works and speeches. Users can simply scroll through and select the particular item from the sidebar menu, or conduct a basic search. The Opinions tab will link to all of Gorsuch's majority opinions, concurrences, and dissents, or users can alternatively select the specific category tab for quicker access. The site also highlights nine of what it considers to be his major decisions, such as the civil rights case *Wilson* vs. *City of Lafayette* from 2013. Within each category, case links are listed alphabetically. Selecting a particular case will link to the PDF of the decision. The Publications tab links to a list of thirteen of Gorsuch's writings, including contributions to legal journals, news outlets, and more. Speeches offers three videos (two with text) showing Gorsuch delivering remarks on Supreme Court justice Antonin Scalia and "Law's Irony." The site does not provide much personal background on Gorsuch, but the materials gathered here offer good insight nonetheless into his thinking and into the work of the 10th Circuit. The site would be very useful for legal scholars, historians, and others.—**ARBA Staff Reviewer**

275. Ryden, David K., and Jeffrey J. Polet. **Church and State: Documents Decoded.** Santa Barbara, Calif., ABC-CLIO, 2018. 284p. index. $81.00. ISBN 13: 978-1-61069-948-8; 978-1-61069-949-5 (e-book).

"Congress shall make no law respecting an establishment or religion, or prohibiting the free exercise thereof." As the editors, professors of political science at Hope College, ably demonstrate, these seemingly straightforward clauses from the 1st Amendment have created decades of controversy and confusion, as public opinion and the changing makeup of the Supreme Court have evolved. This collection of digested documents is divided into five sections that date from the earliest American settlements to the present day. "Church and State in Colonial America" features documents that illustrate how in this era there was no absolute separation of church and state; indeed, the right to freely worship was a collective right for various colonies, not an individual right. Gradually, there developed tolerance for diverse forms of worship (e.g., Rhode Island, under Roger Williams), but even so there were definite limits. In "The Constitutional History of Church-State Relations" the editors trace the impetus behind the Article 1 clauses: the main concern was to ensure that Congress could not mandate an established state church (as the British crown had done with the Anglican Church). At the same time, the framers clearly saw a place for religion in the affairs of state; this has become known as civil religion. In the last three sections, "Civil Religion and Religious Expression in the Public Square," "Public Aid to Religious Institutions and Organizations," and "The Challenge of Religious Liberty," the tension between the "strict separationists" and the "accommodationists" is illustrated. Issues include public aid for private schools, public displays of religious items (e.g., the Ten Commandments), compulsory education imposed on Old Order Amish, the use of peyote in Native American rites, and, most recently, the imposition of Obamacare mandates regarding sexual healthcare on Catholic and Evangelical churches and their adherents. The editors highlight certain passages in these excerpts and provide their commentary or paraphrasing in adjacent sidebars. Their contributions are even-handed and lucid. They also provide an introduction and conclusion, as well as a timeline of events. Recommended for public and academic libraries.—**Jack Ray**

276. **Social Security Handbook, 2017: Overview of Social Security Programs.** Lanham, Md., Bernan Press, 2017. 703p. index. $74.00pa. ISBN 13: 978-1-59888-899-7.

In this book users will find answers to the most common questions regarding the complicated Social Security System. It is designed for ease of use and readability. The book has twenty-seven chapters and an index. Each chapter has its own table of contents which lists topics next to a section number. The first chapter provides a thorough overview of the Social Security system. This is followed by chapters on how to get Social Security insurance, survivor benefits, disability benefits, how to file a claim, underpayments and overpayments, supplemental security income like Medicaid and Food Stamps, information about special benefits for veterans, and a great deal more. The book breaks complex subjects into digestible parts. So, for example, in the chapter on self-employment, users first learn that self-employed people began receiving Social Security coverage in 1951. The next section (eight lines of text) discusses exceptions while other short sections cover partnerships and almost any imaginable self-employment scenario. The work concludes with an index in which subject terms refer to section numbers, not page numbers. This provides users with another, very useful navigation tool. Recommended.—**ARBA Staff Reviewer**

Copyright Law

Handbooks and Yearbooks

277.   **Copyright.gov. https://www.copyright.gov/.** [Website] Free. Date reviewed: 2017.
This site takes on the significant task of clarifying and facilitating the U.S. Copyright Office, which administers U.S. Copyright Law and policies in regards to authorship of creative property such as music, artwork, photographs, literature, computer programs, video games, and movie scripts. The site emphasizes three main procedures related to copyrights: Register, Record, and Research. Users have online access to a registration portal (Register) whereby they can execute the copyright application process. The Record tab provides information on the recordation process specific to transferring copyrights or other documents, such as a breakdown of the Code of Federal Regulations. The Research tab leads to a variety of services allowing access to official documentation including Certificates of Registration, Application copies (completed and in-progress), correspondence, inspections, and much more. In addition to the three main procedural options, there are generous options for research and education. Resources allows users to do such things as search the Copyright Public Records online catalog (kept since 1978), access several different administrative reports (e.g., annual, tech, etc.), and examine a schedule of fees. The Education tab links to the copyright office Fair Use Index database of relevant court opinions (expansive, yet noncomprehensive), FAQs, historical and educational information on copyright law (including a timeline), and other information. Users can also access generous information related to copyright policy—particularly relevant in the age of digitization—and rulemaking, regarding bulk copyright submissions and more. Copyright Quick Links allows easy access to the Copyright Law of the U.S. and the Code of Federal Regulations in addition to a draft Compendium of U.S. Copyright Office Practices (Third Edition), including twenty-four chapters and a glossary. All of these items are downloadable. Latest News updates users on rule changes, new publications, and more. The wealth of information on the site makes it invaluable to those researching American copyright law, issues, and procedures.—**ARBA Staff Reviewer**

278.   **Research Handbook on Copyright Law. 2d ed.** Paul Torremans, ed. Northampton, Mass., Edward Elgar, 2017. 613p. index. (Research Handbooks in Intellectual Property). $275.00. ISBN 13: 978-1-78536-142-5; 978-1-78536-143-2 (e-book).

It should first be explained that this second edition (of a 2007 publication, with the title *Copyright Law: A Handbook of Contemporary Research*) is all new material, by many new contributors, rather than a mere revision of any of the earlier text. The 24 contributors come from 10 countries, although none are from the United States, thus offering an international view of the topic, ranging from the European Union to Vietnam, Albania, and other countries. (Two or three of the chapters, however, do discuss issues in the United States.) The chapters can be very detailed and narrowly focused. For example, one chapter deals with Article 8 of the WIPO Copyright Treaty (1996) and references dozens of cases from the Court of Justice of the European Union among its 245 footnotes. Another explores the role or importance of the French droit d'auteur copyright principle when incorporated into Vietnamese law, from the 1860s to the 1970s, with numerous footnote references in Vietnamese.

This volume is clearly aimed at a specialized audience interested in worldwide copyright issues and history; those readers will be found almost exclusively in law office or academic settings. While the cost may preclude some institutions from purchasing this work, it remains a useful resource for learning about worldwide issues in copyright law, both now and in the past.—**Mark Schumacher**

Criminology and Criminal Justice

Dictionaries and Encyclopedias

279.   **The Criminal Justice System. 2d ed.** Michael K. Hooper and Ruth E. Masters, eds. Amenia, N.Y., Grey House Publishing, 2017. 3v. illus. maps. index. $295.00/set. ISBN 13: 978-1-68217-310-7; 978-1-68217-311-4 (e-book).

Comprised of three volumes, this ready-reference set contains 620 articles on the most important facets of the U.S. criminal justice system with volume 1 focusing on crime and criminal law, volume 2 on law enforcement and the courts, and volume 3 on corrections and special issues. Article subjects range in time from the Salem witch trials (1692) to the extradition of Mexican drug kingpin Joaquin "El Chapo" Guzman to the United States (2016). Each article focuses on one of the 6 Cs of criminal justice: criminals, codes, constitutions, cops, courts, or corrections. Alphabetically arranged, each article contains important definitions, explains the significance of the subject, and elaborates on key issues relating to criminal justice. Throughout the three volumes there are hundreds of photographs, maps, charts, tables, and graphs. Written with the casual reader in mind, each article also contains *see also* references and annotated further readings for more in-depth study.

While the first two volumes focus primarily on articles, the third finishes up the 6 Cs of criminal justice and follows with several other prominent features. Following the articles are over 100 pages of appendixes including an annotated bibliography, a helpful glossary containing over 700 criminal justice terms, and a special section of crime rates and definitions, courtesy of the Federal Bureau of Investigation and the National Crime Victimization Surveys of the U.S. Census Bureau. There is also a chronological listing of key U.S. Supreme Court rulings and their relevance to criminal justice, as well as a chronological listing of well-known American trials and the significance of their outcomes. A complete chronological timeline of all key issues relating to criminal justice is followed by several indexes which provide the reader with quick access to issues. The issues are arranged by subject, court case, laws and acts, and person.

Put together by hundreds of contributors from both the academic world and the criminal justice profession, *The Criminal Justice System* is a valuable one-stop reference work for a quick understanding of some of the most important issues in the U.S. criminal justice system.—**Thomas O'Brien**

280.   West, Nigel. **Encyclopedia of Political Assassinations.** Lanham, Md., Rowman & Littlefield, 2017. 360p. $95.00; $90.00 (e-book). ISBN 13: 978-1-5381-0238-1; 978-1-5381-0239-8 (e-book).

From military historian Nigel West, a specialist in intelligence and security issues, comes this fascinating historical contribution. The pages offer political intrigue, conspiracies, and law enforcement applications. This book is relevant, especially in a time when international relations, terrorism, and security issues are particularly concerning. The *Encyclopedia of Political Assassinations* details well-planned scenarios, motives, consequences, and the backgrounds of assassins. The well-organized book includes abbreviations and a glossary, as well as a chronology, introduction, and appendixes to support readers. Altogether there are more than seven hundred cross-referenced entries on assassinations, intelligence agencies, politics, and foreign relations.

This book offers captivating reading for students, researchers, academics, and general readers. History enthusiasts will benefit from the reader-friendly format. Public and university libraries will consider this contribution an essential resource. Law enforcement agencies, intelligence services, and the secret service will also consider this book an excellent resource.—**Thomas E. Baker**

Handbooks and Yearbooks

281.   Banks, Cyndi. **Prisons in the United States: A Reference Handbook.** Santa Barbara, Calif., ABC-CLIO, 2017. 312p. illus. index. (Contemporary World Issues). $60.00. ISBN 13: 978-1-4408-4437-9; 978-1-4408-4438-6 (e-book).

Prisons in the United States: A Reference Handbook creates a learning environment that encourages reader interest and retention. Offering perspectives from a range of experts, both academic and nonacademic, this reference book examines the development of prisons (both men's and women's) in the United States. It addresses principal contemporary issues and controversies and documents the shift from prisons as reform institutions to "warehouses" for undesired elements. The volume is enhanced by its organization into parts and chapters that use headings and subheadings along with bullet points, tables, charts, and illustrations. Chapters focus on singe topics and utilize content from respected government agencies and other sources. The book also offers a chronology, helpful glossary, well-done index, and resource directories.

The book provides an indispensable resource for students and others and acts as a useful starting point and guide for those who wish to undertake a deeper study of prisons. Designed for high school students, undergraduates, and general nonspecialists, this excellent book presents a current, balanced, and reliable collection of material to understand a sensitive and mutually shared topic in an easy-to-understand and thought-provoking manner. High schools, community colleges, and universities will value this book as an essential addition to their library reference shelves.—**Thomas E. Baker**

282.   **Corporate Prosecution Registry. http://lib.law.virginia.edu/Garrett/corporate-prosecution-registry/index.html.** [Website] Free. Date reviewed: 2017.

This site, a project of the University of Virginia Law School, is home to a database listing of over three thousand corporations prosecuted by the U.S. government since 2001. It also includes a look at nonprosecutorial agreements between corporate entities and the federal government since 1990. The Data and Documents tab provides quick entry to the alphabetical database. Users can simply scroll through the listing or search via company, crime, jurisdiction, total fines, year, and more. Next to each company name, the database categorizes crime (immigration, fraud, antitrust, environmental, etc.), type (e.g., plea), and date. Selecting a company from the database will link to a case profile including detail about the company, the case, and the punishment. Users can also access the unofficial docket with more case details. The data is downloadable via a number of applications, such as Excel. Downloadable copies of the plea agreement or deferred prosecution agreement are available for some but not all cases in the database. The Data and Documents tab provides other resources as well, including a listing of relevant books, articles, and Department of Justice documents. The Visuals feature allows users a graphic look at corporate prosecution penalties by amount and crime. Users can also peruse a Blog carrying data updates and topical essays archived back to March of this year.—**ARBA Staff Reviewer**

283.   **The Dark Web: Breakthroughs in Research and Practice.** Edited by Information Resources Management Association. Hershey, Pa., IGI Global, 2018. 377p. index. $395.00. ISBN 13: 978-1-52253-163-0; 978-1-52253-164-7 (e-book).

The Dark Web: Breakthroughs in Research and Practice offers a groundbreaking resource that addresses the security needs of an interconnected global community. Under the direction of an editorial advisory board, a renowned international cast of contributors provide essential insight into a world that camouflages terrorist communications, threats to homeland security, and clandestine financial transactions—all global threats. The volume is presented in four parts: Cyber Crime and Security, Data Mining and Analysis, Online Identity, and Web Crawling. Chapters cover a broad range of topics by authors from Europe, Asia, the Middle East, and the Americas. This reader-friendly volume includes references, an index system, additional readings, key terms and definitions, graphics, and charts. *The Dark Web* provides essential information for anyone interested in current cyber safety issues. A short learning curve is essential for technology security experts and practitioners. This superior publication provides insightful learning opportunities that enhance detection capabilities and prevent hackers from stealing valuable information. This book has a broad audience that includes law enforcement, consumers, financial institutions, academic programs, businesses, and government agencies. All library acquisition decision-makers will consider this contribution an essential resource. Recommended especially for academic libraries.—**Thomas E. Baker**

284.   Goldstein, Margaret J. **Legalizing Marijuana: Promises and Pitfalls.** Minneapolis, Minn., Twenty-First Century Books/Lerner Publishing Group, 2017. 104p. index. $35.99. ISBN 13: 978-1-4677-9243-1.

Given that almost half the states have legalized marijuana in one form or another, it's important for students to understand both sides of this debate and the possible repercussions for both legalizing and criminalizing the drug. Beginning with a tale of a young girl whose only relief from a severe form of epilepsy was a special strain of cannabis, the book continues on with a history of marijuana from ancient times until now, with particular emphasis on its legal and illegal history in the United States. Goldstein then provides separate chapters outlining the possible benefits and consequences of legalizing it across the country, working hard to present an unbiased review of the debate. She acknowledges that rigorous study of the long-term effects of cannabis is lacking due to federal research laws, and that more information is needed before declaring marijuana safe. She also provides interviews from people on both sides of the argument. Regardless of how the future of marijuana legalization plays out, this is a hot-button topic that will keep this book flying off the shelves. A bibliography and an index round out the work. Recommended.—**Michaela Schied**

285.   **A Guide to Mass Shootings in America. www.motherjones.com/politics/2012/07/ mass-shootings-map/.** [Website] Free. Date reviewed: 2017.

This Web page offers a clear look at gun violence in the United States by presenting a database of domestic mass shootings occurring from 1982 to 2017. The database lists ninety-five gun events, providing general information such as location, date, fatalities, number of injured, and venue. The listing also includes information on the weapon used (type, where obtained, etc.) and the shooter (name, race, gender), along with notes on mental health and a brief description of the event. Additionally users will find media report sources. Data is downloadable in a variety of formats and is up to date with events that have occurred as recently as November of 2017. Users can click the Guide to Mass Shootings in America link to access good contextual analysis of the data in regards to the perpetrators and the weapons they use. Aside from narrative analysis, the page incorporates several data visualizations (e.g., number of shooters who obtained weapon illegally) and provides links to other research related to topics such as mental health and gun legislation. The page also establishes the parameters used to define mass shootings, such as shootings occurring in a public place, etc. With mass shootings appearing all too much in the national conversation, this website is an important receptacle of data that would hold significant appeal for policy makers, mental health advocates, educators, journalists, and others.—**ARBA Staff Reviewer**

286.   Hatch, Alison E. **Campus Sexual Assault: A Reference Handbook.** Santa Barbara, Calif., ABC-CLIO, 2017. 342p. illus. index. (Contemporary World Issues). $60.00. ISBN 13: 978-1-4408-4139-2; 978-1-4408-4140-8 (e-book).

Campus Sexual Assault: A Reference Handbook addresses difficult questions about the widespread incidence of sexual assault among high school and college students. Aimed at high school and undergraduate students, the book is clearly organized in seven sections: Background and History; Problems, Controversies, and Solutions; Perspectives; Profiles; Data and Documents; Resources; and Chronology. Readers will gain a deeper appreciation of the gravity of the problem, grasp the causes of this societal issue, and learn how to initiate successful interventions and solutions. The book is enhanced by the inclusion of case studies, recommended resources, and current references. The use of diagrams, figures, tables, graphs, charts, and pictures, along with a glossary of terms and an index also make this book a good choice.

Recommended for high school, community college, university, and public libraries.— **Thomas E. Baker**

287.   **The Henry A. Wallace Police Crime Database. https://policecrime.bgsu.edu/.** [Website] Free. Date reviewed: 2018.

This free database compiles information on over 9,000 criminal arrest cases from 2005 to 2013 involving approximately 7,500 nonfederal law enforcement officers in 1,402 counties and independent cities in all 50 states and in Washington D.C. The database was developed by and is run by Philip M. Stinson, an associate professor of criminal justice at Bowling Green State University. More about the project, its funding, and its staff can be discovered under the About tab. Users can access information about crimes and their location from the homepage or by clicking on either the Map tab or the Crime tab. Clicking on a state in the U.S. map produces a list of case numbers and an indication of what crime was committed (drug-related, alcohol-related, etc.). The case numbers are clickable and take users to information about the officer involved (name, age, sex, rank, years of service), some details on the case, and case outcome. The Crime tab leads to the same information but allows searches by type of crime. The results list includes a case number, date, state, county, and agency. There are also tabs that take users to tutorials on how to use the information in the database, discussions on data collection and liability, outside resources (limited), a glossary, a blog, and FAQs.—**ARBA Staff Reviewer**

288.   **Justice Statistics: An Extended Look at Crime in the United States 2017.** 3d ed. Hattis, Shana Hertz, ed. Lanham, Md., Bernan Press, 2017. 320p. index. $89.00pa. ISBN 13: 978-1-59888-931-4.

This volume offers insight into numerous criminal activities that lead to the victimization of U.S. citizens. Many statistics are staggering to the casual observer. Topics include criminal victimization, correctional populations, crime in the United States, hate crimes, probation, parole, and law enforcement officers killed and assaulted. The volume provides valuable data accumulated by the Department of Justice, including its partners— The Bureau of Justice Statistics and the Federal Bureau of Investigation. Editor Shana Hertz Hattis highlights the most compelling data at the beginning of each chapter. Additionally, she offers a brief summary of the report's methodology. The third edition includes new sections on crimes against persons, including those with disabilities, and school violence. This comprehensive publication also includes statistics on rape and sexual assault. The content includes tables, line and bar charts, pie charts, general term definitions, and an extensive index system. Appendix A includes sources for tables documented throughout the book. Appendix B documents capital punishment statistics.

Justice Statistics is an essential reference book. Local, state, and federal law enforcement agencies need the information to implement effective crime fighting strategies and tactics planning. This is also an important book for high school, community college, and university libraries.—**Thomas E. Baker**

289.   Melusky, Joseph A., and Keith A. Pesto. **The Death Penalty: A Reference Handbook.** Santa Barbara, Calif., ABC-CLIO, 2017. 372p. (Contemporary World Issues). $60.00. ISBN 13: 978-1-4408-4549-9; 978-1-4408-4550-5 (e-book).

Part of the Contemporary World Issues series, this reference handbook is a highly academic treatment of an issue that is often studied and debated in school and society. The text reads like a legal brief, extensively citing cases to illustrate rulings in federal and state courts within the context of constitutional law. The chapters work together to illustrate how these cases and experiences shaped society's social, legal, and political perspectives. The first chapter provides a historical background from ancient societies to European and American applications. Subsequent sections provide essays on: current controversial issues; profiles of legislation, organizations, and individuals; and data, statistics, and portions of legal documents associated with the development and practice of the death penalty as a means of capital punishment in the United States. Each chapter ends with pages of copious notes. This complex book will work best for sophisticated learners who may appreciate in-depth information for reports, debates, or other projects. The book includes additional resources, a timeline, and an index. Recommended.—**Karen Leon**

290.   **The National Registry of Exonerations. http://www.law.umich.edu/special/ exoneration/Pages/about.aspx.** [Website] Free. Date reviewed: 2018.

This site collects and shares information going back nearly thirty years related to exonerations of criminal defendants in the United States. It maintains a database of over two thousand exonerations with details, explores issues exposed through the collected data, and offers varied resources with the ultimate goal of educating the public and reducing the number of false convictions. Selecting the Browse Cases tab allows users a "summary view" or "detailed view" of the database. The sortable database includes name of exonerated, state, county, year of conviction, year of exoneration, crime, sentence, race, and more. The database also notes factors contributing to exoneration, such as perjury, false confessions, and official misconduct. Selecting an individual entry accesses a detailed narrative of the affiliated crime, conviction, and exoneration. The Issues tab provides educational information on particular questions pertaining to erroneous convictions, such as compensation, false confessions, group exonerations, jailhouse informants, and DNA. Resources are plentiful and include a selection of charts, infographics (e.g., percent exonerations by contributing factors), news items, and reports (e.g., "Race and Wrongful Convictions"). There is also a generous glossary of related terms. The depth of information on this website speaks to the importance of the project. It offers ample material for educators and students of criminal justice, policy makers, social historians, and many others.—**ARBA Staff Reviewer**

291.   Newton, David E. **Marijuana: A Reference Handbook.** 2d ed. Santa Barbara, Calif., ABC-CLIO, 2017. 372p. illus. index. (Contemporary World Issues). $60.00. ISBN 13: 978-1-4408-5051-6; 978-1-4408-5052-3 (e-book).

The updated research and dramatically changing societal attitudes on marijuana over the past ten years have necessitated a new edition of this outstanding book (see ARBA 2014, entry 468), which includes the most recent U.S. laws and medical findings. Many local and state laws are often at variance with the current federal regulation of marijuana. In contrast to federal laws which label marijuana as an illegal substance, some states allow marijuana for recreational use, others only for medical purposes. Pro and con arguments for each position are clearly stated and include data and references. There are also brief descriptions of the role of individuals and organizations in the debates and drafting of laws on marijuana. The book summarizes five thousand years of marijuana history, including cultivation, use, legal status, medical findings, and popularity. This reference work presents unbiased information and provides essential material for students researching this topic for reports or personal knowledge. The book includes a bibliography glossary, and index. Recommended.—**Anitra Gordon**

292.   **Sexual Assault: The Ultimate Teen Guide.** Olivia Ghafoerkhan, ed. Lanham, Md., Rowman & Littlefield, 2017. 200p. index. (It Happened to Me series). $45.00; $44.99 (e-book). ISBN 13: 978-1-4422-5247-9; 978-1-4422-5248-6 (e-book).

This entry in the It Happened to Me series provides an easy-to-read, moving guide to understanding sexual assault. The author begins by discussing the many ways sexual assault happens, followed by the myths that surround the situations and the ways a person can get help if it happens to them. There are sidebars which contain stories or other information that may be pertinent. Many works of fiction and movies dealing with the subject are presented to the reader. I was especially interested in the analysis of the Twilight series, where the author notes the number of occurrences when Bella is ordered to do something by the main male characters, as well as the number of references to suicide, self-harm, and instances of male aggression. The author discusses how important it is to speak up about instances of sexual assault, but that many times the person to whom the victim speaks is a friend who may not be able to help. The book also contains additional resources, a bibliography, an index, and a glossary. Recommended.—**Patricia Brown**

293.   **The Use and Abuse of Police Power: Historical Milestones and Current Controversies.** Gina Robertiello, ed. Santa Barbara, Calif., ABC-CLIO, 2017. 370p. illus. index. $89.00. ISBN 13: 978-1-4408-4372-3; 978-1-4408-4373-0 (e-book).

Modern policing and law enforcement are important social issues that affect each individual across the nation. Law enforcement officials now, more than ever, must adhere to strict departmental policies and personal morals to protect the rights of the citizens they police. *The Use and Abuse of Police Power in America* examines the history of policing in America and the relationships of modern police agencies and their communities. The opening chapters of this authoritative resource provide a brief summary of the 4th, 5th, and 6th amendments and the rights guaranteed to the defendant of a criminal prosecution. This reference book also contains an outline of early policing that includes Sir Robert Peel, the Bow Street Runners, Southern Slave Patrols, Colonial Night Watches, the Pinkerton Detective Agency, and more. After recounting the establishment of policing and early criminal rights, *The Use and Abuse of Police Power in America* highlights organized crime in America and early technology advancements like the advent of the Uniform Crime Reports. The book continues to detail many notable events, persons, and places in American law enforcement history but the most notable sections focus on the recent police shootings that gained media scrutiny and sparked the Black Lives Matter movement. The conclusion focuses on mending the tattered relationships of law enforcement officials and the communities they serve. With an in-depth history of policing in America and police/public relationships, *The Use and Abuse of Police Power in America* provides a effective and complete understanding of police use of force in modern times.—**Trent Shotwell**

294.   Van Gundy, Karen T., and Michael S. Staunton. **Marijuana: Examining the Facts.** Santa Barbara, Calif., ABC-CLIO, 2017. 284p. index. (Contemporary Debates). $63.00. ISBN 13: 978-1-4408-3672-5; 978-1-4408-3673-2 (e-book).

   Marijuana: Examining the Facts is a timely Contemporary Debate series contribution. The book contextualizes the marijuana debate, presenting opposing viewpoints and providing readers with reliable and valid statistics. The book also lends itself to discussions over the differences between fact and opinion, as well as to debates over marijuana use. The book includes timeline events, bullet formatting, and bold font questions followed by succinct descriptions. The question-and-answer format delivers a superior learning and debate curriculum design. Logical organization, graphics, font size, line spacing, and charts offer directional signposts for piloting through relevant data. The volume includes suggestions for further reading and an index.

   Recommended for school and academic libraries.—**Thomas E. Baker**

Environmental Law

Handbooks and Yearbooks

295.   McCall, Duke K., III. **The Clean Water Handbook.** 4th ed. Lanham, Md., Bernan Press, 2017. 342p. $99.00; $94.00 (e-book). ISBN 13: 978-1-59888-818-8; 978-1-59888-819-5 (e-book).

   This is the fourth edition of *The Clean Water Handbook* and the first complete update since the third edition in 2003. This dense book begins by outlining the history, goals and policies, elements, and discharge prohibition of the Clean Water Act (CWA). Clearly aimed at environmental professionals, the book details the National Pollutant Discharge Elimination System permit program, Storm-Water Discharges, Dredge Permits, Enforcement, and other topics. An appendix contains the text of the CWA; a section on resources, notes, and an appendix round out the work. Statutory changes, regulatory enactments, and court decisions have amended this act, originally passed in 1972, so this guide is a valuable resource for those tasked with enforcing compliance.—**Thomas E. Baker**

296.   **Research Handbook on Climate Change and Trade Law.** Panagiotis Delimatsis, ed. Northampton, Mass., Edward Elgar, 2016. 547p. index. (Research Handbooks in Climate Law). $310.00. ISBN 13: 978-1-78347-843-9; 978-1-78347-844-6 (e-book).

   The scientific consensus is that climate change is mainly caused by the emission of greenhouse gasses; thus, constraints need to be imposed globally. How? Any measures used directly involve economics, production of goods, and trade. What is the role of the World Trade Organization (WTO) and WTO law in dealing with climate change? The authors want to protect trade among members, and they want WTO laws to guide members in negotiating contracts to deal responsibly with these emissions. They look at existing WTO law and regulations and adjustments to accommodate ways counties are dealing with climate change. Current challenges to trade are energy security, food security, "plurilateral" agreements, and green paradox. Global and regional perspectives, as well as trade and investment are discussed. The 27 authors are experts from 12 nations. These lawyers and experts are academics or practicing professionals in the arena of international law, world trade, and other international agencies.

Highly recommended for practitioners and for libraries supporting graduate schools and undergraduate seniors studying in this area.—**Ladyjane Hickey**

297.   **Research Handbook on Climate Change, Migration and the Law.** Benoît Mayer and François Crépeau, eds. Northampton, Mass., Edward Elgar, 2017. 490p. index. (Research Handbooks in Climate Law). $240.00. ISBN 13: 978-1-78536-658-1; 978-1-78536-569-8 (e-book).

Anthropogenic climate change has negatively impacted the availability of the natural resources required to sustain life on many continents. That has led to forced migrations to other locales where the newcomers have seen others try to deny their basic human rights. This research handbook, edited by Benoît Mayer, assistant professor in the faculty of law at the Chinese University of Hong Kong, and François Crépeau, Hans & Tamar Oppenheimer professor in public international law at McGill University, Canada, contains twenty-one essays authored by lawyers and policy makers that explore the subject matter from a variety of perspectives. Some offer overviews on the plight of climate migrants. Others focus on specific legal issues, with differences of opinion between authors evident. The final six essays contemplate what the acceleration of climate change portends for the future. While each essay includes an extensive number of footnotes, the volume does not include a cumulative bibliography. It does conclude with a general index. While the handbook's coverage of the subject is exemplary, the level of academic jargon makes it appropriate for libraries supporting graduate-level research in such areas as political science and environmental law. It is also suitable for special libraries serving lawyers and diplomats.—**John R. Burch Jr.**

298.   **Research Handbook on Emissions Trading.** Stefan E. Weishaar, ed. Northampton, Mass., Edward Elgar, 2016. 366p. index. (Research Handbooks on Climate Law). $310.00. ISBN 13: 978-1-78471-061-3; 978-1-78471-062-0 (e-book).

What is emissions trading? According to the *Research Handbook on Emissions Trading,* the term emissions trading typically refers to a cap and trade or allowance trading. The purpose is to reduce pollution and effectively safeguard human health and the environment. In this vanguard book, expert research offers an interdisciplinary approach that draws from law, economics, and political science. This multidisciplinary approach presents relevant research and scientific observations regarding emissions trading and merges theoretical insights with field experiences from existing trading systems. This handbook offers insights that have worldwide applications and identifies significant related issues.

The *Research Handbook on Emissions Trading* contributors bring together views from different disciplinary and geographic perspectives. This multifaceted examination of economic and legal origins, implementation problems, and the emerging international aspect of emissions trading identifies key bodies of research for both upcoming and seasoned academics in the field and highlights future research opportunities. The book's broad and accessible approach touches on climate law, environmental law, and environmental governance and will serve the needs of decision-makers, policy leaders, and development practitioners engaged in the process of climate policy formulation and implementation. University librarians would do well to incorporate this handbook in their acquisition budgets for the coming academic year.—**Thomas E. Baker**

Human Rights

Biography

299.   **Human Rights Innovators.** Hackensack, N.J., Salem Press, 2016. 2v. illus. index. $165.00/set. ISBN 13: 978-1-68217-157-8.

This two-volume work from Salem Press, which appears to be designed primarily for secondary school students and college undergraduates, offers biographical sketches of 208 individuals who were selected for having advanced the cause of human rights since the 1960s. They are in alphabetical order, beginning with U.S. civil rights leader Ralph Abernathy and ending with Pakistani Nobel Peace Prize winner Malala Yousafzai. Many of the subjects are obvious choices, such as Nelson Mandela and Elie Wiesel, while others will be new to most U.S. readers. For example, Yemeni activist and Nobel Prize winner Tawakkol Karman is cited for her work on gender equality and nonviolence; lesser-known selections include Native American educator Ada E. Deer and Kimi Naidoo of Greenpeace International. There is a heavy emphasis on figures from the civil rights movement in the United States and on Africans who have struggled for equality and justice. Although volume two begins with Chinese environmentalist Ma Jun, very few Asians appear in these pages, and seemingly no Latin Americans—surprisingly, not even Oscar Romero, the martyred bishop of El Salvador. As might be expected, the list leans politically to the left, including as it does Black Panthers, a number of prominent feminists, the founders of MoveOn, and radical activist William Ayers. The editorial team—no editor is listed— apparently tried for some balance by also including conservative tax-reform advocate Grover Norquist. Each biography has sections on Early Life, Life's Work, Personal Life, and Further Reading. This last section lists a few works by or about the subject, given in a run-on paragraph and in italics; the format makes the list hard to use. In most cases, a photo of the subject is provided. Three appendixes follow the biographies at the end of volume two: the "Universal Declaration of Human Rights" adopted by the United Nations in 1948, a "Chronology of Human Rights 1946-2016," and a brief "Website Directory." These are followed by a "Human Rights Category Index" and the index proper. It would have been helpful to have an index also at the end of volume one. While it does not fall in the category of essential reading, *Human Rights Innovators* could serve as a useful resource for the study of human rights issues.—**ARBA Staff Reviewer**

Dictionaries and Encyclopedias

300.   Doyle, Thomas E., II, Robert F. Gorman, and Edward S. Mihalkanin. **Historical Dictionary of Human Rights and Humanitarian Organizations.** 3d ed. Lanham, Md., Rowman & Littlefield, 2017. 400p. (Historical Dictionaries of International Organizations).

$110.00; $109.99 (e-book). ISBN 13: 978-1-4422-7617-8; 978-1-4422-7621-5 (e-book).

The *Historical Dictionary of Human Rights and Humanitarian Organizations* begins like other historical dictionaries produced by Rowman & Littlefield—with an annotated chronology that offers the reader a context for the topics, events, and individuals which form the content of the title. The dictionary also offers an extensive quick reference list of acronyms and abbreviations used throughout the title. The content is solid and global, focusing on topics, events, and individuals from around the world. The dictionary features several appendixes including the Universal Declaration of Human Rights, the International Covenant on Economic, Social, and Cultural Rights, and several similar documents pertinent to human rights and which govern and guide humanitarian organizations and movements. The title also contains a rather comprehensive bibliography. While the entries are somewhat more encyclopedic than dictionary-like, the content is nonetheless concise and objective. While illustrations would have been appropriate (such as images of protesters or of critical individuals), overall this title is an excellent quick-reference resource. Recommended for public, school, and academic libraries.—**Megan W. Lowe**

301.   **Encyclopedia of American Civil Rights and Liberties.** Kara E. Stooksbury, John M. Scheb, II, and Otis H. Stephens, Jr., eds. Santa Barbara, Calif., ABC-CLIO, 2017. 4v. index. $435.00/set. ISBN 13: 978-1-4408-4109-5; 978-1-4408-4110-1 (e-book).

Encyclopedia of American Civil Rights and Liberties is a four-volume set which provides an introduction to the issues related to both civil rights and civil liberties. The 2017 edition contains over 75 new entries, which reflect changes in law and society on topics such as gay rights, voting rights, and government surveillance. The 688 entries cover court cases, social movements, historical figures and organizations, legislation, controversial issues, and legal concepts. Each entry also contains a suggested reading list, which provides an entry point for further study. Additionally, this set contains almost 200 pages of primary documents, a table of cases, a bibliography, a guide to related topics, and an index. This is a comprehensive resource, which would be a useful addition to any academic or public library.—**Lisa Schultz**

Handbooks and Yearbooks

302.   **American Civil Liberties Union Papers, 1912-1990.** [Website] Farmington Hills, Mich., Gale/Cengage Learning, 2017. Price negotiated by site. Date reviewed: 2017

The American Civil Liberties Union database is an extraordinary resource for exploring primary source documents of an American institution that has shaped American law in more ways than most Americans realize. The database contains papers related to many of the hot-button issues from 1912 to 1990, including the rights of women, racial minorities, sexual minorities, and individual rights against the federal, state, and local governments. Reading through these papers is like opening a time capsule: one can view correspondence, court filings, telegrams, and legal briefs, among other miscellanea. The database even includes several entries that detail the organization's utility invoices. The database is, in a word, comprehensive.

The database is broken down into two ACLU "generations"—the first generation of the organization under founder Roger Baldwin, spanning from 1912 to 1950, and the second generation as the organization's influence grew and spread spanning from 1950 to 1990. In reviewing the papers, one can almost feel the authors' dedication to their life's work: from a fledgling organization simply trying to gain a foothold to the civil rights juggernaut the ACLU became in time.

The researcher will doubtlessly benefit from the breadth and depth of the papers included in the database. For example, instead of seeing the end product of a court brief of a case that led to significant legal change, the researcher may dive into the internal memoranda and differences of opinion between the ACLU staffers before the brief was filed—what was excluded, why certain portions of the brief were included, and what carried the day internally. This glimpse into the inner workings of the ACLU is as useful as it is rare. The papers contain candid conversations between staffers about what arguments will carry the day with the judges and the public, their research on myriad legal issues, and, to a certain extent, mundane topics such as invoices from court reporters.

While the database is interesting to peruse without a strict roadmap, researchers on a time crunch will appreciate the database's intuitive, searchable features. Additionally, many of the papers link to each other. Further, each paper is searchable, meaning that a 30-page internal memorandum can be targeted for certain keywords; this saves the researcher immense time.

The ACLU papers provide extraordinary insight into a uniquely American institution. Students of American history will find these papers to be a tremendous resource. This database is recommended for academic libraries and law libraries.—**Sara Mofford**

303.   **Anti-Defamation League. https://www.adl.org/.** [Website] Free. Date reviewed: 2017.

The Anti-Defamation League (ADL)—long a champion of human rights and a fighter against discrimination and intolerance—maintains this sophisticated website full of valuable educational materials. From the What We Do tab on the menu bar, users can select from a range of social justice issues (e.g., voting rights, religious freedom, etc.) and challenges (hate crimes, etc.) to learn about the ADL's role. Users will find a generous series of Best Practices, Action Guides, Media Reports, and Model Legislation in addition to specialized Tools & Strategies and much more. Research & Tools offers two unique and compelling databases. The Amicus Brief Database presents 107 briefs filed in various court cases related to some form of discrimination. Users can read a summary of the court case and download the pdf of the filed brief. Users can also search the briefs topically. The Hate Symbols database currently holds 178 graphic symbols known to be associated with hate groups or movements. For each symbol, the database provides one or more images and a brief description of context and affiliation. The Resource Library offers an extensive collection of reports (e.g., "Funding Hate: How White Supremacists Raise Their Money"), Glossary Terms, Podcasts, Fact Sheets ("Global Anti-Semitism: Selected Incidents Around the World in 2017"), Group Profiles, and others, which can be searched via subject and type (medium) filters. The Education tab presents ADL training programs, Lesson Plans, K-12 Discussion Guides, and other materials for families and schools. Materials focus on Holocaust Education, Cyberbullying, and other important topics. The website does well in presenting a wealth of materials that would appeal to a range of educators and researchers across all grade levels.—**ARBA Staff Reviewer**

304. **Freedom in the World 2017: The Annual Survey of Political Rights and Civil Liberties.** Puddington, Arch, ed. Lanham, Md., Rowman & Littlefield, 2018. 700p. $99.00pa.; $94.00 (e-book). ISBN 13: 978-1-5381-0007-3; 978-1-5381-0008-0 (e-book).

Freedom in the World has been published annually for the last forty-five years. For at least forty of those, the volume has managed to remain as bipartisan as possible. But the volume has inched toward a more partisan color over the last few years, certainly in this 2017 installment. For example, the volume opens with a discussion of the 2016 election, and makes the case somewhat against a populist agenda. Any form of government can turn sour, of course, but populist agendas per se are not necessarily as antifreedom as, say, totalitarian ones are unquestionably. Further, under the entry for the United States, the beginning sentences read that while Hillary Clinton won the popular vote, Donald J. Trump won the Electoral College. This is the equivalent of saying that while team A played vigorously, team B won by twenty-one points, obviously not vigorously enough. The point being that elections in the United States are determined, not by popular vote, but by the Electoral College. And this fact is determinedly so from our beginnings, since the prescience of our leaders saw that it would not be fair for the most densely populated cities to have an unfair advantage over our more sparsely populated rural areas.

Apart from these defects, the volume still provides a strong voice for freedom. Moreover, it gives us, at a glimpse, where and in what parts of the globe freedom is under attack, if not very nearly defeated. Again arranged alphabetically by country, each entry provides an annual status overview in key areas: elections, freedom of expression and belief, associational rights, rule of law, and individual rights. Tables, charts, and other graphs provide at-a-glance views of freedom worldwide. Contributor bios close out the volume.—**Mark Y. Herring**

305. **Human Rights Watch. https://www.hrw.org/donate-now?promo_id=1010.** [Website] Free. Date reviewed: 2018.

This database is produced and maintained by the nonprofit, nongovernment, nonpartisan Human Rights Watch organization, established in 1978. The goal of Human Rights Watch is to promote human rights around the world. The bountiful information on the site is available in dozens of languages from Burmese to Dutch to Russian to Tagalog. On the homepage users can access information via a series of drop-down menus under the following headings: Countries, Topics, Reports, Videos/Photos, Impact, Take Action, About, Join Us, and Give Now. The database covers ninety countries, organized by area: Africa, Americas, Europe/Central Asia, Asia, and the Middle East/North Africa. The United States has its own link. There is abundant information in this section of the database, and it is quite current. For example, part of the information available for the United States includes a special feature that profiles 43 recently deported immigrants. Clicking on a country name reveals further links to dispatches, commentary, news links, and more. Entries have links to author profiles, related content, and other information. Topic links are further subdivided into: Arms, Business, Children's Rights, Disability Rights, Environment, Free Speech, Health, International Justice, LGBT Rights, Refugee Rights, Terrorism/Counterterrorism, Torture, United Nations, and Women's Rights. The Reports tab connects users to the 2018 Human Rights Watch Report and reports for every year extending back to 1989. Materials under Video and Photos are searchable by keyword and can be filtered by country, topic, and media type. This material is updated regularly; users can even sign up to get alerts when Human Rights Watch posts new videos on

YouTube. The Impact tab links users to Human Rights Watch success stories. Take Action presents issues like threats to deport Dreamers in the United States and steps people can take to help. The other tabs users to information about Human Rights Watch, how to join, and how to donate.—**ARBA Staff Reviewer**

International Law

Handbooks and Yearbooks

306.   Aronowitz, Alexis A. **Human Trafficking: A Reference Handbook.** Santa Barbara, Calif., ABC-CLIO, 2017. 406p. index. (Contemporary World Issues). $60.00. ISBN 13: 978-1-4408-3484-4; 978-1-4408-3485-1 (e-book).

International in scope, this volume in the Contemporary World Issues provides a greater understanding of the complexities of human trafficking, a crime that forces millions into slavery and generates billions of dollars for traffickers (second only to drug trafficking in terms of profit). The book introduces readers to a number of organizational and individual efforts to combat trafficking and to the factors that facilitate and fuel trafficking, among other subjects. A chronology of the significant events and dates, a glossary of terms, and profiles provide the reader with a starting point for further research as does an annotated bibliography of print and Internet sources.

Human Trafficking: A Reference Handbook is appropriate for public, high school, community college, university, and public libraries. This book will be a welcome addition to research collections and will serve the needs of students, professionals, and many others.—**Thomas E. Baker**

307.   **Research Handbook on International Law and Natural Resources.** Elisa Morgera and Kati Kulovesi, eds. Northampton, Mass., Edward Elgar, 2016. 551p. index. (Research Handbooks in International Law). $310.00. ISBN 13: 978-1-78347-832-3; 978-1-78347-833-0 (e-book).

In a four-part format, editors Elisa Morgera (Univ. of Strathclyde) and Kati Kulovesi (Univ. of Eastern Finland) examine concepts of international law in relation to natural resource exploration and development. Part one of the volume looks at the relationships between international law and natural resources, considering the impacts of national sovereignty, international investment law, international trade, human rights, corruption, conflict, and corporate responsibility. The text continues the focus on international environmental law, human rights, and economic law throughout. Part two targets national jurisdictional issues relevant to land, forest, fishery, wildlife, and genetic resources; energies including oil, gas, renewables, and biofuels; and water, mineral, and Arctic resources. It also explores the development of soft law in relation to natural resource exploitation. Part three covers international law with regard to natural resource issues in areas beyond national control including fishing on the high seas, mining in marine environments, marine genetics, and Antarctic resources. Finally, part four delves into the "actors" (e.g., states, institutions, courts, tribunals, trade bodies, environmental treaty bodies, and various intergovernmental organizations) that help create and implement international natural resource laws. It also explores "problem shifting," looks at international dispute settlement, and offers suggestions for future legal research. The book is text heavy with no figures or tables; however, it includes an index and each chapter is extremely well referenced.— **Jennifer Brooks Huffman**

308.   **Research Handbook on Remote Warfare.** Jens David Ohlin, ed. Northampton, Mass., Edward Elgar, 2017. 502p. index. (Research Handbooks in International Law). $240.00. ISBN 13: 978-1-78471-698-1.

The topic of remote warfare, including drones, cyberwarfare, and autonomous weapons systems, has raised huge legal questions; a burgeoning literature has emerged on the subjects in the last decade. In this contribution in the series, Research Handbooks in International Law, Cornell University law professor and vice dean, Jens David Ohlin, brings together fourteen essays by top international scholars, primarily students of international law, from around the globe. These are weighty essays of deep import. The editor provides an invaluable introduction to the essays, and the appendixes (at the beginning of the volume) provide a table of legal cases from around the world and international legislation relative to the subject. The quality of this volume is without question, but it is a source for a limited number of specialist scholars, particularly in law schools. Few other libraries will find it necessary for their collections.—**Joe P. Dunn**

309.   Shelley, Fred M., and Reagan Metz. **Geography of Trafficking: From Drug Smuggling to Modern-Day Slavery.** Santa Barbara, Calif., ABC-CLIO, 2017. 364p. illus. maps. index. $89.00. ISBN 13: 978-1-4408-3822-4; 978-1-4408-3823-1 (e-book).

Drug smuggling and modern-day slavery are reprehensible acts of monetary greed that poison the core of society. The *Geography of Trafficking* chronicles social, historical, political, and monetary issues that dominate the world economy. The book explores the mystique of trafficking origins, transportation, and destinations of illegal goods and services. The content then transitions into an examination of trafficking facts and geographical issues. Furthermore, the text addresses prevention and legislative strategies. Legal issues are particularly germane to human rights questions. Primary documents present legislative laws that regulate illegal trafficking. The book benefits from common-sense organization, graphics, readable font size, line spacing, and a complete index system. Library acquisition decision-makers will consider this reader-friendly contribution an essential resource. This is a must-read for students in middle and high school. Community college and university libraries would also find this contribution an ideal reference book.—**Thomas E. Baker**

11 Library and Information Science and Publishing and Bookselling

Library and Information Science

General Works

310. Oswald, Godfrey. **Library World Records.** 3d ed. Jefferson, N.C., McFarland, 2017. 3809. illus. index. $65.00pa. ISBN 13: 978-1-4766-6777-5; 978-1-4766-2772-4 (e-book)

Have you ever wondered just what the oldest public libraries in the world are? Maybe you are prepping to teach an information session on African Studies, and you wanted to share with your students, that outside of Egypt, the oldest indigenous alphabet comes from Ge'ez, Amharic, Old Nubian and Berber areas of Africa, with Ge'ez dating back to 1st century B.C. If so, *Library World Records,* third edition, is the resource you will want to have in your library's reference collection or on your personal bookshelf. This resource is more than just a book about libraries and book comparisons, it is a journey through humankind's history of the written word. From the dawn of time, as humans began learning to write, they have been on a journey to communicate and share their ideas, knowledge, and inspirations to the world.

This edition uses a format similar to earlier editions, with the use of entry numbers that are also used in the index. The continued use of italicized type highlights interesting and fun facts. New to the third edition are suggested readings after several entries and detailed information on sources. This, along with the bibliography at the end of the book, provides the researcher valuable starting points for further research. One of the best features is the "How to use this book" section, especially useful if you are a novice researcher. This section explains the format and the arrangement of entries—libraries of the United States and Europe will appear first, followed by libraries of Latin America and Asia, which are then followed by libraries of the Middle East and Africa. The author also provides an email to contact him if the user of this book knows of a country that is missing from this book.

Overall, I found this work to be both informative and interesting. A resource for anyone who is in need of learning not only about libraries and their history, but that of the written word as well. It also is a valuable tool for those in the field of special collections and old books. I mean did you know that the British Library in London is home to the oldest surviving vellum manuscript, the Codex Sinaiticus or that Nieuwe Tijdingen, produced in Antwerp, Belgium, in 1605, is considered the first modern newspaper in the world. I did not know those two particular facts. This book will interest anyone looking to learn more about humankind's written word and our history.—**Lawrence Joseph Mello**

311.   Wakimoto, Diana K. **Easy Graphic Design for Librarians: From Color to Kerning.** Chicago, American Library Association, 2018. 154p. index. $54.00pa. $48.60pa. (ALA members). ISBN 13: 978-1-8389-1593-6.

Diana Wakimoto's *Easy Graphic Design for Librarians* is the how-to manual librarians didn't know they needed. Books, guides, tutorials, videos, and websites dedicated to teaching graphic design for any level of expertise are not difficult to discover. Despite this plethora of information, however, connecting the dots and applying that information in a library setting may not be as easy as it sounds. Enter this book, which takes graphic design and frames it from a librarian perspective.

The book is divided into two parts: part one explaining the fundamentals of graphic design and part two providing examples of specific librarian-related projects. The first part includes seven chapters discussing such topics as the design process itself, structure, typography, color, images, design software, and templates/style guide. This section is a fantastic introduction for new librarians entrusted with design responsibilities or experienced librarians tasked with a new design project. In about eighty pages Wakimoto covers all the foundational and fundamental information that will help to make the graphic design process much more comfortable and productive. The second part, then, is focused on providing detailed discussions about some common library-related projects, such as bookmarks, brochures, Web banners, flyers, etc. These chapters each explain the thought process and design elements to keep in mind while developing a project. This book concludes with an appendix of additional resources, further readings, and an index.

Easy Graphic Design for Librarians accomplishes its stated goal with aplomb. With so many graphic design resources available, it may seem unnecessary to publish yet another resource. However, designing a guide for an audience that is often tasked with graphic design responsibilities without much, if any, training is very insightful. Any librarians tasked with even rudimentary graphic design responsibilities would benefit from absorbing and applying the lessons within this book.—**Tyler Manolovitz**

Libraries

College and Research Libraries

312.   **Affordable Course Materials: Electronic Textbooks and Open Educational Resources.** Chris Diaz, ed. Chicago, American Library Association, 2017. 144p. index. $65.00pa.; $58.50pa. (ALA members). ISBN 13: 978-0-8389-1580-6.

This slim volume examines programs at nine university libraries to improve the textbook options for students and faculty by acquiring online textbooks and investigating Open Educational Resources (OER) options. The schools include North Carolina State, UCLA, Louisiana State University, and the University of Florida. The programs are diverse, engaging various groups on the campuses, from faculty and administrators to, on occasion, students themselves. These initiatives are driven in large part by the need to reduce student expenditures on textbooks, but also to raise general awareness of the diverse options available. Several studies/projects found that faculty were not aware of the possibilities available; many instructors tended to continue with traditional textbooks they had used in the past.

Libraries in academia will certainly want to consider this volume, especially in those institutions which are beginning to explore this topic. The accounts reveal the various ways to enhance the teaching/learning experience for all. (It is ironic, however, that a key word in the title of this 144-page, $65.00 paperback is "Affordable".)—**Mark Schumacher**

313. **Developing Digital Scholarship: Emerging Practices in Academic Libraries.** Alison Mackenzie and Lindsey Martin, eds. Chicago, American Library Association, 2017. 184p. index. $70.00pa.; $63.00pa. (ALA members). ISBN 13: 978-0-8389-1555-4.

Mackenzie, Martin, and their eight coauthors "aim to offer to readers, through a collection of contrasting perspectives, contexts, insights, and case studies, an exploration of the relationships between digital scholarship, contemporary academic libraries, and professional practice" (xiii). The contributors eschew exact definitions of digital scholarship, even for themselves, but generally agree that digital scholarship will utilize new skills and technologies, be more interactive, and transform both the departmental organization and the project workflows of academic libraries.

The book is divided into four parts, comprising ten chapters (three of which are written by the editors). A Review of the Landscape, part one, includes a literature review and reflects on current trends in the field. Part two, The Agile Librarian, discusses collaboration, skill development, and customer service. Next, Digital Spaces and Services examines digital scholarship centers, scalability, and sustainability. Communications and Social Networking, the final section, addresses social media, outreach, and possible future directions for the field.

Developing Digital Scholarship will be of interest primarily to library administrators who already have the context and resources to shape their institutions' digital scholarship initiatives. It will also be useful for students who are still in the process of choosing a specialty or for practitioners desirous of broadening their skill sets. Most readers will respond to the book's optimistic mindset, best captured in its final sentence: "The groundwork for success is rooted in the resilient attitudes and behaviours of individuals in relation to the digital environment."—**Richard Nathan Leigh**

314. **E-Learning and the Academic Library: Essays on Innovative Initiatives.** Scott Rice and Margaret N. Gregor, eds. Jefferson, N.C., McFarland, 2016. 192p. index. $55.00pa. ISBN 13: 978-0-7864-9642-6; 978-1-4766-2441-9 (e-book).

How can academic libraries utilize e-learning tools to effectively promote library resources to students? Editors Scott Rice and Margaret Gregor, from Appalachian State University Libraries, thoughtfully consider this question in *E-Learning and the Academic Library.* Thirteen successful e-learning projects are thoughtfully presented from a host of academic environments.

This volume focuses on four areas: orientations; physical and virtual spaces; technology in the classroom; and enhanced reference. Chapters take a case study approach and are written by the librarians that spearheaded these projects. Sections are direct and accessible, examining projects from their initial conception through their implementation. Case studies are also timely; most e-learning initiatives were completed after 2013. Although images from these projects are rarely provided, an effective reference list is included after each chapter.

Enhancing the classroom is the largest and, arguably, the most innovative section. Several libraries created highly engaging student-centered learning tools. These e-learning projects were often created for large academic programs to serve a broad audience. Throughout the volume a wide variety of technology is examined including: Augmented Reality, Chatbots, Crowdsourcing Software, MOOCs, Pinterest, and QR Codes.

Although *E-Learning and the Academic Library* does not cover every aspect of this substantial topic, the selected projects provide a useful blueprint of the major avenues academic libraries should consider. Additionally, most projects are scalable to smaller libraries without a dedicated systems librarian. This is a promising volume on a valuable topic that should be read by librarians that plan to implement e-learning in diverse and creative ways.—**Joshua Becker**

315.   **The Handbook of Art and Design Librarianship.** 2d ed. Paul Glassman and Judy Dyki, eds. Chicago, American Library Association, 2018. 344p. index. $85.00pa.; $76.50pa. (ALA members). ISBN 13: 978-0-8389-1624-7.

The fact that this book is in its second edition is an indication of its necessity and importance. It is divided into six parts with thirty chapters that explore and explain the intricacies and details of art and design librarianship. The six parts are: Roles and Responsibilities, Materials and Collection Development, Teaching and Learning, Knowledge Creation, the Physical Environment, and Promotion and Sustainability. The chapters discuss topics such as governance and administration, the liaison model, accreditation, visual resources from collection to preservation, artists' books, teaching within the ACRL Framework, metaliteracy, art history research, cultural differences, art librarianship and scholarly communication, creating and renovating library spaces, marketing, and social media, to name a few. The appendix contains a number of profiles and descriptions of art and design libraries around the world. This book is essential for any librarian whose duties include these subject areas.—**Bradford Lee Eden**

316.   **Leading in the New Academic Library.** Becky Albitz, Christine Avery, and Diane Zabel, eds. Santa Barbara, Calif., Libraries Unlimited/ABC-CLIO, 2017. 196p. index. $55.00pa. ISBN 13: 978-1-4408-5113-1; 978-1-4408-5114-8 (e-book).

Edited by librarians from Marist College and Penn State University, *Leading in the New Academic Library* thoughtfully approaches many of the challenges faced by college and university libraries in the postrecession era. This volume engages the reader through a variety of complementary perspectives. Numerous institutions are represented, with most contributors discussing their administrative challenges at large research universities and selective liberal arts colleges. A succinct and engaging initial chapter, "The Academic Library's New Role," accurately frames the major issues facing library leadership.

The volume's sixteen chapters are divided into two parts. Challenges and Opportunities details common management issues including: implementing digital repositories, data driven decision making, technological considerations, dwindling budgets, shifting job responsibilities, and reshaping physical spaces. This is the stronger section and provides the richest practical examples. Leadership in the Face of Transformation emphasizes executive qualities and early career preparation. Interestingly, an executive search consultant provides their perspective on the key qualities of successful library directors. Regrettably, little space is devoted to personnel management or collaborations with campus administration.

Leading in the New Academic Library is brisk and conversational. Chapters clearly stress the practical over the theoretical. Although research studies are occasionally mentioned, the tone is usually anecdotal. A more extensive reading list would have been very useful for specialized topics.

Ultimately, *Leading in the New Academic Library* provides a productive overview of common leadership challenges coupled with sound advice on facing these situations. This title is recommended for early and midcareer librarians interested in pursuing administrative roles.—**Joshua Becker**

317.   **The Library Assessment Cookbook.** Aaron Dobbs, ed. Chicago, American Library Association, Association of College and Research Libraries, 2017. 192p. $50.00pa. ISBN 13: 978-0-8389-8866-4.

The fifth volume in the ACRL Cookbook series explores scores of assessment ideas for academic libraries. The nine various sections include topics such as library instruction, websites, service points, library spaces, and outreach. Each assessment project references particular principles in the ACRL Standards for Libraries in Higher Education (2011). There are 80 "recipes" by 122 "cooks" from across the United States, and each spells out the different aspects of a successful assessment: who should conduct it, how long it will take, how to optimally collect the required data, and how to analyze it once gathered. Some assessment projects are quite simple and fairly brief, while others may take more than a semester to complete. Some involve quantitative data, while others use qualitative data, such as open-ended student responses to questions. Some assessment activities involve obtaining information from other campus offices on individual students, data such as ongoing attendance at the school, grade point averages, and graduation dates. It may be that some institutions may not make those data (linked to individuals) available.

The cookbook component of the format is intense, and sometimes distracting: each brief (1-3 page) item includes sections such as "Ingredients," "Cooking Time," "Cooking Technique," and occasionally "Allergy Warning." Words in the titles of some of the assessment projects include "paella," "spice rack," "taste test," "chicken soup," and so on. Nevertheless, this will certainly be a useful guide for academic libraries interested in analyzing their services and other functions; they should certainly consider it.—**Mark Schumacher**

318.   Luo, Lili, Kristine R. Brancolini, and Marie R. Kennedy. **Enhancing Library and Information Research Skills: A Guide for Academic Librarians.** Santa Barbara, Calif., Libraries Unlimited/ABC-CLIO, 2017. 189p. index. $65.00pa. ISBN 13: 978-1-4408-4172-9; 978-1-4408-4173-6 (e-book).

Luo, Brancolini, and Kennedy are not only the three coauthors of this book, but also the three codirectors of the Institute for Research Design in Librarianship (IRDL), a two-week program held at Loyola Marymount University every summer. The goal of the IRDL is to "assist librarians to develop the skills necessary to complete a research project of their design, as well as assist them in constructing a personal network of possible collaborators for future research projects" (p. 173). This book is designed to help academic librarians who cannot attend the institute achieve similar results, albeit without the synergy observed by interacting with equally motivated individuals.

The book is divided into seven chapters. "Academic Librarians as Researchers" and "Overview of the Research Process" provide an introduction to research, showing why research is important for the professional development of librarians and explaining what good research entails. "Research Question and Literature Review," "Research Design and

Methods," "Research Support," and "Disseminating Research Findings" describe each step of the research process. "Becoming a Librarian-Researcher" provides a blueprint for librarians to transition from their first research project into a career in which scholarship, service, and continuing education will play a vital role.

Enhancing Library and Information Research Skills is an informative book, but it may be too abstract for some readers. The central portion thereof could reasonably be mistaken for a book about general research with occasional examples drawn from librarianship, rather than as a guide for library and information research specifically. There are pull-out boxes in some of the chapters where the authors expand upon existing research findings, focusing primarily on the research process itself rather than the results yielded. These are very helpful, but there are too few of them (one in chapter 3 and eight in chapter 4). The introduction and conclusion of the book are excellent because they empower readers to feel that serious research is both achievable and sustainable for any librarian, regardless of institution or department.—**Richard Nathan Leigh**

319.   Martin, Victoria. **Transdisciplinarity Revealed: What Librarians Need to Know.** Santa Barbara, Calif., Libraries Unlimited/ABC-CLIO, 2017. 214p. $85.00pa. ISBN 13: 978-1-4408-4347-1; 978-1-4408-4348-8 (e-book)

This book attempts to reveal what transdisciplinarity is and why it is important for the academy and for librarians. The foreword provides a concise summary of knowledge creation and organization since ancient times and the dynamic between the four modes of knowledge production (disciplinary, multidisciplinary, interdisciplinary, and transdisciplinarity) in current society. The book is divided into two parts: part one, comprised of nine chapters, is an extensive introduction and discussion of transdisciplinarity. Its origins, its practice in scientific research and societal benefit, its involvement as a collaborative enterprise, its engagement within scholarly communication, its practical applications, and the vision of a transdisciplinary university are all explained. Part two, with six chapters, focuses on how librarianship and transdisciplinarity interact and engage one another in knowledge organization, collection development, research and reference services, learning and information literacy, and how to become a transdisciplinary librarian. Overall, this is a very thought-provoking and timely book for academic librarians interested in and wanting to get involved and knowledgeable about the topic of transdisciplinarity.—**Bradford Lee Eden**

320.   **Peer-Assisted Learning in Academic Libraries.** Erin Rinto, John Watts, and Rosan Mitola, eds. Santa Barbara, Calif., Libraries Unlimited/ABC-CLIO, 2017. 220p. index. $65.00pa. ISBN 13: 978-1-4408-4688-5; 978-1-4408-4689-2 (e-book).

This book provides detailed case studies related to peer-assisted learning partnerships in academic libraries. Research shows that students learn and retain information better from their peers; academic libraries have a long history of hiring student employees to assist in daily operations. Providing these student employees with the appropriate training and guidance to assist the library is a win-win situation. Divided into three parts focused on peer-assisted learning as a part of information literacy instruction, co-curricular outreach, and research services, the fourteen case studies range from Research I universities to small liberal arts colleges, providing detailed guidance and experience for those in academic libraries ready to embark on these initiatives and partnerships. In a time when academic libraries are challenged to show their value to the educational vision and mission of the institution, peer-assisted learning becomes a pathway towards documented success and collaboration.—**Bradford Lee Eden**

321.   Polger, Mark Aaron, and Scott Shiedlower. **Engaging Diverse Learners: Teaching Strategies for Academic Librarians.** Santa Barbara, Calif., Libraries Unlimited/ABC-CLIO, 2017. 165p. index. $60.00pa. ISBN 13: 978-1-4408-3850-7; 978-1-4408-3851-4 (e-book).

The modern college experience can reasonably be said to be built upon the idea of bringing together a diverse group of people to learn and foster new concepts of growth. The ongoing question is how to effectively engage people of different socio-economic, generational, racial, and cultural backgrounds, not to mention those who need different learning styles or are of differing physical and developmental abilities, and teach in a way that the information not only sticks but stays relevant long after the class is over. *Engaging Diverse Learners* seeks to provide librarians with a framework to achieve these goals by helping readers to first identify some of the key differences between generations before moving on to look at some learning groups like LGBTQI, ADA, English learners, and so forth.

From examining the generational and learning groups, *Engaging Diverse Learners* transitions to the primary focus of the book: applying teaching techniques intended to reach as many groups as possible. The techniques mentioned are reinforced with real-world examples from the authors' experience or other librarians while the questionnaire that forms the premise for the book is well constructed and included in the appendix for reference. Focusing on how others apply the techniques and including ways for librarians to engage, and disengage, outside of the classroom helps to illustrate how academic librarians can use the diversity of their student bodies to effectively communicate and teach, regardless of background or development.

Probably the largest omission of the book is the lack of a more in-depth examination of the learning groups mentioned in chapter two. Going into additional detail here would be highly beneficial in helping academic librarians better apply the techniques discussed in the latter portions of the book.—**Ian King**

322.   **The Self as Subject: Autoethnographic Research into Identity, Culture, and Academic Leadership.** Anne-Marie Deitering, Richard Stoddart, and Robert Schroeder, eds. Chicago, American Library Association, Association of College and Research Libraries, 2017. 362p. $70.00pa. ISBN 13: 978-0-8389-8892-3.

This rather fascinating volume examines a relatively new research approach, as applied to the academic library world. (Only a half-dozen articles on the topic appear in the library science databases.) These essays create a challenging text, as editor Deitering points out in her introduction: "Autoethnography demands a lot of the reader." Autoethnography can also be challenging because the material and topics it covers can be difficult."(p. 12)

The 16 chapters vary greatly, from a short story to a combination of transcribed conversations, analysis, and interjected reflections by the authors. Given the focus on the authors' individual experiences, the writing is very personal, introspective, and sometimes even sad, irritated, annoyed, or angry. The variety of situations presented does paint a panorama of settings and experiences that librarians in an academic setting might encounter, and the effects of those moments on that individual. Although one chapter's discussion of noise sensitivity, which then evolves into an analysis of racism in America, seems curious, the chapter, like the others, creates a striking image of the life of librarians in a personal way. Libraries in academia, particularly those supporting library science programs, should find these accounts useful. Other libraries will probably feel this tome is "out of scope."—**Mark Schumacher**

323.   **The Small and Rural Academic Library: Leveraging Resources and Overcoming Limitations.** Kaetrena Davis Kendrick and Deborah Tritt, eds. Chicago, American Library Association, Association of College and Research Libraries, 2016. 246p. $56.00pa. ISBN 13: 978-0-8389-8900-5.

Kendrick, Tritt, and their 26 (!) collaborators endeavor to provide "a voice for librarians at small and rural academic libraries, [exploring] how these information professionals keep up with modern academic library practices and innovate with finite resources" (xiii). The editors acknowledge that most academic libraries are responding to the same trends and reacting to the same pressures, but believe that the professional literature has not sufficiently addressed how small and rural academic libraries have been specifically affected. For the purposes of this book, small academic libraries are defined as having less than 3,000 full-time students (in accordance with the Carnegie Classification Size and Setting Definitions).

The book is divided into 5 sections, comprising 11 chapters and 5 brief interviews with relevant practitioners. Library and Outreach Services discusses collaboration, archives, and distance learning. Human Resources and Professional Development discusses staffing and student workers. Planning discusses succession planning and strategic planning. Instruction discusses information literacy and assessment. Technology discusses library systems, online tutorials, and distance learning. Each chapter is formatted in a similar manner, including literature reviews, best practices, and notes/appendixes.

The Small and Rural Academic Library will be of interest primarily to the 6,000+ professional librarians already working in one of the 2,500+ small academic libraries in the United States. Much of this content will also appeal to anyone trying to do "more with less," overcome bureaucracy, or foster innovation. The book may not be an official entrant in the ACRL Cookbook series, but its numerous case studies could be used in an equally practical manner.—**Richard Nathan Leigh**

324.   **So You Want to Be an Academic Library Director.** Colleen S. Harris, ed. Chicago, American Library Association, 2017. 120p. index. $59.00pa.; $53.10pa. (ALA members). ISBN 13: 978-0-8389-1496-0.

This brief volume offers thirteen chapters, written by academic library administrators (many of them directors) from across the United States and Canada, discussing the various skills required of successful library leaders. Those skills range from understanding one's institutional culture, grasping employment law, and developing teamwork in the library, to ongoing strategic planning, supervision of a diverse library faculty, and the maintenance of community relations, among others. (One essay describes a conflict between a provost and a library director, which led to the latter's termination.) As the editor says in the preface, speaking of the chapters to follow, she hopes that "together they will help you see where you may best apply your strengths, hone your skills, and plan your career." (p. viii)

Institutions with library science programs will want to consider this slim text, despite its surprisingly high cost, particularly given the publisher. Some other academic libraries which support schools of education, or have staff interested in moving into library administration, may also wish to consider it.—**Mark Schumacher**

325.   **Students Lead the Library: The Importance of Student Contributions to the Academic Library.** Sara Arnold-Garza and Carissa Tomlinson, eds. Chicago, American Library Association, Association of College and Research Libraries, 2017. 302p. illus. index. $62.00pa. ISBN 13: 978-0-8389-8867-1.

In separate sections, this book looks at college/university students in academic libraries acting as designers, curators, employees, and ambassadors, and student groups as library leaders. Numerous projects in libraries from Southern California to Guelph, Ontario, and New York City, illuminate the range of possibilities for student engagement—1) peer mentoring in a library context, 2) "niche" collections (science fiction, sustainability, etc. developed by students) within a repurposed library space, 3) peer recruitment for library employment, and 4) students handling the social media activity for libraries, among others. The diversity of the endeavors, and the success which they have had, occasionally following adjustments en route, should inspire libraries to explore the possibilities on their campuses.

Two minor shortcomings: there is no information about the authors or editors (one can guess some of it by the mention of institutions within the articles, but no more) and the title and subtitle do not indicate clearly that student workers are the focus of much of this volume. Colleges and universities will certainly benefit from this volume, as they seek to enhance the position and role of their libraries.—**Mark Schumacher**

326.   **Textbooks in Academic Libraries: Selection, Circulation, and Assessment.** Chris Diaz, ed. Chicago, American Library Association, 2018. 148p. index. $65.00pa.; $58.50pa. (ALA Members). ISBN 13: 978-0-8389-1587-5.

College textbook prices have risen almost 100 percent in the last 15 years, and statistics show that over 65 percent of students do not buy textbooks because they cannot afford them. This book examines the challenge academic libraries face regarding whether or not they purchase textbooks, and provides case studies of various institutions that have conducted pilot projects or are exploring textbook purchasing. Given that the top concern of academic administrators is student recruitment and retention, and that the success of many students hinges on whether or not they purchase class textbooks, academic libraries are struggling with how to justify as well as pay for the purchase of textbooks in order to "show their value" to the academic mission. Nine case studies are presented on this challenge, from implementing a textbook reserve program, to balancing a library's budget where textbook purchases are concerned, to student-funded textbook reserve programs. This book will be of interest to all academic libraries struggling through these questions and challenges.—**Bradford Lee Eden**

327.   **Undergraduate Research & The Academic Library: Case Studies and Best Practices.** Merinda Kaye Hensley and Stephanie Davis-Kahl, eds. Chicago, American Library Association, Association of College and Research Libraries, 2017. 322p. $65.00pa. ISBN 13: 978-0-8389-8908-1.

This book contains a collection of twenty-five best practices and case studies related to the academic library and undergraduate research. In the foreword, the editors describe high-impact practices (HIPs) related to student experiences as documented by the

Association of American Colleges and Universities (AAC&U) which include: first-year seminars, learning communities, common intellectual experiences, writing- and inquiry-intensive courses, collaborative assignments and projects, service- and community-based learning, study abroad and other experiences with diversity, undergraduate research, internships, and other types of field experiences, culminating experiences (capstones, projects), and ePortfolios. Real-life experiments, digital projects, research, colloquiums, collaborations, assignments, awards, and partnerships are described throughout the book, illustrating the many ways that academic libraries can engage and lead in the academic mission of their institution. I highly recommend this book for all academic librarians.—**Bradford Lee Eden**

Public Libraries

328.   DiVincenzo, Salvatore, and Elizabeth Malafi. **Supporting Local Businesses and Entrepreneurs in the Digital Age: The Public Librarian's Toolkit.** Santa Barbara, Calif., Libraries Unlimited/ABC-CLIO, 2017. 118p. index. $50.00pa. ISBN 13: 978-1-4408-5152-0; 978-1-4408-5153-7 (e-book).

Supporting Local Businesses and Entrepreneurs in the Digital Age is a strong entry for business support in the public library arena. Adept with matters of business services, Salvatore DiVincenzo and Elizabeth Malafi impart their knowledge coupled with examples from librarians around the United States.

Following typical front matter, each of the nine chapters stands alone though readers will want to pour over the wealth of resources collected here. White space, text, and figures with pie charts, room layouts, and other engaging visuals are all agreeably paced throughout. Moreover, the two authors write with humor and possibility while incorporating a plethora of resource options. Bulleted lists such as "familiarizing yourself with the small business world…" provide fodder for development of a patron base of small businesses. The book closes with a conclusion, bibliography, index, and information about the authors.

Why bother with your community entrepreneurs? "Economic prosperity for the region can translate into success for library with funding through taxes, donations, grants, jobs, and increased library support from patrons." Business owners, those seeking career change, and entrepreneurs, both beginner and experienced, are another patron base for public libraries. This volume offers basics from what a business librarian is to specific business reference questions and how librarians found information. Additional topics include funding, outreach, program ideas, promotion, physical book purchasing, and networking.

In this adult services title, the greatest value is the compilation of resources. Chapter four, "Deep in Data", is comprised of a reviewed selection of subscription database resources (with contact information) and sample reference questions that each database can answer. Of equal measure is the list of free resources found in chapter five.

Librarians, administrators, and support staff will all benefit from the information found in this book. The assemblage of resources listed, both free and subscription, is significant as libraries seek avenues for patron engagement in the business world.

Highly recommended.—**Janis Minshull**

329.   Hunt, Kyla. **Library Programs and Services for New Adults.** Santa Barbara, Calif., Libraries Unlimited/ABC-CLIO, 2017. 148p. illus. index. $45.00pa. ISBN 13: 978-

1-4408-5171-1; 978-1-4408-5418-7 (e-book).

We've all heard of young adults but what is a new adult? The first chapter of this book—"What is a New Adult?"—clearly answers the question. Generally, for the purposes of this book, new adults are people from age 18 to age 29, who fall into the abyss between young adults and older adults. Traditionally, once young adults turned 18, libraries considered them adults. Comprised of twelve chapters and customary back matter, this book explores the concept of new adult services and makes sense with relevant topics, realistic trials, and pragmatic solutions. Tips from librarians such as a "Think about Book Placement" frame, highlighted information boxes, interviews, surveys, and lists such as examples of curated social media accounts create an interesting and readable design. Visually engrained, the emerging adults may not have their own space in the library but this book encourages digital and in-house aesthetics and visuals. Displays, collections, marketing, and online presence require thinking and seeing with a new adult mind. Practical social topics that target this age include meet-ups, movie screenings, and table-top games. Age appropriate challenges like financial challenges give librarians great opportunity to bridge the gap between the unknown and financial literacy. With a more metropolitan (significant size) library in mind, *Library Programs and Services for New Adults* will be useful for librarians with a new adult population. Information here will also be helpful for academic librarians in college towns seeking engagement and practical life skills for students. Recommended.—**Janis Minshull**

330.   Munro, Karen. **Tactical Urbanism for Librarians: Quick, Low-Cost Ways to Make Big Changes.** Chicago, American Library Association, 2017. 164p. index. $57.00pa.; $51.30pa. (ALA members). ISBN 13: 978-0-8389-1558-5.

This book explores tactical methods for building social capital and the overlay of city and library efforts. Its 164 pages are divided into chapters beginning with an introduction and ending with "Summing Up." Several chapters are comprised of case studies with the principles behind the tactic and the nature of the intervention. While the book lacks visual figures or tables, ample white space divides text with bulleted lists, interviews, and sidebars. Topnotch back matter includes extensive references and subject entries via an index.

Finding new paths to increase library service can be challenging. Munro successfully launches a paradigm for tactical efforts in creating organizational change in metropolitan library environments. Action creates results, and this book provides a framework that is sensible and flexible, even for moderate budgets. Generally, these tactics are a short-term and a low-risk commitment where engagement involves a diversity of stakeholders who value intangible benefits. With extensive examples, this book provides both ideas and inspiration. Munro is realistic, however, about challenges associated with taking on a tactical project.

This ALA title will be useful to public library staff and administrators seeking ways to further their reach in metropolitan communities. Recommended.—**Janis Minshull**

331.   Roberts, Ann. **Designing Adult Services: Strategies for Better Serving Your Community.** Santa Barbara, Calif., Libraries Unlimited/ABC-CLIO, 2017. 180p. index. $45.00pa. ISBN 13: 978-1-4408-5254-1; 978-1-4408-5255-8 (e-book).

Author Ann Roberts, reference librarian at the U.S. Patent and Trademark Office, Public Research Facility, has a background in academic, public, and research libraries.

In this title, she addresses adult services from a different perspective—by age group. Following standard front matter, the first chapter provides strong reason to learn about your community and yourself: "knowing your community, knowing your staff, understanding your users' technology needs, and knowing your strengths and weaknesses make for a better opportunity to grow and expand, both as library professionals and with your library services and programs" (p 9). Chapter 10 provides the other bookend for this philosophy, with a conclusion on the importance of and inspiration for adult library services. The intermediate chapters, which explore library service organized by age group, provide the meat of this dialogue. For example, chapter 5, "Midlife Crisis (or Not): Age Group 40-55" explores common themes for this age: empty nesting, caring for caregivers, midlife career changes, and adult summer reading are some of the potential programs for this age target, though many programs fit for a broader age spectrum. All chapters have general information and detailed programming specifics. Literacy options from family to financial, health to homebound are incorporated into age groupings. Rich with information, online links are provided. For the 19-24 age section, a Pew study, (http://libraries.pewinternet. org/2013/06/25/younger-americans-library-services/), shares that over 60% age 16-29 have used a library at least once a year. Links like this provide information specialists with additional fodder to understand what their library needs in services and to back budgetary requests. Additionally, 6 appendixes offer examples of forms, policies, and surveys that will support changes to adult services. Lacking in this book is a chapter on intergenerational programming where the overlap of groups would be represented. Best suited for public library administrators and staff seeking new vision, *Designing Adult Services* will give ample opportunity to view these services from a different perspective and move forward with tangible ideas.

Recommended.—**Janis Minshull**

332.   Taylor, Nick D. **Raising the Tech Bar at Your Library: Improving Services to Meet User Needs.** Santa Barbara, Calif., Libraries Unlimited/ABC-CLIO, 2017. 120p. index. $50.00pa. ISBN 13: 978-1-4408-4496-6; 978-1-4408-4497-3 (e-book).

In this book, Nick D. Taylor inspires librarians to incorporate technological advancements into modern library services. The 120-page guide has 7 text-only chapters, each commencing with a summary box for ease of use. Five appendixes supplement the text with a library technology plan and visuals. The black-and-white charts are somewhat ineffective due to the limited color gradation. Public libraries evolve and *Raising the Tech Bar at Your Library* offers librarians the tools to understand, assess community need, train staff, market, teach, and evaluate technology services. Business collaboration, the digital divide, makerspaces, personal devices, STEAM prospects, and more are discussed. The nuts and bolts of accessibility, affordability (found at the close of each chapter), data evaluation, digital literacy, hiring tech staff, marketing, program design, and technology evaluation are just some of the hands-on elements found in this book. Training of staff is given priority as is discussion of teaching styles

Raising the Tech Bar at Your Library is best suited for public library administrators and staff seeking to keep in step with the partnership between libraries and technology for improved community services and relevance. Recommended.—**Janis Minshull**

School Libraries

333.   Farmer, Lesley S. J. **Managing the Successful School Library: Strategic Planning and Reflective Practice.** Chicago, American Library Association, 2017. 264p. index. $60.00pa. ISBN 13: 978-0-8389-1494-6.

This is one of those rare professional books that school librarians will want to keep on the shelf and refer to time and again. Farmer packs a lot of information about managing a school library into the book's 12 chapters: from resources to facilities to funding and more. In her chapter on managing communications, Farmer addresses advocacy with insight, and school librarians will welcome the lists of resources and sample letters provided. Included in each chapter are textboxes labeled "Food for Thought" that serve as catalysts for reflection. Sample spreadsheets and forms are plentiful and are easy to reproduce. Lists of references are included at the end of each chapter. Farmer's book will prepare school librarians to become more strategic as well as more reflective in their planning and practice. A bibliography and an index round out the work. Highly recommended.—**Susan Yutzey**

334.   Graves, Colleen, Aaron Graves, and Diana L. Rendina. **Challenge-Based Learning in the School Library Makerspace.** Santa Barbara, Calif., Libraries Unlimited/ABC-CLIO, 2017. 136p. index. $45.00pa. ISBN 13: 978-1-4408-5150-6; 978-1-4408-5151-3 (e-book).

This book is a must-have for librarians who want to build a makerspace from scratch or improve an existing one. It includes a concise yet comprehensive overview of makerspaces, as well as practical advice about what it takes to develop a maker mindset and maintain a vibrant schoolwide makerspace. Drawing on the experience and expertise of the authors, the book offers a clear definition of what a makerspace is and goes on to include strategies for connecting students to both local and global communities, crafting interactive spaces, balancing guided instruction and tinkering, distinguishing between design thinking and design process, and providing concrete examples of design challenges for K-12 grade levels. In addition, insight from leading experts in the field such as Gina Seymour, A.J. Juliani, John Spencer, Jay Silver, Laura Fleming, Ryan Jenkins, and Kristina Holzweiss adds authenticity and credibility to the text. Each chapter includes inclusive strategies suggestions and concludes with a list of action steps and references. The book includes a bibliography and a glossary. Highly recommended.—**Melissa Thom**

335.   **Guided Inquiry Design in Action: High School.** Leslie K. Maniotes, ed. Santa Barbara, Calif., Libraries Unlimited/ABC-CLIO, 2017. 254p. index. (Guided Inquiry Series). $40.00pa. ISBN 13: 978-1-4408-4711-0; 978-1-4408-4712-7 (e-book).

This is the second title in a series that focuses on how to undertake Guided Inquiry Design. For high school practitioners, this book fills a need to see examples of Guided Inquiry Design in action. The first half of the book examines the Guided Inquiry Design process, while the second half provides fully tested exemplar unit plans in a range of subject fields. In chapter five, Carol Kuhlthau focuses on the student's emotional journey and covers the responses that educators can provide to support student knowledge construction through inquiry-based learning. In chapter 11, Leslie Maniotes addresses the challenges of getting started and handling change with Guided Inquiry Design. Whether you are a librarian just beginning the inquiry-based learning journey or a veteran, you will find this title a welcome addition to the professional shelf. Highly recommended.—**Susan Yutzey**

336.   Howard, Jody K. **The School Librarian as Curriculum Leader.** Santa Barbara, Calif., Libraries Unlimited/ABC-CLIO, 2017. 117p. index. (Library and Information Science Text Series). $45.00pa. ISBN 13: 978-1-59884-990-5; 978-1-4408-4407-2 (e-book).

This book, intended for the instructors of preservice school library students, presents a solid introduction to the components and theories necessary for the development and use of curriculum in a school library program. Each chapter begins with an explanation of the desired outcomes and a paragraph that states what the reader should know after finishing the chapter. Beginning with basic definitions of curriculum and leadership, the first chapters present different models and approaches for both. Reflective questions at the end of each chapter are helpful to assess the reader's understanding of the concepts and ideas outlined. The book then discusses applications of curriculum and leadership, providing examples and strategies that contribute to curriculum and collection development in classrooms and school libraries. The importance of learning theory is included as well, with a focus on inquiry and essential questions. This book is recommended for professionals who are searching for a text to use as an introduction to the role of curriculum in the school library. However, preservice school library students will require additional texts to fully grasp many of the concepts and theories included in the book. Recommended.—**Emily Rozmus**

337.   **The Many Faces of School Library Leadership.** 2d ed. Sharon Coatney and Violet H. Harada, eds. Santa Barbara, Calif., Libraries Unlimited/ABC-CLIO, 2017. 184p. index. $50.00pa. ISBN 13: 978-1-4408-4897-1; 978-1-4408-4898-8 (e-book).

For the second edition—for a review of the first edition, (see ARBA 2011, entry 519)—Coatney and Harada have completely revised this primer for both new school librarians and veterans looking to step up their leadership, advocacy skills, and opportunities. The concept of the librarian as a leader is explored as it manifests in the areas of literacy, technology, intellectual freedom, curriculum, professional development, and more. Experts in the field provide not only theoretical discussions but also case studies from school librarians in the trenches. Readers are given questions and checklists for program evaluation and to help guide their own practice. This meaty book is one that could be used as a springboard for PLCs and task forces and also as an inspirational manual for solo school librarians. Each chapter provides numerous detailed references to help interested readers dive deeper. Recommended.—**Michelle Glatt**

338.   Wallace, Virginia L., and Whitney N. Husid. **Collaborating for Inquiry-Based Learning: School Librarians and Teachers Partner for Student Achievement.** 2d ed. Santa Barbara, Calif., Libraries Unlimited/ABC-CLIO, 2017. 134p. index. $45.00pa. ISBN 13: 978-1-4408-5284-8; 978-1-4408-5285-5 (e-book).

This book is a highly academic text that focuses primarily on the process of guiding and assessing learning outcomes of Inquiry-Based Learning (IBL). Chapters cover everything from understanding student needs to reflecting on the project once it is complete and conclude with a particularly useful list of resources for further reading. Despite the title, the authors spend little time explaining how, when, and why school librarians and classroom teachers can partner to achieve IBL, or the many ways that their roles and expertise might differ. Future editions would do well to provide more insight and example projects from real school librarians and classroom teachers across grade levels and content areas who have successfully worked together using this model. While the text is geared toward all educators, high school libraries in communities wanting to learn more about IBL may find it more applicable to their needs.—**Alexandra Quay**

339.   Weisburg, Hilda K. **Leading for School Librarians: There is No Other Option.** Chicago, American Library Association, 2017. 176p. index. $45.00pa.; $40.50pa. (ALA members). ISBN 13: 978-0-8389-1510-3.

School librarians play a number of vital roles in their profession, and this book explores each one succinctly. The sections about leadership, communication, teaching, and developing strengths are highlights. Weisburg offers a bit of history and theory along with plenty of practical advice that new and experienced librarians can read today and use tomorrow. Ideas for ongoing development and what it means to be a professional are explored throughout. Key ideas are bulleted at the end of each chapter. This slim volume is essential reading for all school librarians. An index rounds out the work. Highly recommended.—**C. Ellen Wickham**

Special Topics

Archives

340.   Phillips, Faye. **Creating a Local History Archive at Your Public Library.** Chicago, American Library Association, 2018. 162p. illus. index. (ALA Guides for the Busy Librarian). $57.00pa.; $51.30pa. (ALA members). ISBN 13: 978-0-8389-1566-0.

Public libraries are frequently valuable sources of local and regional history information stressing the unique personal, political, economic, and social aspects of their surrounding areas. This work describes ways of creating an effective local history archive in public libraries.

Chapter contents include defining, creating, and developing a local history archive; collection development policies for these libraries; acquiring and making local history collections accessible; and caring for a local history archive. Specific topics addressed within these chapters include developing institutional mission statements and materials management policies; focusing on user needs; determining gift acquisition and deaccessioning policies; appraising and acquiring collections and setting processing priorities; legally transferring materials from private ownership to a public archive; budgeting; determining levels of collection arrangement and description; copyright; developing finding aids; providing reference service; digitization; preservation; and addressing collection security, disaster awareness, prevention, and recovery.

This is a good introduction to the multiple factors and processes involved in setting up a local history archive. It provides good guidance on types of materials to include in such a collection including personal records and genealogical resources. An area where it falls short, however, is emphasizing the importance of local government records in documenting government history. Such records document legal activities including probate, property taxes, criminal justice, and government policy-making including local ordinance; they also record the activities of agencies as varied as city councils, mayor's offices, commissions, police, parks, fire departments, and emergency management agencies, as well as local government interaction and correspondence with other adjacent local governments, state governments, and federal government agencies and policy-makers. Material as varied as environmental impact statements, land use and educational policy, economic development or retrenchment, election results, demography, births, marriages, divorces, and deaths, and local business conditions will also be reflected in local government information resources and statistics. Failure to include print, microform, and electronic government records in a local history archive is a grievous dereliction of this repository's duty to its users and appropriators.

This is a useful work in spite of its weaknesses but possible future editions of it should place much greater emphasis on the criticality of government information resources in local history collections.—**Bert Chapman**

Careers

341.   **Becoming an Independent Information Professional: How to Freelance, Consult, and Contract for Fun and Profit.** Melissa M. Powell, ed. Santa Barbara, Calif., Libraries Unlimited/ABC-CLIO, 2017. 158p. index. $50.00pa. ISBN 13: 978-1-4408-5540-5; 978-1-4408-5541-2 (e-book).

This book is designed as a how-to for professional librarians who want to pursue self-employment. The germane "Foreword" is written by Loida Garcia-Febo, an international librarian, consultant, and educator. Garcia-Febo states that "today's librarians are driving change, and library consultants are right there with them jointly driving this change in cities, countries, and the world" (p xii).

Editor Powell has aptly interwoven information from experts in the field of library consulting. The book is comprised of eight chapters, starting with "Is Consulting Work For You?" From self-assessment to practical advice on financial, legal, marketing, and management, the advice is from practicing consultants. Insights are experience-based and both the plusses and minuses of working as an independent information professional are addressed. Designed for ease of reading while distributing a wealth of information, this guide includes: bulleted lists, examples, figures, highlighted information boxes and tips, a question-and-answer section, sample forms, and tables. Researchers will find the "Resources" and "Further Reading" concluding sections in each chapter extremely valuable. Whether seeking a full-time independent career or a side hustle, readers will find this to be an exceptional tool. Best use will be for librarians or LIS students seeking independent work.

Highly recommended.—**Janis Minshull**

Cataloging and Classification

342.   Chan, Lois Mai, Sheila S. Intner, and Jean Weihs. **Guide to the Library of Congress Classification.** 6th ed. Santa Barbara, Calif., Libraries Unlimited/ABC-CLIO, 2016. 376p. index. $75.00pa. ISBN 13: 978-1-4408-4433-1; 978-1-4408-4434-8 (e-book).

The first revision/update since 1999, this work presents in great detail the organization and structure of the classification system used by the United States national library (and now by numerous countries around the world). Hundreds of examples showing line-by-line explanations of call number building cover all the classes of items, from decorative arts and international relations to vocal music and internal medicine, among many others. Some examples are rather exotic: Fishing Saskatchewan and Fifty years of Bay Area art, for example. Special categories of materials are explored as well: government documents, publications with corporate authors, translations, comic books, individual maps, and annotated bibliographies, which can fall outside standard classification treatment.

Given its detail throughout, this volume is clearly aimed at readers with a deep interest in the classification process within the setting of the LC system. Universities offering a program in library science will certainly want to have this volume, but other academic institutions may well want to add a copy for their library staff.—**Mark Schumacher**

343.   Joudrey, Daniel N., and Katherine M. Wisser. **Organization of Information.** 4th ed. Santa Barbara, Calif., Libraries Unlimited/ABC-CLIO, 2018. 722p. index. (Library and Information Science Text Series). $75.00. ISBN 13: 978-1-59884-859-5; 978-1-4408-6129-1 (e-book).

For nearly twenty years, *The Organization of Information* has introduced budding technical services librarians to the tools and underlying principles of their profession. When the first edition appeared in 1999, it focused on traditional retrieval tools and well-established standards like MARC (Machine Readable Cataloging) and AACR2 (Anglo-American Cataloging Rules, Second Edition) for describing sources of information. Subsequent years, however, have seen an increase in different encoding standards and controlled vocabularies, even as the basic goals of identifying and enabling the retrieval of resources have remained the same. RDA (Resource Description & Access) has replaced AACR2 as a bibliographic standard, the computing concept of linked data has gained currency, and institutions (most notably, the Library of Congress) have taken on the ambitious task of investigating alternatives to MARC.

The third edition published in 2009 (see ARBA 2010, entry 557). The revised and expanded fourth edition offers a comprehensive survey of the intellectual and practical aspects of organizing information, highlighting the similarities and differences between libraries, archives, and museums and reflecting recent developments. The authors navigate their subject matter with feet rooted in the past and eyes pointed to the future, providing useful historical context on the one hand and a clear yet detailed explanation of linked data and the Semantic Web on the other. They remind the reader why card catalogs were innovative in their day and why controlled vocabularies are so important in the Internet age. They demonstrate the ways technological advances have broken down boundaries between cultural heritage institutions and the computing and library science disciplines. Above all, they affirm the value of the work of organizing information sources, even in the face of rapid changes.

The fourth edition of *The Organization of Information* is an essential text that is worthy of its predecessors.—**Craig Mury Keeney**

344.   Shaw, Marie Keen. **Cataloging Library Resources: An Introduction.** Lanham, Md., Rowman & Littlefield, 2017. 262p. index. $35.00pa.; $33.00 (e-book). ISBN 13: 978-1-4422-7486-0; 978-1-4422-7487-7 (e-book).

Written with all the library jargon defined and explained, this guide to cataloging contains a wealth of information and practical guidance. The book discusses the history of Dewey Decimal and Library of Congress classification systems, the advent of MARC records, the evolution of cataloging as new and different material formats have come on the scene and topics and subjects have expanded or emerged, and current RDA cataloging as well as what's coming in the future. Each chapter begins with one or more ALA-LSSC competency standards and a text box of key terms. A summary, discussion questions, practice activities, notes, and additional resources finish each chapter. Relevant information is condensed and presented in tables. There are numerous black-and-white photos and computer screenshots to illustrate the text, though details are difficult to make out in some. This text would be useful to students in library school or new catalogers in current practice. It would also be helpful to experienced catalogers to bring them up to date or to librarians in settings where they must do their own cataloging from time to time. An index rounds out the work. Recommended.—**Cynthia Ortiz**

Children's and Young Adult Services

345.   Alessio, Amy J., Katie LaMantia, and Emily Vinci. **50+ Fandom Programs: Planning Festivals and Events for Tweens, Teens, and Adults.** Chicago, American Library Association, 2017. 162p. index. $49.00pa.; $44.10pa. (ALA members). ISBN 13: 978-0-8389-1552-3.

An excellent resource for librarians who want to provide their patrons an opportunity to interact with others who share their passion for a series, genre, television show, game, sport, and much more. A variety of fandom events are offered including fan fiction, *Game of Thrones,* big board games, medieval fest, killer Stephen King night, plus many others. The resource provides information on how to run each program including prep time, program length, ideal number of patrons, suggested age range, supplies, activities, and marketing. Depending on the program type, many programs also offer crafts and costume ideas, trivia, other free games, and variations to make the program adaptable for different age groups. In addition, key terms and resources are also provided to keep up with popular fandoms. This is a great guide for anyone wishing to step up their programming for all age ranges.—**Shelly Lee**

346.   Flowers, Sarah. **Crash Course in Young Adult Library Services.** Santa Barbara, Calif., Libraries Unlimited/ABC-CLIO, 2017. 138p. index. $45.00pa. ISBN 13: 978-1-4408-5170-4; 978-1-4408-5171-1 (e-book).

Written by retired librarian Sarah Flowers, who has an extensive background in Young Adult (YA) services, this 138-page guide includes an introduction, 9 chapters, 3 appendixes, a listing for extended reading, and an index. The content will inspire all professionals working with teenagers, though may not be as useful for libraries without YA Staff or space. Chapters are concise and pertain to heading areas. The book uses bulleted listings where relevant and provides examples of forms such as Teen Volunteer Applications. Inclusion of data from the 2010 U.S. Census, Annie E. Casey Foundation, the Association for Library Services to Children (ALSC), Nielsen Surveys, Pew Research, the Young Adult Library Services Association (YALSA), and others provides solid data to support library staff in augmenting teen services. The 9 core values of the teen services profession as determined by YALSA (http://www.ala.org/yalsa/core-professional-values-teen-services-profession) well influence this handbook. Information is timely with practical ideas of how to connect with today's schools and students. Topics of collection development, college readiness, displays, mobile communication, online presence, physical space, and transliteracy complement book talks, reader's advisory, and reference interviews. This all-in-one crash course customarily mentions engagement and listening, key to strong YA library services. "One of the best ways to develop good, positive relationships with teens in the library is to involve them." (p. 18). From how the teen brain works (chapter 1) to programming (chapter 4) and teen informational needs (chapter 5), *Crash Course in Young Adult Services* gives both tangible ideas and ethical philosophies. As a reviewer with vast experience in YA library services, I must note the lack of mention of how students can teach adults the value of teens in the library community. This, too, is an important part of staff training for creating a positive, respectful YA atmosphere and more detail would be pragmatic. This title will be useful for public library YA specialists, school library media specialists, and other library staff seeking to develop, expand, and enhance teen services in library environments as well as in the virtual world. Recommended.—**Janis Minshull**

347.   Huang, Brian, and Derek Runberg. **The Arduino Inventor's Guide.** San Francisco, Calif., No Starch Press, 2017. 360p. $29.95pa. ISBN 13: 978-1-59327-652-2.

Have you thought of purchasing an Arduino for your makerspace but are unsure of what to do with it? This book can give you the first steps and start you and your students off with 10 projects of increasing difficulty. Create a stoplight, a balance beam, or even a tiny electric piano! Readers get not only an overview of Arduino, but also a brief primer on electricity and electronics. Each project includes a list of needed materials and step-by-step directions with color photographs and/or screenshots of code. Tips and directions for soldering and using craft knives and multimeters are covered as well. Beware that there is no index and some of the technical details of the electronics can seem a bit overwhelming to the novice, but the book is very clear on the steps to take within a project. This book assumes that the user knows nothing about Arduino, so it provides a basic starting point to become familiar with and confident in its use. This book would be a great addition for makerspaces that want to take coding and electronics to the next level. Recommended for grades 9 and up.—**Lisa Castellano**

348.   Kepple, Sarah. **Library Robotics: Technology and English Language Arts Activities for Ages 8-24.** Santa Barbara, Calif., Libraries Unlimited/ABC-CLIO, 2015. 157p. index. $22.50pa. ISBN 13: 978-1-4408-3558-2; 978-1-4408-3559-9 (e-book).

This book is a must-have tool for librarians who are interested in developing robotics in their libraries. It is a start-up kit for librarians who are beginners in this area and want to gain general knowledge about library robotics. The main advantage of this book is that the content is divided in logical, coherent chapters. It starts with the simple definition of a robot and ends with a set of activities using robots for technology and English language arts activities. With each chapter a reader develops a systematic, cogent chain of robotics knowledge with the help of detailed information. One of the most important chapters is chapter four because a reader can find valuable tips about how to create a logic model of his or her robotics project. The example of a logic model is transformed each time a new element is added, and it is shown visually in the tables. The elements include an impact statement, outcomes, activities, inputs, outputs, and indicators. The logic model is crucial for a librarian who wants to strategically plan his or her goals and to present them to a funder or a boss. Because buying and installing robots in libraries can be expensive, chapter three provides different agencies and organizations that support and fund robotics projects on a small or large scale. The book has illustrations, an appendix, notes, a glossary, references, a bibliography, and index pages for easier navigation and future studies.

One technical shortage is that chapter three does not have any illustrations of the robots and robot kits. The chapter describes the robots, such as "Bee-Bot," "Cubelets," "Lego WeDo," "Lego Mindstorms," and others, but there is no single illustration that helps a reader distinguish one robot from another.

Despite that, the book is full of valuable insights about library robotics. The examples of ready-to-go activities in the last chapters present for librarians a good start for future inspiration and creation.—**Maria Agee**

349.   McChesney, Elizabeth M., and Bryan W. Wunar. **Summer Matters: Making All Learning Count.** Chicago, American Library Association, 2017. 134p. illus. index. $50.00pa. ISBN 13: 978-0-8389-1561-5.

Want to make your library a welcoming place and your summer learning program better? This book was written by a librarian and a museum director team after they decided to improve their summer reading program. This book discusses what they did, describes the partnership with the Chicago Public Library and the Museum of Science and Industry, and provides suggestions for other libraries to follow.

After deciding to follow research-based practices they settled on STEAM and one big idea from science as a theme each week. STEAM, which originates from STEM, goes a step beyond science, technology, engineering, and math to incorporate the arts. STEAM helps children to be better creative thinkers, problem solvers, and evaluators of information. The authors ultimately wanted their participants to be excited about the libraries and excited about the summer program.

The book provides an excellent blueprint to follow with well-laid-out chapters starting with the rationale for change and ending with managing change. Chapters in between cover the role of STEAM; evaluation, assessment, and continuous improvement; and other topics. The book helps guide the reader through change and assessment, supplies research sources, contains many useful ideas, and answers a multitude of questions, like "what about the mess?" In the forward there is a letter from Mayor Rahm Emanuel and Commissioner Brian Bannon espousing the importance of this type of program to libraries, cities, and ultimately to the children they serve. The book ends with an extremely useful appendix with sample forms; resource, vendor, and store lists; and a bibliography.

I believe the book is a good resource for any library that wants to do a better job with summer programs but also for other institutions that would like to have a quality summer learning program for children.—**Kathy Adams**

350.   Mediavilla, Cindy. **Creating & Managing the Full-Service Homework Center.** Chicago, American Library Association, 2018. 172p. index. $54.00pa.; $48.60pa. (ALA members). ISBN 13: 978-0-8389-1618-6.

Creating & Managing the Full-Service Homework Center supports the findings of a 2013 American Library Association survey which established that practically all U.S. public libraries now offer online and in-person homework assistance. This service is especially important in rural areas because libraries offer high-speed Internet access that many households cannot afford. This imaginative book offers librarians a unique opportunity to fashion creative learning centers.

Material is presented in a workbook format that includes essential tools to initiate the journey towards successful student study centers. The decision making process requires addressing pressing issues early. Model program examples help. This insightful publication offers examples of necessary paperwork and explores essential information including space, location, service hours, funding job duties and training, supplies and equipment, resources, and media and public relations.

Creating & Managing the Full-Service Homework Center may be described as a ready-made kit that paves the road for engaging learners who otherwise may "fall through the cracks" because of circumstances beyond their control. The content is inspiring and offers straightforward advice for professionals interested in developing homework centers that support curriculum needs. Every librarian who strives to meet the learning needs of today's youth needs to read this book. In addition, teachers and trainers would find this contribution to be an essential planning tool to assist in curriculum foundations.—**Thomas E. Baker**

351.   Pierce, Jennifer Burek. **Sex, Brains, & Video Games: Information and Inspiration for Youth Services Librarians.** 2d ed. Chicago, American Library Association, 2017. 202p. index. $57.00pa.; $51.30pa. (ALA members). ISBN 13: 978-0-8389-1548-6.

In its second edition, *Sex, Brains, and Video Games: Information and Inspiration for Youth Services Librarians* by Jennifer Burek Pierce serves as a good introduction for librarians who serve teens, but who may not interact with them daily. Written in six chapters, the handbook begins with basic information about teens including some demographics, the definition of adolescence, and several myths and widely accepted common misconceptions regarding teens. Other chapters cover diversity, sex and sexualities, the science of the adolescent brain, and interacting with different types of media. This resource is a good choice for those who serve teens, but who may not fully understand them. After all, it is imperative for librarians to understand the patrons they serve.—**Shelly Lee**

352.   Williams, Connie Hamner. **Understanding Government Information: A Teaching Strategy Toolkit for Grades 7-12.** Santa Barbara, Calif., Libraries Unlimited/ABC-CLIO, 2017. $50.00pa. ISBN 13: 978-1-4408-4349-5; 978-1-4408-4350-1 (e-book).

There is a wealth of U.S. government information that is available for educators and students, and this book is designed "to help teachers and school librarians uncover the vast array of United States government resources that are mostly available on the Internet but exist largely beyond the reach of typical student search" (p xiii). The book's four primary sections are: Getting Geeky with Government Information; Tools of the Trade: Toolkit; Design Ideas: Classroom Strategy; and Blueprint Agencies and Institutions. Whether group or individual research, lesson plans will support student inquiry. For example, in "The Presidential Brief," students are encouraged "to collate the best information possible from the most reliable sources to guide the best policy decisions" (p. 74), much the same as those in public office might. Branches of government, contemporary issues, and exposure to timely resources make this a solid entry for information studies. Teachers and librarians will need to instruct students initially because of the depth of federal resources found here.

Understanding Government Information is a practical source for educators who work with students in grades 7-12 in the areas of science, history, government, civics, health, and agriculture. Recommended.—**Janis Minshull**

Collection Development

353. **Audio Recorders to Zucchini Seeds: Building a Library of Things.** Mark Robison and Lindley Shedd, eds. Santa Barbara, Calif., Libraries Unlimited/ABC-CLIO, 2017. 271p. illus. index. $65.00pa. ISBN 13: 978-1-4408-5019-6; 978-1-4408-5020-2 (e-book).

This interesting book provides information and case studies on the "things" movement in libraries—library collections centered around lending items other than books. These items include seeds, video game consoles, bicycles, musical instruments, sewing machines, and so much more; items that don't necessarily satisfy an information need but a more practical, material need. In the introduction, the editors define and discuss this movement, also called the sharing economy. They describe why libraries are doing this type of service, the pros and cons, and how both innovation and value are combined in this philosophy. Fourteen case studies follow, detailing services already mentioned (seeds and bicycles) to other fascinating services (tools, toys, board games, curriculum materials, media production equipment, endoscopes, microscopes, telescopes, furs, skulls, and mounts). Best practices for building one's own Library of Things is included, as well as a number of appendixes documenting lending agreements, checklists, return forms, and consent issues. I haven't seen a book like this before, so I highly recommend it for all libraries, given that the case studies include public, special, and academic library examples.—**Bradford Lee Eden**

354. **Public Library Core Collection: Nonfiction. Collection Development Recommendations by Librarians for Librarians.** 16th ed. Wyatt, Neal, Kendal Spires, and Gabriela Toth, eds. Bronx, N.Y., H. W. Wilson, 2017. 3028p. index. (Core Collection Series). $420.00. ISBN 13: 978-1-68217-071-7; 978-0-8242-1462-3 (e-book).

Now in its 16th edition, the *Public Library Core Collection: Nonfiction* continues to aid librarians tasked with purchasing and collection maintenance. The book also serves as a readers' advisory aid, as a place to verify bibliographic data, and as an instructional aid in courses covering literature and book selection in public libraries.

Inside users will find approximately 12,000 reference and nonfiction titles; a star at the beginning of an entry indicates that a book is most highly recommended (1,700 titles in this edition are so marked). A slate of experienced librarians from both academic and public libraries selected the titles for inclusion (the advisory board is listed in the book's acknowledgments). This core collection includes new and old titles, all of which were in print at the time of publication. Older titles have been retained if they remain the best resource in a given area. There have been significant revisions in the areas of STEM, graphic novels, and weeding.

The introduction explains the organization of the book into two parts, the Classified Collection and the Author, Title, and Subject Index. Part one is organized by Dewey Decimal Classification and includes bibliographical information along with book annotations. The section begins with an Outline of Classification that also serves as a table of contents for the first part of the book. The extensive index (which includes *see* and *see also* references) also facilitates searching.

For those who prefer database content, free trial information is available at https://www.ebscohost.com/public/core-collections.

Recommended.—**ARBA Staff Reviewer**

355. Verminski, Alana, and Kelly Marie Blanchat. **Fundamentals of Electronic Resources Management.** Chicago, American Library Association, 2017. 252p. index. (ALA Fundamentals Series). $65.00pa.; $58.50pa. (ALA members). ISBN 13: 978-0-8389-1541-7.

This short introductory book, part of the American Library Association's Fundamentals Series, is meant to provide new information professionals a practical foundation for electronic resources management. Main topics include negotiation and licensing, setting up and maintaining access, usage statistics, questions to ask library vendors, marketing electronic resources, and emerging trends. Although chapters are relatively short and only offer a broad overview, a list of recommended readings at the end of each chapter provides historical context or more complete explanations. The recommended readings include articles from prominent journals in the field of serials management, including *Serials Review, Journal of Electronic Resources Librarianship,* and *The Serials Librarian.* Within chapters are shaded sections highlighting acronyms relevant to the content, key advice, or take-home points. Two appendixes provide a rubric for evaluating open access resources and a license review checklist. The latter is particularly useful as it is very extensive and makes librarians aware of details they may have never considered when examining licenses. Finally, there is a 15-page glossary that helps define jargon regularly used when dealing with electronic resources. Overall, the authors, Alana Verminski and Kelly Marie Blanchat, have done a nice job introducing the most important factors to consider when managing electronic resources. Without the selective reading list at the end of each chapter, the content might be too general to help professionals take leadership for their library's electronic resources. Since these readings are included, this book is a great first step. Recommended for academic libraries, new information professionals, or experienced librarians taking on new responsibilities.—**Kevin McDonough**

Customer Service

356. Marquez, Joe J., and Annie Downey. **Getting Started in Service Design: A How-To-Do-It Manual for Librarians.** Chicago, American Library Association, 2017. 108p. illus. $60.00pa.; $54.00pa. (ALA members). ISBN 13: 978-0-8389-1564-6.

Written by Joe. J. Marquez and Annie Downey, *Getting Started in Service Design* will stand on its own, even though it was designed to supplement to *Library Service Design: A LITA Guide* (2016).

With 108 pages, divided over five chapters, this professional development title endorses understanding library users and empowering them by actively engaging customers in service evolution; involving users in the process of designing, implementing, and assessing library services creates real services. The opening page of each chapter is designed with a right-side margin summarizing details included therein. Further support is found in the back matter—three appendixes, an extended reading list, and bibliographic information. This book lacks an index.

Customer service is central to all types of libraries and this book provides a concrete resource for modification of services. Let's face it, as librarians we believe we are experts in service but evaluation needs to be part of our service design. "When we rethink services, we must reconsider the current inherited ecology to determine what does and does not work. Essentially, we must allow our services to evolve with our users." This manual emphasizes a holistic approach using collaboration, partnership, and service provision in considering user behaviors and expectations. In viewing the library from the user's perspective, design and delivery of services will mirror characteristics inherent to unique community needs.

Lush with tables, figures, worksheets, and visual prompts, this book will benefit library staff in finding a navigational route in what can be a daunting process. Prompts such as the Library Service Design Heuristics actively involve staff in the evaluation process while tables such as Table 3.1, Team Recruitment Form, define persons participating. The multiphase process, described in full earlier in the book, all comes together in chapter four where extensive research tool options from focus groups, journals, and mobile ethnography are provided.

Highly recommended.—**Janis Minshull**

357.   **Protecting Patron Privacy: A LITA Guide.** Bobbi Newman and Bonnie Tijerina, eds. Lanham, Md., Rowman & Littlefield, 2017. 142p. index. $45.00pa.; $42.00 (e-book). ISBN 13: 978-1-4422-6970-5; 978-1-4422-6971-2 (e-book).

Protecting Patron Privacy is a slim but information-packed book which delves into the issues facing a modern library in protecting their patron's privacy. A range of experts on privacy issues contribute to seven sections each focused on a specific privacy issue.

From the historical foundations of patron privacy in libraries, to what that means for libraries in a technology-saturated, modern-day world—think of everything from social networking to RFID library cards and physical materials—*Protecting Patron Privacy* covers the issue in understandable prose. Most chapters have a conclusion as well as a notes section and bibliography.

Protecting Patron Privacy would be an excellent resource for any librarian or information technology person employed at a public or academic library.—**Alicia Brillon**

Digitization and Digital Libraries

358.   Monson, Jane D. **Getting Started with Digital Collections: Scaling to Fit Your Organization.** Chicago, American Library Association, 2017. 192p. index. $69.00pa.; $62.10pa. (ALA members). ISBN 13: 978-0-8389-1543-1.

Getting Started with Digital Collections covers the many areas of digital collections from planning projects to preservation strategies. The preface states that smaller organizations face unique challenges, especially having limited staff to devote to digital collections. The purpose of this book is to provide key information needed to start a digitization project. This book is for the novice beginner who needs a good grounding in the basic skills and vocabulary associated with the many stages of digital collections.

One of the themes of the book is to find solutions that fit your institution. Monson suggests that we refrain from copying the workflow of a large university or cultural heritage institution because each institution has different limitations and assets that it can use in any project. The book contains two parts. Part one is a basic introduction to managing projects. It is possible to skim some of these chapters if the reader is not a true novice and has a basic understanding of project management and collaborations. Part two contains helpful information on varied areas within digital collections with chapters on image conversion (digitization), metadata, copyright, preservation, and content management systems. One of the best features of this book is the list of suggestions on where to look for additional learning and resources.

I would recommend if you are new to the field or are transitioning into digital collections.—**Susan Elkins**

Information Literacy

359.   Broussard, Mary Snyder. **Reading, Research, and Writing: Teaching Information Literacy with Process-Based Research Assignments.** Chicago, American Library Association, Association of College and Research Libraries, 2017. 132p. $40.00pa. ISBN 13: 978-0-8389-8875-6.

The research assignment has become ubiquitous in higher education. The research assignment encourages learning about a topic, while also testing students' skills in reading comprehension and writing; yet, despite its use, faculty, instructors, teachers, and librarians are often unsatisfied with the quality of students' work. In this book, Mary Snyder Broussard, Assistant Professor and Instructional Services Librarian, Coordinator of Reference and Assessment at Lycoming College in Williamsport, Pennsylvania, argues that in order to get higher quality student work, information literacy, a key component of research, cannot be taught completely independent of reading and writing. She challenges the library's traditional role of limiting their teaching information literacy to search and retrieval and instead argues for a more process-based method interconnected with reading and writing. Rooted in teaching pedagogies, research, and psychology, this book encourages bridging the artificial divides between reading, writing, and research to make information literacy instruction more meaningful, thereby increasing students' ability to evaluate and synthesize information, and encouraging a higher quality of student work.

Written in clear language and logically presented, the book's chapters explain and connect process-based information literacy teaching methods with writing, reading comprehension, and information synthesis, as well as provide insight on the implementation of process-based information literacy practices in the library and classroom. Each chapter provides theoretical foundations and practical applications, giving readers insight into how these skills interact to support students' development of critical analysis skills and ends with an extensive list of supporting documentation. Readers will gain a better understanding of the relationships between reading, research, writing, and information literacy along with assignment ideas to support the development of these skills. This book will be appreciated by anyone with an interest in the teaching of information literacy or anyone looking to improve the quality of their students' work. It will, however, be most valuable to school, college, and university librarians looking to improve their teaching and increase promotion of information literacy on their campus.—**Kali A. Rippel**

360.   **Information and Technology Literacy: Concepts, Methodologies, Tools, and Applications.** Edited by Information Resources Management Association. Hershey, Pa., IGI Global, 2018. 4v. $2,495.00/set. ISBN 13: 978-1-52253-417-4; 978-1-52253-418-1 (e-book).

This four-volume book set represents a great scholarly reference about the current trends and issues in information and technology literacy. It consists of seven sections with 115 chapters in total. The first section is Fundamental Concepts and Theories; the section title accurately reflects the content. The second section is Development and Design Methodologies, and it addresses theoretical concepts about design of information and technology literacy. Tools and Technologies is the third section, covering various tools and technologies that can be used by practitioners in the field. The fourth section, Utilization and Applications is full of different topics with case studies, theories, and research methodologies. This section provides a wide range of recommendations and suggestions for further application. Organizational and Social Implications, section five, describes how technologies influence people's personal and professional lives. The sixth section is Managerial Impact. It explains how professionals can use the latest research that is presented in the books to improve their workplaces by making them more functional and productive. The final section, Critical Issues and Challenges, tries to provide answers about important aspects of the field.

Like other IGI Global books I have reviewed this set has many positive qualities: an international cast of scholars that give a more holistic view of an issue or trend; a reference list of reliable scholarly sources after each chapter; a long, comprehensive index; and a format that is clear and easy to read. There are a few negatives, like the lack of organizational consistency and visual graphics. Ideally, each chapter has a reference list, additional readings, and key terms and definitions. Throughout this book set, however, some chapters have only reference lists, others have a reference list and key terms and definitions but not additional readings, and some have only a reference list and additional readings. Moreover, some figures are hard to read or see (e.g., the images on pages 185, 1233, and 1235).

Overall, I think this book set will be a valuable acquisition for academic and special libraries. Technology professionals, instructors, and students will greatly benefit from these books and will find scholarly value in the pages.—**Maria Agee**

361.   Lanning, Scott. **Concise Guide to Information Literacy.** 2d ed. Santa Barbara, Calif., Libraries Unlimited/ABC-CLIO, 2017. 183p. index. $40.00pa. ISBN 13: 978-1-4408-5138-4; 978-1-4408-5139-1 (e-book).

Lanning endeavors to teach the core concepts of information literacy, for a popular audience, in a manner refreshingly free of assumptions. He does not presume that his readers have a specific level of education, or work in a specific field, or that certain sources of information are inherently superior to others. Rather, the author wants to help the reader ask better questions, consult the appropriate sources, and reach valid conclusions.

The book is divided into 11 chapters. The first two chapters provide an introduction, defining and exploring information and information literacy. The next five chapters discuss specific sources of information: libraries, databases, library catalogs, library databases, and the web. The last four chapters discuss specific aspects of information literacy: the research process, managing information, information ethics, and communicating one's results. Each chapter concludes with Vocabulary, Questions for Reflection, and an (optional) Assignment.

Concise Guide to Information Literacy was written by a reference librarian and published by a library-focused imprint, but its primary audience should be older high school students or younger college students. It could easily be used as a textbook, culminating in the writing of a research paper. Librarians could use this book in their own information literacy sessions, of course, especially if afforded multiple sessions. Professionals could also use this book for ready-reference to brush up on specific topics, like citation styles or the tools used to create a bibliography.—**Richard Nathan Leigh**

Information Technology

362.   Curating Research Data: Practical Strategies for Your Digital Repository.
Lisa R. Johnston, ed. Chicago, American Library Association, Association of College and
Research Libraries, 2017. 2v. $110.00/set. ISBN 13: 978-0-8389-8918-0.

This two-volume book is divided into both theoretical and practical strategies around
the topics of data curation, data repositories, data reuse, institutional repositories, cost
recovery and revenue models, outreach and marketing, data life cycles, meta-repositories,
and data dissemination and rescue. Volume one contains an introduction and three sections
divided into twelve chapters centered around the current major issues on these topics;
the introduction in particular provides excellent summaries on the content of each of
the chapters. Volume two is a handbook of current practice around these topics, with
thirty case studies interspersed among the nine steps required around establishing a data
curation service. These steps include: establish your data curation service, receive the
data, appraisal and selection techniques that mitigate risks inherent to data, processing and
treatment actions for data, ingest and store data in your repository, descriptive metadata,
access, preservation of data for the long term, and reuse. This two-volume book is the
most authoritative source for current theory and practice on the curation of research data,
and is an essential tome for any research library involved in these activities.—**Bradford
Lee Eden**

363.   Databrarianship: The Academic Librarian in Theory and Practice. Lynda
Kellam and Kristi Thompson, eds. Chicago, American Library Association, Association
of College and Research Libraries, 2016. 386p. index. $68.00pa. ISBN 13: 978-0-8389-
8799-5.

Four parts divide the chapter articles into themes in this volume, Data Support Services
for Researchers and Learners, Data in the Disciplines, Data Preservation and Access, and
Data: Past, Present, and Future. Overall, the book emphasizes how librarians can support
researchers who use datasets; the section on data support is the most extensive. Services
could be thought of as a studio as described by Samantha Guss in "A Studio Model for
Academic Data Services" or as a village, in the chapter "The Data Management Village"
by Alicia Hofelich Morh, Lisa R. Johnston, and Thomas A. Lindsay. Other chapters in the
data support section describe the potential for how librarians could become involved in
research projects with faculty and how to provide training to fill in educational gaps in data
management and digital preservation for researchers.

According to author Ryan Clement in his chapter "The Data Librarian in the Liberal
Arts College," nearly half of the top 15 doctorate-granting universities in the sciences and
engineering have students coming from eight liberal arts colleges. Although he makes the
argument that having undergraduate students at liberal arts colleges wait until graduate
school to learn about data management and curation would be a disservice, this volume
may not be appropriate for all college libraries because of its focus at an advanced research
level. It would, however, be a welcome addition to the collections of libraries at large
research institutions and in those colleges which do emphasize advanced research for
undergraduate students.—**Kay Shelton**

364.   Hennig, Nicole. **Keeping Up with Emerging Technologies: Best Practices for Information Professionals.** Santa Barbara, Calif., Libraries Unlimited/ABC-CLIO, 2017. 180p. $50.00pa. ISBN 13: 978-1-4408-5440-8; 978-1-4408-5441-5 (e-book).

Central to the book is the ideal that there are different roles for different types of people whose job is to keep up with emerging technologies. Repeated throughout the book is the scale of traits that includes visionaries and implementers. Each person falls at different places on this scale. Personality types and skills are listed for both visionaries and implementers, but the book really only covers the role of the visionaries and handing the project off to the implementation team.

Several chapters of the book are devoted to strategies and possible sources of information about new technologies. Many resources are listed along with techniques to find the information that might be of interest to the reader. Hennig admits that there is too much information to take in, so it is important to direct your consumption of information. The next step is evaluating what you learn for usefulness, then picking out the most useful and relevant information for your users.

The remainder of the book looks at some things to remember when investigating technology such as user needs, technology ethics, and project design. After selecting the technologies that might be useful to the user, Hennig writes about experimenting with technology and designing hands-on projects to test it out. Another limitation of the book is that it assumes that the reader has personnel, money, and time to take on these tasks. Very little is said about smaller libraries with limited support and how the process could be adapted.

I would recommend this book to the visionaries who want to be out there gathering information about the latest technology or for organizations that are creating an Emerging Technologies Librarian position.—**Susan Elkins**

365.   Kennedy, Marie R., and Cheryl LaGuardia. **Marketing Your Library's Electronic Resources: A How-To-Do-It Manual for Librarians.** 2d ed. Chicago, American Library Association, 2018. 218p. index. $65.00pa.; $58.50pa. (ALA members). ISBN 13: 978-0-8389-1565-3.

Spoiler alert: *Marketing Your Library's Electronic Resources* accomplishes exactly what its title forewarns. This 2nd edition, two-hundred-plus page publication from the American Library Association sets out to provide updated information in order to assist librarians who aim to promote and increase usage of electronic resources. Beginning with the (correct) assumption that most users don't have a complete grasp on the information available through their library's electronic resources, this guide was developed in order to facilitate that awareness and understanding.

This book is divided into two parts: How to Design Your Marketing Plan and Sample Marketing Plan Reports. Part 1 is divided into six chapters exploring how to fashion, implement, assess, revise, etc. a marketing plan. These chapters are immensely thorough and dense with practical and helpful information. Part 2, though, is what makes this guide particularly useful. Instead of stopping with the first part, perhaps with a brief example or two, *Marketing Your Library's Electronic Resources* devotes half of the book to seven incredibly detailed marketing plan examples from a variety of institutions. As those familiar with academic citations can attest, written instructions are great, but concrete examples bring those instructions to life.

Increasing the usage and awareness of library resources is an important focus for many libraries, and having an authoritative go-to resource is particularly useful. As with many reference books intended for library purchase the price might be a bit inflated, but the content is very high quality and can be extremely valuable for many libraries.—**Tyler Manolovitz**

366. **Mobile Technology and Academic Libraries: Innovative Services for Research and Learning.** Robin Canuel and Chad Crichton, eds. Chicago, American Library Association, Association of College and Research Libraries, 2017. 270p. $68.00pa. ISBN 13: 978-0-8389-8879-4.

The 17 chapters in this book "explore the responses of academic libraries to [the] maturing of mobile technology" (p. xi). The basic premise is that mobile computing has now surpassed desktop computing as the preferred mode of gathering information, including library information. In the last decade, technology has evolved rapidly, and libraries are working to keep pace with changes, in order to enhance their services to patrons. The authors present a diverse range of programs and services that engage with these recent advances: interactive library tours, provision of a roaming service using iPads and other tablets, use of proximity beacons, enhanced sessions of active learning, and information literacy instruction through various technologies. One chapter explores the use of "augmented reality." The programs span libraries across North America, from North Carolina to Ontario, from Boston to San Diego, with one study from Western Australia.

This book will be welcome in academic libraries, despite a slightly steep price for a paperback of this length. Institutions with library science programs should find it even more useful, as a resource for future librarians. A minor note: a number of the graphics included in this volume were very difficult to read, and thus, to understand.—**Mark Schumacher**

Intellectual Freedom and Censorship

367. Jarvis, Zeke. **Silenced in the Library: Banned Books in America.** Santa Barbara, Calif., Greenwood Press/ABC-CLIO, 2017. 292p. index. $94.00. ISBN 13: 978-1-4408-4394-5; 978-1-4408-4395-2 (e-book).

For the most part, this reference work consists of descriptions of books that have been frequently challenged in America. The entries are divided into subject categories representing the primary focus of the challenges: race, religion, sex, sexual orientation, drugs and alcohol, and bad behavior. There is also a chapter devoted to graphic novels. Each section includes a brief introduction focused on the specific type of challenge discussed in the section and a timeline. The general introduction provides an overview of censorship from a broad, historical point of view including the role of the government, publishers, and the effects on literature for children and young adults.

The entries range from 300 words to over 2,500 words. Each entry includes a brief description of the book followed by examples of censorship attempts and the reasons behind the challenges. The descriptions are interesting and well written. Each one provides a historical and cultural context for the challenged title, including information on the critical reaction to the book, its financial success, and the overall importance of the work in literature. Each entry also includes a brief list of references.

The books range from literary classics to popular titles from the past 20 years. The titles chosen represent a majority of the works on the American Library Association (ALA) lists of the 100 most frequently banned/challenged books from the decades 1990-1999 and 2000-2009. In addition, a few titles on more recent lists are included, but the work is primarily an overview of banned books over time, not an update on the latest books on the most challenged lists. There is an alphabetical list of titles and authors and a list by subject. There is an extensive bibliography and a well-developed index.—**Theresa Muraski**

International Librarianship

368.   **Queer Library Alliance: Global Reflections and Imaginings.** Rae-Anne Montague and Lucas McKeever, eds. Sacramento, Calif., Library Juice Press, 2017. 256p. index. $35.00pa. ISBN 13: 978-1-63400-031-4.

This book contains a number of essays on the topic of queer identities and queerness in libraries, discussing a number of the challenges and critical needs for individuals and services in this area. It is divided into two parts. Part one, which examines library services to meet LGBTQ users' needs, has four chapters examining the Michael McConnell case from 1970 at the University of Minnesota, the state of LGBTQ public library services to children in the United Kingdom, challenges in archiving personal materials in the Democratic Republic of the Congo, and inherent biases in the various library classification systems on LGBTQ topics. Part two, on the queering of professional practice, also has four chapters centered around protection issues in India for LGBTQ individuals, awareness of LGBTQ issues at the Mariestad Public Library in Sweden, the development of a queer collection at the University of South Florida, and concerns over inequitable access and safety for vulnerable users in libraries. I found the range of topics and challenges quite interesting in this volume, and would definitely recommend it for all librarians and libraries.—**Bradford Lee Eden**

Library Automation

369.   **Library Technology Guides. https://librarytechnology.org/.** [Website] Free. Date reviewed: 2017.

This site reflects an intensive effort towards establishing a resource for people interested in integrated library systems (ILSs), trends, and developments. It offers several databases applicable to libraries and the technologies that sustain them, in addition to other helpful resources. The homepage serves as a topical blog and industry news site. However, the databases accessible via the menu bar are the heart of the site. Under the Libraries tab, users can conduct a general search or can focus on a particular library association (based in the United States or the United Kingdom), such as the Association of Research Libraries and the U.S. Presidential Libraries & Museums. Selecting a library will display a summary noting contact information, description, academic statistics, technology profile, and more. A vendor database lists companies offering fully integrated library automation systems, such as Follett or Ex Libris, and shows contact information, ILSs offered, news, a corporate chronology, and other details. Users can also search a variety of documents such as industry reports, ten years of satisfaction surveys, newsletters, and columns. Guides offers a number of graphics (pie charts, tables, etc.) outlining topics such as mergers and acquisitions in the library tech industry and tech implementation by library size. The Jobs and Procurement tabs link to registries of active opportunities for both library technology job seekers and tech companies looking for library business. The bulk of all content—from the databases to the blog to the industry reports—is generated by one man, Marshall Breeding. While Breeding maintains vast experience in the industry, the fact that this is his personal project should be pointed out from an objectivity standpoint.—**ARBA Staff Reviewer**

370.   **Migrating Library Data: A Practical Manual.** Kyle Bannerjee and Bonnie Parks, eds. Chicago, American Library Association, 2017. 251p. index. $56.00pa.; $50.40pa. (ALA members). ISBN 13: 978-0-8389-1503-5.

This strong resource is organized into 13 chapters. Each chapter is outlined succinctly with corresponding page navigation. The first chapter opens the stage to the possibility of technology migration and the importance of team building and collaboration; it also overviews the need for a migration plan, stressing the importance of teamwork and organization for a smooth transition. Further chapters describe staff processes for the various system changes. The process of cleaning data is critical and data types include: bibliographic, acquisitions, holdings and electronic resources, item, and patron and user, with a chapter designated for explanation of this process. Along with format information, the work of standardizing, consolidating, and purging are shown with visual figures throughout the text. Examples of commands to create relevant formatting add to the hands-on nature of this book. Highlighted boxes with a "Pro Tip" give detailed, useable ideas. Common questions are addressed and the sharing of authors' knowledge is apparent. Comparison of new and old computer systems will unveil differences and areas of possible gaps. Critical steps of test load concerns are listed, and topics of authentication, serials, staff training (pre-and-post migration), Electronic Resource Management Systems (ERMS), and MARC records are examined in relation to systems migration. The book includes a list of contributors, a list of acronyms, and an index.

Moving library data can intimidate. *Migrating Library Data* is truly practical and plausible with representation for small libraries, shared systems, larger libraries, institutional repositories, and digital collections. In advance of the transition, this professional development title should be required reading for all library staff, not just those on the migration team.

Highly recommended.—**Janis Minshull**

Library Cooperation

371.   **Library Information and Resource Sharing: Transforming Services and Collections.** Beth Posner, ed. Santa Barbara, Calif., Libraries Unlimited/ABC-CLIO, 2017. 174p. index. $55.00pa. ISBN 13: 978-1-4408-4968-8; 978-1-4408-4969-5 (e-book).

Providing resources is the mainstay of any library and Interlibrary Loan (ILL) is often used as a way for libraries to enhance their collections. This book is a collection of papers that explore innovations in ILL beyond the traditional borrowing and lending of books and media. It explores where ILL and libraries fit into the future of information sharing; how ILL practices can serve as models for other library services; and how ILL departments can build their institution. It is an in-depth exploration of how ILL can be used for advocacy, curriculum, and growth. This book would be an excellent textbook for preservice librarians and could also provide a new perspective to seasoned librarians.

Recommended for libraries with a large ILL department looking for different ways to enhance their department.—**Elizabeth Nebeker**

Library Facilities

372.   Schlipf, Fred, and John A. Moorman. **The Practical Handbook of Library Architecture: Creating Building Spaces that Work.** Chicago, American Library Association, 2018. 1004p. illus. index. $149.00pa.; $134.10pa. (ALA members). ISBN 13: 978-0-8389-1553-0.

This hefty volume is an essential reference book for every library director or librarian tasked with building a new library or renovating an existing library/space. It is divided into six major sections: Introduction, About Library Buildings, Basic Steps, Money, Library Spaces, and Technical Issues. The Library Buildings section discusses construction processes, basic configuration of library spaces, evaluating library buildings by walking around, dysfunctional designs, and converting nonlibrary spaces to public libraries. The Basic Steps section goes through designing for various programs, hiring and working with an architect, site selection, zoning and codes, the construction process and firms, and remodeling and expanding existing buildings. The Money section gets into the issues surrounding building costs and funding. The Library Spaces section is the largest, and tackles issues such as user seating, collection storage, public service desks, program and study rooms, display and exhibit areas, restrooms, staff workrooms, staff facilities, and storerooms. The Technical Issues section deals with lighting, elevators and other constructs for moving between floors, electrical systems, HVAC systems, plumbing, security, and walls and ceilings. The title says it all!—**Bradford Lee Eden**

Library Instruction

373.   Benjes-Small, Candice, and Rebecca K. Miller. **The New Instruction Librarian: A Workbook for Trainers and Learners.** Chicago, American Library Association, 2017. 237p. index. $68.00pa.; $61.20pa. (ALA members). ISBN 13: 978-0-8989-1456-4.

Two experienced instruction librarians, Candice Benjes-Small of Radford University and Rebecca K. Miller of Penn State University, present a trove of practical advice in this engaging volume. *The New Instruction Librarian* succinctly illuminates major issues facing new teaching librarians at academic institutions. By incorporating time-tested teaching practices, personal anecdotes, and solid research, both authors accurately discuss the unique and complex roles instruction librarians have on campus.

This handbook looks at the function of an instruction librarian as a colleague, instructional designer, teacher, faculty partner, manager, and library advocate. True to its form, chapters are pithy and practical. Topic discussions are interspersed with checklists, handouts, common teaching scenarios, and recommended activities in each chapter. Straightforward classroom assessments are also included in relevant sections. Chapter overviews provide an excellent introduction that is perfectly complemented by an extensive reference list.

The two strongest chapters thoughtfully examine faculty partnerships and library advocacy on campus. While teaching remains the prime focus, this volume also tackles weighty matters such as conducting a needs assessment and project planning. The authors wisely include a chapter on the enduring role of professional development in teacher efficacy. Regrettably, very limited attention is paid to the ACRL Frameworks, educational theory, or recent technological trends.

The New Instruction Librarian provides a superior overview of most major topics facing new teaching librarians. As a resource, this volume should be used in tandem with other specialized titles in library instruction. Ultimately, this handbook will be an excellent asset to new librarians and instruction coordinators.—**Joshua Becker**

374.   **Creative Instructional Design: Practical Applications for Librarians.** Brandon K. West, Kimberly D. Hoffman, and Michelle Costello, eds. Chicago, American Library Association, Association of College and Research Libraries, 2017. 384p. index. $72.00pa. ISBN 13: 978-0-8389-8929-6.

Envisioned as a collection of case studies gathered from academic librarians around the country on how they use instructional design to develop everything from individual information literacy sessions to full for-credit courses, *Creative Instructional Design* hits the sweet spot between theory and implementation. Each case study comes off as highly personalized, but the wealth of experiences and variety of situations in which instructional design was integrated helps one get a feel for how an institution's library staff might be able to use instructional design to improve their instruction. The editors chose an excellent selection of librarians for schools ranging in size from Virginia Tech University through Kansas State and Eastern Michigan to Nevada State College and Erie Community College. This diversity aids in selling the title to all librarians, regardless of the size of their library and college.

As a textbook for students interested in instructional design as it pertains to librarians or as a reference book for current librarians looking to integrate design philosophies into their curriculum, *Creative Instructional Design* can fulfill either role. Of particular significance is the fact that while some authors of the included studies used traditional and well-known design tools such ADDIE, Rapid Prototyping, and Backwards Design, others embraced lesser-known models, USER, TILT, ARCS, or even an in-house hybrid of several models. This decision, whether conscious or not, helps to show that instructional design is not a one-size-fits-all approach and that each theory has its own merits and drawbacks. The book also addresses how similar-sized institutions can implement instructional design models in their own projects.—**Ian King**

375.   **The Discovery Tool Cookbook: Recipes for Successful Lesson Plans.** Nancy Fawley and Nikki Krysak, eds. Chicago, American Library Association, 2016. 137p. $35.00pa. ISBN 13: 978-0-8389-8891-6.

In *The Discovery Tool Cookbook: Recipes for Successful Lesson Plans,* the editors, Nancy Fawley and Nikki Krysak, have included a wealth of lesson plans primarily for one-shot instruction sessions in a higher education context. The majority of the title's content is lesson plans of varying length (from short activities to full plans) and plans for group activities. There are a few plans for different audiences such as English language learners, faculty, and K-12 students. Also included are three plans that flip the classroom, which is a recent trend in higher education.

The premise of the book is that with discovery tools, teaching basic database searching skills is no longer necessary, but the editors found that this is not always true. Discovery tools add their own complications but those allow instructors to delve into more theoretical ideas about searching and search strategies. Thus, these plans have a natural fit with the ACRL Framework for Information Literacy for Higher Education, a fact that the editors realized and so each lesson plan includes the frame that it addresses. This is helpful information for those programs that are transitioning from the Standards to the Framework, or for those instructors that are interested in including the Framework in their teaching but are not sure how to approach that since the Framework is theoretical. This book ties the practical to the theoretical in a supportive and effective way.

The book accomplishes what it sets out to do: practical lesson plans for discovery tool instruction. However, it could do so more clearly if the format of the book was not forced into a cookbook theme. For example, the section with full lesson plans is called Meal Plans and the group activities are in the Tapas section. The theme is carried into the individual plans themselves with subheadings such as Nutrition Information (the objectives) and Dietary Guidelines (the Frames). This only confuses rather than clarifies which seems to be known as there is a How to Use this Book section at the beginning. This is part of the Cookbook series published by ACRL so readers of previous books in this series will be familiar with this format and it may not cause as much confusion for them.

Regardless of this format choice, the content of the volume is valuable and would be a strong addition to the teaching librarian's collection.—**Elizabeth Webster**

376.   **The First-Year Experience Cookbook.** Raymond Pun and Meggan Houlihan, eds. Chicago, American Library Association, Association of College and Research Libraries, 2017. 164p. index. $42.00pa. ISBN 13: 978-0-8389-8920-3.

Like its popular predecessors, *The First-Year Experience Cookbook* is a valuable new addition to ACRL's successful library instruction series. Editors Meggan Houlihan and Raymond Pun have compiled a significant array of learning activities submitted by academic librarians from across the United States. While the prospect of acclimating first-year students to library resources can be challenging, this volume successfully offers inventive ways to grab students' attention through imaginative lessons.

The First-Year Experience Cookbook consists of four main sections: Orientations, Library Instruction, Programs, and Assessment. Each section includes a variety of content specific "recipes." These "recipes" are actually learning activities, allowing the "chef" (instruction librarian) to create a succulent "dish" (successful lesson). Each recipe, there are over sixty, concisely summarizes the learning activity in a straightforward step-by-step process.

Gimmickry aside, this volume is well organized with unique and engaging learning activities for the first-year experience. Lessons promote inclusivity, and should work with a range of student abilities. Some recipes originated in research universities, while others were created at community colleges. Section 2, Library Instruction, is the strongest, and offers a particularly eclectic mix of lessons for all learners. Activities are flexible, in terms of class time, ranging from as little as fifteen minutes to several instruction sessions. Although recipes can be taught as prescribed, most examples offer suggestions that allow for adaptation.

The focus of *The First-Year Experience Cookbook* is clearly classroom-based, and many recipes are aligned to the ACRL Frameworks. Images, handouts, and fliers occasionally enliven the text with potential tools for librarians. On a minor note, online links to these activities are usually absent, and there are rarely reference lists for most submissions. Instruction librarians will find substantial value in these lessons. This volume is highly recommended for academic libraries.—**Joshua Becker**

377. Francis, Mary. **The Fun of Motivation: Crossing the Threshold Concepts.** Chicago, American Library Association, Association of College and Research Libraries, 2017. 168p. (Publications in Librarianship series). $48.00pa. ISBN 13: 978-0-8389-8933-3.

Since ACRL's Framework for Information Literacy for Higher Education was introduced in 2015 there have been discussions on effectively implementing these concepts in the library classroom. Mary Francis, a librarian at Dakota State University, has written a worthy addition to this conversation in *The Fun of Motivation: Crossing the Threshold Concepts.* This title, published by ACRL, discusses creative ways to help instruction librarians spur student engagement with these concepts.

The book consists of two sections. The first section examines the theories behind student motivation. Creating intrinsic motivation in the classroom can be difficult, but Francis suggests three useful pathways to spark student engagement. Francis makes good use of seminal and current research to highlight the effectiveness of humor, games, and group work in the library classroom. The central role of fun in the learning experience is also explored. The second section includes a variety of useable lessons for teaching the six threshold concepts. Each threshold concept is given a chapter, with separate lessons that incorporate: games, group work, and humor. Sample rubrics and assessments are provided for these activities. These lessons are well suited for a range of student abilities, and Francis includes suggestions for adaptation. Despite a detailed exploration of student motivation, some relevant topics are not discussed. There are no activities geared towards online students. Similarly, a consideration of faculty partnerships would have also been timely.

Academic librarians should find *The Fun of Motivation: Crossing the Threshold Concepts* a useful source of inspiration when planning lessons. Not every activity is excellent, but quite a few have the potential to gain wide acceptance. While some librarians are very reticent to use humor in library instruction, this volume deserves credit as one of the few titles to discuss humor's role in the classroom. This book will be accessible to both novice and experienced instruction librarians. Highly recommended.—**Joshua Becker**

378. Ippoliti, Cinthya M., and Rachel W. Gammons. **User-Centered Design for First-Year Library Instruction Programs.** Santa Barbara, Calif., Libraries Unlimited/ABC-CLIO, 2017. 187p. index. $60.00pa. ISBN 13: 978-1-4408-3852-1; 978-1-4408-3853-8 (e-book).

Library instruction is one of those areas of librarianship in which one is often thrust or called upon to perform without having had much practice or prior preparation. As important as instruction has become for academic libraries, it can be a wholly overwhelming experience for the new and uninitiated. The goal of *User-Centered Design* is to encourage and motivate those new to the idea of instruction and give them the foundation necessary for success.

The authors have laid out *User-Centered Design* in an intuitive and user-friendly manner with chapters flowing easily from one to another covering the areas of design (curriculum and assessment), implementation (teaching and outreach), and administration (staffing and spaces). This is a well-written and easy-to-read book with excellent case studies in each of the six chapters covering a wide range of library sizes. The inclusion of the case studies and their variety cannot be emphasized enough in the effective portrayal of how academic libraries take the principles explained here and apply them in real-world contexts.

One thing of note is the lack of in-depth discussion on what impact the Framework for Information Literacy for Higher Education will have on library instruction. The framework is mentioned several times through the chapters and there is at least one case study in which the library was implementing it, but with something as groundbreaking and disruptive as the framework, one would appreciate seeing more analysis. Given the relative newness of its release, it is easy to see why less was devoted to the framework; thus, a new edition may be warranted in the near future. Aside from this minor concern, *User-Centered Design for First-Year Library Instruction Programs* is highly beneficial to the reader whether as a standalone textbook in a master's course on creating library instruction, an introductory text for someone new to instruction, or as a refresher for a seasoned instructor looking for new ideas.—**Ian King**

379.   Klipfel, Kevin Michael, and Dani Brecher Cook. **Learner-Centered Pedagogy: Principles and Practice.** Chicago, American Library Association, 2017. 197p. index. $60.00pa.; $54.00pa. (ALA members). ISBN 13: 978-0-8389-1557-8.

This book explores student-centered learning and instructional metamorphosis in librarianship. Authors Klipfel and Cook suggest that learning is humanistic. Emphasis on educational experience navigated by the learner is based in the studies of Carl Rogers; "we follow the pioneering 'person-centered' vision of humanistic psychologist and educator Carl Rogers in placing empathy as central to humanistic education and therapies, by placing the concept of empathy at the heart of learner-centered librarianship" (p. xv).

No longer teaching Dewey with traditional instruction, librarians today instruct in a plethora of study areas. Information literacy has breadth and pedagogy suggests that allowing students primary control in their learning improves outcomes. "The individual learner before us is not a blank slate, but an embodied existential being with a deep desire to express who he is, no matter the context" (p. 25). Authenticity and motivation coupled with abilities cultivated through student choice, effort, and receptiveness to instructional feedback lead to strongest educational autonomy and success. *Learner-Centered Pedagogy* succinctly demonstrates the need for empathy in self-directed learning.

This title is compelling in design; theory and practicality entwine, and infographics generate intentional engagement. Six-chapter content is bookended with standard front and back matter. The index is worthy and concise, and supplemental information such as a list for further reading offers extension of research on learner-centered instruction. Chapters have a clean, crisp design beginning with a highlighted summary box and clear areas of text with black-and-white maps, charts, flow charts, lesson plan templates, and worksheets dispersed throughout offering visual appeal as well as information. Operational paradigms bring this pedagogy to life; librarians will put to use "Six Cognitive Principles for Organizing Information Literacy Instruction" (p. 64) and be able to model technological case studies found in chapter six.

Best suited for librarians who teach or intend to teach, this book is also a wise choice in professional reading for all administrators, educators, and librarians in the changing face of librarianship and pedagogy.

Highly recommended.—**Janis Minshull**

380.   Pitts, Joelle, Sara K. Kearns, and Heather Collins. **Creating and Sharing Online Library Instruction: A How-To-Do-It Manual for Librarians.** Chicago, American Library Association, 2017. 142p. index. $54.00pa.; $48.00pa. (ALA members). ISBN 13: 978-0-8389-1562-2.

Academic librarians will instantly be familiar with the textbook layout of the title. Chapters begin with a definition of terms, chapter learning objectives, and an action item checklist. A summary of critical questions raised by the material ends each chapter along with references. Extensive appendixes present templates and samples along with a comprehensive index. Supporting illustrations and figures increase understanding of presented concepts.

The title implies the information contained is a walkthrough tutorial on how to create library instruction objects along with where and how to share online. The true focus of the book is a case study that follows the experiences, methods, and lessons learned by the New Literacies Alliance (NLA) project setting up and working with an online interinstitutional collaboration. The book demonstrates how to identify and select potential collaborators, establish project roles, establish design parameters, including software and longevity, and launch the learning object.

The book is recommended for academic librarians seeking to work with other institutions on library instruction creation, or with multiple departments within their own institution. Pitfalls, problems, and guess work are largely avoided by following the roadmap to collaborative development in this book. Librarians working alone or in a very small group will get minimal value and should look elsewhere.—**Jeffrey A Jensen**

381.   Puckett, Jason. **Zotero: A Guide for Librarians, Reserchers and Educators.** Chicago, American Library Association, Association of College and Research Libraries, 2017. 206p. index. $54.00pa. ISBN 13: 978-0-8389-8931-9.

Zotero is a free software product that produces a perfectly formatted bibliography from scratch. This book, now in its second edition, provides a wealth of documentation and information for librarians, educators, and researchers on the ins and outs of using Zotero. It is geared towards teachers and users of the software, as well as those who teach Zotero in the classroom and the library. New changes in this edition include information on the new Zotero Standalone, which allows the software to now work with Chrome and Safari along with the original Firefox browser. The author indicates that the Firefox version may be discontinued in the near future. Revisions have been made in chapter five, but the biggest revision is chapter six, which discusses mobile applications and add-ons. A Zotero guide is maintained by the author with up-to-date information at http://research.library.gsu.edu/zotero. I highly recommend this book, both for new and advanced users of Zotero, as well as librarians who teach the use of this product in the classroom.—**Bradford Lee Eden**

382.   **Rewired: Research-Writing Partnerships within the Frameworks.** Randall McClure, ed. Chicago, American Library Association, Association of College and Research Libraries, 2016. 330p. $68.00pa. ISBN 13: 978-0-8389-8904-3.

The 14 essays in this useful text are grouped in three sections: Developing a Shared Understanding, Partnering Research & Writing, and Assessing Writing & Information Literacy. Each chapter either examines a concept concerning cooperation between libraries and writing instruction, or presents the results of a program based on that cooperation, while applying the frameworks created in 2015 by the Association of College and

Research Libraries (ACRL) and in 2011 by the Council of Writing Program Administrators (CWPA). Authors include both librarians and teaching faculty associated with college writing programs from universities across North America. The range of the studies is quite diverse, from the expected English 101 classes and writing center analyses to music and health science course settings. The accounts of collaboration between different units on a college campus were inspiring.

This volume will be quite useful to anyone in academia interested in the interaction between librarians and teaching faculty with the goal of enhancing both writing and research skills, as they implement the recent ACRL and CWPA guidelines. Patrons of school and public libraries are much less likely to be drawn to this work. (Minor note: copyediting of this book could have been more attentive. The contributor list is not quite alphabetical and a couple of bibliographies lack all the needed information such as page numbers, etc.)—**Mark Schumacher**

Library Management

383.   **Academic Library Management: Case Studies.** Tammy Nickelson Dearie, Michael Meth, and Elaine L. Westbrooks, eds. Chicago, American Library Association, 2018. 214p. index. $69.00pa.; $62.10pa (ALA members). ISBN 13: 978-1-8389-1559-2.

Fourteen chapters/studies, by 22 librarians from the United States and Canada, explore a wide variety of topics related to decision-making within academic libraries: user spaces, funding, liaison models, and technical services reorganization, among others. Written by the personnel directly involved in the decision-making and implementation of the tasks described, these studies allow the reader to truly grasp the multiple dimensions of library management. In fact, the personal involvement of the authors certainly enhances the impact and usefulness of this material. The chapter on an incident of violence in a library is the most striking, as to the impact of the event and the difficulties faced by the library staff subsequently. By presenting accounts from a variety of settings, involving units from public and technical services to archives/special collections and facilities management, this tome gives managers and future managers much to ponder.

Again, this reviewer finds the price of this small paperback book (188 pages of text), put out by an American Library Association publisher, to be rather exorbitant. In any case, college and university libraries will want to consider it, especially at schools with library and information studies graduate programs.—**Mark Schumacher**

384.   de Farber, Bess G., April Hines, and Barbara J. Hood. **Collaborating with Strangers: Facilitating Workshops in Libraries, Classes, and Nonprofits.** Chicago, American Library Association, 2017. 144p. illus. index. $55.00pa.; $49.50pa. (ALA members). ISBN 13: 978-0-8389-1542-4.

Another title in the "How-To-Do-It Manual for Librarians" series, *Collaborating with Strangers: Facilitating Workshops in Libraries, Classes, and Nonprofits* is an assemblage of real-life ideas, activities, and promotions for relationship building, not with those already in your network, but those you do not know.

Collaboration, we all do it and have great networks. Or do we? *Collaborating with Strangers,* in eight digestible chapters, exemplifies why alliances may be lacking and how to create collaborative workshops to expand collective efforts. Authors Bess G. de Farber,

April Hines, and Barbara J. Hood describe CoLAB Workshops; facilitating a practicum that guides researchers through the process. "CoLAB-facilitated processes may well be the very best way to quickly and enthusiastically initiate collaborative relationships with new stakeholders" (p. 10). Each chapter accurately covers another aspect of the value of face-to-face conversations with strangers. Figures break up text with useable forms and visual information; floor plans, flowcharts, promotional images, and surveys are some of the offerings. Black-and-white photos and screenshots add to the material. Plenty of white space is balanced with sidebars and highlighted textboxes with additional tips, participant quotes, and recommendations. An index rounds out the work

Collaboration matters and through this well-defined guide, professionals will expand their efforts and potential by charting unknown territory. *Collaborating with Strangers* gives workshop facilitators practical material for developing a successful CoLAB experience. The information here is applicable to a broad range of workshop settings (class, conference, geographical proximity, topic based) where creating a participatory atmosphere is key. Recommended.—**Janis Minshull**

385.   **Digitization Cost Calculator. http://dashboard.diglib.org/.** [Website] Free. Date reviewed: 2017.

Our world is a digital one, and this simple mechanism maintained by the Digital Library Federation Assessment Interest Group's working group on cost assessment collects and offers data on the digitization process to help institutions with "digitization project planning and benchmarking." The project team is led by project coordinator Joyce Chapman of Duke University Libraries. Users can retrieve time and cost estimations by entering the number of scans they will be conducting into the Digitization Cost Calculator, then answering questions about staffing (hourly, salaried, etc.) and processes (prep, quality control, metadata creation, etc.). More precise answers will naturally lead to more accurate cost estimation. For example, an assistant paid an hourly wage of $25 can complete ten scans using a manual DSLR camera in approximately 6.98 minutes at a cost of $2.93 (using minimal parameters). While this may seem quite technical, users can link to a Processes and Definitions document for clarifying information. It is important to note that the site does not save or share the particulars of individual data submitted through the calculator. Users can, however, contribute their own time data by filling out a submission form that asks questions about material to be digitized and the time spent on various aspects, such as scanning or color correction. Users can also examine the raw data collected so far, matching time information to distinct digitization processes and considering variables such as image capture device (e.g., overhead scanner, medium format camera, etc.) and more. Data has been collected from Harvard University, the Smithsonian Libraries, the Center for Jewish History, and many other institutions.—**ARBA Staff Reviewer**

386.   Dugan, Robert E., and Peter Hernon. **Financial Management in Academic Libraries: Data-Driven Planning and Budgeting.** Chicago, American Library Association, Association of College and Research Libraries, 2018. 188p. $56.00pa. ISBN 13: 978-0-8389-8943-2.

This book is written by two well-respected and well-known leaders within librarianship, on a topic of perennial interest to the profession: planning and budgeting. Comprised of ten chapters, the authors delve into areas such as planning techniques, strategic planning, basic steps in financial management, accountability, types of budgets, budgeting and source of funds, data, staff and staffing, collections, technologies, facilities, program budgets, monitoring and managing a budget during the fiscal year, internal and external budget reporting, annual reports, uses of expenditure data, calculating unit costs, library value from a financial perspective, financial metrics for studies on benchmarking and best practices, dealing with budget reductions, library fraud, and financial leadership theories. Each chapter has a number of exercises to go through, with answers at the end of the book. Notes and bibliography are found at the end of each chapter as well. This book is a welcome addition to the toolkit of any library manager or leader.—**Bradford Lee Eden**

387.   Evans, G. Edward, and Holland Christie. **Managerial Leadership for Librarians: Thriving in the Public and Nonprofit World.** Santa Barbara, Calif., Libraries Unlimited/ABC-CLIO, 2017. 380p. index. $65.00pa. ISBN 13: 978-1-4408-4170-5; 978-1-4408-4171-2 (e-book).

This book was put together by a number of well-respected library managers and leaders to help other librarians become better managers and leaders. The term they use is managerial leadership. Through twenty chapters, the reader is provided numerous tips, experiences, case studies, research, and guidance on how to thrive in the public and nonprofit world of libraries. There are numerous sidebars throughout containing pointers to other and additional resources. Some of the many topics include: explanations of what public sector and nonprofit organizations are and do; leadership and management and their differences; using communication successfully; authority and power issues; advisory and governing boards; vision and mission planning; assessment and coordination; fiscal matter; fundraising; project management; advocacy and marketing; public relations; political skills; legal aspects; ethic; understanding oneself and others; training and developing staff; collaboration; negotiation; and long-term career success. This is a great book for those wanting to jump-start or enhance various aspects of their managerial leadership skills.—**Bradford Lee Eden**

388.   Farney, Tabatha. **Using Digital Analytics for Smart Assessment.** Chicago, American Library Association, 2018. 155p. index. $65.00pa.; $58.50pa. (ALA members). ISBN 13: 978-0-8389-1598-1.

The first sentence from the preface of *Using Digital Analytics for Smart Assessment* hints at the very reason this books exists: "Libraries routinely collect massive amounts of data and sometimes even analyze that data to drive the decision-making process." The key word there is "sometimes" because the intention of this book is to help libraries utilize all of that gathered data in useful and practical ways.

The first part explores five steps (chapters) of the digital analytics process. Written by Farney, these chapters go from understanding digital analytics to collecting, analyzing, and utilizing that data. A concluding chapter in this section explores the use of digital analytics in collection development specifically. The second part brings in additional authors and experts to explore, in more detail, topics mentioned in the first part, such as data privacy, digital analytics in social media marketing, etc. This book also includes a great section of further readings and additional resources that are incredibly valuable in supporting this topic.

The content of *Using Digital Analytics* is extremely relevant in today's online world. The chapters are full of broad digital analytics theory, as well as practical and applicable hands-on information. The writing only gets as technical as necessary, but the writing is careful and clear enough to be easily followed. Farney's book is a great resource for libraries trying to better harness the wealth of data they've been collecting. It is also a fantastic introduction and guide for those who have perhaps been too intimidated to truly delve into the field of digital analytics.—**Tyler Manolovitz**

389.   **Feminists among Us: Resistance and Advocacy in Library Leadership.** Shirley Lew and Baharak Yousefi, eds. Sacramento, Calif., Library Juice Press, 2017. 196p. index. (Gender and Sexuality in Information Studies series). $22.00pa. ISBN 13: 978-1-63400-027-7.

This feminist anthology focusing on Library and Information Sciences (LIS) is the 9th title in the Series on Gender and Sexuality in Information Studies. The book includes orthodox opening and closing matter. Some chapters have an introduction and conclusion; all chapters have footnotes and succinct bibliographies. Documentation sources include: books, bulletins, journals, and links to digital content such as blogs, periodicals, and websites. The book has only a few bulleted lists, one chart, and a general lack of white space; the table of contents and index use a small font size. Chapters authored by LIS researchers and practitioners explore feminist theory and practice in the context of library administration. At times, examples and discussion come from the educational realm where deeper information is relatable. Background on the feminist approach, conversations, interactions, interviews, personal narratives, praxis, quotes, research, and theory frameworks represent the challenges and progress of intersectional feminism. Beyond the limitations of strict feminism, *Feminists among Us* addresses class, ethnicity, race, religion, and sexual orientation. An "Ethic of Care" is presented as no longer just a woman's role; traditional patriarchal roles are shifting and contemporary thought evolves to interdependent perspective.

The significance of this social justice collection is its contemporaneousness; articles are timely and offer hope and courage on the journey forward. "The real job of a feminist leader is simple: free yourself in order to free and empower others; free our libraries in order to empower those we serve" (p 40). Perceptible thought and well-documented discussion will support library management intent on making changes in their community and beyond.

Feminists among Us: Resistance and Advocacy in Library Leadership is best suited for advocates, feminists, resisters, and LIS interested in library leadership. Library administrators seeking forward-thinking ideas will gain from this timely discourse as well. Recommended.—**Janis Minshull**

390.   Madden, M. Leslie, Laura Carscaddon, Denita Hampton, and Brenna Helmstutler. **Now You're a Manager: Quick and Practical Strategies for New Mid-Level Managers in Academic Libraries.** Chicago, American Library Association, Association of College and Research Libraries, 2017. 86p. $28.00pa. ISBN 13: 978-0-8389-8787-2.

Despite a wealth of titles geared towards library administrators, *Now You're a Manager* is one of the first books to focus on middle management in academic libraries. This volume is the collaborative effort of four librarians at Georgia State University. These management situations apply to many institutional settings, though the authors' background is in a large research university. This volume serves as an effective introduction to understanding the issues of supervising a team or department within a larger library.

Through a series of ten short chapters *Now You're a Manager* discusses topics as diverse as: professional development, managing change, institutional politics, and running successful meetings. The advice is sensible and provides useful examples to handle a variety of routine management issues. The chapter on mentoring and coaching is among the strongest, offering an eclectic variety of useful tools to acclimate new colleagues. A timely reading list accompanied by suggested exercises are provided at the end of each chapter.

Unfortunately, important management issues are seldom given sustained focus; many recommendations are also observational and rarely grounded in research. Similarly, this volume does not contain case studies or statements from current library managers. While sections discuss supervising librarians, there is little mention of support staff or student workers.

Despite its lack of depth, *Now You're a Manager* may provide modest benefits to librarians aspiring to middle management. This title will also serve as a readable introduction to understanding a library's administrative functions prior to looking at management theory, current scholarship, and case studies.—**Joshua Becker**

Library Outreach

391.   **Engaging Community through Storytelling: Library and Community Programming.** Sherry Norfolk and Jane Stenson, eds. Santa Barbara, Calif., Libraries Unlimited/ABC-CLIO, 2017. 170p. illus. index. $50.00pa. ISBN 13: 978-1-4408-5069-1; 978-1-4408-5070-7 (e-book).

For generations people have engaged in storytelling as a way to share experiences, express individuality, convey ideas and knowledge, and transmit historical information. Personal stories have immense power. They inspire, instill moral values, and preserve culture. Stories even have the ability to grow communities. In *Engaging Community through Storytelling: Library and Community Programming* the editors provide 19 examples of how storytelling programs can be utilized to draw communities together, build relationships, and impact lives.

The book is organized into five chapters, each focusing on a specific target audience. Chapters contain essays detailing model storytelling projects submitted by individuals extensively involved in the creation, design, or implementation of storytelling programs. Venues for these programs include libraries, schools, community centers, shelters, and churches throughout the United States.

The editors describe this book as a "how-to-do-it-guide" due to the fact that in varying degrees submissions discuss such topics as intended purpose, target audience, design parameters, participant and leadership selection, promotional methods, funding source opportunities, venue options, evaluation techniques, supplemental documents, photographs, and bibliographic resources. However, many do not provide a step-by-step guide to storytelling program construction. Rather, many essays supply the reader with project ideas and general benefits of community storytelling programs rather than specific guidelines. Nevertheless, taken as a whole, the book demonstrates the value of community storytelling programs and provides design ideas and valuable implementation suggestions.—**Dianna L. Kim**

392.   **Literacy behind Bars: Successful Reading and Writing Strategies for Use with Incarcerated Youth and Adults.** Mary E. Styslinger, Karen Gavigan, and Kendra Albright, eds. Lanham, Md., Rowman & Littlefield, 2017. 108p. index. $45.00pa.; $42.00. ISBN 13: 978-1-4422-6925-5; 978-1-4422-6926-2 (e-book).

This concise volume presents individual chapters by people currently working with incarcerated youth as English teachers or librarians or the professors teaching upcoming teachers in the field. Broken into three sections, the book covers creative writing, reading curriculum and book groups, and partnerships, which has a more professional development focus than the other two. Well-written and academic in nature, this will most likely be needed in libraries supporting the educational needs of incarcerated teens and adults either to reaffirm what they are already achieving or to convince those in power to try something new.—**Kristin Fletcher-Spear**

393.   Pandora, Cherie P., and Kathy Fredrick. **Full Steam Ahead: Science, Technology, Engineering, Art, and Mathematics in Library Programs and Collections.** Santa Barbara, Calif., Libraries Unlimited/ABC-CLIO, 2017. 240p. index. $45.00pa. ISBN 13: 978-1-4408-5340-1; 978-1-4408-5341-8 (e-book).

Full Steam Ahead: Science, Technology, Engineering, Art, and Mathematics in Library Programs and Collections is an excellent resource for both public and school librarians who are interested in implementing or growing a STEAM (science, technology, engineering, art, and mathematics) program. The resource is written in twelve chapters which include everything a librarian could possibly need to know for a fantastic STEAM program including, but not limited to funding, outreach and collaboration, makerspaces, connecting national standards, evaluation and measurement, and professional development. In-depth information is provided regarding how school and public libraries can collaborate to ensure success, to share programming ideas, and to encourage girls and minorities to become more involved with STEAM. This is a must-have resource for any librarian wishing to incorporate STEAM programming.—**Shelly Lee**

394.   Reed, Sally Gardner, and United for Libraries. **The Good, the Great, and the Unfriendly: A Librarians Guide to Working with Friends Groups.** Chicago, American Library Association, 2017. 158p. index. $57.00pa.; $51.30pa. (ALA members). ISBN 13: 978-0-8389-1498-4.

Written by Sally Reed, executive director of United for Libraries and former executive director of Friends of Libraries, U.S.A., this book advises public and academic librarians on managing their relationships with Friends groups. The work is divided into six chapters, starting with "How to Start a Friends Group (and Why You Should)." Along the way, Reed covers myriad such topics as fundraising, advocacy, ways to engage Friends, and how to motivate those whom she refers to as unfriendly Friends. The use of real-life examples enlivens the text. Seven appendixes cover other important matters like gift giving guidelines and starting a Friends group at an academic library. An index rounds out the work.

This book will inspire those library professionals and community volunteers seeking to enhance library advocacy and community engagement.

Recommended.—**Janis Minshull**

Readers' Advisory

395.   Cart, Michael. **Confessions of a Book Reviewer: The Best of Carte Blanche.** Chicago, American Library Association, 2018. 191p. index. $45.00pa.; $40.50pa. (ALA members). ISBN 13: 978-0-8389-1645-2.

This volume brings together fifty "Carte Blanche" columns from the publication *Booklist,* written by Cart between 1994 and 2017. They are grouped into eight chapters, on topics such as book collecting, historical fiction, the evolution of young adult literature, and "memories and memorials." These pieces are more than book reviews, despite the volume's subtitle. These short pieces explore genres, introduce readers to numerous authors worth learning about, and present those authors from a voracious reader's point of view. Providing a wide range of topics, from an essay on the lack of literary biographies written for young adults to one on the growth of fantasy works for young readers, spurred on by the success of the Harry Potter phenomenon, these columns are always engaging and often amusing or moving. They also capture the atmosphere of books and reading over the last twenty-plus years.

This volume will have wide appeal and will engage teenage and adult readers in all sorts of libraries: high school, public, and academic. Although the price is somewhat high for a modest paperback, it should be considered.—**Mark Schumacher**

396.   **Crossover Readers' Advisory: Maximize Your Collection to Meet Reader Satisfaction.** Jessica E. Moyer, ed. Santa Barbara, Calif., Libraries Unlimited/ABC-CLIO, 2017. 182p. index. $55.00pa. ISBN 13: 978-1-4408-3846-0; 978-1-4408-3847-7.

Moyer, reference and reader services scholar, and editor of previous works including *The Readers' Advisory Handbook* (see ARBA 2011, entry 506) and *Research-Based Readers' Advisory* (see ARBA 2009, entry 513), explains a few reasons for this new resource guide, which focuses on recent and in-print titles but also includes classics. Recent library user trends have indicated a crossover reading interest between adults and young adults. Tight book budgets, together with a "gap in the literature" for crossover advisory guides, has created the perfect basis for this new work, as Moyer explains.

Moyer has assembled a team of 13 contributors (mostly adult or children's services librarians and collection management specialists) to bring this needed resource to busy public librarians. The guide is divided into two main sections (adult books for teen readers, teen books for adult readers). Within each section, chapters are arranged by genres as diverse as horror, science fiction, fantasy, mainstream literature, and graphic novels. Each chapter introduces the genre briefly, describes its appeals to readers, lists several helpful tools and resources for understanding the genre, provides customized advice on collection development, advises how to work with avid readers, and, lastly, comments on future trends. One little-known genre librarians may find interesting is that of "new adult." Growing out of romance, and appearing mostly since 2009, this genre appeals primarily to the 18-25 age group and revolves around the challenges of early adulthood—whether in college, new on the job, or navigating romantic relationships. In total, Moyer presents 14 genres, seven in each half of the book. To demonstrate how Moyer walks a librarian through a genre, the adult section's "Romance" chapter first provides a background (e.g., explaining the difference between "HEA" and "HFN" plots). She then reports that romance accounts for 13% of the books sold every year. Due to their popularity and relatively short shelf life, romance book collections are best stocked in paperback, although readers increasingly read from e-books. Website resources such as "Dear Author" can advise librarians in guiding their readers. They are advised to help teens find new books that will "make them feel the same way" they did with their favorite books.

This guide includes separate author/title and subject indexes, editor and contributor bios, and notes on scope and organization for ease of use. Compare with *The Readers' Advisory Guide to Genre Blends* (see ARBA 2015, entry 447), which includes some discussion of young adult titles across genres.—**Lucy Duhon**

397.   Friesner, Brenna. **The Verse Novel in Young Adult Literature.** Lanham, Md., Rowman & Littlefield, 2017. 209p. index. (Studies in Young Adult Literature). $65.00; $64.99 (e-book). ISBN 13: 978-1-4422-7244-6; 978-1-4422-7245-3 (e-book).

The Verse Novel in Young Adult Literature by Brenna Friesner is a unique professional resource that both teachers and librarians will find useful for reader's advisory. The "handbook" begins with an introduction that includes a definition of a verse novel as well as an exmination into the writing and reading of a verse novel. Subsequent chapters are categorized into teen issues, grief, displacement, diversity, historical narratives, memoirs and biographies, and Australian parallels. Each of these chapters includes verse novel titles and a synopsis to go with each. The resource includes interviews with a variety of authors regarding their experiences and insights into writing a verse novel. This is a great professional resource for both librarians and teachers alike.—**Shelly Lee**

398.   Goldsmith, Francisca. **The Readers' Advisory Guide to Graphic Novels, Second Edition.** Chicago, American Library Association, 2017. 232p. index. $54.00pa.; $$48.60pa. (ALA members). ISBN 13: 978-0-8389-1509-7.

Using formal readers' advisory methods, this guide to graphic novels will be helpful to new and experienced librarians trying to establish a highly used graphic novel area. For beginners, the introductory chapters set the foundation by addressing myths, appeal factors, and different styles of graphic novels (the appendix also features a "Short Course" for those completely new to the genre). Goldsmith offers ideas for displays, programming, book clubs, media tie-ins, and social media tools including blogs and fan sites. Annotated reading lists are organized by age and genre and are a useful tool for collection development. It would be a worthwhile experience to compare each reading list to current inventory. Goldsmith demonstrates the breadth of her research with a list that moves beyond best-sellers and well-known titles; even librarians with well-curated collections will find new titles to add to their next book order. The guide is well-researched with source notes at the end of each chapter, and a thorough index that will help readers find titles and authors easily. Highly recommended.—**Elizabeth Andersen**

Reference Services

399.   Brown, Christopher C. **Harnessing the Power of Google: What Every Researcher Should Know.** Santa Barbara, Calif., Libraries Unlimited/ABC-CLIO, 2017. 134p. index. $55.00pa. ISBN 13: 978-1-4408-5712-6; 978-1-4408-5713-3 (e-book).

Much like Terry Ann Jankowski's recent title, *Expert Searching in the Google Age* (see ARBA 2017, entry 430) (2016) which covered the basics of reference services using

Google as a lens, Christopher C. Brown, veteran reference librarian with a specialty in government information documents, has essentially covered basics of database searching, using Google as a lens. I appreciate the focus on the more academic Google applications—Google web (the general Google search), Google Scholar, and Google Books. With this in mind, this title is more than just for a librarian audience, who through their professional degrees have some background in how Google does (and does not) work like a research database. This book is probably more helpful for the upper level undergraduate or new graduate student transitioning from using Google Web as a default tool for all research to a more nuanced researcher, utilizing many types of tools, including Google Web, as research context dictates. I particularly liked the author's chapter of case studies, looking at scenarios where one might use these three Google applications within one research session.—**Rachel Meredith Minkin**

400.   Cassell, Kay Ann. **Managing Reference Today: New Models and Best Practices.** Lanham, Md., Rowman & Littlefield, 2017. 172p. index. $36.00pa.; $35.99 (e-book). ISBN 13: 978-0-8108-9221-7; 978-0-8108-9222-4 (e-book).

The present state of library reference work is one of upheaval and unease, due to the overall decreasing number of reference questions, staff, and budgets, coupled with the many different sources of available information—some of them quite expensive. This book discusses some alternatives for library administrators and reference staff to consider while figuring out how to best allocate limited resources to achieve the most effective service for their patrons. Here Dr. Cassell, Department of Library and Information Science at Rutgers University, has chapters on the education and training of reference librarians, new ways of offering reference services and utilizing staff, and how the very nature of reference sources influences library operations. She emphasizes the human aspect of the whole issue: how electronic resources can require more individual help, that librarians are mediators and information providers, how we need good communication skills, and the importance of building relationships, collaboration, and partnerships, both within and outside of the institution. (For what it is worth, this reviewer, who has worked in the reference field for over 30 years, feels that knowledge of resources, a good personality and public service attitude, flexibility, and adaptability are most important for a smoothly functioning library. With these attributes, one should be able to deal with almost any question and organizational arrangement; it just all depends on the individual situation.) The author provides chapter endnotes to document her sources and helpful charts to summarize the important points of big issues. This very-reasonably-priced book is easy to read and understand and is suitable for circulating collections, for reference classes in library school, and for practitioners wanting to catch up on current thinking.—**Daniel K. Blewett**

401.   **The Feminist Reference Desk: Concepts, Critiques, and Conversations.** Maria T. Accardi, ed. Sacramento, Calif., Library Juice Press, 2017. 396p. index. $35.00pa. ISBN 13: 978-0-63400-018-5.

Edited by Maria T. Accardi, *The Feminist Reference Desk* is a scholarly compendium of thought on the significance and influence of female reference desk staff in the library setting. This title is the eighth entry in the series Gender and Sexuality in Information Studies. A companion title and another volume in this series, *Feminist Pedagogy for Library Instruction* is authored by Accardi (see ARBA 2014, entry 565). The "Introduction" and

"Prelude" give foundation to the ensuing case studies, discussions, essays, guides, models, and theories with thirty-three contributing authors beyond Accardi. Because of the breadth of ideas, the book is divided into three sections: Emotional Work and Ethics of Care, Ways of Doing and Rethinking the Work, and Intersectional and Collaborative Work. Chapters involve aspects of feminine pedagogy and library service though each is a different spoke connecting to the hub of the feminine reference desk. Contributors include charts, data, and footnotes where relevant, and conclude chapters with bibliographic information. Back matter includes a "Postlude," "Contributor Biographies," and an "Index," all relevant for further research. Information itself includes librarian housekeeping tasks of analysis, assessment, cataloging, databases, models, policy, procedure, and reference interviews to name a few. Feminine perspective is demonstrated throughout.

A research tool for postsecondary students, this book will find greatest applicability in feminist and advanced library studies. It will also be useful for educators with contemporary class studies and academic library staff searching out progressive materials. Recommended.—**Janis Minshull**

402.   Gottfried, John, and Katherine Pennavaria. **Providing Reference Services: A Practical Guide for Librarians.** Lanham, Md., Rowman & Littlefield, 2017. 150p. illus. index. (Practical Guides for Librarians). $65.00pa.; $61.00 (e-book). ISBN 13: 978-1-4422-7911-7; 978-1-4422-7912-4 (e-book).

This is a practical, easy-to-understand guide developed by two veteran librarians at Western Kentucky University. It discusses how traditional reference service has changed due to the presence of so many electronic resources and demands for an increased variety of services. The chapters are concise and the text is well divided, ending with a summary of key points and a reference list. One of the themes of the book is how to understand and satisfy the information needs of your patrons with the resources at hand. Another theme is the unfortunate turmoil that exists for so many institutions with regards to finances: how to allocate limited resources to meet rising prices and changing requirements, within a sometimes hostile government environment—what are the possible options and outcomes in challenging situations? It is pointed out that having a clear vision for reference service and methods of accurate assessment are important in guiding operations for both the library staff and those in oversight positions. Chapter 4, on managing reference staff, is perhaps the most important for those new to reference work, as well as reference managers. Selecting and training individuals with the best combination of knowledge, ability, and personality to work with patrons and colleagues is crucial. Then comes creating a professional and supportive environment (flexible scheduling!), where the librarians can juggle their many obligations and responsibilities (paperwork, desk time, committee meetings, family matters). If there is an understanding and respectful relationship between librarians and administrators, then the other demands and difficulties can be addressed with less tension. There will always be various kinds of threats and competition to reference service, but humans are knowledgeable and should have the flexibility to adapt to changing situations (especially when it comes to explaining how to find and use the resources). This well-structured and informative book is recommended for library science students and collections.—**Daniel K. Blewett**

403.   Imler, Bonnie, and Michelle Eichelberger. **Optimizing Discovery Systems to Improve User Experience.** Santa Barbara, Calif., Libraries Unlimited/ABC-CLIO, 2017.

138p. index. (Innovative Librarian's Guide series). $55.00pa. ISBN 13: 978-1-4408-4382-2; 978-1-4408-4383-9 (e-book).

This volume in the "Innovative Librarian's Guide" series is authored by two experts in the study of discovery and user experience (UX) and addresses the problem of encouraging patrons to use library resources. So how do library professionals improve patron confidence in using singe search systems? Imler and Eichelberger write about processes for developing, promoting, and instructing library discovery systems. Ideas of how to examine UX studies for enhanced performance, instructional focus for more efficient patron searches, and modification for community needs are presented. Evaluation of your current system design is also explored with an end game of modification for greater system efficacy. Examples are primarily drawn from EBSCO's EDS and Proquest's Summon products. The abyss between vendor tool creation and actual needs is discussed in a forward-thinking manner. The "Software and Tools" appendix briefly lists potential options with navigable links in the digital version.

Six chapters create a clear pathway to improving single search discovery systems. Chapter two, "Usability Testing Framework," navigates the process of evaluation from developing a team to final implementation. Chapter three addresses common areas of library searching; catalog records, database content, digital collections, and local depository collections are some of the search options discussed. The authors note relatable resources throughout the text for further research. Highlight boxes, tables, and bulleted points provide critical information throughout. For example, "Ways to Teach Research Grit" offers four practical instruction options. Chapter five includes excellent ideas for promotion of your search system and the final chapter knits all of the earlier chapters together.

Optimizing Discovery Systems to Improve User Experience will be of use to all library administrators and IT staff seeking to enhance their single search system or for professionals seeking to develop such searching in their digital library community.

Recommended.—**Janis Minshull**

Storytelling

404.   **Engaging Teens with Story: How to Inspire and Educate Youth with Storytelling.** Janice M. Del Negro and Melanie A. Kimball, eds. Santa Barbara, Calif., Libraries Unlimited/ABC-CLIO, 2017. 189p. index. $55.00pa. ISBN 13: 978-1-4408-4508-6; 978-1-4408-4509-3 (e-book).

This convincing text promotes the use of storytelling practices with young adults. Editors Janice M. Del Negro and Melanie A. Kimball have garnered both scientific research and hands-on information to substantiate storytelling as a strong means to educate teens today.

The book is comprised of eight chapters following an introduction. The first chapter provides an overview of contemporary practices. Chapter 2 explains the science behind oral tradition. Digital storytelling, with examples from YouTube and other places, comprises chapter 3. The remaining chapters analyze folk and fairy tales, telling stories to young adults, storytelling to at-risk students, the connections between storytelling and writing, and more.

Engaging Teens with Story pairs well with *Out of This World Library Programs: Using Speculative Fiction to Promote Reading and Launch Learning,* another Libraries

Unlimited title by Joel A. Nichols (2017). The potential for a robust young adult storytelling program, whether in a library or school, is evident in these resources.

Engaging Teens with Story is best suited for library programming staff, secondary teachers, scholars, and storytellers that seek to promote listening, teaching, telling, and writing in the oral tradition..

Highly recommended.—**Janis Minshull**

Technical Services

405.   Schmidt, Krista, and Tim Carstens. **The Subject Liaison's Survival Guide to Technical Services.** Chicago, American Library Association, 2017. 95p. index. $40.00pa.; $36.00pa. (ALA members). ISBN 13: 978-0-8389-1502-8.

Technical services are an integral part of the library; however, subject liaisons tend to focus on collection development without a keen understanding of how technical services affects operations. *The Subject Liaison's Survival Guide to Technical Services* provides an overview of technical services and what a subject liaison should know. The book is targeted toward new subject liaisons or those with little experience.

Seven chapters are organized in a logical sequence covering the topics of collection development, budgets and budgeting, submitting orders, acquisitions ordering, receiving and processing, cataloging, and collection maintenance. Each section throughout the title provides a list of thought-provoking questions for information gathering and conversation starters with technical services. The questions are intended to be used as the need arises, not as a to-do checklist to answer all at once. Terminology, job duties, and tasks vary from one library to another. A comprehensive glossary clarifies how each term is used in the book and an index is provided.

Purposefully excluded are specific details on how technical services works. Each library has its own organizational structure, job titles, and functional differences. Communication is crucial to learning the specifics and that is exactly what this book seeks to establish. The book avoids diving into philosophical discussions or best practices, choosing to promote information-gathering on the complexities of technical services.

Recommended to academic librarians seeking methods to instigate communication channels with technical services.—**Jeffrey A. Jensen**

Publishing and Bookselling

Handbooks and Yearbooks

406.   Herr, Melody. **Writing and Publishing Your Book: A Guide for Experts in Every Field.** Santa Barbara, Calif., Greenwood Press/ABC-CLIO, 2017. 140p. index. $50.00. ISBN 13: 978-1-4408-5875-8; 978-1-4408-5876-5 (e-book).

What appears to be an innocent new book on getting published is actually a solid contribution for aspiring authors, especially academics. Divided into ten chapters ranging from the early development of a publishing project to the book contract to the final manuscript, the writing is crisp and concise. Herr's experience with academic publishers shines through with honest and thoughtful suggestions and ideas. The chapter on presentation of evidence explores how to use quotations, maps, visuals, and tables is just one example of simple yet highly useful ideas on the publication process. Two thoughts come to mind in evaluating this small book—practical and no-nonsense. The book also includes a brief introduction, list of references, and index, but the real value is as a how-to guide for authors and researchers.—**Boyd Childress**

407.   Matarese, Valerie. **Editing Research: The Author Editing Approach to Providing Effective Support to Writers of Research Papers.** Medford, N.J., Information Today, 2016. 244p. index. $49.50. ISBN 13: 978-1-57387-531-8.

This exceptional book will provide great help to persons involved in editing research articles and also to researchers attempting to ready their manuscripts for publication in scholarly journals. Author Valerie Matarese, an experienced editor who currently specializes in the biomolecular sciences, explains that an author's editor is one who works directly with the author rather than for a publisher or journal. In this book she has covered the many aspects of helping a scholar translate his or her research into a form that will be accepted by a journal in the scholar's field. Matarese opens with a prologue telling the story of a researcher sitting at her computer starting to put her article onto the screen and goes through all the steps she and her editor go through in their electronic correspondence, until finally the article is ready to submit. Topics include the challenges of writing for publication in today's global research environment, editing in the sciences and other scholarly disciplines, editing research articles, and how to manage the business of working as an author's editor. She deals with the particular challenges of editing articles in English written by scholars from other language backgrounds and editing for other genres, such as grant applications, press releases, theses and dissertations, and for the web. There are two appendixes, the first one describing membership associations relevant to author's editors. The second appendix provides the name and online address, scope, and frequency of publication of 11 peer-reviewed journals relevant to author editing. The book also includes an annotated list of references and a competent index. Highly recommended for academic libraries.—**ARBA Staff Reviewer**

12 Military Studies

General Works

Autobiography

408. Harold Innis Reflects: Memoir and WWI Writings/Correspondence. William J. Buxton, Michael R. Cheney, and Paul Heyer, eds. Lanham, Md., Rowman & Littlefield, 2016. 260p. index. (Critical Media Studies: Institutions, Politics, and Culture). $95.00; $94.00 (e-book). ISBN 13: 978-1-4422-7399-3; 978-1-4422-7400-6 (e-book).

The editors of this volume have brought together a variety of writings from the early life of Canadian economic historian and media scholar Harold Adams Innis (1894-1952). Included are a memoir, written in the last year of Innis's life, covering the first 26 years of his life, 44 letters written in 1916 and 1917 (many from France), and miscellaneous documents, including his 1918 master's thesis at McMaster University, which examined the condition of Canadian soldiers returning from World War I and what could be done to help them. This topic of course remains important today. While not exploring the fields of expertise for which Innis became known and respected, these items present the youth of an important Canadian scholar.

Clearly a specialized collection of documents, this book will be of interest to Canadian readers and people interested in a personal view of World War I. Libraries without that user population can forego this title.—**Mark Schumacher**

Dictionaries and Encyclopedias

409. Afghanistan at War: From the 18th-Century Durrani Dynasty to the 21st Century. Tom Lansford, ed. Santa Barbara, Calif., ABC-CLIO, 2017. illus. index. $100.00. ISBN 13: 978-1-59884-759-8; 978-1-59884-760-4 (e-book).

All ABC-CLIO reference volumes are first rate, and this one is no different. Few nations have witnessed as much warfare as Afghanistan—from the British Empire, through Russia's long involvement in the nineteenth century and the decade of Soviet occupation in the 1980s, to what has become America's longest war. Internal violence, civil war, and terrorism also have prevailed throughout the country's history. The 317 alphabetically arranged encyclopedia entries by 48 contributors address individuals, groups, wars, battles, treaties, weapons, military forces, biographies, and larger essays on individual wars. Fifteen primary documents, an introductory essay, an extensive chronology, a bibliography, and a list of contributors augment the individual entries. Since past history would indicate that wars in Afghanistan are not likely to cease in the future, this volume is a very good summation of where we stand at this point in time.—**Joe P. Dunn**

410.   **Encyclopedia of Invasions and Conquests: From Ancient Times to the Present.** 3d ed. Paul K. Davis, ed. Amenia, N.Y., Grey House Publishing, 2016. 642p. illus. maps. index. 165.00. ISBN 13: 978-1-68217-100-4; 978-1-68217-101-1 (e-book).

The third edition of this major work has been updated with new articles, the Russian incursion into Ukraine, and seven section introductions. The book is divided into four major sections: section one is the largest, comprising seven parts divided into the following time periods: the Ancient World, the Classical World, the Dark and Middle Ages, the Renaissance and the Age of Exploration, the Age of Revolutions and Napoleon, the Age of Empires, and the 20th-21st Centuries. Each of these seven parts has numerous entries that describe the event, followed by *see also* references and a short bibliography. Section two provides a number of primary source materials for reading and additional background to the entries in section one. Section three is a chronological timeline of all of the entries contained in the book, and section four is the bibliography. There are a large number of maps (over 100), which provide excellent visual references to all of the content. This volume is a necessary reference work for any high school or academic library.—**Bradford Lee Eden**

411.   Kowner, Rotem. **Historical Dictionary of the Russo-Japanese War.** 2d ed. Lanham, Md., Rowman & Littlefield, 2017. 842p. illus. maps. (Historical Dictionaries of War, Revolution, and Civil Unrest). $190.00; $180.00 (e-book). ISBN 13: 978-1-4422-8183-7; 978-1-4422-8184-4 (e-book).

The Rowan & Littlefield Historical Dictionary volumes, in several series, are well into the hundreds of publications. This contribution is the second edition in the group on "War, Revolution, and Civil Unrest." It follows the fairly standard format for all volumes—preface, acknowledgments, readers notes, acronyms and abbreviations, maps, chronology, introduction, lengthy dictionary entries, appendixes, and an extensive bibliography under country and subject headings. The author, the world's leading authority on the subject, contributed all the entries, rewriting every one of the original six hundred in the first edition and adding more than two hundred new ones for this edition. The essays range from two hundred to two thousand words. With its equally impressive data in the appendixes, no question exists that this is a monumental accomplishment.

However, the author's own words indicate why it is not necessary for libraries to purchase the book. Kowner explains that Wikipedia, "the most important and elaborate website dealing with the war," draws its extensive material from this book. The free and constantly updated Wikipedia source, as well as the five other comprehensive Internet sites that the author lists in the bibliography, serve most purposes that a reader would ever need.—**Joe P. Dunn**

412.   **The SAGE Encyclopedia of War: Social Science Perspectives.** Paul Joseph, ed. Thousand Oaks, Calif., Sage, 2017. 4v. index. $650.00/set. ISBN 13: 978-1-4833-5989-2.

At four volumes, this encyclopedia almost seems too small to be considered a resource on war itself. However, a closer look reveals the density and diversity of the information retained in these four books. Each volume begins with an alphabetical list of entries that covers the entirety of the four volumes, which is then followed by a reader's guide, grouping the entries in general categories that include such things as Concepts and Theories, Nations, and Gender, just to name a few. These categories each relate to social sciences, some blatantly—Psychology, for example—and some a little more subtly, such as Opposition and Resistance. The list of contributors, in the first volume, is reassuringly robust. It includes not just professors from world universities, but independent scholars, professors from military universities, and members of militaries from around the world. This reflects the in-depth and diverse nature of the research held in this encyclopedia.

While some entries do not require multiple parts—see Alamo, The—most entries are composed of several sections, working to explain the chosen entry from various angles. Looking at the entry for Camp Followers, it is divided into five sections, which define the idea of camp followers as noncombatants, explain their place in premodern armies, and look at their historical significance, before wrapping up with a thought on the possibility of "camp followers" in the modern era. This organization into explanatory sections is indicative of the entries throughout the encyclopedia, and each entry ends with a list of further readings, should the reader want more information.

This resource is exceptionally text-heavy, with readings broken only by the occasional table. Illustrations or photographs would have been appreciated to add a bit of visual interest. However, this title is an excellent resource for academic libraries, and for those scholars who study war, the social sciences, or both.—**Mary Rebecca Yantis**

413.   Smith, Joseph, and Simon Davis. **Historical Dictionary of the Cold War.** 2d ed. Lanham, Md., Rowman & Littlefield, 2017. 388p. (Historical Dictionaries of War, Revolution, and Civil Unrest). $95.00; $90.00 (e-book). ISBN 13: 978-1-4422-8185-1; 978-1-4422-8186-8 (e-book).

Authors Joseph Smith and Simon Davis have captured the essence and madness of the "balance of terror" of the Cold War in the second edition of *Historical Dictionary of the Cold War.* Covering an extensive period and much of the globe, this dictionary presents a year-by-year chronology and alphabetical entries on civilian and military leaders, crucial countries, and peripheral conflicts, the increasingly lethal weapons systems, and the various political and military strategies. While both authors are specialists in American foreign policy and diplomacy, Smith has a particular interest in United States relations with Latin America, and Davis in Anglo-American relations. This broader focus is helpful, since it enables the authors to have a comprehensive view of the Cold War and to provide a more neutral perspective. The first entry is for the September 1, 1939, invasion of Poland by Germany, and the last is for the formal dissolution of the U.S.S.R. in December, 1991. This book is an excellent resource for students, researchers, and anyone wanting to know more about this crucial period in history and is appropriate for high school, community college, university, and public libraries.—**Thomas E. Baker**

414.   **Vietnam War: A Topical Exploration and Primary Source Collection.** James H. Willbanks, ed. Santa Barbara, Calif., ABC-CLIO, 2017. 2v. illus. maps. index. $198.00/ set. ISBN 13: 978-1-4408-5084-4; 978-1-4408-5085-1 (e-book).

The list of Vietnam War reference volumes is so extensive that one has to ask how many more do we need? I have contributed to a half dozen of them, professionally reviewed in print more than twice that many, and have more than two dozen large and multiple-volume references on the war on my personal bookshelf (out of hundreds of Vietnam War reference sources in print, not even counting a whole other genre of pictorial histories). Each offering justifies itself with a slightly different focus. James Willbanks is one of the best Vietnam War chroniclers. Besides his several excellent monographs on the war, his *Vietnam War Almanac* (2nd ed., 2013) and *The Vietnam War: The Essential Reference Guide* (see ARBA 2013, entry 582) remain standards. This latest two-volume set emphasizes topically organized primary sources and documents.

The work contains the normative encyclopedia entries, written by a number of academic, military, and independent scholars, most of which were published earlier in Spencer Tucker's *Encyclopedia of the Vietnam War* (see ARBA 2001, entry 490). Rather than alphabetically arranged through the entire volume, the clustering of entries by period and event and linked with relevant documents makes the reference more useful for individuals who wish to focus on a particular period or topic. The documents are pertinent.

Other features include a listing of the reference entries and documents, a preface and introduction, chronology, a lengthy selected bibliography, and an index. Typical of ABC-CLIO, the publication is colorful and attractive. Whether another such source is needed or not, this is one more very good one.—**Joe P. Dunn**

415.   **War and Religion: An Encyclopedia of Faith and Conflict.** Jeffrey M. Shaw and Timothy J. Demy, eds. Santa Barbara, Calif., ABC-CLIO, 2017. 3v. illus. $310.00/set. ISBN 13: 978-1-61069-516-9; 978-1-61069-517-6 (e-book).

This set is ambitious and exciting in scope. Investigating the "great" or "major" religious traditions and their intersection with war and conflict is not only important, but timely. As with most such aspirational projects, however, there is a tendency to overreach, and this undertaking is no exception. A disclaimer indicating that these volumes are predominantly skewed toward the Abrahamic faiths would ease any confusion in the reader looking for a more global focus. This narrowed vision leads to generalizations ("Egypt was relatively isolated in ancient times") and omissions (while there are four and a half substantive pages on the impact of a "vow" on the Crusades, the four paragraphs on "Native American Warfare" do injustice to the history of a continent). A chronology is found in volume one, and the final volume contains the referenced primary documents. Each entry is short (a page or two at most), quite readable, and provides related indexed entries and further reading suggestions. Not intended for the specialist in the field, this is a good introduction to the topic, and provides a jumping-off point for interested students. However, the cultural focus of the entries should be reflected in the title, and in the mind of the purchasing librarian.—**Stephen J. Shaw**

Handbooks and Yearbooks

416.   **Civil War Soldiers and Sailors Database https://www.nps.gov/civilwar/soldiers-and-sailors-database.htm.** [Website] Free. Date reviewed: 2018.

This database, developed by the National Park Service (NPS) and several partners, provides information about soldiers and sailors who served in the Union and Confederate armies during the Civil War. The database is easy to navigate by a series of clickable images: Soldiers, Sailors, Regiments, Cemeteries, Battles, Prisons, Medals of Honor, and Monuments. All these sections allow users to do a basic search or to search using filters that can include first name, last name, war side, battle unit, and state, among other categories. Clicking on soldiers will take users to an index of those millions who served. Records indicate the war side, state, unit function, battle unit, and alternate name(s) if necessary. There is also a link to the soldiers' full service records at the National Archives and Records Administration. Sailors offers information on 18,000 African American servicemen. The information was derived from enlistment records and quarterly muster rolls of Navy vessels; a team from Howard University curated the information. Users will find amazing details in this section of the database. Clicking on the record of George E. Church, for example, reveals his hometown (New York, New York); occupation (farmer/ waiter); age (18); rating (1st class boy); height (5'3"); complexion (Negro); date, place, and term of enlistment; and detailed muster records. Other sections of the database will provide users details about more than 4,000 Union and Confederation regiments, burial information, and 400 of the more than 10,000 Civil War battles. Information discoverable under Prisons links to details about prisoners of war or political prisoners at Confederate-run Andersonville and Union-run Fort McHenry. This information can include historical notes in addition to basic facts like name, unit, and date of registration. For example, users will find that Union prisoner of war William Lewis was part of a prisoner exchange on April 1, 1865. Medals of Honor contains information on 1,500 recipients. A large amount of the information on the honorees comes from a Senate committee report. Monuments not only provides descriptions but also images. There is also further information available at the NPS Civil War site, https://www.nps.gov/civilwar/index.htm, of which this database is a part.—**ARBA Staff Reviewer**

417.   **The Cold War Chronicles.** New York, Cavendish Square Digital, 2018. 8v. illus. maps. index. $42.79 (individual title).

This eight-volume series discusses the issues that led to the Cold War and its impact on world events from its inception to its end in 1991. Volumes cover the Bay of Pigs and Cuban Missile Crisis, The Marshall Plan and the Truman Doctrine, NATO, Sputnik, and more. Each volume in this highly readable and visually appealing series has chapters with an introduction that explains the crisis being discussed, people who were major players during the perilous times, an overview of the negotiations and innovations that took place during the dispute, and the legacy of the crisis into the 21st century. The chapters highlighting people involved in the topics cover featured players such as Edward Teller, Klaus Fuchs, Joseph Stalin, and Buzz Aldrin. The books are replete with numerous color and black-and-white photographs and graphs. The books provide a bibliography, glossary, timeline, and websites. Recommended for grades 9-12. [Editorial note: see publisher site for individual ISBN numbers]—**Augie E. Beasley**

418.   **The Cold War through Documents: A Global History.** Edward H. Judge and John W. Langdon, eds. Lanham, Md., Rowman & Littlefield, 2018. 366p. $45.00pa.; $42.50 (e-book). ISBN 13: 978-1-5381-0926-7; 978-1-5381-0927-4 (e-book).

The first Cold War between the United States and its allies and the former Soviet Union and its allies lasted from World War II's concluding days in 1945 until approximately 1991. This historical epoch saw many significant military confrontations and near confrontations including the Korean and Vietnam Wars, the Cuban Missile Crisis, Soviet interventions in Hungary, Czechoslovakia, and Afghanistan, and eventually the collapse of the Soviet bloc and German reunification.

This compendium of documents includes excerpts from significant documents during the first Cold War along with contextual introductions to the background and policy developments resulting in the production of these documents. Work contents are broken into sections covering the Origins of the Cold War, 1945-1950; the Global Confrontation, 1950-1960; Crisis and Conflict, 1961-1969; The Era of Détente, 1969-1979; Renewal of the Cold War, 1979-1985; and The end of the Cold War, 1985-1991. Examples of document excerpts, including speeches and policy documents, are Churchill's March 1946 Iron Curtain speech at Westminster College; a 1950 telegram from Mao Zedong to Joseph Stalin on sending Chinese troops into North Korea; portions of the 1963 Nuclear Test Ban Treaty; an August 1966 Chinese document launching the Cultural Revolution; the 1975 Helsinki Final Act; a 1989 letter from Iran's Ayatollah Khomeini to Mikhail Gorbachev; remarks by U.S. secretary of state George Schultz on the 1983 Soviet shootdown of Korean Airlines flight 007; and the text of Ronald Reagan's 1987 "Tear Down This Wall Speech in Berlin."

This compilation is a useful introduction to some Cold War documents for undergraduate students, and the study questions presented at the end of each document are very beneficial. Most of the contextual introductory remarks are straightforward and objective; however, the editors fall for the superficial rhetoric criticizing Reagan's Strategic Defense Initiative (SDI) as "Star Wars" and falsely maintain that the system did not work (p. 312). In reality, SDI helped the Soviets realize they could not compete technologically with the United States; this initiative also began the system of ballistic missile defense which is becoming increasingly important to defenses against weapons of mass destruction from various rogue nations. The editors should also mention that the west is now in a second cold war due to the mounting aggression of the Russian Federation and China in a variety of global arenas.—**Bert Chapman**

419. Collins, Darrell L. **The Army of Tennessee.** Jefferson, N.C., McFarland, 2017. 266p. index. $49.95pa. ISBN 13: 978-1-4766-6821-5; 978-1-4766-2750-2 (e-book).

The history of the American Civil War has continually been a popular research topic for both scholars and family historians. Because the Civil War involved so many facets of American life, research on any specific topic can often seem overwhelming. Information on a specific person, regiment, or state army of the Civil War would better serve the researcher if it were conveniently arranged and easy to access. The purpose of *The Army of Tennessee: Organizations, Strength, Casualties, 1862-1865* is to concisely organize the records on the Army of Tennessee for scholarly research and family genealogy. This is the third volume on Civil War Armies by Darrell L. Collins. The author's previous works focused on the Army of the Potomac and the Army of Northern Virginia (see ARBA 2016, entry 443). The information in this book is compiled primarily from the 128 volumes of *War of the Rebellion: A Compilation of the Official Records of the Union and Confederate Armies. The Army of Tennessee* is handily arranged by three sections that include organization reports, present for duty reports, and casualty reports. The book also contains a brief introduction to the Army of Tennessee with its origins, commanding officers, and significant battles during the Civil War. The author has included a section of military abbreviations to assist the reader along with a commander and unit index at the end of the book. Because of its convenient arrangement and reliable information, *The Army of Tennessee* is a must-have reference book for anyone interested in the Army of Tennessee and Civil War history.—**Trent Shotwell**

420. **D-Day: The Essential Reference Guide.** Spencer C. Tucker, ed. Santa Barbara, Calif., ABC-CLIO, 2018. 280p. illus. maps. index. $89.00. ISBN 13: 978-1-4408-4974-9; 978-1-4408-4975-6 (e-book).

D-Day, the largest amphibious operation in world history took place on June 6, 1944. It is an understatement to claim that this single event changed the course of world history and allowed the Allies to achieve the foothold required to ultimately invade occupied France and to then defeat Nazi Germany a mere year later. The risk of failure by the Allies was ever present and the question of success took nearly a month to realize, but the invasion was truly an Allied effort that brought together the British, the Americans, the French, and the Canadians and made names like Eisenhower, Howard, Cota, and Winters famous. The planning to go into this event was tremendous, as were the logistics and the political wrangling, not to mention the issue of the weather and the Germans.

Dr. Tucker, the master encyclopedist, has provided the reader with a simple, but useful reference guide to all things D-Day. A list of signed entries that covers over two hundred pages along with numerous primary and secondary documents, a bibliography, maps, a chronology, and several pieces that place this event into context with events prior and after D-Day make this a useful guide to the novice and to the scholar alike.—**Scott R. DiMarco**

421. **Enduring Controversies in Military History: Critical Analyses and Context.** Spencer C. Tucker, ed. Santa Barbara, Calif., ABC-CLIO, 2017. 2v. $198.00/set. ISBN 13: 978-1-4408-4119-4; 978-1-4408-4120-0 (e-book).

The way we view events, people, and subjects differs from person to person. The filter they interpret with is based upon their biases, information, and experiences. The 64 topics explored in this work, edited by acclaimed encyclopedist Dr. Spencer Tucker, range from ancient history to the modern topics of today. Seven major eras are examined: The world of the Greeks and Romans; the Middle Ages; Modern Europe and the Americas; The Rise if Imperialism and Nationalism; The World Wars; The Cold War; and Post-2000. Each section has a brief introduction and two or three authored perspective essays that offer differing points of view in a creative and informative manner. A detailed further reading list is provided for each topic.

An example of a topic is in the Modern Europe and the Americas (1500- 1825) section—Topic 15—which asks if taxation without representation was the primary cause of the American Revolution. Three points of view are provided by scholars—one says yes, one says no, and the other provides a different primary cause for the American Revolution. This book is well-argued, provides detailed rationales, and is concise.—**Scott R. DiMarco**

422. **Modern Conflict in the Greater Middle East: A Country-by-Country Guide.** Spencer C. Tucker, ed. Santa Barbara, Calif., ABC-CLIO, 2017. 421p. illus. index. $94.00. ISBN 13: 978-1-4408-4360-0; 978-1-4408-4361-7 (e-book).

Distinguished encyclopedist Dr. Spencer C. Tucker edits this 421-page guide on the 22 countries that make up the Middle East. He provides for each country: a narrative history; a timeline; a further reading list; sidebars; documents; and photographs. A second section contains 18 primary documents. Many of these countries from Morocco in the West to Pakistan in East acknowledge World War I as a turning point for this region; other turning points include World War II, the rise of Israel, and the aftermath of September 11, 2001. Lebanon is a perfect example of an entry. Ranging from page 189 to page 199, it contains: a map, a dense narrative, a black-and-white photograph from the 1982 Israeli invasion; a four-page timeline; and a detailed further reading list. The contributors who wrote the sections are well-respected historians and scholars. This work is excellent.—**Scott R. DiMarco**

423. **National World War I Museum and Memorial. https://theworldwar.org.** [Website] Free. Date reviewed: 2018.

This website provides access to a vast archive of materials related to World War I. While only a small portion of the museum's holdings, the digital archive is nonetheless rich with globally sourced artifacts which attest to the long reach of what some consider the first modern war. The Explore tab at the top of the homepage leads to the Online Collection Database holding a large array of artifacts. Users can conduct a Keyword or Advanced Search, Search by Term (people, term, subject) or go through the document Archives of material. Users can separately explore the archive Photos, Objects (e.g., medals, plaques, prints, etc.), or Libraries (books, periodicals, etc.). Users can also view a display of Random Images. It is important to note that items within each of the larger searchable categories seem to be randomly organized, which could make browsing a bit challenging. Items are simply displayed via a thumbnail image, catalog number, and item type (letter, report, photo, etc.). Selecting an item will generally provide a description, object name, date, people, subjects, and more. A translation may be included if the item's original language is not English. The archive includes diaries, training schedules, postcards, maps, newspaper articles, personal sketches, advertising posters, and other items. Users may wish to examine the five Online Exhibitions located under the Exhibitions link also found underneath the Explore tab to get a good sense of the digital archive and what can be done with it. "The Christmas Truce, Winter 1914," for example, is an excellent multimedia presentation melding museum artifacts with scholarly essays, first-hand accounts, and other materials. Back on the homepage, the Learn tab offers a detailed Interactive WWI Timeline, using artifacts to establish the chronology of the war from Franz Ferdinand's 1914 assassination in Sarajevo to the 1920 Treaty of Sevres. The timeline notes events both on and off the frontlines, from trench battles to women's suffrage protests to influenza outbreaks. The U.S. Enters the War link connects a series of essays with video content and select artifacts to address America's initial hesitation to fight followed by the events which led to American mobilization.—**ARBA Staff Reviewer**

424. **The National WWII Museum. https://www.nationalww2museum.org/.** [Website] Free. Date reviewed: 2018.

While mainly focused on museum activities, the site nonetheless contains quality digital material devoted to upholding the history of the World War II from the American perspective and educating about the particular events of the devastating global conflict and the people who experienced them. Users will find excellent resources under The War tab at the top of the homepage. Articles cover topics inspired by the museum artifacts. Profiles present sixteen essays discussing people notable for their actions in and around the war, such as Harlan Twible who survived four days adrift at sea after the sinking of the *USS Indianapolis*. Users can search the profiles by Branch of Service or Theater of Operation. The Research a Veteran link offers resources to help users find information about individuals buried overseas, missing in action and more, while the WWII Veteran Statistics link provides data about remaining veterans. There is also a link for Students & Teachers to find resources for a range of digital learning opportunities.

It is the From the Collection link, however, which offers the most compelling material via a large and growing archive of oral history videos and photographs which collectively help to tell the story of American involvement in the war. Users can Browse by Branch of Service, Theater (e.g., Home Front, Pacific, etc.), or Vocabulary (keyword or phrase) such as Tank Warfare, Terrain, Friendships, Postwar Life, Escape and Attempts. Although there are currently no transcripts to accompany the oral histories, most videos are annotated for context and indexed for quick access to particular information. Users can also browse the large collection of photographs via the parameters mentioned above. Information accompanying the photographs may include description, donor, location, subjects, and other identifying information.—**ARBA Staff Reviewer**

425.   Pollack, David. **World War II Posters.** Atglen, Pa., Schiffer Publishing, Ltd., 2016. 352p. $50.00. ISBN 13: 978-0-7643-5246-1.

World War II Posters is comprised of 504 full-color plates of posters produced by Australia, Canada, France, Germany, Great Britain, Italy, Japan, and the United States. While an impressive compilation, the catalog is not comprehensive. David Pollack, Past-President of the International Vintage Poster Fair, selected the posters for inclusion on the basis of historical and artistic merit. Among the artists whose work is presented are Abram Games, Newell Convers Wyeth, Norman Rockwell, and Thomas Hart Benton. Also included is a short introduction and an essay that discusses the evolution of poster art from World War I to World War II. The work concludes with a section entitled "Plate Identification," that contains information such as the name of each poster, who produced it, and the dimensions of the poster as published. Since this work is designed primarily as an art catalog, its reference use is very limited. Libraries should instead consider acquiring a copy of this highly recommended and reasonably priced work for their art or military history collections.—**John R. Burch Jr.**

426.   Roberts, Priscilla. **Arab-Israeli Conflict: A Documentary and Reference Guide.** Santa Barbara, Calif., Greenwood Press/ABC-CLIO, 2017. 350p. index. $108.00. ISBN 13: 978-1-4408-4390-7; 978-1-4408-4391-4 (e-book).

This excellent resource source employs 91 documents, divided chronologically into five chapters, to tell the story of the Arab-Israeli conflict. The documents cover a wide range of sources, including Arab, Israeli, Palestinian, U.S., UN, and Soviet/Russian. Although only a tiny portion of the record, and the inclusions are almost all excerpted, the selected documents still provide an incredible introduction to one of the most complex historical conflicts on record. Each document is placed in context and is followed by an analysis of its importance. Scattered throughout the volume are "Did You Know" sidebars on persons, places, and events central to the story. The volume also contains an introduction which explains the collection, a bibliography, websites and blogs, and an index. In sum, it is a superb source. Were it not for the expense, it would be a wonderful textbook for an advanced course specifically on the Arab-Israeli conflict. More practically, given the high profile and interest in the topic, many libraries will find the volume quite useful.—**Joe P. Dunn**

427.   **Russian Revolution of 1917: The Essential Reference Guide.** Sean N. Kalic and Gates M. Brown, eds. Santa Barbara, Calif., ABC-CLIO, 2017. 258p. maps. index. $94.00. ISBN 13: 978-1-4408-5092-9; 978-1-4408-5093-6 (e-book).

The Russian Revolution of 1917 was one of the defining events of the twentieth century. It saw the end of more than four centuries of Romanov rule and set the stage for the founding of the Union of Soviet Socialist Republics. Editors Sean N. Kalic and Gates M. Brown, both in the Department of Military History at the United States Army Command and General Staff College, are joined by forty-two scholars in producing an excellent introduction to not only the conflict referenced in the title, but also the 1905 Revolution and the Russian Civil War (1917-1922).

The guide begins with three introductory essays, one on each of the conflicts. The essays serve to both provide an overview of the distinctive periods of violence and also to contextualize them in regards to Russia's instability from 1905 to 1922. The bulk of the work consists of alphabetically arranged entries on individuals, groups, and events. Each is signed and includes suggestions for further research. The final and arguably most valuable section is the collection of twenty-three documents, including Lenin's View on Bloody Sunday (1905), Abdication of Nicholas (1917), and Trotsky Insists on Stalin's Recall (October 4, 1918). Supplementary materials include maps, black-and-white pictures, a chronology, a bibliography, and an index. Public and undergraduate libraries should strongly consider acquiring this resource for their reference collections.—**John R. Burch Jr.**

428.   Tucker, Spencer C. **The Roots and Consequences of Civil Wars and Revolutions: Conflicts That Changed World History.** Santa Barbara, Calif., ABC-CLIO, 2017. 529p. illus. maps. index. $100.00. ISBN 13: 978-1-4408-4293-1; 978-1-4408-4294-8 (e-book).

This book contains 30 detailed essays on various civil wars and revolutions presented chronologically, from the Peloponnesian Wars of 460-404 B.C.E. to the Libyan Civil War from February 15-October 23, 2011. Each essay is an extended commentary and historically accurate description of the events, most of which occurred over multiple years and often had multiple antagonists and players. That the book is successful is due to the chronological presentation of each conflict within each event, and the author assists the narrative by providing a detailed timeline at the end of each essay, along with a further reading list. Some of the other civil wars and revolutions discussed include the Wars of the Diadochi (323-275 B.C.E.), the Hussite Wars (1419-1434), Pugachev's Rebellion (1773-1775), the Taiping Rebellion (1851-1864), the Irish War of Independence and Civil War (1919-1923), the Greek Civil War (1946-1949), the Cambodian Civil War (1967-1975), and the Sri Lankan Civil War (1983-2009), to name a few. The fact that the entries are representative of both historical and country/regional conflicts is another plus. An excellent detailed reference work for the conflicts that it covers.—**Bradford Lee Eden**

429.   Welch, David. **World War II Propaganda: Analyzing the Art of Persuasion during Wartime.** Santa Barbara, Calif., ABC-CLIO, 2017. 198p. illus. index. $79.00. ISBN 13: 978-1-61069-673-9; 978-1-61069-674-6 (e-book).

David Welch, professor of modern history and director of the Centre for the Study of War, Propaganda, and Society at the University of Kent and co-editor of *Propaganda and Mass Persuasion: A Historical Encyclopedia from 1500 to the Present* (see ARBA 2015, entry 518), proffers forty-six examples of propaganda produced during World War II. The media selected for inclusion include excerpts from leaflets and speeches, newspapers, postage stamps, and posters. The primary sources derive from such disparate countries as Canada, Germany, Great Britain, Italy, Japan, Union of Soviet Socialist Republics, and the United States. Each of the items, reproduced in black and white, is accompanied by an analysis that includes the intended purpose of the document and its actual effect. The work concludes with a short bibliography and general index. This work is highly recommended for libraries that collect books about World War II. One caveat is that libraries serving younger patrons should be aware that racist stereotypes abound, such as an image of the cover of the March 1943 issue of Action Comics where "Superman Says: You can Slap a Jap with War Bonds and Stamps!"—**John R. Burch Jr.**

430.   **World War I Document Archive. https://wwi.lib.byu.edu/index.php/Main_ Page.** [Website] Free. Date reviewed: 2017.

Assembled from a large array of sources by volunteers of the World War I Military History List (WWI-L) and housed on the Brigham Young University Library server, this site organizes links to numerous primary source documents related to World War I. Simply structured, the site lists eight categories of document links, with an additional category offering a listing of links to other notable subject area sites. Thematic categories include Conventions and Treaties and Official Papers; Diaries, Memorials, Personal Reminisces; Books, Special Topics and Commentaries; The Maritime War; and The Medical Front. There is also a World War I Biographical Dictionary offering brief profiles of noteworthy individuals of the era, and a World War I Image Archive. Alternatively users can choose to examine documents by year, ranging from just before the war's opening salvos in 1914 to just after the war's official end of 1918. Materials within each category may be structured differently depending on types and amounts held within them. They may include A-Z listings, direct links, and more. Within each category, users will find a compelling and diverse collection of materials. Users can view such items as each article of the 1919 Treaty of Versailles, U.S. Congressional Testimony regarding American POW's, Fleet Deployments of the Imperial German Navy, and diaries of trench soldiers and dignitaries. While the site itself offers no bells or whistles, historians, educators, and students would find it to be an excellent gateway to a wealth of unique artifacts on the first true global conflict.—**ARBA Staff Reviewer**

431.   **World War II, 1939-1949: A Collection of U.S. Government Documents. https:// www.nlm.nih.gov/news/incunabula_ww2_gov.html.** [Website] Free. Date reviewed: 2018.

This digital collection is comprised of nearly 1,400 U.S. government publications providing information on U.S. involvement in World War II and its aftermath. The publications include government reports, pamphlets, recruitment materials, health manuals, and more, and deal with U.S. domestic health issues as well as health concerns abroad. The collection shares its homepage with the Incunabula project of early European medical texts. To access the collections, users click on the WW2 1939-1949: A Collection of U.S. Government Documents link near the bottom of the page. This will produce materials listed with thumbnail photograph and basic identifying detail such as format, author, and subject(s). Clicking on the title link allows users to closely examine or download the item and note further identifying detail. Highlights of the collection include a 24-page manual on Army Autopsy Procedure, the illustrated "What You Should Know About the Atomic Bomb" guide, Notes on Air-Raid Damage and Health in Germany, and much more. The publications were produced by local, state, and federal government agencies, and would be of interest to military or government historians, among others.—**ARBA Staff Reviewer**

Weapons and Warfare

432.   **Arms Trade Treaty Database. www.att-assistance.org/.** [Website] Free. Date reviewed: 2017.

The Arms Trade Treaty (ATT), enacted in December of 2014 and signed on by over 100 nations, is a vital yet complex example of international diplomacy. This website aims to increase and enhance cooperation between signatory nations via its two searchable databases which provide information on activities related to the treaty and its implementation, with an emphasis on developing regions.

Created in partnership between the United Nations Office of Disarmament Affairs and SIPRI, an international think tank researching global conflict and arms control, the straightforward, easily navigable site essentially contains two databases, accessible via the menu bar. The Activity Database allows access to nearly 400 "activities" concerning arms trade and control issues which were conducted by ATT partners in Sub-Saharan Africa, Latin America, and the Caribbean in the five years spanning 2012-2017. Activities can refer to a number of things including workshops, roundtable meetings, seminars, and trainings. Selecting the "Find Out More" tab underneath an activity title links to a map which highlights the participating nations, a summary description of the activity, focus, type, implementer(s), links to activity media (reports, etc.), contact information, and related activities. The database is searchable by a number of categories and subcategories, such as focus, donors, region, and partners. Activities are organized chronologically, and include a 2016 Strategic Planning Workshop for ATT Implementation in East Africa and the Horn of Africa, a 2016 Regional Meeting on Improving Arms Control and Violence Prevention in Bolivia, Colombia, Ecuador, and Peru, and much more. Users can also access a Document Database, which currently houses one 149 documents related to ATT implementation. Documents can be model laws, guidelines, reports, etc., and include "Border Controls and Law Enforcement," "Southern African Development Community Firearms Protocol Guidelines," and more. Documents are searchable by year, publisher, focus, and type, and are generally downloadable in PDF format. The site encourages feedback and the submission of new activities, and is hoping to include materials from additional regions into its databases.—**ARBA Staff Reviewer**

433.   **The CNS North Korea Missile Test Database. http://www.nti.org/analysis/ articles/cns-north-korea-missile-test-database/.** [Website] Free. Date reviewed: 2018.

This database tackles the timely subject of North Korean missile testing. Tracking tests conducted by the secretive Asian nation since 1984, the database notes a variety of information that would appeal to those interested in military studies, global nuclear policy, and other affiliated topics. The database appears as an interactive map whereby users can examine data in a number of ways. Users can choose Missile Type (e.g., Scud-B, KN-02, etc.), Missile Family (e.g., Medium Range Ballistic, etc.), and Test Results (Failure, Success, Unknown), then view tests as they have been conducted over time (April 1984-September 2017). The full dataset is downloadable as an Excel spreadsheet. The database has tracked 116 tests, and employs a qualifying standard for the missiles it tracks—500 kilogram minimum payload and 300 kilometer minimum distance traveled. The size of the pin marker on the map notes number of launches by site. Alternatively, clicking on a pin accesses launch location-affiliated data in graph format, including Test Results, Launches over Time, Most Recent Recorded Test, number of Tests, and Facility Activity. Users can also note missile types per facility. Supplementary material includes analytical essays and infographics on database specifics and related topics (e.g., "North Korea's Hwasong-12 Missile: Stepping Stone to an ICBM").—**ARBA Staff Reviewer**

434.   Garrett, Benjamin C. **Historical Dictionary of Nuclear, Biological, and Chemical Warfare.** 2d ed. Lanham, Md., Rowman & Littlefield, 2017. 376p. $95.00; $90.00 (e-book). ISBN 13: 978-1-5381-0683-9; 978-1-5381-0683-9 (e-book).

Expanded by nearly 70 pages, this important addition to the publishers' Historical Dictionaries of War, Revolution, and Civil Unrest is both timely and more comprehensive than the first edition published 10 years ago (see ARBA 2008, entry 601). The only volume in the series not targeting a specific war or military action, the second edition updates entries in light of 10 years of scientific developments, both describing weapons and their uses and how such weapons are countered. A list of acronyms and abbreviations, a brief chronology, and an introduction precede the 500 plus alphabetical entries ranging from a paragraph to two to three pages. The who, what, and where are covered, and *see* and *see also* references are interspersed throughout the volume. Bold print is utilized for cross-references. Chemical names are included and the volume is not burdened with excessive statistics. An extensive bibliography includes sections for historical and technical works. Handy as a ready reference tool, the volume will interest students and specialists. One curious omission is an index, noted in reviews of the first edition yet absent in the revision. An example is Tinian in the Mariana Islands, an important test site for nuclear weapons during the Second World War and mentioned in several entries but without its own entry. Even with this flaw, the volume is a must purchase for larger reference collections.—**Boyd Childress**

435.   Lepage, Jean-Denis G.G. **Military Trains and Railways: An Illustrated History.** Jefferson, N.C., McFarland, 2017. 206p. illus. index. $45.00pa. ISBN 13: 978-1-4766-6760-7; 978-1-4766-2764-9 (e-book).

Who can forget the image of the military train in movie extravaganzas such as *Dr. Zhivago, Lawrence of Arabia,* or *The Bridge on the River Kwai?* Indeed, popular media is replete with the image of the train in warfare. What the helicopter came to symbolize in visions of the Vietnam War, the train was for more than a century earlier. A whole field of historical scholarship concentrates on trains and railroads. Lepage, historian and illustrator who resides in the Netherlands, is the author of at least a dozen illustrated histories that include military vehicles, aircraft, fortifications, and castles and fortified cities.

This book, which describes how the railroad transformed the nature of warfare, features 256 drawings, as it treats wars such at the Boer Wars, American Civil War, Austro-Prussian

War, Franco-Prussian War, Russo-Turkish, War, World War I, Finish Civil War, Spanish Civil War, World War II, and the French-Indochina War, with a brief note on conflicts such as the Korean War and the U.S. War in Vietnam. Written for a popular lay audience rather than specialists, the concise text is interesting and full of useful information. As a reference source, the volume would have quite limited audience, most likely best suited for high school student reports and papers. However, as general circulation reading, the book is most engaging for military buffs and train enthusiasts.—**Joe P. Dunn**

13 Political Science

General Works

Handbooks and Yearbooks

436.   **CQ Press Library. http://library.cqpress.com/.** [Website] Thousand Oaks, Calif., CQ Press / Sage, 2017. Price negotiated by site. Date reviewed: 2017.

   While historical context and discussion of recurring issues play roles in library research about Washington politics and activity in the United States Congress (including interaction with the executive and judicial branches), some questions can be answered only by having very recent information. *Congress.gov* publishes official texts as they appear, but lacks independent analysis. The combination of current reporting with analysis is the mission of CQ Press. *CQ Press Library* is an omnibus online resource to keep track of proposals, debates, and voting; it also provides a rich archive of older and related materials.

   CQ Press Library has multiple parts each with a specific role. The weekly *CQ Magazine* (until 2016 known as *CQ Weekly*) covers recent issues and debates and the progress of legislation. In addition to articles about current Capitol Hill business, this is a source for a detailed record of roll call votes on the floor of the House of Representatives and the Senate. For October 2017, for example, the tally tracks 96 different votes ranging from confirmations of federal officials, to procedural votes, to final passage of bills into acts of law. *CQ Researcher* is another weekly, focusing on one major topic in each issue, such as abortion, climate change, or refugee policy. Recent issues looked at sexual harassment and cyberwarfare. *CQ Almanac* is an annual summary of Congressional business, extending back to the 79th Congress in 1945. Reports are grouped by topic, such as appropriations, defense, or science. Appendixes list new public laws, and record the most important floor votes. *Politics in America* provides profiles for all members of Congress, with contact information and a short biography. For each individual, there is a timeline of "key votes" and voting scores from interest groups such as Americans for Democratic Action (ADA: liberal), the Chamber of Commerce of the United States (CCUS: business interests), and the American Conservative Union (ACU: conservative). Appendixes identify members of caucuses and congressional committees. An archive extends back to the 106th Congress in 2000. The *Supreme Court Yearbook* summarizes the work of the top court since 1989, with lists of cases, notes about key cases by topic, and biographies of recently serving justices. Texts of court opinions can be found using the Supreme Court website at https:// www.supremecourt.gov/. The *Voting and Elections Collection* provides numerical election results for presidential, senatorial, congressional, and state gubernatorial elections, in some cases extending back to 1789. Interpretive maps include Electoral College results and results of House races by district in the states. *Political Handbook of the World* looks at overseas politics, with summaries for all world states (including the Palestinian Authority and China: Taiwan). The emphasis is on politics: identification of ruling figures or cabinet officers and summaries of recent political developments.—**Steven W. Sowards**

437.   **The Palgrave Handbook of Political Elites.** Heinrich Best and John Higley, eds. New York, Palgrave Macmillan, 2018. 688p. index. $239.00. ISBN 13: 978-1-137-51903-0; 978-1-137-51904-7 (e-book).

The introduction addresses the definition of political elites and changes in the scholarly treatment of political elites since the mid-twentieth century. Political elites, as explained by the book, are business executives, government officials, and military leaders, but they can also be people or groups who hold strategic positions in such entities as trade unions, political parties, media enterprises, and religious institutions with enough influence to affect political decisions nationally and internationally. The handbook is divided into six sections comprised of forty chapters. The sections are as follows: Theories of Political Elites, Research Methods for Studying Elites, Political Elite Patterns in the World's Main Regions, Differentiation & Integration of Elite Sectors, Elite Attributes and Resources, and Elite Dynamics and Dilemmas. Chapters within these sections allow readers to understand important topics like how to identify political elites, changes in political elite behavior in the West since World War II, and elites beyond the nation state. The book includes with an extensive, cross-referenced index.

This is a scholarly enterprise. The writing level reflects the target audience, college students and above. Highly recommended.—**ARBA Staff Reviewer**

438.   **Political Handbook of the World 2016-2017.** Lansford, Tom, ed. Thousand Oaks, Calif., Sage, 2017. 2v. index. $415.00/set. ISBN 13: 978-1-5063-2718-1.

The *Political Handbook of the World* has been a foundational resource in the reference collections of medium to large-sized libraries for decades. The 2016-2017 edition under review continues to reflect this quality. The work contains detailed, up-to-date information about the governmental and political conditions within two hundred countries and territories arranged in alphabetical order. Entries are organized in a consistent format and include a detailed synopsis of significant events, issues, and political or social crises and controversies that have emerged during the past couple of years. Particularly useful are the descriptions of both major and minor political parties. Entries also include a brief description of legislature bodies and the key ambassadors and the key international memberships of each country. Embedded in the entries of specific countries is recent coverage of important events, such as the Brexit referendum and the installment of a new British prime minister, the impeachment of Brazil's president, the impact of the Panama Papers scandal, and the migrant and refugee crisis across Europe, alongside obscure events like the unconstitutional declaration of Gambia as an Islamic State. Of particular value are the in-depth descriptions of more than thirty intergovernmental organizations and UN agencies. These entries focus on examining the origins, development, and recent activities of each organization. Note that the Palestinian Authority/PLO is listed here. Front matter includes a comprehensive table of contents and a list of intergovernmental organization abbreviations. Back matter in volume two includes a chronology of major political events from 1945 to 2016, an important descriptive chronology of major international conferences sponsored by the UN from 1946 to 2016, a table of country memberships of the UN and its agencies, and a source list of serial publications. The text is very dense and there is no index, so finding specific information across entries can only be done in the online edition. The handbook represents a time capsule of the political landscape of the world. The annual *Europa Year Book* and its regional editions serve a similar function. However, the handbook focuses almost exclusively on describing political systems, the nature of political parties within those systems, and their transitions and, therefore, remains a uniquely valuable resource for students and researchers.—**Robert V. Labaree**

439.   **Russia Matters. https://www.russiamatters.org/.** [Website] Free. Date reviewed: 2017.

Launched in 2016 by Harvard Kennedy School's Belfer Center for Science and International Affairs, this database aims to explain the importance of Russia (now and in the future) to U.S. policy-makers, students, and members of the U.S. public. Russia Matters also hopes to further policies that simultaneously advance U.S. interests while reducing and/or mitigating conflict and to create a new generation of Russia experts.

Russia Matters (RM) has a number of institutional partners and a distinguished editorial board, which can all be found under the About link at the bottom of the home page. Other material is discoverable under a series of tabs on the top of the home page. Under the Analysis tab, there is a choice of what the database calls RM Exclusives, Recommended Reads, Partner Posts, and works by upcoming scholars and policy thinkers (Future Policy Leaders). The RM Exclusives are original pieces, while the Partner Posts first published elsewhere. RM exclusives and Future Policy Leaders pieces are searchable back to 2016; Recommended Reads and Partner Posts are searchable to 2012. As of August, 2017, when this reviewer accessed the site, there were RM Exclusives on whether or not giving Ukraine lethal weapons would serve U.S. vital interests, the role of Russia in solving the crisis in North Korea, a roadmap to U.S.-Russia relations, and much more. Clicking on the News tab reveals a weekly digest of Russia-related items like trade and investment, Russian domestic news, and foreign affairs. This too is searchable to 2016. Material from Analysis and News are both easily shareable via social media. There is also a Blog tab that pulls up interesting posts like one that hypothesizes about Donald Trump's affection for Vladimir Putin and a Facts tab that links to vetted quantitative data on Russian demographics, education and science, military and security, and more. Under the Contested Claims tab, the database indicates the truthfulness of claims (e.g., Russian life expectancy fell in 2014 and 2016) using a stoplight rating system; red for false, green for true, and yellow for partially correct. Users will also find interesting quotes, information about upcoming events, and more by clicking the links on the bottom of the home page. This is also where users will find a Search link that reveals a basic search box alongside filter and refine options.

This is a valuable tool for anyone interested in Russia, its place in the world, and its relations with the United States. It will be a useful source for policy-makers, journalists, scholars, students, and members of the general public.—**ARBA Staff Reviewer**

440.   **UN Climate Change Newsroom. http://newsroom.unfccc.int/about/.** [Website] Free. Date reviewed: 2018.

The United Nations Framework Convention on Climate Change has created this website to report on its work in particular relation to Climate Action and the Paris Agreement. Users can find articles, reports, announcements, meeting synopses, and other resources which could be useful to researchers studying climate change or connected issues like international relations, education, and media. The page reflects a diverse range of topics and media. Users can scroll through the page to examine a gallery of tagged topics or can organize the material by Climate Action or Paris Agreement categories. Users simply click on a title to access information. Under the Paris Agreement category alone, users can access a statement from the UN Climate Change head on Nicaragua's recent accession to the agreement, a meeting synopsis in preparation of formal Paris Agreement progress accountability, a video encouraging G20 leaders' support of the agreement, and background on the social media initiative #Faith4Paris which asks for Paris Agreement support among global faith leaders. An efficient use of color photography lends the site a professional look. Supplemental information is available on the right-hand column of the page under Featured Links and Resources, such as Policies and Actions up to 2020, Sustainable Development Goals and a Climate Funding Snapshot.—**ARBA Staff Reviewer**

Ideologies

441.   **Socialism on Film: The Cold War and International Propaganda. https://www.amdigital.co.uk/primary-sources/socialism-on-film.** [Website] Chicago, Adam Matthew Digital, 2017. Price negotiated by site. Date reviewed: 2017.

The first module of this extensive database provides access to 435 films from the ETV-Plato Films collection, now in the archives of the British Film Institute. Two other modules— *Newsreels & Magazines* (2018) and *Culture and Society* (2019) will follow. Subcategories include "Lenin & the Russian Revolution," "The Vietnam War & Southeast Asia," and "The Holocaust & War Crimes," among others. The subjects are quite diverse, from a movie about an 1877 battle of Russians and Bulgarians against Ottomans, and a film about the 1905 Potemkin Mutiny, to films about Latin America in the 1970s. The films come from 23 countries, dominated by the USSR [219], with others from Japan, North Vietnam, China and other countries around the world. Only five are from the United States. Some films have English narrators, while others have subtitles. All are presented as originally made.

Given the chronological breadth of the collection, the subtitle, *The Cold War and International Propaganda* seems somewhat misleading (or unduly restrictive). This collection will be useful for any library whose patrons study modern world history. Because cost is based on a number of variables, that aspect should be examined carefully.—**Mark Schumacher**

International Organizations

442.   Fomerand, Jacques. **Historical Dictionary of the United Nations.** 2d ed. Lanham, Md., Rowman & Littlefield, 2018. 784p. $170.00; $161.50 (e-book). ISBN 13: 978-1-

5381-0970-0; 978-1-5381-0971-7 (e-book).

This book, now in its second edition (see ARBA 2008, entry 659), is part of the Historical Dictionaries of International Organizations series published by Rowman & Littlefield. It is the most extensive and comprehensive dictionary available on the United Nations (UN). The introduction provides a concise history of the UN, and the chronology (included in the front matter) is itself a detailed document listing major UN decisions from 1864 through January 2017. The entries vary in size, providing in-depth coverage of many topics related to the UN; entries include *see* references in bold within the text and *see also* references in all caps at the end of each article. This particular volume has ten appendixes, providing key documents such as the Charter of the UN, the membership of the UN, current peacekeeping operations, core UN treaties, major environmental treaties, and major disarmament and arms control agreements. As is usual in this series, the bibliography is both broad and deep in its coverage and detail. I highly recommend this volume as a reference work in academic and government libraries.—**Bradford Lee Eden**

443.   **InterAction.org. www.interaction.org.** [Website] Free. Date reviewed: 2917.

InterAction is a 180-member-strong global community of nongovernmental organizations (NGOs), both secular and faith-based, hosting a range of programs and resources targeting issues like poverty, gender equality, and health. Their website educates users on their work and the many issues facing the world today. The home page features a topical video and listing of recent blog posts and InterAction news items. The page also includes a number of easy-to-navigate tools, such as the NGO Aid Map—an excellent way for users to examine over 2,000 InterAction projects around the world. Selecting a pin on the map will highlight a singular country, showing the location of over 100 NGO efforts and profiling each of them with their name, a brief description, applicable sectors (e.g., agriculture, social services, etc.), target groups (e.g., extreme poor, women, etc.), and more. These maps are updated constantly and include recent examples of NGO assistance with hurricane response in the U.S. Virgin Islands and earthquake response in Mexico. The mapped projects are also available to view as a list. Our Members is a directory listing NGO members by Issue Area or Country. Users can also search by member name. The directory includes a brief member profile with contact information. The directory cross-references to the NGO Map if applicable. Our Work outlines the four areas of InterAction work: International Development (Gender Equality, Environment & Climate, etc.), Accountability and Learning (Leadership Development, Mapping, etc.), Humanitarian Action (Protection, Current Crisis, etc.), and Policy & Advocacy (G7/G20 Summit, Food Aid Reform, etc.). Our Resources displays a variety of tools which serve to both assist member NGOs in their work and educate the general community. Tabs allow access to such things as InterAction Annual Reports, training materials, and a searchable document library of reports. Other links report on the annual InterAction Forum, the agenda of the G7/G20 summits, and other issues. Recommended.—**ARBA Staff Reviewer**

International Relations

444.   Braveboy-Wagner, Jacqueline, and Clifford Griffin. **Historical Dictionary of United States-Caribbean Relations.** Lanham, Md., Rowman & Littlefield, 2017. 201p.

(Historical Dictionaries of Diplomacy and Foreign Relations). $85.00; $80.00 (e-book). ISBN 13: 978-1-5381-0222-0; 978-1-5381-0223-7 (e-book).

The relationship with the small Caribbean nations and their bigger neighbor to the North has been both a source of conflict and enlightenment. While U.S. culture and manufactured goods dominate the region, the relationship between the two parties has been a rocky one over the past three centuries. This excellent historical dictionary treats each topic in a uniform, unbiased fashion. Topics include, among others: Bay of Pigs Invasion, Eric Matthew Gairy, Papa Doc, Guantanamo Bay, Congress of Vienna, Jimmy Carter, Donald Trump, Che Guevara, and the Caribbean Diaspora. Also included is a collection of topics under the theme "United States, Interventions in ..." which chronicles more direct attempts by Washington to influence local political outcomes in the region. In addition to the historical dictionary section, the authors have provided a map, acronyms and abbreviations, a chronology, a twenty-one-page introduction, a bibliography, and the text of historical documents: Monroe Doctrine, Platt Amendment, Roosevelt Corollary, Ronald Reagan's speech on the Caribbean Basin Initiative, George H.W. Bush's Speech on the Enterprise for the Americas, and Barack Obama's Normalization of Relations with Cuba. The map unfortunately is so small that the reader will need magnification to view the names of the islands/countries. The chronology fails to mention the arrival of Columbus in the New World. The bibliography is up to date and provides a jumping off point for future research. There is no index or table of contents/topics so you sort of have to guess what entries you might be interested in. Overall this is a handy guide to United States-Caribbean relations that will provide basic information on topics of interest.—**Ralph Lee Scott**

445.   Keithly, David M. **The USA and the World: The World Today Series 2017-2018.** 13th ed. Lanham, Md., Rowman & Littlefield, 2017. 282p. illus. maps. (The World Today Series). $23.00pa; $21.00 (e-book). ISBN 13: 978-1-4758-3520-5; 978-1-4758-3521-2 (e-book).

The central theme of this volume on the United States and the world is the maintenance of global connections to manage the worldwide prosperity and security for itself and all nations. The goals for the future are fourfold: support a more secure world by the encouragement of settling negotiated disputes and agreements to lessen the event of wars; stimulate the U. S. economy by creating markets abroad and creating jobs to promote growth here in the United States; advance democracy, economic growth, and human rights around the world; and gain control over narcotics and simultaneously promote world health education and housing through financial assistance programs and contributions to international institutions.

There is a "Recommended Reading" list and a list of "Web Sites." There is no index, but black-and-white photographs and maps are provided. This volume is recommended for public, academic, business, and corporate libraries for their political science and economics collections.—**Kay Stebbins Slattery**

446.   Lamb, Peter, and Fiona Robertson-Snape. **Historical Dictionary of International Relations.** Lanham, Md., Rowman & Littlefield, 2017. 376p. (Historical Dictionaries of International Organizations). $95.00; $90.00 (e-book). ISBN 13: 978-1-5381-0168-1; 978-1-5381-0169-8 (e-book).

As part of the Historical Dictionaries of International Organizations series from Rowman & Littlefield, this book focuses on the history of international relations. As an academic discipline, it first appeared immediately after World War I as a university degree centered around the problems of war and peace among the great powers so that another war could be avoided. The foundation of international relations goes back several centuries to the writings of Machiavelli and Hobbes, and the editors offer a concise history of the study from the early Greek city-states up to modern times, explaining the Westphalian Era, the twentieth century, the post-Cold War era, and the twenty-first century. A list of acronyms and abbreviations, chronology, and extensive bibliography are included. Entries consist of biographies of important persons, events, wars, treaties, and related topics. Boldface type within individual essays indicates other entries, and *see also* references are included at the end of each entry. Recommended for high school and academic libraries.—**Bradford Lee Eden**

Politics and Government

Canada

447.   **Canadian Parliamentary Guide 2017/Parlementaire Canadien 2017.** Toronto, Grey House Publishing Canada, 2017. 1251p. index. $299.00. ISBN 13: 978-1-68217-524-8; 978-1-68217-525-5 (e-book).

This latest edition of the *Canadian Parliamentary Guide* is published the year of the 150th anniversary of Canada's Confederation. The text is in English and in French. This excellent research source contains more than 2,800 biographical sketches and begins with an introduction, a photo gallery of the Maclean's Parliamentarians of the Year, an illustrated section of the history of Canada, including a timeline and maps, and the history of the Parliament of Canada. The bulk of the book follows, with biographical information of Queen Elizabeth II and senior members of the royal family; biographical information on the Governor General; and biographies of members of the Senate, Privy Council, House of Commons, and of those politicians representing the Provinces. Each biographical entry includes date of birth, education, political career, private career, address, phone number, fax number, email address, and projected date of retirement. Additionally, election results are included by provinces and districts. The appendixes are comprised of: Table of Precedence; Table of Titles; Acronyms and Abbreviations; Canadian Representatives Abroad; and Alma Maters. A Name Index is also provided. The *Canadian Parliamentary Guide* is a thorough source of information about Canada and its history and government. It is highly recommended to academic and larger public libraries. It can be used for "quick reference" questions and as a starting point for research about Canadian history and politics.—**Lucy Heckman**

448.   **Governments Canada 2017.** Toronto, Grey House Publishing Canada, 2017. 1160p. index. $449.00pa. ISBN 13: 978-1-68217-240-7; 978-1-68217-553-8 (e-book).

Governments Canada provides directory information and direct contact details for the federal/provincial government and municipal governments. The introduction includes an essay and guide to the Canadian Parliament, including how laws are enacted; highlights of significant changes, describing major changes and events in Canada since the last election; government statistics; and a quick reference guide. Under each topic, federal agencies are listed first, followed by provincial and territorial agencies. Each entry contains name, address, phone, fax, and email. The section on federal government features directory information for the Office of the Prime Minister; the Governor General and Commander-in-Chief of Canada; officers of the Privy Council plus a list of members; House of Commons; Senate of Canada; the Canadian Ministry/The Cabinet; Members of the Forty-second Parliament; the Bank of Canada; Canadian Space Agency; Employment and Social Development; the Royal Canadian Mounted Police; and the Royal Canadian Mint, among other agencies. Directory information is also provided for provinces and territories. The municipal section is arranged by provinces and by municipal type (counties, major municipalities, and municipal district). The diplomats section features a directory of Diplomatic Representatives in Canada and also Canadian Diplomatic Representatives Abroad. Additionally there is an acronyms index, containing those used for departments, ministries, and agencies; and a contact index of approximately 20,000 key contacts. Each listing includes title, phone number, and page where listed in book. *Governments Canada* is a quick reference guide to locating agencies and specific government contacts. It also is an excellent starting point to research. It is highly recommended to larger public and academic libraries.—**Lucy Heckman**

United States

Dictionaries and Encyclopedias

449.   Conley, Richard S. **Historical Dictionary of the Reagan-Bush Era.** 2d ed. Lanham, Md., Rowman & Littlefield, 2017. 488p. (Historical Dictionaries of U.S. Politics and Political Eras). $110.00; $109.99 (e-book). ISBN 13: 978-1-5381-0180-3; 978-1-5381-0181-0 (e-book).

This second edition (see ARBA 2008, entry 626) addresses the 1980s and early 1990s and the presidencies of Republicans Ronald Reagan and George H.W. Bush, whose victories were complemented by the electoral successes of conservatives Margaret Thatcher and Brian Mulroney in Great Britain and Canada, respectively. The Reagan-Bush era witnessed some of the most dramatic events of the latter half of the 20th century: the collapse of the Soviet Union, a presidential assassination attempt, political scandal, a stock market crash, military invasions, and the explosion of the space shuttle *Challenger.* This dictionary relates these events and provides extensive political, economic, and social background on this era through a detailed chronology, an introduction, appendixes, a bibliography, and several hundred cross-referenced dictionary entries on important persons, events, institutions, policies, and issues. The author, Richard S. Conley, is an associate professor of political science.

The *Historical Dictionary of the Reagan-Bush Era* is appropriate for high school, community college, university, and public libraries. The dictionary also serves the needs of history buffs and enthusiasts—perhaps a suitable gift for a special occasion.—**Thomas E. Baker**

450.   **The SAGE Encyclopedia of Political Behavior.** Fathali M. Moghaddam, ed. Thousand Oaks, Calif., Sage, 2017. 2v. $395.00/set. ISBN 13: 978-1-4833-9116-8.

This 2-volume encyclopedia contains 365 alphabetically arranged entries that examine various economic, psychological, sociological, and theoretical aspects of political behavior related to processes of resource allocation, civic engagement, and bureaucratic decision-making. The selection of topics is based on "classic" subjects or theories in political behavior studies such as feminism, as well as "important cutting edge topics" that reflect emerging issues like the entry on Internet Jihadism. Contributors are associated with institutions throughout the world and are profiled in the front matter of the first volume. Their profiles reflect the multidisciplinary treatment of political behavior found in this work. Entries vary in length depending on the topic, but most clearly define the topic, outline its development, and examine its relevance to the political behavior. Entries conclude with a list of *see also* references and further readings that consist primarily of books, both foundational and more recent, and selected articles form scholarly journals. Tables of information that summarize key points accompany a few entries. Both volumes include a complete list of entries and a reader's guide that arranges entries under 11 general categories. Although each essay stands alone in covering a particular topic, the reader's guide is helpful in locating, for example, all entries that describe social political movements or all entries that related to examining voting behavior and political campaigns. The second volume concludes with a comprehensive index that facilitates locating terms throughout the work. Entries are written for a wide audience of teachers, beginning researchers, and students. Overall, this work takes a comprehensive approach to describing political behavior among groups and individuals and the underlying theories and concepts that form the basis for exploring the complex relationship between politics and human behavior. It is highly recommended.—**Robert V. Labaree**

Directories

451. **The California Directory. cold.govops.ca.gov.** [Website] Free. Date reviewed: 2017.

From the California Department of Technology comes The California Directory, which offers state government and public service information useful to a broad audience. Simply structured, users can conduct a basic search of entities or employees or select from the State Entities or Employees tabs at the top of the home page. Selecting State Entities leads to an extensive alphabetized list of agencies, boards, departments, offices, and more. The Board of Forestry, State Council on Developmental Disabilities, Courts of Appeal, Office of the Lieutenant Governor, Department of Motor Vehicles, Prison Industry Authority, Sierra Nevada Conservancy, and the Office of Traffic Safety are just a few of the hundreds of entities listed. Hovering over or clicking on a particular entity will bring up a limited profile with address, executive names, phone numbers, and email addresses, although it is important to note the available information varies. Employees can be searched by name or keyword which can be a bit cumbersome, as the search term applies to any aspect of the employee entry (e.g., first or last name, portion of name, email address, and entity). Information that appears alongside employee names includes emails, phone number, city, and entity. It would be helpful to also include job titles in this listing. There is no browse function for employees. While there are no bells and whistles to this site, it nonetheless provides useful and accessible information relevant to the most populous state in the union.—**ARBA Staff Reviewer**

Handbooks and Yearbooks

452.   **Archives of Maryland Online. www.aomol.msa.maryland.gov/.** [Website] Free. Date reviewed: 2017.

This site has collected over 470,000 documents reflecting the course of government of the state of Maryland. Many of the documents precede Maryland's union with the United States. Site users can examine the documents that serve as evidence of the state's legal, fiscal, and general administrative systems. Users simply scroll down through a listing of particular document groups—mostly organized into numbered volumes—on the left sidebar to select their area of interest. They will find Early State Records, Land Records, Fiscal Records, Probate Records, and much more. Additionally, users can access the eighteenth-century Charter of Maryland, the Current Maryland Constitution, and a number of city directories. Some of the volumes are works-in-progress, such as the Slavery Commission listing which compiles documents detailing the history of slavery and emancipation in Maryland. These documents include manumission records and certificates of freedom. The page provides several tools to assist users in their search, like a glossary of historic terms and navigation and image viewing tips. The wealth of information and straightforward organization of the site makes it a must-stop for those interested in the rich administrative history of a state which holds such a prominent place in American history.—**ARBA Staff Reviewer**

453.   Brandus, Paul. **This Day in Presidential History.** Lanham, Md., Bernan Press, 2018. 386p. illus. index. $40.00; $38.00 (e-book). ISBN 13: 978-1-59888-943-7; 978-1-59888-944-4 (e-book).

In this attention-grabbing book, award-winning White House journalist, Paul Brandus, organizes little-known historical anecdotes about the presidents of the United States. He offers a fascinating reading experience that relates narratives about scandal, sex, and tragedy and explores social, political, and historical intrigue. The book is formatted to resemble a calendar with historical entries. The book poses questions such as "why did Abraham Lincoln have a beard" that satisfy curious readers. Moreover, the clarity and ease of the author's writing style makes this a fun read. The book is enhanced by timelines, bullet-point formatting, bold font, presidential photographs, quotations, and appendixes. One particular appendix, "How Do Historians Rate the Presidents on Greatness" is thought provoking but might be considered controversial by some. A substantial index rounds out the work. Recommended.—**Thomas E. Baker**

454.   Burch, John R., Jr. **The Great Society and the War on Poverty: An Economic Legacy in Essays and Documents.** Santa Barbara, Calif., Greenwood Press/ABC-CLIO, 2017. 436p. index. $89.00. ISBN 13: 978-1-4408-3387-8; 978-1-4408-3388-5 (e-book).

Lyndon Johnson's Great Society was America's second economic revolution of the twentieth century. In some ways modeled on the New Deal, the Great Society and accompanying War on Poverty were initially governmental attempts to address poverty among African Americans and in Appalachia but expanded to other problems in the nation. A wide sweeping set of reforms and legislation targeted economic and social issues, including civil rights, equal pay, education and health care, housing and urban ills, and legal protections. Programs begun during the Kennedy Administration were expanded and new efforts tackled long-standing social problems. This useful historical volume provides concise entries on programs, legislation, organizations, and individuals from that era of American history. Over eighty alphabetically arranged entries include *see also* references and a list of readings. A set of twenty-six documents provides original resources of the Great Society, each with a useful introduction placing the document into historical perspective. It is within these "hidden" introductions where some of the best information in the volume is provided. Examples are the Kerner Commission and Johnson's state of the union address in 1965 which created Medicare and Medicaid. The introduction and epilogue are excellent historical essays but the index lacks a comprehensive approach. Overall the volume is a solid contribution to American history.—**Boyd Childress**

455.   **CQ Press Guide to U.S. Elections.** Deborah Kalb, ed. Thousand Oaks, Calif., CQ Press / Sage, 2016. 2v. illus. index. $390.00/set. ISBN 13: 978-1-4833-8036-0.

This comprehensive two-volume set provides information on the U.S. electoral process for elections through 2015. The first volumes provides an overview, and covers such topics as campaign finance, political parties, and presidential elections. The second volume covers congressional and gubernatorial elections, as well as such reference materials as related websites, a bibliography, abbreviations, and constitutional and population information. The thirty-one chapters contain tables, black-and-white photos and illustrations, and references. Researchers will find the content and analysis of interest, while general readers may appreciate the historical and background details.—**Denise A. Garofalo**

456.   **Digital Maine. www.digitalmaine.com.** [Website] Free. Date reviewed: 2017.

This site serves as the online library for publications relating to the large variety of state and community organizations in the state of Maine. Users can browse through the lengthy list of Maine state agencies such as the Maine Department of Environmental Protection, The Arts Commission, Health & Human Services, etc. Selecting an agency affords users a brief explanation of agency duties in addition to document submissions— many in PDF format—related to that agency. Documents may include certifications, annual reports, newsletters, activity summaries, agency recommendations, educational guides, and financial statements. Users can also conduct a basic or advanced search or link to other Maine historical libraries, museums etc. for further information on the New England state. An interactive map shows the types of documents downloaded by users, and where the users are located throughout the globe. There are no bells or whistles, but users such as students, business owners, community organizations, and many others interested in the governing processes of Maine will be treated to an easy-to-navigate and thorough website.—**ARBA Staff Reviewer**

457.   **Documentary History of the First Federal Congress of the United States of America, March 4, 1789-March 3, 1791. Correspondence: Third Session, November 1790-March 3, 1791. Volume 21.** Charlene Bangs Bickford, Kenneth R. Bowling, Helen E. Veit, and William Charles DiGiacomantonio, eds. Baltimore, Md., Johns Hopkins University Press, 2017. 1060p. illus. $125.00. ISBN 13: 978-1-4214-1606-9.

458. **Documentary History of the First Federal Congress of the United States of America, March 4, 1789-March 3, 1791. Correspondence: Supplement. Volume 22.** Charlene Bangs Bickford, Kenneth R. Bowling, Helen E. Veit, and William Charles diGiacomantonio, eds. Baltimore, Md., Johns Hopkins University Press, 2017. 1136p. illus. maps. index. $125.00. ISBN 13: 978-1-4214-2019-6.

These are the final volumes in a widely honored project that began in 1972, to document the activities of the first U.S. Congress (March, 1789-March, 1791), considered by many as the most important Congress in our history. Earlier volumes presented documents on debates, the "Senate executive journal and related documents," legislative histories, and correspondence in the earlier sessions held in New York. These volumes, focused on the final session of the First Congress, begin with a discussion of Congress's move to Philadelphia, and the role of the city as a temporary national capital. The introductory material lists the members of the two units (House and Senate), bills being discussed, and topics that appear regularly in the correspondence to follow. "These letters and other documents bring the official record to life, illustrating the often informal political negotiations of a young nation's earliest leaders . . ." [publisher]. The second volume in this set contains the index, of subjects and individuals, for the two volumes, as well as letters from the entire two-year period, discovered after the publication of earlier volumes.

According to OCLC, over 98 percent of the libraries holding this set are academic or historical society libraries. Scholars whose focus is on the early years of United States government and the activities of our early national leaders will surely find this resource useful, although possibly a bit frustrating on rare occasions, given the vast number of topics being addressed in these letters, and the references in footnotes to earlier volumes in this long-running set.—**Mark Schumacher**

459. **FDSys. https://www.gpo.gov/fdsys/.** [Website] Free. Date reviewed: 2017.

The U.S. Government Publishing Office hosts the Federal Digital System responsible for providing free online access to official publications from the Legislative, Judicial, and Executive branches of American government.

The homepage currently features two documents up front: the Fiscal Year 2018 Budget and the 2017 Economic Report of the President. It also features a Moments in History tab on the right sidebar which offers access to collections of historically significant documents, such as the Warren Commission Report, President Nixon's Watergate Grand Jury Testimony Transcripts, and the 9/11 Commission Report. Each collection is introduced with a brief contextual essay.

For other documents, users can conduct a basic or advanced search or can browse through the 13 categories of government documentation listed on the right sidebar. Categories include U.S. Court Opinions, Congressional Record, Economic Indicators, Congressional Hearings, Public & Private Laws, Compilation of Presidential Documents, and much more.

Also listed here is the extensive Code of Federal Regulations (CFR) which comprises all published rules established by each department, agency, commission, etc. of the federal government. Users are able to view and/or download each or all of the 50 annually updated titles in the code going back to 1996. Titles in this vast collection include, among others, *The President, Domestic Security, Animals & Animal Products, Energy, Federal Elections, Aeronautics & Space, Customs Duties, Food & Drugs, Internal Revenue, Labor, National Defense,* and *Public Health.* Each title in the code is further divided into chapters. For example, Title 22, *Foreign Relations,* lists 17 chapters related to publications from the Department of State, the Foreign Service Grievance Board, the Peace Corps, the Agency for International Development, and others. Chapters are further organized by part, subpart, and section. For clarification, the Department of State chapter alone consists of 199 parts, while the entire foreign relations title contains 1,799 parts. This page also provides a link to the e-CFR (Electronic Code of Regulations) which is the unofficial daily update for the standard legal CFR, compiling CFR material with Federal Register Amendments and a link to the List of CFR Sections Affected (LSA), which shows proposed, new, and amended regulations since date of the last full CFR title revision.

As a whole, the Federal Digital System site would definitely appeal to researchers in the broadly historical sense, particularly through its Moments in History collections. But the site's greatest appeal would be for users looking for the absolute fundamentals of government workings—from rules and regulations to records, bills, reports, opinions, and more.—**ARBA Staff Reviewer**

460. **The Institute for Local Self-Reliance. https://ilsr.org.** [Website] Free. Date reviewed: 2018.

The Institute for Local Self-Reliance (ILSR) focuses on empowering local and regional entities with strategies and information aimed at sustainable and fair community development. This website details several ILSR initiatives in addition to providing a wealth of resources that community leaders, policy makers, educators, and others would find immensely helpful. The Initiatives tab on the menu bar lists seven categories of ILSR work, including Banking, Broadband, Energy, Independent Business, The Public Good (emphasizing the preservation of public assets like libraries or the military), and Waste to Wealth (e.g., turning recycling into jobs). Users can choose an ILSR initiative to explore resources and information related to that topic or browse more broadly through the Rules Library, Reports & Resources, or Archives. For each ILSR initiative, users will find an overview in addition to various topical resources, such as articles, videos, podcasts, data, and affiliated companies. For example, the particularly timely category of Broadband provides a round-up of articles (e.g., "EPB Fiber Optics Reaffirms Network Neutrality Commitment in Chattanooga"), podcasts (the Building Local Power podcast episode "Internet Connectivity in Indigenous Communities"), and factsheets (e.g., "Net Neutrality Repeal: By the Numbers Maps & Data"). Under the Broadband Rules tab, the site lists a nationwide range of local/regional codes, acts, and more concerning issues of telecommunications, such as the 1999 Iowa Act Authorizing Municipal Networks or the Ammon, Idaho Fiber Optic Network Ordinance. Users can search generally through resources and initiatives or can search within each initiative via local, state, and federal filters. Users can find newly added materials under the Recent Updates tab, and note frequently viewed materials under the Most Popular tab. In addressing a range of issues from the simple act of composting to the hot-button topic of Net Neutrality, the site offers an excellent way to examine local/regional motivations and resources.—**ARBA Staff Reviewer**

461. LeMay, Michael C. **The American Political Party System: A Reference Handbook.** Santa Barbara, Calif., ABC-CLIO, 2017. 368p. illus. index. (Contemporary World Issues). $60.00. ISBN 13: 978-1-4408-5411-8; 978-1-4408-5412-5 (e-book).

Political parties and partisanship make up much of our news cycle at present, and civics lessons regarding the development of our nation's party systems may be long past. For those just learning or who need a refresher, *The American Political Party System: A Reference Handbook* explains the history of political parties in the United States from the consensus election of Washington to the turbulent years of rising minor parties through the establishment of the modern two-party system we know today.

This history comprises approximately one-third of the volume. To cover so much information in just over one hundred pages certainly means some topics are compressed; however, each chapter contains a significant reference list for further reading, and the book closes with an annotated resource list for more context. Also included are first-person perspectives on many issues related to the party system and American elections, including activism, ballot access, and modern third parties. This title is timely, including the outcome of the 2016 election, and provides additional context for the shakeup of traditional party politics in its aftermath. A "Profiles" chapter covers the major organizations and people in contemporary national politics, and a ready reference "Data and Documents" chapter provides quick facts including the full details of the presidents and state primary systems.

For lower division students or those needing a primer on the foundations of our electoral process, this volume will be of great use. The significant reference lists will allow novices to seek out further resources to expand their understanding of this key aspect of our democracy.—**Emily Lauren Mross**

462.   Lindner, Dan. **A Guide to Federal Contracting: Principles and Practices.** Lanham, Md., Bernan Press, 2017. 622p. index. $95.00pa.; $90.00 (e-book). ISBN 13: 978-1-59888-965-9; 978-1-59888-966-6 (e-book).

The author of this work brings more than 30 years of practical experience to this text, having worked in the departments of Homeland Security and Defense (Navy), as well as in the private sector. He organizes this volume using "5 Ps": principles, planning, placement, pricing, and post-award. The information is quite detailed from the very beginning. Scores of terms and acronyms need to be defined or spelled out. Many sections also have references to the corresponding texts of the Uniform Commercial Code (UCC) and the Federal Acquisition Regulation (FAR). (The latter is a 1,900-plus-page document.) The detailed complexity of the entire process is pointed out when the author lists 41 strategies to keep in mind during a certain kind of contract negotiation process! And similarly, following the signing of a contract, "contract administrative officers" and their teams may have as many as 76 functions to perform. It is clear, however, that the author's background in this world allows him to present the many steps in the contract process clearly to those who require the information.

Given the nature of the information presented here, specialized libraries will be most interested in acquiring it: business school and law school libraries, corporate libraries of companies dealing with the federal government, and possibly some academic libraries at institutions which teach related courses outside their professional programs. Others will not need this text.—**Mark Schumacher**

463.   Misiroglu, Gina. **The Handy American Government Answer Book: How Washington, Politics, and Elections Work.** Canton, Mich., Visible Ink Press, 2018. 372p. illus. maps. index. (Handy Answers series). $21.95pa. ISBN 13: 978-1-57859-639-3; 978-1-57859-674-4 (e-book).

This book delivers excellent insight that stimulates political curiosity, providing

a. reader-friendly explanation of how Washington politics function and increasing understanding of the basic requirements of American citizenship. The straightforward soft-cover book answers basic questions regarding the workings of a complex system. The cloaked world of power brokering and bureaucratic stealth comes to life, as the author explains behind-the-scenes political practices and the responsibilities of citizens. The clarity of the author's writing style encourages active rather than passive citizenship. This volume includes a substantial index system. Moreover, the book provides a timeline of events and uses both bullet formatting and questions and answers highlighted in bold font. The question-and-answer format helps learners prepare for examinations and enhances motivation to continue reading. Appendixes offer further readings, a copy of the Declaration of Independence, and more. Recommended for public, school, and academic libraries.—**Thomas E. Baker**

464.   **The Papers of James Monroe: Selected Correspondence and Papers, April 1811-March 1814. Volume 6.** Daniel Preston, ed. Santa Barbara, Calif., Greenwood Press/ABC-CLIO, 2017. 628p. index. $195.00. ISBN 13: 978-0-313-31983-9.

Continuing a massive project begun in 2003, and now totaling more than 4,000 pages, this volume presents documents from a period that James Monroe was the Secretary of State under President James Madison; that also included much of the War of 1812. Most of the 503 documents are letters, both to and from Monroe. Correspondents include Madison, John Quincy Adams, Secretary of the Treasury Albert Gallatin, politician Henry Clay, Sr., and the lawyer and son-in-law, George Hay. The documents have been drawn from a large number of repositories in the United States and abroad. Each item includes notes and annotations to explain references in the text. A 22-page index guides the reader to individuals, places, and events of the period, as they appear in the letters. The editors stress that there is very little "personal correspondence" included, so as to focus on texts pertinent to the social, political, and military events taking place.

Academic historians and their students with an interest in the early years of the United States will be the primary readers of this volume. A previous knowledge of the period will certainly enhance the usage of this set. Colleges and universities will be the home of this title.—**Mark Schumacher**

465.   **The Prague Spring Archive. www.scalar.usc.eduworks/prague-spring-archive/ index.** [Website] Free. Date reviewed: 2017.

Presenting select records from the larger Lyndon Baines Johnson Presidential Archive, this website offers an introductory look at U.S. interest in the events of the Prague Spring—the brief period of Czechoslovakian rebellion against Communist control. This particular project has digitized two boxes of archived materials, and acts as a portal to the larger Texas ScholarWorks repository which houses the full collection of items concerning the U.S. interest in the era. Users can simply click on corresponding buttons for each box (numbered 179 and 180) to examine its contents, or select from the drop down menu. For each box, users will see a listing of contents organized into folders. Folders are marked by total pages, years covered, and a brief description, and may include maps, reports, memos, meeting notes, telegrams, and more issued by a variety of foreign and domestic agencies. Photographs of select folder items appear on the right sidebar. Clicking on a folder link will generate a more detailed description of contents with highlights and links to several key documents. For example, Folder One of Box 180 contains a "State

Department Telegram re: The Czech Ambassador to the United States" and a "CIA Report on the Future of Czech Leadership." Clicking the folder link here will then redirect to the larger Texas ScholarWorks website where individual items can be examined. The home page offers additional features to provide context and navigation assistance. Key Figures lists individuals from the United States (e.g., Secretary of State Dean Rusk) and abroad (e.g., General Secretary of the Soviet CCCP Leonid Brezhnev) relevant to the era. Key Documents highlights and links to notable papers from boxes 179 and 180. A Timeline allows users to select key dates or events throughout the Prague Spring. And the Guide and Finding Aid tab provides searching assistance for this somewhat composite site. More document boxes will be digitized and profiled in the Prague Spring Archive in the future. Still, the contents here are certainly enough to help scholars initiate study of the era, its people, and events.—**ARBA Staff Reviewer**

Public Policy and Administration

Handbooks and Yearbooks

466.   **Civios. https://civios.umn.edu/.** [Website] Free. Date reviewed: 2018.
      Civios employs a digital platform to disseminate public affairs research to a broader audience. The site hosts a state-of-the-art collection of videos, podcasts, case studies, and mixed media presentations that address topics of domestic and international concern, such as Gender, Education, Race & Identity, Migration, Labor Policy, Strategic Planning, and much more. Users can conduct a basic search or browse by format or subject, which can relate to historical or current events. Alternatively, they can click on a particular format to browse its contents. Mixed Media uses photo galleries, interactive maps, timelines, and other tools in its three offerings, one of which explores "Deportation in the U.S." Six Video offerings include a feature on "Policy and Planning Opportunities of Self-Driving Vehicles." Case Studies includes eight projects dealing mostly with the processes and practices of Public Affairs work, such as its "Applying Design Thinking to the Social Sector" study. And the particularly accessible Podcast category contains nine programs, such as "Jordan's Youth: Effects of the Syrian Refugee Crisis." The homepage highlights Recent Additions and Trending Topics. Although the content may seem a bit limited in number, the projects are professional and focused on diverse topics with both local and global impact. The site does a good job of demonstrating the relationship between digital media and those topics. It holds much promise as it should easily expand on its fine foundation of topical offerings in the future. Civios would appeal to both users with a general interest in public affairs or a particular focus on issues of the day.—**ARBA Staff Reviewer**

467.   **FactCheck.org. http://www.factcheck.org/.** [Website] Free. Date reviewed: 2017.
      The nonpartisan, not-for-profit FactCheck.org is a free website whose aim is to inform the general public of the accuracy of the information coming out of Washington, D.C. by key players in U.S. politics. The site was launched in 2003 by reporter Brooks Jackson and is a project run by the University of Pennsylvania's Annenberg Public Policy Center.

The site is divided up between eight different tabs (Home, Articles, Ask a Question, Viral Spiral, Archives, About Us, Search, and More). The homepage features a rotating banner comprising a handful of featured articles that check the accuracy of a range of policy-related topics. Below this banner is a list of recently published articles (with the most recently published article listed first). Users can access the full article by either clicking on the image associated with each article or the article title. The menu bar to the right-hand side of these articles contains an "Ask FactCheck" question-and-answer; includes an easy-to-find "Donate Now" button; and includes links (with useful visual graphics) to various other site features, like "SciCheck" and "Health Watch," among others. This bar is a permanent feature of the site and remains in place as the user navigates between pages.

Some of the tabs offer pull-down menus to different pages related to that tab. For example, the Articles tab consists of links to the "Featured" articles page, "The Wire," and "SciCheck," which is related specifically to science policy. The Ask a Question tab is a Q&A forum that allows users to submit questions and which features answers to questions posed by users (with both a "FactCheck" and "SciCheck" option). Viral Spiral is a portion of the site dedicated to investigating and analyzing the credibility of widely disseminated—"viral"—stories. The Archives tab allows users to browse archived articles by month, section, people, location, and other tags. And the About tab gives information about the organization: its mission, process, funding, and staff. There's a search tab that allows for a custom Google search and a More section which features a pull-down menu of additional resources.

The organization of the site isn't immediately intuitive and takes some scrolling around in order to get a good feel for its organization and breadth of content. Even then, it's not always clear what distinguishes some pages from others. While the writing is clear and informative, the site is probably best suited for an older audience already familiar with some of the material, as the nature of the content itself might be difficult for younger users. Nevertheless, this reliable site is recommended to school, public, and academic libraries.—**ARBA Staff Reviewer**

468.   **Handbook of Public Policy Agenda Setting.** Nikolaos Zahariadis, ed. Northampton, Mass., Edward Elgar, 2016. 487p. index. (Handbooks of Research on Public Policy). $240.00. ISBN 13: 978-1-78471-591-5; 978-1-78471-592-2 (e-book).

The *Handbook of Public Policy Agenda Setting* describes a complex process with many important humanitarian applications. Why is this handbook important to the reader? The answer is pure and simple. Government corruption harms everyone, especially those in most need of effective leadership and meaningful agenda setting. When government policy fails under the control of unethical manipulators and actors, they often enhance personal wealth and power, and do not provide effective policy agenda setting. That is, there is as much evidence that the government agenda drives the public as there is for the reverse condition. Because public policies are in place to address the needs of people, they are often broken down into different categories as they relate to society. As a collection of laws and rules used to manage a society, public policy can often be controversial or passionately debated. Depending on a person's perception or point of view, public policy can seem unfair, oppressive, or even inhumane. Getting scholars to agree on a single, all-inclusive definition of public policy is not an easy task. Public policy is generally not a tangible concept but a term used to describe a collection of laws, mandates, or regulations, established through a political process. This handbook provides an excellent description of the public policy pathway and positive government mandates. It provides a comprehensive overview and analysis of the perspectives, individuals, and institutions involved in setting the government's agenda at subnational, national, and international levels. Drawing on contributions from leading academics across the world, this handbook has five distinct parts: People and Context, Theoretical Developments, Institutional Dimensions, Comparative Applications across Levels of Government, and Agendas and Crises.

In this work, editor Zahariadis introduces students and scholars alike to the most up-to-date and important research in agenda setting. The aim is to cover as many topics and dimensions of agenda research as possible in a comprehensive way. Given that such a project is the first of its kind, the editor sees the handbook as a reference tool and as tasty "food for thought." Succeeding admirably, this handbook will be the definitive reference tool in public policy agenda setting for scholars, students, and practitioners in political science, public policy, public administration, and mass communication. Colleges and universities will value this handbook as an essential addition to their library reference shelves.—**Thomas E. Baker**

469.   Madigan, Michael L. **HAZMAT Guide for First Responders.** Boca Raton, Fla., CRC Press, 2017. 326p. illus. maps. index. $64.95. ISBN 13: 978-1-1380-3629-1.

This is an authoritative text by an author currently working as a master instructor at the Department of Homeland Security. During his more than forty-year career, he has gained expert knowledge in weapons of mass destruction, terrorism, and other areas. The text is divided into nineteen chapters starting with "What Is a Hazardous Material Responder" and concluding with "National Information Management System and Incident Command System." Other chapters provide extensive information on decontamination methods and procedures, equipment needed if responding to a situation with hazardous materials, weapons of mass destruction and biological agents, what is needed when response involves meth labs, mass casualties and fatalities, hazardous waste, and much more. Four case studies included near the end of the book showcase different types of incidents: a 1989 gasoline tanker crash in Virginia, a runaway train and derailment that occurred in Québec in 2013, the 2011 earthquake and tsunami in Japan followed by the Fukushima nuclear disaster, and a 2004 pipeline accident that took place in Ghislenghien, Belgium. The book includes a bibliography and an index. It is highly recommended to academic and public libraries and those agencies responsible for responding to crises involving hazardous materials.—**ARBA Staff Reviewer**

14 Psychology, Parapsychology, and Occultism

Psychology

Dictionaries and Encyclopedias

470. DeBord, J.M. **The Dream Interpretation Dictionary: Symbols, Signs, and Meanings.** Canton, Mich., Visible Ink Press, 2017. 464p. index. $21.95pa. ISBN 13: 978-1-57859-637-9; 978-1-57859-658-4 (e-book).

The average person spends one third of their lifetime in sleep mode. Analyzing dreams offers opportunities to scrutinize insightful observations. Readers are the best interpreters of their dreams, but they need to know how. Anyone can do it—it is not as difficult as it might appear to novice interpreters. The entries encourage the analysis of dream messages and serve as entertaining journeys during the course of ageless interpretations. Readers will find the alphabetical entries fascinating and intriguing. The introduction orients the reader and explores how to benefit from the book. One section entitled Figuring Out Your Dreams assists readers in self-exploration. Some entries serve as a hub for related entries and further readings. The Dream Interpretation section offers a *see also* list that thoroughly explores topics.

The Dream Interpretation Dictionary is a hypnotic read and is recommended for public and academic libraries as well as personal collections.—**Thomas E. Baker**

471. **The SAGE Encyclopedia of Abnormal and Clinical Psychology.** Amy Wenzel, ed. Thousand Oaks, Calif., Sage, 2017. 7v. index. $1,300/set. ISBN 13: 978-1-4833-6583-1.

An alphabetical listing of terms presenting established concepts and modern concerns (such as diversity) are arranged within twenty-six categories, most of which are aligned with the DSM-5. A list of these categories with the corresponding entries helps to group similar topics together. Entries about disorders further discuss some, if not all, of eleven different aspects: biological factors, cultural factors, diagnosis, epidemiology, gender and sex differences, lifespan perspectives, psychological factors, risk for, social factors and treatment. The well-researched and organized information is meant to be an overview and not a thorough examination, with text that is nontechnical. There are cross-references and brief bibliographies after each entry and some black-and-white illustrations. The final volume includes a resource guide that lists sources arranged by major topic and includes books, journals, organizations, agencies, and videos—and an index to the entire set. Information about the editors and the contributors is available in volume 1. This collection would serve as an excellent source for students and the general public and as a quick reference for professionals.—**Martha Lawler**

472.   **The SAGE Encyclopedia of Industrial and Organizational Psychology.** 2d ed. Steven G. Rogelberg, ed. Thousand Oaks, Calif., Sage, 2017. 4v. index. $655.00/set. ISBN 13: 978-1-4833-8689-8.

The second edition of Sage's *Encyclopedia of Industrial and Organizational Psychology* provides an excellent update to 2006's first edition (see ARBA 2007, entry 652). The encyclopedia now includes 550 articles in four volumes of work and remains appropriate for experts and students alike. Entries are organized alphabetically beginning with "abusive supervision" and concluding with "workplace spirituality and spiritual leadership"; articles are designed to be an introduction to all topics researched in industrial and organizational (I-O) psychology. The most notable addition to the second edition is a collection of essays discussing the pursuit of I-O psychology as a profession as well as success as a professional. Coverage is expanded in the areas of history of I-O psychology, ethics at both corporate and individual levels, contemporary legal issues such as gay rights and data privacy laws, and advances in research methodologies. While articles are organized alphabetically with cross-references and further readings lists included at the end of each article, there is also a reader's guide that organizes content thematically into 28 sections creating a readily accessible cross-referenced list of content. The encyclopedia would be suitable for a wide variety of readers, ranging from PhD level academics to undergraduate and graduate students as well as practitioners and lay audiences seeking an introduction to I-O psychology topics.—**Alexandra Hauser**

473.   **The SAGE Encyclopedia of Marriage, Family, and Couples Counseling.** Jon Carlson and Shannon B. Dermer, eds. Thousand Oaks, Calif., Sage, 2017. 4v. index. $650.00/set. ISBN 13: 978-1-4833-6955-6.

This four-volume set provides authoritative and comprehensive coverage of the history, theories, therapeutic approaches, clinical techniques, and important people in the field of marriage and family counseling. There are over 500 signed articles, each accompanied by a current bibliography. The editors also provide cross-references to related articles. Each volume begins with an alphabetical list of entries, as well as a topic-based reader's guide that provides the reader with the articles related to a given concept, such as intimacy, and articles that fit into a certain category, such as assessments. There are over 150 articles dealing with diagnosing disorders and models, interventions, and techniques used in therapy. The currency of the set is apparent by the articles on the relevant new disorders in the DSM-5, including hoarding disorder, gender dysphoria, and disinhibited social engagement disorder, as well as many references to the DSM-5 within the articles. The first volume includes a list of contributors, who are primarily from academic institutions, and the introduction provides additional in-depth background on the editors. There are three appendixes: a history of the field, a resource guide with information on professional associations and important journals, and a short list of additional selected readings. There is an extensive, detailed subject index in the fourth volume. The articles are clear and concise and would be an excellent starting point for undergraduate research. This work would both update and complement the *International Encyclopedia of Marriage and Family* (see ARBA 2003, entry 823), especially by providing a focus on current clinical diagnoses and therapies in the field.—**Theresa Muraski**

474.   **The SAGE Encyclopedia of Psychology and Gender.** Kevin L. Nadal, Silvia L. Mazzula, and David P. Rivera, eds. Thousand Oaks, Calif., Sage, 2017. 4v. index. $550.00/ set. ISBN 13: 978-1-4833-8428-3.

The first thing that one takes in when encountering *The SAGE Encyclopedia of Psychology and Gender* is its size: four fairly dense and sizable volumes comprise the encyclopedia. Each volume begins with a list of entries represented across the entirety of the work; it might have perhaps been useful to have divided this list into volumes—this list format comes across as a wall of text barely relieved by spacing. The first volume alleviates this by listing which letters are represented in each volume, though one questions the necessity of the entry list, especially given the presence of the index. This minor quibble aside, the encyclopedia comes with a reader's guide which is arranged into twenty general topics, primarily focusing on topics related to age, biology, health, and social issues (e.g., adolescence, developmental and biological processes, mental health and gender, and gender and society). Given the complexity of the issues that fall within this discussion, this reader's guide is far more useful to an individual encountering these issues for the first time.

The entries themselves are fairly lengthy and include *see also* cross-referencing and further reading suggestions. Some entries are subdivided into sections but not all of them. That practice should have been applied across the board, given the sheer comprehensiveness of the entries themselves. Without the subdivisions, some of the entries come across as walls of text. This is not a make-or-break aspect of this text—simply something to consider when presenting certain material in such a fashion.

In terms of content, the thoroughness and diversity of topics and viewpoints is breath-taking and laudable. The notion of psychology and gender is not an easy one to unpack and is often affected by a variety of factors ranging from social values to spiritual/ religious beliefs to politics to education. The editors and authors of the encyclopedia have attempted to be as honest and unbiased as possible with a powder keg of a topic, for which they should be commended. They do justice to the diverse range of issues and concepts represented by psychology and gender, incorporating historical viewpoints as a means of showing the development of ideas as well as recent research to challenge popular misconceptions of ideas.

While the price tag is admittedly steep, this title is worth the price. The encyclopedia does a great job trying to tackle all the meaningful dimensions of psychology and gender and provide users with a grasp on the topic and a resource for delving deeper. This title is highly recommended for academic libraries, especially at institutions with significant psychology/marriage and family therapy programs as well as sociology and related programs.—**Megan W. Lowe**

Handbooks and Yearbooks

475.   **Depression Sourcebook.** 4th ed. Keith Jones, ed. Detroit, Omnigraphics, 2017. 567p. index. (Health Reference Series). $95.00. ISBN 13: 978-0-7808-1498-1; 978-0-7808-1499-8 (e-book).

This fourth edition is an ideal all-in-one educational tool that addresses a sensitive topic, offers multiple insights into human behavior, and serves as an incentive to help those who suffer in silence.

The book effectively communicates insights that address diagnosis and treatment—including therapies, medications, and brain stimulation techniques. In addition, it offers suggestions and evidence about alternative and complementary therapies used to improve depression symptoms. The academic content provides information about frequency, symptoms, and types of depressive mood disorders, including major depression, dysthymia, atypical depression, bipolar disorder, depression during and after pregnancy, depression with psychosis, and seasonal affective disorder. In addition, chapters discuss genetic, biological, and environmental risk factors for depression and examine the impact of depression among the chronically ill, minority populations, children, adolescents, college students, men, women, and older adults. Anyone seeking preventative guidance, information about depression warning signs, and suicide risk factors, will likely find answers to their inquiries. This volume is not intended to replace the advice of a trained professional.

The book is organized into nine parts: The first eight are: Introduction to Mental Health Disorders and Depression, Types of Depression, Who Develops Depression?, Causes and Risk Factors for Depression, Depression and Chronic Illness, Diagnosis and Treatment of Depression, Strategies for Managing Depression, and Suicide. Part ten, Additional Help and Information, provides a glossary of important terms related to depression and a directory of organizations that help people with depression and suicidal thoughts. Usability is enhanced by the use of headings and subheadings. An index rounds out the work.

The *Depression Sourcebook* provides basic medical information for patients, families, caregivers, and the public. Recommended for school, community college, and university libraries.—**Thomas E. Baker**

476.   Hill, Valerie, and Tennille Nicole Allen. **Hanging Out: The Psychology of Socializing.** Santa Barbara, Calif., Greenwood Press/ABC-CLIO, 2018. 196p. index. (The Psychology of Everyday Life series). $38.00. ISBN 13: 978-1-4408-4392-1; 978-1-4408-4393-8 (e-book).

This addition to the Psychology of Everyday Life series analyzes socialization, an essential part of cognitive, physical, social, and emotional well-being. The material is presented in three parts: Socializing in Everyday Life; Scenarios; and Debates and Controversies. Chapters in the first part delve into the negative and positive effects of socializing, psychological theories, changes in socializing during the life cycle, various forms of socializing, and socializing around the world. In the second part, the authors present five case scenarios that include a teen coping with peer pressure and the experiences of older adults as their social circles shrink or change due to the deaths of friends and other factors. The last part addresses controversies and debates, such as nonromantic social relationships between men and women. These sections are followed by a directory of resources, glossary, bibliography, notes about the contributors, and an index. This interesting discussion about the psychology of socializing would be appropriate for high school, academic, and public libraries.—**Thomas E. Baker**

477.   Minetor, Randi. **Blowing Up: The Psychology of Conflict.** Santa Barbara, Calif., Greenwood Press/ABC-CLIO, 2017. 200p. index. (The Psychology of Everyday Life). $38.00. ISBN 13: 978-1-4408-4467-6; 978-1-4408-4468-3 (e-book).

Conflict can be positive or negative—constructive interpersonal skills help prevent the latter. The book offers constructive steps to create better understanding between people and groups. The book unfolds in perfect learning progressions over the course of three parts: The Conflict of Everyday Life, Scenarios, and Controversies and Debates. The author assembles contributors that offer unique conflict solution perspectives. The writing clarity enhances understanding. The dialogue bypasses complex psychological jargon and addresses emotional traffic in the fast pace of modern society. A resources directory, glossary, and bibliography offer further clarification for readers. *Blowing Up* is an excellent anger management book. This exceptional contribution offers practical advice to a diverse readership; however, it targets teenager and young adult audiences. Writing to a well-defined readership is an excellent approach for reaching out to those experiencing the turmoil of erratic emotions while transitioning towards adulthood. Every high school, community college, and university library should consider adding this book to their resource collections.—**Thomas E. Baker**

478. Reel, Justine J. **Filling Up: The Psychology of Eating.** Santa Barbara, Calif., Greenwood Press/ABC-CLIO, 2017. 216p. index. (The Psychology of Everyday Life). $38.00. ISBN 13: 978-1-4408-4089-0; 978-1-4408-4090-6 (e-book).

The Psychology of Everyday life series of books addresses many different psychological issues and areas. This installment on eating is authored by Justine Reel and is divided into three sections: Eating in Everyday Life, Scenarios, and Controversies and Debates.

The six chapters in part one are divided into the what, why, how, who, when, and where of food and the history, issues, and culture of eating. Each chapter concludes with extensive resource details. Part two creates five situations with food-related issues, and part three includes information on both sides of food controversies (e.g., The Paleo Diet, Sugar Addiction, and the Freshman 15). The title concludes with a useful "End Directory of Resources" as well as standard back matter.

The text examines the central role of food; food crises, poverty, and hunger; and such food issues as dieting, fast food, genetically modified organisms (GMOs), nutrition, obesity, and overeating. Chapter four examines different models of food choice; developmental models, cognitive models, and psychological models explain the psychology behind food theory. Food lifestyle and preferences include Mediterranean, pescatarian, vegan, vegetarian, and others. Integrated into this work are modern food movements like the locavore movement. Geographically, the book focuses on the United States though chapter six will fascinate as it explores eating patterns around the world. In today's "foodie" culture, understanding the process of eating and the emotion associated with it is useful to all. As an introduction to the biological, cultural, social, and psychological aspect of food, *Filling Up* offers students a starting point for development of research.

Recommended.—**Janis Minshull**

479. **Sigmund Freud Papers.** https://www.loc.gov/collections/sigmund-freud-papers/. [Website] Free. Date reviewed: 2017.

This website from the U.S. Library of Congress offers digital access to over 2,000 items from its Sigmund Freud collection. The archive captures the essential Freud—famed neurologist and founder of psychoanalysis—through his correspondence, legal documents, interviews, patient files, newspaper clippings, notes, and much more. The site provides limited but good reference material alongside the collection. Articles & Essays discuss the history of the large collection in addition to the challenges of material preservation and digitization. There is also a timeline that tracks the signature events in and around Freud's life. About this Collection discusses the organization and contents of the archive, offers links to Expert Resources, and displays several featured items from the collection, such as an oil painting of Freud himself. Users can conduct a general or advanced search in consideration of a number of parameters, including subject, contributor, location, date, original, or online format. Items can be displayed in a variety of ways (list, gallery, etc.) and can be arranged by title, date, etc. Selecting an item from the collection allows users to examine the image alongside reference information such as genre, source collection, language, date, contributor, and subject headings. Overall, the site is an excellent source of primary source material for students, educators, medical professionals, and others interested in the life and work of Sigmund Freud.—**ARBA Staff Reviewer**

15 Recreation and Sports

General Works

Handbooks and Yearbooks

480. **Careers in Sports & Fitness.** Hackensack, N.J., Salem Press, 2017. 307p. illus. index. $125.00. ISBN 13: 978-1-68217-322-0; 978-1-68217-323-7 (e-book).

Careers in Sports & Fitness is an easy-to-read guide to the major careers in the sports and fitness industry, aimed at informing high school and college students about career possibilities, including many that would not immediately jump to mind.

Each of the 21 chapters is devoted to one career—from the well known such as "Coach" to the lesser known "Fundraiser/Fundraising Manager" and everything in between. Each chapter delves into the career and provides information such as the salary that can be expected, whether the field is growing, what skills can be transferred to other job categories, etc.

Other features include interviews with professionals working in the specific field. These interviews contain a wealth of information such as what they like most and least about their job and what they wish they had known when they first started. It is this kind of practical information that would be very valuable to someone considering a particular career.

Each chapter also contains information on the best schools to attend for a particular field and industry associations that can be contacted for more information.

Careers in Sports & Fitness is an excellent resource for those who are thinking about a career in any sports oriented field and would be a valuable addition to any high school or college library.—**Alicia Brillon**

481. **Fitness and Exercise Sourcebook.** 5th ed. Keith Jones, ed. Detroit, Omnigraphics, 2016. 538p. index. (Health Reference Series). $95.00. ISBN 13: 978-0-7808-1534-6; 978-0-7808-1535-3 (e-book).

This title in Omnigraphics' Health Reference Series offers general information on a wide range of topics related to fitness and exercise. The reference, while taking a medical approach, is designed to assist nonmedical professionals, patients, families, and others who are not fluent in these topics but may take a genuine, personal interest in them. Eight parts organize the material, beginning with an overview of the Health Benefits of Physical

Activity. Following parts provide general guidelines for promoting fitness in diverse groups (children, elderly, pregnant women, etc.), encouraging a fitness plan, basics of different exercise approaches, safety, special circumstances (e.g., exercising with a disability), and trends. The closing section offers a glossary of specialized terms and a helpful directory of organizations offering information and support regarding fitness and health, from the National Institutes of Health to the American Running Association and beyond.

Each part is further divided into detailed chapters addressing the particulars of its subject. Part two, Guidelines for Lifelong Physical Fitness, for example, describes how much exercise various groups of people need, how to motivate each group, benefits of exercise per group, and more. Part four, Exercise Basics, discusses a range of activities, such as kickboxing, walking, bicycling, core-strengthening exercises, and boot camps, while part five, Fitness Safety, looks at warming up, equipment, nutrition, injuries, and other issues. Beyond basic topic information, chapters may also examine mental health issues, latest research, risks, gear, dietary supplements, and how physical activity affects particular health issues, as well as other topics. All this information is presented clearly and concisely. Chapters make strong use of headers, subheaders, tables, bullet points, and tools for ease of navigation.

This fifth edition provides the most up-to-date information in regards to fitness and exercise relative to the rapid advancements in research and technology (such as online fitness training or fitness wearables). The reference is not produced to replace professional medical counsel; however, it succeeds at providing intelligent, basic information about the impact of fitness and exercise on overall health to a general audience.—**ARBA Staff Reviewer**

482.   Lumpkin, Angela. **Modern Sport Ethics: A Reference Handbook.** 2d ed. Santa Barbara, Calif., ABC-CLIO, 2017. 396p. illus. index. (Contemporary World Issues series). $60.00. ISBN 13: 978-1-4408-5115-5; 978-1-4408-5116-2 (e-book).

Modern Sport Ethics begins by acknowledging that some enthusiasts refer to sport ethics as possibly foolish because many believe sport and ethics are opposing philosophies. This insightful book supports the premise that coaches, players, administrators, parents, and fans need to teach, role model, and reinforce character development—including positive values.

The book is divided into seven sections: Background and History; Problems, Controversies, and Solutions; Perspectives; Profiles; Data and Documents; Resources (print and nonprint); and Chronology. Included in these sections is a wealth of information on ethical theories, the differences between morals and winning, how to teach values in youth sports, controversies like the scandal surrounding Lance Armstrong and the Tour de France, sports luminaries like Jackie Robinson and Lou Gehrig, data regarding the race, ethnicity, and gender of college athletes, and much more. A glossary and index round out the work.

Recommended for public, high school, and college libraries.—**Thomas E. Baker**

483.   **The Routledge History of American Sport.** Linda J. Borish, David K. Wiggins, and Gerald R. Gems, eds. New York, Routledge/Taylor & Francis Group, 2017. 466p. index. (The Routledge Histories). $240.00. ISBN 13: 978-1-138-78675-2; 978-1-315-76712-3 (e-book).

This volume presents 33 articles/chapters on sport grouped around social, cultural, and psychological themes such as politics, gender, race/ethnicity, business, and material culture. Readers seeking a straightforward history of, for instance, basketball or golf in America, will not find that information here. Characteristic chapter titles include "Sport and Italian-American Identity," "Sport, Television, and the Media," and "Active Radicals: The Political Athlete in the Contemporary Moment." As an example of the theoretical approaches adopted by contributors, one chapter is based in part on the work of Gilles Deleuze and Félix Guattari, a French philosopher and a French psychiatrist, scholars not usually associated with this area of study. The studies found in this book reveal key (and often little-known) moments in American sport history and probe the nuances of that history by linking events to broader happenings in the United States.

Chapters are well documented: a Further Readings section at the end of the volume supplements the chapter footnotes. This book is clearly aimed at academic libraries. And while the cost is fairly high, institutions with programs or courses in sport history should consider adding this research to their collections, as it examines both content and methodologies in a variety of useful ways. (Given the approaches applied to the topics explored here, the reviewer is not surprised that there are no images in the book.)—**Mark Schumacher**

Baseball

484.   Edmonds, Ed, and Frank G. Houdek. **Baseball Meets the Law: A Chronology of Decisions, Statutes and Other Legal Events.** Jefferson, N.C., McFarland, 2017. 319p. index. $39.95pa. ISBN 13: 978-1-4766-6438-5; 978-1-4766-2906-3 (e-book).

This book investigates the historical origins of sports litigation and our national pastime, baseball. This lengthy historical chronology of decisions, statutes, and other legal events provides a resource of case review regarding legal concepts and their interrelationship with sports.

As the book shows, baseball and law have intersected from the early stages of the sport in America. For example, in 1791, a Pittsfield, Massachusetts, ordinance prohibited ball playing near the town's meetinghouse while a 1794 Pennsylvania statute barred ball playing on Sundays. Further examples include a federal court's 2015 decision to uphold baseball's exemption from antitrust laws applied to franchise relocations. Another federal court overturned the conviction of Barry Bonds for obstruction of justice. A third denied a request by rooftop entrepreneurs to order the construction of a massive video board at Wrigley Field.

Written by Ed Edmonds, emeritus professor at the Notre Dame Law School, and Frank Houdek, emeritus professor at Southern Illinois University School of Law, *Baseball Meets the Law* makes a convincing case that knowledge of when and how baseball and law came together is essential for anyone wishing to understand not only the game's past and present, but also its future. This is a recommended purchase for school, public, community college, and university libraries ass well as private individuals.—**Thomas E. Baker**

485.   Weeks, Jonathan. **Latino Stars in Major League Baseball: From Bobby Abreu to Carlos Zambrano.** Lanham, Md., Rowman & Littlefield, 2017. index. $36.00; $34.00 (e-book). ISBN 13: 978-1-4422-8172-1; 978-1-4422-8173-8 (e-book).

The book begins with a list of Latin American baseball players in alphabetic order by country. A short introduction discusses not just the talent of Latin American players but also the struggle of these players to get to the United States to play. Each section begins with brief comments on the origin of baseball in the following places: the Dominican Republic, Puerto Rico, Venezuela, Cuba, Panama, Mexico, Colombia, Nicaragua, Curacao, Honduras, and Brazil. Player entries are presented in alphabetic order in two sections, Major Players of the Past and Notable Active Players. Entries vary in length but include biographical details, the position played, and ample information on the player's career. The book is not arranged alphabetically. The Dominican Republic, with 41 players, comes first; Brazil, with one player, appears last. Altogether, there are approximately 150 biographies. The book does not include references or further readings within each entry or section, nor does it include photographs of players. It does, however, include an 8-page bibliography and an index. There are many familiar names in this book—Fernando Valenzuela, Juan Marichal, Jose Abreu, and Sammy Sosa to name a few. Recommended for school and public libraries.—**ARBA Staff Reviewer**

Football

486.   **The All-America Football Conference: Players, Coaches, Records, Games and Awards, 1946-1949.** Kenneth R. Crippen and Matt Reaser, eds. Jefferson, N.C., McFarland, 2018. 361p. index. $45.00pa. ISBN 13: 978-1-4766-7095-9; 978-1-4766-3107-3 (e-book).

This painstakingly researched encyclopedia includes players, coaches, records, awards, and statistics associated with the short-lived All-America Football Conference (AAFC). The data was gathered and analyzed by members of the Professional Football Researchers Association (PFRA), an organization with four hundred members. The book is divided into nine sections. The first seven sections provide readers with a history of the AAFC, lists of PFRA all-pro and all-time teams, individual statistics by year, awards and statistical records, conference statistics, line scores, and the names and colleges of players drafted each year. The eighth part, Player Register, is by far the longest. Here users will find players listed alphabetically by name. Entries include player position, height and weight, college attended, life dates, and game statistics during AAFC tenure. National Football League statistics are also included if the athlete played in both leagues. The last part, Coach Register, is much shorter but is arranged in the same format. The book includes a bibliography of the books, newspapers, magazines, website, and other sources (e.g., press guides) consulted. An index rounds out the work. This book would give anyone interested in researching the AAFC a strong foundation. Recommended for public libraries and other libraries looking for a reliable source on this important slice of football history.—**ARBA Staff Reviewer**

487.   **NFL History: Record & Fact Book. http://www.nfl.com/history/randf.html.** [Website] Free. Date reviewed: 2017.

American football is certainly exciting to watch, and, for many, even more exciting to talk about. This Web page of the greater National Football League site is home to historical numbers, dates, and personnel behind the action that enthusiasts need to know (if they don't already). Simply organized, users can select from three categories of information. Records provides statistics covering individual, team, and defensive efforts across a large variety of measures. Individual Records examines the numbers of leaders in passing, scoring, rushing, PATs, and more alongside the less-celebrated records of fumbles, interceptions, etc. Team Records looks at championships, games won, and games lost in addition to total team numbers in scoring and rushing, and other categories. Defensive Records tally turnovers, interceptions, sacks, and kick returns, among other statistics. Statistics in the Records section are generally recorded up to the year 2007. History offers a chronology of the game from 1869 to 2000, spotlighting domestic and world football events occurring both on and off the field. Information is mainly grouped by decade, and offers brief synopses of game development (in 1912, for instance, a touchdown counted as six points as opposed to five), setbacks (the 1982 players' strike shortened the season by seven games) and, of course, record-breaking moments. Rules help explain the mechanics of the game to the layman (but should not be considered on par with the official rulebook). The section addresses thirty-four categories of game play and other details, with information about Officials' Jurisdictions, Positions and Duties; a Summary of Penalties; Definitions for common terms; and rules about the field of play, the ball, sudden death, and more. The NFL Record and Fact Book would definitely appeal to sports historians, journalists, and other professionals in addition to the average fan of the game.—**ARBA Staff Reviewer**

Hunting

488.   Biscotti, M. L. **Six Centuries of Fox Hunting: An Annotated Bibliography.** Lanham, Md., Rowman & Littlefield, 2017. 500p. illus. index. $85.00; $80.00 (e-book). ISBN 13: 978-1-4422-4189-3; 978-1-4422-4190-9 (e-book).

This is easily the definitive work on literature of fox hunting available to the general public. M. L. Biscotti, author of several books on American sports, treats the reader to a particular luxury, though an acquired one—the world of fox hunting. This annotated bibliography exhaustively explores six centuries of books printed in Great Britain and the United States that either "pertains to or mentions fox hunting with hounds." Obviously a labor of love for the retired antiquarian, Biscotti includes over two thousand titles and his level of detail into each title is painstaking. This alphabetically arranged work contains: a guide to using this book; four appendixes, several timelines; a further bibliography; an author index, a title index; numerous black-and-white illustrations, and some biographical details on famous or noteworthy authors. Recommended.—**Scott R. DiMarco**

16 Sociology

Aging

489. **Improving the Quality of Life for Dementia Patients through Progressive Detection, Treatment, and Care.** Jinglong Wu, ed. Hershey, Pa., Information Science Reference/IGI Global, 2016. 353p. index. (Advances in Psychology, Mental Health, and Behavioral Studies (APMHBS) Book Series). $205.00. ISBN 13: 978-1-52250-925-7; 978-1-52250-926-4 (e-book).

This book provides a thorough overview of emerging research on various neuroscience methods for the early diagnosis of dementia and focuses on the improvement of health care delivery to patients. With dementia affecting nearly 10 percent of individuals aged 65 and older, the need for an accurate diagnosis has become more compelling than ever. Although dementia is far more common in the geriatric population, it can occur during any stage of adulthood.

Dementia is an umbrella term for a number of neurocognitive disorders, encompassing not only Alzheimer's Disease (AD) but also Vascular Dementia, Lewy Body Dementia, Parkinson's Dementia, and Frontotemporal Dementia (FTD). Dementia is usually chronic or progressive in nature. Dementia is the result of a variety of diseases and injuries that primarily or secondarily affect brain function. Dementia is a major cause of disability and dependency among older people. A lack of awareness and understanding of dementia results in social stigma and obstructs intervention, diagnosis, and care. The impact of dementia on caregivers, family members, and society, can be physically exhausting, psychologically draining, socially constraining, and financially stressful.

Improving the Quality of Life for Dementia Patients through Progressive Detection, Treatment, and Care promotes the premise that appropriate and supportive legislative environments based on internationally accepted human rights standards are required to ensure the highest quality of service for people with dementia and their caregivers. The book attempts to bring researchers and practitioners together, including engineers, medical doctors, health professionals, and neuroscientists, computer scientists, and individuals who want to solve real world problems. The academic areas covered in this publication include, but are not limited to: AD; cognitive training; emotional stability; human-computer interaction; nutritional status; stimulation devices; and unobtrusive vs. obtrusive detection. The handbook is well-organized and well-written and features useful graphs, tables, charts, and figures, as well as a glossary, key terms and definitions, current references, and an index.

Highlighting relevant issues on health information systems, behavioral indicators, and treatment methods, *Improving the Quality of Life for Dementia Patients through Progressive Detection, Treatment, and Care* is a pivotal reference source for health professionals, neuroscientists, upper-level students, practitioners, and researchers interested in the latest developments within the field of dementia treatment. Library acquisition decision-makers responsible for the selection and purchase of materials or resources will consider this book a welcome addition to their collection.—**Thomas E. Baker**

Death

490.   **Death and Dying Sourcebook.** 3d ed. Keith Jones, ed. Detroit, Omnigraphics, 2016. 525p. index. (Health Reference Series). $95.00. ISBN 13: 978-0-7808-1496-7; 978-0-7808-1497-4 (e-book).

This third edition (see ARBA 2007, entry 696) provides information about end-of-life perspectives and the medical management of symptoms that can occur as death approaches. This excellent resource book helps support individuals who are swept up in the complicated emotions that hamper informed decision-making skills. One key feature of the sourcebook is the broad scope of sensitive and complex information. The volume offers a wide variety of articles from authoritative sources to inform and educate readers about a particularly difficult subject. It gives comprehensive information that increases understanding and helps readers cope with challenging decisions and emotions.

The chapters are devoted to single topics in nine easy-to-navigate parts: End-of-Life Perspectives, Medical Management of End-of-Life Symptoms, End-of-Life Care Facilities, End-of-Life Caregiving, Death and Children: Information for Parents, Legal and Economic Issues at the End of Life, Final Arrangements, and Mortality Statistics. Authoritative content from respected government agencies and institutes, along with selected original material is incorporated in the text. Tables, charts, and illustrations enhance usability. Part ten, Additional Help and Information, includes a glossary of end of-life terms, a directory of support groups for end-of-life concerns, and a directory of organizations able to provide more information about death and dying. A professionally prepared master index rounds out the book.

Death and Dying Sourcebook provides basic medical information for patients, families, caregivers, and the public. Designed for undergraduates, high school students, and general nonspecialists, the content presents a current, balanced, though-provoking, and reliable collection of material. Recommended for school, community college, and academic libraries, as well as nurses, hospice staff, school counselors, and others.—**Thomas E. Baker**

491.   Gay, Kathlyn. **Dealing with Death: The Ultimate Teen Guide.** Lanham, Md., Rowman & Littlefield, 2017. 200p. illus. index. (It Happened to Me series). $45.00; $42.50 (e-book). ISBN 13: 978-1-5381-0274-9; 978-1-5381-0275-6 (e-book).

This excellent resource book helps support teens swept up in the complicated turmoil of confused emotions that hamper healing and survivorship following the death of a loved one. The chapters and passages assist readers in understanding cultural rituals and religious beliefs regarding death. Most young people face the pain of losing a pet early in life.

However, the vigor of youth sometimes promotes a sense of immortality until forced to grieve the loss of a friend or family member. This easy-to-read book presents information in a compassionate and logical way; the content offers current information that relates to teen viewpoints. Visuals illustrate concepts and build bridges to balance the author's fundamental purpose and premise. Special boxes highlight additional facts and website information provides additional support. The book also includes a glossary of terms.

Dealing with Death delivers outstanding reading for teachers, school counselors, parents, and teen populations. It is highly recommended for high school, community college, and university libraries.—**Thomas E. Baker**

492. **Suicide Information for Teens.** 3d ed. Jones, Keith, ed. Detroit, Omnigraphics, 2017. 329p. maps. index. $69.00. ISBN 13: 978-0-7808-1490-5; 978-0-7808-1489-9 (e-book).

This third edition (See ARBA 2011, entry 743) is updated with current data about young adult suicide risk, causes, and prevention. The book is part of the Teen Health Series, a straightforward reference collection for middle and high school students. Titles in the health series offer preventative guidance, information about disease warning signs, medical statistics, and risk factors.

The teenage years are challenging and teens are not always understood by their family, peers, and teachers. Suicidal behavior can be the culmination of myriad challenges and is often influenced by alcohol, drugs, gender factors, grief, mental illness, peers, and trauma, some of the topics discussed. For example, chapter 29, "Coping with Stress," gives clear definition to stressors and highlights how to manage them.

While teen suicide is a disconcerting topic, this volume provides crisp design of information in layman's terms. Data is current with much of it relating to people of all ages. Learning to recognize signs of those considering suicide, primary facts, and nine chapters on preventing suicide all provide constructive information for research or concerned individuals.

The layers of information peel back as each of the fifty chapters is short and succinct and offers visual data in the form of bar graphs, pie charts, and highlighted textboxes such as the extremely relevant information that "suicide is the second leading cause of death for adolescents and young adults 10 to 24 years of age in the United States. Firearms, used in 44 percent of the cases, are the most common method of suicide" (p. 42).

This volume is well suited for middle and high school students, parents, educators, and school health care professionals seeking introductory information. Recommended.—**Janis Minshull**

Disabled

493. **Annual Disability Statistics Compendium. https://disabilitycompendium.org/.** [Website] Free. Date reviewed: 2017.

This site consolidates a vast amount of research and data on issues affecting people with disabilities in an effort to organize, enhance, and disseminate knowledge of the disabled community, with the ultimate goal of improving the quality of life for disabled people. The website presents an annually updated compendium—a large report sharing statistics on disability across a number of topics, including employment, poverty, veterans, health insurance coverage, special education, and other categories. Users can simply select from the options prominently displayed on the homepage to Download the 2016 Compendium, Download the 2016 Supplement or Download the 2016 Annual Report, or to Request Copies by Mail. The materials are available to view and download in PDF or HTML format. Statistics for each topic are preceded by brief contextual information, including source material (e.g., U.S. Census Bureau), definitions, and more. Sample statistics include such things as "Poverty—Civilian Veterans with Disabilities Ages 18-64 Living in the Community for the United States and States," "Health Insurance Coverage—Civilians with Disabilities Living in the Community for the United States and States by Type of Coverage," and "Vocational Rehabilitation—Applicants." The 2016 (current) version of the compendium has been updated significantly from the prior edition. The online-only supplement adds further categorized tables whereby users can examine comparative data by age, gender, and race/ethnicity. The Employment Policy section is new, while several sections have been removed due to a lack of updated information. Additional information on the site includes the archives of all compendiums reaching back to 2009 (including media releases and more), an A to Z glossary of common terms used throughout the work, and FAQs. The annual report works as a complement to the larger compendium, focusing on particular areas (e.g., "to what extent are people with disabilities employed?") and mapping particular state or trend data to note variability. Reports and presentation slides for 2016 and 2015 may also be downloaded. The information on this well-organized site would strongly appeal to disability advocates, students, educators, and others.—**ARBA Staff Reviewer**

Philanthropy

494.   **Annual Register of Grant Support 2018: A Directory of Funding Resources.** 51st ed. Medford, N.J., Information Today, 2017. 1200p. index. $359.00pa. ISBN 13: 978-1-57387-539-4.

This 51st edition compiles information about 2,554 grant making organizations that support 3,967 grant programs. The register makes every effort to be comprehensive and current. The introduction discusses the different types of grants: private foundations, corporate giving, federated giving, and public money. This is followed by a key to using the register and a list of the new listings in the current volume. The entries are arranged by category: multiple special purpose, humanities, international affairs and area studies, special populations, urban and regional affairs, education, social sciences, physical sciences, life sciences, and technology and industry. Entries cross-reference if they fall into more than one category. There are four indexes that further facilitate searching: an entry listing by chapter, a subject index, an organization and program index, a geographical index, and a personnel index. Entries contain a wealth of information that includes the name of the foundation, contact information, the purpose of the foundation, eligibility, application information, foundation publications, financial data, and much more. This is a valuable resource for researchers and many others. Highly recommended for academic and public libraries.—**ARBA Staff Reviewer**

495.   **Charity Navigator. https://www.charitynavigator.org/.** [Website] Free. Date reviewed: 2017.

This site offers objective performance evaluations of nearly nine thousand U.S.-based charities. Charity Navigator examines each organization's Financial Health and Accountability & Transparency, and bestows a star rating with the ultimate goal of enlightening potential donors. Site users can conduct a basic or advanced search or browse the A to Z directory. In the database, each charity is listed with its location, category, cause, and star rating. Users can then access more detail, such as executive personnel and contact information, by clicking on the charity name. They can also access a detailed Rating Profile, with Financial Charts, Income Statement, Mission, Comment Forum, Historical Ratings, and more. Users can also donate directly to the charity from this page. Charity Navigator has also created a number of Top Ten Lists and Hot Topics which may draw even the casual user's attention. Top Ten Lists include Most Frequently Viewed, Celebrity-Related, and Worth Watching. Hot Topics point to current events and issues in the news, such as Civil Rights, the Syrian Crisis, Immigration & Refugees, and, of course, the recent disasters in the Caribbean and Mexico. As of this review, two prominent banners on the homepage link directly to pages listing charities aiding with Hurricane Maria and Mexico Earthquake relief. The page also provides an up-to-the-minute Donation Ticker so users can see where money is going, a list of Today's Featured Charities, and a blog. This site would be very helpful to potential donors, large and small, but would also appeal to business students, educators, community advocates, and others.—**ARBA Staff Reviewer**

496.   **Foundation Center. http://foundationcenter.org/.** [Website] Free. Date reviewed: 2017.

The Foundation Center has created a smart and generous website that gathers and disseminates a large amount of data and resources in an effort to increase and facilitate philanthropy. Specifically, the site offers a vast set of tools that help users Gain Knowledge, Find Funding, and Improve Your Skills. While users have free access to much of the information on the site, some premium features are only available by paid subscription or product purchase.

Users can conduct a basic search from the prominent bar on the homepage, or select from the substantial list on the drop down menus underneath the titles noted above. The Gain Knowledge tab leads to a selection of links connected to Foundation Center's Knowledge Services, which employ state-of-the-art data visualization tools, web portals, shareable reports, custom research, and much more. For example, the Foundation Map link allows paid subscribers to visualize what is funded around the world, where money is going, and from where money originates. Foundation Research offers free access to downloadable reports, and Foundation Benchmarkers highlights projects which take a broad, comparative view of philanthropic performance as they examines boards, salaries, and more. The Find Funding tab allows users free access to Foundation Directory Online Quick Start, a search tool that lists basic profiles (address, fiscal information, fields of interest, etc.) of thousands of foundations. Paid subscribers can utilize the larger Foundation Directory Online, a more detailed, constantly updated database of over 140,000 companies, foundations, and other grant makers. Also free is the 990 Finder search tool, allowing users a look at grant maker tax documents, and Foundation Stats, offering general donation statistics by year. Improve Your Skills hosts a selection of online and in-person training courses, webinars, and more related to leadership, grant writing, and other aspects of fundraising. The GrantCraft link offers a large, curated collection of other resources (e.g., blog posts, events, videos, etc.) related to many topics around philanthropy, such as civic engagement, media, and youth. The GrantSpace link offers resources to help grant seekers/nonprofits enhance their applications and create a stronger, more vital organization.

With an abundance of free options in addition to its quality premiums, this stylish website would appeal to educators, students, entrepreneurs, civic leaders, and many others interested in the power of philanthropy.—**ARBA Staff Reviewer**

497.   **The Routledge Companion to Philanthropy.** Tobias Jung, Susan D. Phillips, and Jenny Harrow, eds. New York, Routledge/Taylor & Francis Group, 2016. 532p. index. (Routledge Companions in Business, Management, and Accounting). $240.00. ISBN 13: 978-0-415-78325-5; 978-1-315-74032-4 (e-book).

Philanthropy, the use of private resources for public purposes, is experiencing a transformation, both in practice and as an emerging field of study. Prospects regarding philanthropy have increased significantly in recent years. *The Routledge Companion to Philanthropy* examines fluctuations and additional challenges that philanthropists and philanthropic organizations may experience. Philanthropists still want to make their mark. In addition, experiments with entrepreneurial and speculation philanthropy are producing novel intersections of the public, nonprofit, and private spheres, accompanied by new kinds of partnerships and hybrid organizational forms. As stated in Helmut Anheiers foreword, this companion "recognizes and demonstrates the spread of philanthropy scholarship: it offers reflection, admiration, and critical engagement with philanthropy as a vital area of practice and scholarship. To this end, it provides both theoretical and empirical insight on which we are able to further build, amend, refresh–and sometimes discard–our understanding and perceptions of philanthropic actions and organizations."

This book contains contributions from an international team of leading contemporary thinkers on philanthropy. Moreover, this companion provides an introduction to, and critical exploration of, philanthropy. Contributors discuss current theories, research, and diverse professional practices within the field from a variety of disciplinary perspectives. Divided into seven parts, the book anticipates the needs of philanthropists: anyone who gives anything—time, money, experience, skills, and networks, in any amount, to create a better world. This excellent book empowers individuals to practice philanthropy more effectively and make giving more meaningful to themselves as well as those they strive to help. Classroom and online offerings in philanthropy and nonprofit leadership provide opportunities to build skill sets and increase fund raising effectiveness.

The Routledge Companion to Philanthropy is a valuable resource for students, researchers, practitioners, and policy-makers working in or interested in philanthropy. Library acquisition decision-makers responsible for the selection and purchase of materials or resources will consider this book a welcome addition to their research collection. This superior and scholarly book arrives at its destination at just the right moment in time.—**Thomas E. Baker**

Sex Studies

498.   Gowen, L. Kris. **Sexual Decisions: The Ultimate Teen Guide.** 2d ed. Lanham, Md., Rowman & Littlefield, 2017. 223p. illus. index. (It Happened to Me series). $45.00;

$42.50 (e-book). ISBN 13: 978-1-4422-7783-0; 978-1-4422-7784-7 (e-book).

This book covers such important topics as body basics, gender identity, sexual orientation, sexually transmitted diseases, and contraception. The book incorporates recent information, imperative teen viewpoints, and visuals; it also uses special boxes to highlight important points. Reading lists, websites, and a substantial index system enhance content navigation. Moreover, the writing style helps engage a hard-to-reach audience. The expert information assists parents, guardians, and librarians in their understanding of a variety of teen and lifestyle problems. *Sexual Decisions: The Ultimate Teen Guide* may help teens consider postponing activities and emotional behaviors that have life-altering consequences. The succinct information alerts teens regarding consequences of sexual activities in the midst of emotional decisions and the normal flow of intense new feelings. This book may serve as an incentive for teens to pause and think. Recommended for high school and academic libraries.—**Thomas E. Baker**

499. McNabb, Charlie. **Nonbinary Gender Identities: History, Culture, Resources.** Lanham, Md., Rowman & Littlefield, 2018. 284p. index. $75.00; $71.00 (e-book). ISBN 13: 978-1-4422-7551-5; 978-1-4422-7552-2 (e-book).

This book is a compilation of resources for nonbinary gender identities: individuals who are not exclusively male or female. It is an umbrella term, as the author states in the preface: other terms include genderfluid, bigender, and genderqueer. These individuals have existed in society for centuries, but have often been marginalized and even persecuted. This book is meant to be a pathfinder book for nonbinary people as well as a guide for those who wish to educate themselves on this topic, and is a point-in-time publication given the resources cited. It is divided into two parts: Part 1, (Hir)stories, has five chapters on issues such as definition and introduction, visibility in the United States, culturally specific genders, nonbinary genders in popular culture, and notable nonbinary people. Part 2, Resources, has eight chapters which focus on places to find information such as archives and special collections, nonfiction books, journals, theses and dissertations, fiction books, organizations and associations, online resources, and multimedia. Four appendixes provide a glossary, pronoun usage, a sexuality and gender primer, and Library of Congress subject headings, along with a bibliography and index. Given that there are very few print resources in this area, I highly recommend this book for high school and academic libraries.—**Bradford Lee Eden**

500. Newton, David E. **Sex and Gender.** Santa Barbara, Calif., ABC-CLIO, 2017. 362p. illus. index. (Contemporary World Issues series). $60.00. ISBN 13: 978-1-4408-5479-8; 978-1-4408-5480-4 (e-book).

Sex and Gender proposes the need for additional research regarding the two distinguishable terms. This book does not imply that it addresses all the issues and problems associated with sex, gender, and society. It touches on topics that include the biology of sexual development, development of gender roles, transvestism, transgenderism, and affectional orientation. In his frank analysis, author David E. Newton acknowledges that confusion persists about related terminology and that disagreement and little research has led to misunderstandings and the need to explore historical perspectives, problems, issues, and solutions. The book offers an excellent, reader-friendly format, including bulleted paragraphs, charts, graphics, and bold chapter photographs that signal what's to come. It also offers readers an extensive resource section that includes books, articles, reports, and websites. There is also a glossary and an index. Recommended for school, public, and academic libraries.—**Thomas E. Baker**

Social Work and Social Welfare

501.   **Routledge International Handbook of Social Work Education.** Imogen Taylor, Marion Bogo, Michelle Lefevre, and Barbra Teater, eds. New York, Routledge/Taylor & Francis Group, 2016. 415p. index. (Routledge International Handbooks). $210.00. ISBN 13: 978-1-138-89023-7; 978-1-315-71253-6 (e-book).

The purpose of *The Routledge International Handbook of Social Work Education* is to augment academic research and scholarship for social work education. This book addresses international social work education as well as social work education as practiced. This informative collection of professional articles written by experts provides educational content that stimulates the reader to pursue its persuasive discourse. Moreover, this is an exceptional anthology that provides a convincing overview of current understanding by addressing key debates, exploring the state of play in particular social work education fields, and reflecting on possible future associated pursuits.

Professional contributions address the theory and practice of social work education at all levels. They are concise, conceptually clear, research based where appropriate, critically reflective, and properly supported. The following six sections reflect proposed themes and subthemes: Social Work Education in Context: The Western Drivers; Emerging and Re-emerging Social Work Education; The Scholarship of Learning and Teaching; New Insights into Field Education; New Directions in Learning and Teaching; and Future Challenges for Social Work Education. The content is well organized; the book uses both bullet points and question-and-answer formats. In addition, there are black-and-white illustrations, extensive references, and a solid index.

This scholarly contribution is an important resource for all social work educators preparing students for practice in our global community. This handbook is ideally suited for undergraduate and graduate students.—**Thomas E. Baker**

Substance Abuse

502.   Standora, Joan E., Alex Bogomolnik, and Malgorzata Slugocki. **Steroids: History, Science, and Issues.** Santa Barbara, Calif., Greenwood Press/ABC-CLIO, 2017. 218p. index. (The Story of a Drug series). $58.00. ISBN 13: 978-1-61069-723-1; 978-1-61069-724-8 (e-book).

Steroids provides a holistic overview of this controversial class of drugs; gives readers an understanding of the function of natural steroids in the human body; clarifies the differences between natural and synthetic steroids and their legal use in medicine and their illegal use in recreational activities; supplies an overview of current legislation and federal regulation of steroids and steroid-like chemicals; projects the continuum of use of steroids as medications and as recreational drugs based on current research, governmental attitudes, and social perceptions of the acceptability of such substances; and features an introductory case-study chapter about two young people whose lives were significantly impacted by steroids, putting the material into a real-world context. Chapter headings and subheadings facilitate navigation, as does the index. Readers will also benefit from an effective use of tables, charts, and other visuals. In addition, there is a glossary, compilation of references, directory of resources, and a list of abbreviations.

Readers will come away from this volume with a comprehensive understanding of the pros and cons of steroid use based on current research. It is specifically tailored to address the questions and concerns of young people, providing readers with an accessible and balanced source of information. The book is appropriate for the public, high school, community college, university, and public libraries. Recommended.—**Thomas E. Baker**

17 Statistics, Demography, and Urban Studies

Statistics

Canada

503. **Statistics Canada. https://www.statcan.gc.ca/eng/start.** [Website] Free. Date reviewed: 2017.

This well-organized and easy-to-use site offers statistical detail about the nation of Canada across a range of topics. Users can conduct a basic search or browse via a list of thirty-two subjects accessible straight from the homepage or by selecting the Browse by Subject tab. Subjects include Energy, Agriculture, Crime & Justice, Government, International Trade, Population & Demography, Science & Technology, Transportation, and many others. Selecting a subject link brings up a database of applicable data, analysis, and reference. Databases are generally searchable by keyword, data publication year, type of data, and originating program. Broad subject categories may also be further focused. For example, the general subject of Children & Youth can be segmented by Child Care, Child Development & Behavior, Crime & Justice (youth), Education, and more. From the homepage, users can also Browse by Key Resource, such as articles, data tables, and surveys. A variety of tools enhance the site. The Daily blog presents subject-marked posts on indicator updates and more. My StatCan allows users to subscribe to subject updates. Key Indicators lets users go directly to the particulars, such as CPI, Quarterly Population Estimates, and Retail Sales for a snapshot of trends and numbers. Users can choose indicators for a particular province or for the whole of Canada. The Canada and the World Stats Hub is a resource for contextualizing Canada's economic relationship with the United States (more countries to be added in the future). Other links include a Statistics Canada Library; Infographics; Definitions, Data Sources & Methods, among others.—**ARBA Staff Reviewer**

United States

504. Scardamalia, Robert L. **Millennials in America 2017.** 2d ed. Lanham, Md., Bernan Press, 2017. 406p. maps. index. (County and City Extra Series). $110.00; $104.50 (e-book). ISBN 13: 978-1-59888-933-8; 978-1-59888-934-5 (e-book).

This book, following the first edition published in 2015, presents scores of detailed tables concerning various social and economic topics, such as ethnicity, place of birth, education, native language, housing, employment and income, and mobility and migration. Statistics are drawn from the American Community Survey (ACS) using microdata among other numbers, and organized by states, counties, metropolitan/Micropolitan Statistical Areas and "places," within each of the eleven chapters of data. Each of the sections opens with a brief discussion of the information provided in the tables that follow.

The opening pages provide a useful explanation of the ACS, including how readers can access its data online. Millennials are defined as those born between 1982 and 2000; they now represent the largest generation in the United States. These twenty-five pages are crucial to readers' utilization and interpretation of the many tables that follow. Dozens of links to online information on the www.census.gov website are also provided. (There is also repeated mention, within these pages, of "margin of error," indicating that readers must pay attention to the accuracy of the various data set.)

There are issues, however, with this volume. There are occasional numerical discrepancies between tables, and charts with unclear headings (see p. 31, concerning Native American populations). More importantly, readers cannot manipulate the data in this print format. Working directly with the Census Bureau's site, on the other hand, permits researchers to do that. This book is more useful for looking up a particular place (state, county, city) to see what the characteristics of the Millennials living there are. Libraries should weigh these factors when considering this title.—**Mark Schumacher**

505.   **State and Metropolitan Area Data Book 2017.** 2d ed. Deirdre A. Gaquin and Mary Meghan Ryan, eds. Lanham, Md., Bernan Press, 2017. 462p. maps. index. $110.00pa.; $104.50 (e-book). ISBN 13: 978-1-59888-920-8; 978-1-59888-921-5 (e-book).

The *State and Metropolitan Area Data Book* (SMADB) is described in the preface as "a convenient summary of statistics on the social and economic structure of the states, metropolitan areas, and micropolitan areas in the United States. It is designed to serve as a statistical reference and guide to other data publications and sources." This resource includes a "Guide to Tabular Presentation," with an explanation of symbols and terms and "Major Federal Data Contacts," a list of contacts (names, addresses, phone numbers, and websites) of federal agencies with major statistical programs. Statistical tables are arranged as follows: A. States; B. Metropolitan Areas; C. Metropolitan Counties; and D. Micropolitan Areas. Part A. States contains tables with data for each state including Area and Population; Population by age Group and Sex; Households; Deaths and Death Rates, by Race and Hispanic Origin; Health Care Services, Physicians and Nurses; Violent Crime and Crime Rates; Civilian Labor Force and Employment; Personal Income; Gross Domestic Product per State; Wholesale and Retail Trade; Elections; and Energy Consumption. Part B. Metropolitan Areas (metropolitan statistical areas and divisions) includes tabular data on Area and Population; Components of Population Change; Migration and Community; Housing Units; Personal Income and Earnings by Place of Work; and Civilian Labor Force. Part C. Metropolitan Counties (encompassing metropolitan statistical area, division, and component county) contains data on Population and Population Characteristics; Population Characteristics and Housing Units; Personal Income and Earnings by Industry; and Labor Force and Private Business Establishments and Employment. Part D. Micropolitan Areas contains data on Population and Personal Income for Micropolitan statistical area component counties. There are several appendixes.

Appendix A, "Source Notes and Explanations," presents General Notes on population and economic and government censuses followed by source note and explanations of the data items; Appendix B, "Limitations of the Data and Methodology," describes how data is collected by agency; Appendix C, "Geographic Concepts," includes maps of Core Based Statistical Areas (CBSAs) and counties; and Appendix D is a "Guide to State Statistical Abstracts and State Information," with names, addresses, phones, and websites of state statistics sources. An index is included for the publication. *State and Metropolitan Area Data Book* is a source of statistics and a guide to other data sources. Highly recommended to academic and larger public library collections.—**Lucy Heckman**

506.   **State Profiles: The Population and Economy of Each U.S. State.** 9th ed. Lanham, Md., Bernan Press, 2018. 555p. index. $175.00. ISBN 13: 978-1-59888-941-3; 978-1-59888-942-0 (e-book).

Energy production, health care, conservation, national defense, and homeland security decision makers use statistical data in their efforts to implement legislation that affects the lives of state and local citizens. Government officials and policy makers who endorse necessary expenditures require accurate demographic information. This 9th edition offers comprehensive data on individual states and the District of Columbia. Profiles include population, state size, principal cities, state song, state symbols, state motto, and the number of senators and representatives. Furthermore, this 554-page hardbound volume serves as a reader-friendly assemblage of population composition, by age, sex, and language. The content is well organized. Topics include population, health, marital status, crime, state ethnicity, migration, origin, voting, and other important factors that offer state portraits for inquisitive readers. Each chapter relies on the same standard set of federal data sources. Sources include the Bureau of Economic Analysis, Bureau of Labor Statistics, Federal Bureau of Investigation, National Center for Education Statistics, and the U.S. Census Bureau. Readers have opportunities to peruse 10-page profiles for each U.S. state plus the District of Columbia. The profiles include up-to-date information on a variety of topics. The book offers an extensive index system, tables, pie charts, graphics, notes, and definitions. Moreover, the editor commences by inserting clear explanations on the most effective way to use the book. Informative guideposts clarify the book's organization and contents for improved research and speedy information retrieval. *State Profiles* is an essential reference book. The book is important for local and federal government agencies. Recommended to public and academic libraries.—**Thomas E. Baker**

507.   **Statistical Abstract of the United States 2018: The National Data Book.** Lanham, Md., Bernan Press, 2018. 1061p. maps. $199.00. ISBN 13: 978-1-59888-945-1.

This, the best-known statistical reference publication in the country, is a comprehensive collection of data that covers the social, political, and economic conditions in America. The volume offers a selection of data from many statistical sources, both government and private. Moreover, the 1,016-page hardbound volume serves as a convenient assemblage of vital information from many statistical sources. The volume's organization enhances improved research and speedy information retrieval. New features include data on health insurance enrollment and coverage, use and misuse of prescription drugs, presidential pardons, foodborne disease outbreaks, household electronics, characteristics of employer firms, young adult living arrangements, high school English as a second language programs, organic farms, cost of attendance of undergraduate education, and Freedom of Information

Act requests. The volume offers extensive tables, 30 sections with astute introductions, and a convenient index system. The publisher printed the book on acid-free paper that extends shelf life. Moreover, the volume has a reinforced Smyth-sewn binding that holds up to heavy use. Statistics in this edition are generally for the most recent year or period available, as of early September 2017. This volume is an ideal research tool for scholars, government officials, and students. Publications cited as sources offer supplementary statistical detail and comprehensive discussions of definitions and concepts. Four appendixes address (1) a guide to sources of statistics, state statistical abstracts, and foreign statistical abstracts, (2) metropolitan and micropolitan statistical areas: concepts, components, and population, (3) limitations of the data, and (4) weights and measures.

Highly recommended to school, public, and academic libraries. Rowman & Littlefield achieved its goal—to maintain the integrity and tradition of a long-standing and celebrated reference contribution.—**Thomas E. Baker**

International

508.   **Atlas of Sustainable Development Goals 2017. http://datatopics.worldbank.org/sdgatlas/.** [Website] Free. Date reviewed: 2017.

This site from the World Bank measures 17 Sustainable Development Goals (SDG) in context with information within its extensive database of over 1,400 global development indicators for over 200 countries with the purpose of tracking progress and pinpointing challenges in meeting these goals. The simple homepage features a numbered listing of 17 goals with corresponding icon, including No Poverty, Good Health and Well-Being, Gender Equality, Affordable and Clean Energy, Zero Hunger, and Quality Education. Selecting a goal from the list allows access to a summary report detailing specific objectives, status, and general solutions/methods toward achieving the goal. For example, with the goal of Zero Hunger, the report outlines more specific objectives of ending hunger, achieving food security/improved nutrition, and promoting sustainable agriculture. It provides figures and percentages related to worldwide trends within these objectives, such as the number of stunted children, prevalence of undernourishment, and regions of food deficit. It also offers brief general detail on solutions used to address these issues, such as improving yield growth, climate resilience, and enhanced trade. Reports include maps, tables, graphs, and other resources. For users who would like a closer look at data on individual indicators or countries, the site links to the World Development Indicators 2017, where one can examine or download the most current data and estimates. There is also a link to the Interactive Dashboards of SDG data where users select a goal (such as Achieve Gender Equality), choose a target (e.g., end all forms of discrimination against all women and girls everywhere), and an indicator (e.g., proportion of women subjected to physical and/or sexual violence in the last 12 months—percentage of women age 15-49). The simple focus of the website, coupled with its generous information, makes it a good resource for policy makers, educators, students, business leaders, and others with an interest in improving the global community.—**ARBA Staff Reviewer**

509. **Data.gov.uk. https://data.gov.uk/.** [Website] Free. Date reviewed: 2017.

This site makes it easy to find a wealth of data on a good variety of topics applicable to life in the United Kingdom. Larger public or smaller local agencies, in addition to the U.K. government, have issued the data, which encompasses a broad range of themes. Users can conduct a basic search or browse by the themes, which include Business & Economy, Crime & Justice, Defence, Education, Environment, Government, Government Spending, Health, Mapping, Society, Towns & Cities, and Transport. Selecting a theme brings up a sortable listing of relevant data. Users can scroll through the listing or search via a number of parameters on the left sidebar, such as status, API, publisher, format, and other technical specifications. Choosing the Environment theme, for example, allows access to over 14,000 results with such titles as "Historic Flood Map," "Conservation Areas," "Environmental Pollution Incidents," "Tree Preservation Orders," and "Crop Map of England, Complete." Each entry is listed with publishing agency and a brief description. Some titles are available for preview. Selecting a data set will provide a map with range of data, links to the data (variable formats), and metadata. The site offers a generous amount of information on the broader idea of this data, as well. Selecting the Data tab provides such things as publisher info, site analytics, maps, and listings of data requests. The Interact tab connects users to a Blog on government data collection and downloadable Library resources on a number of topics, including policy, administration, and more through relevant sectors (academia, private, etc.). Clearly constructed, the site offers excellent insight into data collection processes in addition to a diverse range of data which would appeal to myriad researchers.—**ARBA Staff Reviewer**

510. **UNESCO Institute for Statistics. www.uis.unesco.org.** [Website] Free. Date reviewed: 2017.

This website reflects the drive of the UNESCO Institute of Statistics (UIS) to inspire collaborative progress on a number of globally impactful issues. The site shares a significant collection of data coalescing around five major areas of UNESCO interest: Science, Technology & Innovation, Culture, Communication & Information, and, most significantly, Education & Literacy. Users can select the Explore Themes tab to find data tracking literacy skills, quantitative and qualitative information about women in STEM fields, trade flows of cultural goods and services, access to technology in the classroom, and more. Selecting the View Indicators tab allows users to search specific data points or to select from a topical listing (e.g., school resources and teaching conditions in Africa). Users can also Browse by Country to find data for a specific area. A number of innovative tools help users easily access, interpret, and work with the data. The Document Library holds over four hundred downloadable papers, brochures, reports, fact sheets, and other items. A Visualization Gallery offers a select number of interactive data representations, and the substantial A to Z glossary defines phrases and terms relevant to site information. Users can also scroll through the latest news related to UIS research, read posts from the UIS blog, and note a listing of new and upcoming data releases. This website, available in English or French, would be an excellent resource for students, researchers, policy-makers, and others looking for insight on the broader educational, scientific, cultural, and communicative development of the global community.—**ARBA Staff Reviewer**

Urban Studies

511.   **Atlas of Urban Expansion. http://www.atlasofurbanexpansion.org/.** [Website] Free. Date reviewed: 2017.

This atlas offers a state-of-the-art look at the quantity and quality of urban expansion across many diverse cities around the world. Specifically, it maps and measures important components of urban expansion, such as population density, and compares the quality of city areas and peripheries across different time periods. Users can select from pinned locations on the global map display, or can select from the Cities tab to access a city profile. The project has organized two hundred cities by region, noted by color on the map. Eight unique regions include East Asia & The Pacific (Shanghai, Seoul), Europe & Japan (Vienna, Osaka), Land-rich Developed Countries (Los Angeles, Sydney), Latin America & the Caribbean (Guadalajara, Buenos Aires), South and Central Asia (Kabul, Dhaka), Southeast Asia (Palembang, Bangkok), Sub-Saharan Africa (Kinshasa, Johannesburg), and Western Asia and North Africa (Istanbul, Algiers). The profile highlights the country, region, population, urban extent measured in hectares, and density (number per hectare). Users can then scroll through each metric (such as population, extent roads, etc.) for charts, graphs, maps, and more. The Data tab lists the cities alphabetically alongside their individual data sets. Information on the site is downloadable across several applications. The Historical Data tab presents animations of changing urban extents for thirty cities (representing the genesis of this project). The site currently reflects the work of two parts of a three-phase project, and would appeal to educators, students, urban planners, historians, and many others.—**ARBA Staff Reviewer**

512.   **City Health Dashboard. http://www.cityhealthdashboard.com/.** [Website] Free. Date reviewed: 2017.

This innovative tool allows users to examine select health data for cities (population 70,000 plus) across a variety of metrics. As of this review, the site has amassed data for four U.S. cities: Flint, Michigan; Waco, Texas; Kansas City, Kansas; and Providence, Rhode Island. The project aims to include data for 500 cities by mid-year 2018. Users can enter a city into the bar, then choose from one of five domains: Social & Economic Factors, Physical Environment, Health Behavior, Health Outcomes, and Clinical Care. Twenty-six metrics, such as air quality, poor mental health, teen births, unemployment, etc. are examined within these domains.

When selecting a metric to examine, users will see a description noting source, years of data collection, and how measure is calculated. A colored bar graph notes the percentage per 100 for both the profiled city and national average. Below, a city map breaks down the neighborhood percentages if known (colored to align with the bar graph). Users can also scroll through the city demographics. Selecting the Tabular button transposes the map data into a listing of neighborhoods alongside metric percentages. Users who select the Explore Metrics tab will see similar graphics for each metric, but for all four cities in the database, with the options to examine by map, listed percentages, or demographics. The Compare Metrics tab allows users to examine the correlation between selected metrics for each city. City Overviews provide a brief city description next to a tabular report on all metrics. Metrics Background restates the descriptive profile for each metric across the five domains.

While not at its full potential, the dashboard nonetheless offers a good idea of its future capabilities and will be an excellent source for key municipal-level health information valued by policy-makers, health care professionals, students, educators, and more.—**ARBA Staff Reviewer**

513.   **County and City Extra, 2017: Annual Metro, City, and County Data Book.** Deirdre A. Gaquin and Mary Meghan Ryan, eds. Lanham, Md., Bernan Press, 2018. 1472p. maps. $180.00. ISBN 13: 978-1-59888-939-0; 978-1-59888-940-6 (e-book).

Published annually, *County and City Extra* "provides the most up-to-date statistical information available for every state, county, metropolitan area, and congressional district, as well as all cities in the United States with a 2010 census population of 25,000 or more." The resource includes national data maps in color of the United States which shows population change, 2010-2016; Black, not Hispanic or Latino, population 2016; Hispanic or Latino Population 2016; Population under 18 years old 2016; Population 65 years and over 2016; population density 2016; unemployment rate 2016; educational expenses per student 2013-2014; population with high school diploma or less 2011-2015; earnings from manufacturing 2015; employment in management, business, science, and arts occupations: 2011-2015; land in farms 2012; persons under age 65 with no health insurance 2015; median household income 2015; and percent in poverty 2015. The resource is arranged in parts: A. States contains State Highlights and Rankings with a figure showing Fastest Growing States; tables of selected rankings by variables such as median household income, birth rate, and number of immigrants. The second part, States and Counties, provides highlights and rankings of states and tables with statistics on such topics as housing, labor force, and employment; population, vital statistics, health and crime; health care and social assistance, other services, nonemployer businesses and residential construction; personal income; and land area and population. C and D provide rankings for metropolitan areas and cities of more than 25,000, respectively. The final section is Part E. Congressional Districts of the 115th Congress. The appendixes contain Geographic Concepts and Codes; Metropolitan Statistical Areas, Metropolitan Divisions and Components; Core Base Statistical Areas (Metropolitan and Micropolitan, Metropolitan Divisions and Components; Maps of Congressional Districts and States; Cities by County; and Source Notes and Explanations. The appendixes also provide references and URLs of resource materials. *County and City Extra* is a major resource and would benefit researchers of economics and business; social studies; criminal justice; and sociology, among other topics. It should be purchased by public and academic libraries. Recommended.—**Lucy Heckman**

514.   **Global Human Settlement Layer. http://ghsl.jrc.ec.europa.eu/.** [Website] Free. Date reviewed: 2017.

This site offers a technical overview of the Human Planet Initiative that studies centuries of human presence around the globe. The site appears highly targeted to those familiar with the initiative, with references and information which may not resonate with casual users. However, all users have the ability to download two major projects using the Global Human Settlement Layers (GHSL), whereby maps are layered with enhancing data, from the global initiative: the 2016 Mapping Human Presence on Earth Atlas, and the 2017 Global Exposure to Natural Hazards Atlas. Constructed from diverse sources such as satellite imagery and census data, the atlases offer a host of such data related to urban expansion. The website displays data examples for each of the two atlases which may be of interest to users. For the 2016 Atlas, users can read an overview, examine graphs and maps for 27 Key Findings, and note mapping showcases. Key Findings include data on "Vegetation in Urban Clusters," "Global Built-up by Income Class," "Degree of Urbanization by Country," and more. Users can download any or all of the full 2016 Atlas, an Executive Summary, the GHSL Basic Facts, and Atlas Key Findings. For the 2017 Atlas, users can download the same reports as for the 2016 Atlas, minus an Executive Summary. They can also read an Overview, note the Methodology whereby researchers overlay particular hazard maps with population and built-up data, and examine 13 Key Findings such as "Population and Built-up Potentially Exposed to Cyclone Storm Surge," "EU Countries with More Than 50,000 People Potentially Exposed to Flood in 2015," and "Population and Built-up within 100 K of Volcanoes." Site navigation is a bit cumbersome, with technical language, many overlapping organizations/projects (e.g., Joint Research Center, UN Technology Facilitation Mechanism, etc.) to track, an array of acronyms, and a busy homepage. Nonetheless, the information on the site would appeal to a range of researchers, educators, urban planners, and others.—**ARBA Staff Reviewer**

515.   **Handbook of Cities and the Environment.** Kevin Archer and Kris Bezdecny, eds. Northampton, Mass., Edward Elgar, 2016. 464p. illus. index. $230.00. ISBN 13: 978-1-78471-225-9; 978-1-78471-226-6 (e-book).

The eighteen chapters in this work examine the diverse facets of today's urban environments, exploring climate change, sustainability, and other topics in cities from Seattle (and other American cities) to Europe and Australia, and even the Mekong Delta. By placing urban areas in a focused examination of the environment, these authors seek to analyze the problems facing an increasingly urban population having to deal with environmental change. Some chapters are rather theoretical while others report studies in specific urban settings. Some pieces require a background understanding of the issues involved; the vocabulary includes terms like "capitalocene," "metropolocene," "counterurbanization," and "urban informality." Each chapter includes a useful reference list for readers to pursue earlier discussions of these topics.

As the book itself states, this volume will interest "urbanists, geographers, planners, sociologists, economists, anthropologists, policy-makers, public administrators and environmental scientists." Libraries serving these groups, or advanced students in these fields should consider it, all the while factoring in its high cost.—**Mark Schumacher**

516.   **The SAGE Handbook of the 21st Century City.** Hall, Suzanne and Ricky Burdett, eds. Thousand Oaks, Calif., Sage, 2018. 706p. illus. maps. index. $160.00. ISBN 13: 978-1-4739-0756-0.

This book is organized around nine themes: hierarchy; productivity; authority; volatility; conflict; provisionality; mobility; civility; and design. Analysis is done through aligned and opposing forces, infrastructures, and inhabitations. Sociological complexities and race, class, and gender differences; public services and welfare; risk strategies and risk management; global and national violence and how cities are part of that; borders and mobility; and construction and deconstruction are all brought into the light in these nine issues related to "collective life."

All the signed essays are looking for a humane way to make cities work better in every land, in every culture, and at every level. These authors are experts in their field; a number of them are in urban studies or sociology, while others are in politics or law. Most of them are professors in prestigious academic institutions from the United States, Europe, Great Britain, and Africa. A few of them are actually working in urban studies in India, Great Britain, and China, as architects, anthropologists, or urban planners.

Written for practitioners and upper-level undergraduates, this title is recommended for public libraries located in cities and urban centers and for academic libraries supporting urban studies in sociology.—**Ladyjane Hickey**

18 Women's Studies

Biography

517. Her Hat Was In The Ring! U.S. Women Who Ran for Political Office before 1920. http://www.herhatwasinthering.org/index.php. [Website] Free. Date reviewed: 2018.

Her Hat Was In The Ring takes an important look at the history of women in politics via its database of over three thousand women who ran local or statewide campaigns before the passage of the 19th Amendment and the allowance of full suffrage. From the homepage, users can conduct a Search or browse in a number of ways. The Women by Name tab lets users browse an alphabetical (last name) listing of all currently known candidates. Users can alternatively browse Women by State, Women by Office, or Women by Party. For each candidate, the database provides a biographical page with personal (e.g., birthdate, state, marital status, occupation, etc.) and campaign-related (e.g., office, party, etc.) information. There may also be a brief essay, a photograph, and a listing of related resources. Users will learn of the many women who ran for office out of fervent commitment to their local communities, such as Mrs. C.A. Curtis who ran a successful campaign for school board in 1890s Kansas. They will also learn about the leaders who truly wanted change on a larger scale, like Marilla Ricker, an attorney who championed equal rights and full suffrage, won admission to the Washington D.C. and U.S. Supreme Court bar, and nearly became the first female U.S. Ambassador abroad. Ricker also ran for Governor of New Hampshire even though, as a woman without a vote, she could not legally run. The site also contains supplementary essays about political parties (there were quite a number, such as the Single Tax, Prohibition, Equal Rights, Union Labor, and others both familiar and obscure), political offices, and regional campaigns. Her Hat Was In The Ring is a work in progress, with the hopes of both fleshing out the information on the women already in the database and finding more intrepid candidates to add. Nonetheless, the ample available information would appeal to many users from local historians and educators to equal rights activists and others.—**ARBA Staff Reviewer**

518. Women in Congress, 1917-2017. https://bookstore.gpo.gov/products/women-congress-1917-2017. Office of the Historian, U.S. House of Representatives. Free. Date reviewed: 2017.

This massive tome (more than 1,000 pages) is available via the Government Printing Office as a free download or for sale as a cloth-bound book. The material comprises four generations of women members of Congress starting with Jeannette Rankin in 1917. The 2006 (third) edition differs from the former two in scope, structure, and concept. These differences reflect the dramatic growth, changing characteristics, and increased influence of women House and Senate members. Another difference is the organization in chronological order of the material in part one. Moreover, individual profiles have been expanded and more emphasis within profiles has been placed on congressional service. The profiles are typically 1,500 words; some exceed 2,000 words in cases where House and Senate service has been exceptional. The book includes shorter entries (approximately 550-750 words) for widows who served brief terms or for those congresswomen about whom there is only a small amount of information. Each entry has information on a woman's precongressional career and an analysis (where possible) of the first election campaign. Also covered are reelection efforts, major legislative initiatives, and brief summary comments on the member's postcongressional career. The first part is separated into four sections: "I'm No Lady, I'm a Member of Congress": Women Pioneers on Capitol Hill, 1917-1934, with a contextual essay and 20 profiles; Onto the National State: Congresswomen in an Age of Crisis, 1935-1954, with a contextual essay and 36 member profiles; A Changing of the Guard: Traditionalists, Feminists, and the New Face of Women in Congress, 1955-1976, with a contextual essay and 39 profiles; and Assembling, Amplifying, and Ascending: Recent Trends Among Women in Congress, 1977-2006, with a contextual essay and 150 member profiles. An advantage of chronological order is that it allows readers to gain a fuller perspective of the era. In the print book, a much shorter part two covers current women members of the House and Senate. A series of appendixes follow the main content, and an index rounds out the work.

The website and 2017 e-book edition are based on the 2006 book; however, the material is updated to 2017. Through the table of contents, users can link to a series of clickable portraits of all women members of Congress. Once an image is accessed, users will find further information (political party affiliation, links to external research collections, etc.) There are also a series of Historical Data links, including "Women Representatives and Senators by Congress, 1917-Present," "Women of Color in Congress," "Women in Party Leadership Positions, 1949-Present," and many others. A final section, Artifacts, links to paintings, photographs, election pins, and other items, all of which have annotated explanations.

This is a highly recommended work (in either print or electronic format) for public, school, and academic libraries.—**ARBA Staff Reviewer**

Dictionaries and Encyclopedias

519.   Snodgrass, Mary Ellen. **American Colonial Women and Their Art: A Chronological Encyclopedia.** Lanham, Md., Rowman & Littlefield, 2018. 384p. illus. index. $110.00; $104.50 (e-book). ISBN 13: 978-1-4422-7096-1; 978-1-4422-7097-8 (e-book).

This volume examines the creative endeavors of women in the American colonies from 1607 to the inauguration of President George Washington in 1789. It is a year-by-year encyclopedia based on extensive research of archival and newspaper collections, illustrating the varied and dynamic lives, arts, and concerns of colonial women. For instance, some of the topics which the encyclopedia brings to the fore are: patriot vs.

loyalist sentiments, diatribes against issues such as slavery and oppression, fears related to battles and conflicts, travelogues and protests, anecdotes and memoirs, and new forms of expression within social and economic situations, to name but a few. Some of the arts represented include painting, musical composition and performance, writing and storytelling, dancing and acting, and stitchery and quilting. Two appendixes, "Art Genres" and "Artists by State" are perhaps the most important part of the book because they allow the user to quickly find information related to particular interests and research. An extensive glossary and bibliography are also included. I highly recommend this volume given its unique focus along with its usability and attention to detail.—**Bradford Lee Eden**

520.   **Women's Lives around the World: A Global Encyclopedia.** Susan M. Shaw and others. Santa Barbara, Calif., ABC-CLIO, 2018. 4v. illus. index. $415.00/set. ISBN 13: 978-1-61069-711-8; 978-1-61069-712-5 (e-book).

Women's Lives around the World is a four-volume global encyclopedia, organized by regions of the world: Africa and the Middle East, The Americas, Asia and the Pacific, and Europe. The encyclopedia includes entries on 150 different countries including some territories. Such women's and feminist issues as education, employment, children and teens, health, family, sexuality, politics, religion, LGBTI matters, climate change, and social media are covered. Each entry includes a country overview and primary resource data, plus a further resources bibliography for researchers wanting to probe deeper. The substantial essays are discernible for high school and adult researchers. Sidebars in each essay include primary sources and explorations into the lives of real people and real issues worldwide. There are color photographs in the middle of each volume illustrating the lives of women from the countries examined. While each volume includes unique information, the authors attempted to cover nearly the same information in all countries. The researcher can easily find a topic in the index and comparisons can be made between countries for critical analysis. *Women's Lives around the World* strengthens any sociology and/or women's studies collection in public, high school, or academic libraries.—**Amy B Parsons**

Handbooks and Yearbooks

521.   **Handbook of Research on Women's Issues and Rights in the Developing World.** Nazmunnessa Mahtab and others. Hershey, Pa., IGI Global, 2018. 452p. index. $245.00. ISBN 13: 978-1-52253-018-3; 978-1-52253-019-0 (e-book).

This volume in the Advances in Electronic Government, Digital Divide and Regional Development (AEGDDRD) book series shines a light on the changing roles of and continuing pressures on women in developing nations. The book shares the scholarly research of numerous contributors covering an expanse of topics in an efficient and digestible way.

The volume's preface along with its detailed table of contents lays out its organization and explains its highly specialized focus. Twenty-four chapters fall into six sections: Women & Work, Women's Education & Health, Vulnerability & Women, Equality & Empowerment, Gender & Media, and Emerging Challenges & Inclusion of Men on

Women's Issues. Information may address both longstanding issues, such as patriarchy and gender violence in addition to issues only recently brought to the forefront, like female entrepreneurship and the media's role related to gender equality. Chapters stress the importance of including men in the dialogue ("Engaging Men in Women's Economic Empowerment in Butiama District, Mara Region, Tanzania") and track the development of women's issues from the crowded public bus ("Women's Commuting Environment in Public Buses in Dhaka City: A Case of Men's Perspectives") to the corporate board room ("Role of Women Empowerment in Public and Corporate Leadership"). Each chapter opens with an abstract to establish the impetus and methodology of the research that follows. Chapters are generally well structured and may provide an introduction, background, future research directions, and conclusion sections; they may also incorporate the use of data tables, headers, subheaders, key terms and definitions, and more. References are listed at the end of each chapter and compiled again at the end of the book, alongside brief contributor biographies and an index. The material in this volume would have a broad appeal to women's rights advocates, global policy makers, business leaders, educators, students, and many others.—**ARBA Staff Reviewer**

522.   **International Women's Library. http://intlwomenslibrary.org/about.** [Website] Free. Date reviewed: 2018.

The International Women's Library gathers information from around the globe about issues affecting women and girls in order to enhance female learning opportunities and address particular learning challenges. The site has collected over six hundred government reports, policy briefs, NGO studies, social media campaigns, organizations, digital tool kits, blogs, and other resources in a rich and accessible resource of otherwise hard-to-find publications and alternative media. Casual users may choose to first peruse the Featured Collection, Featured Item, or list of Recently Added Items displayed on the homepage. Alternatively, users can conduct a basic or advanced search from the bar on the top right corner of the page, or can Browse Items which are listed by title, creator, or date added. Listings include a brief description, tags, and a thumbnail photograph. Users can browse all or browse by tags. Item metadata includes such things as title, subject, description, creator, source link, publisher, date, and collection. Items reflect a diverse array of domestic and international issues, and include the Nordic Women in Film website, Women for Action oral history interviews, Black Womanhood university course syllabus, Wisconsin Women Make History digital resource, a Brazil-based study on "Feminist Perspectives towards Transforming Economic Power: Agroecology," and much more. Browse Collections organizes materials into fifty-nine thematic groups, with information on Food & Agriculture, Reproductive & Sexual Health, Law & Justice, Film, Politics, History, STEM, and other categories. Users can alternatively find nearly five hundred of the items on the Google Map by selecting a pinned location.—**ARBA Staff Reviewer**

523.   **It's My Country Too: Women's Military Stories from the American Revolution to Afghanistan.** Jerri Bell and Kayla Williams, eds. Dulles, Va., Potomac Books, 2017. 330p. illus. $32.95. ISBN 13: 978-1-61234-831-5.

Observing that "too often women were viewed as incidental," Jerri Bell, retired naval officer and managing editor of *O-Dark Thirty,* and Tracy Crow, a former Marine Corp Officer, endeavored through this anthology to highlight the service of women in the military conflicts in which the United States has engaged from the American Revolution to

Operation Iraqi Freedom. For the Civil War, this meant including individuals who served the Confederate States of America. Since the military did not enlist or commission women during most of those conflicts, some, like Deborah Sampson Gannett during the American Revolution, disguised themselves as men to serve their country. Others were engaged in tasks like medical care or spying. In order to capture the voices of those who are no longer living, the editors relied on memoirs and military records for source material. The tone of the work changes somewhat in the latter chapters as veterans of recent conflicts provide detailed and visceral narratives of their experiences in the field. All of the first-hand accounts are deftly contextualized by the editors. While the work does include a bibliography, there is no index. As a reference work, it has limited utility as it was not designed for that purpose. It is a unique title that should be strongly considered for acquisition by academic and public libraries.—**John R. Burch Jr.**

524.   Owen, Patricia R. **Gender and Patriarchy in the Films of Muslim Nations.** Jefferson, N.C., McFarland, 2018. 235p. illus. index. $49.95pa. ISBN 13: 978-1-4766-6787-4; 978-1-4766-8260-8 (e-book).

As the subtitle of this fascinating volume indicates, this is a filmography of twenty-first-century feature films from eight Muslim-majority countries: Afghanistan, Algeria, Bangladesh, Egypt, Iran, Iraq, Pakistan, and Turkey. The author indicates that all films presented are accessible to U.S. viewers and all have English subtitles. All of the films present/explore issues concerning gender status and gender relationships, seen within the setting of everyday life in the country being portrayed. A total of fifty-six films made between 1999 and 2015 are analyzed, following a similar format for all: synopsis, traditional and nontraditional gender portrayals, elements of patriarchy, and other topics as applicable to an individual film. Each of the eight country chapters begins with a two- or five-page "country profile," including an introduction and a section on sociopolitical and religious issues related to gender. A brief introduction and a similar summary do a very good job of framing the presentation of these films, providing context for Islam and Sharia law within daily life and artistic creation. Male domination and female subjugation are prevalent, and resistance against this situation appears in several of the films. Generally, these are moving (and depressing) films that often present the constant struggles of females despite their strength of character.

This book is designed for, and recommended for, academic libraries, predominantly those that support cinema studies, international studies, and women's studies. It will certainly introduce readers to important themes in films that are little known in the United States.—**Mark Schumacher**

525.   **Women's Rights: Reflections in Popular Culture.** Savage, Ann M., ed. Santa Barbara, Calif., Greenwood Press/ABC-CLIO, 2017. 192p. illus. index. (Issues through Popular Culture). $37.00. ISBN 13: 978-1-4408-3942-9; 978-1-4408-3943-6 (e-book).

The editor, a professor at Butler University, is joined by contributors who are primarily PhD candidates and professors from across the United States, and together they have produced a collection of articles that chronicle how women's rights have been depicted across media. The first four sections cover television, music, film, and literature. The two final chapters cover women's rights in the news media and on the Web. While some documentaries are included in the film section, and some autobiographies are in the literature section, the first chapters primarily describe fictional works. Articles are written for a general audience, with clear and understandable language. They are enhanced by black-and-white images, and accompanied by brief recommendations for further reading. Many of the suggested items are monographs, but the occasional article, website, and documentary round out the lists. Within each section, works and issues are listed chronologically, which allows the reader to place them within the broader and evolving cultural context. The section covering women's rights on the Web provides some surprising dates, however. While a number of contributors to the volume may recall a time before the Internet was ubiquitous, younger researchers have never experienced a pre-Web world, so seeing a section titled "Our Bodies Ourselves (ourbodiesourselves.org) (1969-)" may be confusing, as it appears the website was started in 1969. Although the section's introduction somewhat explains the use of dates, it is unusual to see URLs followed with years of introduction that long predate the Web. Despite this irregularity, this volume provides succinct background on a variety of major films, television shows, writers, and musicians that have explored and advanced women's rights in the modern United States. Recommended for public, high school, and college libraries.—**Amanda Izenstark**

526.   **Women's Studies Archive: Women's Issues and Identities.** [Website] Farmington Hills, Mich., Gale/Cengage Learning, 2017. Price negotiated by site. Date reviewed: 2017.

Gale's Women's Studies Archive provides a remarkable look at primary source materials focusing on women's issues in the nineteenth and twentieth centuries. The archive includes deeply personal information including diaries, letters, photographs, news clippings, organizational records, and journals. It provides insight into large, history-making events, while also providing details on the minutia of the lives of ordinary women called to extraordinary tasks. By reading these primary source documents, the women are humanized in a unique way.

The archive is broken down into fifteen collections, including women's periodicals, feminist organizations, Planned Parenthood records, and records of the Women's Trade Union (WTU). For example, one area with an extensive archive is the Women's Trade Union League and Its Leaders. The WTU existed from 1903 to 1950, securing many important victories for women during its almost half century of existence. Interestingly, the WTU was founded in the early part of the twentieth century to combat sweatshop conditions in the nation's largest cities. The organization simultaneously advocated for women's rights and for labor rights simultaneously. Advocacy included awareness campaigns, union organizing, and labor strikes. By reading through the organization's documents, the researcher can see the internal struggle, the difficult decisions, and the unplanned situations that led to tremendous triumphs. The organizers of the WTU learned the system as they organized for change; the archive documents that process of learning as well.

The WTU represented the first phase of women's liberation. Representing the second phase, and well represented in the Gale's archive, is the San Francisco Women's Building (SFWB)/Women's Centers. The SFWB, an organization still in existence, advocates self-determination, gender equality, and social justice. As is evident to the researcher, the WTU represented the first wave of feminism and the most basic of needs: the ability to work in a safe environment. The second wave of feminism, as represented by SFWB, represents the second wave of feminism that advocates for equal pay, access to contraceptives, and other second wave goals. As with the archives of the WTU, the archives of the SFWB detail a legacy of struggle, including two fire bombings at the organization's San Francisco building located in the Mission district.

The Gale's Women's Studies Archive is doubtlessly valuable to researchers who are investigating the history of the women's liberation movement. As new generations of leaders in the women's studies movement emerge, they can use the Gale's Women's Studies archive to look back on the movement for research, inspiration, and useful lessons. Recommended for academic libraries.—**Sara Mofford**

Part III

HUMANITIES

19 Humanities in General

General Works

527. **Digital Bodleian.** http://digital.bodleian.ox.ac.uk/. [Website] Free. Date reviewed: 2017.

As the preeminent research library of England's Oxford University, the Bodleian Library is home to over twelve million artifacts including books, prints, drawings, manuscripts, and more. Digital Bodleian is the well-organized and generous digital archive of well over half a million items from various Bodleian Library collections. Users can search from the bar or browse by twenty-four specific collections. A drop down menu from the Filter Collections bar allows users to browse by theme, such as Maps, Ephemera, Early Printed Books, and Prints & Portraits. Users can also access eight External Collections from the site, such as the John Johnson Collection of Printed Ephemera. It is important to note that some external collections may be password protected.

Selecting a collection allows access to the specific database offering a choice of list or grid item views. Users can further filter the database by language or source. Users can scroll through the collection to select an item for examination and then select the "open" icon or double click the image for access. The item may be accompanied by a narrative description (some can be quite lengthy) and metadata which may include item condition, contributor, format, rights, and language. Collections are quite diverse, and include Western Manuscripts, Educational Ephemera and Children's Games of the 18th and 19th Centuries, Burmese Life and Devotion, Cobbett's Parliamentary History, Exploring Egypt in the 19th Century, and others. Notable items include papers of writer Lewis Carroll (Charles Dodgson), Napoleonic-era satirical cartoons, illustrated works on Botanical Theology (proving the existence of God through nature), illuminated manuscripts, a Boer War board game, and the Gough Map—the oldest road map of Great Britain. The site also allows users to curate their own annotated and tagged collections upon simple site registration. The ease of navigation makes the esteemed collections of the Bodleian Library accessible to an array of researchers and casual users alike.—**ARBA Staff Reviewer**

528. Dooley, Patricia L. **Freedom of Speech: Reflections in Art and Popular Culture.** Santa Barbara, Calif., Greenwood Press/ABC-CLIO, 2017. 167p. illus. index. (Issues through Pop Culture). $37.00. ISBN 13: 978-1-4408-4339-6; 978-1-4408-4340-2 (e-book).

This short introduction to the myriad ways free speech has been challenged is a broad entry point for beginning researchers. Written by a professor of communication at Wichita State University, coverage begins with challenges to literature during the colonial period in the United States, and moves through successful and unsuccessful expressions of and challenges to free speech in art and media of all forms to the present day.

Chapters include instances in fashion, broadcast and online media, sports, and arts, and address these chronologically within each area. Researchers exploring recent clothing and dress code issues, for example, will also find information about the Zoot Suit Riots—violent incidents based on dress that took place in the 1940s. The chapter on the visual arts starts with a nineteenth-century uproar over a naked statue and concludes with visual arts censorship in schools.

Relevant black-and-white images enhance the text throughout. Each chapter begins with an overview and concludes with a list of additional readings, including primary sources from newspapers as well as academic and mainstream monographs. Websites are occasionally included in the readings, but it's worth evaluating their quality (and continued existence). For example, a WordPress site developed by a masters' degree student is included in the list of readings for the literature chapter, but the author of the site is not listed in the reference, and it's a free site—neither a scholarly work nor reviewed by an editor.

Despite this, this volume is written in a readable, accessible style, and would be well suited for high school and academic libraries supporting students examining current as well as historical free speech and censorship events.—**Amanda Izenstark**

529. **Ebsco eBooks & Audiobooks. https://www.ebscohost.com/ebooks/schools.** [Website] Birmingham, Ala., EBSCO Publishing, Inc., 2017. Price negotiated by site. Date reviewed: 2018.

This site, representing one in a suite of EBSCO's academic research databases, covers eBooks which span a wide range of topics and genres that would generally appeal to high school students for research or entertainment purposes. Easy to navigate, the site allows users to browse in several ways, or conduct a basic or advanced search from the bar in the upper left corner of the page. The Browse by Category tab on the left hand side of the page lists thirty-one genre choices such as True Crime, Philosophy, Education, Fiction, History, and Literature & Criticism. Users can alternatively examine the Highlights section in the center of the page, which allows users a look at a good sampling of genres from short stories to poetry. Featured eBooks displays several titles within a genre (e.g., Business & Economics). Users can click on the thumbnail photograph of the eBook cover to access the eBook and its record, which will generally include author(s), publication information, resource type, subject(s), database identification information, publisher permissions, and more. There will also be a brief description of eBook contents. Users can view an eBook's full text via the eBook viewer, click a link to a specific chapter, search specific text, and make notes to save within the EBSCO host folder. Users may also be able to print, download, save, copy/paste, and perform other functions depending on the particular eBook publisher agreement. Users new to the eBook format can select the Learn More link at the bottom of the page to learn how to navigate the viewer. With a generous and diverse selection of titles, and ample research tools, EBSCO's E-Book site would be a valuable student resource.—**ARBA Staff Reviewer**

530. **Sahapedia. https://www.sahapedia.org/.** [Website] Free. Date reviewed: 2017.

This site is designed as a hub of Indian culture and heritage education, offering access to a rich virtual exhibition of commentary, interviews, photo galleries, and more. This virtual exhibition presents the unique traditions of the vast and somewhat mysterious country over many disciplines, such as language, archaeology, performing arts, and material arts. Users can conduct a basic search, select a category of interest from the left sidebar, or choose from a number of featured and tagged exhibitions, like "Post-partition Sindhi Literature in India," "Documentary and Censorship in India," "The Qutb Complex: An Overview," and "Mapping Indian Textiles: Applique." Users can also learn about the current collaborative projects pursued by the site with other organizations (such as Paramparik Karigar—An Association of Craftspersons) to broaden accessibility to some of the more rare materials. Users can conduct research on the site's diverse exhibits via the Library, which offers access to good source material (books, journals, etc.) for further contextual background. The News feature updates users on the latest issues of Indian culture and preservation, such as financing, education, and recent discoveries. This site would strongly appeal to students of Indian culture, armchair travelers, and others.—**ARBA Staff Reviewer**

531. Walker, Barbara L. E., and Holly E. Unruh. **Funding Your Research in the Humanities and Social Sciences: A Practical Guide to Grant and Fellowship Proposals.** New York, Routledge/Taylor & Francis Group, 2018. 198p. index. $39.95pa. ISBN 13: 978-1-61132-320-7; 978-1-315-15903-4 (e-book).

Early on, the authors of this book clearly spell out their goal: "This book will walk you through the process of finding the best funding opportunities for your research and career goals" (p.14). Chapter by chapter, the book lays out the steps in the entire endeavor. The first section explores finding the proper agencies to approach and creating a plan for the proposal. The next section, the heart of the book, discusses the writing of the various sections of the proposal, and is followed by sections on collaboration, rebounding from rejection of a proposal, and other print and online resources worth exploring. Given the diverse types of research funding sources in the humanities and social sciences, a key aspect of this book is its focus on understanding which agency or foundation will be most interested in a scholar's project. A number of contributors share their real-life experiences on both sides of the process, with excerpts from actual successful proposals, which are useful additions to the text.

This book is clearly aimed at academics and the libraries that serve them. In fact, the authors mention that having "an affiliation with an accredited institution" is necessary in almost every case. Stylistically, the authors' decision to use the second person (you/your/yours) throughout the book reinforces their connection with and support of the readers of the work. The approach enhances the reading of the text. Highly recommended.—**Mark Schumacher**

20 Communication and Mass Media

General Works

Dictionaries and Encyclopedias

532.   Willis, Jim, and Anthony R. Fellow. **Tweeting to Freedom: An Encyclopedia of Citizen Protests and Uprisings around the World.** Santa Barbara, Calif., ABC-CLIO, 2017. 370p. illus. index. $89.00. ISBN 13: 978-1-4408-4004-3; 978-1-4408-4005-0 (e-book).

The goal of this volume is to analyze "how freedom-loving people in 32 countries around the world are harnessing the power of the Internet for greater liberties . . . " (p. vii). Those countries range from the United States and the United Kingdom to diverse countries such as India, Egypt, Vietnam, and Brazil. Each of the 32 chapters uses the same set of subdivisions: general overview, economic conditions, social conditions, media and Internet activity, and threats to journalists, followed by a "Further Reading" bibliography. The chapters range in length from seven pages (Singapore, UAE) to 20 pages (United States). There are a dozen or so photos as well. The 25-page introduction examines the development of the political use of the Internet, referencing several movements around the world which employed tools on the web to put forth their views and battle opposing factions. From smog to black lives and political oppression around the world, this book presents the evolution of cyberspace as a powerful tool for social and political justice.

One minor matter: the references in the bibliographies often include URLs of 100 or more characters; they are a bit easier to access in the e-book version, where the address can usually be copied and pasted. Given the topic of this volume, it is not surprising that a high percentage of the references provided are Internet items. A variety of libraries should find this source of use to their readers. Although academic libraries may be the most interested, others should consider it as well.—**Mark Schumacher**

Handbooks and Yearbooks

533.   **Al Jazeera. http://www.aljazeera.com/.** [Website] Free. Date reviewed: 2018

The Al Jazeera network launched in 1996 as the first independent news channel in the Arab world; in 2006, the network launched the Al Jazeera English version. The database associated with Al Jazeera is a true treasure trove for those looking for international news and much more. The News tab sorts information by region: Africa, Asia, US & Canada, Latin America, Europe, and Asia Pacific. The news from the Middle East is accessible under its own tab. The Documentaries tab is further subdivided by Featured Documentaries, Witness, Al Jazeera World, 101 East, People & Power, Fault Lines, My Tunisia, Al Jazeera Selects, Al Jazeera Correspondent, and REWIND. The last group of documentaries, REWIND, updates information on issues and people profiled in earlier films. Shows gives users several different ways to access Al Jazeera programming. One of the links under this tab, The Stream, provides information on times for live viewing. The Investigations tab focuses on Al Jazeera staff research into doping in sports, the sex abuse of young players in the British football system, Myanmar's campaign against the Rohingya, Pakistan's official report on the killing of Osama bin Laden, and many other topics. Information includes contact information for reporters and producers as well as links to the documents associated with the investigations. Editorials appear under the Opinions tab; the lead editorial story at the time of this review was on the Oxfam sex abuse scandal and the lack of legal accountability on the part of human aid organizations. In Pictures links to worldwide images like those covering the people displaced from the old city of Sanaa, Yemen, due to the ongoing civil war. These photographs are captioned, attributed, and contextualized. The More tab links to features, human rights, sport, weather, and other materials. The Live tab allows people to watch or listen (live). There is a wealth of information on this site, and it will prove an invaluable resource for those looking for a different and/or more international take on the news.—**ARBA Staff Reviewer**

534.   **AllSides. https://www.allsides.com/.** [Website] Free. Date reviewed: 2017.

The mission of this resource is to "free people from filter bubbles so they can understand the world and each other." Educators and librarians teaching the topic of media literacy will find this to be a solid resource for discussing bias, balanced news, and the difference between fact and opinion in the media world. This website is a news aggregator that helps facilitate discussions and teaches essential skills related to inquiry, collaboration, critical thinking, and evaluation. Students and teachers can search for topics such as healthcare, gun rights, and immigration, and view current event articles from popular news sources from the left, right, and center in order to better understand media bias. The site provides its own bias ratings for the articles, which provides a helpful way for teachers to introduce the topic of bias to younger students. AllSides For Schools, a part of AllSides.com, is a free nonprofit resource which schools can sign up for in order to receive more educator tools, lessons, and assessments, such as civil dialogue starters and individual teacher pages to post articles and discussions. This is a powerful resource that social studies, language arts, and school librarians will find invaluable for teaching media literacy and critical thinking skills.

Highly recommended.—**Angela Wojtecki**

535.   **Applying the Actor-Network Theory in Media Studies.** Markus Spöhrer and Beate Ochsner, eds. Hershey, Pa., Information Science Reference/IGI Global, 2017. 315p. index. $175.00. ISBN 13: 978-1-52250-616-4; 978-1-52250-617-1 (e-book).

This volume in the Advances in Media, Entertainment ,and the Arts (AMEA) series offers research aimed at understanding processes, innovations, and challenges across a number of media manifestations from gaming to television to film production.

Specifically, the volume considers the effects of the Actor-Network Theory (ANT), which confines relationships to networks between humans and nonhuman processes, ideas, and objects. The well-structured volume's preface along with its detailed table of contents lays out its organization and explains its highly specialized focus. Chapters establish the concepts and general applications of ANT, present case studies across a variety of media, and explore the theory in its approach to media studies from a skeptical perspective. The opening chapters provide an overview of the essential accumulated research in addition to foundational information on the ANT and media studies in general. The following case studies explore ANT theory in connection to film ("Applying Actor-Network Theory in Production Studies: The Formation of the Film Production Network of Paul Lazarus' Barbarosa"), video games ("The Home Console Dispositive: Digital Games and Gaming as Socio-Technical Arrangement"), and other media. Four concluding chapters seek to poke holes in ANT, criticizing its lessening of human value ("ANTi-Human: The Ethical Blindspot"), comparing it to the competing German Media Theory and more. Each chapter opens with an abstract to establish the impetus and methodology of the research that follows. Chapters make generous use of headers and subheaders, and may incorporate the use of key terms and definitions and other tools. References are listed at the end of each chapter and are compiled again at the end of the book, alongside brief contributor biographies and an index. The material in this volume would likely appeal to educators and students in media studies or the social sciences. Recommended for academic libraries. Those not able to afford the entire book can purchase chapters separately in electronic format.—**ARBA Staff Reviewer**

536.   Burns, Kelli S. **Social Media: A Reference Handbook.** Santa Barbara, Calif., ABC-CLIO, 2017. 398p. index. (Contemporary World Issues). $60.00. ISBN 13: 978-1-4408-4355-6; 978-1-4408-4356-3 (e-book).

This single-volume ABC-CLIO (Contemporary World Issues) book, edited by University of South Florida professor Kelli S. Burns, provides a broad and easily understandable discussion of the evolution of social media. The book is organized into seven sections: Background and History; Problems, Controversies, and Solutions; Perspectives; Profiles; Data and Documents; Resources; and Chronology followed by a glossary and an index. Social media addiction; hoaxes, rumors, and scams; cyberbullying; the deleterious affect social media can have on personal relationships; and privacy concerns are among the many issues addressed. This volume also includes a succinct account of the meteoric rise of social media and includes profiles of movements like the 2010-11 Arab Spring and people like Snapchat cofounder Eric Spiegel. Graphics, charts, illustrations, tables, and the inclusion of current resources enhance the book's usefulness.

This one-stop, authoritative reference is recommended for high school, community college, university, and public libraries.—**Thomas E. Baker**

537.   **Documenting Hate News Index. https://projects.propublica.org/hate-news-index/.** [Website] Free. Date reviewed: 2018.

This page from the independent news organization Pro Publica presents a chronological listing of media reports on hate crimes or other bias incidents. The index lists reports of specific incidents (e.g., vandalism, physical altercations, etc.), statistical reviews, legislation, analysis, and more. The index is a part of the larger Documenting Hate project which gathers and verifies personal stories of bias and hate for use in the creation of a national database (a work in progress). In a straightforward, two-column display, the page lists the dated articles and their source next to a keyword listing of names and places mentioned in the articles. Keywords are sized in accordance with their frequency of use within the articles. Users can initiate a search for other articles by using time-frame parameters. Then users can select a keyword to create the listing of relevant articles within the selected time-frame, in addition to a new set of keywords which relate specifically to the narrowed list of articles. Users can click on a selected article to redirect to the original source. Article listings reflect a diverse media—newspapers, public and commercial television, websites, public radio, and more—from across the ideological spectrum. They include local, national, and some international media outlets as well. Users can also click a link to Download Data and receive free access to updated information on collected news stories, such as article title, publisher, location, keywords, and a short item synopsis. In allowing quick access to information from a wide variety of sources, the site would be an excellent facilitator in regards to research for journalists, students, policy makers, civil rights advocates, and others.—**ARBA Staff Reviewer**

538.   Evergreen, Stephanie D. H. **Presenting Data Effectively: Communicating Your Findings for Maximum Impact.** Thousand Oaks, Calif., Sage, 2018. 226p. illus. index. $56.00pa. ISBN 13: 978-1-5063-5312-8.

Evergreen discusses and presents practical advice on how to create an effective presentation while avoiding pitfalls. The author includes reports, slideshows, handouts, posters, and data displays. The book covers the use of graphics and their various types, the varieties of typefaces and how to select fonts and font size, the use of color for "legibility, decoration, and spotlighting critical information," the cohesive arrangement of photos, text, and graphs, and how to make data presentation design more efficient, saving time and money in the process. Each chapter provides a list of learning objectives and a bibliography for further information. The appendixes include a "Report Layout Checklist," a diagnostic guide identifying elements of reports that can be "enhanced using graphic design best practices and/or the assistance of a graphic design expert," and "Data Visualization Checklist," with specific guidelines regarding arrangement, text size, and color scheme, among other factors. An index is included and illustrations in color are presented throughout the book. *Presenting Data Effectively* is a very practical and helpful source. This how-to title belongs in academic and public libraries and in the offices of teachers, businesspeople, researchers, medical professionals, students, and anybody who needs to prepare a presentation. Highly recommended.—**Lucy Heckman**

539.   **Hoaxy. https://iuni.iu.edu.** [Website] Free. Date reviewed: 2017.

As our reliance on social media as a news source increases, it is important to understand the ways in which news—real or "fake"—travels through it. Currently in beta stage, Hoaxy is a website designed to help organize and visualize how claims and fact checks spread via social media. First-time users can watch a brief video tutorial, or simply enter a news-related term or phrase in the search bar. Choosing either "all relevant" or "most recent" information will then display a list of affiliated news articles (claims) and/ or fact check articles. These are listed with title, source, date, and numbers of social media shares; users can also check a box if they would like to track it with a visualization. Clicking the article title will link to it. Selecting the Visualize tab allows users to chart those claims and/or fact checks over time vis-à-vis the social media site Twitter. In addition, users can observe accompanying "diffusion networks," showing the way claims and fact checks move from person to person. Clicking on a node of the visualization allows users to access specific Twitter users and their tweets. The Stats tab on the homepage offers insight across several topics, including most popular claims and fact check articles, most influential Twitter users, and most active Twitter users. Simply structured, Hoaxy takes a smart look at the relationship between facts and social media, and would appeal to researchers across a number of disciplines.—**ARBA Staff Reviewer**

540. **The SAGE Encyclopedia of Communication Research Methods.** Mike Allen, ed. Thousand Oaks, Calif., Sage, 2017. 4v. index. $695.00/set. ISBN 13: 978-1-4833-8143-5.

The SAGE Encyclopedia of Communication Research Methods is the first reference work exploring methods specific to communication and media studies. Communication research originally started as the most primitive of communication methods, but has since evolved with the use of the Internet. As society's communication methods have become more complex and varied, so has the field of communication research methods. The entries in the encyclopedia are authored by respected luminaries in the field of communication research, and, as such, are tailored to communication research.

While the researcher may read the encyclopedia from cover to cover, this is likely not how the encyclopedia was meant to be used. Rather, the encyclopedia is a useful desk reference for both established professionals and upcoming scholars. In addition to the entries, the encyclopedia also contains a useful reader's guide. The purpose of the reader's guide is to direct the attention of the researcher to entries devoted to an area, rather than to force the researcher to explore the entire encyclopedia in search of entries that may fit the research topic. The reader's guide is broken down into eight topics, including creating and conducting research and statistically analyzing data. While the reader's guide is not intended to substitute for the judgment and skill of a learned researcher, it can significantly cut down research time.

Overall, the encyclopedia is a useful, readable, and accessible addition to the library of any communication research professional or student. It is a welcome addition to an area where scholarly literature has been scant. This book is recommended for academic libraries.—**Sara Mofford**

541. Sergy, Lauren. **The Handy Communication Answer Book.** Canton, Mich., Visible Ink Press, 2017. 416p. illus. index. $21.95pa. ISBN 13: 978-1-5785-9587-7; 978-1-5785-9652-2 (e-book).

With depth and breadth, Sergy offers up this comprehensive answer book on communication. Leaving nothing to chance, she strategically organizes chapters to build knowledge and confidence around all facets of communication, beginning with what it is. She then moves on to rhetoric, written communication, emails, social media, public speaking, body language, audience, technology, and types of communication including business, social, and academic. Each chapter includes subtopics, images, and text boxes to add style to its substantive approach. Headings transition between ideas and provide easy referencing. The book is not for entertainment purposes, but is rather a manual for understanding the psychological and sociological characteristics of communication from past to present. The content is contemporary, featuring examples such as the current president and popular social media. Sergy's approach contextualizes each part of communication and serves to educate and inform, not preach. Here, knowledge is power and Sergy emboldens her readers to act with the information she has provided in one concentrated tome. She answers questions about why writing in all capitals is bad practice and pinpoints how Steve Jobs revolutionized business communication. The book includes additional resources, an appendix, and an index. Where is the "like" button for this book? It is a solid purchase for all libraries. Highly Recommended—**Alicia Abdul**

542.   **Under-Told Stories Project. https://www.stthomas.edu/give/whattosupport/ stories/.** [Website] Free. Date reviewed: 2018.

The Under-Told Stories Project from St. Thomas University in Minnesota provides an outlet for international media coverage of less familiar but nonetheless vitally important stories to a public television and online audience. This website holds an extensive video archive of news features from around the world. Selecting the Stories tab allows users to search by locations or tags, or scroll through a listing of recent stories, which users can view upon clicking the play button. Users can alternatively select to read the transcript. Related stories are displayed beneath the content. Topics groups stories into ten categories: Global Health, Human Rights and International Justice, Religion and Ethics, Food Security, Development, Infectious Disease, Social Entrepreneurship, Environment, Global Trade, and the local topic of Minnesota. Within the Religion and Ethics category, for example, users can view stories on "Rebuilding Nepal's Temples," the "India Beef Ban," or the compelling story of the "Last Jews of Cochin." In the Classroom offers a topical listing of Case Study Resources which organize the stories for quick, easy reference. The Archives tab presents the story collection going back to 2002. The Under-Told Stories Project brings to light stories that may not otherwise gain broad exposure, and would appeal to educators, students, and others interested in global issues, media studies, and more.—**ARBA Staff Reviewer**

Authorship

Style Manuals

543.   **The Chicago Manual of Style.** 17th ed. Chicago, University of Chicago Press, 2017. 1145p. index. $70.00. ISBN 13: 978-0-226-28705-8.

This is the first update to this venerable reference since the last edition in 2010 (see ARBA 2011, entry 819). Many changes and additions reflect the massive increase in access to electronic information and the overwhelming reliance in publishing on digital. Chapters 1 and 2 reflect these changes with expanded coverage of keywords and metadata; chapter 4 provides information on open-access publishing and distribution. In chapters 14 and 15, users will find expanded information on how to identify and consult sources online, including tips on choosing the best form of a link to cite, new coverage on how to cite such things as apps and blog posts, and much more. Other changes throughout the book were made in response to reader questions and answers. One notable change, also mentioned in the preface, is the recognition of "they" as a gender-neutral singular pronoun. The bibliography has also been updated. The manual remains an essential resource and should be purchased by all public and academic libraries. Publishing houses will also want to purchase the new edition.—**ARBA Staff Reviewer**

544.   Heard, Stephen B. **The Scientist's Guide to Writing: How to Write More Easily and Effectively Throughout Your Scientific Career.** Princeton, N.J., Princeton University Press, 2016. 306p. index. $21.95pa. ISBN 13: 978-0-691-17022-0.

Stephen B. Heard's *The Scientist's Guide to Writing* offers the reader a means by which to take some of the blood, sweat, and tears out of the scientific writing process. Through engaging writing and practical writing advice, Beard attempts to guide the young science professional through the writing process to avoid common pitfalls, such as writer's block and a lack of motivation, and make the most of the writing process, such as emphasizing the importance of revision. The book is divided into seven parts which address different facets of the process. The first part, entitled What Writing Is, represents a kind of philosophical or theoretical view on the process, grounding it in the work of Bacon and Hobbes. The second part, entitled Behavior, addresses different aspects of the writer's process and how to avoid "bad" habits. The third part, Content and Structure, offers ways of organizing one's writing based on what one hopes to accomplish and covers all the major parts of scientific-style writing, from abstract to appendixes. The fourth part, Style, discusses paragraphs, sentences, words, and brevity, the last of which is a critical element in the kind of concise but thorough writing necessitated by scientific research. The fifth part, Revision, focuses on revision and the review process. The sixth part, entitled Some Loose Threads, addresses various aspects of writing and publishing, focusing on the diversity of writing forms and types and dealing with co-authorship. The final part, Final Thoughts, brings it all together while tackling the question of whether or not scientific writing can be enjoyable—spoiler alert, Heard thinks it can be, but acknowledges that this is not a universally held belief. While perhaps overall the writing is a bit informal, it is nonetheless useful and applicable, and would even make for an excellent textbook in scientific or technical writing classes. In conclusion, this book is highly recommended, especially for academic libraries supporting applied sciences and research-heavy programs.—**Megan W. Lowe**

545.   Mills, Elizabeth Shown. **Evidence Explained: Citing History Sources from Artifacts to Cyberspace.** 4th ed. Baltimore, Md., Genealogical Publishing, 2017. 892p. index. $59.95. ISBN 13: 978-0-8063-2040-3.

This work updates the third edition published in 2015, although its length matches that of the earlier volume. The focus is on primary resources, such as court, cemetery and church documents, archives, and other institutional records. Information about citing books and periodical articles starts on page 643. Although its major role is to serve as a citation guide for scores of types of sources, it also seeks to help readers locate diverse sources and to analyze/evaluate them for their value within the research project at hand. The diverse citations generally follow the *Chicago Manual of Style's* "Humanities Style" format. Twelve of the fourteen chapters start with a section called "QuickCheck Models," where simple citation examples of the sources discussed in the chapter are given. As throughout this volume, categories can be very narrow: "Local Records—Vital records, Amended" and "Lineage-Society Records, Archived In-House" are two such examples.

This work will be useful to genealogists and other historians using these (often esoteric) sources in their work and their publications. Public libraries and academic libraries will have patrons who could find this resource useful, especially at a reasonable price for so much information.—**Mark Schumacher**

Newspapers and Magazines

Handbooks and Yearbooks

546.   **Historical Jewish Press www.web.nil.org.il/JPress/English/Pages/.** [Website] Date reviewed: 2018.

This site maintains a large collection of internationally published Jewish newspapers spanning over 200 years. Users can conduct a basic search from the bar at the top of the homepage, or can select from several browsing options on the menu bar. Users with more complicated searches may consult the User Guide from the menu bar for assistance. The All Titles tab lists newspapers currently available to view (145 at the time of this review). The listing includes a thumbnail image, brief description, and identifying information such as country of origin, time period, and language. Users can click the blue View Newspaper button to access the digital edition. While most (but not all) newspapers are published in the Hebrew language, limited translation may be available for some issues. On the listing page, users can also find newspaper Sections or sort by Languages, Publication Countries, Publication Years, or Tags. A Titles Map shows a visualization of publication countries. Papers such as the "clandestine" *Ashnav* from Israel or the *Daily Jewish Herald* from turn-of-the-century United States provide an excellent historical look at both the local and regional coverage offered by mainstream and small-press Jewish publishers. The website would appeal to users from a variety of disciplines including history, journalism, and Jewish studies.—**ARBA Staff Reviewer**

547.   **Newspapers SG. www.eresources.lb.gov.sg/newspapers.** [Website] Free. Date reviewed: 2017.

Newspapers SG is an online archive devoted to newspapers of Singapore. The site offers information about nearly two hundred newspapers published since 1831, listing titles held on microfilm at the Singapore National Library. The site allows free online viewing access to various editions of approximately forty of these titles. It is highly recommended that users first select the Q&A tab in the top right corner of the page for background information on site usage. "What are the Titles in the Digitized Newspaper collection?" charts the dates of the editions available for computer viewing and those that are only available to view in person at the Singapore National Library. Users must also consent to the site's terms and conditions before viewing the digital editions. Users can conduct a basic or advanced search, or can browse through the titles (and/or dates) available for home viewing, such as the *Malaya Tribune, Singapore Standard, Straits Chinese Herald, Sunday Standard,* and the *Singapore Free Press.* Selecting a newspaper will bring up a page noting publisher, frequency of publishing, language, and more. Users can manipulate a timeline to hone in on a particular date range of interest. A color-coded calendar graphic will note editions available to view for the chosen range. Clicking the date on the calendar brings up a transcription of the newspaper with masthead or title articles serving as links to the digital rendering. A table of contents runs the length of the left sidebar. Users can note microfilm reel number here, and "star" the article for citation use. The homepage offers several other features of note. This Week in History matches today's date with a particular newspaper page from Singapore's past. Most Viewed Articles allows users to view the current top five ("Python at Raffles" takes the number one slot at the moment). The Search Term Visualizer is a good tool for tracking keywords/phrases over decades. Users can enter a maximum of five keywords and incorporate several filters (newspaper title, date, range, and content type) to generate a graphic. For example, the term "war" appears with marked frequency during the two great global conflicts of the twentieth century. Microfilm Catalog helps users search all newspaper titles in the Singapore National Library's collection, filtered by date range, language of publication, and place of publication and identifying reel number, date range, and reference library location. Saved Citations collects starred citations throughout the length of a browsing session. Users can print or email the citations, but not the articles.—**ARBA Staff Reviewer**

Radio, Television, Audio, and Video

Directories

548.   Complete Television, Radio & Cable Industry Directory 2017. Amenia, N.Y., Grey House Publishing, 2017. 1600p. index. $350.00pa. ISBN 13: 978-1-61925-938-6.

The *Complete Television, Radio & Cable Industry Directory,* formerly published as the *Broadcasting & Cable Yearbook* provides "current, comprehensive television, radio and cable industry information for both U.S. and Canadian markets." The directory is arranged as follows: Introduction; Chronology of Electronic Media; The FCC and Its Regulatory Authority; Glossary of Terms; List of Abbreviations; Broadcast Television-U.S.; Broadcast Television-Canada; Radio-U.S.; Radio-Canada; Cable-U.S.; Cable-Canada; Programming and Production Services; Equipment Manufacturers and Production Services; Professional Services; Associations, Events, and Awards; and Government. The section on Broadcast Media in the U.S. provides market research including the top market areas of various regions in the country based on Designated Market Areas (Nielsen Media Research); Top 50 Shows, 2015-2016 season; sales of television receivers; an essay on the future of television; a directory of major broadcast networks (ABC, CBS, NBC, etc.); U.S. TV group ownership; TV stations in the US; U.S. television stations by call letters; U.S. television stations by analog channel; and U.S. television stations by digital channel. Each entry in the directory section includes: name, address, fax, phone, management, and, for major broadcasting networks, the names of its programs. The section on Broadcast Television-Canada includes a directory of major networks and stations by province and city in addition to market data. The Radio-U.S. section contains statistics on sales of home and clock radios; an essay on a look at the future of radio and directories of national radio networks among which are National Public Radio, CNN Radio, and CBS Radio; regional radio networks; U.S. radio group ownership; radio stations listed by state and city; U.S. based international radio; U.S.-based satellite radio; U.S. AM radio stations by call letters; U.S. FM radio stations by call letters; US AM stations by frequency; U.S. FM stations by frequency; glossary of radio format terms; and programming on radio stations by genres (among which are: adult contemporary, Christian, country, news/talk, and sports). The Radio-Canada section includes statistics and trends, radio stations in Canada by province and city, Canadian AM stations by call letters, Canadian FM stations by call letters, radio stations by frequency, and directory of stations by genre. The section on Cable TV for both the United States and Canada contains a directory of National Cable Networks (AMC, BBC America, CNBC, etc).The additional sections in the directory (for the United States and Canada) contain national associations, equipment manufacturers and distributors, trade shows, and a directory of regulatory agencies. The *Complete Television, Radio & Cable Industry* is a thorough and comprehensive source for professionals involved in the industry, for students in media related courses, and for anybody who seeks directory information on radio and television organizations. Highly recommended.—**Lucy Heckman**

Handbooks and Yearbooks

549.   **Video Source Book: A Guide to Programs Currently Available on Video.** 59th ed. Farmington Hills, Mich., Gale/Cengage Learning, 2017. 9v. index. $1,100/set. ISBN 13: 978-1-4103-2499-3.

Now in its 59th edition, this title is comprised of 9 volumes. The 1st volume includes an introduction followed by a user's guide and list of abbreviations; the user's guide and list of abbreviations are printed in each volume. Volumes use guide words to facilitate searching. The first six-and-a-half volumes contain the alphabetic list of more than 170,000 videos covering many topics, such as business and industry, fine arts, health and science, and sports and recreation. There are videos for various formats: VHS, 8mm, CD-I, ¾" U-matic, DVD, UMD, Blue-Ray Disc, and HD-DVD. Six indexes comprise the remaining volumes. The first index covers alternate titles (e.g., *Hunchback see*The Hunchback of Notre Dame). The second is an awards index that includes 6,000 films in 90 categories. There is also an index for special formats and one for program distributors. The 8th volume contains the subject index (with nearly 500 subject headings), and the 9th volume contains the credits index. Recommended for large public libraries and academic libraries, particularly those with film schools.—**ARBA Staff Reviewer**

21 Decorative Arts

Collecting

Coins and Paper Money

550. **Corpus of Early Medieval Coin Finds. http://www-cm.fitzmuseum.cam.ac.uk/ emc/.** [Website] Free. Date reviewed: 2018.

The Fitzwilliam Museum in England has conceived the Corpus of Early Medieval Coin Finds as a digital database of coins found throughout the British Isles that were minted during the years 410-1180. The database focuses on "single find" coins (as opposed to larger hoards) which possibly represent accidental deposits and can create a view of everyday coin usage and circulation. The homepage is straightforward, allowing users a choice of three link options. Users should first click the Introduction tab, where they will learn the parameters of the database with the option of supplementary information on The Importance of Single Finds, Recording New Finds, and a Note on Findspots. Search the Corpus accesses a default search form that users can edit with personal specifications. Users can select parameters such as Dates, Kingdom (e.g., Norman England), Ruler (e.g., Aethelred of East Anglia), Mint Location, and County Found. Users can apply more specific information such as "findspot" location if known. Via boxes at the bottom of the form, users can customize the coin(s) display. There are images available for most coins. It is recommended that casual users follow the Instructions link on the search form page before beginning their search. Search results will be displayed with as much reference information as is known. Users will also be able to view a rudimentary map of the findspots and a histogram of the search results if applicable. The Checklist of Coin Hoards links to a listing with supplementary information on the larger documented coin hoards. The absence of any browsing capability may somewhat limit the site's functionality.—**ARBA Staff Reviewer**

551. Friedberg, Arthur L., and Ira S. Friedberg. **Gold Coins of the World: From Ancient Times to the Present.** 9th ed. Williston, Vt., Coin & Currency Institute, 2017. 800p. illus. index. $39.99. ISBN 13: 978-0-87184-009-7.

The first updated edition in eight years (see ARBA 2010, entry 865) serves as a basic discussion of coin types rather than a complete listing of individual coins and serves as a basic guide, rather than a determination of the latest values. The preface presents an overview of the history of coinage and gold and of the format used to provide the information in this reference. The first part examines coins of the ancient world, specifically Ancient Greece and the Roman, Byzantine, and Nicaean empires, with information about the coins discussed chronologically, roughly following the historic path of the development of coinage. The second part forms the majority of the text and examines coins throughout the world from 600 A.D. to the present. The information is arranged alphabetically by country, using the most recent name for that country (e.g., coins of the Soviet Union are listed under Russia) and then arranged chronologically. Included in the descriptions are the date of issue, a brief description of what is on the obverse and reverse of each coin, and an indication of possible values for each of the best two states or conditions of the coins (which may or may not be the available value). Most entries have black-and-white illustrations that are actual size. At the back is a brief section with helpful information about weights and measures, the Mohammedan calendar, and a table of alphabets. A list of general references for further study and an index of place names completes the volume. One somewhat annoying feature is the fifteen pages of glossy, color advertisements at the front of the volume, which seem somehow inappropriate for a reference volume. However, this resource serves as a very good, very knowledgeable starting place for the historic, social, and political significance of coinage—**Martha Lawler**

552.   Friedberg, Arthur L., and Ira S. Friedberg. **Paper Money of the United States: A Complete Illustrated Guide with Valuation.** 21st ed. Williston, Vt., Coin & Currency Institute, 2017. 308p. illus. $67.59. ISBN 13: 978-0-87184-721-8.

Paper Money of the United States: A Complete Illustrated Guide with Valuations is a first-rate assemblage of United States currency. This book is the standard reference that documents paper money from colonial times to the present. The authors based this edition on Robert Friedberg's original research. Furthermore, this all-inclusive, 308-page volume describes large-size notes, fractional currency, small-size notes, and encased postage stamps. In addition, colonial and continental currency, Confederate state notes currency, error notes, and postage envelopes receive substantial coverage. It chronicles historical events and provides pathways to timely information and factual explanations. Examples of the fine art of engraving are remarkable. The production and design team used color to reproduce every illustration. All currency image presentations are accurate, vibrant, and well documented.

Initial paper money under the United States Constitution dates from 1861. All currency issued by the U.S. government remains valid. Since 1935, the one-dollar note, the most familiar denomination of paper currency, has carried the Great Seal of the United States. Interestingly, old and obsolete notes depicted in the book remain legal tender at face value. Banks or the government will exchange it for current paper money. Sometimes, the actual redemption value is higher than the face value.

Highly recommended.—**Thomas E. Baker**

553.   **Numismatics. http://numismatics.org/search/.** [Website] Free. Date reviewed: 2017.

This page from the American Numismatics Society (ANS) offers free access to over 600,000 objects in their vast collection of coinage, paper money, tokens, medals, and other currency. Users can simply select from the links underneath the coin display or from the Departments category links on the left sidebar. Users can also choose to browse all departments together. Departments include Greek, Roman, Byzantine, Islamic,

East Asian, South Asian, Medieval, Modern, United States, Latin America, and Medals & Decorations. Within each department page, users can conduct a keyword search with generous filter capabilities. Users can view the database with or without coin images (users must select "with images" in order to actually see them). Descriptive information on the items is generous and may include object date, measurements, denomination, material, geography, authority, identifying notes, and ANS references. There may also be a Google Map of the item's originating location. Notable items in the database include the 1792 half disme—the first coin minted in the United States, and a silver Olympic medal from the first modern games held in 1896. The page also contains a Featured Object which highlights a random item from the collection. Several links on the left sidebar may also appeal to researchers. The Publications link hosts the ANS Digital Library of monographs, dissertations and other numismatic scholarship, and Online Resources links to a page listing other digital coin collection projects of note, such as CRRO (Coinage of the Roman Republic Online) and PELLA (Coinage of the Macedonian Kings).

This reliable site will appeal to a wide variety of users. Recommended.—**ARBA Staff Reviewer**

Crafts

554.   Muno, Frieda. **Troubleshooting for Jewelers: Common Problems, Why They Happen and How to Fix Them.** New York, Firefly Books, 2016. 176p. illus. index. $16.95pa. ISBN 13: 978-1-77085-735-3.

This book is written for amateur and professional jewelers. It is divided into an introductory chapter and five major sections: Shaping, Decoration, Wirework, Casting, and Stone Setting. Each section also has two divisions: Best Practice and Fix-Its. What is nice about this book is that it is extensively illustrated in color, and that it is quite detailed in its descriptions. Step-by-step procedures are the norm, with both color pictures and textual guidelines. Unfortunately, because the book is jam packed with so much content, the print is quite small and can be a challenge for those who have visual difficulties. The book is definitely geared towards the how-to-do-it-yourself (DIY) crowd, and would probably fit in well in most public libraries and technical colleges who have curriculum in this area.—**Bradford Lee Eden**

Fashion and Costume

555.   Moore, Jennifer Grayer. **Street Style in America: An Exploration.** Santa Barbara, Calif., Greenwood Press/ABC-CLIO, 2017. 382p. illus. index. $94.00. ISBN 13: 978-1-4408-4461-4; 978-1-4408-4462-1 (e-book).

One aspect of the pop culture of the 1950s was the emergence of street style in which fashion evolves from grassroots, everyday dress styles rather than runway shows and fashion salons. The author of this book that explores street style has also written a companion volume, *Fashion Fads through American History* (Greenwood, 2015). Coverage in the present volume is centered on the United States and begins in the 1940s with entries on such topics as "bobby socks" and "zoot suits" and ends with the 2010s and material on, for example "steampunk hipster" and "Coachella Festival." The book begins with four introductory chapters that explore the meaning and origin of street style, its socioeconomic background, different forms, and its impact on the fashion and business world. There follows, in alphabetical order, 34 entries that explore specific topics related to street style. In addition to the subjects listed above, other examples are "American street gangs," "goth," "hippie," "punk," "skin head," and "snowboarding." In each article, there is extensive historical and background information on the subject followed by dress practices and fashion statements associated with the topic. Each entry is about five or six pages in length and includes an extensive (usually about 12 to 15 items) bibliography of books, articles, and websites "for further reading." In general, the writing style is simple and direct although, at times, it seems somewhat pretentious. Part three, called Gallery of American Street Style contains about 30 pages of photographs (one per page) illustrating some of the street styles described in the text. For example, there are pictures of street gang dress, punk garb, goths, and kids in bobby socks. These photographs are arranged alphabetically by topic and have accompanying explanatory descriptions. Unfortunately, there are no cross-references either from the main text to the pictures or from the pictures to the main text. This severely limits the value of both the text and the pictures. After a brief concluding essay in which the author speculates on the future of street style there is an extensive 25-page bibliography of books and articles, many dated as late as 2016, followed by a brief index principally of basic subjects. In spite of the flaw mentioned above, this remains an important, thoroughly researched work that is recommended for large collections where material on contemporary fashion is needed.—**John T. Gillespie**

556.　Sterlacci, Francesca, and Joanne Arbuckle. **Historical Dictionary of the Fashion Industry.** 2d ed. Lanham, Md., Rowman & Littlefield, 2017. 708p. illus. (Historical Dictionaries of Professions and Industries). $150.00; $142.00 (e-book). ISBN 13: 978-1-4422-3908-1; 978-1-4422-3909-8 (e-book).

This book, part of the Historical Dictionaries of Professions and Industries series, is in its second edition. Given the fact that humans have been wearing clothing from their ancient beginnings, the chronology ranges from 50,000 B.C.E. (Cro-Magnons making clothes out of animal skins and plants) up to the present. The introduction focuses on the rise of the fashion industry in the nineteenth century, discussing various important trends and individuals. Each of the entries in the dictionary is concise, with bolded terms pointing to other entries and fully capitalized terms pointing to *see also* references. Eight appendixes provide information on fashion magazines and periodicals, trend and forecasting services, trade periodicals and newsletters, trade shows, major trade organizations and associations, fashion and textile museums, top fashion schools, and size ranges. The extensive bibliography has many subdivisions detailing resources in history, influences, designers and brands, business, and apparel categories. A good introductory reference work for K-12 and academic libraries.—**Bradford Lee Eden**

Interior Design

557.　Fitzgerald, Oscar P. **American Furniture: 1650 to the Present.** Lanham, Md., Rowman & Littlefield, 2018. 622p. illus. index. $130.00; $123.50 (e-book). ISBN 13: 978-

1-4422-7038-1; 978-1-4422-7040-4 (e-book).

This lavishly illustrated volume contains over eight hundred photographs, of which forty-eight are in color. This book combines and expands information from the author's previous publications *Three Centuries of American Furniture* and *Four Centuries of American Furniture* with additional content into the twenty-first century. As a result, it is probably the most extensive and comprehensive volume on American furniture from the seventeenth century up to the present. Twenty-one chapters provide in-depth analysis of various types and histories of American furniture such as Queen Anne, Federal, American Empire, Shaker, Gothic, Rococo, Eastlake, Mission, Revival, Post-Modern, and Avant-garde, to name but a few. Each chapter has numerous black-and-white photographs referred to in the content. The color photographs feature a number of re-created and historical rooms from around the United States, in order to show how Americans decorated rooms in various time periods, from rich mansions to humble rural dwellings. A wonderful addition to any public or academic library's holdings.—**Bradford Lee Eden**

558.   Ott, Jennifer. **1000 Ideas for Color Schemes: The Ultimate Guide to Making Colors Work.** New York, Firefly Books, 2016. 288p. illus. index. $29.95pa. ISBN 13: 978-1-77085-752-0.

This book, put together by Jennifer Ott of Houzz and HGTV.com fame, is extremely useful. Ms. Ott is an interior designer and architectural design specialist and an excellent one if the book is any indication.

While using the book the reader cannot help but be inspired. There is a short explanation of the colors from the color wheel and after that the book quickly proceeds into the 1,000 ideas. The book is extremely well laid out and indexed with different palettes from fashion, nature, jewelry, home design, and more. Colored side tabs make it easy to find desired color schemes quickly.

I can see this book not only used by designers, sewers, decorators, and artists but by teachers and individuals as well. I have already used it multiple times. Recently my young granddaughter had decided on a new grey bedspread for her room but could not decide on the color of curtains. She and I looked at the book and found eye-catching teal colors were displayed in the grey section. A beautiful combination with grey and one we would never have considered without the book.

Whether this book is used every day to make decisions and choices for work, to help with making personal choices, or used for display on a coffee table, the user will never be disappointed.—**Kathy Adams**

22 Fine Arts

General Works

Biography

559.   **Essay'd: Short Essays on Detroit Artists. http://essayd.org/.** [Website] Free. Date reviewed: 2018.

The Essay'd website currently hosts eighty-five essays on individual artists who have created in and around Detroit, Michigan. The simple mission of Essay'd—to gather and share writing on these artists and their work—belies the rich and complex view of the Detroit art environment it describes. Users will find information on creators of paintings, metalwork, performance, textile, photography, jewelry, street art, and much more. To select an artist, users can simply choose from a numbered listing of entries running through the right sidebar. Users can scroll through the most current entries features on the left side of the page. Entries for each artist contain an essay, offering an objective assessment of the artist's approach and intent, with general descriptions of the particular art, its themes, and its elements (composition, color, medium, etc.). The entry also includes several thumbnails of the artist's work. Clicking on a thumbnail affords a larger view with title, date, medium, and piece dimensions. Essays are notably brief, providing just enough to elicit a general understanding of the artist and their work, and cleverly encouraging users to browse through the essays as if in a gallery of art writing. The site does an excellent job of calling out the diversity of the art and artists in the area. Certainly a number of artists are keenly tuned into the issues of the city, from racial justice to economic struggles. Other artists focus on their own inner landscapes, or take a broader view of worldly concerns. Thus the effect of the website is to both highlight a range of talented artists, but to also emphasize the wealth of ideas behind a robust art scene. The site would appeal across a number of cultural disciplines from writing to art to regional culture studies.—**ARBA Staff Reviewer**

Dictionaries and Encyclopedias

560.   **The Eerdmans Encyclopedia of Early Christian Art and Archaeology.** Paul Corby Finney, ed. Grand Rapids, Mich., William B. Eerdmans, 2017. 3v. illus. maps. $495.00/set. ISBN 13: 978-0-8028-3811-7.

The Eerdmans Encyclopedia of Early Christian Art and Archaeology (EECAA) is fittingly dedicated to Ernst Kitzinger, the German American historian of late antique, early medieval, and Byzantine art, whose work sought to integrate the visual with the conceptual. The discipline of early Christian art has become more differentiated in recent years, and students new to the field will find this conceptually expansive book a true pleasure for both its aesthetic qualities and its rich and authoritative content. The EECAA is the product of more than 50 years of conceptualizing, writing, and editing, and in it, editor Paul Corby Finney draws on an international and methodologically diverse list of specialists: the editorial board includes scholars from both art and archaeology, while the list of contributors reveals the worldwide interest in the topic and underscores the editor's intent to stretch the boundaries of the discipline. Indeed, the editor notes a connection between this methodological expansion and recent archaeological findings, which have challenged the notion that art and architecture in late antiquity were strictly urban in character. Just as rural artifacts have influenced our understanding of the period, so too must a wider range of contemporary perspectives.

While this three-volume set is an investment at $495, the contents provide real value with the quality of scholarship, the suggestions for further study, and the striking images and illustrations found throughout the encyclopedia. The first two volumes hold the encyclopedic entries (distributed in entries A-J and K-Z, respectively), while volume three offers plates and maps to illustrate many of these entries, with clear instructions to the reader for navigation and map plots for pieces of art, archeological dig, place, and other data points. Other helpful front matter includes two forewords, a preface by the editors, and an abbreviations section of more than 20 pages, which is duplicated in volumes one and two. The works listed in the abbreviations are not repeated in bibliographies. The editor has employed periods and commas to indicate where the citation will be found. Additionally, cross-references in the text follow an in-line arrow. Finally, at the back of volume one, one finds a list of terms, jargon, and definitions in the glossary. These terms are not actually glossed or embossed in the text, however, offering a point for revision if a second edition appears.

As regards the contributors, the list in the front matter provides little information. But some exploration in the entries reveals participation from archaeologists, art historians, historians, epigraphers, and theologians, who take as their audience students of Christianity and the art and archaeology of Africa, Asia, and Europe from 200-650 C.E. They rely on archaeological findings from urban and rural areas. Their essays cover a broad range of subject matter, from insects to saints, and show a large path of development in Christian art, from its most diverse beginnings to the more formal use of iconography in architecture, sculpture, painting, mosaic, and portables. Per the editor's guidance, there is consistent use of terminology and prose throughout these entries, which is clear and accessible. In each entry, Christian evidence is presented first, followed by the background of non-Christian parallels and precedents.

This beautiful set provides the student with an authoritative guide to the art and archaeology of a vibrant and eclectic time in Christian art, which incorporated elements and motifs from many cultures, traditions, and media. I highly recommend the EECAA for college, university, and seminary libraries.—**Amy Koehler**

561.   Morgan, Ann Lee. **Historical Dictionary of Contemporary Art.** Lanham, Md., Rowman & Littlefield, 2017. 531p. (Historical Dictionaries of Literature and the Arts).

$120.00; $119.99 (e-book). ISBN 13: 978-1-4422-7667-3; 978-1-4422-7668-0 (e-book).

The *Historical Dictionary of Contemporary Art* is an excellent quick-reference resource for the art student and art enthusiast alike. The title offers an annotated chronology of pertinent historical events prior to the beginning of the dictionary proper which offers the reader an appropriate context for the concepts, events, and individuals contained in the dictionary. The entries are often more encyclopedic than dictionary-like, but the information is solid and otherwise concise, offering the highlights and providing extensive cross-referencing. Unfortunately, this volume is not illustrated which seems strange for a dictionary focused on a visual phenomenon. Nevertheless, this title is an excellent and well-written resource, and it offers an excellent bibliography at the end. Recommended for public, school, and academic libraries.—**Megan W. Lowe**

562.   **Pharos http://pharosartresearch.org/.** [Website] Free. Date reviewed: 2017.

Pharos brings together 14 European and North American photo archives documenting a renowned selection of art, architecture, photography, and more. Archives include, among others, The Getty Institute, National Gallery of Art, Bildarchiv Foto Marburg, Frick Art Reference Library, The Netherlands Institute for Art History, and Villa I Tatti. Currently, the website allows direct access to 8 of the archives representing over 61,000 artworks and nearly 100,000 images of them. The other archives are available via link to the holding institution database. More images will be added to the archive in the future. Selecting the Visual Search tab from the menu bar allows users to conduct a basic search or an image search whereby users can upload an image file (to find similar images in the archive). Users can also browse by entire Pharos collection or individual institute collection. Once within a collection, users can filter their search by date, type (mosaic, painting, sculpture, etc.), and more. Item photographs are accompanied by identifying information such as artist, location of original artwork, type, date, and category(ies), each of which link to similarly classified photographs. Users may also be able to Compare Images if there are similarities within the archive. Users can select Institutions from the menu bar for information on them, such as location, archive structure, archive provenance, etc. This is also where users would access those archives not directly incorporated into the Pharos database. Pharos News and Initiatives is also available from the menu. The photos in this archive document the history of art in its many forms, from the humble fragment of Roman architecture to the regal eighteenth-century portrait in oil. The site is a valuable resource for art historians and others.—**ARBA Staff Reviewer**

Handbooks and Yearbooks

563.   **Collaboration and Student Engagement in Design Education.** Richard Tucker, ed. Hershey, Pa., Information Science Reference/IGI Global, 2017. 411p. index. $195.00. ISBN 13: 978-1-52250-726-0; 978-1-52250-727-7 (e-book).

This volume in the Advances in Higher Education and Professional Development book series offers new research on collaborative relationships in the design field with the emphasis on instilling the notion of teamwork as a student and developing it in preparation for the challenges of the profession. The volume structures most of its chapters as case studies—exploring a singular example in relation to its topic. It should also be noted that while many of the chapters use the profession of architecture to model the research, the volume assumes a relevance to the greater design profession. The volume's preface along with its detailed table of contents lays out its organization and explains its highly specialized focus. The volume organizes its chapters into three sections which address the teaching, evaluation, and professional preparation of collaboration. Early chapters propose a framework for measuring students' collaboration effectiveness, discuss cognitive challenges of design teams, and explore peer assessment bias. Several chapters in section two discuss "participatory design thinking" which engages design students with the greater community, while chapter nine examines the use of mobile technology within collaboration. Concluding chapters in section three connect the group learning idea to the reality of the emerging professional. All chapters open with an abstract that summarizes the research that follows. Chapters make good use of headers, subheaders, data tables, key terms and definitions, and more, and will generally organize the material via background, conclusion, future research directions, and other parts. References are listed at the end of each chapter and are compiled again at the end of the book, alongside brief contributor biographies and an index. Educators and advanced students of design as well as professionals affiliated with the design field would be interested in this volume.— **ARBA Staff Reviewer**

564.   **Images of Rome: The Rodolfo Lanciani Digital Archive. https://exhibits. standford.edu/lanciani.** [Website] Free. Date reviewed: 2018.

This archive includes roughly four thousand handmade drawings, prints, photographs, and more from the personal collection of Italian archaeologist Rodolfo Lanciani, a "pioneer in the systematic, modern study of the city of Rome." In works created primarily between the seventeenth and nineteenth centuries, the archive examines the city through of number of lenses, including topographical, architectural, historical, and artistic. The site allows users to explore the collection in several ways. The Explore tab lets users view thirty-six distinct galleries of materials arranged by subject, such as Colosseo (Colloseum), Foro Romano (Forum), and Fontane (fountains). Users can additionally search via the bar in the upper corner of the page. Alternatively, users can select from the listing of terms on the left side of the page, which allow searches by Topic, Author, Medium, Century, Publisher, and Date Range. Users can zoom in and download each digital image, and note identifying information such as title, type (medium or perspective), date, format (size, etc.), creator, and other descriptive information. Users can also examine a current map of Rome showing the subject's location. The Collection tab links to several scholarly essays on such subjects as "Lost Rome" or "The Domes of Rome," as well as a statistics graphic showing the number of images digitized by medium. In its portrayals of this rich and historic city, the site would appeal to students and educators within a broad range of the humanities discipline.—**ARBA Staff Reviewer**

565.   **J. Paul Getty Museum. http://www.getty.edu/museum/.** [Website] Free. Date reviewed: 2017.

This website provides excellent access to one of the premier art collections in the United States. Digitizing thousands of items held at both campuses of the Getty museum, the site allows close examination of marble busts, Roman mosaics, Impressionist paintings, ornate furniture, illuminated manuscripts, Renaissance sketches, photographic portraits (including several of J. Paul Getty himself), and much more. Users can conduct an advanced search or can search through individual or combined "collection areas" as displayed on the page. Collection areas include Antiquities, Drawings, Manuscripts, Paintings, Photographs, and Sculpture & Decorative Arts. Users can incorporate keywords as well. For example, matching the term "landscape" with the Paintings collection area will display the appropriate portion of the larger database. Items appear as thumbnails with title, artist, and date noted beneath (although it is important to note that images are not available for every cataloged item). Items can either be viewed as a grid or list. Object Details are generous and may include medium, country/culture, item dimensions, a narrative description of the item, provenance, exhibitions, bibliography, and related media if applicable. Other site features include a gallery of Recent Acquisitions and the multimedia Collection Channels which connect the researcher with extensive videos and tutorials on the art, artistic techniques, exhibits, and more. These resources enhance the remarkable digital galleries and make this website valuable for educators, students, and others.—**ARBA Staff Reviewer**

Indexes

566.   **The Bezalel Narkiss Index of Jewish Art. http://cja.huji.ac.il/browser.php.** [Website] Free. Date reviewed: 2018.

The simplicity of the Jewish Art Index's homepage belies the vast, varied, and vital archive tracing the rich artistic history of the Jewish people. Myriad browsing options pop out over bright geometric backgrounds. Users need only choose one to begin to explore the archive. The left-hand side of the page displays eight distinct mediums of historical works of Architecture, Modern Art, Illuminated Manuscripts, Funerary Art, Sacred Objects, Ancient Art, and Printed Books. There is also a category of Comparative Material and Miscellaneous Objects. The index, in total, contains over 270,000 images. Browsing through the more general categories leads users to several search fields which can narrow the focus in addition to a thumbnail catalog of category contents. The right side of the page allows for browsing within the more precise categories of Artist, Object, Community, Collection, Location, Subject, or Origin. Choosing any of these browsing categories leads users to the applicable section of the index or "tree." To examine an individual item, users can either select from the index or from the thumbnail catalog. Images may be enlarged and are accompanied by a variety of identifying details as outlined in the advanced searching options (e.g., origin, subject, etc.) in addition to digitization information such as photographer and photograph date. The archive covers an expansive, broadly sourced (Yemen, Romania, Russia, etc.) collection of Jewish artistic skill and style as displayed in homes, gravesites, synagogues, memorials, paintings, furniture, photographs, coins, burial artifacts, sculpture, graphic art, and much, much more.—**ARBA Staff Reviewer**

Architecture

567.   Greene, Elizabeth B. **Buildings and Landmarks of 19th-Century America: American Society Revealed.** Santa Barbara, Calif., Greenwood Press/ABC-CLIO, 2017. 325p. illus. index. $100.00. ISBN 13: 978-1-4408-3572-8; 978-1-4408-3993-1 (e-book).

This work is part of a Greenwood Press series of topical, architectural-themed volumes. The series portrays important themes in national history through the use of buildings and landmarks. This volume describes forty-five key buildings that chronicle the westward expansion of the United States and the Industrial Revolution. The building descriptions are divided into architectural classes: civic, commercial, domestic, religious and funerary, and fortifications. Readers will find an introduction to nineteenth-century U.S. history, an historical chronology of the United States, an essay on "How to Evaluate Buildings and Structures," a glossary, a bibliography, and an index.

The Commercial Architecture section relates the story of six important, nineteenth-century commercial buildings: Boott Mill, Ford's Theatre, Madison Square Garden, Wainwright Building, Marshall Field Department Store, and the Bradbury Building. The author places each building in its historical context and describes the building and key architectural features. Additionally, the author provides information on the lasting significance of each building. Buildings are accompanied by short bibliographies and some structures have extra informational inserts. For example, the section on New Harmony, Indiana, has an insert on Millennialists. Some of the further information references are rather basic or poorly edited. The New Harmony essay suggests that the reader go to Leland Roth's *Concise History of American Architecture,* a website on Utopians, a National Park Service pamphlet on the Amana Colonies, and an article "Reprinted from Indiana Magazine" for more information on the Shaker Colony (the citation fails to tell where the article is reprinted!). Not cited are any number of good books available on New Harmony. Each building essay is accompanied by a black-and-white photograph of the structure. The glossary contains a number of odd choices for a work on architecture: apotheosis, autodidact, a long paragraph on bridge failure, didactic, erudition, lunacy, phrenology, sociology. Overall the book is an interesting collection of essays on important nineteenth-century American buildings placed in their historical context. The essays are easy to read and introduce the reader to a variety of basic historical ideas through the use of buildings of the period. The cover and binding make the book a very attractive work to use. The book will appeal most to high school and lower-division college students.—**Ralph Lee Scott**

Painting

568.　**Clyfford Still Museum. https://clyffordstillmuseum.org/.** [Website] Free. Date reviewed: 2018.

The Clyfford Still Museum in Denver, Colorado, contains a significant collection of artworks and personal artifacts of one of the foremost Abstract Expressionists. Still's career spanned decades and this collection traces its evolution in relation to themes and mediums and helps illustrate the national reaction to external events of his time. The Clyfford Still Museum homepage allows access to the extensive digital collection of his work, in addition to a rich archive of research materials. Users can scroll to the bottom of the homepage to select the From the Online Collection tab to access the art. Users will see a color catalog of over two thousand items with the oldest works displayed first. Users can browse the catalog, conduct a basic search, or add filters such as object type, material, decade, subject/color, and creation space. Users will explore an array of watercolors, oil paintings, woodcuts, pastels, and more covering a wide range of subjects conveyed through portraits, landscapes, and groundbreaking abstracts. Information accompanying each artwork may note relevant exhibitions, dimensions of piece, related objects, and other details. Users can zoom in/out and use the innovative "slowlooking" tool to methodically examine a full-screen image. The From the Archives tab allows users access to the research database of Still's correspondence, studio materials, photographs, exhibition records, and other materials. After clicking on the Launch the Research Database link users can browse the complete archive alphabetically or browse by Category Pages, which refer to locations, dates, people, or subjects. Users can closely examine the item with identifying information such as title, creation date, and general description. Specific items include a letter from the Los Angeles County Museum of Art to Still's widow announcing the installation of a memorial exhibit, and early photographs of Still in a scout's uniform. Researchers and educators will appreciate the ease in which they can navigate between the two essential resources of the Still collection and archive within this one website.—**ARBA Staff Reviewer**

569. Webb, David. **Painting in Watercolor: The Indispensible Guide.** New York, Firefly Books, 2016. 256p. illus. index. $35.00. ISBN 13: 978-1-77085-738-4.

From the moment you see the book with its colorful cover and title you know there are more awesome things inside. The book begins with a short autobiography followed by examples, illustrations, and techniques. It becomes apparent early that the author is not just an artist but also a teacher. The book is an inspiration for beginners but also experienced painters. The author provides everything you could think of from the different ways to hold brushes to paper types to wet technique. Clear guidance is given; readers will learn the basics and so much more. The last chapter in the book ends with accomplished guest artists who provide variety and life lessons for the reader. From the cover to the end of this book the art illustrated is just awe-inspiring. Until reading this book I never knew that watercolor paintings could be so rich. Watercolor would be a great medium for anyone who wanted to start painting.—**Kathy Adams**

Sculpture

570. Loe, Hikmet Sidney. **The Spiral Jetty Encyclo: Exploring Robert Smithson's Earthwork through Time and Place.** Salt Lake City, Utah, University of Utah Press, 2017. 342p. illus. maps. $34.95pa. ISBN 13: 978-1-60781-541-9.

This book is a celebration of the life of Robert Smithson (1938-70), an artist of the minimalist movement in the early 1960s and his major piece of art, *Spiral Jetty,* made atop Rozel Point on the Great Salt Lake in Utah in 1970. *Spiral Jetty* still survives today, made out of some 6,500 tons of basalt, earth, and salt, but is often submerged by the ebb and flow of the Great Salt Lake. The book is divided into two parts: the first contains a reprint of Smithson's essay "Spiral Jetty" (1972) along with transcriptions of the films *Spiral Jetty* and *Mono Lake.* The second part is an encyclopedia which draws its title from an early drawing by Smithson titled "Encyclo." It is a compilation of artwork, places, people, ideas, and influences on both Smithson and his art, both a tribute and a colorful reflection of photographs and thoughts by Smithson's colleagues, his era, and himself. This book would be appropriate for anyone interested in art, specifically the earthworks in Utah or the minimalist movement of the 1960s.—**Bradford Lee Eden**

571.   Poyner, Fred F., IV. **Seattle Public Sculptors: Twelve Makers of Monuments, Memorials and Statuary, 1909-1962.** Jefferson, N.C., McFarland, 2017. 230p. illus. index. $35.00pa. ISBN 13: 978-1-4766-6650-1; 978-1-4766-2866-0 (e-book).

The city of Seattle has a rich history of public art and sculpture, much of which was generated before and after the Alaska-Yukon-Pacific Exposition of 1909. This "golden age" was dominated by an emphasis on figurative sculptures of famous individuals of regional, national, and even international reputation. During the 1920s to 1940s, public memorials to the dead were the focus. The 1950s saw the emergence of sculpture inspired by the water and woods of the Pacific Northwest, while the 1960s brought the World's Fair/Century 21 Exposition back to Seattle. This book tells the story of 12 public sculptors in Seattle history during the twentieth century, with numerous black-and-white photos throughout of their contribution to Seattle's art scene. These individuals were: Lorado Taft (1860-1936), Richard E. Brooks (1865-1919), Finn Haakon Frolich (1868-1947), Max P. Nielsen (1864-1917), James A. Wehn (1882-1973), Allen George Newman (1875-1940), Herman Atkins MacNeil (1866-1947), Alonzo Victor Lewis (1886-1946), John Carl Ely (1897-1929), Alice Robertson Carr (de Creeft) (1899-1996), James FitzGerald (1910-1973), and August H. Werner (1893-1980).—**Bradford Lee Eden**

23 Language and Linguistics

English-Language Dictionaries

General Usage

572. **Cambridge Dictionary. http://dictionary.cambridge.org/US/.** [Website] Free. Date reviewed: 2017.

The Cambridge Dictionary allows quick keyboard access to millions of words in addition to a variety of helpful tools that can facilitate the understanding and use of them. The dictionary is available in 11 languages, and addresses English usages in both the United Kingdom and the United States.

Users can simply type a word into the prominent search bar to access its definition(s). The word will be displayed accompanied by the figure of speech, phonetic and syllabic transcription, definition(s), and sample sentence. Users can also click the red sound button to hear how the word is pronounced. If the word is incorrectly spelled in the search bar, the site will present a list of similarly spelled or pronounced words from which to choose. Users can also browse or search a large variety of focused dictionaries by clicking the Dictionary tab at the top of the page. These include several English dictionaries (Essential American, Essential British, Learners, etc.) and several translation dictionaries (e.g., English to Korean, etc.). Selecting a dictionary to search will bring up a list of popular searches, allow alphabetical browsing, and list key features of the particular dictionary. The Translate tab offers easy and free translations between languages of up to one 160 characters in a field (up to 2,000 per day). The Grammar tab allows users to search, note popular searches, browse alphabetically, and scroll through a list of seven topics such as Adjectives & Adverbs, Easily Confused Words, and Verbs. Other features on the site include a posted Word of the Day, New Words, and a link to the About Words Blog offering detailed breakdowns of word usage ("Peering and Gawking—Synonyms for the Word 'Look'"), tips on "Describing Landscapes," and much more.

Registering (free) with the site allows users to create, save, and share word lists, quizzes, and other items. Advertisements do slightly affect the browsing experience, especially those using similar typefaces and interruptive placement on the page. Nonetheless, this site offers an important and easy-to-use resource for researchers and writers across a range of disciplines. Recommended for public, school, and academic libraries.—**ARBA Staff Reviewer**

573.   **Eighteenth-Century English Phonology Database (ECEP)**
       https://www.hrionline.ac.uk/ecep/. [Website] Free. Date reviewed: 2017.

The ECEP is an academic resource for the advanced study of linguistics, focusing on the standardization of English pronunciations in the eighteenth century. The site is one of several digital projects created by the University of Sheffield's Humanities Research Institute, the stated goal of which is "supporting the innovative use of technology in arts, humanities and heritage research as both a method of inquiry and a means of dissemination." Most of the database's content is comprised of primary sources in the form of eighteenth-century English dictionaries. It also includes metadata (summaries, biographies, and external links) about the dictionaries and their authors. There are currently eleven dictionaries featured, all accessible via links on the home page.

Both the names of the authors and the titles of their works are linked. Clicking an author name takes you to a page focused on biographical information about the author. Clicking on a title takes you to a more detailed run-down of the work itself, including metadata (the intended audience, publication information, and editions) and a section titled "Lexical Sets in this Work." This section allows you to view or download lexical sets for individual works; however, in this reviewer's experience, the functionality of this feature was spotty.

The main utility of the site is its niche focus on phonology. The creators of the database are trained linguists, and have categorized the contents of each dictionary according to their relevant lexical features. The user can search the contents of all eleven dictionaries for various phonological elements, by clicking "Lexical Sets" in the site header. The proceeding search can be customized according to the following criteria: Lexical Categories, Lexical SubSets, Lexical Keywords, IPA, IPA Variant, Attitudes, and Labels. Matching results are displayed in a table format, with columns organized according to these same criteria. The site also contains a footer with a ready-made citation, making it a streamlined source for academic research.—**ARBA Staff Reviewer**

Sign Language

574.   **ASL-LEX. http://www.asl-lex.org/.** [Website] Free. Date reviewed: 2018.

This database helps inventory the building blocks of American Sign Language (ASL), the visual language mainly used by deaf communities in the United States and Canada. A large visualization of colored nodes indicates the roughly one thousand signs in the database, and tracks representations of sound, meaning, parts of speech, and other elements. Users can closely examine the visualization or download a spreadsheet of the gathered data. Users can select either the About ASL-LEX tab at the top of the homepage or the Learn More tab at the bottom to access a listing of what the visualization depicts. A brief, helpful video further explains this and demonstrates the ways in which users can explore the visualization. More specific information on how to navigate, search, or download data from the visualization is found when selecting the Instructions tab, also at the top of the homepage. The Explore the Visualization tab at the bottom of the homepage accesses the graphic, with each node representing an individual sign. Users can click on a node to zoom in on its "neighborhood" of signs (signs that look similar when made) and Sign Data, which includes information on sign frequency (generally depicted by the size of the node), iconicity (does the sign look like its meaning?), lexical properties (parts of speech), phonological properties (where or how the sign is made on the body), neighborhood density, and more. Users can also observe a brief video demonstration of the sign. Selecting the About Sign Data link provides a list of definitions regarding these highly technical data terms and ratings. The site will continue to add information on the signs it has incorporated into the database and hopes to add more signs as well. ASL-LEX would be enormously useful to ASL educators and students in terms of vocabulary instruction and/or acquisition.—**ARBA Staff Reviewer**

Terms and Phrases

575.   Grothe, Mardy. **Metaphors Be with You: An A-to-Z Dictionary of History's Greatest Quotations.** New York, HarperCollins, 2016. 480p. index. $19.99. ISBN 13: 978-0-06-244533-9.

Those who love language in general and metaphors in particular have come to the right place. Dr. Mardy Grothe, a quotation anthologist, has compiled metaphors from A to Z on 250 topics, starting with ability and ending with zeal. Each topic has 10 of what the author considers the best metaphors (his selection rationale is enumerated in the introduction). The engagingly written introduction covers the importance of metaphor, the definition of metaphor, similes and analogies, and how the book came into being. A navigation guide follows. Here, readers will find an explanation of how to use the QR codes found throughout the book. These codes link users to the book's companion website, which can also be accessed at http://www.drmardy.com/. In addition to ability and zeal, there are metaphors for apology, blues, death & dying, genius, love & hate, politics & religion, science & scientists, technology, and so many more. An author index completes the work. This fun and informative read is recommended to public libraries.—**ARBA Staff Reviewer**

Visual

576.   Adelson-Goldstein, Jayme. **Oxford Picture Dictionary.** 3d ed. New York, Oxford University Press, 2016. 288p. illus. index. $32.00pa. ISBN 13: 978-0-19-450529-1.

This is the go-to dictionary for English-language learners, now in its third edition. Author Jayme Adelson-Goldstein organizes the content into 12 sections: Everyday Language, People, Housing, Food, Clothing, Health, Community, Transportation, Job Search, The Workplace, Academic Study, and Recreation. Based on the words people need to use most, as well as on real-life situations, users will find the necessary vocabulary for shopping, childcare and parenting, household repairs, eating out, a garage sale, a medical emergency, buying a car, looking for a job, sports and recreation, and much more. There are more than 4,000 words and phrases in total. Pages contain several color illustrations. Sections also include practice activities to reinforce what has been learned. For example, in the third unit on words associated with the home, a two-page color picture of a home with numbers that correlate to 14 vocabulary words from attic to basement begin the unit. The activities on these pages ask users to practice such things as pointing to different rooms and using phrases like "It's on the floor."

For English-language learners, this is an easy-to-use, effective resource by an experienced English for Speakers of Other Languages professional. This resource is also a good place for English-language teachers to find curriculum materials. Highly recommended for public, school, and academic libraries.—**ARBA Staff Reviewer**

Non-English-Language Dictionaries

Spanish

577.   **Spanish English Bilingual Visual Dictionary.** New York, DK Publishing, 2017. 360p. illus. maps. index. $14.95pa. ISBN 13: 978-1-4654-5981-2.

This is a revised and updated edition—earlier versions published in 2009 and 2015. The dictionary was previously published as part of the *5 Language Visual Dictionary.* Front matter includes a table of contents, information about the dictionary, and usage directions for both the dictionary and the free audio app that provides pronunciations by native Spanish and English speakers for all the words and phrases in the book. There are chapters on people, appearance, health, home, services, shopping, food, eating out, study, work, transportation, sports, leisure, environment, and reference. The reference chapter covers time, geography, phrases, weights and measures, and more. There are thousands of words, phrases, and colored photographs. A word index follows the heart of the book, starting with Spanish words. From learners of Spanish or English to teachers to leisure and business travelers, this will be a valuable resource. Recommended.—**ARBA Staff Reviewer**

24 Literature

General Works

Dictionaries and Encyclopedias

578.   **Supernatural Literature.** Thomas Riggs, ed. Farmington Hills, Mich., St. James Press/Gale Group, 2017. 3v. illus. index. $488.00/set. ISBN 13: 978-1-41033-905-8; 978-1-41033-907-2 (e-book).

This three-volume set includes three hundred essays on novels, novellas, short stories, poems, plays, and works of nonfiction that fall under the supernatural category. Each volume has one hundred essays. The first volume, *The Dead,* contains five chapters: "Ghosts," "Possession," "The Returned," "Vampires," and "Zombies." Eight chapters comprise the next volume, *Magic*: "Bargains and Curses," "Fairies," "Magical Places," "Potions," "Prophecies," "Quests," "Witches," and "Wizards." *Monsters and Beasts,* the last volume includes six chapters: "Demons and Devils," "Dragons," "Hybrid Monsters," "Manmade Monsters," "Monstrous Transformations," and "Sexual Predators." The essays were selected based on several criteria: inclusion in university courses, genre, region, country of the author and text, and time period. Works covered date from ancient times to the present. The title includes works from the Americas, Europe, Africa, and Asia. Users will find a list of advisory board members, an introduction to the set, an editor's note, a list of contributors and academic reviewers and their affiliations, a thematic outline, and a table of contents for all three volumes. Each volume has its own table of contents included in the front matter. To enhance readability, each essay uses the same structure with the following elements: overview, historical and literary context, themes and style, critical discussion, sources, further readings, and media adaptations (if applicable). In addition, readers will find either an excerpt of the original text or a related discussion topic within a shaded sidebar. All volumes conclude with an inclusive subject, author, and title index. This work is highly recommended for academic libraries.—**ARBA Staff Reviewer**

Handbooks and Yearbooks

579.   Anderson, Earl R. **Friendly Fire in the Literature of War.** Jefferson, N.C., McFarland, 2017. 222p. index. $49.95pa. ISBN 13: 978-1-4766-6721-8.

"Friendly fire" was coined in the mid-1970s to describe incidents where military personnel were accidently wounded or killed by members of the same force or allies. While the phrase is of recent vintage, it describes a phenomenon in warfare that has existed since the first projectiles were introduced as weapons. Earl Anderson, professor emeritus and former dean of Arts and Sciences at Cleveland State University and author of Folk Taxonomies in Early English, utilizes friendly fire as a narrative trope in examining such disparate works as *The Persians,* by Aeschylus, Stephen Crane's *Red Badge of Courage,* and *The King's Gold,* by Yxta Maya Murray. What emerges from his copious research is a heightened sense of tragedy when combatants are not maimed or killed by their opponents, but rather by those on their side of the conflict. The text is supplemented by chapter notes, a bibliography, and index. This work will be of interest to academic institutions supporting programs in U.S. history or literature.—**John R. Burch Jr.**

580.   **The Bloomsbury Handbook of Electronic Literature.** Joseph Tabbi, ed. New York, Bloomsbury Academic, 2018. 450p. illus. index. $136.00. ISBN 13: 978-1-4742-3025-4; 978-1-4742-3026-1 (e-book).

This is a fascinating look at today's world of literature beyond the printed page. Starting with hypertext works created a few decades ago and coming up to the latest endeavors, 26 contributors from a number of countries explore a wide range of literary creations, their past and their future. The range of works explored in this volume is incredible. For instance, *Pry* (2014), by Samantha Gorman and Danny Cannizzaro, combines film and gaming with text. Other works of vast diversity engage participants in a wide variety of ways: for example, *Mimesis* (2012), created by Fox Harrell and others, is a "computationally driven narrative" which challenges readers/players to explore social identity, modes of communication in social settings, and related topics.

Much of this volume is aimed at a relatively narrow, specialized audience. For some chapters, readers need to be familiar with expressions such as "glitch-incision," "multidirectional scrolling," "universalization and normalization of affordances and potentials," and "poetic implications of the associationist paradigm." The topic of one chapter is described this way: "the mesh of the 'materials, ideologies, and structures' that surround and subtend instances of broken or faulty language." (p. 238) Other chapters, however, explore topics in ways that are much more accessible to a broader readership. The audience is thus a diverse group: both literary scholars and those interested in the technology that can be used for literary creation. Academic libraries will certainly be the only institutions interested in this material; recommended for institutions with a serious interest in the evolution of literature and/or cybernetics.—**Mark Schumacher**

581.   **Critical Approaches to Literature: Moral.** Robert C. Evans, ed. Hackensack, N.J., Salem Press, 2017. 282p. index. $125.00. ISBN 13: 978-1-68217-274-2; 978-1-68217-275-9 (e-book).

This volume in the Critical Insights series presents a number of scholarly essays which examine literature from an ethical perspective. It references a broad selection of creative media, including poetry, short fiction, contemporary television, novels, and films. It examines an equally diverse list of moralistic approaches to this media. Tracking works from as far back as the Renaissance through to the modern day, this essay collection is also able to follow the evolution of the moralistic approach to literature study.

An opening essay by James S. Baumlin entitled "On Moral Criticism: A Feminist

Approach to Caring" establishes the umbrella theme for the book, i.e., the need to "do justice to oppressed or marginalized groups." The following fifteen essays may touch on that theme in individual ways.

Four essays fill the Critical Contexts section of the book, and include an examination of historical perspectives, a survey of modern thought on the connections of morality in the narrative art, and more.

The eleven essays in the Critical Readings section offer a diverse array of moral approaches across a spectrum of authors and media. Two essays focus on Shakespeare's *King Lear* as it is conveyed in film. Robert C. Evans' "The Blinding of Gloucester: Trauma and Morality in Some Films of Shakespeare's *King Lear*" examines the particularly horrific implications of seeing Gloucester's vicious blinding on screen. R. Kent Rasmussen later writes of the somewhat overshadowed notion of greed running the length of Mark Twain's evocative *The Adventures of Huckleberry Finn.* Susan C. W. Abbotson looks at a number of Arthur Miller's plays as a study of the playwright memorialized as "the moral voice of [the] American stage." The works of writers John Steinbeck, Zadie Smith, Anton Chekhov, and Edgar Allen Poe are also studied, while closing essays address the television series *Breaking Bad* and its complex view of morality and the relationship between morality and the emerging genre of creative nonfiction.

Resources include an excellent piece applying different moralistic approaches to Ben Johnson's (1572-1637) "On My First Son," a chronology of key moments in the evolution of moral thought vis-à-vis literature, a list of additional works on the subject, and a glossary.—**ARBA Staff Reviewer**

582.   **Critical Approaches to Literature: Psychological.** Robert C. Evans, ed. Hackensack, N.J., Salem Press, 2017. 320p. illus. index. $125.00. ISBN 13: 978-1-68217-272-8; 978-1-68217-273-5 (e-book).

The examination of psychological aspects of literature ranges over various periods of time and techniques of authorship. An introduction on the format and intention of this collection precedes a basic introduction on the significance and development of psychological approaches in literature. The main text is a selection of essays that examine topics such as the focus on psychology in the critical examination of literature, evolutionary psychology (i.e., how humans first developed psychologically), cognitive psychology, crowd psychology, and psychological scholarship. The discussions examine such aspects as misogyny, familial relationships, suicide, empathy, depictions of the mentally ill, etc., with Freud and Freudianism being the main influence, but also considering the theories of others such as Jung and Lacan. The last section looks at the mythical and folkloric characteristics of popular characters, such as those found in the Star Wars series, and in the overall story development, such as in the Harry Potter series. Each essay ends with a brief bibliography and, in some cases, endnotes. A chronology of developments in the study of psychology, additional bibliographies, information about the editor and the contributors, a glossary, and an index complete the volume. The essays offer an interesting, informative, well-researched array of material, with some black-and-white illustrations.—**Martha Lawler**

583.   **Critical Insights: Flash Fiction.** Michael Cocchiarale and Scott D. Emmert, eds. Hackensack, N.J., Salem Press, 2017. 250p. index. $105.00. ISBN 13: 978-1-68217-270-4; 978-1-68217-271-1 (e-book).

With roots in the distant past, flash fiction, or the short, short story, is nevertheless only recently emerging as a target of genuine scholarship. This volume in the Critical Insights series takes on the literary genre of flash fiction with essays offering a range of perspectives on the works of a number of flash fiction practitioners.

Opening essays provide readers with essential foundational material, establishing a flash fiction history in fables and parables, its early critical dismissal, and the varying ways the genre is conceived and considered. The four essays in the Critical Contexts section expand on that foundation. Pamelyn Castro presents a survey of flash fiction anthologies going back to the 1920s and extending into today's multimedia world. Megan Giddings, in "The Destroyer and the Rotten Heart: Comparing and Contrasting Donald Bartheleme's 'The Baby' and Amelia Gray's 'The Heart,'" focuses on narrative technique in the genre. Ten essays bring diverse topics and points-of-view to the Critical Readings section. Robert C. Evans examines renowned writer Kate Chopin's meticulous approach to her short, short stories. Several pieces like Laura Hatry's "Latin American Flash Fiction: Julio Cortazar and Luisa Valenzuela" examine both contemporary and classic examples of international flash fiction. And Eric Sterling takes a look at the work of Isaac Babel, whose fleeting stories served (dangerously) as a vehicle of protest. Other essays explore the mechanics of flash fiction character development, style, and wordplay; look at an author's ability to create tension in a short piece; and more. Essays touch on the work of Franz Kafka, Lou Beach, Lydia Davis, Amy Hempel, Kathy Fish, and others. A Resources section rounds out the volume and includes a good listing of additional works of flash fiction (collections, anthologies, literary journals, etc.) and a bibliography.

Overall, the volume is a thoughtful collection that will engage anyone new to or already interested in the significant, if less known, genre of flash fiction.—**ARBA Staff Reviewer**

584.   **Critical Insights: Paranoia, Fear and Alienation.** Kimberly Drake, ed. Hackensack, N.J., Salem Press, 2017. 230p. index. $105.00. ISBN 13: 978-1-68217-126-4; 978-1-68217-127-1 (e-book).

Critical Insights: Paranoia, Fear and Alienation is a collection of essays discussing the presence and prevalence of these components in a variety of pieces of literature and film. Instead of focusing on a specific work, author, or even genre, this essay collection focuses on a set of separate, but related, ideas and explores their importance to different stories, novels, and films.

Paranoia, Fear and Alienation is comprised of twelve essays in two main parts: Critical Contexts and Critical Readings. A bonus thirteenth essay written by the editor is included in the introduction in order to set the stage for what follows. The essays range from "'Filthy Air' and the 'Heat-Oppressed Brain': Fear in Macbeth" to "The Horror of the Camera in The Blair Witch Project" to "Fear, Guilt, and Paranoia in Patricia Highsmith's Strangers on a Train." Also included are additional works on the theme, a bibliography, contributor information, and an index.

Collecting essays by a shared topical theme, instead of by author, time period, or genre, is perhaps a bit of an unorthodox choice, but one with great results. The themes discussed are so relatable and personal that being taken on this exploration proves fascinating and intriguing. The essays themselves are well-written, focused, and as interesting as they are diverse. This unique blend of breadth and focus makes this book a great addition to literature collections.—**Tyler Manolovitz**

585.   **Critical Insights: The Diary of a Young Girl.** Ruth Amir and Pnina Rosenberg, eds. Hackensack, N.J., Salem Press, 2017. 257p. index. $105.00. ISBN 13: 978-1-68217-262-9; 978-1-68217-263-6 (e-book).

This book explores in detail, through critical readings and essays, the diary of Anne Frank. Anne's tragic story, first brought to the world by her father immediately after World War II, has become a major vehicle for discussion and education surrounding the Holocaust of the mid-20th century. The Critical Contexts section contains four essays focusing on various aspects of the diary, Anne's personal journey of various locations, her self-portrait and ethical evolution, the idea of "coming of age," and children's literature of atrocity. The Critical Readings section contains nine extended explorations of how Anne's diary has been transformed into different mediums, media, and receptions, related to confessional writing, deconstructive reading, other children's wartime writings, teaching the Holocaust, Anne's diary and story on stage and screen, Japanese reception of Anne's story, graphic novels, and the Anne Frank House in Amsterdam as a memorial. Under the Resources section, there is a very nice chronology of Anne's life as well as the postwar life and influence of her diary, and a listing of various dramas, graphic novels, nonfiction works, short fiction, diaries and memoirs, novels, young readers, fiction, and poetry based around the life of Anne Frank. I highly recommend this resource for all libraries.—**Bradford Lee Eden**

586.   **Critical Insights: The Woman Warrior.** Linda Trinh Moser and Kathryn West, eds. Hackensack, N.J., Salem Press, 2016. 245p. index. $105.00. ISBN 13: 978-1-68217-394-7; 978-1-68217-395-4 (e-book).

Critical Insights: The Woman Warrior is a collection of essays about Maxine Hong Kingston's influential 1975 book *The Woman Warrior: Memoirs of a Girlhood Among Ghosts.* Intended to convey the importance of Kingston's work, this book attempts to highlight its major themes and stylistic features, while also exploring the debates and controversies surrounding the work.

Critical Insights: The Woman Warrior is divided into three sections about the book and author, critical contexts, and critical readings. The first section includes three essays: a discussion of *The Woman Warrior,* a biography of Kingston, and a conversation with Kingston herself. The second section includes four critical essays surrounding the work and its cultural context. The final section of eight critical readings explores such topics as the power of discourse, the role of talk-story, existentialism, etc. The book concludes with a chronology of Kingston's life, a catalog of her works, a bibliography, information about the editors and contributors, and an index.

This publication is an excellent compilation of quality essays exploring Maxine Hong Kingston, *The Woman Warrior,* and its enduring critical and cultural importance. Many other writings about Kingston and *The Woman Warrior* exist, but this book serves as a great introduction and collection for those truly interested in Kingston's work. Academic collections that include important twentieth-century or multicultural literature would benefit from its inclusion.—**Tyler Manolovitz**

587.   O'Reilly, Édouard Magessa, Dirk Van Hulle, and Pim Verhulst. **The Making of Samuel Beckett's** *Molloy.* New York, Bloomsbury Publishing, 2017. 407p. illus. index. $43.95pa. ISBN 13: 978-1-4725-3256-5.

This book is volume four of the Beckett Digital Manuscript Project, which is comprised of two parts: a digital archive of Samuel Beckett's manuscripts organized into twenty-six research modules (with digital facsimiles and transcriptions of all extant manuscripts), and a series of twenty-six published volumes analyzing the genesis of the texts contained in the corresponding research modules. This volume focuses on *Molloy* (1946-50). Chapter 1 describes all of the extant manuscripts of this work, from autograph manuscripts to typescripts, prebook publications, editions, broadcasting scripts, and a genetic map. Chapter 2 describes the genesis of the French original of *Molloy* and its two parts, while chapter 3 details the English translation of the book and all of the complexity which that entails. There are a number of nice photographs of the various manuscripts and typescripts throughout the book. This highly specialized volume/series would be of interest to scholars of modern literature and Beckett specialists.—**Bradford Lee Eden**

Children's and Young Adult Literature

Bibliography

588.   **Cooperative Children's Book Center. http://ccbc.education.wisc.edu/default. asp.** [Website] Free: Date reviewed: 2017.

The Cooperative Children's Book Center (CCBC) is a good site to visit for educators, librarians, and others with interest in literature for children and young adults. It offers a host of resources this audience can use to promote books and inform themselves about pressing topics and ideas related to the genre. Users can select from many links according to their interest. Those who select the Authors & Illustrators tab will note examples of websites, fan sites, publisher sites, and institutional sites to explore. Through CCBC Publications users can find links to bibliographies and book lists organized by reader age. Books for Children & Young Adults offers guidance relative to the great numbers of these books in existence. Links here include the "CCBC Bibliographies and Booklists," which creates thematic lists, "CCBC Choices," hosting an annual Best-of-Year list, "Graphic Novels," offering resources on this burgeoning area of youth and young adult interest, "Multicultural Literature," by and about people of color, and much more. The site also offers access to information and resources (such as the "What If...Forum" and a Q & A) concerning Intellectual Freedom and the roles and responsibilities of educators and librarians. Links alphabetically organizes all lists in one simple place. The Cooperative Children's Book Center is based out of the University of Wisconsin-Madison and some site information may have a limited appeal, such as local book signings, local literacy programs, Wisconsin themed booklists, etc. However, the amount and quality of material on the site is still likely to interest a broader, remote audience of teachers and librarians.— **ARBA Staff Reviewer**

589.   **The Newberry & Caldecott Awards: A Guide to the Medal and Honor Books, 2017.** By Association for Library Service to Children. Chicago, American Library Association, 2017. 178p. illus. index. $34.00pa.; $20.60pa. (ALA members). ISBN 13: 978-0-8389-1567-7.

This edition of a title that should be purchased often by every library that collects children's literature includes information about the winners and honors recipients for each of these premier children's literature awards since their inception through 2017. Each entry, arranged chronologically, includes the title, author, illustrator, publisher, and a brief description of the book. The Caldecott entries also include notes on the type of illustrations. Other features of the volume include an essay on the history, terms, definitions, and criteria for each of these awards; an interview with four-time Caldecott honoree Bryan Collier; and separate author/illustrator and title indexes. It is surprising that the Association for Library Service to Children (ALSC) has not included a subject index to these most revered books as not all users of this book are entirely submersed in the history of these awards, and librarians or teachers may wish to search for award winners by subject. Still, regular purchase of this reasonably priced title for professional or reference collections should be considered essential.—**Rosanne M. Cordell**

590.   Pawuk, Michael, and David S. Serchay. **Graphic Novels: A Guide to Comic Books, Manga, and More.** 2d ed. Santa Barbara, Calif., Libraries Unlimited/ABC-CLIO, 2017. 719p. illus. index. (Genreflecting Advisory Series). $65.00. ISBN 13: 978-1-59884-700-0; 978-1-4408-5136-0 (e-book).

Graphic Novels: A Guide to Comic Books, Manga, and More, 2d edition, by Michael Pawuk and David S. Serchay is a guide intended for the selection of graphic novels that have been enjoyed the most by readers of all age groups. Although it is not intended to be a beginner's guide, it does provide a wealth of information that the beginner needs to make informed selections regarding graphic novels. The guide includes over 3,000 original and collected graphic novel titles encompassing a wide range of publishers and authors, mostly published in the last 10 years. Although the guide is global, the focus is on titles published in North America and Asia. The guide begins with a graphics section that explains what graphic novels are, how the author came to value them, graphic novel award information, and how the term graphic novel was coined. It also includes information on how to find recommendations and reviews, ideas on displaying and promoting, and precautions about using good selection practices because each graphic novel, like regular novels, have an intended audience and may not be appropriate for all age groups. Broken down in nine chapters based on fundamental genres, the criteria for inclusion includes popularity, suitability, age level, writing quality, artistic quality, artistic style, reputation, awards, recognition received, and format. Age appropriateness for each title is indicated: A for all ages, Y for youth ages 7-12, T for teens ages 13-15, and so on. The guide utilizes the right panel of the book to make searching for genres easier. The panel is numbered in conjunction with chapter numbers from the index. Icons are utilized to denote awards or recognition received, relation to core collections, associations with film, television, gaming, and anime. For ease in location, the listings are by graphic novel title, series, or featured character. Each listing includes the title, writer, illustrator, publisher, publication year, ISBN, and annotation. Content indicators such as violence, sex, language, and others are not included. However, this guide is an excellent resource for anyone interested in increasing their collection of graphic novels and is highly recommended to all.—**Shelly Lee**

Drama

Handbooks and Yearbooks

591. Snodgrass, Mary Ellen. **A Literary Brian Friel Companion.** Jefferson, N.C., McFarland, 2017. 206p. index. $39.95pa. ISBN 13: 978-1-4766-6574-0; 978-1-4766-2781-6 (e-book).

Sometimes called "the Irish Chekov," Brian Friel (1929-2015) was the author of two dozen plays, two volumes of short stories, numerous translations of Russian plays, and many essays on literary topics. In the United States, he is best known for his plays including *Philadelphia, Here I Come* (1954) and *Dancing at Lughnasa* (1990), which was also made into a successful motion picture. Many of his works take place in the fictional Irish town of Ballybeg (literally "small town") and deal with basic social and family problems and relationships.

The author of this volume is a prolific, award-winning writer of books on literary history and criticism. This work begins with a brief introduction to Friel's accomplishments followed by a detailed 24-page chronology of his life and work and an extensive bibliography of general articles and essays on the author. The body of the work consists of 65 alphabetically arranged entries averaging two or three pages each. Most of them deal with subjects and themes important in his work such as betrayal, alcohol consumption, hypocrisy, symbolism, irony, and male and female characters. The remaining two dozen articles deal with individual plays and include brief background information, a plot analysis, a list of characters—their nature and relationships—and, most important, a thorough discussion of themes, subjects, and literary devices used. All entries end with extensive bibliographies. Appendixes include a glossary of distinctive Irish words and expressions (and in what plays they appear), a timeline of historical events as they are referred to in his plays, and lists of topics for further study. The book ends with an extensive bibliography that is broken down by format including electronic devices and an excellent general index. This is a fascinating literary reference work exhibiting a high level of scholarship. It is highly recommended for both academic and large public libraries.—**John T. Gillespie**

Fiction

Crime and Mystery

592. Mazzeno, Laurence W. **James Lee Burke: A Literary Companion.** Jefferson, N.C., McFarland, 2017. 284p. index. $39.95pa. ISBN 13: 978-1-4766-6281-7.

The 16th volume in the publisher's Literary Companion series, which began in 2004, this book follows the series' standard format: brief introduction, brief biography, chronology of the author's works, then an A-Z series of entries which discuss individual novels and characters, explore diverse themes and writing styles, and explain events (such as Hurricane Katrina) that appear in Burke's fiction. Among the longer entries are those for the individual novels, a number of which have won Burke literary prizes and honors. Given the importance of the (now twenty-one-volume) series of novels involving police detective Dave Robicheaux, numerous entries discuss topics relevant to those works. Most entries have cross-references to other topics, and selected texts for "Further Reading." A thirty-eight-page glossary following the A-Z list of entries explains varied terms found in the main section of the book. The entries Auschwitz, Beach Boys, Calgary Stampede, Norman Rockwell, and Hmongs indicate the vast range of topics mentioned in this volume. Finally a ten-page "Works Cited" section provides further resources, many of which are newspaper articles.

Given the popularity of this author, there will be interest in this work, probably mostly in public libraries. Academic institutions with programs or courses in popular fiction will also find this useful to their students.—**Mark Schumacher**

593.   Young, Laurel A. **P.D. James: A Companion to the Mystery Fiction.** Jefferson, N.C., McFarland, 2017. 276p. illus. index. (McFarland Companions to Mystery Fiction). $39.95pa. ISBN 13: 978-0-7864-9791-1; 978-1-4766-2890-5 (e-book).

Fans and researchers of P.D. James' work will appreciate this recent addition to McFarland's encyclopedic companion series. The front matter includes: a brief summation of James' writing style in the preface; a list of her works in chronological order, followed by the same list in alphabetical order; a brief biography; a career chronology; and a list of abbreviations used throughout the book. The back matter contains an annotated bibliography and index. The bibliography is particularly useful for researchers seeking material about specific viewpoints or aspects of James' writing career due to the brief descriptions of referenced publications, except those authored by James.

The remainder of the volume contains over seven hundred entries that describe James' works, major themes in her works, and contributing articles, reviews, and introductions written by James for other publications. Entries appear in alphabetical order, and each named character has an entry, no matter how small a role they played within a story. Descriptions of locations are also included. An especially useful facet of this companion is that it contains entries for adaptations of James' work, which may well be useful for those interested in how James' written words have been interpreted into other formats such as television and film.

Overall, the entries are written in a clear and objective style, and include references to quotations in specific printings of James' work. Anyone interested in exploring the range of James' authorship will appreciate this comprehensive companion book.—**Cynthia Goode**

Science Fiction, Fantasy, and Horror

594.   **Critical Insights: Isaac Asimov.** M. Keith Booker, ed. Hackensack, N.J., Salem Press, 2017. 262p. index. $105.00. ISBN 13: 978-1-68217-254-4; 978-1-68217-255-1 (e-book).

This volume of the Critical Insights series essentially serves as an introduction to the life and works of the author Isaac Asimov. Through a collection of informative and expansive essays, this book explores Asimov and his writings from a number of angles and vantage points. From bird's eye analyses to detailed studies, M. Keith Booker has brought together a number of writings to help flesh out and define the character and importance of perhaps the most famous and prolific science fiction author in history.

Critical Insights: Isaac Asimov begins, as one would expect, with a biography and discussion of Asimov. Following these biographical writings are fourteen essays divided into two main areas: Critical Contexts and Critical Readings. The four essays in the first section look at Asimov and his writings from a more encompassing vantage point, discussing such topics as his cultural and historical context, critical reception, etc. The second section delves into more detailed and specific analysis of Asimov's writings. Contributions in this section explore such topics as race and robotics, morality, gender, and Asimov's Shakespeare writings. This book also includes a chronology, a list of Asimov's books, a bibliography, contributor information, and an index.

Compiling an exhaustive collection and analyses of all Asimov's writings would be nigh impossible. Fortunately, this book does not attempt such a feat, and instead focuses on laying a foundation for further research and understanding of Asimov, his works, and his importance to literature and culture. The essays are interesting and informational, doing an admirable job of exploring a variety of perspectives. Any collection including Asimov's works would benefit from adding this title to its collection.—**Tyler Manolovitz**

595.   **Horror Literature through History: An Encyclopedia of the Stories That Speak to Our Deepest Fears.** Cardin, Matt, ed. Santa Barbara, Calif., Greenwood Press/ABC-CLIO, 2017. 2v. $189.00/set. ISBN 13: 978-1-4408-4201-6; 978-1-4408-4202-3 (e-book).

This two-volume history of horror literature has a unique, three-part structure that encompasses the breadth and depth of the topic. After an introduction which defines the topic and the encyclopedia, along with a timeline of horror literature through history, the first part contains eight essays which provide a comprehensive history of horror literature from ancient times to the present. The second part, Themes, Topics, and Genres, contains twenty-three essays on interdisciplinary and intertwining subjects within horror literature such as ghost stories, Gothic poetry, eco-horror, horror literature and science fiction, Shakespearean horrors, and occult fiction, to name a few. The third part has over four hundred alphabetically arranged entries on authors, works, and specialized topics. Supplementing these entries are seven original interviews with important contemporary horror authors and editors plus one hundred fifty sidebars with mini-analyses, excerpts, timelines, media adaptations, and trivia. Overall, this encyclopedia does an excellent job of presenting the topic historically, broadly, and definitively in its three-part division of content. I highly recommend this resource as a reference work in high school and academic libraries.—**Bradford Lee Eden**

National Literature

American Literature

Biography

596.   **Critical Survey of American Literature.** Kellman, Steven G., ed. Amenia, N.Y., Grey House Publishing, 2016. 6v. illus. index. $499.00/set. ISBN 13: 978-1-68217-128-8; 978-1-68217-147-9 (e-book).

This 6-volume survey of 412 significant American and Canadian writers is arranged in alphabetical order, and offers a brief but thorough essay about each author covering a standard set of information points: most commonly used form of name, birth date, death date, and further biographical information; a general analysis of the author's body of work and its context; a closer critical examination of a selection of the author's most notable works; a summary discussing the author's overall importance to the literary landscape; suggested discussion topics; and a bibliography of the author's works as well as suggested analysis and criticism. The selection of featured authors ranges from short story writers to poets to playwrights to novelists, from the very beginnings of American literary history to writers as recent as Ta-Nehisi Coates.

The essays are cogent and accessibly written, varying in length from 6 to 13 pages, and would serve as an excellent starting point for any middle school, high school, or college student researching a particular author. But there is also plenty of useful content here for teachers preparing assignments, book clubs looking for contextual details and discussion prompts, and even general readers pursuing more information about authors that interest them.

Further research tools include a glossary of literary terms, an index of all work titles referenced, and a categorization of authors by genre, ethnic descent, sexual orientation, and gender. The latter is a less common but important inclusion, and an appreciated step toward information literacy. For a work as definitive as this survey sets itself out to be, information about the demographics involved are crucial for context. (For instance, the category list provided allowed the reviewer to determine that about one third of the included authors are women, about 6 percent are LGBTQ, and about 22 percent are people of color.) It is of course impossible for any such survey of literature to escape its native framework of historical and cultural bias; rather, tools like this allow readers to acknowledge and further explore that framework.—**Autumn Faulkner**

Handbooks and Yearbooks

597.   **Critical Insights: Adventures of Huckleberry Finn by Mark Twain.** R. Kent Rasmussen, ed. Hackensack, N.J., Salem Press, 2017. 280p. illus. index. $105.00. ISBN 13: 978-1-68217-122-6; 978-1-68217-123-3 (e-book).

Guided by an esteemed Mark Twain scholar, the fourteen authors in this fine collection explore both familiar ground and new territory in their analyses of this famous novel, from traditional topics such as the language of the book and the topic of slavery to areas such as the picaresque novel, identity switching, and parenting. The unusual diversity of subjects enhances this book. One chapter presents the author's creation (in 2011) of a version of the novel with euphemistic terms replacing Twain's original vocabulary, so as to make the work more palatable to young readers of all backgrounds. Another chapter describes the creation of a novel about Huck's father Pap, set within the context of examining Twain's minor attention to that character in the original text. A thirteen-page chronology of Twain's life and the "life" of Huckleberry Finn provides a useful history of the novel, while references in most chapters offer further reading options, albeit a small fraction of the literature on this classic text.

Given that this volume examines one of the iconic works in American literature, this book will be of interest to patrons of all kinds of libraries, although the price may force some libraries (and their patrons) to rely on interlibrary loan services to make it available. Both scholars and more casual readers will find this book fascinating.—**Mark Schumacher**

598.   **Critical Insights: Billy Budd, Sailor.** Brian Yothers, ed. Hackensack, N.J., Salem Press, 2017. 261p. index. $105.00. ISBN 13: 978-1-68217-569-9; 978-1-68217-570-5 (e-book).

This volume of the Critical Insights series takes a close look at Herman Melville's posthumously published novella, *Billy Budd, Sailor.* Revered as a shining example of American literary distinction, *Billy Budd, Sailor* has had a worldwide impact, making it a prime target of scholarly criticism. The volume gathers 13 essays which collectively illustrate the thematic depth as well as the creative and editorial processes behind the short, but resonant piece of fiction.

Brian Yothers opens the discussion with two chapters of good foundational material that paint a portrait of Melville and his works within the context of American letters. These opening chapters also set up the particular discussion of *Billy Budd, Sailor* as they describe the author's last years working on the story.

The Critical Contexts section of the book offers essays which speak to the process and reception of the novella. In two essays, Yothers describes the importance of Melville's sources related to both the novella's content and style, and the evolution of its critical focus. Mary K. Bercaw Edwards, in her essay "Performing the Sailor in *Billy Budd, Sailor*," emphasizes Melville's grasp of the tangible reality of the sea over its metaphor in heightening the story's impact.

The larger Critical Readings section explores the wide range of thematic elements put forward by *Billy Budd, Sailor,* whether intentionally or interpretively. Jonathan A Cook's "Legends of the Fall: Genesis, Paradise Lost, Schopenhauer, and Billy Budd" looks at the relationship between Melville's work and theological influence, both in terms of the story and the readings of it. Nicole De Fee points to Cold War influence on Peter Ustinov's 1962 film *Billy Budd,* and David Greven discusses the neglect of early critics to properly address the theme of sexuality. Other essays point to the impact of new technologies on the creation and dissemination of *Billy Budd, Sailor* analysis, the relevance of *Billy Budd, Sailor* to the philosophy classroom, and its contribution to the discussion on capital punishment.

The volume is rounded out by the Resources section, which provides a timeline of notable events in the life of Melville, an inventory of the volumes that make up the anthology *The Writings of Herman Melville,* and a bibliography. With its varied and thoughtful discussion, *Critical Insights: Billy Budd, Sailor* is a testament to the quality of the author and his final creation.

Recommended.—**ARBA Staff Reviewer**

599.   **Critical Insights: Civil Rights Literature, Past & Present.** Varlack, Christopher Allen, ed. Hackensack, N.J., Salem Press, 2017. 370p. index. $105.00. ISBN 13: 978-1-68217-268-1; 978-1-68217-269-8 (e-book).

For those libraries looking for a book that contains information and essays related to issues on civil rights, this book covers quite a bit of ground. After an introduction which encompasses a succinct overview of the content, there are four essays under the Critical Contexts section that examine free speech and racial rhetoric in relation to African American writers, a look at the inadequate conception of human complexity, a discussion of the 1961 play *Purlie Victorious* by Ossie Davis, and racial identity and otherness in civic society. Fifteen essays follow in the Critical Readings section, which are subdivided by the topics of literature of the civil rights era and beyond; womenhood, civil rights, and the politics of identity; representations of the LGBTQ rights movement; economic mobility and class stratification in the civil rights debate; and contemporary civil rights literature. Three separate chronologies are provided under the Resources section, with emphases on race, gender, and sexual orientation. A substantial bibliography is included. I highly recommend this volume for all libraries.—**Bradford Lee Eden**

600.   **Critical Insights: Of Mice and Men.** Barbara A. Heavilin, ed. Hackensack, N.J., Salem Press, 2017. 257p. index. $105.00. ISBN 13: 978-1-68217-266-7; 978-1-68217-267-4 (e-book).

Like many of the other volumes in this useful series, this book explores a single work, one of John Steinbeck's best-known fictional works, usually described as a novella. Twelve scholars present sixteen studies of diverse aspects of this text: racism, feminism, international reception of the work (in Slovenia!), morality, and the work as novel, play and film, among others. Easily read and full of clear, insightful analysis, the essays will enlighten readers about the creation of a male community within the narrative, the function of the bunkhouse in the evolution of the story, as well as more general analyses of the world of Steinbeck. Useful chronologies of Steinbeck's life and the publication of his works add to the value of this volume.

Any student of American literature who has read, or plans to read, this novella (or other works by Steinbeck) will benefit from the insights and explanations of the text provided here. High school, college/university, and public libraries should consider it for their collections.—**Mark Schumacher**

Individual Authors

601.   **Willa Cather at the Modernist Crux.** Ann Moseley, John J. Murphy, and Robert Thacker, eds. Lincoln, Nebr., University of Nebraska Press, 2017. 384p. illus. index. $40.00pa. ISBN 13: 978-0-8032-9699-2.

The 11th volume in the Cather Studies series (begun in 1990 and with recent volumes increasingly focused on a single theme/topic in her work) explores the development of the modernist elements in Cather's writing, with a portion of the book focused on her novel *The Song of the Lark* (1915). Other works examined include her poetry, *The Professor's House* (1925) and *Death Comes for the Archbishop* (1927). Most of the chapters here were papers first presented at the 14th International Willa Cather Seminar held in 2013. They proceed in a generally chronological manner: the three parts of this volume are titled "Beginnings," "Presences," and "Articulation: The Song of the Lark." The chapters explore diverse topics related to modernism: one explores the theme of prostitution in *A Lost Lady* (1923), another examines thematic parallels between Cather and Longfellow, others examine the works of painters Ernest Blumenschein and Fred Demmler and their connection to Cather's writing. In a variety of ways, these studies map Cather's shift from a "nineteenth-century writer" to an "emergent modernist." An epilogue, written by the editors of the book in question, presents a useful look at the value of the recently published *Selected Letters of Willa Cather* (Knopf, 2013) for those studying her writings.

These studies are aimed at readers with some previous exposure to Cather's writings, and to the scholarly criticism of her work. Academic libraries supporting programs in literature should consider this volume, especially, of course, if they have earlier volumes in the series. Other kinds of libraries will probably find it too specialized for their audience.—**Mark Schumacher**

British Literature

Dictionaries and Encyclopedias

602.   Sabatier, Armelle. **Shakespeare and Visual Culture: A Dictionary.** New York, Bloomsbury Arden Publishing, 2017. 295p. illus. index. (Arden Shakespeare Dictionary Series). $145.99. ISBN 13: 978-1-4725-6805-2; 978-1-4725-6807-6 (e-book).

This book, part of the Arden Shakespeare Dictionary series, explores references to visual arts and vision in Shakespeare's drama and poetry. The technical term for this scholarship is called "ekphrasis": the verbal depiction of a work of art. In the introduction, the author spends a considerable amount of time discussing Elizabethan prejudices around images and the description and use of colors in Shakespeare, along with an extensive literature review and opinions surrounding the coverage and scholarship on this topic in recent years. Each entry in the dictionary is divided into three sections. Section A gives general definitions and a brief overview of the meanings of the term in Shakespeare's texts. Section B examines the different ways in which the term is used by Shakespeare, often showing the evolution of the term throughout one single work or its use in different works. Section C provides secondary readings which explore different interpretations and approaches to the term. The bibliography includes both primary and secondary sources.—**Bradford Lee Eden**

Handbooks and Yearbooks

603.   **Critical Insights: Romeo and Juliet.** Robert C. Evans, ed. Hackensack, N.J., Salem Press, 2017. 311p. index. $105.00. ISBN 13: 978-1-68217-264-3; 978-1-68217-265-0 (e-book).

A collection of essays from various authors examines both contextual criticism and interpretations of different aspects of the writing and presentation of Shakespeare's most famous play. A section describing the background of the play and the life of Shakespeare begins the text, followed by two main sections describing critical contexts and critical readings. The critical contexts section examines significant aspects of characters, scenes, critical reception, and film presentations. The critical readings section looks at such considerations as use of imagination, artificiality, soliloquies, inclusion of trauma, and examples of parodies. Notes and a bibliography complete each essay and black-and-white illustrations enhance the text. The essays feature extensive research and present topics that are of interest and, perhaps, are outside the usual scope. A chronology of Shakespeare's life, a list of Shakespeare's works and a survey of recent editions (1997-2017), a bibliography and index, and information about the editor and the contributors complete the whole collection.—**Martha Lawler**

604.   **The Historian's Heart of Darkness: Reading Conrad's Masterpiece as Social and Cultural History.** Mark D. Larabee, ed. Santa Barbara, Calif., Praeger/ABC-CLIO, 2018. 180p. illus. maps. index. (The Historian's Annotated Classics). $37.00. ISBN 13: 978-1-4408-5106-3; 978-1-4408-5107-0 (e-book).

The third volume in the publisher's series (Mark Twain and Frederick Douglass were the earlier authors), this work connects Joseph Conrad's tale of the Congo, based on his own experiences, with the often brutal realities for native Africans in central Africa. After an 11-page chronology there is a 10-page biographical sketch and a 33-page, illustrated account of later nineteenth-century Congo history and discussion of "fact and fiction" in Conrad's depiction of the period in *Heart of Darkness* (first published in 1899, in magazine form).

The central section of the volume is comprised of the annotated texts of *Heart of Darkness* and *The Congo Diary*. A total of 223 annotations analyze and explain the two works; some are single words or short phrases, while others are substantial paragraphs. They may clarify language, or elaborate references to places, people, and events, or provide broader contextual history for a passage in Conrad's text. The major exploration in this book is the interlinking of Conrad's on-site observations during his visit to the Congo in 1890 (first published in 1925) with elements in his novella

The preface mentions the book's value to instructors, but it certainly has a broader audience. This book will be most appreciated in academic libraries, whose readers, whether studying history or literature, will appreciate the interweaving of the two disciplines. Given its rather reasonable price and its readability, other libraries should also consider it if their patrons are interested in British literature or African history.—**Mark Schumacher**

Individual Authors

605.   **Critical Insights: Geoffrey Chaucer.** James M. Dean, ed. Hackensack, N.J., Salem Press, 2017. 255p. index. $105.00. ISBN 13: 978-1-68217-256-8; 978-1-68217-257-5 (e-book).

There are hundreds of books on Geoffrey Chaucer, ranging from the introductory to the specialized examination of his numerous publications and works. This book falls in between, providing both a concise introduction to Chaucer and his works, while also including critical essays devoted to specialized topics. The critical essays focus on topics such as satire in Chaucer, his use of language, his transnational character, various perspectives such as Robertsonian and Boethian, his international presence, specific works such as *The Monk's Tale* and *Canterbury Tales,* comparisons with other authors such as John Donne and John Gower, and his role as a sociolinguist. A chronology of Chaucer's life, a listing of his works, and a bibliography round out the content. Overall, it is difficult to categorize this book for a specific audience; it tries to please both the novice and the researcher. As such, it is more appropriate as an addition to an academic library's medieval literature/authors collection.—**Bradford Lee Eden**

606.   **Critical Insights: Joseph Conrad.** Jeremiah J. Garsha, ed. Hackensack, N.J., Salem Press, 2016. 248p. index. $105.00. ISBN 13: 978-1-68217-114-1; 978-1-68217-115-8 (e-book).

Joseph Conrad (1857-1924) has been called one of the greatest novelists in the English language. He was a personification of Europe at the turn of the twentieth century:

a Polish-born Russian citizen of the Ukraine, who thought in French, wrote in English, and incorporated his native Polish language into the English literary tradition. He influenced numerous writers through his works, which were explorations of the effects of colonization, globalization, and conquest by European nations on Third World nations. This book is both an introduction to and new exploration of Conrad's writings and influence, so that both novices and Conradian experts can find something of interest and insight. As with other books in the Critical Insights series, a succinct biography as well as chronology and bibliography of Conrad's life and work frame a number of essays that focus upon Conrad's major writings and influences, delving into critical contexts and readings which illustrate Conrad's immense depth and breadth of literary topos. An excellent guide to the life and works of this important writer.—**Bradford Lee Eden**

607.   **Critical Insights: Neil Gaiman.** Joseph Michael Sommers, ed. Hackensack, N.J., Salem Press, 2016. 245p. index. $105.00. ISBN 13: 978-1-68217-260-5; 978-1-68217-261-2 (e-book).

Neil Gaiman (1960-) and his writings and music are currently front and center with the release of the TV series *American Gods* based on his 2001 book. Gaiman maintains that his local library in West Sussex in England was his haven and intellectual progenitor, where he spent considerable time from the age of four reading anything having to do with magic, especially the works of C.S. Lewis, Lewis Carroll, and J.R.R. Tolkien. This book contains fourteen essays on Gaiman's writings and influences, separated into two major sections titled Critical Contexts and Critical Readings. Prior to the essays, an introduction to Gaiman is provided as well as a short biography. The essays delve into many of Gaiman's writings, including *The Graveyard Book, The Wolves in the Wall, The Sandman,* and many others, including *American Gods* for which he won numerous awards including the Hugo, the Nebula, the Locus, and the Bram Stoker. A chronology of Gaiman's career along with a listing of his published works is included with a bibliography at the end. A fascinating collection of essays on one of the most interesting writers of the twenty-first century.—**Bradford Lee Eden**

608.   **The Definitive Shakespeare Companion: Overviews, Documents, and Analysis.** Rosenblum, Joseph, ed. Santa Barbara, Calif., Greenwood Press/ABC-CLIO, 2017. 4v. illus. index. $415.00/set. ISBN 13: 978-1-4408-3444-8; 978-1-4408-3445-5 (e-book).

This set provides an incredible amount of information for those wishing to learn more about the life and works of William Shakespeare. (It is an updated, enlarged, and enhanced version of a similar 2005 set, also published by Greenwood Press and edited by Dr. Rosenblum.) Sixty-two scholars from the United States and England have contributed chapters on the histories, comedies, tragedies, romances, and many of the poems. The format for the 37 plays is similar throughout: plot summary, publication history, literary sources (and excerpts), historical context (and historical excerpts), "devices and techniques," main characters, themes, critical controversies, production history, reviews, and bibliography. Such a standard structure makes it easier for readers to find the information they might be seeking for multiple plays. Individual entries for the plays range from 26 (Love's Labor's Lost) to 66 pages (King Lear) and 70 pages (Henry IV, Parts 1 & 2), while poems like Venus and Adonis receive 15 to 25 pages, and the sonnets have briefer entries. Annotated bibliographies, with added references in many cases, accompany each chapter and guide readers to further useful reading.

Clearly, this set will enhance any library's literature collection. Although there is detailed analysis throughout, the organization of each chapter will provide a clear setting for readers of all kinds, from high schoolers to scholars in the field. All libraries should consider it; for nearly 2,000 pages of information on a subject of widespread interest, the price is not unreasonable.—**Mark Schumacher**

609.   **The Reception of Alfred Tennyson in Europe.** Leonce Ormond, ed. New York, Bloomsbury Publishing, 2017. 424p. index. (The Reception of British and Irish Authors in Europe). ISBN 13: 978-1-4411-1419-8; 978-1-3500-1253-0 (e-book).

One of the recent volumes in a long-running series exploring the European reaction to writers from the British Isles, this book presents and analyzes the impact of the work of Alfred Tennyson (1809-1892) in France, Spain, Italy, Portugal, Greece, Germany, Russia, and Bulgaria. A 34-page, 3-column timeline, covering 1830 to 2015, identifies translations, studies, and other events (such as art and music) in those countries, while a 48-page bibliography, arranged chapter-by-chapter, takes readers to references in numerous languages.

In her quite useful introduction, editor Ormond points out the challenges of Tennyson's poetic forms, which could create a barrier to foreign readers and often led to prose translations. She also cites *Enoch Arden* as the work which introduced the poet to European readers. The 11 succeeding chapters provide detailed looks at the individual countries' approach to Tennyson, discussing the European translators and scholars, such as France's Hippolyte Taine, who introduced his work to their compatriots. One interesting chapter explores the European impact of Gustave Dore's illustrations, in the 1860s, for *The Idylls of the King.*

Given the specialized focus of this volume, it will be most interesting for academic scholars in English and comparative literature, or possibly Victorian historians. Colleges and universities will be the place for this volume, as well as others in the series.—**Mark Schumacher**

Japanese Literature

Handbooks and Yearbooks

610.   **Critical Insights: Modern Japanese Literature.** Frank Jacob, ed. Hackensack, N.J., Salem Press, 2017. 293p. index. $105.00. ISBN 13: 978-1-68217-258-2; 978-1-68217-259-9 (e-book).

This volume in the Critical Insights series focuses its essays on the enigmatic genre of Modern Japanese Literature. The concept of Modern Japanese is borne on the opening of the insular Japan to Western commercial and cultural trade in the late nineteenth century. This book provides contextual and critical essays which ultimately act as an excellent (yet noncomprehensive) survey of the genre, working mainly to encapsulate an author's most important themes and aesthetics.

The essays in the Critical Contexts section provide a good foundation for discussion, pointing to the origins of what is considered Modern Japanese Literature. Two pieces discuss writers Mori Ogai and Futabatei Shimei, who were both influenced by travels abroad and were the first to blend Western ideas with Japanese sensibilities. The other essays in this section examine the geographical development of the new literature through the lens of two very different locations: the bustling capital of Tokyo and the outlying island of Okinawa.

The eleven essays in the Critical Readings section explore a range of writers and topics. Katharina Schmolders examines the works of diarist Nagai Kafu ("Nagai Kafu: The Unwilling Modern Writer") and his reflections on a rapidly changing Tokyo. Schmolders later looks at Shiga Naoya ("Shiga Naoya: Modern Observer of Human Nature") whose writings buckled against contemporary Japanese social issues. Other essays examine the unique aesthetics of Modern Japanese Literature, such as George T. Sipos' review of Nobel Prize winner Kawabata Yasunari and the development of the New Sensationists, or Frank Jacob's piece on Mishima Yukio and his treatment of the themes of beauty and death. The volume also looks at the works of female writers Kirino Natsuo and Oba Minako, the unique character of Okinawan literature and more.

Resources include a listing of Modern Japanese Literature in English translation, a bibliography, and information on essay contributors (although a chronology would have been a helpful addition). Overall, the volume does an excellent job of opening eyes to the genre melding modern literary thought and style with the deep cultural traditions of an ancient nation.—**ARBA Staff Reviewer**

Poetry

Handbooks and Yearbooks

611.   **The Collected Poetry of Mary Tighe.** Paula R. Feldman and Brian C. Cooney, eds. Baltimore, Md., Johns Hopkins University Press, 2016. 640p. illus. index. 69.95. ISBN 13: 978-1-4214-1876-6.

Only recently "rediscovered," Mary Blachford Tighe (1772-1810) was a key figure in British Romanticism, inspiring Keats and others. This comprehensive volume presents her complete poetic works, including recently discovered poems. (Her novel *Selena,* completed in 1803, but only published recently, is not included.) There is a considerable critical framework surrounding the poems: a 55-page introduction, textual notes throughout, several appendixes, including false attributions and nineteenth-century "poetic responses" to Tighe's work. A major portion of the volumes presents Tighe's "Psyche; or, The Legend of Love" (1805). An added feature is the inclusion of scores of Tighe's drawings, taken from her notebooks, throughout the volume.

Academic libraries, especially those with strong English and Women's Studies departments, will have readers interested in the work contained in this volume. Other types of libraries will have less need for the contents of this book.—**Mark Schumacher**

612.   **First World War Digital Poetry Archive.** [Website] Free. Date reviewed: 2018.

This site is home to two complementary archives of materials related to World War I: The First World War Poetry Digital Archive and the Great War Archive. Together, the collections capture both the tangible and the emotional realities of the first armed conflict to touch all corners of the globe. Users can examine and download myriad materials including manuscript and published writings, contextual items, and a generous offering of supplemental resources.

The First World War Poetry Digital Archive homepage allows users to Browse the Collections in several ways. The collections include items from ten individual British poets of the era, including Siegfried Sassoon, Wilfred Owen, Vera Brittain, and Isaac Rosenberg. Selecting a poet displays a biographical essay in addition to links to items in the collection. Users can Find A Specific Poem, search poems by title or first line, and can access images of manuscripts and/or text. Other poet-related items may also be available to examine, such as correspondence, photographs, related publications, and official documents. Supplementary materials in the poetry archive provide context and include a Photographic Collection from the Imperial War Museum Archive; an Audio Collection of oral history interviews; a Film Collection of war footage, early feature films and more; and Publications of War, including wartime journals affiliated with Sassoon and Owen and propaganda newsletters. Back on the homepage, the Education tab offers links to excellent resources for educators and students alike, such as several tutorials ("An Introduction to World War I Poetry"), Film & Audio Clips, and First World War Timelines. First-time users may also wish to view the Archive Showreel—a seven-minute YouTube video introducing the archive. Users can also access The Great War Archive, primarily sourced from small family collections, from this page. Users can search the diverse archive via the link or Browse by Keyword (e.g., Autograph Books, Interviews, Maps, Memoirs, Paintings, Music, etc.). Information for each item may include title, author, notes, item date, creation place, and more. The Editor's Pick highlights a particular item from the archive. Other highlights include hand grenade lecture notes from a young Lance Corporal, audio recordings of veterans singing their favorite war ditties, and hand-painted postcards.

As the war affected Britain so directly, it is vital that researchers understand the British perspective of the era. Each archive here is a testament to that perspective and both the primary artifacts and supplementary materials provide an excellent basis for World War I scholarship.—**ARBA Staff Reviewer**

613.   **Poetry & Short Story Reference Center. https://www.ebsco.com/products/ research-databases/poetry-short-story-reference-center.** [Website] Birmingham, Ala., EBSCO Publishing, Inc., 2017. Price negotiated by site. Date reviewed: 2018.

This site from EBSCO, well suited to high school students and educators, is an excellent online source of materials concerning the poetry and short story mediums. Easy to navigate, the site allows users to browse in several ways or conduct a basic or advanced search from the bar in the upper left corner of the page. Users can scroll through select e-Books within the poetry and short story genres or explore examples from Featured Writer, Featured Interview, or Featured Video categories. Poetry off the Page is designed for educators, allowing them to browse lesson plans and individual assignments that help maximize the impact of poetry. Users can alternatively browse the database using one of the links from the left side of the page, which include Periods, Movements & Schools (e.g., American Romantic, Age of Goethe, etc.), Poetic Forms, Themes & Techniques (e.g., Ballad, Love, Blank Verse, etc.), Most Studied Poets (Auden, Frost, etc.), Most Studied Poems ("Annabel Lee," "Song of Myself," etc.), and much more. The Infographics link, recently added to the page, shows word cloud graphics of select poetry such as Edgar Allen Poe's "The Raven" in addition to short story plot points for works such as Jack

London's "To Build a Fire" and Guy de Maupassant's "The Necklace." Information included alongside selected poems may include first line, last line, author, poetic form, poetic theme, poetic technique, and keywords. An audio link allows users to hear selected works (although it is important to note that the recording is phonetic and may not realize the ideal reading of the poem). Short stories may appear in pdf, html, or audio format and include author, source, publication, lexile, full text word count, and other information. Users may also find More about This Work, More About this Author, and Related E-Books links. Students can take advantage of several tools within this site to help manage their research. They can save files, email, notate, cite, and perform other operations.—**ARBA Staff Reviewer**

25 Music

General Works

Bibliography

614. **A Basic Music Library: Essential Scores and Sound Recordings, Fourth Edition, Volume 1: Popular Music.** 4th ed. The Music Library Association, comp. Edward Komara, ed. Chicago, American Library Association, 2017. 360p. index. $258.00pa.; $232.20pa. (ALA members). ISBN 13: 978-0-8389-1039-9.

The fourth edition of this popular reference work has moved from one to three volumes, in order to better represent the variety and changing needs of library selectors in public and small academic libraries. Volume one deals with popular music, while volume two will focus on world music, and volume three will encompass classical music. Besides printed music materials (books and scores) and sound recordings, this edition has greatly expanded outside of the classical music arena into a global reference work. Volume one, then, has popular music as its objective, and is divided into eleven topic areas: Music of Colonial North America and the United States to about 1900; Blues; Jazz; Mainstream Popular and New Age; Country and Western; Rock; Rhythm and Blues and Soul; Rap and Hip-Hop; Gospel Music and other Popular Christian Music; Children's Music; and Holidays, Special Occasions, Patriotic Music, and Miscellaneous. Each area is subdivided into various categories as well, and each entry is fairly concise in providing a title, publisher, pressing information, and format. Those entries with a star indicate a high priority for acquisitions. The index is comprehensive and provides the easiest way to use this resource. Highly recommended now that it encompasses much more than classical music.—**Bradford Lee Eden**

Biography

615. Pfitzinger, Scott. **Composer Genealogies: A Compendium of Composers, Their Teachers, and Their Students.** Lanham, Md., Rowman & Littlefield, 2017. 616p. $150.00; $142.00 (e-book). ISBN 13: 978-1-4422-7224-8; 978-1-4422-7225-5 (e-book).

This large volume documents the genealogies or pedigrees of musical composers from the eighteenth century to the present. One of the ways that musicians establish credibility and public interest in their music is through the teachers under whom they studied, as well as those teachers under whom their teachers studied. The author of this book has documented, as much as possible, the genealogies of musical composers who have taught other composers; it thus does not try to be comprehensive regarding other musical disciplines or instruments and their pedigrees. Just focusing on musical composers has produced a book of over 600 pages. The entries are listed alphabetically, starting with the composer's name and dates, the primary countries where they lived, their teachers, and their notable students. The book serves as an index with comprehensive cross-referencing. One can follow a composer's musical pedigree both backwards through their teachers and forwards through their students, so this volume is a fantastic quick reference source for learning who influenced whom in the musical composition world in the last 350 years.—**Bradford Lee Eden**

Handbooks and Yearbooks

616.   **British Sound Library. https://sounds.bl.uk/.** [Website] Free. Date reviewed: 2018.

This archive compiles a large and unique assortment of audio recordings encompassing music, natural sounds, spoken words, and more. Users can listen to over fifty thousand recordings organized into different collections for ease of reference, including Accents & Dialects; Arts, Literature & Performance; Classical Music; Environment & Nature; Popular Music; and Oral History. Collections may be further organized into distinct categories—the Environment & Nature collection alone has ten categories, including Soundscapes, Weather, Amphibians, and Early Wildlife Recordings. Users can conduct a keyword search or search by collection. Users can browse by collection as well via the specific links located throughout the homepage. Within each collection, users can read a description of contents, listen to select highlights, and view individual sound recording selections in various ways. The Listen to Nature category within the Environment & Nature collection, for example, lets users approach recordings by Animal Group, Habitat, or Species. Descriptive information for each recording varies, but may include type, duration, recording date, recording location(s), and recordist. Highlights of the British Sound Library include music recordings from each continent, oral histories on a wide range of subjects (women's suffrage, jazz in Britain, etc.), field recordings of weather systems, the extensive Survey of English Dialects, and much more. Other site features include a listing of the Most Shared sounds, a Tag Cloud of popular searches, interactive Sound Maps which pin locations where sounds are recorded, and Case Studies which provide various examples of how the British Sound Library has been used in research.—**ARBA Staff Reviewer**

617.   **English Broadside Ballad Archive. https://ebba.english.ucsb.edu/.** [Website] Free. Date reviewed: 2017.

The broadside ballad, finding its heyday within the British Isles throughout the seventeenth century, marks a significant point along the evolution of popular music. This project from the University of California, Santa Barbara gathers several significant collections of broadside ballads in one electronic archive. Hailing from prestigious libraries in England, Scotland, and the United States, the archive has digitized close to eight thousand ballads. Users will appreciate the easy access to original text and woodblock illustrations, and enjoy modern recordings of many of the ballads in the archive.

From the homepage, users can search by identification number, title, publication date, standardized tune title, author, text, and more. The page also features amusingly curated collections, such as "The Bachelor," with ballads about love and courtship, "Orange is the New Black" on crime and punishment, "Pretty Little Liars" on youthful indiscretions, "Shark Week," "Game of Thrones," and so on. Users can examine a selected item in several ways: as an Album Facsimile, a Ballad Sheet Facsimile, a Facsimile Transcription, and a Text Transcription. In many cases, the item will be accompanied by a recording, which enables users to hear its associated tune. All of these options are available by tab on the item page. Users can also select the Citation tab for publication date, author, collection, location, keyword categories, first lines, and more.

Features on the left sidebar include three data Visualizations (e.g., Geography of the London Ballad Trade 1500-1700) and generous Resources which include a glossary of terms and essays covering technical, cultural, and historical information. While the site could benefit from more browsing capabilities (e.g., library collection, tune, etc.), it is nonetheless richly enlightening and thoroughly engaging, and does well by this robust example of seventeenth century popular culture.—**ARBA Staff Reviewer**

618.   **The Great 78 Project. www.great78archive.org.** [Website] Free. Date reviewed: 2018.

The days of vinyl recordings in the mass market are gone, but the devotion music aficionados, historians, and others show towards them is telling. These records brought music to many for over fifty years spanning the first half of the twentieth century. The Great 78 Project helps to preserve these treasures via digitization, allowing researchers and general fans access to the authentic sounds and stories of over forty thousand 78 rpm records, with an emphasis on more obscure recordings (noncommercial reproductions, less popular genres, etc.). Users can select the Listen tab to access the full digitized archive which can be sorted in several ways and viewed either as a list or a thumbnail gallery. Each recording is marked by number of views, title, archive date, and creator. Users can search the collection via filters such as genre, collection, and recording date. Selecting a particular recording allows users to listen to it and view an image of the record label alongside known recording and digitizing information, such as record publisher. Users will also note affiliated Collections, Download options, User Reviews, and other material. The Discovery tab offers tips and links on ways to explore the archive by language, genre, or timeframe and also includes thumbnails of select recordings. Research accesses two scholarly essays on topics related to the project: "Listening to the 78rpm Collection," which relates to the type of information researchers can glean from the recordings, and "Stylus Size and Speed Selection in Pre-1923 Acoustic Recordings," which discusses some technical aspects of the 78 rpm medium. Hopefully the site will add more essays along these lines. The appeal of preserving such a large and historical audio collection, and making it easy to access, is enormous. The Great 78 Project will interest a range of users from the casual music lover to the music historian.—**ARBA Staff Reviewer**

619. **Open Music Library. http://openmusiclibrary.org.** [Website] Free. Date reviewed: 2018.

The Open Music Library encompasses a broad array of digital resources for use in music research across orchestral, operatic, folk, classical, popular, and other musical genres. Although there is some information available to all users, select content requires site registration enabled by an academic or institutional affiliation. Users can search from the prominent search bar on the homepage or narrow their search by category. Tabs running along the top of the page link to the archive. People provides information on roughly two hundred prominent figures in music, such as Romantic composer Frederic Chopin, singer Maria Callas, and conductor Herbert von Karajan. Users can follow links to affiliated materials including videos, scores, journal articles, and more, although the amount of materials will vary between individuals. Journals offers an alphabetical listing of close to seven hundred individual publications, such as *ArtCultura, Beethoven Forum, The Hungarian Quarterly* and *Vibe*. For each publication, the listing notes ISSNs and country of origin, and displays a lock/unlock icon to signify whether content is restricted to subscribers (most are locked). Users can organize the listing by theme, such as music history, popular music, etc. Works presents over one hundred thousand pieces/compositions (Beethoven's "Ode to Joy," and more) with descriptive information, tags, and affiliated categories of available material. In regards to Scores, the site helps focus the search by displaying featured composers and popular tags (e.g., "violin," "20th Century," and others). Over four thousand Videos, accessible to all users, range from singular performances to feature documentaries and lectures. The Audio tab helps users search roughly eight thousand ensembles, highlights featured performers, and allows registered users to listen to and create thematic playlists ("Musique Macabre," etc.). Users who wish to browse can scroll down the homepage to select from Popular Topics, Featured Scores, Featured People or Featured Videos. While there is certainly enough on this website to engage the casual user, researchers with academic affiliations would definitely benefit from its many diverse sources of music scholarship.—**ARBA Staff Reviewer**

620. **Pittsburgh Symphony Archive. https://archive.pittsburghsymphony.org/.** [Website] Free. Date reviewed: 2018.

This archive captures the history of the storied Pittsburgh Symphony and its home, Heinz Hall. The site allows digital access to years of photographs, concert programs, posters, and other ephemera. In addition, users can listen to audio highlights of the symphony's significant performances. The site would be of particular interest to regional historians, music historians, and others who appreciate the symphony. Users can conduct a general search from the bar or can use the Discover tab to search the archive in a number of ways. Choosing Subject organizes available items into seventeen topical categories, emphasizing particular aspects of the Pittsburgh Symphony (e.g., programs, musicians, posters, tours etc.). There is also an A-Z category filter option. Users who select Season will find symphony materials organized chronologically going back to its 1896 debut. Conductor presents an alphabetized listing of hundreds of maestros from Claudio Abbado to Pinchas Zukerman, and Composer offers a generous list of both classical and contemporary creators from J.S. Bach to Sara Bareilles. Users can also browse by specific item collections under the Communities and Collections tab, such as the Public Affairs Department collection which houses photographs, the Pittsburgh Symphony Orchestra Program Collection, which holds both Tour and Grand Classics concert programs, and more. The website allows for good study of a work's performance history at Heinz Hall and the many relationships that the symphony has nurtured with composers, conductors, performers, and others.—**ARBA Staff Reviewer**

Instruments

621.   Dempf, Linda, and Richard Seraphinoff. **Guide to the Solo Horn Repertoire.** Bloomington, Ind., Indiana University Press, 2016. 605p. index. $68.00. ISBN 13: 978-0-253-01929-5.

This is a comprehensive guide to music for solo horn, also called the French Horn in some literature. The scope includes music originally composed for the horn, and excludes arrangements, with the exception of piano reductions of works originally for horn and ensemble. Most works listed are published.

The book has three sections: Music for Unaccompanied Horn, Works for Horn and Keyboard, and Works for Horn and Ensemble; each section is arranged by composer. Entries include vital information for the purchase or location of the music: composer name, primary country of residence, title, date of composition, publisher and publication date, and a brief description of the work; the authors identify technical details, durations, and the range of most pieces, using the Standard found in D. Kern Holoman's *Writing About Music.* Dempf and Seraphinoff add five indexes: "Title index"; "Name Index for Premieres, Commissions, and Dedications"; "Index-Music for Horn with Band"; "Index-Music for Horn with Small Instrumental Ensemble"; and a "List of Composers by Nationality." Most of the composers appear to be late 19th and 20th century in their lifespans.

This timely resource updates and enhances information found in *The Hornist's Compendium,* by John D. K. Brisbin (Calgary, Alberta: Brisbin, 1977) and *Horn Bibliographie,* by Bernhard Brüchle (Wilhelmshaven: Heinrichshofen, 1970-75). Reference librarians who have appreciated the various volumes on piano music by Maurice Hinson will likewise find *Guide to the Solo Horn Repertoire* useful for brass performers.—**Ralph Hartsock**

622.   Siek, Stephen. **A Dictionary for the Modern Pianist.** Lanham, Md., Rowman & Littlefield, 2017. 285p. illus. $99.00; $89.99 (e-book). ISBN 13: 978-0-8108-8879-1; 978-0-8108-8880-7 (e-book).

Siek opens with two considerations: new technologies of digital keyboards are evolving at a quick pace and colleges or conservatories increasingly emphasize music on instruments constructed during the composer's lifetime—period instruments.

Pianists are geared more toward personality than terminology, so a majority of entries focus on major teachers and performers. Some twenty entries present modern parts of the piano and its components. The author also presents "A Brief Word about Recordings" (p. xv-xvi) that highlights technological developments in the recordings of sound. For a fuller view and narration, readers should look to *Vinyl: a History of the Analogue Record,* by Richard Osborne (Burlington, Vermont: Ashgate, 2012) and *Why Jazz Happened,* by Marc Myers (Berkeley: University of California Press, 2013).

The entries for pianists include those who perform, compose, and teach classical (art music), jazz, and popular styles. This resource is not intended as a repertoire guide; users will find the volumes by Maurice Hinson more instructive on specific works. Siek also omitted pianists who became primarily known as composers (Johannes Brahms, Claude Debussy, Sergei Prokofiev), unless the pianist maintained/sustained a long concert career (Duke Ellington, Franz Liszt, George Gershwin, Sergei Rachmaninoff).

"Space did not permit the inclusion of more general music terminology," but Siek presents a bibliography of more general sources. The author uses the Acoustic Society of America (ASA) standard for pitch identification, outlined on page ix. The Modified Hemholtz system is presented for comparison, as many museums use Hemholtz.

Entries include well-placed cross-references in the articles (as bold print) to guide users to relevant entries. These prove especially useful in the biographies (linking pianists to their teachers), piano manufacturers, such as Aeolian Company and Knabe (linking these to mergers or competitors), and genres, such as rag or ragtime (linking to composers and notable performers). Piano competitions are entered under the full name most known (the Cliburn competition is under Van Cliburn International Competition, while the biography of the pianist is under Cliburn, Van).

Appendix A displays entries by category; Appendix B is an overview of the acoustic piano's action, with a diagram. Essays in the appendixes C-E highlight historical pianos (Edmund Michael Frederick), digital pianos (S. David Beryl), and the Player Piano (Robert J. Beckman). Siek presents quick access to major piano manufacturers and performers.—**Ralph Hartsock**

623.   Strain, James A. **A Dictionary for the Modern Percussionist and Drummer.** Lanham, Md., Rowman & Littlefield, 2017. 313p. illus. index. $100.00; $95.00 (e-book). ISBN 13: 978-0-8108-8692-6; 978-0-8108-8693-3 (e-book).

This book by Strain, a professor of music at Northern Michigan University, historian of the Percusive Arts Society (PAS), and principal percussionist of the Marquette Symphony Orchestra, is intended for use by percussionists and nonpercussionists at all levels. Even at approximately three hundred pages (including appendixes), the book cannot cover every aspect of percussion. Instead, the scope is limited to percussion terms related primarily to music in orchestra, concert band, marching band, drum corps, opera, musical theater, and film scores as well as instruments and terms commonly found in jazz and popular music styles. Ethnic instruments and terms typically found in university or public school settings are also included. The dictionary utilizes black-and-white illustrations of instruments and detailed parts of instruments throughout. Slang terms related to real-life performance situations or technical issues are defined and the biographies of percussionists, drummers, and composers from the PAS Hall of Fame are included in the body of the dictionary. The entries range in length from one word to several sentences and employ cross-references when necessary. Users will also find a series of useful appendixes (fifteen in total), such as "Philosophies and Approaches to Teaching Percussion," "List of Drum Set Styles," and "Standard Ranges for Tuned Percussion Instruments." A list of further readings rounds out the work. Recommended for academic libraries with schools of music and for public libraries.—**ARBA Staff Reviewer**

Musical Forms

Band

624.   Cicconi, Christopher M. **The Band Music Handbook: A Catalog of Emerging Band Repertoire.** Lanham, Md., Rowman & Littlefield, 2017. 178p. index. (Music Finders series). $85.00; $84.99 (e-book). ISBN 13: 978-1-4422-6863-0; 978-1-4422-6864-7 (e-book).

This book supplements the volumes of William Rehrig, *The Heritage Encyclopedia of Band Music: Composers and Their Music* (see ARBA 93, entry 1283). Cicconi has compiled data on 1,500 works of younger composers. His data for each entry includes the composer's name, life dates, nationality, and composition titles. For each work listed, he adds the year composed, duration, publisher, and instrumentation, conveyed in a numerical standard.

Eleven appendixes enhance the catalog's value: the works listed by title, then an index by duration. Composers are indexed in a brief alphabetical list, then by nationality. Other appendixes list works with choruses, or for unusual instruments; one lists the arrangements under their original composers. Four additional appendixes list transcriptions by Mark Hindsley, and the marches of James Henry Fillmore, Karl King, and John Philip Sousa.

Bands, wind symphonies, and similar ensembles will find this source useful for programming. Libraries will find it useful for locating editions of music. Both will find Appendix K useful for publisher information.—**Ralph Hartsock**

Popular Music

625.   Abjorensen, Norman. **Historical Dictionary of Popular Music.** Lanham, Md., Rowman & Littlefield, 2017. 654p. (Historical Dictionaries of Literature and the Arts). $145.99; $137.00 (e-book). ISBN 13: 978-1-5381-0214-5; 978-1-5381-0215-2 (e-book).

One of the many books in the Historical Dictionaries of Literature and the Arts series from Rowman & Littlefield, this book focuses on the topic of popular music. This series is unique, in that each book includes an extensive chronology of the topic (in this case, from 1827 to the present), as well as a fairly comprehensive bibliography that is quite thorough and nicely subdivided (in this case, into regions, major popular music artists, genres, and significant artists by genre). This volume also includes appendixes that list notable songs and artists from 1920 to 2015, as well as selected Grammy Award winners from 1958 to 2015. Each entry is fairly short, with cross-references in bold type. No visuals are included (since it is a dictionary), and the entries are not meant to be comprehensive but to provide the reader with basic information to begin further research. This quick guide to popular music is appropriate for school libraries as well as libraries in colleges and universities.—**Bradford Lee Eden**

626.   Sullivan, Steve. **Encyclopedia of Great Popular Song Recordings.** Lanham, Md., Rowman & Littlefield, 2017. 2v. illus. index. $200.00; $190.00 (e-book). ISBN 13: 978-1-

4422-5448-0; 978-1-4422-5449-7 (e-book).

Continuing where his inaugural two volumes left off (see ARBA 2014, entry 958), Steve Sullivan explores additional selections of great but underappreciated song recordings in volumes three and four. Added are some 1,700 records and artists omitted from the earlier volumes for lack of space to complete Sullivan's review of over a century and a quarter of Anglo-North American pop music. But as music writer Dave Marsh explains in his foreword, what sets Sullivan apart as a music critic is not his vast knowledge of what was recorded, but his passion for seeing how the songs connect across time. Calling it the "Smithsonian of Soul," Marsh praises Sullivan's work for its ability to bring long-forgotten, soul-stirring songs back to life. While it is impossible to read an entry for a familiar song and not "hear" it playing, it is equally possible to read an entry for an unfamiliar song and begin to "hear" it playing—thanks to Sullivan's exquisite descriptions.

Sullivan's criteria for selection do not appear to differ from that of his earlier volumes, as he again presents songs from 1890 through today using playlists. However, this time he dispenses with a hierarchical arrangement, presenting the songs in straight chronological order instead. True to his mission, Sullivan again focuses on "undeservedly neglected" recordings. For example, while "Arthur's Theme" was undoubtedly a fantastic 1980 hit, the song he chooses to highlight in volume four is Christopher Cross' "Sailing" (the former does get a mention). New in these volumes also is the occasional inclusion of "news bulletins" to complete an entry (e.g., mention of the space shuttle *Challenger's* explosion following The Bangles' "Manic Monday" January 1986 entry).

This heavily footnoted music guide includes an extensive, themed bibliography and separate title and subject/name indexes. Volumes three and four are paged and indexed separately from volumes one and two. Entry recordings are indexed in "all caps" while recordings referenced in the text are listed in uppercase and lowercase. Also provided is a list of music resource abbreviations used throughout the work. Entries include record label information and recording and charting dates. Authoritative and a joy to browse, this goldmine will be an indispensable resource in pop culture collections and college libraries supporting music departments. Nearest comparable titles include *1,000 Recordings to Hear Before You Die* and *1001 Songs: The Great Songs of All Time and the Artists, Stories and Secrets Behind Them.*—**Lucy Duhon**

Rock

627. Luhrssen, David, and Michael Larson. **Encyclopedia of Classic Rock.** Santa Barbara, Calif., Greenwood Press/ABC-CLIO, 2017. 431p. illus. index. $89.00. ISBN 13: 978-1-4408-3513-1; 978-1-4408-3514-8 (e-book).

The *Encyclopedia of Classic Rock* by David Luhrssen and Michael Larson covers rock artists who emerged or became prominent during the period 1965–1975. Unique in this work is the discussion of the musical and cultural importance of rock groups from outside the United States and United Kingdom, including significant artists from continental Europe, Africa, Asia, and Latin America. Rock music played a critical role in the cultural shifts occurring during 1965-1975, with rock reaching new heights of innovation and expressiveness, thereby fitting the term classic. Prior to 1965, rock and roll was primarily viewed as entertainment, and after 1975 elements from classic rock diminished to appease commercial radio formats. The encyclopedia provides an A to Z listing of over 300 classic rock articles. Ranging in length from more than five pages for significant artists like The Beatles or Bob Dylan to a single paragraph for less-known groups like Brewer and Shipley, the reviews place artists in historical context and explain the impression they made at the time. Readers will find a list of historically important albums. Although much of the book focuses on artist profiles, there are short essays on topics germane to the period such as genres or rock in a particular geographical area. Pictures are scarce, and the few included are black and white. Extra sections include a recommended reading list of more serious rock scholarship that influenced the authors and a chronology of important events from 1965 to 1975. Although much of the information contained within the *Encyclopedia of Classic Rock* can be found on the Internet, fans of the genre will enjoy paging through the entries, stirring their nostalgia for a time long past. Recommended for public libraries.—**Kevin McDonough**

26 Mythology, Folklore, and Popular Culture

Folklore

Handbooks and Yearbooks

628. **The Book of Greek & Roman Folktales, Legends, & Myths.** William Hansen, ed. Illustrated by Glynnis Fawkes. Princeton, N.J., Princeton University Press, 2017. 549p. illus. index. $35.00. ISBN 13: 978-0-6911-7015-2.

This comprehensive, wide-ranging anthology of materials from Greece and Rome also covers some content from Egypt and Persia. The title includes a list of illustrations and tables and of abbreviations, as well as an appendix of ancient terms, beliefs, and relative numbers. A glossary, index, bibliography, ancient sources, and a list of international stories, with legend type and select motifs, are also included. The stories are feats of merchants, sages, soldiers, etc. rather than the tales of deities. Edited by William Hansen, a professor emeritus of classics and folklore at Indiana University, the entries vary in length, with a commentary or summary following most content. Scholars and general readers alike will find this title useful and entertaining.—**Denise A. Garofalo**

629. Elswit, Sharon Barcan. **The Caribbean Story Finder: A Guide to 438 Tales from 24 Nations and Territories, Listing Subjects and Sources.** Jefferson, N.C., McFarland, 2017. 308p. index. $45.00pa. ISBN 13: 978-1-4766-6304-3; 978-1-4766-3001-4 (e-book).

These stories present the history and everyday existence of exploited people as a way of preserving their culture and history, which was often recorded within an oral tradition and often told within an incomprehensible, private language. An introduction gives an overview of the history and the layout of the information—i.e., the reasoning behind the choice of tales; the various aspects of the culture from which they came; the characteristics, themes, etc. that weave in and out of the stories; and the presentation of the material within the collection and how to use it. The main text is mostly an annotated subject guide in which the tales are arranged by basic categories such as musical tales, sparing with gods and spirits, justice, courtship, tricksters, fools, magical beings, and supernatural creatures. Each entry includes various versions of the title (including various languages), the author or origin of the story, a brief synopsis (with variations), and a collection of connector terms that are found within different stories (e.g. anger, bird, captivity, etc.). At the end are a geographical lexicon of story sources, a separate source listing for stories told in creole or patois dialects, a glossary and list of characters, an extensive bibliography, and indexes of story title and subjects. This collection serves as a place to begin a more advanced study of a culture that is often neglected or misunderstood.—**Martha Lawler**

630.   **The Sorcerer's Apprentice: An Anthology of Magical Tales.** Jack Zipes, ed. Illustrated by Natalie Frank. Princeton, N.J., Princeton University Press, 2017. 404p. illus. index. $35.00. ISBN 13: 978-0-691-17265-1.

Rather than focusing on one story, this collection of essays, short stories, and folk tales (from the earliest centuries through the nineteenth & twentieth centuries) offers several versions of the basic tale of an apprentice and his master, examining such topics as child exploitation and the master/slave dynamic. An extensive preface outlines the purpose and intent of the collection, including a discussion of the ideas of subjugation, cruelty, and triumph over evil intentions, all of which are concepts that are as apparent and relevant today as they have been throughout history. The introduction goes into more depth about the definition of magic and the interpretation, presentation, and application of the idea of magic in stories such as the Sorcerer's Apprentice and the Harry Potter series. The main part of the collection includes humiliated apprentice tales (in which the apprentice remains subjugated to the master's will), rebellious apprentice tales (the majority include tales in which the apprentice fights back and often wins against the master), and Krabat tales (which are a particular type of tale from a region in Central Europe). Biographies of the authors, editors, collectors, and translators; a filmography and a selective, chronological listing of variations of the basic tale; an extensive bibliography; and an index complete the collection. Eerie, bizarre black-and-white illustrations serve to enhance the mysterious and ethereal nature of the main topic. Although the examples included in this collection tend to be a bit repetitious, they serve to highlight the main purpose of examining the concept of the abuse and transference of power.—**Martha Lawler**

Popular Culture

Dictionaries and Encyclopedias

631.   Danesi, Marcel. **The Concise Dictionary of Popular Culture.** Lanham, Md., Rowman & Littlefield, 2017. 308p. illus. index. $90.00; $89.99 (e-book). ISBN 13: 978-1-4422-5311-7; 978-1-4422-5312-4 (e-book).

The slimness of this volume most definitely reflects the "concise" in the title. Strangely, the book begins with a listing of the entries in the book, an odd way to start off a dictionary of any sort. However, this list of entries provides a quick overview of the title's contents which range from concepts/genres—such as "A movie" and "indie"—to people like Madonna and the Lumière brothers to characters like James Bond and products like Coca Cola. This list demonstrates the broad range of things encompassed by the notion of popular culture. The book also provides a thematic arrangement of contents which allows the user to jump quickly to genres, theories/critics, music, fads, and other topics. There are some photographs included which are usually of musicians, actors, characters, icons, and the occasional concept, such as advertising. The entries are unsurprisingly brief and include *see also* cross-referencing. There are several appendixes which seem like little more than listings of the contents based on additional thematic arrangements such as superheroes, best-selling books, and cartoon characters. Several brief timelines/chronologies of different types are included in this section such as a radio timeline, a television timeline, and the Internet timeline. This is followed by the index.

This book is concise, just as the title suggests. However, it seems rather thin on the ground in terms of actual content and seems intent on reflecting the current Internet media taste for lists. It does not necessarily provide any information that could not easily be found on the Internet itself and in reputable sources no less. It is not clear what the author hoped to accomplish by creating such a volume in the electronic age, and given pop culture's increasing interconnectedness with the Internet, it seems strange that a print volume of this kind would be published. The e-book seems more appropriate though truly no more affordable than its print counterpart.

As a quick-reference resource, *The Concise Dictionary of Popular Culture* delivers. As a competitive, ground-breaking contribution to the discipline of popular culture, it does not accomplish much of anything. Public libraries looking to add to their quick-reference collections would benefit from such a title, and that is the venue for which this title would be recommended.—**Megan W. Lowe**

Handbooks and Yearbooks

632.   Giordano, Ralph G. **Pop Goes the Decade: The Fifties.** Santa Barbara, Calif., Greenwood Press/ABC-CLIO, 2017. 361p. illus. index. $89.00. ISBN 13: 978-1-4408-3666-4; 978-1-4408-3667-1 (e-book).

Pop Goes the Decade: The Fifties by Ralph Giordano gives its readers an overview of life and times in the 1950s and provides context for historical research of the time. This robust yet accessible collection includes a table of contents, timeline, background and introduction, bibliography, and index. Each chapter focuses on a specific topic and its status during the decade of the fifties. Entries include topics like film, literature, sports, and controversies. Chapters are then broken down into sections and focus on subjects like Be-Bop Jazz, Howdy Doody, Walt Disney, the TV Children's Market, and Building a Thermonuclear Arsenal. A shortened bibliography for further reading is included at the end of each section. The background and introduction gives a good overview of historical relevance and subject matter that the book encompasses. It provides context for the chapters and prepares researchers for study of the decade. The timeline is short but inclusive and includes major events, important dates, and population growth for the decade. The full bibliography is sound and broken down by type of resource. Relevant charts, figures, and photographs are included in the book and convey necessary information with succinct captions. Concise, informative, and inclusive, *Pop Goes the Decade: The Fifties* would be an appropriate addition to any library collection and particularly useful for undergraduate students doing historical research.—**Jessica Crossfield McIntosh**

633.   Hammond, Andrew. **Pop Culture in North Africa and the Middle East.** Santa Barbara, Calif., ABC-CLIO, 2017. 319p. illus. index. (Entertainment and Society around the World). $97.00. ISBN 13: 978-1-4408-3383-0; 978-1-4408-3384-7 (e-book).

Pop culture is shaped by several factors including culture, political movements, economic stature, and religion. This single volume work tries to define pop culture through Arab eyes and present it in a way that the general reader can understand it. The Arab World has witnessed the Arab Spring (a movement that has tried to incorporate democratic ideals in Arab culture) as well as the jihadist movement (that has tried to incorporate fundamentalist strands in contemporary culture). Arab pop culture reflects both, and other influences. Not surprisingly, a large part of the material references Egypt or Saudi Arabia and its immediate neighbors.

A long introduction tries to define how Arabs see their culture, and some of the issues of defining what makes an Arab, and what makes pop culture within an Arab context. The substantive chapters cover the gambit of media used to give pop culture its form. These include the traditional forms of print media, music, and television. It also includes other forms of cultural expression such as sports and fashion. Included also are other more contemporary forms such as the Internet and social media and video games.

Each chapter is fairly lengthy (about thirty pages), but chapters are not meant to be read in their entirety (although highly interested readers may read entire chapters). Each chapter starts with an introduction that serves to frame the media within an Arab and contemporary context. Following the introduction are about a dozen subheadings, each with a specific focus on the topic. While the topic list is not complete, it does cover the main areas with sufficient depth for a more-than-causal understanding. Appendixes include a timeline from Napoleon's invasion of Egypt (in 1798) to 2016, and a selected "Top Ten" list.

A unique feature of this book is that it does try to present pop culture as Arabs see it, rather than as Westerners see it. However given strong Western influence it is difficult to decouple a Western perspective from an Arab one when Western influences are among those shaping that aspect of pop culture. Given this work's depth and coverage, it would make a good initial reference work for undergraduates studying Arab pop culture.—**Muhammed Hassanali**

634.   Harrison, Thomas. **Pop Goes the Decade: The Eighties.** Santa Barbara, Calif., Greenwood Press/ABC-CLIO, 2017. 283p. illus. index. $89.00. ISBN 13: 978-1-4408-3666-4; 978-1-4408-3667-1 (e-book).

This set of essays authored by a professor at the University of Central Florida examines 1980s popular culture in the United States, through the lenses of the arts, media, technology, and sports. Each essay describes both significant individuals and their particular impacts on the field; the essay on technology describes the main inventions and advances. Essays include black-and-white pictures that complement the text and end with a list of further readings. Most of these books are mainstream and easily acquired, but some scholarly materials are also listed. Many of the topics provide background into some of today's hottest topics, including the rise of cable news channels and the birth of the mobile phone and personal computers. The essays are in clear and readable language that is accessible to a wide variety of learners. The final essays cover major cultural controversies of the decade, including those in art, health, business, and religion, and profile significant cultural figures.

There are a few issues with the references, however. In the visual arts chapter, for example, Robert Mapplethorpe's book has the title and publisher information incorrectly listed in the chapter's further reading list (it is not listed in the book's bibliography), and an item cited as being written by "Redden and Stadler" in 1987 is not listed in either. This may present some challenges for researchers interested in digging deeper into quotations in hopes of learning more on the topic.

A timeline at the beginning as well as the bibliography and index at the end complete the volume. Recommended for high school and public libraries.—**Amanda Izenstark**

635. **Pop Culture Universe. http://pop.greenwood.com/.** [Website] Santa Barbara, Calif., ABC-CLIO, 2017. Price negotiated by site. Date reviewed: 2017.

This is an excellent database. The home page offers access to separate sections about each decade from the 1900s to the 2000s, an Explore the Library feature, a Tools for Students section (Getting Started, Research Tips, Research Lists, and Ask the Cybrarian), and a News You Can Use feature. Each decade section has subheadings that include Explore, Analyze, Research, and Library sections. Explore contains subheadings for the Arts, Sports & Recreation, Everyday Life, and Communications, each containing links to articles about various related topics. The Analyze section has topics that can be explored in depth, which include a key question, background essay, points of view/ pros & cons/ defining moments, and an assignment for students related to the topic. The Research section contains links to reference articles, biographies, timelines, a glossary, and various types of primary sources related to the decade listed by type. Each primary source contains a detailed description, citation, and can be closely analyzed. The Library section contains additional related resources. The site works well on tablets and computers. Helpful features include save, email, cite, translate, article read-aloud, and site search. Students will find this visually appealing resource to be easy to use and understand, while teachers will value the comprehensiveness and the ability to create class assignments using the Research Lists feature. Highly recommended.—**Darshell Silva**

636. Sheumaker, Helen. **Artifacts from Modern America.** Santa Barbara, Calif., Greenwood Press/ABC-CLIO, 2018. 348p. (Daily Life through Artifacts series). $100.00. ISBN 13: 978-1-4408-4682-3; 978-1-4408-4683-0 (e-book).

Okay, this book makes me feel old, as half of the objects described I know about or grew up with. It is part of the Daily Life through Artifacts series. The forty-eight objects described are organized into ten sections; the sections are listed alphabetically although the objects under the sections are not. The sections are: Communications; Cooking, Food, and Drink; Entertainment; Grooming, Clothing, and Accessories; Health and Medicine; Household Items; Political and Civic Life; Religion; Tools and Weapons; and Transportation. Some of the objects described include Bob's Big Boy, Coffee Percolator, Atari 2600 Video Console and Packaging, Schick Electric Razor, Hoover Vacuum Cleaner, First Fordson Tractor, and Pullman Railroad Car, to name just a few. Each entry includes an introduction to the object, a detailed description, its significance, and a short reference section. For those libraries and librarians that want to date themselves (given that most of these objects were in use in the last fifty years), this book would probably generate a few laughs from today's university students.—**Bradford Lee Eden**

637. Tzvetkova, Juliana. **Pop Culture in Europe.** Santa Barbara, Calif., ABC-CLIO, 2017. 414p. illus. index. (Entertainment and Society around the World). $97.00. ISBN 13: 978-1-4408-4465-2; 978-1-4408-4466-9 (e-book).

Tracing the advent and history of pop culture is a monumental task in an era when the term pop—or popular—culture is in everyday use, and can refer to anything from music to clothing to technology. Indeed, a full examination of what constitutes "pop culture" would likely fill several thick volumes. As such, I was worried about the size of *Pop Culture in Europe* by Juliana Tzvetkova. Considering Europe's position as a cultural powerhouse, confining Europe's contributions to pop culture in a single volume seems risky, and perhaps a bit too minimalist. However, in her preface, Tzvetkova is quick to acknowledge this, and explains that this encyclopedia is "designed to offer a brief introduction to the most important developments of twentieth-century popular culture in the European continent" (p. xi). This reference is meant to provide a general overview of Europe's major trends in pop culture as a whole, rather than an in-depth examination of each cultural area. To this end, the book provides informative articles and extra resources for future research; most entries are written by Tzvetkova, but contributions by a varied group of scholars are included.

The introduction provides an examination of the rise of popular culture, as well as an explanation of the term as used in various eras of history. There is a chronology that charts important points in European cultural history, starting in 1804 and ending at 2016. The information in the book is organized into chapters focusing on a particular area of pop culture—*see* Video Games or Fashion and Couture—complete with chapter introductions that give the reader a historical and cultural overview of that particular area. Entries are sorted into the relevant chapters and organized alphabetically, finished with a short bibliography of suggested readings. Scattered throughout the book are photographs, as well as small features on various specifics deemed important (*see* Rowan Atkinson as a feature underneath the Comedy section in the BBC Best entry).

While not meant for in-depth research, *Pop Culture in Europe* is an excellent reference tool for those who wish to gain an overview of Europe's pop culture landmarks and trends.—**Mary Rebecca Yantis**

638.   **Vine Archive. https://vine.co.** [Website] Free. Date reviewed: 2018.

Even though it was only here for four years, the Vine social media phenomenon engaged millions with its short, looping videos. This archive creatively organizes the Vine video collection, allowing distraught teens and others the ability to once again fall down the rabbit hole of contemporary popular culture. Site users can explore the archive in a number of ways from the homepage. Those in-the-know can Search for a Profile of a particular "viner" by typing in their Vine username. Alternatively, users can access Vine highlights by selecting one of four tabs, each indicating a year in which Vine operated. Users can also select a thematic category under Channel Highlights, including Animals, Art, Comedy, Edits, Music & Dance, Sports, and Weird. Editors' Picks offers individually curated video groupings. Playlists work off a particularly popular (i.e., viral) Vine which inspired further video creations of similar theme. The archive offers additional curated Vine categories as well, including "Most Revined," "Most Looped Magic," "Most Followed Viner," "Most Revined Collab," and more. While it is easy to navigate around these categories, it may be helpful for site users to familiarize themselves with the specialized language of the medium. For example, a "collab" refers to one Vine created by two "Viners." A "remix" is a Vine that is reused creatively in another Vine, and so on. Under these categories, Vines can be viewed in several modes: grid, timeline (users scroll downward) or tv, which fills the screen and allows an autoplay option. Each Vine is accompanied by username, date, number of "loops," and other identification information such as title or tags. Viewers can also note the number of "likes" and "revines." The Vine Archive offers a snapshot of an era that not only captures the pop culture trends of the time, but examines the way people create and tell stories.—**ARBA Staff Reviewer**

27 Performing Arts

General Works

Biography

639.   Lentz, Harris M., III. **Obituaries in the Performing Arts, 2016.** Jefferson, N.C., McFarland, 2017. 440p. illus. $49.95pa. ISBN 13: 978-1-4766-7031-7; 978-1-4766-2912-4 (e-book).

This yearly serial offers a one-stop reference source of all deaths and obituaries for individuals in the performing arts. The 2016 edition covers big names such as Carrie Fisher, Prince, Muhammad Ali, and Gene Wilder, to name but a few. Celebrities, actors, performers, behind-the-scenes people, musicians, cult film stars, television stars, cartoonists, and reality television personalities, as well as those associated with and/or related to important celebrities are all included. Each obituary includes a black-and-white photograph of the personality, a career description, and a note on the person's importance to the performing arts, along with birth and death dates and place of death. A short reference bibliography of books and Internet resources is included. As long as one knows which year a performing arts person died, an obituary can be found within this series. Most academic libraries would find this book important enough to include in their collection.—**Bradford Lee Eden**

Directories

640.   **The Grey House Performing Arts Directory 2017/18.** Amenia, N.Y., Grey House Publishing, 2017. 1188p. index. $195.00pa. ISBN 13: 978-1-61925-939-3.

This latest edition of *The Grey House Performing Arts Directory* (see ARBA 2015, entry 778) is a reference guide to 9,453 performing arts organizations in America. Directory listings are arranged by five performance categories: Dance, Instrumental Music, Vocal Music, Theatre, and Series & Festivals; within each of these categories the listings are subdivided by state and city. There are additional listings by Facilities (by state) and Information Resources, including Associations, Newsletters, Magazines and Journals, Trade Shows, Directories and Databases, and Industry Web Sites. Each entry includes name, address, phone, fax, email, website, officers, date founded, specialized field, budget status (e.g., professional, nonprofit), staff, mission, where group performs, and organization type. In entries for theaters, seating capacities are included. The resource includes indexes by Entry Name, Executive Name, Facilities, Specialized Field, Geographic location, and Information Resources. Through this very thorough resource, researchers can locate information ranging from listings of magazines and journals for the performing arts, to opera companies in California, Broadway theaters, and music festivals in Pennsylvania. Entries are found for larger, famous institutions such as the Metropolitan Opera and the New York Philharmonic as well as local organizations such as the Choral Arts Society of New Jersey, the Illusion Theater in Minneapolis, and the Lucille Ball Little Theatre of Jamestown in New York. *The Grey House Performing Arts Directory* is highly recommended for public, academic, and special libraries. It not only serves as a reference to those locating information about specific organizations, but as a first stop for researchers in the arts needing to locate specific resources such as websites and journals. This should prove to be of great help to students and faculty of performing arts, performers, and those looking for career opportunities.—**Lucy Heckman**

Film, Television, and Video

Biography

641.   Aaker, Everett. **Television Western Players, 1960-1975: A Biographical Dictionary.** Jefferson, N.C., McFarland, 2017. 478p. index. $49.95pa. ISBN 13: 978-1-4766-6250-3; 978-1-4766-2856-1 (e-book).

This comprehensive title provides information on about a thousand actors and actresses in regular roles on Western series on American television from 1960 through 1975. Arranged alphabetically, each entry contains birth and death dates, family information, an overview of the career, and the sources used for the entry. Occasional black-and-white photographs are also included. The index contains entries for people and television program names, while the appendix lists 89 television series, including the dates the program ran on television, the studio, the number of episodes, whether it was color or black and white, the length of each episode, the star or stars, a brief synopsis of the story, and the day and time the program was broadcast. Researchers and fans of Western television series will find the content of interest.—**Denise A. Garofalo**

642.   **Critical Insights Film: Alfred Hitchcock.** Douglas A. Cunningham, ed. Hackensack, N.J., Salem Press, 2017. 306p. illus. index. $105.00. ISBN 13: 978-1-68217-110-3; 978-1-68217-111-0 (e-book).

This essay collection examines the Master of Suspense's extensive body of work and his legacy as a filmmaker. Written primarily by academicians, the reference begins with a brief biography of Alfred Hitchcock. He saw firsthand the history of film as it happened, from the first introduction of movies, just four years before his birth in 1899, to the early days of his career in silent films and all the way up to *The Family Plot* in 1976—the last of his 60 films. In the essays, we discover the historical and biographical background that shaped Hitchcock's genius; how the critical reception of his films varied over the course of his career; his conflicting attitudes to women; in-depth analysis of this gifted director's iconic themes, images, and filming techniques with specific references from many of his movies; and the profound and enduring influence he still exerts on the art today. An example of one of Hitchcock's thematic "trademarks" is his use of birds. Often in his movies they are a symbol of malevolent force and agents of chaos. One essayist attributes Hitchcock's fascination with birds to his high regard for the artist Paul Klee. Both Klee, who often painted birds, and Hitchcock were modernists and symbolists, emphasizing form and visual effects over content. Melanie's ordeal in *The Birds* bears a striking resemblance to Klee's painting, *A Young Lady's Adventure*—interestingly Klee's young lady is also a blonde. As an example of his impact on the industry, Hitchcock's 1940 movie, *Rebecca,* marked the end of the classic Hollywood era of producer as creative force and established the director as the creative driver of a film. Features include a chronology of Hitchcock's life and a filmography of his oeuvre. This reference provides an accessible look into the expanse of contemporary Hitchcock scholarship and explains why we continue to watch—and rewatch—his films decades after their initial release.—**Adrienne Antink**

643.   Erickson, Hal. **Any Resemblance to Actual Persons: The Real People Behind 400+ Fictional Movie Characters.** Jefferson, N.C., McFarland, 2017. 403p. illus. index. $49.95pa. ISBN 13: 978-1-4766-6605-1; 978-1-4766-2930-8 (e-book).

This book uniquely ties real-life people to the films that were made about them. There are 220 entries covering almost 400 individuals. There are also 80 shorter entries that are like thumbnail sketches, which the author has included for personal reasons. All of the films discussed are theatrical releases, and only English-language films are included. Entries are listed alphabetically by the "real" people fictionalized in the film, not by the character name. The most significant film in which the person is fictionalized appears first, followed by other films if there are any. Production company and release date are in parenthesis and bold italics. Various cross-references are in bold and/or italics. To give an example, Randall "Duke" Cunningham, one of the most highly decorated Navy pilots of the Vietnam War, was the inspiration for Tom Cruise's character Pete "Maverick" Mitchell in the movie *Top Gun.* The author provides extensive biographical material on Cunningham, all the way down to his 2005 charges on corruption as a California congressman. For those interested in linking "real" persons to their film counterparts, this book is for you!—**Bradford Lee Eden**

644.   Liebman, Roy. **Broadway Actors in Films, 1894-2015.** Jefferson, N.C., McFarland, 2017. 308p. index. $49.95pa. ISBN 13: 978-0-7864-7685-5; 978-1-4766-2615-4 (e-book).

Broadway Actors in Films contains biographies of 300 actors who, with a few exceptions, were first Broadway players who moved from the theater to the cinema. It chronicles the few who made films in the 1890s to those still active in theater and film. Each entry contains name, place of birth, date of birth and, where applicable, date of death, with a biography, a list of selected stage highlights, and a filmography. Among actors and actresses included are: Julie Andrews, Judith Anderson, Tallulah Bankhead, John Barrymore, James Cagney, Bette Davis, Ossie Davis, Jeanette MacDonald, the Marx Brothers, Katharine Cornell, Helen Hayes, Al Jolson, James Earl Jones, Henry Fonda, John Garfield, Montgomery Clift, George M. Cohan, Spencer Tracy, Humphrey Bogart, and Marlon Brando. Appendixes include "More About the Performers" with information about the actors who have won the Oscar, Tony, Emmy, and Grammy; those who are on postage stamps; those who have had songs written about them; and those who have played presidents, among other facts. An index of titles of shows and films is provided. The bibliography lists additional biographies about the actors and actresses. Some autobiographies are included in the list. For future editions, I would recommend including more autobiographies among which are *We Barrymores* by Lionel Barrymore; *The Lonely Life,* by Bette Davis; *Steps in Time* by Fred Astaire; and *Me: Stories of My Life* by Katharine Hepburn. *Broadway Actors in Films* is a very informative biographical source of actors and actresses who moved from Broadway to film and some who made it big in Hollywood. It belongs in public, academic, and research libraries and is an excellent starting point for research. Highly Recommended.—**Lucy Heckman**

Dictionaries and Encyclopedias

645.   Aveyard, Karina, Albert Moran, and Errol Vieth. **Historical Dictionary of Australian and New Zealand Cinema.** 2d ed. Lanham, Md., Rowman & Littlefield, 2018. 404p. illus. $100.00; $95.00 (e-book). ISBN 13: 978-1-5381-1126-0; 978-1-5381-1127- (e-book).

This book, in its second edition and part of the Historical Dictionaries of Literature and the Arts series, focuses on cinema and films produced, directed, and/or filmed in the countries of Australia or New Zealand. Australian entries take up about 75 percent of the book, while New Zealand takes up around 25 percent of the content. Each country begins with a chronology of the cinema followed by an introduction/history of cinema in that country. Essays focus on actors, directors, films, companies, and locations, with cross-references in bold and *see also* references in capitals after the essay. As is common with this series, an extensive bibliography related to the topic for each country is provided. For instance, in the New Zealand section, there are essays related to the hugely successful films *The Hobbit* and *The Lord of the Rings,* which brought international and tourist attention to New Zealand almost immediately after their releases. An interesting and focused volume for public and academic libraries.—**Bradford Lee Eden**

646.   Green, Paul. **Encyclopedia of Weird War Stories: Supernatural and Science Fiction Elements in Novels, Pulps, Comics, Film, Television, Games, and Other Media.** Jefferson, N.C., McFarland, 2017. 232p. illus. index. $39.95pa. ISBN 13: 978-1-4766-6672-3; 978-1-4766-2874-5 (e-book).

This encyclopedia focuses on war stories that feature elements of fantasy, horror, or the supernatural. Not included are alternate histories, such as the show *The Man in the High Castle,* since they pose the "what if" question rather than incorporating fantastical aspects. This is similar to the approach utilized by Paul Green in his earlier work *Encyclopedia of Weird Westerns: Supernatural and Science Fiction Elements in Novels, Pulps, Comics, Films, Television and Games* (see ARBA 2010, entry 975).

The entries in the encyclopedia are alphabetically arranged and document novels, pulps, comics, film, television, games, and other media. Due to the variety of source material, the entries vary greatly in the information included. For films, television shows, and the like, the entries include the main cast and a synopsis. The date of release, game platforms, and description are provided for video games. Entries for print media include date of publication, name of author and publisher, and overview of the plot. Interspersed among the entries are black-and-white photographs and illustrations. The appendix includes the respective stories organized by medium. The work concludes with a short bibliography and index. Recommended for public libraries.—**John R. Burch Jr.**

647.   Hutchings, Peter. **Historical Dictionary of Horror Cinema.** 2d ed. Lanham, Md., Rowman & Littlefield, 2018. 408p. (Historical Dictionaries of Literature and the Arts). $100.00; $95.00 (e-book). ISBN 13: 978-1-5381-0243-5; 978-1-5381-0244-2 (e-book).

Part of the Historical Dictionaries of Literature and the Arts, this book focuses on the history of horror cinema. This second edition brings the genre up to date since the 2008 edition by providing new entries on horror film cycles such as *Resident Evil, Saw,* and *Final Destination,* as well as on key creative personnel such as directors and producers. Previous entries have also been expanded or updated, and historically important films not included due to space in the first edition are now available. A chronology of horror and horror films from 1764 to 2017 is provided, followed by a short introduction which explains the format of the dictionary. Entries are bolded, as are words and individuals which point to other entries. *See also* references are capitalized. Two appendixes list horror films and Oscar awards, and winners of the Saturn Award (from the Academy of Science Fiction, Fantasy, and Horror Films) from 1972 to 2015. As is typical with this series, an extensive bibliography follows the dictionary.—**Bradford Lee Eden**

648.   Kinnard, Roy, and Tony Crnkovich. **Italian Sword and Sandal Films, 1908-1990.** Jefferson, N.C., McFarland, 2017. 250p. illus. index. $39.95pa. ISBN 13: 978-1-4766-6291-6; 978-1-4766-2704-5 (e-book).

This book is a compendium of the "peplum" genre in the Italian film industry from 1958 to 1965, also known as "sword and sandal." "Peplum" refers to the Greek/Roman-style tunic worn by the heroes of the films, since the drama was often placed into these time periods. The large-scale success of huge Hollywood movies like *The Ten Commandments* and *Spartacus* compelled the Italian film industry to produce a large number of spinoffs and secondary plots that featured strongmen, supermen, and superheroes along with scantily clad females. These movies were produced at a fraction of the cost of Hollywood movies, yet still starred the big-name actors with obvious vocal dubbing. The "peplum" genre was replaced in the 1960s by Hollywood spaghetti westerns and Eurospy films. "Peplum" had a resurgence in the 1980s due to the popularity of Arnold Schwarzenegger and his Conan the Barbarian movies. The encyclopedia is divided into three sections: the silent era of films, the sound era, and the 1980s revival. Each section has films listed alphabetically, with each entry having both the Italian and English title, film company, and date of release, followed by a listing of credits, cast/role, and comments/plot. Black-and-white photos are in abundance, along with interesting information on various stars such as Orson Welles, Sophia Loren, and Jack Palance, to name but a few.—**Bradford Lee Eden**

649.   Lobrutto, Vincent. **TV in the USA: A History of Icons, Idols, and Ideas.** Santa Barbara, Calif., Greenwood Press/ABC-CLIO, 2018. 3v. illus. index. $325.00/set. ISBN 13: 978-1-4408-2972-7; 978-1-4408-2973-4 (e-book).

The purpose of *TV in the USA* is "to inform students, teachers, scholars, and other interested readers about the history and scope of American television from its inception into the 21st century." The encyclopedia is comprised of three volumes that cover the 1950s-present. Each volume includes an introductory essay. The essay in volume 1, "Introduction: The Emergence of Television" discusses the origins of television, key players in its founding, the manufacture of the first television sets, and early television stars such as Lucille Ball, Jack Benny, Red Skelton, Milton Berle, and Arthur Godfrey. Volume 2 contains "Introduction: The Evolution of Television from Color to Satellite Broadcasts" and discusses the introduction of remote control, the videocassette, cable television, and controversial shows among which were *All in the Family* and ground breaking miniseries like *Roots*. Volume 3 features "Introduction: The Rise of Technology and Internet Television" and covers such topics as digital satellite dishes, the DVD, Pay per View; High Definition television, and shows including *The Sopranos, Game of Thrones,* and *Mad Men.* Entries in the encyclopedia are arranged alphabetically and among categories are television networks, iconic television stars, and historic events (e.g., Watergate) covered on television. Cross-references are provided, as well as a list of further resources or bibliographic references. The coverage of television shows is not totally complete (i.e., hit shows such as *Dallas, Knots Landing, Rhoda,* and *The Young and the Restless* are not included). Among the shows included are *Gilligan's Island, Jeopardy, American Bandstand, Bonanza, Batman, I Love Lucy, the Jack Benny Program, 60 Minutes, Twin Peaks, Frasier, Cheers, Sesame Street, The Fugitive, Perry Mason, Sex and the City, M*A*S*H, The Mary Tyler Moore Show, Seinfeld, The Twilight Zone,* and *Star Trek.* Biographical entries are provided for such personalities as Lucille Ball, Norman Learn, Barbara Walters, Sid Caesar, Jackie Gleason, Milton Berle, Rod Serling, and Walter Cronkite. In addition to the entries, the title includes a series of essays about various television themes and shows. Among these are "The Greening of the Late Night Talk Show," "From Outer Body to Inner Mind: The Evolution of the Medical Drama," "The Ethics and Frenzy of Game Shows during the 1950s and 1960s," "Reality and Artifice in 1950s and 1960s Soap Operas," and "Zombies and Vampires Invade Television in the 21st Century." Each volume includes a glossary of terms, the index for all three volumes, and a list of shows grouped by category. Highly recommended resource for public and academic libraries. For anybody interested in television and its history and for students researching television history for media courses.—**Lucy Heckman**

650. Mayer, Geoff. **Encyclopedia of American Film Serials.** Jefferson, N.C., McFarland, 2017. 308p. illus. index. $75.00pa. ISBN 13: 978-0-7864-7762-3; 978-1-4766-2719-9 (e-book).

According to the author Geoff Mayer, the film serial is "a coherent, aesthetic system that embraces many sub-genres, categories and types of stories"; these include westerns, reporters, superheroes, spacemen, jungle princesses, soldiers, and spies. Children and their parents would watch cliffhangers and return the following week to see how the crisis or imminent danger was resolved. Serials are still popular with viewers through movie channels and DVDs. Included in this encyclopedia are entries for every Republic Studio serial (66 total) and "representative selections from other studios." Mayer describes the history of the serial and key serials and actors and actresses. Entries in the encyclopedia are names of serials, major actors and actresses, directors, and studios such as Mascot pictures and Universal Studio and the aforementioned Republic. Legendary serials, their plots, and their production, are described (some with illustrations of posters and stills); among these are: *Flash Gordon, Flash Gordon's Trip to Mars, Buck Rogers, Zorro, Batman,*

Superman, Dick Tracy, The Lone Ranger, The Green Hornet, and *The Perils of Pauline.* Plots are described and biographies are also featured for iconic serial stars among which are: Larry "Buster" Crabbe (*Flash Gordon* and *Buck Rogers*); Kirk Alyn (*Superman*); Charles Middleton (*Ming the Merciless*); Ray "Crash" Corrigan; Clayton Moore (*The Lone Ranger*); Noel Neill (Lois Lane); Tom Mix; Jean Rogers (Dale Arden); John Wayne; Pearl White (*The Perils of Pauline*); and Dick Purcell (*Captain America*).

The Encyclopedia of American Film Serials is a treasure trove of information and trivia about film serials and their performers, directors, and producers. It is recommended to just about anybody interested in these films, to academic libraries supporting a film history and/or popular culture curriculum, and to public libraries. Highly recommended.—**Lucy Heckman**

651.   Pohle, Robert W., Jr., Douglas C. Hart, and Rita Pohle Baldwin. **The Christopher Lee Film Encyclopedia.** Lanham, Md., Rowman & Littlefield, 2017. 378p. illus. index. $95.00; $90.00 (e-book). ISBN 13: 978-0-8108-9269-9; 978-0-8108-9270-5 (e-book).

In the film industry, Sir Christopher Lee was a rarity among his peers. Widely considered to be one of the most versatile and prolific actors of all time, Lee's career spanned nearly seven decades, and is comprised of various film roles, spoken in a variety of languages and viewed by audiences from around the globe. Despite Lee's reputation and typecast as a master of suspense and fantasy films, his roles encompassed a plethora of characters that reflect all manner of disposition and psyche. Accordingly, through sheer talent and necessary flexibility, the actor ostensibly re-created entire genres through his roles, without the benefit of the multimillion-dollar production budgets and luminous special effects that ensconce today's filmmaking.

The 2017 encyclopedia is an updated version of a 1983 catalog of Lee's movies, researched and written by the same authors, with an additional author for this latest edition. Of particular note is Lee's involvement in providing commentary in both this and the earlier version; these are the only encyclopedias of Lee's films that garnered his formal approval. The current encyclopedia contains all of Lee's films, with each entry providing typical information (e.g., director, cast) and synopses, reviews, notes, and comments by Lee. Entries are arranged alphabetically, ranging in detail from a single page to two pages. Front matter includes short forwards by actors Tim Burton and Johnny Depp; Douglas Fairbanks, Jr.; and by Lee himself; and acknowledgements and an introduction by the authors. Rounding out the encyclopedia is an appendix of ephemera describing Lee's television appearances and voice work; alternate and foreign language film titles; a bibliography and index; and a smattering of black-and-white photos. The authors purposely excluded Lee's films that have received extensive coverage elsewhere so as to ensure enough space for his lesser-known films.

The encyclopedia presents a comprehensive record of Lee's films in such a way that it functions somewhat loosely as a primary source. To wit, many entries include Lee's recollections about a particular film. While some commentary is more detailed than other, it nevertheless lends an unexpected but decidedly amicable tone to the entries in which the commentary appears. On that last note, the authors' inclusion of personal forwards from actors who worked with Lee, and from Lee himself, renders the encyclopedia more conversational than is the usual case with encyclopedic sources. Entries typically are one to one-and-a-half pages each, but do give enough information as to be all-inclusive. Finally, the detailed and thoughtfully written introduction by the authors, and their noticeable inclusion of a rationale for updating their original book of the same content, offer significant insight into why the encyclopedia is necessary.—**Sheri Edwards**

652.   Terrace, Vincent. **Encyclopedia of Television Shows: A Comprehensive Supplement, 2011-2016.** Jefferson, N.C., McFarland, 2018. 222p. index. $75.00pa. ISBN 13: 978-1-4766-7138-3; 978-1-4766-3094-6 (e-book).

As a mass medium that has been iconic to modern American life for more than a half-century, television continues to adapt itself to audience demands and to advances in technological capabilities. While television programming typically reflects the social mores and cultural interests of adults and children alike, shows increasingly have become more nuanced as those mores and interests evolve and diversify. So, too, has accessibility to television shows flourished, with Web-based programming providing yet another avenue for audiences to be both entertained and informed. What has remained constant, however, is written, documented evidence of our national collection of television shows, no matter how broadcasted, and their singular, circumstantial characteristics.

This supplement updates the second edition of *Encyclopedia of Television Shows, 1925-2010* (see ARBA 2012, entry 1080). Entries in this edition span the years 2011 to 2016. All 1,612 entries are alphabetized by title of television show, with each entry accompanied by a corresponding cardinal number. Descriptions within each entry include casts and characters and years of broadcast, as well as story lines and respective genres. Also included with each entry is its show's broadcast network; nearly sixty are represented, ranging from classic broadcast networks (NBC) to current cable channels (OWN) or those that are now defunct (FearNet), and Internet streaming channels (Netflix). The supplement also contains an appendix that lists television shows by title according to respective decades, beginning in the 1940s and continuing through 2010, in keeping with the content of the encyclopedia. Of note is a performer index, populated with both commonly known and obscure names of actors, actresses, voice artists, hosts, mentors, and other featured performers, although, as pointed out on the first page of the index, the numbers beside each name are entry numbers, and not page numbers.

The supplement is a concise, user-friendly guide that emphasizes what likely is the information most television audiences care about concerning a television show. While some descriptions of shows are much more detailed than others, and without explanation, this difference could be a natural effect of the storied nature of fictional programming versus the straightforward nature of reality-based shows. On that note, the presence of shows accessible by digital platforms (e.g., Internet streaming) inadvertently lends insight into the ways in which television as a medium is taking shape in the Information Age. Meanwhile, the performer index is a convenient accessory, as is its organization (alphabetized listings with cognate entry numbers), and lends a distinct usefulness to the supplement, given that audiences are likely most interested in cast names than in, say, genre or network. In short, the supplement is as it should be: comprehensive, inclusive, and complementary.—**Sheri Edwards**

Filmography

653.   Budnik, Daniel R. **'80s Action Movies on the Cheap: 284 Low Budget, High Impact Pictures.** Jefferson, N.C., McFarland, 2017. 252p. illus. index. $45.00pa. ISBN

13: 978-0-7864-9741-6'; 978-1-4766-8687-1 (e-book).

This book clearly reflects the author's fascination with action films, a genre that came into its own in about 1980. He introduces the reader to many films they may not be familiar with, in contrast to the major hits of the decade, some of which were also action films: *Raiders of the Lost Ark, Terms of Endearment, Top Gun,* and *Rain Man.* Many subgenres are presented: ninja movies, cop movies, war movies, and fantasy movies, among others. Entries usually run less than a page; cast and crew are listed, and some entries include a poster of the movie. The language is informal and easy to read; sometimes the author will point out the shortcomings of a film—for instance, "There are also too many characters" or "fight scenes that range from good to jaw-droppingly silly." The goal of this work seems to be making film lovers aware of enjoyable, but less-well-known movies. There is clearly not sophisticated analysis intended. Public libraries with "film buffs" among their clientele, and possibly colleges with film departments, will want to consider this volume.—**Mark Schumacher**

654.   Sculthorpe, Derek. **Brian Donlevy, the Good Bad Guy: A Bio-Filmography.** Jefferson, N.C., McFarland, 2017. 210p. illus. index. $35.00pa. ISBN 13: 978-1-4766-6657-0; 978-1-4766-2658-1 (e-book).

From the 1930s to the 1960s, Hollywood experienced its Golden Age. As the Great Depression took hold, and as audio technology heralded new film genres, audiences sought reprieve from their troubles in movie houses across the nation, driving up ticket sales and film popularity. Financial backers took serious note and invested accordingly, bringing forth a competitive studio system that introduced new generations of actors and new roles for them to play, including supportive roles. At the outset of the Golden Age, supportive roles were considered pedestrian and inconsequential, but many actors were able to parlay their supportive roles into characterizations that made invaluable contributions to the film industry. A biography devoted to one such actor provides key documentation of that ability.

The book contains thirteen chapters, the first of which describes Donlevy's birth and childhood. All subsequent chapters chronicle Donlevy's adulthood, including his early forays into modeling, followed by his voice and acting careers, which spanned three decades, and, as the title implies, the latter of which consisted mostly of so-called "bad guy" roles. Chapters are ordered chronologically, with most written in a conversational style that combines formal description with present-tense anecdote. Similarly, each chapter alternates between Donlevy's personal and professional lives, and frequently delves into how each influenced the other. Rounding out the contents of the book is a two-page epilogue, in which the author remarks on Donlevy's ever-present self-consciousness; appendixes, comprised of a filmography and listings of theater, radio, television, and miscellaneous recordings; chapter notes; a bibliography; and an index.

According to the author, the book is the first that focuses exclusively on Donlevy's professional career as a model, voice artist, and actor. As noted, most of Donlevy's roles were as a "bad guy"; however, rather than shackle Donlevy to those roles alone, the author masterfully intertwines editorialized critiques of Donlevy's entire career with qualitative and descriptive details of his private life, producing a two-sided portrait of Donlevy that lends a welcomed depth to biographical writing. Notably absent, however, is a rationale for why the book was written or is needed; even a sentence or two to justify its presence could go a long way toward instructing readers on the importance of studying Hollywood's Golden Age as a microcosm of a unique era in U.S. history.—**Sheri Edwards**

655. Senn, Bryan. **The Werewolf Filmography.** Jefferson, N.C., McFarland, 2017. 408p. illus. index. $55.00pa. ISBN 13: 978-0-7864-7910-8; 978-1-4766-2691-8 (e-book).

Werewolf films have generally received less attention than those of other classic horror icons such as vampires, but psychometrist and horror film critic Senn gives them their due here in this well-done new guide to the genre. Covering three-hundred-plus international feature films (including direct-to-videos and made-for-tvs) dating from 1925's *Wolfblood* to the contemporary age, *Werefwolf Filmography* gives the reader the best guide available to the best and worst of lupine mayhem. Each alphabetically arranged entry includes brief cast and production information; a page or two of plot summary and critique; and a concluding and most helpful "Morphology" (what the critters look like), "Demise" (e.g., silver bullet), and "Full Moon Rating." Concluding sections on "Pseudowolves" (minimal werewolf elements) and "Other Were-Beasts" (e.g., Cat People, Hyenas) only add to the quality of the overall collection. Black-and-white photos are scattered throughout for those readers interested in comparing werewolf makeup or poster art from film to film. An excellent companion volume to Stephen Jones' hard-to-find *The Illustrated Werewolf Movie Guide* (Titan Books Ltd., 1996) and a must-have for all horror film fans and comprehensive public library film collections.—**Anthony J. Adam**

656. Solomon, Aubrey. **The Fox Film Corporation, 1915–1935: A History and Filmography.** Jefferson, N.C., McFarland, 2016. 385p. illus. index. $35.00pa. ISBN 13: 978-1-4766-6600-6; 978-0-7864-8610-6 (e-book).

Aubrey Solomon's modest volume *The Fox Film Corporation, 1915-1935: A History and Filmography* does exactly what it sets out to do according its title. In part one, the book presents the history of the Fox Film Corporation from its beginnings, helmed by William Fox, through its development, and its eventual merger with 20th Century Pictures. Solomon provides an engaging narrative that not only shows how the corporation changed over the course of its development but also discusses the careers of its many stars and actors. Solomon makes good use of images, most of them stills or lobby cards from Fox-made movies. The narrative also reveals how movie-making changed over the years, including how movie budgets grew as the economy changed and movies gained more and more popularity. Part two is a filmography of the movies made at Fox during the 1915-1935 time period. It is arranged chronologically. Each movie entry provides main credits and a brief synopsis. No pictures are included in this section which, strictly speaking, is not surprising, but it might have been nice to have a few more of the wonderful kinds of pictures Solomon used throughout part one.

Overall, this is a great title—a must-have for public libraries and academic libraries, particularly those at schools with film/media and/or history of film/media programs. Film buffs would also appreciate such a title, and the price tag is not bad for what one gets! Highly recommended.—**Megan W. Lowe**

Handbooks and Yearbooks

657. Bagnato, Dominick. **Making Your First Feature Film: Lessons I Learned the Hard Way.** Jefferson, N.C., McFarland, 2017. 2289. illus. index. $29.95pa. ISBN 13: 978-1-4766-7034-8; 978-1-4766-2949-0 (e-book).

This book provides tools for independent filmmaking in a way that attracts readership. The first- and second-person dialogue personalizes the writing style. Writing to the readers is an excellent tool that allows them to identify with the author's personal story. For example, the preface serves as a letter to his audience. The author documents personal experiences in parts that include practical production steps, scene-by-scene breakdown, and transferable lessons learned during the production and postproduction phases. Many appealing photographs appear throughout the chapters. *Making Your First Feature Film* provides essential information for anyone interested in screen production. This fascinating book may inspire future film and theater career opportunities. Every high school, community college, and university should consider adding this book to their resource collections.—**Thomas E. Baker**

658. **Books to Film: Cinematic Adaptations of Literary Works.** Barry Keith Grant, ed. Farmington Hills, Mich., Gale/Cengage Learning, 2018. 450p. illus. index. $205.00. ISBN 13: 978-1-4103-3842-6; 978-1-4103-3843-3 (e-book).

This volume, the first of an annual series on the topic, aims to provide a standard reference work for the fields of literary studies and film. Its objectives include providing important information and facts regarding a literary work and its adaptation into film; at this time, literary works with multiple film adaptations are not included. This first volume contains eighty essays, each beginning with a "Key Facts" box containing the following information: title of the literary work, year of publication, author(s), publisher, genre(s), title of film, year of release, production company, director(s), screenwriter(s), and main cast and character names. The essay then proceeds to discuss various similarities and differences between the book and the film. Each essay also contains a sidebar with a short biography of the author and concludes with five "Questions for Discussion" for pedagogical use. Some of the books/films featured include *Beowulf, Catch-22, Fahrenheit 451, I am Legend, Planet of the Apes,* and *Watchmen,* to name a few. Black-and-white photographs are interspersed throughout; a glossary and index are included. A great guide for film and literary studies. Recommended.—**Bradford Lee Eden**

659. Lenig, Stuart. **The Bizarre World of Reality Television.** Santa Barbara, Calif., Greenwood Press/ABC-CLIO, 2017. index. $89.00. ISBN 13: 978-1-4408-3854-5; 978-1-4408-3855-2 (e-book).

Television reality shows are nothing new and are likely to remain with us for some time. The definition of "reality show" in the present volume is stretched to include the familiar (e.g., *Jersey Shore*) and those that would arguably fall into categories such as game shows (*The Newlywed Game*) or talent shows (*American Idol*), but for the most part the selections are recognizable as episodic series focusing on a family (*The Osbournes*) or contest (*The Bachelor*). Overall, Lenig critiques 130 reality shows, including a handful of non-U.S. productions, with interspersed entries on personalities (e.g., Guy Fieri) and brief essays to open each of the five thematic chapters. Because of the thematic organization, readers should use the index for quick access to specific entries. The entries vary in length from one to three pages, with suggestions for further reading after each. Not every reality show is included—Gene Simmons' *Family Jewels* is absent, for instance—but apparently Lenig was seeking breadth rather than comprehensiveness. The quality of each entry varies significantly, although all are written by Lenig. Basic information such as length of run and host network is included throughout, but whereas some entries will list all participants, as with Duck Dynasty, others neglect to name even those individuals who gained some infamy, such as the *Jersey Shore* crew. The author's critiques are fairly objective, and he quotes other sources as necessary to underscore his arguments. Even with these caveats, libraries will want to purchase this unique volume to complement standard media reference works such as Terrace's *Encyclopedia of Television Shows, 1925 through 2010* (see ARBA 2012, entry 1080).—**Anthony J. Adam**

660.   Mooney, Darren. **Opening The X-Files: A Critical History of the Original Series.** Jefferson, N.C., McFarland, 2017. 228p. index. $19.99pa. ISBN 13: 978-1-4766-6526-9; 978-1-4766-2880-6 (e-book).

Opening The X-Files offers a critical examination and overview of The X-Files television series, as well as the series' two feature films and three semi-related series by the show's creator. This thoroughly researched volume delves into *The X-Files'* themes, influences (cinematic, literary, and cultural), and impact; in addition, it examines the historical context of both the series as a whole and individual episodes of the show.

Opening The X-Files is an informative companion to the series that should interest die-hard fans, casual viewers, and those new to the series. Die-hard fans will find things to quibble with, which is to be expected, but they will also very likely find information and insights that are new to them. Through its examination of *The X-Files,* the book also provides a look at American culture in the 1990s; as Mooney notes in the preface, *The X-Files,* which aired from 1993 to 2002, is one of "those shows that define a moment in time; television series that seem to perfectly encapsulate a certain cultural moment" (though its themes remain relevant today).

The text of *Opening The X-Files* is scholarly but not overly complex. Actor and X-Files Files podcast host Kumail Nanjiani provides a foreword, followed by a preface by Mooney giving a brief overview of the historical and pop culture context of the 1990s. The book then begins with a chapter discussing the cultural context of *The X-Files* and Ten Thirteen, the production company of series creator Chris Carter. The following chapters are broken up by season; the series' first film is discussed along with the fifth season, the second film is covered in its own chapter, and some chapters cover a season of the show along with Carter's companion series (Millennium, Harsh Realm, and The Lone Gunmen). Discussion of the 2016 revival of *The X-Files* is not included as the book was in the works before the series aired. *Opening The X-Files* includes extensive notes, a bibliography, and an index.

Mooney assembled *Opening The X-Files* from work published on his blog, the m0vie blog, and while the book doesn't include the reviews for each individual episode as the blog does (to do so would require thousands of pages), the broader overview found in the book still provides valuable insight. As an abridged version of the m0vie blog's discussion of the series, *Opening The X-Files* is accessible, whereas the body of 200-plus reviews on the blog can be a bit overwhelming (the m0vie blog is worth visiting for those who wish to delve even deeper into The X-Files than the deep dives *Opening The X-Files* provides, particularly for reviews of episodes dealing with complex themes and history, e.g., "Nisei" and "731.")

Recommended for libraries with collections on film and television.—**ARBA Staff Reviewer**

661. Orwig, Gail, and Raymond Orwig. **Where Monsters Walked: California Locations of Science Fiction, Fantasy and Horror Films, 1925-1965.** Jefferson, N.C., McFarland, 2018. 370p. illus. index. $49.95pa. ISBN 13: 978-1-4766-6840-6; 978-14766-2797-7 (e-book).

This is the book for fans of old science fiction, fantasy, and horror movies who have wondered about the places where the films were made. The authors of this book have always been fascinated by this question, and this book is the result. Over 160 movies from 1925 to 1965 are featured. Each entry has the film's title, year, studio, director, cast, a synopsis of the plot, and locations used in the film. What follows are actual photographs by the authors (between 2000 and 2016), side by side with the clip in the film. Some locations either exist no longer, or were unable to be found, and they are designated as such. Most of the locations are in California and adjacent states, given the budgets and time constraints of many early movie studios. This book was a labor of love for the authors, and it will bring back many benefits for those wanting to reconnect to the movies of their youth or the early history of Hollywood movies. Recommended for public libraries.—**Bradford Lee Eden**

662. **Oscars Awards Databases. http://www.oscars.org/oscars/awards-databases-0.** [Website] Free. Date reviewed: 2017.

This site is home to information covering the Oscars—the annual awards given out by the Academy of Motion Picture Arts and Sciences. The page allows access to a database of past award winners and nominees in different categories, and a database of over 1,500 award acceptance speeches. Users click the Search link under the corresponding database for access. For the acceptance speeches, users can conduct a keyword search and incorporate affiliated information such as the name of the award winner/acceptor, Film Title, Award Category, or Award Year. Users can consult alphabetical Film Title, Award Category, and Award Year lists should they require search assistance. This database includes a transcript of the winner's speech alongside identifying information such as Year, Award Category, Film Title, Winner Name, Presenter, and Date & Venue. There may also be a link to a YouTube video clip of the speech. The more general database allows users to conduct a basic or advanced search. They can also examine a listing of nearly 40 award categories including special awards (e.g., the Jean Hersholt Humanitarian Award), Scientific and Technical Awards, and Discontinued Categories (e.g., Dance Direction) in order to narrow their search. The Statistics tab within this database adds further perspective; sharing facts and trivia such as Oscar firsts, films or actors most nominated, and more. With the Academy Awards considered by many to be the most prestigious honors in film, the information on this website reflects an essential record of the industry that would interest film historians, educators, and others.—**ARBA Staff Reviewer**

663. Sherman, Fraser A. **Now and Then We Time Travel: Visiting Pasts and Futures in Film and Television.** Jefferson, N.C., McFarland, 2017. 270p. illus. index. $39.95pa. ISBN 13: 978-0-7864-9679-2; 978-1-4766-8643-7 (e-book).

Time travel has long been a fantasy of humankind. While Einstein, Galileo, and other notable scientists brought us theories that changed our notions of time and space, time travel continues to inspire literature, film, and television, absent of scientific rules or logic. Accordingly, our fascination with time travel, and its impact across cultural, historical, and philosophical contexts, allows us to endlessly visit and revisit alternate histories and parallel universes. Drawing on history as the overriding context, the book reviews elements of time travel as they occur within selected films and television series (heretofore "series").

The book provides countless examples of films and series centered on time travel; the author lists "every" time travel-related film and series made in the United States, Canada, the United Kingdom, and Japan at the time of the book's writing. Front matter includes a preface, in which the author briefly discusses the history of time travel in film; cinematic and series approaches to time travel (e.g., the logic of time travel); and criteria for inclusion of films into the book. Eleven chapters follow, each focused on one of several themes (e.g., attempts to alter history) and fused with the films' and series' plots. Rounding out the structure of the book are eight appendixes, including film and television series credits, short films, and porn films, as well as chapter notes, a small bibliography, and an index.

The book is an excellent source for scholars and consumers alike who wish to study and explore time travel in film and, to a lesser extent, television. Rather than provide a mere descriptive catalog, the author categorizes selected films and series according to universal, romanticized themes typically associated with stories and storytelling (e.g., love across time). Each of the eleven chapters contains a plethora of details, leaving no stone unturned. The book contains a sprinkling of well-placed, visually-enticing photographs and advertisements, although additional photographs of older time travel films (and series if applicable) from the 1960s and earlier would further elucidate the historical context in which the book is located. Moreover, as noted, the author does include a comprehensive set of selection criteria; however, a rationale for the criteria could provide valuable insight into how the book took shape and, thus, its usefulness as a catalog of time travel in film and television.—**Sheri Edwards**

664.   Terrace, Vincent. **Television Series of the 1970s: Essential Facts and Quirky Details.** Lanham, Md., Rowman & Littlefield, 2017. 242p. illus. index. $40.00; $38.00 (e-book). ISBN 13: 978-1-4422-7828-8; 978-1-4422-7829-5 (e-book).

This book is part of a series of books that details trivia aspects of mostly American television programs by decade. Two books in the series, dealing with the 1950s and 1960s, have already appeared. It is important to understand that this book (and series) is not about opinions or essays; it is a presentation of trivia facts, little details that most people have no idea about. Television series are presented alphabetically, with a listing of cast members and their personas, and then individual details about each persona. For instance, under *The Partridge Family,* Daniel "Danny" Partridge has a number of subheadings: Age, Trait, Obsession, Favorite Reading Material, Favorite Colors, Bank, Stock, Hobby, School, Sports, Hangout, and Girls. Under *Laverne and Shirley,* Shirley Wilhelmina Feeney's subheadings are: Heritage, Religion, Political Party, Money, Plush Cat, Catchphrases, Idol, Famous For, Favorite Foods, Favorite Novel, Favorite Reading Matter, Favorite Christmas Song, Favorite Prayer, Favorite Soap, Author, Performer, Least Favorite Childhood Memory, Boyfriend, and Siblings. For those interested in trivia about 1970s television series, this book is for you!!—**Bradford Lee Eden**

665.   Terrace, Vincent. **Television Series of the 1980s: Essential Facts and Quirky Details.** Lanham, Md., Rowman & Littlefield, 2017. 246p. illus. index. $40.00; $38.00 (e-book). ISBN 13: 978-1-4422-7830-1; 978-1-4422-7831-8 (e-book).

This collection of 1980s television trivia is fourth in a series of volumes that take a microlevel look at television programs of the 1950s through the 1980s. This book covers 56 programs that premiered between January 1980 and December 1989. For each program there is a cast list, a brief summation of what the show is about, and a list of facts about each major character: birthplace, parents, occupation, education, marital status, spouse, children, hobbies, pets, and so forth (the precise details given depend upon the character). Diane Chambers (of *Cheers*), for example, named her cat Elizabeth Barrett Browning after her favorite poet and Alex Keaton (of *Family Ties*) had an IQ of 137. It is puzzling that such popular eighties programs as *L.A. Law, Pee-Wee's Playhouse,* and *Thirtysomething* are not included. Equally odd is the lack of an explanation about the compiler's selection criteria. Were these 56 programs selected because they are thought to in some way define the eighties or are they simply the compiler's favorite shows? There are a number of editorial glitches as well: some program entries abruptly switch from an itemized list presentation of the facts to narrative paragraphs (*St. Elsewhere, Dear John, Hill Street Blues*); many shows are missing a section called "Overall Series Information"; and occasionally a cast list is incomplete (*Miami Vice, Cagney and Lacey*). While this trivia compilation is easy to use and may be a rich resource for trivia-obsessed pop culture fans, it will probably be of limited use outside this narrow audience.—**Cynthia Knight**

Theater

Dictionaries and Encyclopedias

666.   Dietz, Dan. **The Complete Book of 2000s Broadway Musicals:.** Lanham, Md., Rowman & Littlefield, 2017. 498p. index. $125.00; $118.00 (e-book). ISBN 13: 978-1-4422-7800-4; 978-1-4422-7801-1 (e-book).

As the world turned its attention to a new millennium, New York City found itself at the center of grim, unchartered territory. Shaken and aggrieved by the worst foreign terrorist attack on U.S. soil, New York became a stark symbol of resolution and grit as it persevered in the ensuing months. Accordingly, New York's theater industry found itself in the dubious position of embodying resilience and hope while facing plummeting ticket sales and attendance. Nonetheless, marketing and advertising strategies, designed around the age-old philosophy that the "the show must go on," found the Broadway musical adapting to post-9/11 economic and political realities, and raising audience expectations for more challenging and provocative shows. Given the evolution of Broadway theater as it continues to push boundaries and find a voice in the modern age, a catalog of musicals of the early 2000s is necessary for understanding Broadway musical theater's current transformation.

The book covers theater seasons 2000-2009, and contains a total of 213 revues and musicals, including shows that closed prior to premiering on the New York stage. The author presents a myriad of entries that range by number and type (e.g., "21 personality revues and concerts," "6 return engagements"). Each entry is accompanied with an etymological description, as well as numerous correlative details, including opening and closing dates; total number of performances; cast; and musical numbers. Moreover, the author notes top-level Tony awards for each musical as those awards apply. The book contains an appendix of an alphabetized list of musicals and their page numbers, although entries are formally organized in the table of contents according to one-year seasonal increments (e.g., 2001-2002 Season, 2005-2006 Season). Similarly, 9 appendixes offer a variety of accompanying details, including chronologies by season and classification; a discography of musical scores; and Black and Jewish revues and musicals. Bibliography, index, and about the author sections are additional ephemera.

The book is a comprehensive, finely detailed compilation of early 2000s Broadway, originating On, Off, and Off-Off Broadway, each with its own rich and varied history as a meaningful backdrop to a wide range of accompanying minutia. These historical descriptions, when taken together, present a textual timeline of the passing of some recent eras in musical theater (e.g., mega-musicals in the 1980s, commercial presentations of revivals in the 1990s) and the debut of new eras (e.g., the musical comedies found throughout the book). An antecedent to the main contents is a brief introduction, well-stocked with explanations for the layout of the contents and of the author's goals in writing the book. Similar to the author's The Complete Book of 1980s Broadway Musicals, (see ARBA 2017, entry 692) this book does not contain photographs, the addition of which would lend vibrancy to an otherwise robust and spirited book. Still, the book is thorough and well-written, and a stellar example of how a cataloging of Broadway musicals ought to be done.—**Sheri Edwards**

667.   Fisher, James, and Felicia Hardison Londré. **Historical Dictionary of American Theater: Modernism.** 2d ed. Lanham, Md., Rowman & Littlefield, 2018. 776p. $170.00; $161.50 (e-book). ISBN 13: 978-1-5381-0785-0; 978-1-5381-0786-7 (e-book)

The latest volume in the publisher's Historical Dictionaries of Literature and the Arts series explores theater in the United States between 1880 and the early 1930s. It is the middle volume (chronologically) on the American theater, between Beginnings (covering the sixteenth century to 1880) and 1930-2010. This second edition adds two hundred pages and approximately six hundred entries to the first edition (see ARBA 2010, entry 1077) and now offers readers a total of two thousand entries, focusing on individuals (actors, playwrights, producers), plays, theaters across the country, and events that affected the evolution of theater. A fifteen-page chronology and a ten-page introduction provide a context for the A-Z list of entries. Most of those entries have multiple cross-references, clearly indicated in bold type. In addition, there are indications when a name or topic also appears in one of the other two volumes in the set. Little attention is paid to either musical theater or vaudeville, although there are brief entries on each. The introductory essay is quite useful. It discusses the evolution of "modernism" within the theater setting, including the roles of several major international figures. It points out that Eugene O'Neill is the most important playwright of the period. (Fifteen of his plays have entries in this volume.)

This book will be useful, most of all, in academic libraries, where readers will need (or want) to research details of the history of theater in the United States. Other kinds of libraries—school or public—will benefit from more general narrative histories.—**Mark Schumacher**

668.   Mason, Fran. **Historical Dictionary of Postmodernist Literature and Theater.** 2d ed. Lanham, Md., Rowman & Littlefield, 2017. 553p. (Historical Dictionaries of Literature and the Arts). $130.00; $129.99 (e-book). ISBN 13: 978-1-4422-7619-2; 978-1-4422-7620-8 (e-book).

In the second edition of the *Historical Dictionary of Postmodernist Literature and Theater* (see ARBA 2008, entry 789), Fran Mason presents 553 pages of a necessarily dense and complex reference work that begins with a chronology spanning 1939-2015 charting the subject matter as an international phenomenon heavily based in written and performed works. The introduction is divided into distinct sections: Defining Postmodernism, Postmodern Culture and Postmodernity, Postmodernist Literature and its Antecedents, Postmodernist Literature and Postmodern Culture, Histories and Geographies of Postmodernist Literature, Postmodern Poetry and Theater, and Postmodernism in the 21st Century. In a mere 25 pages Mason manages to present in a clear and direct manner what could be impenetrable topics that will be essential reading for the novice researcher. Mason points out that the dictionary is explicitly described as being postmodernist and does not refer to postmodern literature, which Mason sees as being a far more nebulous category. Mason argues that if a distinction is not made between these terms that the result is a "version of postmodernist literature and cultural expression that is so generalized and extensive in its operation that it becomes meaningless," because all forms of contemporary cultural production could then be considered within the definition. In further justification of his approach, Mason states that "…postmodernist textual devices are often articulated within a cultural, rather than a philosophical, framework and are not, therefore, expressing an author's viewpoint. Instead, they are being self-consciously used as a means to refract or configure postmodern cultural processes." Following the introduction are 450 pages with over 400 entries in alphabetical order each enriched with cross-references in bold. These entries cover "writers, movements, forms of writing, textual strategies, critical ideas, and texts that are significant in relation to postmodernist literature." The collection of writers covered has been expanded from the previous edition to include cutting-edge writers from an international perspective such as Jenny Erpenbeck, Georgi Gospodinov, Andrei Kurkov, Dimitris Lyacos, Tom McCarthy, Ben Marcus, Marie NDiaye, Tommaso Pincio, Mikhail Shishkin, Michal Ajvaz, László Krasznahorkai, Yuri Andrukhovych, and Chiru Nivedita. The exhaustively researched bibliography is 73 pages long and has its own table of contents consisting of five major sections: General, Postmodernist Aesthetics, Postmodernist Literature (Fiction, Drama, and Poetry), Postmodernist Literature (Critical Works), then Journals and Websites. This dictionary is an indispensable guide for students of postmodernist literature and would be a worthy addition to any reference collection.—**Todd Simpson**

669.   Pavis, Patrice. Andrew Brown. **The Routledge Dictionary of Performance and Contemporary Theatre.** New York, Routledge/Taylor & Francis Group, 2016. 295p. $160.00. ISBN 13: 978-1-138-85435-2; 978-1-315-72115-6 (e-book).

Patrice Pavis with the aid of Andrew Brown serving as translator has written an essential reference text for any student, critic, or theater professional navigating contemporary critical discourse on theater and performance. Immediately, Pavis confidently grounds his work in an explicit modern historic context "…it was after the fall of the Berlin Wall (1990) and the collapse of the Twin Towers in New York (2001) that theatrical activity changed its nature, both in economic and philosophical and aesthetic terms." Timing is everything in performance, and Pavis demonstrates an informed perspective that is uniquely able to guide the reader through traditional definitions and how they have been disrupted by current events. He is assembling definitions within a time seemingly intent on disassembling meaning. Pavis states that the intention of this work is to address an identity crisis within the world of performance that ultimately intimidates spectators. He asks: "If experts and critics and erudite academics in every faculty can no longer agree about the subject of their enquiries and the object of their desires, how can mere theatre lovers find their bearings?... My one hope is that this book comes neither too late nor too early. Too late, because the current theatre is so volatile that it will have vanished before we can become aware of its nature; too early, because we cannot encompass, in our gaze or our thoughts, its endless metamorphoses, and we would need to project ourselves into the next century—if indeed the theatre is still felt to be necessary."

Throughout there is a palpable immediacy both in the choice of terms defined and how they are written about. When reading an entry on "Spectator" or "Performativity," for example, the reader is not just given a definition but instead learns about the history of the concept, how that concept evolved influenced by advances in theory, and what meaning it currently holds within the world of performance theory and theater practice. Pavis somehow provides the definition and at the same time shows the reader how to think critically about the concept. The work concludes with 12 pages of a rich bibliography and a subject index. For 278 pages he relentlessly pins down and defines the intangible weaving throughout references to theorists and practitioners falling across a spectrum from literary theory to cinema and the stage, in what is ultimately a fascinating treatise. This work is highly recommended for any collection in support of a performance studies or theater arts program.—**Todd Simpson**

Handbooks and Yearbooks

670.   Kabatchnik, Amnon. **Blood on the Stage, 1600 to 1800: Milestone Plays of Murder, Mystery, and Mayhem.** Lanham, Md., Rowman & Littlefield, 2017. $150.00; $142.00 (e-book). ISBN 13: 978-1-5381-0615-0; 978-1-5381-0616-7 (e-book).

This volume is part of a seven-volume series that chronicles murder, mayhem, and other forms of violence and intrigue as depicted in world drama from 480 B.C.E. to 1900. The present volume contains analyses of forty-seven plays (arranged chronologically) and covers two centuries (1600-1800) from Marlowe's *Lust's Dominion* of 1600 to M. G. Lewis's 1797 drama, *The Castle Spectre.* Most originated in the English language but four, like Schiller's 1782 *The Robbers,* appear because of their popularity in translation. Thomas Godfrey's *The Prince of Parthia* (1767) and two others from the American colonies are included. Eight plays by Shakespeare are also included from *Richard II* (1601) to *Cymbeline* (1609) and the major tragedies written in between. After a brief introduction, each entry contains a detailed (about seven pages in length) plot summary. Although cast lists are not provided, all characters are introduced as are generous snippets of dialogue. After the plot summary, there is a lengthy section which gives extensive information on important past productions and actors associated with key roles. There is also material on foreign productions and translations, spinoffs, film and/or musical adaptations, and an assessment of the play's importance in world literature. The coverage is up to date (e.g., Daniel Craig's Iago in a 2016 production of *Othello* is included). Footnotes are covered at the end of each entry. Most are for print sources (books, articles, etc.) but, otherwise, there are no bibliographies. As in other volumes in the series, the scholarship is thorough and impressive and the presentation accessible, informative, and entertaining. The seven appendixes present a strange assortment of facts and tables (e.g., a list of early "trial" plays and one for courtroom dramas). By far most valuable and longest (nearly fifty pages) is an overview of important revenge tragedies from Aeschylus's *Oresteia* (458 B.C.E.) through Shakespeare's *Titus Andronicus* (1594) (when coverage in the main text begins). There is also an index by name (playwrights, actors) and play title (no subjects). This book is a gold mine of entertaining and valuable information. The author deserves congratulations on the completion of an excellent series which will be useful in academic as well as medium- and large-sized public libraries.—**John T. Gillespie**

671.   Kabatchnik, Amnon. **Blood on the Stage, 1800 to 1900: Milestone Plays of Murder, Mystery, and Mayhem.** Lanham, Md., Rowman & Littlefield, 2017. 720p. index. $150.00; $142.50 (e-book). ISBN 13: 978-1-5381-0617-4; 978-1-5381-0618-1 (e-book).

    This volume is a completion of a seven-volume series on this topic: theater's scariest and bloodiest plays from the dawn of time to the year 2000. This volume covers the nineteenth century. Fifty-one dramas are described, from Holcroft's *A Tale of Mystery* (1802) through Gillette's *Sherlock Holmes* (1899). The author, a retired professor of theater, provides fairly complete historical and plot descriptions of each of the dramas. Six appendixes are included: "Lethal Poison," "Early Trial Plays," "Classic Revenge Tragedies," "*Arden of Faversham* (1592), by Anonymous (England)," "The Witches of John Masefield and Arthur Miller," and "Modern Versions of 'Jane Eyre.'" All of the books in this series would be appropriate for any undergraduate/graduate academic library and for most academic theater programs.—**Bradford Lee Eden**

28 Philosophy and Religion

Philosophy

Dictionaries and Encyclopedias

672. Blackburn, Simon. **The Oxford Dictionary of Philosophy.** 3d ed. New York, Oxford University Press, 2016. 531p. illus. $17.95pa. ISBN 13: 978-0-19-873530-4; 978-0-19-179955-6 (e-book).

This is the third edition by Simon Blackburn, retired professor of philosophy at the University of Cambridge and a research professor at the University of North Carolina, Chapel Hill. Blackburn has made some changes since the last edition in 2008. He left out some of the more obscure figures (of interest mainly to specialists) and substituted philosophical details and a number of entirely new entries. The material removed from the printed text is still available in the online version of the book. According to the author, these new entries reflect happenings in the contemporary world. For instance, in light of the 2008 financial collapse and crisis, Blackburn chose to include discussions of economic terms and principles. Another feature new to this edition is the inclusion of icons that either identify terms as core ideas with which students in a philosophy course should be familiar or as specialist terms that are important for philosophy majors and scholars to understand. Fatalism, egoism, and tabula rosa are indicated as key terms, for example, while Blackburn identifies hereditary property and zero-sum game as two of many specialist terms. The entries are arranged A to Z; some are quite short (one sentence) while others are several pages long. Entries use *see* references. There are three appendixes: "Logical Symbols," "Key Introductory Terms," and "Specialist Terms." The book ends with a chronology from 10,000 B.C.E. to 2014, which includes broadly philosophical events and cultural, scientific, or political events. This very modestly priced source is an ideal reference for students in introductory philosophy courses. There are well over three thousand entries. It is highly recommended to public and academic libraries.—**ARBA Staff Reviewer**

673. **The Encyclopedia of Diderot & d'Alembert. Collaborative Translation Project. https://quod.lib.umich.edu/d/did/.** [Website] Free. Date reviewed: 2017.

This ongoing, collaborative project offers English translation of the expansive—thirty-two volumes in total—Enlightenment period encyclopedia overseen by Denis Diderot and Jean le Rond d'Alembert. Users can browse and search translated articles in a number of ways, browse original illustration plates, explore related material, and more. Users can select from three links on the left column of the homepage to conduct a Simple, Proximity, or Boolean Search. From the central column, users can choose to browse articles by translated English title, original French title, Category of Knowledge (e.g., Anatomy, Logic, Turkish History, etc.), or Author. In either language, users can browse an alphabetical listing of such things as terms, places, people, and events, before clicking on one to view the full entry. Entries vary in length and convey the knowledge/bias of the Enlightenment period. The entry page also lists title, encyclopedia volume, page, entry author (if known), translator, subject, URL, citation information, and other information. Users can collect translation entries in a "Bookbag" for future use. Users can also browse encyclopedia plates by English translation (captions) or original French. Plates are also listed alphabetically by title and provide identifying information. A third column on the homepage offers additional Resources, including an excellent Chronology of the Encyclopedia, a bibliography of relevant works, and Teaching Resources.—**ARBA Staff Reviewer**

Handbooks and Yearbooks

674.   **The Research Ethics Library. https://www.etikkom.no/en/library/.** [Website] Free. Date reviewed: 2017.

The Norwegian National Research Ethics Committees employs this website, available in English and Norwegian, to promote understanding of current ethical guidelines relative to academic research across an array of scientific and humanistic disciplines. The page primarily hosts an A to Z listing of topics—over eighty of them—related to ethical matters within these disciplines. Topics concern both general matters, including Environment, Bias, Data Protection, etc., to the more particular DNA, Genetic Material, and Prison Inmates. It is important to note that the same topic may appear under different topic headings. Selecting a topic allows users to view a cited and clearly outlined article relaying such things as definitions and most recent standards. Articles vary in length and come with links to additional sources on the subject. Aside from the topic articles, the page also presents guidelines/protocols as outlined by both Norwegian national and international administrative agencies (e.g., the National Committee for Medical and Health Research Ethics). These protocols cover everything from manuscript submissions to the treatment of human or animal research subjects. The library is by no means definitive; rather it was established to provide a general outline of ethical standards in research and to promote further study and discussion. The issues covered make the material applicable to scholars worldwide. All users will appreciate the site's ease of use and singular ethics mission.—**ARBA Staff Reviewer**

Religion

General Works

Dictionaries and Encyclopedias

678. Benowitz, June Melby. **Encyclopedia of American Women and Religion.** 2d ed. Santa Barbara, Calif., ABC-CLIO, 2017. 2v. $198.00/set. ISBN 13: 978-1-4408-3986-3; 978-1-4408-3987-0 (e-book).

The second edition of ABC-CLIO's *Encyclopedia of American Women and Religion* makes significant improvements to the award-winning reference work first published in the late 1990s (see ARBA 199, entry 1265). More than three dozen essays help to expand the work into two volumes totaling nearly eight hundred pages. These additional essays, as well as the updated originals, utilize recent scholarship and benefit from the digitization of primary sources that in 1998 were not easily accessed. In fact, fifteen primary source documents have been included in the volume and are found adjacent to relevant articles. These include speeches, letters, and legal documents.

While an expanded chronology provides helpful dates and figures, there is no indication of which entry in the chronology corresponds to an essay in the encyclopedia, something that could have easily been done through bold face. A very short preface outlines the scope of the entire book. The scope of the biographical entries extends to women who made contributions to the history of American religion, either as leaders or as lay women who made a difference in their spheres of influence, however large or small. Accordingly, the entries depict women at varied ecclesiastical and social ranks, from high church denominations all the way to ecofeminists. Likewise, essays included describe a wide range of devotional cultures, from Native American traditions to the African American to the Hawaiian. Other entries explore topics (such as abortion) or movements (such as Holiness) that pertain to the history of American religion and women. The nineteenth to the twentieth centuries have left the most documentation and are therefore allotted the most space. Each entry ends with cross-references, a *see also* section, and short bibliographies for further reading. Though some entries have pictures, there is no list of images to help the reader navigate them. A bibliography of more than seventy pages is a gold mine of material for the student jumping into this field, while the twenty-six-page index provides keyword access to names, places, themes, and topics. Bold-face numerals indicate an index entry that has a corresponding entry in the encyclopedia.

For a third edition, a shortened table of contents and separate alphabetical list of entries by person, document, movement, and topic might enhance ease of use. As mentioned above, bold face in the chronology, a list of images, and perhaps even a lengthier introductory essay would expand the benefits for the reader. That said, the easy-to-read prose and wealth of sources documented makes this a worthy expenditure for colleges, universities, and seminaries with courses on American history, women, and religious studies.—**Amy Koehler**

675.   **End of Days: An Encyclopedia of the Apocalypse in World Religions.** Wendell G. Johnson, ed. Santa Barbara, Calif., ABC-CLIO, 2017. 381p. index. $89.00. ISBN 13: 978-1-4408-3940-5; 978-1-4408-3941-2 (e-book).

This essay collection offers both the theological and historical views of eschatology ("end of things") from a variety of faiths, but also its influence as seen in film, literature, and art. A brief introduction explains the definitions of eschatology and apocalypse and their representation in various faith traditions. The individual entries, arranged alphabetically, include traditional beliefs of various groups (e.g., Native American, Chinese, etc.), major concepts (e.g., Gnosticism, tribulation, etc.), individuals and groups who included eschatological components in their views and writings (e.g., Jerry Falwell, Dante, People's Temple, etc.) and examples from pop culture (e.g., The Hunger Games, Left Behind Series, etc.). The selection of entries crosses many centuries and includes many lesser-known topics. Some entries also discuss subtopics and some have sidebars with excerpts or additional information. Brief bibliographies and *see also* references provide further resources. Information about the editor and contributors and an index complete the text. The selection of topics covers a lot of material in one volume. It serves as a very good overview and starting point for further research and serves this purpose well.—**Martha Lawler**

676.   Fieldhouse, Paul. **Food, Feasts, and Faith: An Encyclopedia of Food Culture in World Religions.** Santa Barbara, Calif., ABC-CLIO, 2017. 2v. illus. index. $189.00/set. ISBN 13: 978-1-61069-411-7; 978-1-61069-412-4 (e-book).

Food is an integral part of life, so it follows that there are cultural and religious traditions connected to it. Paul Fieldhouse, a nutritionist and adjunct professor of human nutritional sciences at the University of Manitoba, has created a basic encyclopedia that examines food-related customs and laws in the world's major religions. The 226 alphabetical entries range in length from 250 to 2,500 words. They are listed at the beginning of each volume. A subject guide groups them so that users can easily find related articles. Eighty-six sidebars offer interesting facts and historical anecdotes related to the articles. Black-and-white photographs and charts augment the text.

The entries cover a wide range of topics: customs (cannibalism, Potlach); feasts and feast days (agape feast, Thanksgiving); food and drink (airline food, coffee, food certification on Judaism and Islam); people (Guru Nanak, John Harvey Kellogg); religion or belief (African Indigenous Religions, paganism); religious festivals and seasons (Ashura, Holi); religious practices (animal slaughter, fasting); rituals (marriage, rites of passage); and texts and scriptures (Bible, Hadith). There is an interfaith festival calendar for 2017 listing the most important religious holidays for the major world religions, which along with articles on sacred time and sacrifice, will help readers understand the significance of these holidays.

This is a very good resource for high-school and undergraduate students seeking information about food and nutrition, social studies, religion, history, geography, and folklore. The primary source documents, resource list, and detailed index in the second volume provide further insight. By providing accessible information about esoteric subjects such as Candomble and Durga Puja, this encyclopedia will be useful for general readers as well.—**Barbara M. Bibel**

677.   **Great Events in Religion: An Encyclopedia of Pivotal Events in Religious History.** Curta, Florin and Andrew Holt, eds. Santa Barbara, Calif., ABC-CLIO, 2017. 3v. index. $310.00/set. ISBN 13: 978-1-61069-565-7; 978-1-61069-566-4 (e-book).

Along with economics and culture, religion has had a profound effect on the course of human events both throughout history and into modern times. The study of religion therefore has become an important aspect to understanding why societies have taken certain paths, and as such can help students to understand the reasons for those historical choices as well as how they have led to the events of today. *Great Events in Religion* is a reference work designed to provide students with knowledge of the pivotal moments in the history of religion and how they were intertwined with the world around them.

This encyclopedia is divided into three chronological volumes ranging from prehistory to the present day. All entries are likewise listed chronologically as opposed to alphabetically and include either exact dates when available or approximations in cases of uncertainty or when events cover a span of time. Each volume begins with a complete chronological list of entries for the entire set followed by an alphabetical list and a separate topical list of entries in each individual volume. Individual entries vary in length depending on a combination of available source material and their impact on history. Entries are cross-referenced to lead readers to related events in history and also have suggestions for further reading. Authors are listed for each entry and many contain sidebars with additional information such as important people, publications, languages, and concepts that provide context to surrounding topics. Each volume ends with a bibliography and the final book in the set contains an extensive index and a list of contributors.

The strengths of this set are many. Entries are highly informative and well researched while maintaining accessibility for newer students to the subject. Extensive bibliographic listings provide excellent potential for academic research by undergraduates. Organization allows readers to easily focus on topics of interest while the chronological listing of entries actually provides context for a cover-to-cover reading for those who may wish. One flaw with this work is that while it does possess information on various world religions the vast bulk of the entries focus on Western or Judeo-Christian topics. While this is stated in the work's introductory text it may not be readily apparent based on the title and cover art. Therefore, academic libraries that are looking for a more global treatment may wish for an alternative.—**W. Cole Williamson**

679.   Willis, Jim. **Ancient Gods: Lost Histories, Hidden Truths, and the Conspiracy of Silence.** Canton, Mich., Visible Ink Press, 2017. 4002p. illus. index. $19.95pa. ISBN 13: 978-1-57859-614-0; 978-1-57859-643-0 (e-book).

Using a folksy voice, Willis takes the reader through a compendium of ancient ancestors, astronomers, catastrophes, civilizations, mysteries, mythologies, religions, and technologies. Each of these topics receives quick treatment, making this book more amenable to skipping around than to reading it from cover to cover. Willis claims that these histories are lost to the conspiracy of silence—an establishment of scientists and religious leaders who pick and choose the facts that are most deserving of preservation. Interspersed throughout are black-and-white photographs of poor quality and from sources such as Wikicommons. While direct quotes include a bibliographic citation, the book does not have a bibliography. The book does provoke analysis of the status quo and for that reason some of his assertions might lend themselves to student research using inquiry-based learning. The book includes additional resources, an index, and a timeline.—**Susan Yutzey**

Handbooks and Yearbooks

680.   **Milestone Documents of World Religions.** 2d ed. David A. Fahey and Aaron Gulyas, eds. Amenia, N.Y., Grey House Publishing, 2016. 3v. illus. index. $325.00/set. ISBN 13: 978-1-68217-171-4; 978-1-68217-172-1 (e-book).

Religion is a very powerful force in today's world. It influences our daily lives, our political arenas, and our culture. This second edition set (see ARBA 2011, entry 1108) uses documents to focus on five major religious traditions, Christianity, Buddhism, Hinduism, Islam, and Judaism. The first document is the "Pyramid Documents," dated 2404 B.C.E.; the last is "Calling Humanity" created by Jose Hipolito Triguerinho Netto, a Brazilian spiritual leader in 2002. The documents define and illustrate the scriptures, the history, and the tenets of these religions. The extracts are chosen to highlight the essential aspects of a specific spiritual path, and the quotes are chosen to single out the pithiest statements of the document.

The 112 document entries range from 250 words and provide explanations of the document, its impact in the world, and questions for further study. A chronology, illustrations, and photographs accompany the text. There is an index of documents by "Religious Tradition" and a cumulative subject index.

I would recommend this set of religion documents to academic and public libraries.— **Kay Stebbins Slattery**

681.   Olson, Carl. **Sacred Texts Interpreted: Religious Documents Explained.** Santa Barbara, Calif., ABC-CLIO, 2017. 2v. index. $198.00/set. ISBN 13: 978-1-4408-4187-3; 978-1-4408-4188-0 (e-book).

While there is something to be said for simple and direct explanations for complicated and often hotly debated concepts, Carl Olson's two-volume *Sacred Texts Interpreted* raises the question of how meaningful the author's interpretations of such texts can be, given how thin the two volumes are. Furthermore, a close reading of the preface raises other questions regarding the accuracy of the interpretations. The set purports to address both Eastern and Western traditions, which is honestly reflected in the contents: Olson arranges the set by belief systems, and a goodly mix of the major religious traditions. However, both the preface and chapter 1 seem skewed towards the Abrahamic religions. This is interesting, given Olson's critique in the preface regarding the influence secularism exerts on the ignorance of ordinary people regarding understanding other religions.

Another point of concern emerges from Olson's assertion that this anthology represents a much-needed comparative and comprehensive resource. One cannot argue with the comparative nature of this anthology; it does, in fact, offer the reader the ability to understand the sacred texts within their own contexts and in the contexts of other traditions and their texts. But to call this resource comprehensive is dangerous, especially given the ways in which several of these belief systems give way to distinguishably different sects or denominations which are often based on highly variable interpretations of the foundational, revelatory texts that Olson includes. These critiques aside, the anthology is well written and includes a good chapter on the different natures or facets of sacred texts—e.g., the performative and iconic natures of such documents. Olson's selection of belief systems is admirable, though it neglects certain ethnic and pagan traditions and belief systems which, though perhaps not as major or established as the traditions covered in the anthology, are no less meaningful or spiritual (e.g., Wicca).

This title is recommended for public libraries.—**Megan W. Lowe**

682.   **The Routledge Handbook of Muslim-Jewish Relations.** Josef Meri, ed. New York, Routledge/Taylor & Francis Group, 2016. 521p. illus. index. ISBN 13: 978-0-415-64516-4; 978-1-315-67578-7 (e-book).

Muslims and Jews have lived side-by-side since the early days of Islam. Given their close proximity and frequent interactions, they have influenced each other in several areas, and sometimes in unexpected ways. While popular portrayals of Muslim-Jewish relationships stem primarily from the lens of the Palestinian-Israeli conflict, this book seeks to showcase the rich diversity of their interaction that goes beyond politics and religion.

The 24 essays cover all major social areas of interaction, and in most cases need to be read in groups. Meri's introductory essay outlines some of the nuances and potential pitfalls of teaching Muslim-Jewish relations in academia. He addresses the Christian influence on Muslim-Jewish relations, and also takes pains to separate anti-Semitism and Islamophobia and urges readers not to confound the two. While this essay is geared towards university level courses, large portions of it can be used for high school level discussions as well.

The first two chapters provide an overview of Muslim-Jewish relations during Medieval and modern times. The next two chapters cover common themes in scripture and theology, and how the two religions influenced each other. Chapter 5 outlines the contributions of Jewish physicians in the Medieval Christian and Islamic world. The next two chapters explore common themes in literature and their influence on each other. Law, philosophy, education, and mysticism each claim a chapter that outlines its trajectory from medieval to modern times, and their influences on each other.

The next nine chapters focus on the modern era and explore themes such as identity, nationalism (both Arab and Jewish), anti-Semitism, Islamophobia, the Holocaust and Nakba, and the on-going Palestinian-Israeli conflict. The last four chapters trace the trajectory of the fine arts (specifically cinema, music, art, and culinary arts) from Medieval to modern time. While it is not the intent of this work to cover all facets of Muslim-Jewish relations, it serves as an excellent introduction of the major themes in this discussion, and outlines the major fault lines in contemporary academia. It is well suited for a college survey course or as a reference that outlines the background and current major areas of Muslim-Jewish relations.—**Muhammed Hassanali**

683.   **The U.S. Religion Census.** http://www.usreligioncensus.org/. [Website] Free. Date reviewed: 2017.

This website hosts the 2010 publication of U.S. religion data gathered in affiliation with the Association of Statisticians of American Religious Bodies (ASARB). Following studies done in 1952, 1971, 1980, 1990, and 2000, the census helps point to trends and changes across the great variety of denominations representing religion in the United States today. The report has expanded coverage since the 2000 study in significant ways, such as providing county-level statistics, incorporating counts of Buddhist and Hindu congregations, enhancing reporting on Muslim and Orthodox Christian faiths, and focusing on smaller, more exclusive traditions like the Amish. Notably, the 2010 release has nearly doubled the number of congregations and adherents reporting.

From the introductory paragraph on the homepage, users can select the A Quick

Overview is Available Here link for access to the PDF U.S. Religion Census 2010 Summary Findings published in May, 2012. Otherwise, users can select from the links on the sidebar. While they could perhaps be better organized to emphasize the current report, they will nonetheless allow users to navigate through the census with general ease. It should also be noted that users must download data (free) to view. 2010 Maps & Charts allows users to search 236 entities by Religious Group, Series (Major Metro or Largest Group), or all groups in conjunction with their desired data. Datasets include Adherent 50%, Adherent Change, Adherent Quintile, Community Type Charts, Locations, and Penetration. From this page, users can also link to a PDF list of all religious groups (name only) used in the study, in addition to listings of counties with most adherents per religious group, largest ratio of adherents per group, largest number of congregations, and largest population penetration. Lists and Rankings is where users can download data sets for all years collected regarding Total Adherents and Congregations and Individual (religious) Groups. The former category includes 24 data sets ranking Groups, Metros, Counties, and States in regards to congregants, adherents, and more. Individual Groups provides related information on each particular religious group. 2010 Errata links to any corrected data made to the current census information after publication. Reports and Analyses offers links to some of the studies referencing the U.S. Religion Census. Methods presents links to the appendixes which follow the census data tables. The appendixes clarify general information regarding definitions, procedures, etc. for all groups, but also address the unique markers applicable to data collection methods for particular groups (e.g., Amish, Hindu). Other links on the sidebar include FAQs, 2000 Maps (good for comparison), Resources (noting where to purchase bound report, wall maps, etc.) and Religion and Congregational Research Links (e.g., Gallup: Religion Section, Congregational Resource Guide, etc.).

The wealth of new and historical data would appeal to students, educators, social scientists, and many others. Highly recommended to public, school, and academic libraries.—**ARBA Staff Reviewer**

Buddhism

684.   Wang, Youru. **Historical Dictionary of Chan Buddhism.** Lanham, Md., Rowman & Littlefield, 2017. 360p. (Historical Dictionaries of Religions, Philosophies, and Movements). $100.00; $95.00 (e-book). ISBN 13: 978-1-5381-0551-1; 978-1-5381-0552-8 (e-book).

This book, part of the Historical Dictionaries of Religions, Philosophies, and Movements series, focuses on the history of Chan Buddhism, or Zen Buddhism as it is known to the West. The history of Zen Buddhism, as detailed in the chronology and introduction, extends from 148 C.E. to the present, and encompasses a number of key events and individuals. Each essay is concise and brief, with related terms bolded for additional reference. A glossary of Chinese terms is included, along with an extensive bibliography subdivided into Reference Works, Primary Texts, General and Historical Studies, Textual Studies and Translations, Philosophical and Doctrinal Studies, Studies on Various Chan Sects/Schools and Lineages, Studies on Monastic Institutions and Practices, and Social-Political and Cultural Studies. This book would be an excellent addition and introductory reference work in K-12 and academic libraries.—**Bradford Lee Eden**

Christianity

Dictionaries and Encyclopedias

685.   **Encyclopedia of Martin Luther and the Reformation.** Mark A. Lamport, ed. Lanham, Md., Rowman & Littlefield, 2017. 2v. illus. $250.00/set. ISBN 13: 978-1-4422-7158-6; -1-4422-7159-3 (e-book).

Five hundred years have passed since the German professor and priest Martin Luther incited and led the revolution in the Catholic Church that permanently transfigured the medieval ecclesial and political landscape. To commemorate what has been known since then as the Protestant Reformation, publishers Rowman & Littlefield and editor Mark A. Lamport has masterfully selected and arranged a 941-page encyclopedia with articles informed by deep expertise on the life and work of Martin Luther and the Reformation. Four hundred seventy-five entries reflect the work of 180 contributors from 25 countries; roughly 14 percent are women and a handful originate outside the North Atlantic world of scholarship. The authors communicate their expertise with precise, succinct language, producing easily digestible essays that offer on average five references and resources for additional study.

For readers new to Luther and Lutheranism, several editorial materials help to set out a conceptual framework for the historical figure and the time period. A Timeline (which dates and describes historical events from Luther's life, the Reformation, and Global Lutheranism), Appendix A, and the 28 entries under the themes "Lead-In Introductions" and "Why the Reformation Matters" prove especially helpful. These serve to frame the answers to the five, pivotal questions about Martin Luther and the Reformation that the editors, as stated in the preface, promise to explore. The five questions revolve around: the interpretation of Martin Luther; the impact of the reformation on nations, peoples, and cultures; and how religious institutions and other bodies have been influenced by Protestantism and the effects of the Reformation.

Looking forward to a second edition, the editors might consider providing cross-references or markup such as bold face to facilitate navigation between volumes. Another consideration would address the scope of the encyclopedia. How might the addition of more entries about countries outside the North Atlantic region with millions of confessing Lutherans influence our understanding of Luther's legacy and the global impact of the Reformation? Likely additions could include countries such as Ethiopia, Tanzania, and Indonesia, each of which is home to millions of Lutheran worshippers, not to mention historic Lutheran churches, which are absent from the current edition. Finally, this volume includes many new publications, reflecting the boom of scholarship to mark this year of commemoration. Much work will be required for a subsequent edition to evaluate and add the steady flow of works that have appeared, and will continue to appear, surrounding the anniversary.

That said, this new reference work is a must have resource for all seminaries and for most universities and colleges.—**Amy Koehler**

686.   **Evangelical America: An Encyclopedia of Contemporary American Religious Culture.** Timothy J. Demy and Paul R. Shockley, eds. Santa Barbara, Calif., ABC-CLIO,

2017. 515p. index. $94.00. ISBN 13: 978-1-61069-773-6; 978-1-61069-774-3 (e-book).

Since the 2016 U.S. presidential election, there has been a growing scholarly and public interest in the presence of evangelicalism in politics and culture. Beginning with the founding of American Scientific Affiliation in 1941, this newest addition to the literature explores the rich tapestry of American evangelicalism in its regional variation and diverse expressions of social and political thought up to the present. As Timothy Demy and Paul R. Shockley point out in the introduction, American evangelicalism is far from monolithic. The fluidity and vibrancy of the movement is reflected in the construction of the encyclopedia, from African American Evangelicalism to Wycliffe Global Alliance. However, connecting each term into a cohesive historical narratives manifests in a *see also* at the end of each entry to facilitate searching and cross-referencing. Moreover, as a topical overview, each entry allows for a breadth of coverage spanning individuals, musical genres, and political movements. However, theological concepts are carefully contextualized within the biblical interpretation from which they arose, and always include a small bibliography. For example, the entry on Dispensationalism, a core theological tenant in American evangelicalism is carefully articulated through its references in Epheisans 3:2, Colossians 1:25-26, and Daniel 9:25-27. Perhaps most impressive about this encyclopedia is the extensive list of reprinted primary source documents, from 1942 to 2017. Whereas Randall Balmer's *Encyclopedia of Evangelicalism* has been a serviceable A-Z list of American evangelicalism for the last decade, Demy and Shockley have successfully managed to contextualize the key figures, documents, and evangelical organizations into the larger fabric of contemporary American culture. Recommended for both public and academic libraries.—**Josh Eugene Finnell**

687.   **Historical Dictionary of The Salvation Army.** 2d ed. John G. Merritt and Alan Satterlee, eds. Lanham, Md., Rowman & Littlefield, 2017. 749p. (Historical Dictionaries of Religions, Philosophies, and Movements). $155.00; $147.00 (e-book). ISBN 13: 978-1-5381-0212-1; 978-1-5381-0213-8 (e-book).

First published in 2006 (see ARBA 2007, entry 1112) and reissued under a slightly different title in 2009, this edition is now updated and slightly reworked, with the removal of several no longer relevant entries, as well as the sixteen pages of plates and illustrations found in the first edition. There is clearly a great deal of information about the development and evolution of this organization/denomination/evangelical movement, from its founding by William Booth (1829-1912) in England in 1865 to the present. Topic areas include important figures in the history of the Salvation Army, the hierarchy of leadership, and the group's activities in its numerous "territories": Eastern Europe, Sri Lanka, Spain and Portugal, and South Africa to name a few. Numerous appendixes providing basic tenets of the Army, lists of leaders, a sixty-five-page bibliography divided into twenty-five sections, and other information. An eleven-page chronology, now covering events through 2015, also assists readers to understand the steady growth and dispersion of the group.

The text is clearly written by dedicated, committed members of the Salvation Army. For instance, in the chronology, Booth's death is described thus: "General William Booth promoted to Glory." This volume will be most useful in libraries serving readers with a serious interest in religious topics, such as seminary schools. Other academic libraries might consider it for history programs.—**Mark Schumacher**

688.   **The Jonathan Edwards Encyclopedia.** Harry S. Stout, Kenneth P. Minkema, and Adriaan C. Neele, eds. Grand Rapids, Mich., William B. Eerdmans, 2017. 616p. illus. $60.00. ISBN 13: 978-0-8028-6952-4.

The Jonathan Edwards Encyclopedia presents its prolific and influential subject (1703-1758) as a more complex and surprising figure than one might glean from a cursory reading of *Sinner in the Hands of an Angry God* (1741). Indeed, the Jonathan Edwards Center staff produced this community-sourced encyclopedia in order to dispel myths and uncover truths about the frequently misunderstood historical pastor, theologian, college president, and philosopher. Harry S. Stout, along with coeditors Kenneth P. Minkema and Adriaan C. Neele, selected and vetted more than 400 encyclopedic entries authored by about 170 contributors from across the globe. These entries cover relevant biographies, topics, events, and works and serve as entry points into Jonathan Edwards' family, theology, and Zeitgeist. The summaries of topics describe how Edwards interacted with the doctrines of the Reformed Puritan Congregationalist Christian faith that he inherited. As Edwards biographer George Marsden writes in the foreword, these entries will assist both novices and experts concerning Edwards in studying his "vision of the beauty of God's love in Christ," and this is the framework through which users are guided to apprehend Edwards' life and work. Beyond the editors' empirical goal of correcting myths and errors, this is the guiding, interpretive logic of the encyclopedia.

Because the encyclopedia is not a closed work, and will be expanded in its next, online iteration, the print version is not comprehensive. The coverage is minimal when it comes to some basic but necessary context, such as the Puritan background preceding Edwards. Here the editors assume the reader has knowledge about the "New England Way," for example, and what Puritanism was. This may become problematic when the reader encounters the terms in the Cotton Mather entry, for example. Additionally, one misses typical navigation helps such as an index, cross-references, and bold face text mark-up indicating the existence of a helpful *see also* entry. These and the lack of a comprehensive bibliography limit the accessibility of the print edition (e.g., Was Susan Stinson's novel *Spider in a Tree* cited?). Online tools and functions will resolve these problems.

Still, the one-volume, 616-page book has many beautiful features, such as the reproduced end sheets from Edwards' "Blank Bible"; a portrait of Edwards; and newly drawn historical maps of New England and the surrounding areas. The introductory material and list of contributors demonstrates the level of expertise that went into this volume. The Grand List of Edwards' works as well as the bibliographies for further reading that follow each entry provide the reader with ample primary source and current and seminal secondary source material. The latter illustrate Edwards' renewed popularity in the academy and the church. An alphabetical list of entries provides the conceptual map of the encyclopedia. If the editors envision a second printed edition, however, they might consider organizing the entries by type: biography, topic, and work.

In summary, this volume is highly recommended for seminaries and college/ universities with American religious history and theology programs.—**Amy Koehler**

689.   Paterwic, Stephen J. **Historical Dictionary of the Shakers.** 2d ed. Lanham, Md., Rowman & Littlefield, 2017. 433p. illus. (Historical Dictionaries of Religions, Philosophies, and Movements). $100.00; $95.00 (e-book). ISBN 13: 978-1-5381-0230-5; 978-1-5381-0231-2 (e-book).

This volume is a second edition installment in Rowman & Littlefield's Historical Dictionary of Religions, Philosophies, and Movements series. *Historical Dictionary of the Shakers* provides a comprehensive overview of the Shaker movement from its origins with founder Mother Ann Lee in eighteenth-century England through its spread into colonial America and into the modern era. In addition to the dictionary itself which includes a thorough chronology, the volume offers several appendixes which present different aspects of the Shaker experience including a list of those who served in the Gospel ministry; the Covenant or Constitution of the Church of the United Society in the Town of New Gloucester, 3 December 1830; a copy of the form individuals seeking to become novitiates of the modern organization must sign; the rules which currently govern how the Shakers live; the daily schedule of a Shaker; and an outline of a Shaker worship service. It should also be noted that the current Shaker organization in America has an endorsement in the volume, acknowledging the importance and accuracy of the contents of the dictionary. The dictionary itself contains many historically relevant photographs which enhance the dictionary, providing depth and dimension to the entries which bring the Shakers' history to life. The dictionary is heavy on entries regarding individuals and locations, though it does justice to concepts and artifacts as well, providing meaningful insight to Shakerism.

Between the volume's well-written thoroughness and photographic illustrations and its $100 price tag, this title is highly recommended. Its historical and geographical overview of the Shaker movement and the organization's endorsement of their representation in the title give significant weight to its credibility as a resource. Highly recommended for public libraries and academic libraries at schools with religion and American history programs.—**Megan W. Lowe**

Handbooks and Yearbooks

690.   **Catholic News Archive. http://thecatholicnewsarchive.org.** [Website] Free. Date reviewed: 2017.

This site amasses a good collection of newspaper pages culled from a variety of Catholic news sources throughout the United States, including the Catholic News Service feed, the National Catholic Reporter, and the Catholic World in Pictures. The collection represents nearly 200,000 pages from 5,000 newspaper issues.

Users can conduct simple or advanced searches or can browse by news service Titles, Dioceses, or Dates. The digital archive generally covers the years between 1920 and 1973, with the exception of one issue of the *Shepherd of the Valley* (St. Louis, Missouri) from August of 1832. Users can also browse by Tags; however, this feature is currently limited to only nine tags. Selecting a title offers general information about the publication in addition to the available digital run. Users can then select the issue they would like to examine. Users can examine the entire page or focus on a particular article. Article or advertisement text may be transcribed on the left sidebar. Today in History features a page from the archive which highlights news from a distant year. Historians, students, journalists, and many others will find this site of interest.—**ARBA Staff Reviewer**

691.   **New Testament Apocrypha: More Noncanonical Scriptures. Volume One.** Tony Burke and Brent Landau, eds. Grand Rapids, Mich., William B. Eerdmans, 2016. 585p. index. $75.00. ISBN 13: 978-0-8028-7289-0.

New Testament Apocrypha: More Noncanonical Scriptures (MNTA), along with others projected, represents a collaborative effort by the editors and contributors to unravel and document mainly early Christian writings related to Gospel narratives on the life and times of Jesus. The volume does not comment on apocrypha books in the Vulgate nor those found in Nag Hammadi texts nor texts available in up-to-date English translations. The 30 scarcely known apocryphal books in this volume, including the Jewish apologetical/polemical, *Toledot Yeshu,* span the first centuries of Christian apocrypha to the Middle Ages. Chapters of various length are scrupulously presented: introduction, annotation (detailed sidebar scriptural references and voluminous footnotes), translation (English from the original tongues), and detailed bibliography. MNTA presents a cross panorama of Christian belief, practice, prayer, ethics, etc., parsed in apocryphal gospels, acts and related texts, epistles, and apocalypses exhibited among diversified Christian communities in late antiquity which are neither mentioned nor accepted in canonical scriptures and so-claimed authorized Church tradition. The objective is 1) to provide critical issues of scriptural Jesus, John the Baptist, Apostles, and Christology that noncanonical scriptures, texts, and tradition bring to nascent Christianity; 2) to present the necessary textual and interpretive tools to read and appreciate their indispensable value in the formation of Christian centuries; and 3) to expound apocryphal inclusion in classical Christian thought, polemics, and apologetics indispensable for the common interest of Christians and Jews.—**Zev Garber**

Hinduism

692.   Vemsani, Lavanya. **Krishna in History, Thought, and Culture: An Encyclopedia of the Hindu God of Many Names.** Santa Barbara, Calif., ABC-CLIO, 2016. 333p. illus. index. $89.00. ISBN 13: 978-1-61069-210-6; 978-1-61069-211-3 (e-book).

For many western readers there is a great interest in the study of eastern religion. Hinduism, the most ancient among these, is of particular interest with its extensive collection of writings and its great host of deities. Chief among these deities is Krishna, a figure that has managed to affect many aspects of Indian culture including art, literature, and architecture. *Krishna in History, Thought, and Culture* seeks to serve as a beginner's reference to this fascinating piece of Hinduism for students in high school, undergraduates, and the general public.

This encyclopedia contains over three hundred pages of alphabetically listed entries. Each entry contains in addition to its standard informational text a list of cross-references to refer the reader to related topics within the work as well as suggestions for further reading into those topics. Many entries also possess sidebars with special notes on subjects as well as black-and-white captioned illustrations consisting of photographs, artifacts, and artwork. Entries cover a range of content from the most ancient texts available all the way to the modern day. Geographically, they cover primarily India but also include information on other locations of importance to the work's overall topic. Many entries will also discuss modern artistic adaptations of ancient stories such as literature or film. The work's contents possess both an alphabetical listing of all entries as well as a separate topical list for those who wish to focus their study. This organization is additionally supplemented by an easy-to-use index and a glossary for unfamiliar terms at the end.

This work would serve as a good beginning reference for general enthusiasts and lower level students as intended. Organization is well-maintained and individual entries cross-reference well with each other for an engaging experience. One small flaw lies in an incomplete glossary as the reader will notice some italicized terms in the entries lack definition. For this reason higher-level students or universities with large world religion programs would likely be best served by a more comprehensive resource.—**W. Cole Williamson**

Islam

Almanacs

693.   **World Almanac of Islamism 2017.** 2d ed. By the American Foreign Policy Council. Lanham, Md., Rowman & Littlefield, 2017. 1149p. $145.99; $137.50 (e-book). ISBN 13: 978-1-4422-7344-3; 978-1-4422-7345-0 (e-book).

The 2017 edition of the *World Almanac of Islamism* is very similar in format to its 2014 edition (see ARBA 2015, entry 838). Since 2014, Iran has struck a nuclear deal with the West and has experienced some easing of sanctions that were imposed on it. The conditions in Syria, due to its civil war, have worsened, and the United States government strikes a tone that makes it appear to be less tolerant of minorities. As a result, the 2017 edition has added two new entries (Argentina and Islamic State), and dropped two entries (Senegal and Sudan).

Like the 2014 edition, country entries provide an overview of Islamic activities in that country. Following the overview are sections that outline salient Islamist activities, Islamist influences on society, and, finally, Islamist interactions with the government. Entries of Islamist groups that are profiled begin with a summary, an outline of that organization's history and ideology, followed by its global reach, and its recent activities. While the summaries of most entries have been rewritten, the major content of these entries largely remains the same. Three years is not long enough for substantial changes for most entries. The almanac provides a uniquely American perspective on Islamist activities throughout the world. If one were to acknowledge its bias, it serves as an excellent starting reference on Islamist ideology and activity.—**Muhammad Hassanali**

Dictionaries and Encyclopedias

694.   Adamec, Ludwig W. **Historical Dictionary of Islam.** 3d ed. Lanham, Md., Rowman & Littlefield, 2017. 623p. (Historical Dictionaries of Religions, Philosophies, and Movements). $145.00; $149.99 (e-book). ISBN 13: 978-1-4422-7723-6; 978-1-4422-7724-3 9 (e-book).

Adamec, eminent scholar and leading international authority on Afghanistan (see ARBA 2012, entry 95), has spent decades compiling histories of Islam. Since publication of his previous edition of the historical dictionary (see ARBA 2010, entry 1120), the estimated worldwide Muslim population has grown to an estimated 1.7 billion, equating to 23 percent of the world's population. The purpose of this authoritative reference work is to continue to survey Islam today as well as provide an overview of how this major world religion has evolved over centuries—although the geographical focus of this book is on the Middle East, Africa, and the Arab world. Adamec doesn't shy away from the current conflict in the Islamic world between "literalists" and "modernists" and includes both "radical Islamists and their opponents" in his sometimes brutally honest, yet fair and objective, survey.

Meant to be "a concise dictionary of Islamic history, religion, philosophy, and political movements," this third edition contains many new entries and expands on existing ones. With more than 700 entries (or approximately 480 pages), this edition appears to contain approximately 40 percent more information than the last (at over 340 pages of entries). The dictionary contains generous cross-references, easily distinguished by their boldface type. Main entries for universal terms are generally in English (e.g., "Jannah" directs to "Heaven," "Salat" directs to "Prayer"). Where there is a potential conflict or ambiguity with a Muslim term, Adamec purposely relies on Webster's dictionary, so that spellings like "Koran" make his work more accessible to casual Western readers.

Changes to the third edition include a newly updated chronology through 2015, adding major events from the last decade. Other features include an appendix containing population statistics by region and country, both in absolute numbers and as a percentage of the total population for each country and world region; however, no source or access date is provided. This edition also contains a quick-reference glossary of Islamic terms, and it closes with an extensive, updated themed bibliography listing over 125 new sources covering the major Muslim geographic areas and a variety of subtopics. These will be useful to the serious scholar. As observed in the previous edition's review, other than in the bibliography, readers will find little about Islam in Southeast Asia or other regions of the world; this is of note, since Southeast Asia alone is home to more Muslims than all other regions of the world combined.—**Lucy Duhon**

695.   Guidère, Mathieu. **Historical Dictionary of Islamic Fundamentalism.** 2d ed. Lanham, Md., Rowman & Littlefield, 2017. 608p. (Historical Dictionaries of Religions, Philosophies, and Movements). $140.00; $133.00 (e-book). ISBN 13: 978-1-5381-0669-3; 978-1-5381-0670-9 (e-book).

The past five years have seen tremendous changes in the Islamic fundamentalism landscape, and hence an updated historical dictionary is in order. This second edition (see ARBA 2013, entry 1126) has updated the main entries and added several more. The acronyms, editor's forward, preface, chronology, and bibliography have also been updated. The bubble charts depicting relationships among the various fundamentalist groups have not been updated. In some instances, these have been shrunk to further challenge bespectacled readers. It is difficult to believe that since the first edition there have been no new groups to add to the bubble charts, or that these relationships have not evolved—especially in Egypt and Syria or among splinter groups of some of the more well-known fundamentalist groups.

In addition to the bubble charts, this edition has a series of ideological genealogies. By themselves (i.e., without text to place these charts in context), they have little utility, and could in some cases lead to misinterpreting the relationships they depict. The narrative continues to be challenging as the text contains long sentences with complex structures. However, the work with its focus on fundamentalist groups (both well-known and obscure), key personalities (both contemporary and classical), major contemporary events, country profiles, and ideas of governance and Islamic concepts as interpreted through a fundamentalist lens is still an excellent resource for undergraduate or graduate students.— **Muhammed Hassanali**

696.   **Islam: A Worldwide Encyclopedia.** Çakmak, Cenap, ed. Santa Barbara, Calif., ABC-CLIO, 2017. 4v. illus. index. $415.00/set. ISBN 13: 978-1-61069-216-8; 978-1-61069-217-5 (e-book).

This four-volume set contains over 700 entries on the topic of Islam. The editor makes clear in the preface that the focus of the entries is determined by a Western perspective rather than an Islamic one, so that objectivity is the key factor. Basic concepts, history, persons of importance, and geography related to Islam provide the basis of the information. Most of the entries vary in length from 1,000 to 1,500 words, with *see also* references as well as further readings. An alphabetical list of entries, chronology of events, and a guide to related topics is provided for the entire set at the beginning of each volume. Each of the four volumes contains a color photo section which is identified on the contents page. A glossary and select bibliography is provided at the end of the fourth volume. This extensive reference work will be a key text for any college or university library.—**Bradford Lee Eden**

Judaism

697.   Broyde, Michael J. **A Concise Code of Jewish Law for Converts.** Jerusalem, Urim Publications/Independent Publishers Group, 2017. 180p. index. $24.95. ISBN 13: 978-965-524-249-2.

Classical Halakhah (Jewish Law) in religio-theological terms to understand the dynamics of a Jew by choice when conversion commences is presented by Rabbi Michael J. Broyde (Professor of Law at Emory University). Broyde presents a balanced, nonjudgmental synopsis of rabbinical opinion on what is and what is not permissive religious behavior by a ger/geyoret (proselyte) in the everyday practice of traditional Judaism. The volume deals with four basic sections according to the order found in the standard Shulchan 'Arukh ("Set Table"): Orach Chaim (daily, Sabbath, holiday laws, prayers); Yoreh Deah (Kashrut, idolatry, circumcision, nidda [female hygiene], charity, agrarian living, mourning); Even Haezer (marriage, divorce, procreation, Levirate marriage); and Choshen Mishpat (business and financial issues adjudicated in rabbinical courts). Minutiae-laden rabbinic exegesis and eisegesis perforate the text and footnotes and this may prove burdensome to the noninitiate in rabbinic argumentation. Summary appendixes and supplemental topical essays help overcome rabbinical impasse. Nonetheless, struggling the synchronic structure and composition of the halakhic sources (questions–answers–reflections) are worthwhile. The end is the beginning of an erstwhile venture into the will and way of the Dual Torah to bring home the seeking stranger into House of Israel, proclaimed in the sacred Torah: "The ger [stranger, proselyte] that sojourns with you shall be unto you as the home-born among you, and you shall love him as yourself; for you were gerim [strangers] in the land of Egypt–I am the Lord your God," [Lev 19:34].—**Zev Garber**

698.   **Jewish Women's Archive. https://jwa.org.** [Website] Free. Date reviewed: 2018.

This site shares information on historical and contemporary Jewish women via an abundance of well-researched essays, biographies, and various multimedia resources, many of which are gathered into quality thematic exhibits which highlight both the strong community of Jewish women and the issues important to them. Users can find much to explore under the Profiles and Collections tabs at the top of the home page. Profiles accesses a searchable A-Z directory of prominent Jewish women from first century Queen Helene of Adiabene to poet Rajzel Zychlinksy. Entries generally include a summary biography and photograph and list date of birth, date of death, occupation(s), tags, and related site resources. Under Collections, the encyclopedia provides over two thousand A-Z entries— more extensive than the Profiles—on Jewish women and Jewish women's themes including Jewish women in the Bible, the American Birth Control Movement, Anglo-Jewish Writers, Peace Movements in Israel, and much more. Entries generally consist of substantial, cross-referenced essays, photos, and bibliographies. Other links under Collections lead to a series of excellent exhibits. Women Rabbis shares the unique perspectives of women rabbis on such things as faith and family through its collection of oral histories on video. This section also includes a Timeline of Women in the Rabbinate. Power Couples offers comparative profiles of Jewish women related through life achievement, like Olympic Fencers Ilona Elek and Sada Jacobson; suggesting a legacy of connection and inspiration. Women of Valor expands the biographies of sixteen women, including Bella Abzug, Beatrice (Madame) Alexander, and Emma Goldman, who overcame particular hurdles in achieving their life's work. This section may incorporate timelines, photo galleries, audio, and other primary source documents. The Feminist Revolution exhibit lets users browse a gallery of women who impacted the feminist movement via unique avenues like Art & Culture, Education, and Diversity & Tolerance. Users can also follow a Timeline and explore extensive Resources. Community Stories looks at groups of Jewish women (e.g., Washington D.C. Stories, (Hurricane) Katrina's Jewish Voices) via oral histories, videos, artifacts, and more. Other exhibits include This Week in History, We Remember, and Western Pioneers. The Multi-media Gallery tab accesses the site's vast collection of primary sources outside the context of the curated exhibits. Users can explore by topic, type (advertisement, art, memoir, etc.), format (photo, video, etc.), and other filters. There are also teaching materials underneath the Education tab.—**ARBA Staff Reviewer**

699.   Levy, Steven, and Sarah Levy. **The JPS Rashi Discussion Torah Commentary.** Philadelphia, Jewish Publication Society, 2017. 195p. index. $19.95pa. ISBN 13: 978-0-8276-1269-3.

Rashi (acronym for Rabbi Shlomo ben Isaac, 1040-1105), a leading commentator on the Bible and the Babylonian Talmud, is universally known in rabbinic circles as the Parshandata ("the commentator par excellence") for his commentary on the Pentateuch recognized as the first printed Hebrew volume (1475), and ever since the printed chumash ("Five Books of Moses") with Rashi has appeared for Jewish learning and religious guidance. Reading Rashi to prepare for the Sabbath Torah reading (parsha) is standard in traditional Jewish circles. Contemporizing select Rashi exegesis and eisegesis on the weekly parsha for a Shabbat family table talk and study group learning exchange is the goal of this reader friendly guidebook. The yearly Torah cycle is represented by chapters which contain Hebrew and English sentences reflected upon in three short architectonic essays which provide inspirational reading and understanding of text, context, and intertext of the cited Rashi commentary on ethical and moral issues of today. Additionally, chapter questions initiate meaningful and relevant discussion. For example, Israel and the Nations is extracted from Rashi on Gen 1:1a ("When God began to create") explicitly creation of heaven and earth and implicitly the allotment of land, specifically, the heritage of the land of Israel then (Crusaders) and now (Zionist state) and Rashi on Gen 10:9 expounding on

Nimrod's power of speech, Tower of Babel, and United Nations today. In the tradition of classical rabbinic tradition, the written Torah of Moses is eternal and mandated to be interpreted (Exod 24:12, 34:27; Lev 26:46; Deut 33:4) due to forever changing historic situations, which continues to uncover new levels of depth and meaning and thus make new facets of Judaism visible and meaningful in each generation. So marks the scholarship of Rashi and transmitted in contemporary variations by the authors.—**Zev Garber**

700.   Shulman, Daniel H. **Personal Midrash: Fresh Insights into the Torah.** Jerusalem, Urim Publications/Independent Publishers Group, 2017. 158p. $23.00. ISBN 13: 978-965-524-267-6.

Midrash, in the Rabbinic mind, is hermeneutics derived from biblical inquiry; an attempt to explain the text in as many ways as seems possible to the inquiring mind of the Jewish sage. In Jewish and Christian dialogue on sacred texts, the term also embraces doctrinal, ethical, religious, and social concerns. Shulman is neither an academic, educator, or clergy member; rather, he is an accomplished lawyer and involved traditionalist Jew, who takes seriously and personally two of Judaism's ultimate concerns, Torah and Israel. That is to say, Torah revealed at Sinai by divine yad (hand) and affirmed by kol (voice). Yisrael is the lasting heritage of 'am (People) Yisrael to wit he is inspired to add his own midrashic interpretation. Shulman's fifty-two chapters reflect the fifty-four parashiyot (parasha, sing), consecutive Torah portions covering Genesis-Deuteronomy read proportionally in public Shabbat synagogue service in a cycle of a year. The chapters are terse (one-two pages), expounding on a textual thought intrigued by word study and gematria (letter numerology). Each chapter topic is not examined from its historical and cultural background and in the fullness of Jewish sacred texts, halakhic jurisdiction, and extra-halakhic sources. However, contemporary traditionalism characterizes Shulman's methodology and style. Though some may question if Shulman's conservative Jewish approach can persuade the twenty-first-century rationalist Jew to live in the image of God, there is no doubt to his optimism and sincerity. The evidence is in the reading.—**Zev Garber**

701.   Weiner, Jason. **Jewish Guide to Practical Medical Decision-Making.** Jerusalem, Urim Publications/Independent Publishers Group, 2017. 368p. index. $25.95. ISBN 13: 978-965-524-278-2.

The intent of *Jewish Guide to Practical Medical Decision-Making* is to present traditional Halakhah (Rabbinic law) on contemporary medical information and practice. It introduces the reader to biblical and Talmudic sources and a wide range of religious response and ethical insight relevant to birth- and death-related issues, such as surrogacy and egg donation, shared decision-making decisions on assisted suicide, extended and terminal life, organ donations, death, and afterlife. Six sections are parsed into minichapters where Weiner (senior rabbi and director of the Spiritual Care Department at Cedars-Sinai Medical Center in Los Angeles) synthesizes medicine and rabbinics in confronting medical dilemmas. Weiner's read of rabbinic sources emphasizes word study, elements of style, conceptual clarification, and heightened emphasis; and all are accompanied by a concise detailed explanation to help clarify nuances of Halakhah and diversity of rabbinic opinion within the broader medical discussion and practice. Thus Jewish teaching on the sacredness of life may differ from medical practice of extended life; physical pain is in the realm of medical science but suffering in the realm of spiritual care, and so forth.

Personal vignettes introduce the chapters and help actualize theory into practice. In sum, a resourceful rabbinic guide to tedious medical queries birthed in mezuzah-laden operating, recovery, and parking spaces where some of Hollywood's elite die or survive.—**Zev Garber**

Part IV
SCIENCE AND TECHNOLOGY

29 Science and Technology in General

Dictionaries and Encyclopedias

702. **Encyclopedia of Information Science and Technology.** 4th ed. Mehdi Khosrow-Pour, ed. Hershey, Pa., IGI Global, 2017. 10v. index. $4,556.00/set. ISBN 13: 978-1-52252-255-3; 978-1-52252-256-0 (e-book).

This 4th-edition work in 10 volumes includes more than 700 new entries. The work is easily accessible via the tables of contents (one by volume and one in alphabetic order) or from the index in volume 10. Executive editor Mehdi Khosrow-Pour spearheaded this effort that includes the work of more than 1,400 worldwide scholars and researchers; the set also has an editorial advisory board and an editorial review board.

Coverage is broad and includes sections on artificial intelligence, big data, business information systems, cloud computing, cyber and network security, digital literacy, educational technologies, electronic commerce, environmental science and agriculture, gaming (an entirely new section), healthcare administration, human-computer interaction, IT security and ethics, library science and administration, medical technologies, mobile learning, networking and telecommunications, robotics, social networking and computing, sports and entertainment, systems and software engineering, urban and regional development, and Web technologies. Articles vary in length, and each section contains a different number of articles. The section on sports and entertainment has 2 articles, for example, while the one on systems and software engineering has 22. Altogether readers will get more than 15,000 sources of additional information over the 10 volumes.

While the price tag for the entire set is high, individual articles are available for purchase. Recommended for academic libraries.—**ARBA Staff Reviewer**

703. **Encyclopedia of Nanotechnology.** 2d ed. Bharat Bhushan, comp. New York, Springer Publishing, 2016. 4v. illus. $2,999.99. ISBN 13: 978-94-017-9779-5; 978-94-017-9780-1 (e-book).

Advances and developments in nanotechnology necessitated the publication of this second edition under the editorship of Bharat Bhushan. The first edition contained 325 essays in 4 volumes; this edition has 426 entries in 4 volumes. Original entries have been updated. Signed entries, authored by academic subject specialists, vary in length from 4 pages to 10 pages. They are cross-referenced and conclude with a list of sources. There are thousands of illustrations throughout the set. The intended audience is graduate students, researchers, and practitioners, and the writing level reflects this.

This book is highly recommended to university libraries. Those that own the first edition will even want to consider this title because of the amount of new material. Those who purchase the ebook version will benefit from periodic updates—**ARBA Staff Reviewer**

704. **Science Online. www.online.infobase.com.** [Website] New York, Infobase Publishing, 2017. Price negotiated by site. Date reviewed: 2017.

This database features topics ranging from biology to weather and climate. Information is divided into five major learning areas: eLearning Modules; Featured Videos and Animations; Interactive Experiments; Featured Diagrams; and Featured People. In each article users have the option to save to Google Drive, print, share, and view citation formats. The articles also contain bibliographic information and subject heading tags. Navigation is very user friendly. I can see students doing STEM research and completing learning modules with curriculum-oriented information for projects in their science classes. I would recommend this resource for school libraries that need to enrich student research learning needs with reliable, easy-to-find information that is well presented and will provide students with the skills necessary to explore any database. Recommended.—**Deb Grove**

Handbooks and Yearbooks

705. **Analyzing the Role of Citizen Science in Modern Research.** Luigi Ceccaroni and Jaume Piera, eds. Hershey, Pa., IGI Global, 2017. 354p. index. (Advances in Knowledge Acquisition, Transfer, and Management (AKATM) Book Series). $148.00. ISBN 13: 978-1-52250-962-2; 978-1-52250-963-9 (e-book).

Public participation in scientific research is not new. Throughout the twentieth century, thousands of public volunteers have participated in projects to monitor water quality, document the distribution of breeding birds, and scour the night skies for new stars and galaxies. The current concept of citizen science, however, with its integration of explicit and tested protocols for collecting data, vetting of data by professional biologists, and inclusion of specific and measurable goals for public education, has evolved primarily over the past two decades. Developing and implementing public data-collection projects that yield both scientific and educational outcomes requires significant effort and planning.

Analyzing the Role of Citizen Science in Modern Research focuses on analyzing data on current initiatives and best practices in citizen engagement and education programs across various disciplines. The book makes generous use of headings and subheadings as well as diagrams, tables, and charts. The index and table of contents facilitate navigation, and a list of key terms and definitions ensures reader comprehension of technical terms.

Highlighting emergent research and application techniques within citizen science initiatives, *Analyzing the Role of Citizen Science in Modern Research* appeals to academicians, researchers, policy-makers, government officials, technology developers, advanced-level students, and program developers interested in launching or improving citizen science programs across the globe. While there are many books about how the Internet is changing business or the government, this is the first book about something different and fundamental: how the Internet is empowering citizens in transforming the nature of science. Recommended for academic libraries.—**Thomas E. Baker**

706. **bozemanscience. http://www.bozemanscience.com/.** [Website] Free. Date reviewed: 2017.

Over the past several years, Paul Andersen has created hundreds of videos aligned to Next Generation Science Standards. In addition to earth science, biology, chemistry, physics, statistics, and graphing, he has videos geared for AP biology, environmental science, and physics. He also has professional development videos for teachers on the Next Generation Standards, as well as educational theory and practice. Videos can be found by browsing the topics or through use of a search box. Each video is on a discrete topic, such as Biological Molecules or Proper Group Size for Learning. It would be helpful if the video descriptions included the length of the video. Most videos include diagrams that Andersen annotates as he explains the topic. He does a great job of defining terms and relating the scientific concepts to students' background knowledge. For example, the introduction to anatomy and physiology uses a crescent wrench to explain the terms, then moves on to human hands as concrete examples of form and function. The sheer number of topics covered ensures that almost any middle or high school teacher will be able to find a video to help explain the topic he or she is exploring with students. Teachers at both of my schools love this resource.—**Suzanne Libra**

707. **Cutting Edge Careers.** San Diego, Calif., Reference Point Press, 2017. 7v. illus. index. $279.51/set ($29.95 individual title).

The series is like the Department of Labor Statistics' Occupational Outlook Handbook on steroids. It covers many of the same topics but in much greater depth. There are seven books in total, covering the careers of big data analysts, biomedical engineers, cybersecurity analysts, robotics engineers, software engineers, video game designers, and virtual reality developers. Each book covers basic categories in the same order. For example, in Robotics Engineer, readers learn exactly what a robotics engineer does along with possible steps to follow in order to become one, including formal education, volunteer work, and internships that will bolster a resume. There's a section on skills and personality qualities needed as well, allowing students to get a feel for whether or not they'll like a specific career. A particularly helpful feature of these books is a description of a typical day in the life of a person doing each job, including an interview with someone working in that field. This series is relatively inexpensive and would be a good addition for schools that focus on career development, although they will have a short shelf life. A bibliography and index round out the work. Recommended for grades 7-12. [Editorial Note: see publisher site for individual ISBN numbers].—**Laura Younkin**

708. **ECHO. http://echo.gmu.edu/.** [Website] Free. Date reviewed: 2018.

ECHO, or Exploring and Collecting History Online, is a directory of over five thousand websites that offer a historical perspective on science, technology, and industry. The straightforward site allows a basic or advanced search as well as several focused browsing options. From the left side of the page, users can Browse by Category (Earth Sciences, Mathematics, Consumer Technology, etc.), Browse by Historic Period (Ancient, Early Modern, etc.), and Browse by Content (e.g. Video, Artifacts, Images, etc.). Websites may appear under more than one of these browsing options. Users may also examine the Tag Cloud via the link at the top of the page, and the Featured Site (which appears to change daily) for a good look at the optimal ECHO directory entry. Selecting a specific category, period, or content type links to an alphabetical listing of the Web page title, some of which are accompanied by an ECHO annotation—a helpful reference for the casual site user. Presumably ECHO will continue to annotate sites. Clicking on a title leads to the entry, which may include relevant tags, the URL, site author, a brief excerpt, and annotation if available. A wide range of websites are included in this directory, representing museums, universities, archives, small projects, and more. It should be noted that some URLs in the directory may be incorrect or may no longer exist.—**ARBA Staff Reviewer**

709. **Federal Science Library. https://science-libraries.canada.ca/eng/home/.** [Website] Free. Date reviewed: 2017.

This no-frills portal from the Canadian government allows access to the collections of seven agencies and/or departments that are focused on scientific endeavors. Agency libraries include the Canadian Agriculture Library, Environment and Climate Change Canada Library Services, Fisheries and Oceans Canada (DFO) Library, Health Library, National Science Library, and the Natural Resources Canada (NRCan) Library. Users of the portal can conduct a basic or advanced search from the bar, or can click on one of the above links to access particular information about the library, including a brief description of its affiliated agency(ies) and the make-up of its collections. Users can also click the links within the Guides and Help textbox on the right side of the homepage for information on accessing some of the materials. Of the six main homepage links, three of them provide further links connecting directly with those collections. The NRCan link describes its holdings as including publications, maps, photos, and more, and its page includes further links to the Canadian Forest Service Publications Repository (books, articles, and downloadable reports like "The State of Canada's Forests Annual Report" 2017), GEOSCAN (research from the Geological Survey of Canada and more), and the NRCan Photo Database (over twenty-five thousand photographs). Users can also access several archives under the National Science Library page, including the National Research Council Archives which consists of peer-reviewed health and life sciences research publications, technical reports, conference publications, historical records, photographs, and other resources. The DFO library provides a link to a Staff Publications Bibliography, which includes several citation databases (updated as of 2013) covering journals, articles, technical reports, and more from various institutes or monitoring stations throughout Canada .While some library material may be a bit difficult to access (some libraries may continue to redirect users), there is ample information available through this portal to make it a good tool for researchers across a variety of scientific or governmental areas.—**ARBA Staff Reviewer**

710. **The Institute for Data Intensive Engineering and Science. http://idies.jhu.edu/ research/datasets/.** [Website] Free. Date reviewed: 2018.

In affiliation with Johns Hopkins University, the Institute for Data Intensive Engineering and Science (IDIES) website offers resources to aid with data-driven solutions to issues within the science and engineering realms. It offers networking opportunities, technical and administrative resources, and access to a variety of data sets within their specific applications. While most resources are available to IDIES members—educators, research staff, and some others can apply for an IDIES membership at various levels— this website highlights several data applications that may be of interest to general users. The Member Resources tab provides a number of links to training and computing centers in addition to tools and services aligned with big data needs, such as SciServer and

DataScope. There are also links regarding grant funding and online education. Scientists, researchers, graduate-level educators, and others can apply to Join IDIES from the tab on the menu bar to capitalize on these resources. General users can examine several public databases through the Research & Data tab which encompasses astronomy (Sloan Digital Survey), neuroscience (Open Connectome), ecology (Life Under Your Feet), genetics, and more. The Sloan Digital Sky Survey, with its three-dimensional maps of the universe, and Life Under Your Feet, using a large network of sensors to record soil temperature, pressure, content, and other data, would work well with educators of middle school, high school, and undergraduate students. More information on these projects is found under the Education and Outreach tab.

Although somewhat limited to its membership audience, the website is nonetheless helpful in displaying the creative possibilities of big data management and application.—**ARBA Staff Reviewer**

711.   Morris, Iwan Rhys, ed. **The Oxford Illustrated History of Science.** New York, Oxford University Press, 2017. 463p. illus. index. $39.95. ISBN 13: 978-0-19-966327-9.

This beautifully illustrated history of science reflects the work of thirteen historians and editor Iwan Morris, a history professor at Aberystwyth University, Wales. The writing is very accessible, starting with the introduction, which discusses the history of science, as well as the historiography. The book is divided into two sections. The first is chronological, moving from chapters on science in the ancient Mediterranean world and ancient China to science in the medieval Christian and Islamic worlds to science in the premodern east to the Scientific Revolution and Enlightenment science. The second part focuses largely on the period since the eighteenth century and provides thematic coverage. Chapters discuss the rise of experimental cultures, new ways of thinking about the origins and meaning of life, mapping the universe, the development of a distinct culture of highly technical theoretical speculation, and the ways scientists and scientific institutions have developed to communicate findings to a larger audience. It is hard to overstate the importance of the color and black-and-white illustrations throughout this book; many are full page (9 x 7). The illustrations underpin the narrative and help focus reader attention. This book is modestly priced and a great value for public and academic libraries. Highly recommended.—**ARBA Staff Reviewer**

30 Agricultural Sciences

Food Sciences and Technology

Atlases

712.   Hoalst-Pullen, Nancy, and Mark W. Patterson. **National Geographic Atlas of Beer.** Washington, D.C., National Geographic Society, 2017. 304p. illus. maps. index. $40.00. ISBN 13: 978-1-4262-1833-0.

This book, devoted to one of the world's most popular beverages, takes readers on a historical international tour, starting in Europe and moving through North America, South America, Asia, Australia and Oceania, and Africa. The book's introduction includes a historical discussion of beer consumption as well as an examination of the role of geography in the production of beer. The introduction also touches on different tastes and styles. Chapters are subdivided. For Europe, there are separate sections for Belgium, Germany, the United Kingdom, the Czech Republic, France, Ireland, Italy, Austria, Denmark, the Netherlands, Poland, Russia, and Spain. Estonia, Finland, Norway, and Sweden are treated in one section. The same pattern is repeated for North America, South America, Asia, and Australia and Oceania. The Africa chapter is the shortest—South Africa and Tanzania are the only countries included in this book. Chapters contextualize the production and consumption of beer and include such things as guides to beer in each country. All of this information is enhanced by the one hundred maps and more than two hundred color illustrations. The book concludes with a glossary, list of maps by continent, further resources (books and websites), and an index (boldface page numbers in the index refer readers to illustrations). This book will appeal to general readers and would also be a good basic resource in academic libraries. Recommended.—**ARBA Staff Reviewer**

Dictionaries and Encyclopedias

713.   **The Chicago Food Encyclopedia.** Haddix, Carol Mighton, Bruce Kraig, and Colleen Taylor Sen, eds. Champaign, Ill., University of Illinois Press, 2017. 344p. illus. index. (The Heartland Foodways Series). $34.95. ISBN 13: 978-0-252-08724-0; 978-0-252-09977-9 (e-book).

The editors designed this encyclopedia to serve as a reference source to the Chicago food scene and as a place to find cultural and historical perspectives. The introduction provides the scaffolding on which to hang the pieces of information found in the encyclopedia. Here readers will find a food-focused historical timeline; sidebars with things like recipes and literary excerpts; discussions of the impact of both world wars on the food scene; the development made possible by transportation and infrastructure; the affect of different waves of migration and immigration; and other information. There are 375 cross-referenced entries in total, ranging from 100 to 1,500 words. Due to space limitations, the editors confined the content to the current city limits of Chicago. The use of 30 color and 91 black-and-white photographs throughout enhances the work which covers the people, places, concepts, companies, food, and more important to telling the story of Chicago's food. Readers will also find a bibliography, a topical list of entries, short biographies of the contributors, and an index. This well-written, well-researched, and well-priced title is highly recommended for public and academic libraries.—**ARBA Staff Reviewer**

714.   **The Cook's Thesaurus. http://www.foodsubs.com/.** [Website] Free. Date reviewed: 2018.

Simple in design, this website acts as an encyclopedia of the foods we eat and the tools we use to prepare them. It offers a generous amount of basic information with an emphasis on food equivalents or substitutions (e.g., dried pasta for fresh pasta, evaporated milk for fresh milk, etc.). Users can enter a simple search term in the bar or select from seventeen category links in the box on the left side of the homepage, including Vegetables, Flavorings, Legumes & Nuts, Baking Supplies, Equipment, Grains, and Liquids. The homepage also features a brief description of an Ingredient of the Month.

Clicking a category link leads to a generous listing of individual topic links. For example, the Grains category lists rice, wheat, barley, oats, spelt, and much more in addition to grain forms such as flakes, meal, whole, pearled, etc. The Equipment category covers such things as measuring, cleaning & cutting tools, outdoor cooking equipment, bowls & containers, bar, and stovetop & baking equipment. Topic entries may generally include a photo(s) and/or illustration alongside such summary information as ingredient usage in global cuisine, medicinal attributes, cultural information, types, equivalents, substitutes, and varieties in addition to hyperlinks to recipes and other information. The straightforward site offers accessible information that would appeal to home cooks, culinary students, food professionals, and others.—**ARBA Staff Reviewer**

715.   Lakshmi, Padma, and Judith Sutton. **The Encyclopedia of Spices and Herbs.** New York, HarperCollins, 2016. 352p. illus. index. $39.99. ISBN 13: 978-0-06-237523-0.

Authors Padma Lakshmi of *Top Chef* fame and Judith Sutton have written a beautifully illustrated book on spices and herbs from around the world. The spices and herbs are presented A to Z. Entries vary in length, but cover provenance and uses (including medicinal uses, if applicable). Users will find the name of the spice or herb, any alternate spellings or other names, the botanical name, and a description of appearance. There is also generous use of sidebars throughout on such things as curing salts, grinding and toasting spices, recipes for tea, and storing herbs and spices. Widely known spices and herbs are included, like peppers, chiles, basil, and parsley, but this book also includes herbs and spices that may be less familiar to an American audience, like quatre epices, a French four-spice mix, or Panch Phoron, a Bengali five spice that complements lentils and other legumes. The book concludes with a bibliography of books and websites and an index that uses italicized page numbers to indicate illustrations. This easy-to-read and informative spice and herb encyclopedia is recommended for public libraries and academic libraries with culinary programs.—**ARBA Staff Reviewer**

Handbooks and Yearbooks

716. **Agri-Food Supply Chain Management: Breakthroughs in Research and Practice.** By Information Resources Management Association. Hershey, Pa., Information Science Reference/IGI Global, 2017. 528p. index. $300.00. ISBN 13: 978-1-52251-629-3; 978-1-52251-630-9 (e-book).

As demands for high quality and customized agri-food products have increased, the design, development, and operation of efficient agri-food supply chains have enjoyed increased interest in modern management science. Furthermore, the volatility of weather conditions, perishability of goods, complex food safety regulatory environment, changing consumer lifestyle trends, environmental concerns, and overabundance of stakeholders pose significant challenges regarding the development of robust supply chains within the agri-food sector. Agri-food supply chain or food system processes include production, processing, distribution, consumption, and disposal. Supply chain managers require a skill set that allows them to streamline the flow of materials, finances, and information for a company. This text by an international cast of scholars helps experts and practitioners stay informed regarding up-to-date research and provides insight into emerging trends and future opportunities within the discipline. The material is divided into four sections that provide comprehensive coverage of important topics: Fundamental Concepts and Design Methodologies; Technologies and Applications; Organizational and Social Implications; and Critical Issues and Emerging Trends. The material is well supplemented by such tools as tables, graphics, and diagrams, key terms and definitions, clear organization, and a compilation of references.

University librarians would do well to incorporate this book in their acquisition budget for the academic year.—**Thomas E. Baker**

717. **Early American Cookbooks Database. https://wp.nyu.edu/early_american_cookbooks/.** [Website] Free. Date reviewed: 2018.

This database examines a century of American cooking via its collection of nearly 1,500 cookbooks published mainly over the course of the nineteenth century. Users can explore full-text versions of the cookbooks in addition to a good selection of supplementary resources that would be valuable in a number of research scenarios. Users can search the curated collection via the Hathi Trust Digital Library hyperlink, where they will find the cookbooks listed alphabetically by title, author, or publication date alongside a thumbnail of cookbook cover. Clicking the full view link allows access to the digital document, where users can search text, view full catalog records, and perform other functions. From the homepage, users can explore a sampling of topical scholarship on such subjects as cookbooks for men, Fannie Farmer, vegetarian cookbooks, regional cookbooks, and unusual recipes. Users can also access a number of data visualizations such as an authors chart, books by year, a timeline which illustrates the notable usage of the word "frugal" in cookbook titles, and more. The site also demonstrates the use of topic modeling in calling out various trends or patterns throughout cookbook text. The Resources tab lists useful links, bibliographies and other online resources. This material would appeal strongly to those interested in nineteenth century diet, cooking techniques, nutrition, and other topics.—**ARBA Staff Reviewer**

718.   **The International Organisation of Vine and Wine. http://www.oiv.int/en/.** [Website] Free. Date reviewed: 2017.

The International Organisation of Vine and Wine (OIV) has created this website to present its extensive science-based work concerning wine and its related attributes (vines, grapes, etc.). The site presents news of OIV activities in addition to reams of industry standards, codes, statistics, and other material. Users can scroll down the page for featured OIV News articles (e.g., "Bulk Wines: Moving towards a better understanding of markets") in addition to items from the OIV Agenda (such as the Black Sea Region Wine and Spirits Contest 2018), which takes the organization across the world for symposiums, competitions, and more. Users can also access these items from the menu bar at the top of the homepage. Researchers interested in the detail of OIV work can select the Standards and Technical Documents tab from the bar, where they will find the OIV corpus. This material includes such things as official OIV Resolutions, Product Definitions & Labeling, Description of Grape Varieties, Methods of Analysis, and Good Practice Guidelines. Documents are presented as expert reports, compendiums, regulatory codes, and more, and are available for viewing or downloading as a pdf. The Databases & Statistics tab produces data related to Geographical Indications, Vine Varieties, and Training. The Geographical Indications database, for example, allows users to track thirty-one countries that produce wine and related products (e.g., vinegar, grape juice). This section also displays graphs which track and compare wine and related product exports, imports, consumption, and other data. Comparisons can be made between countries and/or regions. The technical focus of the site alongside its expansive repository of information makes it ideal for researchers whether tracking larger issues of wine's global trade or the finer points of a vinegar's acid content.—**ARBA Staff Reviewer**

719.   **International Wine Research Database. http://iwrdb.org/.** [Website] Free. Date reviewed: 2018.

This straightforward database helps users access a range of research on wine from sources around the globe. Its broad variety of both print and electronic media would appeal to both the wine novice and the academic researcher. The homepage allows users to search by author, article title, journal title, or subject. Users can also employ an advanced or authority search. The site will preserve a user's search history, which is accessible from a tab in the upper right corner of the homepage. There is also a Tag Cloud tab which, as of this review, does not seem functional. Browsing capabilities seem limited to a list of sixteen selected sources (there are others in the database) that users may reference in their research, such as the technical journal eViticulture (with direct link), and the familiar *Wine Spectator* magazine (no link). Users can generally ascertain the range of economic ("Valuing Vineyards: A Directional Distance Function Approach"), technical ("Using Grow Tubes in Vineyards"), and aesthetic ("History and Style at Artesa Vineyards") topics the literature covers from this selection. Selecting a particular article from the database provides bibliographical information such as publication date, author, publisher, subject(s), and call number. Some entries include a brief article summary as well. Despite limitations, the diversity of the material contributes to the site's broad appeal to experts in the wine industry, students of oenology, and casual wine lovers alike.—**ARBA Staff Reviewer**

720.   Moreno, Maria Paz. **Madrid: A Culinary History.** Lanham, Md., Rowman & Littlefield, 2018. 204p. illus. index. (Big City Food Biographies Series). $38.00. ISBN 13: 978-1-4422-6640-7; 978-1-4422-6641-4 (e-book).

Part of the Big City Food Biographies series, this book focuses on the culinary history and delights of Madrid, Spain. The first three chapters are a history of food and cuisine in Madrid from its origins up into the twenty-first century. The sixteenth century and the influences of the New World take center stage in this history, along with the transition from famines to abundance that occurred in the second half of the twentieth century. The last four chapters provide details on twenty-first century Madrid with its markets and retail food industry, historic cookbooks, historic restaurants and cafes, and its traditional dishes. Sprinkled throughout with black-and-white photographs of various time periods in Madrid's history in the last two centuries, along with specific recipes and ingredients of famous cuisines, this book illustrates the vibrant food of one of Spain's premier cities.— **Bradford Lee Eden**

721.   **The Poultry Site. www.thepoultrysite.com.** [Website] Free. Date reviewed: 2017.

This site talks all things poultry, sharing a wealth of photographs, reports, forums, articles, recipes, and more dedicated to the care, trade, and processing of chickens, eggs, and turkeys. It presents a busy homepage, with abundant information displayed in a variety of ways. Users can select a topic from the menu bar, or scroll down through the page for featured content. Headlines & Analysis presents the most newsworthy items in the world of poultry ("Study Shows Whole Eggs Better for Muscle Buildup Rather Than Egg Whites") with further categories corralling similarly themed information, such as Poultry News, Poultry Articles, and Company News (focusing on Poultry-affiliated businesses). Market Reports lists most recent stock reports from the USDA (e.g., Cold Storage, Broiler Hatchery, Feed Outlook) in addition to reports from around the world. The homepage also displays a Book of the Month, Poultry Photos, and a collection of Poultry Recipes like Chicken and Mushroom Lasagne. Alongside these numerous links is an abundant display of industry sponsor, event, and promotion buttons which contribute to an informative, albeit, visually cluttered homepage. Some of this information is refashioned into categories along the menu bar, while other information is new. News & Analysis offers categorical organization of poultry-related news (e.g., News by Country, etc.). The Knowledge Center offers information on poultry health and disease (e.g., Avian Flu), an Egg Quality guide, information on different breeds, and a Quick Disease guide, among other things. The Business Directory groups industry-related organizations by region and product/service types. While the site can be visually overwhelming, the generous and clearly demarcated categories make it relatively easy to find information that would appeal to commercial and small poultry farmers, traders, students of agricultural science, and others in the business of poultry.—**ARBA Staff Reviewer**

722.   Smith, Andrew F. **Food in America: The Past, Present, and Future of Food, Farming, and the Family Meal.** Santa Barbara, Calif., ABC-CLIO, 2017. 3v. $294.00/ set. ISBN 13: 978-1-61069-858-0; 978-1-61069-859-7 (e-book).

This is a well-bound set with a consistent layout in each of the three volumes. Each volume is about four hundred pages. There are few photos or other illustrations, charts, or graphs. Overall this set is a thorough historical perspective with a wide range of support documentation, but it is also rooted in today with chapters that focus on very important relevant topics of our time. A subject approach is used for the set—volume one, *Food and the Environment;* volume two, *Food and Health and Nutrition;* and volume three, *Food and the Economy*—which provide extensive information about the transition of American agriculture over time. An historical introduction to each volume's subject gives excellent background, followed by several topical "Controversies: Going Forward." These chapter topics (such as climate change, food waste, and water in volume one; antibiotics, diets, sugar in volume two; and advertising and marketing, genetically modified food, and mega grocery chains in volume three) are discussed and have numerous citations in each chapter's further readings. The final third of each volume contains important historical documents, which range from Benjamin Franklin to International Agreements, and legislative acts (such as the Food Stamp Act of 1964). Each volume has an index of more than forty pages. This is a good acquisition for university libraries, any agricultural office or college, or for large public libraries.—**James W. Agee**

723.   **USDA   Aquaculture   Data.   https://www.ers.usda.gov/data-products/ aquaculture-data/.** [Website] Free. Date reviewed: 2018.

This page from the USDA Economic Research Service presents data on U.S. aquaculture (generally defined as the "production of aquatic animals and plants under controlled conditions") endeavors including catfish and trout inventories, sales, and prices as well as trade related to aquaculture-affiliated products of salmon, oysters, shrimp, and more. The page allows access to several data sets regarding these topics which users can download as Excel files. The Aquaculture Trade Tables file contains eight tables noting value and quantity information for Atlantic salmon, tilapia, and shrimp in addition to a broad variety of fish and shellfish annual imports and exports over a number of years. Production and Inventory tables include information on inventory, sales, prices, and processor types for catfish and grower sales for trout. Zipped CSV Files also contains data related to catfish and trout import/export data. It is highly recommended that users click on the Documentation link found in the upper left corner of the page as it provides essential information regarding the data: its collection, definitions, updates, etc. There are also two additional links here that users may find helpful: the 2013 Census of Aquaculture and the National Marine Fisheries Service with data on domestic wild seafood. While limited to these data sets, this page could nonetheless appeal to those conducting environmental, economic, and other research, particularly in relation to the rapid growth of aquaculture.—**ARBA Staff Reviewer**

724.   **What's on the Menu? http://menus.nypl.org/.** [Website] Free. Date reviewed: 2017.

French gastronome Brillat-Savarin, who is said to have quipped "tell me what you eat and I will tell you what you are," would have been kept impossibly busy if he had What's On the Menu? at his fingertips. The project from the New York Public Library has so far digitized nearly eighteen thousand menus from the United States and abroad and over a half million restaurant dishes spanning decades. Selecting the Menus tab at the top of the page accesses thumbnail images which also list the year of menu publication and number of dishes listed upon it. Thumbnails display a "Done!" banner if they are fully transcribed. Browsers can arrange the menu display by date, name, or dish count. Alternatively, users can explore the vast range of restaurant Dishes, which can be any item served on a menu, from common hors d'oeurves to a particular vintage of wine. This extensive listing can be sorted by dish popularity, date of menu, or obscurity of dish. Users can also examine dishes by decade. Selecting a dish will link to price information, related dishes, restaurant(s), and a listing of outside links to recipes, photos, and more. The Data tab provides behind-the-scenes information regarding the enormous undertaking of this digital project, and the Blog shares light but informative pieces with themes drawn from the menu trove, such as "History on the Half-Shell: The Story of New York City and Its Oysters." The homepage also features select menus (currently a seafood theme) and dishes, while enthusiastically encouraging user participation in transcribing more menus to add to the delicious digital undertaking. Seemingly whimsical, the project tells a fascinating story of relevance to many types of research—historical, gastronomic, social, and more.—**ARBA Staff Reviewer**

Horticulture

Dictionaries and Encyclopedias

725.   Disabato-Aust, Tracy. **The Well-Tended Perennial Garden: The Essential Guide to Planting and Pruning Techniques.** 3d ed. Portland, Oreg., Timber Press, 2017. 416p. illus. index. $34.95. ISBN 13: 978-1-60469-707-0.

This, the third edition of a beautifully illustrated book, features more than fifty new plant encyclopedia entries, nearly the same number of cultivators, new photographs and illustrations, and updated garden design projects. The book is divided into three main sections. The first, Basic Perennial Garden Planting & Maintenance, discusses the selection of the right spot, soil, light, and plants; best practices for preparing garden beds, including much necessary information on amending soils; spacing plants, mulching, watering, weed control, and fertilizing; renovating already-established perennial gardens; pests and diseases; staking; and division. The next section, Pruning Perennials, walks readers through the reasons for pruning, the tools necessary, various pruning techniques (deadheading, cutting back, pinching, etc.), and pruning for winter and for spring. The last section is an encyclopedia of perennials, an A to Z that starts with a user guide and includes color photographs of the plants, as well as common names, planting zones, pruning information, related plants, and more. The encyclopedia section also provides information on which perennials to select by characteristics. Here, for example, users can select from a list of plants listed under a variety of categories: deer resistant, clay busting, dry soil tolerant, and so on. The section concludes with a "Perennial Garden Planting and Maintenance Schedule" by season. A metric conversion scale, bibliography, and index are included in the back matter. This complete guide to all things perennial is highly recommended for public libraries.—**ARBA Staff Reviewer**

726.   **Encyclopedia of Landscape Design: Planning, Building, and Planting Your Perfect Outdoor Space.** Chris Young, ed. New York, DK Publishing, 2017. 392p. illus. index. $35.00. ISBN 13: 978-1-4654-6385-2.

The editor crafted this nine-by-eleven-inch, hardcover book to assist readers with every phase of planting a garden, from first ideas to assessing the soil to choosing a style to planting. The book, at nearly four hundred pages, achieves its stated aim of putting everything one needs to know to plant a garden successfully in one convenient place. It starts with a How to Design section that covers such things as inspirations, use, creating play areas and views and vistas, light and shade considerations, lighting and heating, and basic plant varieties, among other things. This section even provides step-by-step directions on how to create your own garden plan, from the most basic to ones much more complicated. Part 2, Choosing a Style, discusses the rules, "how tos," plans, plants, and design elements for a number of different garden styles: formal gardens, cottage gardens, Mediterranean gardens, modernist gardens, Japanese gardens, foliage gardens, productive gardens, family gardens, natural gardens, urban gardens, country gardens, and cutting-edge gardens. The third section, Making a Garden, is about the hands-on labor it will take to put in your dream outdoor landscape. The section begins with a checklist of considerations from getting official permissions and moves through every phase to completion. Next come instructions for building garden structures, planting techniques, and a plants and materials guide. This last part has hundreds of color photographs of different trees, shrubs, climbers, and bulbs, and details on sun/shade/water requirements, what plants will give you color in a particular season, and so much more. The book also provides information on tiles, stones, decking, and other materials. A resource guide to suppliers and other useful information, along with an index, round out the work. It is hard to overstate the quality of the color photographs in this work, which will inspire gardeners everywhere. Highly recommended for public libraries.—**ARBA Staff Reviewer**

727.   Stockwell, Robin. **Succulents: The Ultimate Guide to Choosing, Designing, and Growing 200 Easy-Care Plants.** Birmingham, Ala., Oxmoor House, 2017. 288p. illus. index. $24.95pa. ISBN 13: 978-0-8487-4947-7.

This book showcases a wide variety of succulents, which are ideal for arid regions. The beginning of the book features a variety of inspirational succulent gardens, showing that these versatile plants are ideal for roof gardens, side yards, containers, entryways, sloped terrain, accent gardens, etc., and that they also grow in different regions from beaches to high deserts. The book also discusses mixing colors and planting patterns. For those who love to craft and create, the book devotes an entire section to projects that can be done with succulents. Basic directions instruct readers on how to make wedding bouquets, table dressings, gift toppers, wreaths, and more. This is followed by a two-page guide to selecting succulents for different situations—basic landscaping, special situations (seacoasts, shade, etc.), and special effects like blooms. Next comes an A to Z list of the plants themselves, starting with Aeonium. The book includes color photographs of each variety. The end of the book is devoted to gardening basics: buying plants, choosing the right spot, preparing the soil, planting, watering, pruning, feeding, dividing, and keeping pests and diseases in check. An index rounds out the work. This visually stunning book will inspire gardeners everywhere, especially those who love the look of succulents. Highly recommended for public libraries.—**ARBA Staff Reviewer**

Handbooks and Yearbooks

728. Alexander, Rosemary, and Rachel Myers. **The Essential Garden Design Workbook.** 3d ed. Portland, Oreg., Timber Press, 2017. 392p. illus. index. $34.95. ISBN 13: 978-1-60469-661-5; 978-1-60469-811-4 (e-book).

This well-titled book, now in its third edition, has been thoroughly revised by authors Rosemary Alexander and Rachel Myers. Alexander founded and is the principal at the English Gardening School, Chelsea Physic Garden, London. Myers, a garden designer in Oxfordshire, also lectures at the English Gardening School. Concern for sustainability and for reducing carbon footprints influenced this revised edition and is apparent throughout the work. This is not a book for casual gardeners. It is, instead, aimed at potential designers, design students, newly qualified designers, and professional gardeners. The book is organized in three sections. The first, Design Phase, is comprised of three chapters on such topics as starting a garden design business and starting work in the studio. This section includes several examples of documents, like job bid sheets, that will be useful templates for garden designers. It is important to note, however, that these sample forms and some of the legal advice was created for designers in the United Kingdom. The information nevertheless translates to other countries. The second section, Design Phase, provides step-by-step directions on starting the design process, drawing/creating plans, and more. The last section, Post-Design Phase, discusses plant sourcing, construction, and other topics. All illustrations and diagrams are easy to read and bring to life the concepts discussed. The book ends with a generous further reading section and an index. Recommended.—**ARBA Staff Reviewer**

Veterinary Science

729. **Merck Veterinary Manual. http://www.merckvetmanual.com/.** [Website] Free. Date reviewed: 2017.

The Merck Veterinary Manual is an extensive online resource covering a wide range of topics relevant to the health care of numerous and varied animals from the domesticated to the exotic. Matching closely to the 11th print edition, the online version offers additional multimedia content and continually updated information, such as new research on heart disease, wound management, and aquaculture. The use of specialized language and a trade point-of-view mainly targets site material to professionals and students in the veterinary field. However, there is a fair amount of information here that would appeal to regular pet owners as well.

Even with its abundance of information, the site is easy to navigate. Users can conduct a basic search from the bar, scroll through the featured items within the page, or select from several tabs on the menu bar. Veterinary Content lists 22 general categories such as Behavior, Digestive System, Exotic & Laboratory Animals, Pharmacology, and Poultry. Selecting a category under this tab leads to a summary "textbook" layout with related topics presented in a section/chapter format. For example, the category Exotic & Laboratory Animals is separated into 22 sections related to specific (e.g., ferrets) and nonspecific (e.g., marine mammals) animal types and issues pertaining to them. These sections are then further divided into individual topical chapters of varying length. For example, the section on Pet Birds contains 14 chapters including an Overview of Pet Birds, Bacterial Diseases of Pet Birds, Nutritional Diseases of Pet Birds, Toxicoses of Pet Birds, and more. Chapters are well organized and may incorporate headers, bullet points, links to affiliated information, illustrations, and video content. The left sidebar will simultaneously scroll through chapter headers as users read through it for easy reference. The right sidebar notes the chapter subject within the context of the main section. The information included underneath the Pet Health tab is similarly structured to Veterinary Content; however, its categories and topics are more attuned to the pet owner/consumer. Categories here are simplified, and include Dog, Cat, Horse, Bird, All Other Pets, and Special Subjects. Sections within each category generally address an animal's Description and Physical Characteristics, Routine Care and Breeding, Behavior, and individual disorders. A user guide provides important information about the organization of the material, and an A to Z glossary assists with frequently used terms and specialized language. Quizzes & Cases presents a searchable listing of quick subject quizzes on a number of topics from animal behavior to disease. Users can also read one case study which follows the examination, testing, diagnoses, treatment, and more of a dog with external wounds. Hopefully, more case studies will be added in the future. The Resources tab links to an extensive collection of audio recordings, videos, images, figures, tables, reference guides, abbreviations, and other material. News & Commentary links to a variety of topical articles and current commentary on veterinary information relevant to the field, such as the "AHS Recommends Best Practices to Prevent Heartworm Transmission" or "Rates of Food Allergies in Pets are Not Generally Known." These articles and others are also featured throughout the homepage, in addition to a topical Infographic, a listing of Trending Veterinary Topics, a listing of Popular Resources, and a link to the Veterinary Student Stories website which offers personal impressions of veterinary student life.

While the site offers ample information, it is meant for educational purposes only and would not take the place of individual veterinary counsel. Nevertheless, the quality, range, and presentation of the material make the site a valuable resource for professionals, students, and consumers alike.—**ARBA Staff Reviewer**

31 Biological Sciences

General Works

Dictionaries and Encyclopedias

730. **Principles of Biology.** Christina A. Crawford, ed. Hackensack, N.J., Salem Press, 2017. 613p. index. $165.00. ISBN 13: 978-1-68217-324-4; 978-1-68217-325-1 (e-book).

This is the 6th volume in Salem's Principles of... series. (The other volumes cover chemistry, physics, astronomy, computer science, and physical science). An encyclopedic work, it contains 112 articles, alphabetically arranged by subject from Activation Energy to Zoology. Each entry includes a list of fields of study, a brief summary of the topic, principal terms, 2-7 pages of text, and a bibliography, sometimes descriptive, of 4-6 books or periodical articles. Most entries contain black-and-white illustrations. Some entries include graphs, websites, and a sample problem. Also included are a 12-page glossary, a list of Nobel Prize Winners in Biological Studies from 1996 to 2016, 2 illustrated pages of body systems, a descriptive bibliography of more than 400 items, and a subject index. Contributors are listed for most of the articles, usually without affiliation. The editor, Christina Crawford, is Assistant Directory for Biology and Life Sciences of the Rice Office of STEM engagement.

The text is generally readable for college biology majors. It is rather daunting for the general reader or the average student. There are several obvious typos (e.g., "Principals" for "Principles" in at least two places). Libraries in higher education institutions may find this title useful for its text and graphs. Other libraries can give it a pass.—**Jonathan F. Husband**

Handbooks and Yearbooks

731. **Comparative Approaches to Biotechnology Development and Use in Developed and Emerging Nations.** Tomas Gabriel Bas and Jingyuan Zhao, eds. Hershey, Pa., IGI Global, 2017. 592p. index. (Advances in Bioinformatics and Biomedical Engineering (ABBE) book series). $205.00. ISBN 13: 978-1-52251-040-6; 978-1-52251-041-3 (e-book).

This volume in the Advances in Bioinformatics and Biomedical Engineering (ABBE) book series takes a comprehensive and comparative look at the growth of biotechnology in both developed and emerging countries. It examines a number of factors that weigh on the success of biotechnology in each type of economy, such as biotech production, government support and promotion, development capabilities and competencies, competition in biotech, and more.

The volume's preface along with its detailed table of contents lays out its organization and explains its highly specialized focus. Fifteen chapters share a variety of scholarly perspectives as they examine global biotechnology development in Chile, Turkey, Canada, China, Mexico, and other countries. Chapter 3 describes the "Influence of Star Bioscientists on Obtaining Venture Capital for Canadian Dedicated Biotech Firms," while chapter 5 asks "Is Collaboration Important at All States of the Biotechnology Product Development Process?" Other chapters assess the stability of Turkish biotechnology development, the role of institutional support in Mexican biotechnology industries, and China's biotechnology evolution in regards to healthcare. Each chapter opens with an abstract to establish the impetus and design of the research that follows. Chapters are generally well structured and may provide background, methodology, discussion, future research directions, and conclusion sections. Chapters may also incorporate tables, graphs, headers, subheadings, and other tools. References are listed at the end of each chapter and compiled again at the end of the book, alongside brief contributor biographies and an index. The material in this volume would appeal to global policy makers, educators, students, and professionals in the biotechnology sphere.—**ARBA Staff Reviewer**

732.   **Handbook of Biology and Politics.** Steven A. Peterson and Albert Somit, eds. Northampton, Mass., Edward Elgar, 2017. 544p. index. $315.00. ISBN 13: 978-1-78347-626-8; 978-1-78347-627-5 (e-book).

This book explores the field of biopolitics, known also as biology and politics. The main focus of the discipline is the interconnections and multiple ways that the life sciences and politics are interlinked. Divided into five parts with thirty chapters, it is a fairly comprehensive examination of the topic. The five parts are: Introduction, Biological Approaches to Politics, Biology and the Fields of Political Science, Biopolicy, and Reflections on Biology and Politics. The first part discusses the history of the topic, evolution and climate change, and Michel Foucault's perspective. The second part examines the political side of the topic, from genes and the brain to evolutionary and political psychology. The third part revolves around philosophy, international relations, research methodology, ethics, political behavior, public administration, media, and policy making. The fourth part details policy, toxicology, human nature, environmental security, women and children, and new frontiers. The last part looks at the future of the discipline and its challenges. An excellent book for those whose main focus is within this topic. Recommended for academic libraries.—**Bradford Lee Eden**

733.   **The Palgrave Handbook of Biology and Society.** Maurizio Meloni, John Cromby, Des Fitzgerald, and Stephanie Lloyd, eds. New York, Palgrave Macmillan, 2018. 941p. illus. index. $189.00. ISBN 13: 978-1-137-52878-0; 978-1-137-52879-7 (e-book).

This handbook attempts to bridge the traditional gap between social sciences and biological sciences, serving as a comprehensive overview that incorporates both. The lengthy introduction discusses the history of the field and introduces the six sections that feature the work of approximately fifty international scholars. The six sections begin with History of the Biology/Society Relationship, comprised of eight chapters.

Section two, Genomics, Postgenomics, Epigenetics and Society, focuses on key changes in contemporary molecular biology that have shifted perspectives in such chapters as "Assembling Biomedical Big Data." Seven chapters comprise Neuroscience: Brain, Culture and Social Relations, section three. Section four, Social Epidemiology, details developments in a field that started to emerge in the 1960s. The five chapters in this section include "Health Inequalities and the Interplay of Socioeconomic Factors and Health in the Life Course." The fifth section, Medicine and Society (six chapters), is followed by Contested Sites/Future Perspectives, which looks at controversies and future directions in six chapters. An index rounds out the work. This handbook is highly recommended for academic libraries.—**ARBA Staff Reviewer**

734.   **Timetree: The Timescale of Life.** [Website] Free. Date reviewed: 2018.

This Timetree is an extensive project which maps the biodiversity of life on earth and allows a visual representation of species development against the backdrop of time. Users can note species divergence, track a single species through time, or examine the genealogy of a whole plant or animal kingdom. From the homepage, users employ one of three options to access the information. The Node Time search visualizes the divergence of two species (such as cats and dogs). Users enter species they wish to compare to bring up the timeline segment illustrating separation time estimates and climate information (e.g., oxygen levels) accompanied by a listing of relevant research. The Timeline search allows a view which traces the development of one species (e.g., human), showing divergence estimates with other species groups, associated environmental factors, and more. The Timetree field lets users build their own visualization after entering group and taxonomic rank information, or after uploading a list of species from another file. Other links from the homepage menu bar provide good foundational material for the somewhat complex Timetree. The Book tab provides access to pdf chapters of The Timetree of Life, with detail organized by species group (e.g., Amphibians, Fungi, etc.) in addition to further explanatory material. Studies presents a listing of links to over three thousand scientific studies which cumulatively serve as the foundation of the Timetree. Users click the PubMed identification number to access the full study. The listing includes author, title, journal name, publishing year, and PubMed identification number. Resources is well supplied with links to websites, software, and journal articles which a range of users could appreciate, like the FishBase search engine, the Arkive online encyclopedia, and the Mega7 divergence time estimator. News contains links to articles about the Timetree project which are helpful in providing clear, easy-to-follow explanations of how the Timetree works to a layman audience. While the project's specialized language and sophisticated material gears the project towards advanced researchers, the quantity of resources and ease-of-use could interest a wider audience as well.—**ARBA Staff Reviewer**

Anatomy

735.   **Gale Interactive: Human Anatomy.** [Website] Farmington Hills, Mich., Gale/Cengage Learning, 2017. Price negotiated by site. Date reviewed: 2017.

Anatomy is an increasingly in-demand college course. Though growing in popularity, the subject matter has traditionally intimidated students, especially those who need better visuals in order to understand complex subject matter. Gale's Human Anatomy database addresses the need for a different type of learning tool with this authoritative and complete resource that follows the progression of a typical college course. Within the database, 3D models give students the ability to magnify, pull apart, or manipulate different body systems; furthermore, the detail provided in these models makes it easy identify anatomical structures down to the smallest detail. The database additionally offers an auditory component, hyperlinks, and the ability to search across concepts, along with clear written descriptions by subject authorities. An added bonus is the ability to download units to a personal computer, which allows students flexible study options. Another plus is the option to jump back and forth through units and to take advantage of the self-testing option at the end of a session. Instructors will also appreciate the database, as material can be used for class discussions, in lieu of a time-consuming or expensive lab. The database is obviously a valuable flipped instruction tool.

This is a highly recommended purchase for academic libraries.—**ARBA Staff Reviewer**

Botany

Handbooks and Yearbooks

736.　Ennos, Roland. **Trees: A Complete Guide to Their Biology and Structure.** Ithaca, N.Y., Cornell University Press, 2016. 128p. illus. maps. index. $19.95pa. ISBN 13: 978-1-5017-0493-2.

This book is a wonderful introduction and guide to the history, structure, biology, and diversity of trees. Basic questions are answered such as: How do trees lift water? How do trees stand up? What are some of the limits to their height? In addition, trees of different climates and hemispheres are discussed, along with survival strategies that many trees incorporate based on their locations. Specialist trees, as well as the relationships that have developed over time between trees and people are examined. There are many color illustrations, photographs, and maps throughout, along with a glossary and further information section. This book is an excellent first book on the topic for K-12 education, and would be a nice coffee table addition as well.—**Bradford Lee Eden**

737.　Munroe, Doug. **The Trees of Ashe County, North Carolina.** Jefferson, N.C., McFarland, 2017. 250p. illus. index. (Contributions to Southern Appalachian Studies). $29.95pa. ISBN 13: 978-1-4766-7252-6; 978-1-4766-3151-6 (e-book).

This striking book, with 160 color photographs, describes over 80 kinds of trees found in Ashe County, which is bordered by both Virginia and Tennessee in northwestern North Carolina. The author traces the history of these trees, across thousands of years at times, and the disappearance of certain species, such as the American chestnut, due to blight and other diseases. For each tree, we learn where they can be found in the county, what they look like, and their possible commercial value (wood, dye, syrup, for instance). The final section of the book discusses "tree culture," exploring topics such as maple syrup, landscaping, and Christmas tree farming.

The language of this book is aimed at all sorts of interested readers, not just botanists—humorous, straightforward, and clear. The photos, taken by a number of the author's friends and colleagues, are beautiful and striking. As the latest volume in the Contributions to Southern Appalachian Studies series, this volume adds to a collection, begun in 1998, that has examined the life, culture, environment, and history of the region. Given the narrow geographical focus, libraries, with readers interested in this region or readers likely to visit Ashe County, should certainly consider adding this volume. Libraries with holdings of the series will find this book a useful addition, as will some science libraries in academic settings.—**Mark Schumacher**

738.   Pope, Ralph. **Mosses, Liverworts, and Hornworts: A Field Guide to Common Bryophytes of the Northeast.** Ithaca, N.Y., Cornell University Press, 2016. 368p. illus. index. $24.95pa. ISBN 13: 978-1-5017-0078-1.

This volume, richly illustrated with color photographs, occasional line drawings, AND range maps, covers most of the species found from Maryland to Maine, as well as regions of maritime Canada and Ontario. Each entry includes a description and a list of similar species. Given the small size of many of these plants, numerous photographs have been enlarged, with indications such as "5x" or "10x" to reflect the magnification. Before presenting the four main categories of these plants, a helpful introduction presents information on biology, taxonomy, and ecology. Within the four main sections—three types of mosses and the liverworts/hornworts—an overview of the group is presented before presenting individual species. There are also "keys" to the genera of each group, which seemed complex to this reviewer.

The author describes the target audience for this field guide as "hikers, amateur naturalists, nonbryologist botanists, and, possibly, sophisticated gardeners." (p. 1) Given the narrow focus of this book, however, and the often highly specialized language employed, it seems to be most usefully acquired by academic libraries, although public libraries may also be interested, as their patrons would be the population that the author seems to be focusing on.—**Mark Schumacher**

739.   Small, Ernest. **Cannabis: A Complete Guide.** Boca Raton, Fla., CRC Press, 2016. 567p. illus. maps. index. $119.95. ISBN 13: 978-1-4987-6163-5.

This book attempts to place the often-contentious debate over cannabis in a scientific context. The book provides an extremely detailed table of contents in addition to an extensive index, so users can quickly find topics of interest. The book is broken into 18 chapters, including an introduction, that comprise approximately 550 pages. The chapters, including "Prehuman and Early History of *Cannabis sativa*," "Shoot and Foliage Architecture," "Oilseed," "Nonmedical Drug Usage," "Medical Marijuana: Production," "Sustainability," and "Botanical Classification and Nomenclatural Issues," provide a view of the topic that is both broad and deep. There are a plethora of illustrations, both in color and in black and white, along with maps and diagrams. The literature cited takes up more than 60 pages. This book is a good place for all kinds of users to find scientific information about a debate colored by political and cultural views. Recommended for public and academic libraries.—**ARBA Staff Reviewer**

740.   Stubbendieck, James, Stephan L. Hatch, Neal M. Bryan, and Cheryl D. Dunn. **North American Wildland Plants: A Field Guide.** 3d ed. Lincoln, Nebr., University of Nebraska Press, 2017. 510p. illus. index. $35.00pa. ISBN 13: 978-0-8032-9965-8.

This volume is the third edition of this title, and the eighth iteration of a guide first published, as *North American Range Plants,* in 1981. Numerous enhancements and refinements have been made. It is quite comprehensive, covering two hundred species of "grasses, forbs, and woody plants." Each entry includes a distribution map of North America, multiple illustrations of key parts of the plant, vegetative, cone, floral, and fruit characteristics, inflorescence, and forage value, along with other information. Although this reviewer recognized a few of the plants—yarrow, sedge, dandelion—most were quite unknown. This book is designed to be used as a field guide, to be supplemented by texts which focus on smaller geographical regions. Included is a thirteen-page list of additional resources and an excellent index. The authors, from the University of Nebraska and Texas A&M, have decades of research experience in this field.

Libraries with patrons interested in ecology, botany, and environmental studies will find this volume, quite reasonably priced, of value in their collections. School libraries will be less likely to have users who would benefit from this detailed and specialized text, but other libraries should consider it.—**Mark Schumacher**

Zoology

General Works

Dictionaries and Encyclopedias

741.   Dohner, Janet Vorwald. **The Encyclopedia of Animal Predators.** North Adams, Mass., Storey, 2017. 280p. illus. maps. index. $24.95pa. ISBN 13: 978-1-61212-699-9.

This book begins with a discussion of coexistence, the beginnings of conservation and preservation movements in the United States, the growth of environmental awareness, and more. Chapter 2, "Who's Out There," focuses on animal threats to livestock and poultry. The second part of the book, Predators Up Close, begins with profiles of wolves, coyotes, and foxes and has chapters on cats, bears, weasels, raccoons, skunks, opossums, rats, domestic and feral animals, birds of prey, true owls, crows, snapping turtles, gators and crocodiles, and snakes. Chapters vary in length; wolves get nearly forty pages, while owls are allotted approximately four. Chapters provide range maps and color photographs and can include information on the species and range, behaviors, life cycle, human interaction, predation patterns, and habitat. Information is also provided on an animal's favored prey, active time of day, kill methods, gait, scat, and tracks. In addition, the author provides tips on how to handle interactions with different types of predator animals or how to avoid them altogether. The last part of the book covers prevention and protection methods, which include fencing, secure housing for animals like chickens, night lighting, and livestock guardian animals. An appendix includes a list of guides on predator control for home, recreation, farm, and ranch, URLs for organizations on predator control, a bibliography, and other online resources. An index rounds out the work. Recommended for public libraries.—**ARBA Staff Reviewer**

742.   **Humans and Animals: A Geography of Coexistence.** Julie Urbanik and Connie L. Johnston, eds. Santa Barbara, Calif., ABC-CLIO, 2017. 466p. illus. index. $89.00. ISBN 13: 978-1-4408-3834-7; 978-1-4408-3835-4 (e-book).

Humans and Animals: A Geography of Coexistence is a one-volume encyclopedia offering comprehensive coverage of the field of human-animal relations. There are approximately 150 entries, arranged alphabetically, that cover such aspects as biological or philosophical concepts, social movements, types of human-animal relations, and specific species. Each entry provides an overview of a topic with a short list of citations for further study. Entries are free of jargon and written at a level that is accessible to general audiences. Effort was taken to provide a global perspective when possible, since the way animals are viewed varies greatly from culture to culture. At the end of the volume is a supplementary section of primary sources representing key documents that include government legislations, court decisions, and international treaties which illustrate the different interpretations of human-animal relationships. This section may prove especially useful for students requiring the use of primary documents when writing papers or for those looking to explore the widely varied approaches to the governance of human-animal relations. This book would be a welcome addition to library collections of all types due to its ease of reading, broad examination across the entire spectrum of human-animal relations, and coverage of a multifaceted topic that appeals to diverse category of audiences.—**Andrea C. Kepsel**

Handbooks and Yearbooks

743.   **Acoustic Atlas. http://www.acousticatlas.org/.** [Website] Free. Date reviewed: 2018.

This website from Montana State University holds over 2,500 audio recordings made in natural environments of the western United States. The project captures a large variety of species and helps to expose the relationship between their sounds and the land, water, and air around them. Users can conduct a keyword or advanced search from the bars on the homepage, or can browse the atlas in several ways. The Recordings by Species tab on the right side of the homepage lets users scroll through a listing of species presented alphabetically by common name (American Bison) and accompanied by scientific name (Bison Bison). Users can filter text or arrange list by species classification. The Listen tab at the top of the homepage provides similar access options to the sound database but also lets users select from lengthier ambient creations. Descriptive information for each recording is generous and may include recording date, recording time, creator, notes, location, recording equipment, and more. There may also be a stock photo of the recording subject and a Google Map of recording locations. The Sound Map offers an excellent visualization of the library, showing its emphasis on sounds collected from the western United States (in particular the Northern Rocky Mountain corridor), but also pointing to outlying recording locations in New England, Hawaii, Florida, and other locations. Clicking on a pin accesses affiliated Acoustic Atlas records. Special features highlight interesting ways to use these recordings including a selection of 12 ringtones (free) and an exhibit titled the "Soundscapes of Ivan Doig" that pairs sounds with locations found in works by the writer. Yellowstone National Park arranges sounds captured in the park in one collection. This showcase of the iconic sounds of natural America—the bison, the bald eagle, the bighorn sheep, and many others—will appeal to many.—**ARBA Staff Reviewer**

744.   Cheshire, James, and Oliver Uberti. **Where the Animals Go: Tracking Wildlife with Technology in 50 Maps and Graphics.** New York, W. W. Norton, 2017. 174p. illus. $39.95. ISBN 13: 978-0-393-63402-0.

This book presents fifty maps and graphics based on the movements of animals worldwide. The map data comes from tags, tracking devices attached by scientists. As the introduction explains, technological advances have led to new ways to track animals and to exponential increases in the amounts of data available. Much of this data is open data and much is produced and curated by people other than biologists. The authors of this book are a case in point. Cheshire is a geographer, and Uberti is a designer.

There are sections on land animals, sea animals, and animals that fly. Each section opens with a brief introduction followed by discussions of the movements of specific animals: elephants, zebras, bees, humpback whales, sea turtles, ants, pythons, owls, coyotes, mountain lions, sea otters, and more. Maps based on the tracking data of tagged animals are the key feature of each of these discussions. In the case of sea otters, for example, users will find a map of the preferred locations of four otters in the Elkhorn Slough near Monterey Bay.

It is hard to overemphasize the quality and impact of the range maps in this book. The book's engaging narrative is accessible to a wide range of readers. Highly recommended to public, school, and academic libraries.—**ARBA Staff Reviewer**

745.   Chester, Sharon. **The Arctic Guide: Wildlife of the Far North.** Princeton, N.J., Princeton University Press, 2015. 542p. illus. maps. index. $27.95pa. ISBN 13: 978-0-691-13975-3.

Sharon Chester has written a neat guide to the "wildlife of the far North." It is a one-stop compendium of everything related to the Arctic. Very few books match the coverage of their topic as this author does. Designed as a guide for the Arctic traveler, the book deals primarily with wildlife, but also contains many useful sections on other topics. The book starts off with a one-page list of the geographic coordinates of major Arctic land features. Next follows a glossary of terms used in the study of the Arctic, and a small essay on the role of the North in Ancient Greece (Arktos). The author next defines the Arctic in a series of map/sections: bioclimatic zones, geomorphic provinces, permafrost, glacial ice, polar seas, circulation/currents, sea ice, and atmospheric phenomena. The main portion of the work consists of section about individual groups of wildlife: mammals, birds, fishes, lizards/frogs, flies/bees/butterflies, and flora. The book has a small select bibliography and an index. Overall the author has done an outstanding job of covering the topic. The illustrations and the handy portable format make this work essential for those working/traveling in the Arctic. Most reference collections will want to have this book in their collection because of its comprehensive coverage of the topic.—**Ralph Lee Scott**

746.   Krausman, Paul R. Henke, Scott E., ed. **Becoming a Wildlife Professional.** Baltimore, Md., Johns Hopkins University Press, 2017. 208p. illus. index. $85.00. ISBN 13: 978-1-4214-2306-7; 978-1-4214-2307-4 (e-book).

The editors provide a navigational compass that defines how to shape a successful future working with wildlife. Chapter contributors describe over 100 diverse career options that require engaging the world from an open-air perspective. Careers include wildlife biology, conservation, forestry rehabilitation, ranching, photography, and refuge management. In addition, the content explores challenges, as well as educational and technical requirements for entry-level positions and career advancement, providing interested students with necessary information on how to transform themselves into qualified applicants. Every high school, community college, and university library should consider adding this book to their resource collections.—**Thomas E. Baker**

747.   **Wildscreen Arkive. http://www.arkive.org/.** [Website] Free. Date reviewed: 2017.

This online encyclopedia, brimming with both narrative and multimedia content, brings the natural world to a range of users. Users can conduct a basic or advanced search from the homepage or select the Random Species tab to see a featured entry. Alternatively, users can browse from one of the tabs on the menu bar. Species presents a gallery of animal groups (mammals, birds, reptiles, etc.) in addition to a display of Popular Species through which users can scroll. These are marked with a color thumbnail photo, a brief description, and multimedia content icons. Individual entries provide a thorough Description of the selected animal, which may include information about its range, habitat, biology, and more. There is good emphasis on the animal's status, threats, and conservation efforts made on its behalf. In fact, the entry is clearly marked with a status icon, pointing to the animal's classification on the IUCN (International Union for Conservation of Nature) Red List. The entry will also include a specialized glossary and reference information, in addition to links to animals found in similar habitats. A starred Top Facts section presents quick highlights of the animal's story. Places profiles twenty different global locations, such as the Antarctic, Mediterranean Basin, and North Pacific Islands. These entries, though more general in nature, are structured similarly to the Species entries with detailed narrative, visual content, glossaries, and other information. Users can also click on the World Map image to access a directory of countries by region. Selecting a country accesses an alphabetical database of encyclopedia entries affiliated with it. Topics presents a visual gallery of numerous topic pages organized within several broader categories: Conservation & Science, Threats to Biodiversity, Behavior, Animal Groups, and Habitats. Many of the individual topics address timely environmental issues of climate change, deforestation, invasive species, and more. The narrative and visual content within this section, including Plants in Peril, Newly Discovered Species, Pollination, and Forests, is generous and well-organized. The wealth and import of the content, in conjunction with the quality of its presentation, makes the Wildscreen Arkive an essential resource for educators, students, and armchair naturalists alike.—**ARBA Staff Reviewer**

Birds

748.   Jiguet, Frédéric, and Aurélien Audevard. Tony Williams. **Birds of Europe, North Africa, and the Middle East: A Photographic Guide.** Princeton, N.J., Princeton University Press, 2017. 448p. illus. maps. index. $29.95pa. ISBN 13: 978-0-6911-7243-9.

Originally published in French as *Tous les oiseaux d'Europe* (Niestlé, 2015), this excellent photographic field guide represents a mammoth achievement: providing the first pocket-sized photographic field guide to every known bird species in Europe. Practical, accessible, and visually pleasing, the book will appeal to professional birders as well as to casual or simply curious learners. Like any good field guide, this one describes key identification features, voice, habitat, and distribution. It also provides well-done range maps with color coding and 2,200 high resolution color photographs of 860 species.

Birding has become a very popular pastime and one of the best things about it is that it requires little equipment. Beginning birders simply need a basic pair of binoculars and a good field guide to get started. *Birds of Europe, North Africa, and the Middle East* makes an excellent contribution to the field. Recommended for public libraries.—**Thomas E. Baker**

749.   Wells, Jeffrey V., and Allison Childs Wells. Illustrated by Robert Dean. **Birds of Aruba, Bonaire, and Curaçao: A Site and Field Guide.** Ithaca, N.Y., Cornell University Press, 2017. 474p. illus. maps. index. $39.95pa. ISBN 13: 978-1-5017-0107-8.

This guide to the more than 280 bird species seen on Aruba, Bonaire, and Curaçao is accessible to both beginners and experts. In this work that serves as both a site guide and a field guide to the islands' birds, readers will find excellent maps and illustrations along with detailed bird descriptions. The section on conservation adds awareness of the threats to the birds and to the habitats on which they rely. This reliable and enjoyable resource is recommended to public libraries.—**Thomas E. Baker**

Mammals

750.   **The Princeton Field Guide to Prehistoric Mammals.** Donald R. Prothero, ed. Princeton, N.J., Princeton University Press, 2016. 240p. illus. $35.00. ISBN 13: 978-1-69115-682-8.

This comprehensive reference to prehistoric mammals includes hundreds of species; it discusses behaviors and how mammals interrelated. Hundreds of full-color illustrations enhance the descriptions. The book is divided into eighteen chapters, starting with "The Age of Mammals" and concluding with "Mammalian Evolution and Extinction." Chapters are divided into subsections (the number of subsections varies). Broad coverage includes the origin and early evolution of mammals; marsupials; elephants, hyraxes, sea cows, aardvarks, and their relatives; and so much more. The book includes suggestions for further reading.

The writing style makes the topic accessible to general readers and to students in high school and college. The modest price enhances the book's appeal. Highly recommended—**ARBA Staff Reviewer**

Marine Animals

751.   Carrier, Jeffrey C. **Sharks of the Shallows: Coastal Species in Florida and the Bahamas.** Baltimore, Md., Johns Hopkins University Press, 2017. 198p. illus. index. $34.95. ISBN 13: 978-1-4214-2294-7; 978-1-4214-2295-4 (e-book).

The author, along with three accomplished animal photographers, has created a fascinating look at sharks in the waters around Florida. Following a very useful forty-page introduction which covers topics such as modes of identification, sharks' senses, types of food, mating, and threats to shark survival, the author presents twenty-two species found in the waters mentioned in the title. The entries follow a specific format, with five sections after a brief introduction: range and distribution, size and growth and reproduction, feeding, behavior and interactions with humans, and conservation of the species. The third section of this book presents related animals: skates, rays, and sawfish. Ten species of these animals are presented in the same format as the sharks. The photographs for all these animals are quite striking.

A seventeen-page bibliography provides readers with numerous other texts to further their reading on sharks in general or on specific species. Although the focus is on a particular area and its sharks, this book serves as a useful and readable introduction to sharks, for all kinds of readers. At a reasonable price, it should be considered by all sorts of libraries.—**Mark Schumacher**

752. Dipper, Frances. Illustrated by Marc Dando. **The Marine World: A Natural History of Ocean Life.** Ithaca, N.Y., Comstock Publishing Associates/Cornell University Press, 2016. 544p. illus. maps. index. $59.95. ISBN 13: 978-1-5017-0989-0.

This book is a plethora of color for the eye. Illustrations (many being photographs) are mostly in color. The foreword describes the book as "authoritative, though not too scientific; easy to read, though not dumbed down; and comprehensive, though far from overwhelming (p. 8)." The book is divided into three parts: the physical ocean; the living ocean; and marine life. The biggest part is marine life, with every type of oceanic animal phyla represented. The book is impressive. Phyla are broken down and explained in a straightforward manner. Illustrations of an animal and how its body works are fascinating. Good for the lay person interested in the world's oceans. Highly recommended.—**Michael W. Handis**

753. Ellis, Richard, and James G. Mead. **Beaked Whales: A Complete Guide to Their Biology and Conservation.** Baltimore, Md., Johns Hopkins University Press, 2017. 194p. illus. index. $79.95. ISBN 13: 978-1-4214-2182-7.

The authors of this work explore the world of the twenty-two species of beaked whales, "the least known of all the large animals in the world." Until quite recently, these animals were seen more often washed ashore than alive in the world's oceans. In fact, this book contains only two photographs accompanying the excellent illustrations of marine artist Ellis. Each of the twenty-two species has an entry, from three to ten pages, with a color painting by Ellis. A physical description (often focusing on the head and jaw), the areas of sightings of the species, and history of the discovery and identification of each species are found in each entry. Some species, such as True's beaked whale, are known from as few as six individuals!

One important section (approximately twenty-two pages), entitled "Beaked Whales Versus the Navy," examines in considerable detail the dangerous effects on these whales of sonar activity, mostly by military ships. Apparently the sound waves from these machines interrupt the whales' echolocation activity and disrupt their normal behavior. Scarring of beaked whales due to their protruding teeth and frequent fighting among males is also discussed.

This volume will best serve academic readers with an interest in biology, ichthyology, and environmental studies. Institutions with marine science or related programs will benefit most from this information. A thirty-one-page bibliography provides the readers leads to hundreds of other texts, from 1758 (Linnaeus) to 2014!—**Mark Schumacher**

Reptiles and Amphibians

754. Powell, Robert, Roger Conant, and Joseph T. Collins. **Peterson Field Guide to Reptiles and Amphibians of Eastern and Central North America.** 4th ed. New York, Houghton Mifflin Harcourt, 2016. 494p. illus. maps. index. $21.00pa. ISBN 13: 978-0-544-12997-9.

The *Peterson Field Guide to Reptiles and Amphibians of Eastern and Central North America* has been the standard work since its first publication in 1958. This update to the expanded third edition (see ARBA 92, entry 1587) sets out to incorporate numerous new taxa which have resulted from, often molecular, study of native taxa and from recently introduced species. Space has been gained by removing most of the natural history description in the species accounts and concentrating on identification. The original plates of species paintings which had been all in one initial section are now broken up so that the snake paintings are adjacent to the snake species accounts, etc. There is now convenient color coding of the page edges to identify both paintings and species accounts for each group (frogs, salamanders, snakes, etc). "Central" in the title means ND-TX and east.

The main competitor is the *Audubon Society Field Guide to Reptiles and Amphibians* (1979 only) (see ARBA 81, entry 1487) which covers all North America and is entirely photograph-based but is now taxonomically out-of-date. There are numerous more specialized books on particular groups (frogs, turtles, etc.) which have abundant natural history information.

An essential book for any academic or public library in its range.—**Frederic F. Burchsted**

32 Health Sciences

General Works

Dictionaries and Encyclopedias

755. **The American Influenza Epidemic of 1918. A Digital Encyclopedia. https://www.influenzaarchive.org/.** [Website] Free. Date reviewed: 2017.

This website is home to a digital archive of roughly 16,000 documents related to the 1918-1919 U.S. influenza epidemic. Taking the lives of over 600,000 Americans, the epidemic was a wake-up call in the realm of public health as it tested health care and civic response systems throughout the country. This archive collects medical journal articles, newspaper clippings, personal accounts, photographs, military reports, and more. The site is well organized and researched. Users can browse generous listings via title, cities, organizations, people, places, publications, and subjects. Organizations, for example, lists hundreds of both national (American Medical Association, American Red Cross) and local (Anti-Mask League of San Francisco, Denver Tramway Company) groups—all with a stake in the epidemic. Subjects range from the scientific to the social as they cover such topics as preserving order, signs of illness, vaccines, funding, therapies, and funeral arrangements. All items are arranged alphabetically within the categories. Users can also conduct a quick or basic search. Each item is represented by a full-page digital image marked by identifying information—keyword listing, author, title, publication source, and date. Medical journal articles may also be accompanied by an abstract summary. Users can also browse an Image Gallery organized alphabetically by representative city. In addition to the documents and images, the site offers 44 city essays (more to come) accessible via the City Essays tab or by the prominent listing along the right sidebar. Each profile includes a narrative essay describing the crisis response from city and health officials and issues unique to the particular community. City leaders in Los Angeles, for example, had to appease many in the budding film industry as they weighed whether to close theaters and other public places. Profiles also come with photographs and an event timeline. This easy-to-use archive tells a compelling story that would appeal to a broad range of historians or researchers studying public health, crisis response, and other subjects.—**ARBA Staff Reviewer**

Directories

756. **Health Guide Canada. 2017-2018.** 3d ed. Toronto, Grey House Publishing Canada, 2017. 1002p. index. $249.00pa. ISBN 13: 978-1-68217-530-9; 978-1-68217-531-6 (e-book).

Health Guide Canada "offers a comprehensive overview of 107 chronic and mental illnesses from Addison's to Wilson's disease...each chapter includes an easy-to-understand medical description plus a wide range of condition-specific support services and information resources that deal with the variety of issues concerning those with a chronic or mental illness." Chronic and mental illnesses covered include chronic fatigue syndrome, eating disorders, hypertension, schizophrenia, tuberculosis, cancer, arthritis, heart disease, suicide, and visual impairment. The guide is arranged within the sections: Chronic and Mental Illnesses; General Resources (among which are national associations, provincial associations, national libraries, and local hospitals and health centers); Appendixes (charitable foundations, death and bereavement, homeopathic medicine, indigenous health issues); Statistics (regional health trends and median wait times) plus Sources for Disease Descriptions, Entry Name Index, and Publication Index. The introduction to the guide includes a chart, Chronic and Mental Illness—Body System which lists the illness and its body system or disorder category. For instance hypertension would fall within the Body System/Disorder Category Cardiovascular. In addition, the introduction features educational material including a glossary and two reports: "Health Status of Canadians 2016" and "A Focus on Family Violence in Canada" by the Public Health Agency of Canada. This resource should prove very helpful regarding specific chronic and mental illnesses. For instance the Addison's disease section contains a definition, the cause, symptoms, prevalence, treatment options, and directory information for The Canadian Addison Society. Each association listing contains name, address, telephone, email, website, overview, chief officers, and publications. *Health Guide Canada* is a very thorough reference source that not only provides overviews of chronic and mental illnesses but also statistics, special reports, and a directory of associations. Highly recommended.— **Lucy Heckman**

757. **Medical Device Market Place 2017.** Amenia, N.Y., Grey House Publishing, 2017. 2v. $465.00/set. ISBN 13: 978-1-68217-389-3.

The Medical Device Market Place is a buying and marketing guide to medical devices and manufacturers in North America. As described in the Publisher's Note and User Guide, "this work fills an information gap in the medical device industry with detailed profiles of FDA-registered medical device manufacturers and their products." Volume one is comprised of six sections. Part 1, The Medical Device Specialty Index, lists devices under one of 19 medical specialty categories and includes a 3-character code, the unique FDA code for each medical device, and some manufacturer services. Categories include Anesthesiology, Clinical Chemistry, General Hospital, Dental, and Radiology. Under each major category, the subdivisions are assigned the 3-character codes. Keyword Index, part 2, lists products alphabetically by over 1,100 keywords; for example, under the Dental category, there is a list of various types of dental equipment. The third part, Product Directory, alphabetically lists the 4,406 medical devices included in this work and provides its medical specialty category, the 3-character FDA code number, and the manufacturer's name, address, and phone number. Geographical Index, part 4, lists companies by geographic location. Next comes a list of trademarked products alphabetically by trademarked name followed by manufacturer information. The last part, Subsidiary Index, lists owner/parent companies alphabetically followed by their subsidiaries. Volume 2 is comprised of 2 sections. Part 1, Manufacturer Profiles, provides an alphabetical list of the 13,098 FDA-registered manufacturers of medical devices and provides company information. Each entry includes name, address, telephone, fax numbers, FDA registration number, website and social media addresses, annual revenue, total number of employees, type of ownership or parent company, stock information (if applicable), quality system adherence, key executives, and product line and medical specialty areas. Executive Name Index, the second part, is comprised of an alphabetical list which includes company affiliation and page number on which it appears in the directory. *The Medical Device Market Place* is an excellent source for practitioners, faculty in medical schools, and medical school students. This should be a staple in hospital libraries and in medical practitioners' offices. Highly recommended.—**Lucy Heckman**

Handbooks and Yearbooks

758.   Davidson, Tish. **Vaccines: History, Science, and Issues.** Santa Barbara, Calif., Greenwood Press/ABC-CLIO, 2017. 259p. index. (The Story of a Drug). $60.00. ISBN 13: 978-1-4408-4443-0; 978-1-4408-4444-7 (e-book).

Vaccines: History, Science, and Issues, part of The Story of a Drug series, provides historical and very current data about medical developments with the immune system, disease, and inoculation. The nine chapters are followed by a glossary of terms, bibliographic resources for further study, and a thorough index. Each book in the series begins with a fictional case study. Chapter 1 in *Vaccines* reads with bias. The remaining chapters provide accurate and balanced presentation with extensive data included in the text as well as such tables as Table 2.1, "Preventable Diseases." Clear writing offers medical terminology in laymen's terms and with informative details for research. Inclusion of the most current data is impressive. "Today, scientists understand how vaccines work to prime the body's immune system against certain diseases. As of 2017, vaccines to immunize against 26 illnesses were available in the United States." Chapter nine explores contemporary information with current discovery in the uses of therapeutic vaccines including autologous vaccines where a patient's immune system cells are used to combat certain types of cancer. The trajectory for vaccines of the future is considered and the depth of scientific study exposed (beginning with the history in chapter three).

The inoculation controversy is also discussed. Beyond the medical continuum, vaccination is often met with skepticism and a perception of risk (chapter six). While the U. S. Centers for Disease Control and Prevention (CDC) and the World Health Organization put out annual vaccination recommendations, many find these recommendations to be under the umbrella of government and pharmaceutical pressures and choose to opt out. Opposing viewpoints are well presented in this book.

Recommended for high school and academic libraries.—**Janis Minshull**

759.   **EWGTap Water Database. www.ewg.org/tapwater/index.** [Website] Free. Date reviewed: 2018.

This free-to-use site from the Environmental Working Group (EWG) advocacy organization helps educate consumers on water "health," as it distills millions of records from fifty thousand water utilities throughout the United States to provide national, regional, and local information on contaminants, pollution sources, and more. Users can either enter a zipcode in the homepage bar to access local information or select the Find Your State link for a broader report. Entering a zipcode provides a listing of relevant water utilities by name. Users can select a utility to find information on the utility, population served, water source, years of data coverage, and a statement on compliance with federal health standards. The report also presents a two-columned listing of water contaminants detected above health guidelines and other contaminants. The listing offers a brief description of the contaminant (e.g., bromate, chloroform, etc.) and a graphic measuring contaminant levels in comparison to state and national levels. Finally, the report links contaminants to originating source: Agriculture, Industry, Treatment Byproducts, Runoff & individual state water information via a national map (this information is also accessible via the menu in the top left corner of the homepage). They can also examine a gallery of topical resources, including information on Farming and Tap Water, Radioactive Tap Water, Lead 101, a summary report on the State of American Drinking Water, and a link to Consumer Resources such as an EWG safe Sprawl or Naturally Occurring. Users can alternatively scroll through the homepage to examine an introductory video and access drinking water tip sheet and the EWG Water Filter Buying Guide, explaining technology, maintenance, and other issues. Details about data collection and other issues can be found in the FAQs accessible from the menu on the homepage.—**ARBA Staff Reviewer**

760.   **Handbook of Migration and Health.** Felicity Thomas, ed. Northampton, Mass., Edward Elgar, 2016. 544p. index. $255.00. ISBN 13: 978-1-78471-477-2; 978-1-78471-478-9 (e-book).

The *Handbook of Migration and Health* provides a comprehensive overview on migration and the related issues by bringing together the contributions of fifty-eight leading researchers and draws on case studies and examples from across the globe. Editor Felicity Thomas intended this handbook to be a scholarly, yet accessible, reference tool for researchers, students, and practitioners interested in the field of migration and health. This book offers an authoritative and comprehensive overview of key debates underpinning migration and health in a contemporary global context. Thomas organized the book into six thoughtful sections in addition to a generous introduction: Theories and Models of Migration, Rights and Deservingness, Vulnerability and Precarity, Specific Healthcare Needs and Priorities, Healthcare Provision, and Transnational and Diasporic Networks. The overall work is enhanced by the use of tables, figures, and boxes and also includes generous references and an index.

This is a significant research handbook that explores the complexity of world health issues. Present and future health challenges related to migration operate most effectively when addressed through collaborative global undertakings. This book provides pathways to initiating positive migration health outcomes.—**Thomas E. Baker**

761.   **Health, United States, 2016. https://www.cdc.gov/nchs/data/hus/hus16.pdf.** [Website] Free. Date reviewed: 2017.

The *Health, United States, 2016* report addresses a range of health issues and topics affecting Americans, with particular attention given to changes and trends since 1975.

Produced by the Centers for Disease Control, the U.S. Department of Health and Human Services, and the National Center for Health Statistics, this annual publication includes a Chartbook looking at long-term health trends falling into four general subject areas: Health Status and Determinants, Health Care Utilization, Health Care Resources, and Health Care Expenditures. There are over 100 Trend Tables associated with these broad subject areas as well. Good supplemental material is also included in this 40th edition of the large report.

The downloadable PDF report is well organized so readers can immediately find what they are looking for and/or move through the whole report easily. A brief opening section provides an At a Glance Table and Highlights which puts the more significant points within each broader category (see above) onto one table, cross-referenced to the corresponding table following later in the report. The Highlights portion offers a brief narrative summary of reported trends within the same subject areas and also appropriate tables and figures.

The Chartbook (68 pages) is organized into five sections, with the first section providing a series of figures encapsulating elements of the previous categories. The opening section notes influencing Population Characteristics, such as sex, age, race, and poverty. The second section presents information on mortality & natality (e.g., life expectancy at birth, birth rates, etc.), health risk factors (cigarette smoking, etc.), and more. A third section—Utilization—emphasizes elements of care such as prescription drugs, hospital stays, and screenings. Health Care Resources looks at hospitals, physicians, and nursing homes. And the last section examines personal expenditures ranging from insurance issues to types of costs (e.g., prescription drugs, hospital stays, etc.). Comparative data tables for each figure listed prior immediately follow.

Trend Tables make up the bulk of the report, and display 114 areas where particular data has been collected over the years, providing an excellent window into past data and changes over time. Some examples include Contraceptive Use, Leading Causes of Death, Obesity Rates, Vaccination Coverage, Death Rates per factor (drug poisoning, car accidents, cancer, etc.), Health Risk Behaviors, and much, much more. The document comes in at nearly 500 pages. The Table of Contents includes links to the corresponding topic/section for ease of navigation, and readers can, of course, bookmark the document. Supplemental information in *Health, United States, 2016* includes Technical Notes and extensive References for the Chartbook information, a List of Chartbook Figures, and a List of Trend Tables (by topic and all). The lists also include links to the affiliated location in the report. Additionally, there is an appendix noting each data source (alphabetical) and supplying references. A second appendix provides definitions of specialized terms and phrases (e.g., hearing trouble, home visit, health care contact, etc.) and information on the methods used in gathering data. A detailed, cross-referenced index completes the report.

The information in this report would be of great interest to many: health care advocates, medical professionals, students, educators, policy makers and others, particularly as people live longer and new health and health care challenges arise.—**ARBA Staff Reviewer**

762. **Institute for Health Metrics and Evaluation. http://www.healthdata.org/.** [Website] Free. Date reviewed: 2018.

This site takes health care data and analyses from a variety of sources and applies specialized tools to track and articulate essential topics in the global health care forum. Much of the Institute's (IMHE) work is centered around the Global Health Data Exchange, which site users can access from the GHDx tab in the upper left corner of the homepage. The exchange serves as a catalog of IHME accumulated health datasets, surveys, censuses, etc., such as the Nepal Demographic and Health Survey 2016-2017 and the U.S. Longitudinal Study of Aging 1994-2000. Users can search the exchange by data or country. The information gathered from this exchange makes up a significant part of the extensive Global Burden of Disease Study (GBD), which serves to educate about the health risk (disease, injury, etc.) across countries, gender, and more. Information about the study is available under the Projects tab on the homepage menu bar, and users can access the many tools used in and around it such as GBD Compare (a broad visualization of GBD data), the Mortality Visualization, Causes of Death Visualization, the EPI Visualization, and the GBD Data Input Sources Tool. Users can select the Results tab to examine the good variety of resources working to maximize the impact of accumulated data. The GBD Results Tool allows a data search of the broader study through the application of particular parameters (location, age, sex, context, etc.). Other items on the drop down menu include Data Visualizations (e.g., "Child Growth Failure"), Policy Reports (e.g., "India: The Health of the Nation's States"), Research Articles ("Factors Associated with Increases in U.S. Health Care Spending 1996-2013"), Infographics ("U.S. Spending on Global Health in 2016"), detailed Country and U.S. County Profiles, and other materials. Users can also find definitions of specialized vocabulary, topic summaries, and other foundational material under the Results tab. Site users can also scroll through a display of featured research and reports on the homepage. The IMHE could have a tremendous impact on health research via the data it gathers and creatively presents. The site would be useful for educators, policy makers, practitioners, and others who are engaged in global health.—**ARBA Staff Reviewer**

763.   **The Internet of Things and Advanced Application in Healthcare.** Catarina I. Reis and Marisa da Silva Maximiano, eds. Hershey, Pa., IGI Global, 2017. 349p. index. (Advances in Medical Technologies and Clinical Practice (AMTCP) book series). $240.00. ISBN 13: 978-1-52251-820-4; 978-1-52251-821-1 (e-book).

The Advances in Medical Technologies and Clinical Practice (AMTCP) book series covers the latest research on new and emerging medical technologies within clinical studies, diagnostics, and more. This volume in the series focuses specifically on the networking and technological potential of the Internet within the healthcare industry. The volume's preface along with its detailed table of contents lays out its organization and explains its highly specialized focus. Ten chapters examine different topics relating to the innovations and challenges of the Internet of Things (IoT) and the way they relate with various healthcare needs and capabilities. Chapters discuss the IoT in the context of such things as Assistive Technology (AT), wearable health monitoring systems, and air quality. They additionally address technical issues of synchronicity, reliability, and efficiency. Chapter 7, for example, examines how the IoT can help to gather and assimilate blood flow and heart rhythm data into one accurate health monitoring system. Each chapter opens with an abstract to establish the impetus and methodology of the research that follows. Chapters are generally well structured and may provide introduction, future research directions, and conclusion sections, and may incorporate the use of case studies, data tables, graphs, headers, subheaders, illustrations, and more. References are listed at the end of each chapter and compiled again at the end of the book, alongside brief contributor biographies and an index. Individual chapters are available for purchase in an electronic format. Recommended for academic libraries.—**ARBA Staff Reviewer**

764.   Moise, Ana Maria R. **The Gut Microbiome: Exploring the Connection between Microbes, Diet, and Health.** Santa Barbara, Calif., Greenwood Press/ABC-CLIO, 2017. 200p. index. (The Story of a Drug series). $58.00. ISBN 13: 978-1-4408-4264-1; 978-1-

4408-4265-8 (e-book).

The overwhelming impact of trillions of microbes on the human body is not within the realm of common knowledge. By reading this book curious readers will become acquainted with contemporary information on the gut microbes that regulate our immune systems and determine the risk for developing chronic diseases, such as type 2 diabetes and heart disease. Moreover, microbes may have implications for neurological disorders like autism, multiple sclerosis, and Parkinson's disease. Most intriguing—the link between gut microbes and brain functions. The author's experience and expertise provides an insightful approach that informs and motivates positive lifestyle changes. The book also includes references for further readings, a glossary, a bibliography, and an extensive index. Sidebar boxes emphasize important information.

This book is an information gem! Recommended for public and academic libraries.—**Thomas E. Baker**

765.   **Patient Care and Health Information. https://www.mayoclinic.org/patient-care-and-health%20information.** [Website] Free. Date reviewed: 2018.

The Patient Care and Health Information page from the Mayo Clinic offers consumer access to fundamental medical information. Simply structured, the page presents four A-Z directories covering Diseases & Conditions (e.g., cancers, gallstones, laryngitis, etc.), Symptoms (back pain, shortness of breath, etc.), Tests & Procedures (amniocentesis, otoplasty, talk therapy, etc.), and Drugs and Supplements (Baby Orajel, Epipen, Metformin, etc.).

Topics within these categories can be quite extensive. Entries for each topic, which will vary in length, are well-organized essays which make a good use of headers, subheaders, bullet points, illustrations, related topics, and more. Many of the topics are cross-referenced to entries in other directories.

Within the Drugs & Supplements category, entries can be searched by either brand name or drug name, and will generally provide a description of drug, U.S. brand name, dosage forms, a description of use, prescription information, and method of delivery. Treatments & Procedures may touch on risks and complications, types, preparations, expectations, results, and more.

Aside from the directories, users can select the Research tab at the top of the page to find an A-Z listing of Mayo Clinic Research Labs which provides information on current research projects, including project goals, background information, project history, and publications. Users can learn about research regarding Aerospace Medicine and Vestibular Research, Airway Biology, Alzheimer's Disease and Inflammation, the Artificial Pancreas, Mitochondrial Genetics, and other topics. Users can also search through Clinical Trials by condition, treatment, or drug name.

As the Mayo Clinic is among the preeminent medical research organizations in the world, this website would be an excellent resource for consumer health information in addition to information on medical research advancements. It would appeal to consumers, health practitioners, medical students, educators, and others.—**ARBA Staff Reviewer**

766.   Rosner, Lisa. **Vaccination and Its Critics: A Documentary and Reference Guide.** Santa Barbara, Calif., Greenwood Press/ABC-CLIO, 2017. 312p. $110.00. ISBN 13: 978-1-4408-4183-5; 978-1-4408-4184-2 (e-book).

This is a collection of documents on vaccination, historical and contemporary. Eight chapters explore the efficacy, safety, cost, policies, practices, values, and beliefs surrounding vaccination. Types of documents include but are not limited to: personal experiences, data on foundations such as the March of Dimes, research studies, government bills, autobiographical reflections from an FDA employee, law cases, and ethical questioning. Highlight boxes give additional information, an analysis section encourages deeper thought, and further readings provide options for extended research. The multiple documents included in each chapter provide perspective and a springboard and allow readers to trace themes and trends. Research students seeking information in the area of inoculation history will find this book thorough and compact. Because of the breadth of documentation, linear correlation is straightforward. Extending historical aspects to current topics such as the autism debate, homeopathic medicine, and contemporary experimentation brings discussion full circle. Authors of the works here are doctors, scientists, lawmakers, regulators, philanthropists, healthcare professionals, and patients.

Bibliographic references and an index close out the material and a chronology dated from 900 B.C.E. to 2014 provides historical context. This title is recommended for public, school, and academic libraries.—**Janis Minshull**

767. **Salem Health: Community and Family Health Issues.** Amber Bruggman and Kimberly Ortiz-Hartman, eds. Amenia, N.Y., Grey House Publishing, 2017. 3v. illus. index. $395.00/set. ISBN 13: 978-1-68217-337-4; 978-1-68217-338-1 (e-book).

This three-volume encyclopedia is the latest addition to the Salem Health series, and combines more than 130 newly written articles written with nearly 370 updated articles from other Salem Health titles. It focuses on major areas that typically influence the health and well-being of individuals, families, and communities: biological illnesses, mental health disorders, and environmental stressors. The work is edited by licensed clinical social worker Amber Bruggman and doctor of psychology Kimberly Ortiz-Hartman. Contributors include social workers, therapists, nurses, physicians, and researchers. While the introduction by Ortiz-Hartman states that this resource is aimed at readers who may be experiencing one or some of the above issues, many of the essays clearly provide information aimed at social work practitioners. This is only one of several inconsistencies that may indicate inadequate editing of previously published material.

Each volume begins with tables of contents for all three volumes. Articles are arranged alphabetically and range from one to eight pages in length, with the exception of 24 overviews that are usually longer and more detailed. All articles, including overviews, are signed by writers and reviewers and follow similar formats. Overviews—on topics like adoption, schizophrenia, workplace violence, juvenile delinquency, and divorce—provide some or all of these subtopics: definitions and descriptions; facts and figures; risk factors; signs and symptoms; assessments and assessment tools; treatments and interventions; laws and regulations; services and resources; food for thought; red flags; and next steps. Of special interest is the food for thought subtopic because it often goes outside the box to shine a different light on the topic. Standard articles may contain some of those subtopics or only a few with subheadings like: what we know, what can be done; and services and resources. Although all articles include a list of up-to-date references, not all articles contain in-text citations, indicating another inconsistency in editing. Lack of in-text citations complicates further reading and research, as one tries to somehow decide which citation in the list of references goes with an interesting article described in the entry. The third volume contains a glossary of terms; categorized list of articles; and a subject index. Schools and libraries that purchase the print version also get complimentary access to the e-book through the publisher's online database.

Despite needing tighter editing, this encyclopedia contains good material and is a worthwhile resource for a variety of audiences, including undergraduate and graduate students, health and social services professionals, and the general public.—**Madeleine Nash**

768. **Salem Health: Nutrition.** Ortiz, Dawn, ed. Hackensack, N.J., Salem Press, 2016. 3v. illus. index. $395.00/set. ISBN 13: 978-1-68217-135-6; 978-1-68217-146-2 (e-book).

Salem Health: Nutrition is a three-volume reference set designed to help consumers focus on the nutritional value of dozens of foods and food groups. The editor, a registered dietitian nutritionist, states in the introduction that her goals for this set are to help consumers see beyond fad diets and food trends and also to provide quality nutritional information for both healthy people and those with health challenges, illnesses, and unique medical conditions. The set can be used as a tool and guide in making healthy food choices and considering the role of food and health.

Volume one (Food Groups) analyzes the nutritional value of foods via food groups: fruits, vegetables, grains, protein, dairy, beverages, herbs/spices, and fats/oils. Each entry gives nutrient content, dietary intake guidelines, and current research findings. References for further reading are also presented. There are occasional photos within entries. The volume concludes with nutrition information (over 30 info-charts) from the USDA, covering a wide range of dietary guidelines.

Volume two (Medical Nutrition Therapy for Various Disease States) focuses on medical nutrition therapy (MNT) for specific diseases and disorders, including cancer, diabetes, gastrointestinal disorders, heart disease, and mental health concerns. Entries cover what is known about the diet/disease connection, research findings, and a summary with references for further reading. Specific MNT information may also be included.

Volume three (Dietary Considerations) offers entries on healthy diet topics, such as eating breakfast, avoiding fast food, and getting sufficient sleep. There are also entries related to nutrition and aging, as well as micronutrients: vitamins and minerals. Volume three concludes with two appendixes and a detailed index.

There are 255 entries across all three volumes. Each entry is between one and eight pages in length. Entries are signed and also have been reviewed. Writing style is entry-level for the topics presented. Graphics and photos are black and white; color graphics and photos would have been preferred by this reviewer.

Salem Health: Nutrition is a useful reference source for introductory research on selected nutrition topics. Emphasis on health and nutrition is noted, and signed and reviewed entries offer extra value of information. Most appropriate for high school and public library collections that support nutrition or introductory health courses.—**Caroline L. Gilson**

769. Selby, Christine L. B. **The Body Size and Health Debate.** Santa Barbara, Calif., Greenwood Press/ABC-CLIO, 2017. 210p. index. (Health and Medical Issues Today). $40.00. ISBN 13: 978-1-4408-4805-6; 978-1-4408-4806-3 (e-book).

This book by Certified Eating Disorder Specialist and Certified Sport Psychology Consultant Christine L. B. Selby, PhD, addresses sensitive topics with dignity, compassion, and understanding. This book is an easy read with well-developed chapters. The book is broken into three main parts: Overview of the Body Size Health Debate, Controversies and Issues, and Case Illustration Scenarios. The book presents a balanced perspective on body image and health care. It covers information related to body weight, shape, and size explicitly as well as the degree to which body size reveals a person's health status. The book offers a glossary, timeline, sources for further information, bibliography, and extensive index system.

This superior contribution rings controversial bell tones that contradict many negative self-image beliefs, motivate positive acceptance, and enhance self-esteem. Every high school, community college, and university should consider adding this book to resource collections.—**Thomas E. Baker**

770.   Subramanian, Sunny, and Chrystle Fiedler. **The Compassionate Chicks Guide to DIY Beauty: 125 Recipes for Vegan, Gluten-Free, Cruelty-Free Makeup, Skin & Hair Products.** Toronto, Robert Rose, 2016. 272p. illus. index. $24.95pa. ISBN 13: 978-0-7708-0547-2.

This 2016 publication from Robert Rose provides recipes (125) for affordable makeup and skin care products made from natural ingredients like aloe, jojoba, essential oils, and arrowroot powder. In addition to a natural lip plumper, there are recipes for facial peels, tooth whitening, sunscreen, foundation, vegan mascara, and blush, among many other products. Recipes include easy-to-follow instructions and extra features about top tips and superstar ingredients. Color photographs accompany most of the recipes. Appendixes list places to find ingredients, the key properties of different ingredients, beauty routine ideas, and other information. This reviewer had great success with the Fruity AHA Facial Peel, made from a mixture of papaya, pineapple, and jojoba oil, and the flawless powder foundation (arrowroot powder, unsweetened cocoa, and lavender oil). This book is highly recommended to public libraries and would be a great source for librarians looking for tween and teen activities.—**ARBA Staff Reviewer**

771.   **Transformative Healthcare Practice through Patient Engagement.** Guendalina Graffigna, ed. Hershey, Pa., Medical Information Science Reference/IGI Global, 2017. 382p. index. (Advances in Medical Diagnosis, Treatment, and Care (AMTDC) Book Series). $215.00. ISBN 13: 978-1-52250-663-8; 978-1-52250-664-5 (e-book).

This volume in the Advances in Medical Diagnosis, Treatment, and Care series from IGI Global focuses on ways to improve health through better interaction between medical personnel and their patients. Editor Guendalina Graffigna is a professor of Social Psychology at Catholic University of the Sacred Heart in Milan and most of the 34 other contributors are from Italian and other European institutions. Thus the book primarily reflects research in European health care practices related to patient engagement, though there are significant contributions from the United States and Canada. The book has two thematic sections. The chapters in the first section, Best Practices in Promoting Patient's Participation and Engagement, cover patient engagement in relation to kidney transplants, the engagement of patients with COPD (chronic obstructive pulmonary disease) in the Italian health system, decision-making in chronic care situations, and patient and family engagement in end-of life care. The second section, on the use of new technologies to facilitate the patient's participation in health management, includes a chapter on how new technologies can encourage better health care while lowering costs, the use of multimedia and interactive voice technology to humanize communication, and the use of technology to assess the quality of prostate cancer websites. An intriguing chapter in this section discusses the effectiveness of a virtual reality tool called Virtual Worlds with individuals and groups to reinforce positive feelings and actions. Another contribution deals with in-home physical therapy, delivered by various personal and electronic means. Each chapter in this volume includes extensive references and a list of key terms and definitions. The scholarship is thorough and the contributions have been peer reviewed. Recommended as a resource for libraries serving health care providers, students, and policy-makers in public health, hospital management, nursing, and physical therapy. A noteworthy feature is that the individual chapters can be purchased electronically through the IGI Global website.—**ARBA Staff Reviewer**

Medicine

General Works

Atlases

772.   Agur, Anne M. R., and Arthur F. Dalley. **Grant's Atlas of Anatomy.** 14th ed. New York, Wolters Kluwer, 2016. 896p. illus. index. $89.99pa. ISBN 13: 978-1-4698-9068-5.

Now in its 14th edition, *Grant's Atlas of Anatomy* has upgraded the material in response to the needs of students and educators without sacrificing its easy-to-use layout and its tried-and-true organization. The most important changes to the 14th edition are in the realm of illustrations. The entire collection of carbon-dust illustrations has been remastered and recolored leading to high-resolution images. The schematic illustrations have also been overhauled with a modern uniform style and consistent color palette. This is in addition to the pictures of real cadavers in the classic illustrations. In terms of written material, users will find clinical comments in blue next to illustration legends. These clinical notes provide information about real-life medical applications of the anatomical concepts being presented. The work has also reordered body regions to correspond to the sequence used in the more recent editions of *Grant's Dissector.*

What has not changed is the uncluttered presentation of material and the excellent organization. The detailed table of contents is followed by a list of tables that are grouped by chapters. Chapters themselves begin with a table of contents, and chapters follow the same format, moving from more general overviews, to specific information, and concluding with diagnostic images. There are nine chapters on the following regions: back, upper limb, thorax, abdomen, pelvis and perineum, lower limb, head, neck, and cranial nerves. For those who prefer to search a specific topic without going to the table of contents or individual chapters, the extensive index has *see* and *see also* references; tables are also indexed and clearly marked as such.

Highly recommended for public and academic libraries.—**ARBA Staff Reviewer**

Dictionaries and Encyclopedias

773.   **Mosby's Dictionary of Medicine, Nursing & Health Professions.** 10th ed. San Diego, Calif., Elsevier Science, 2017. 2,064p. illus. index. $44.95pa. ISBN 13: 978-0-323-22205-1.

Following a forward, list of consultants, and pronunciation key are a series of color atlases of human anatomy: skeletal system, muscular system, circulatory system, endocrine system, lymphatic system, nervous system, respiratory system, digestive system, reproductive system, urinary system, and special senses. The guide to the dictionary provides direction on alphabetization, cross-referencing policies, the elements of an entry, word etymology, and more. Inside users will find more than 56,000 definitions and nearly 2,500 full-color photographs and illustrations that facilitate comprehension of a disease or syndrome. Three hundred of these color illustrations are new to this edition, while new developments in health care have led to 11,000 new terms (some of these are revised from older editions). Unlike *Dorland's Illustrated Medical Dictionary, Mosby's* does not make use of subentries. Users will also benefit from numerous appendixes such as: "Nursing Interventions Classification (NIC) Definitions, 1924"; "Nursing Outcomes Classification (NOC) Definitions, 1934"; "Language Translation Guide, 1949"; "Normal Reference Values, 1961"; "Nutrition, 1966"; "Range of Motion, 1974"; "Infection Control CDC Isolation Guidelines, 1992"; and "Diagnosis-Related Groups, 1994."

This is highly recommended to public and academic libraries as well as medical professionals.—**ARBA Staff Reviewer**

Handbooks and Yearbooks

774.   Bell, Edward A. **Children's Medicines: What Every Parent, Grandparent, and Teacher Needs to Know.** Baltimore, Md., Johns Hopkins University Press, 2018. 146p. index. $22.95pa. ISBN 13: 978-1-4214-2375-3.

This handy reference book meets the public's demand for medical information that supports in-home childcare. Sometimes, the abundance of conflicting information from numerous media sources causes confusion. This book helps caregivers enhance their ability to make better decisions regarding the application of childhood medicines and other therapies with its insightful answers to everyday questions.

The book discusses the art of giving medicine to children, over-the-counter herbs, supplements, and vitamin products; how medicines affect adults and children differently; vaccine safety; and other topics. Reference citations, bullet formats, outlines, tables, and graphics represent effective illustrative communication strategies. Summary points at the conclusion of each chapter serve as content reminders and learning tools. The last chapter offers suggestions regarding inquiries about obtaining reliable information from the Internet and the local pharmacist. One appendix discusses maternal medication and breastfeeding. Another addresses giving medication in a child's nose, ear, and eye.

The author is a pediatric pharmacist and professor of pharmacy practice. His expertise and delivery reflects understanding and a sincere effort to assist individuals charged with caring for children. This book is recommended for public libraries.—**Thomas E. Baker**

775.   **Current Medical Diagnosis & Treatment, 2017.** 56th ed. Maxine A. Papadakis, Stephen J. McPhee, and Michael W. Rabow, eds. New York, McGraw-Hill, 2017. 1902p. illus. index. $85.00pa. ISBN 13: 978-1-259-58511-1.

This is the 56th edition of this venerable reference work designed as a ready reference and/or refresher for medical students and medical professionals. The book covers more than one thousand diseases and disorders. Among its many features are coverage of medical advances up to the time of publication, recent references with PubMed and PMID numbers, and detailed presentation of primary care topics. There are several new updates for 2017, such as new information on the Zika virus; updates on vaccines for influenza, MMR, and HPV; the latest options for obesity treatment; updates and new treatments for HIV; and information on the increase in deaths due to opioid overdose. Chapters utilize such subheadings as General Considerations, Clinical Findings, Differential Diagnosis, Treatment, Prognosis, and When to Refer, which facilitates navigation. There are also textboxes which list the essentials of diagnosis and tables that list such things as drugs and dosages or illustrations of what tests to perform to diagnose a knee injury. Perhaps most importantly, the chapters are signed by one of the many medical professionals listed in the front matter. This vast source of information, under the editorship of three esteemed medical doctors, is highly recommended for medical libraries and for public libraries.— **ARBA Staff Reviewer**

776.　**Disease Management Sourcebook.** 2d ed. Keith Jones, ed. Detroit, Omnigraphics, 2017. 584p. index. (Health Reference Series). $95.00. ISBN 13: 978-0-7808-1545-2; 978-0-7808-1546-9 (e-book).

Disease management has emerged as a promising strategy for improving care for those individuals with chronic conditions. People with chronic conditions usually use more health care services, which often are not coordinated among providers, creating opportunities for overuse or underuse of medical care. Disease management generally requires using a multidisciplinary, integrated team of providers (for example, physicians, pharmacists, nurses, dieticians, psychologists) to assist individuals in managing their condition(s).

The sourcebook is divided into eight parts: Facts about Serious and Chronic Illnesses; Working with Healthcare Providers and the Healthcare System; Health Literacy and Making Informed Health Decisions; Prescription (Rx) and Over-the-Counter (OTC) Medications; Managing Chronic Disease; Children and Chronic Disease; Legal, Financial, and Insurance Issues That Impact Disease Management; and Additional Help and Information. Like other titles in the Health Reference Series, this one is organized in a logical and thoughtful way with a detailed table of contents and a straightforward, easy-to-understand writing style. Headings within the chapters help readers understand the material and find the facts they need, while illustrations, charts, graphs, and other features break up the text and convey facts in different ways. A helpful glossary provides definitions of technical terms, resource directories highlight organizations that can supply further information and support, and a professionally prepared master index facilitates navigation.

Designed for undergraduates, high school students, and general nonspecialists, this excellent book presents a current, balanced, and reliable collection of material and is a recommended purchase.—**Thomas E. Baker**

777.　Fabbri, Christiane Nockels. **From Anesthesia to X-Rays: Innovations and Discoveries That Changed Medicine Forever.** Santa Barbara, Calif., Greenwood Press/ABC-CLIO, 2017. 246p. index. $58.00. ISBN 13: 978-1-61069-573-2; 978-1-61069-574-9 (e-book).

This well-researched compendium of medical techniques and inventions begins each chapter with a short summary covering the inventor, date, and location of the invention, as well as the medical significance of the advancement. From CPR to modern psychopharmacology, this text provides in-depth information about less familiar, yet impactful developments in the medical field. The text is academic and coverage is thorough, though it might give lower-level readers some difficulty. To be considered for collections with a special medical focus or for student researchers.—**Shanna Shadoan**

778.   Friedman, Karen A., and Sara L. Merwin. **The Informed Patient: A Complete Guide to a Hospital Stay.** Ithaca, N.Y., ILR Press/Cornell University Press, 2017. 228p. index. (The Culture and Politics of Health Care Work). $19.95pa. ISBN 13: 978-1-5017-0995-1.

The Informed Patient serves as a reader friendly introduction to a hospital stay that can be both intimidating and stressful as patients and their families are faced with difficult decisions associated with procedures, assessments, and protocols. Chapters explore meaningful discussions from both the patient's viewpoint and the viewpoint of the medical professionals responsible for their care. The entire book is devoted to supporting patients. Topics include a variety of frequently encountered issues and uncertainties. Authors Karen A. Freidman, MD, and Sara L. Merwin, MPH, strive to offer excellent content on how patients can protect themselves and receive improved health care. The accurate information provided is useful when dealing with a system that can easily cause concern once individuals depart from routine comfort zones. The book offers tips, a glossary, and an extensive index system. Every public, high school, community college, and university library should consider adding this book to resource collections.—**Thomas E. Baker**

779.   **Human Medical Experimentation: From Smallpox Vaccines to Secret Government Programs.** Frances R. Frankenburg, ed. Santa Barbara, Calif., Greenwood Press/ABC-CLIO, 2017. 322p. index. $89.00. ISBN 13: 978-1-61069-897-9; 978-1-61069-898-6 (e-book).

Why does *Human Medical Experimentation* make a significant contribution? The road from human research to social benefits is long, uncertain, and often disappointing. Modern medical research focuses on the possibility and anticipation of possible cures for many devastating diseases. Ethical and professionally controlled medical trials offer possible cures for disease sufferers and hope for future generations, but ignorance can lead to human experiments based on poor research, poor methods, and other abuses.

This text offers insight into the laborious struggle to cure life-threatening illnesses. As editor Francis R. Frankenburg, MD, Boston University School of Medicine, comments in the introduction: "The experiments described in this encyclopedia offer moments in medical history that lend themselves to storytelling." The book is organized into six eras: Pre-19th Century; 19th Century; 20th Century to World War II; World War II; Cold War; and Post-Cold War to the Present. Sections include introductions and timelines of major experiments, discoveries, and important scientists. The book offers a comprehensive index system, scholarly contributions, and essential historical perspectives and summaries. Chapters offer documents and further readings. This encyclopedic volume also features an overview of the gradual development of regulations, practices, and research.

This captivating volume is recommended for public and academic libraries.— **Thomas E. Baker**

780.   **Immune System Disorders Sourcebook.** 3d ed. Keith Jones, ed. Detroit, Omnigraphics, 2017. 599p. index. (Health Reference Series). $95.00. ISBN 13: 978-0-7808-1468-4; 978-0-7808-1467-7 (e-book).

This volume in Omnigraphics' Health Reference Series is an excellent resource on the expansive topic of immune system disorders. Written and organized in a straightforward, plain English way, the book allows patients, caregivers, and others access to basic, comprehensive information on the range of immune system disorders, their symptoms, treatments, and more.

Nine parts organize the essential topics, beginning with a general overview of how the immune system functions and the areas of research around it. Following parts include the Diagnosis of Immune System Disorders, Inherited Immune Disorder Diseases, Acquired Immune Disorder Diseases, Autoimmune Diseases, Other Altered Immune Responses, and Treatments. The closing two parts are Coping with Immune Disease and Additional Help and Information, which includes two glossaries and a directory of supportive organizations.

Each part is further divided into clear and concise chapters addressing the particulars of its subject. Part five—the largest section—holds 38 chapters which essentially survey the range of autoimmune diseases such as Celiac Disease, Guillain-Barre Syndrome, Lupus, Myocarditis, Scleroderma, and Vitiligo. Topics within each chapter may include symptoms, causes, risk factors, tests, complications, associated conditions, treatments, and latest research.

The volume incorporates a generous use of headers (many in question format), subheaders, bullet points, lists, tables, diagrams, and more for ease of navigation. Information is copious, but never overwhelming as this reference is clearly targeted to the average person, not the medical professional.

This third edition (see ARBA 2006, entry 1436) presents the most up-to-date information in regards to immune system disorders, treatments, diagnosis, etc., relative to the rapid advancements in medical research and implementation. The reference is not produced to replace professional medical counsel; however, it succeeds at providing intelligent, basic information about immune system disorders to a general audience.— **ARBA Staff Reviewer**

781.   **Incunabula: A Collection of Books and Broadsides Printed in Europe before 1501. www.nlm.nih.gov/news/incunabula_ww2_gov.html.** [Website] Free. Date reviewed: 2018.

The National Library of Medicine has created this small but special database displaying over fifty items of Incunabula—western civilization's earliest printed (via movable type) material connected to medicine and science. The collection shares this homepage with a link to the newly digitized World War II materials collection, but selecting the Incunabula: A Collection of Books and Broadsides Printed Before 1501 link moves users straight to the appropriate database. Items are displayed with a thumbnail photograph and identifying information such as title, language, author, genre, etc. The collection can be searched via a selection of filters corresponding to an item's identifying features. Highlights include *De pollutione nocturne* from 1466, known to be the oldest medical book of western civilization, the beautifully illustrated 1494 almanac broadsheet by Jacobus Honiger, and works by Hippocrates and St. Thomas Aquinas. Users can closely examine or download the digital documents. Within the texts, users will observe hand-colored and woodcut illustrations, consider medieval thought on medical concerns such as mental illness or the plague, draw connections between medicine, astrology, and philosophy, and much more. The library will likely add to the digital collection in the future, but even now there is much to learn for medieval and early renaissance scholars, medical historians, and others.—**ARBA Staff Reviewer**

782.   **Medical Services and Warfare, 1850-1927. http://www.amdigital.co.uk/m-products/product/medical-services-and-warfare/.** [Website] Chicago, Adam Matthew Digital, 2017. Price negotiated by site. Date reviewed: 2017.

This database provides rich content on the evolution of medicine within the setting of warfare, from the middle of the nineteenth century to the late 1920s. As with its other 50-plus databases, this Adam Matthew resource draws on multiple institutions for its content. In this case, the sources are five U.S. libraries, museums, and archives; three British organizations, including the British Library and the National Archives; and the Library and Archives of Canada. The focus is on three conflicts during this period: the Crimean War, the United States Civil War, and World War I, although some documents related to the Boer War, the Spanish-American War, and other conflicts are also included. There are multiple ways to explore the documents' twelve broad themes, such as hospital care, surgery, personal experience, and nursing. Users can also limit their results at any time by one or more of the twenty-four document types—hospital record, diary, military record, printed book, etc. The "advanced search" option allows for searching of multiple terms, each limited to particular fields within records, as well as to dates and document types, and even a particular library or archive.

Fascinatingly, this database offers handwritten text recognition technology for the numerous documents in script connected to Florence Nightingale's life and career. It allows researchers to look for words and phrases that might not be easily decipherable at first glance in the documents. (The technology does not, however, provide a transcription of the complete text for handwritten documents.) This resource is clearly designed for advanced researchers and will be best used by academic libraries, in numerous countries, with scholars exploring these various topics.—**Mark Schumacher**

783.   **Merck Manual Consumer Version. http://www.merckmanuals.com/home.** [Website] Free. Date reviewed: 2017.

The comprehensive Merck Manual brings a wealth of information regarding a large range of medical topics to online consumers. This version differs from the Professional version (www.merckmanuals.com/professional) in that it specifically targets patients, nonprofessional caregivers, and others with a general interest in the information. The site employs simplified, nonspecialized language to examine a wide range of topics from a consumer-friendly perspective.

The website, available in several languages, is easy to navigate and explore. Users can conduct a basic search from the bar, scroll through featured topics within the page, or browse several categories through the menu. Medical Topics lists over two dozen general categories such as Blood Disorders, Children's Health Issues, Fundamentals, Infections, and Immune Disorders. Selecting a category under this tab leads to a summary "textbook" presentation with related topics presented in a section/chapter format. For example, the category Blood Disorders is separated into 16 sections offering both basic educational and specific disorder material, such as Biology of Blood, Blood Clotting Process, Blood Transfusion, Leukemias, and Anemia. These sections (e.g., Anemia) are then further divided into individual topical chapters of varying length. Chapters (e.g., Overview, Anemia of Chronic Disease, Iron-Deficiency Anemia, etc.) are well organized and make excellent use of headers, bullet points, links to affiliated information, illustrations, and more. The tone, language, and detail of the material is clearly geared toward the average consumer. The left sidebar will simultaneously scroll through chapter headers as users read through it for easy reference. The right sidebar notes the chapter subject within the context of the main section. Affiliated quizzes, videos, news, and other material may also be included within the article page. The Symptoms tab allows users to browse a list of roughly 100 medical symptoms. Symptoms can be general (e.g., pain) or specific (e.g., joint pain, single joint) and are organized into categories such as Chest & Respiratory, Children's Symptoms, Abdomen & Digestive, and Eye. Selecting a specific symptom will provide information organized similarly to that under the Medical Topics tab, with ample and effective use of headers, links to affiliated information, and other tools. Common topics addressed with symptoms include causes, treatment, warning signs, and when to see a doctor. The Emergencies tab allows for quick access to 20 topics which reflect incidents which may necessitate immediate medical response, such as drowning, choking, burns, cardiac arrest, wounds, and more. The information here is similarly organized to material in other areas of the website, and also found underneath the broader Medical Topics tab. The Drug Information tab allows users to conduct a basic search for downloadable and printable information within the categories of drug information, natural products (e.g., ginseng), and drug interactions. Users can also browse an extensive alphabetized list of generic and brand names to access ample material regarding dosage, storage, warnings, and side effects. The Pill Identifier searches medications by imprint, shape, color, or generic drug name. News & Commentary links to a variety of topical articles and current commentary on medical and health information relevant to consumers, such as the "Use of Acetominophen During Pregnancy" or "Keep Halloween Spooky, but Safe." These articles are also featured throughout the homepage, in addition to a topical Infographic which illustrates a particular health issue (male breast cancer as of this review). The Resources tab links to an extensive collection of self-assessment tools, quizzes, pronunciations, videos, medical terms, first aid information, and much more, all geared toward the consumer.

As the site is directed to consumers, it is important to note that the information within it is meant for educational purposes only and would not take the place of individual medical advice. Nonetheless, the quality and range of the material, in conjunction with the site's easy-to-navigate format, makes this an excellent online resource for consumers. Recommended for public and academic libraries.—**ARBA Staff Reviewer**

784. **Merck Manual Professional. http://www.merckmanuals.com/professional.** [Website] Free. Date reviewed: 2017.

This site represents the Professional version of the comprehensive Merck Manual— the online resource that defines and discusses a large range of medical topics. This version differs from the Consumer version (www.merckmanuals.com/home) in that it specifically targets the medical community of doctors, medical students, and other health care professionals via relevant topics, specialized language, and an industry point-of-view. Regardless of this difference, the website, available in several languages, is easy to navigate and explore.

Users can conduct a basic search from the bar, scroll through featured topics within the page, or browse several categories through the menu. Medical Topics lists two dozen broader categories such as Clinical Pharmacology; Hematology and Oncology; Infectious Diseases; and Nutritional Disorders. Selecting a category under this tab leads to a summary "textbook" description with related subtopics presented in a chapter format. For example, the category Critical Care Medicine is separated into six chapters which are further divided into individual topical articles of varying length. Articles are well organized and may incorporate headers, bullet points, cross-reference links, videos, and illustrations. The tone, language, and detail of the articles is clearly geared toward the medical community. The left sidebar will simultaneously scroll through section headers as users read through the article for easy reference. The right sidebar notes the chapter subject within the context of the main topic. Affiliated quizzes, videos, news, and more may also be included within the article page. The Drug Information tab allows users to browse an extensive alphabetized list by generic or brand name. Selecting a drug brings up ample information organized by topic, such as Pregnancy Risk Factor, Medication-Safety Issues, Administration, Use, Dosing, and Brand Names. The Pill Identifier searches medications by imprint, shape, color, or generic drug name. News & Commentary links to a variety of blog posts, articles, and current event commentary on the latest procedures, environmental factors, medical devices, therapies, and other research. Several of these items are featured on the home page under the Latest News banner. The Resources tab links to an extensive collection of audio recordings, figures, images, podcasts, abbreviations, and much more. Medical students, in particular, would greatly benefit from several features on the page, including the searchable video collection of 125 of the latest Procedures & Exams (e.g., How to Apply a Knee Immobilizer). The Quizzes & Cases tab offers 10 case studies of real-life medical scenarios and over 300 short quizzes ideal for the student. A featured Med Student Stories link to the Merck Manual Student Stories site offers a genuinely appealing look at the novice experience. And the site's social media connections, quick access to Popular Resources, and other features establish it as a bona fide learning hub.

Even as the site is directed to professionals, the information within it is meant for educational purposes only. The quality and range of the material, in conjunction with its solid organization, makes this a vital online resource for the medical community. Recommended to public and academic libraries.—**ARBA Staff Reviewer**

785.   **NICHSR   ONESearch.   https://www.nlm.nih.gov/nichsr/onesearch.html.** [Website] Free. Date reviewed: 2018.

The National Information Center for Health Services Research (NICHSR) allows users to explore all U.S. National Library of Medicine databases through one portal. Users have access to data, reports, clinical studies, consumer health information, and more. Entering a general term in the bar searches several NICHSR database projects, including the Health Services Research Projects (HSRProj), Health Services and Sciences Research Resources (HSRR), Health Research Information Central (HSRIC), and Public Health Workforce Partners (PHPartners), to produce an extensive listing of relevant materials such as datasets, websites, training materials, citations, software, and research-in-progress. These listings include title, source, associated text, and URL. Users can access other National Library of Medicine Databases from the menu bar as well, including PubMed/ Medline (biomedical citations), MeSH (medical subject headings), ClinicalTrials.gov, and TOXNET (toxicology database). Because the information accessible here is so extensive, it is advised that first-time users examine the NICHSR One Search Video and the FAQs from the links underneath the search bar.—**ARBA Staff Reviewer**

786.   Zorea, Aharon W. **Finding the Fountain of Youth: The Science and Controversy behind Extending Life and Cheating Death.** Santa Barbara, Calif., Greenwood Press/ABC-CLIO, 2017. 390p. index. $89.00. ISBN 13: 978-1-4408-3798-2; 978-1-4408-3799-9 (e-book).

This book begins with some potentially debatable statements: "In the 21st century, the fountain of youth is no longer a myth" or "the possibility of finding immortality on this earth [is] believable." The author then provides a detailed account of the history of the quest for longer life in five chapters, exploring mythology and science from circa 3,000 B.C.E. to the present century. Taoism, Buddhism, Islam, and western monotheism are all explored. But, the "first science-based antiaging movement" began in the late 1500s, growing out of alchemy, and greater detail is provided from that time on. One important attribute of this book is that it does provide a lot of history of science over the last 100-150 years. Genetics (e.g., The Human Genome Project), biochemistry, and related fields are discussed in detail, as they relate to the antiaging movement. Brief biographies of some of the leading figures in the movement are provided: Aubrey de Grey, S. Jay Olshansky, and Michael Fossel, among others.

The next section examines "paths to the fountain of youth," exploring the different ways that life extension can be achieved. By better understanding the process of biological aging, researchers can look for methods of prolonging life, through medicines or other approaches, from supplements to exotic diets. The final section presents differing viewpoints on several of the key issues within this broad topic.

Diverse reading populations are likely to find this information of interest, even if they question some of the premises put forward here. The biomedical history in particular is worth reading. All but school libraries serving young children should consider it.—**Mark Schumacher**

Dentistry

787. **Dental Care and Oral Health Sourcebook.** 5th ed. Keith Jones, ed. Detroit, Omnigraphics, 2016. 581p. index. (Health Reference Series). $95.00. ISBN 13: 978-0-7808-1530-8; 978-0-7808-1531-5 (e-book).

Why is *Dental Care and Oral Health Sourcebook* an authoritative reference source? Many Americans are uninformed or hesitant about addressing dental care needs. Unfortunately, individuals who ignore annual dental cleanings and examinations frequently seek intervention only when they experience severe pain or suffer an accident or emergency. Dental care neglect may enhance the likelihood of oral cancer, as well as cardiac and stroke complications. Moreover, the lack of dental care for the public represents a significant public health challenge. This fifth edition (see ARBA 2013, entry 1264) addresses dental and oral health care issues. Chapters include guidance on such topics as routine care guidelines; fluoride, sealant, and tooth whitening systems; cavities, root canals, extractions, implants, and veneers; dentures, orthodontic, and orofacial procedures; periodontal (gum) disease; temporomandibular joint disease and muscle disorders (TMJ); and oral cancer and other conditions. The glossary of terms, directory of organizations, and information regarding financial assistance solutions are valuable resources. The book is enhanced by an extensive index system, support documents, a concise writing style, and a reader-friendly format.

Recommended for high school, public, and university libraries.—**Thomas E. Baker**

Obstetrics and Gynecology

788. **Pregnancy Information for Teens.** 3d ed. Keith Jones, ed. Detroit, Omnigraphics, 2017. 440p. index. $62.00. ISBN 13: 978-0-7808-1557-5.

This clearly written, comprehensive book provides information on all aspects of pregnancy, from preventing and terminating pregnancy to being pregnant, giving birth, newborn care, and being a teen parent. Within each section, chapters provide details on what to expect and also answer questions readers may have. The pregnancy section includes material on proper nutrition, possible health problems, medicines and drugs, risk factors, insurance, miscarriage, labor, and birth. Bold headings facilitate locating specific concerns. This is an excellent resource for teens, parents, counselors, and social workers. The book includes additional resources and an index. Recommended.—**Anitra Gordon**

Opthamology

789.   **Eye Care Sourcebook.** 5th ed. Keith Jones, ed. Detroit, Omnigraphics, 2017. 638p. index. (Health Reference Series). $95.00. ISBN 13: 978-0-7808-1532-2; 978-0-7808-1533-9 (e-book).

Those with the gift of eyesight often take it for granted while others with eye conditions struggle with ordinary daily activities. Recent statistics indicate more than 30 million people have poor vision or a disorder that can contribute to the problem. There seems to be one common thread that weaves itself through childhood classrooms to adult workplaces and into social settings—those who are visually impaired do not "look" like they are struggling. Moreover, it is common for people to bypass annual eye examinations, seeking interventions only when they experience pain, discomfort, or loss of vision.

This fifth edition (see ARBA 2013, entry 1257) offers clear explanations regarding how the eye works. It also suggests guidelines for recognizing and treating eye emergencies. The book describes basic protective measures people can take at work, home, and during recreational activities. Suggestions aimed at supporting nonprofessional caregivers who assist those with eyesight-related disabilities will prove beneficial. Book features include a glossary of terms, further resources, diagnostic tests, a comprehensive index system, a reader-friendly format, and a concise writing style.

The *Eye Care Sourcebook* is well organized and accessible. It is recommended for high school, public, and university libraries.——**Thomas E. Baker**

Pediatrics

790.   **Childhood Diseases and Disorders Sourcebook.** 4th ed. Keith Jones, ed. Detroit, Omnigraphics, 2017. 772p. (Health Reference Series). $95.00. ISBN 13: 978-0-7808-1538-4; 978-0-7808-1539-1 (e-book).

Childhood Diseases and Disorders Sourcebook, 4th edition, provides up-to-date information about common disorders that affect the physical, mental, and developmental health of school-age children. Even though diseases differ, children and families dealing with any chronic condition have much in common. Learning to live with a chronic condition can be extremely challenging for a child, for parents, and for siblings and friends.

The sourcebook offers five parts and related chapters. Part one, Introduction to Children's Health and Safety, provides basic information on routine and emergency medical care for children, as well as guidelines for childhood wellness. Part two, Childhood

Infections and Related Concerns, focuses on foodborne, bacterial, viral, parasitic, and fungal infections that can occur in childhood, as well as other diseases associated with infections. Part three, Medical Conditions Appearing in Childhood, discusses a wide range of conditions and disorders generally diagnosed in childhood. It includes facts about allergies, cancer, diabetes, growth disorders, and disorders affecting the blood and heart, ear, nose, and throat, gastrointestinal tract, endocrine system, kidneys, liver, muscles and bones, brain, lungs, skin, and eyes. Part four, Developmental and Pediatric Mental Health Concerns, details mental health disorders than can affect children as well as common developmental and learning disabilities. Part five, Additional Help and Information, provides a glossary of terms related to childhood diseases and disorders and concludes with a list of resources for parents and caregivers. Information is based on authoritative sources. Moreover, chapters feature a generous use of headings and subheadings, a question-and-answer format, and tables, charts, and illustrations. An index rounds out the work.

Designed for undergraduates, high school students, and general nonspecialists, the sourcebook presents a current, balanced, and reliable assemblage of material. Community colleges and universities as well as health organizations and school counselors will also benefit.—**Thomas E. Baker**

Specific Diseases and Conditions

AIDS

791.   Cichocki, Mark. **Living with HIV: A Patients Guide.** 2d ed. Jefferson, N.C., McFarland, 2017. 295p. index. $35.00pa. ISBN 13: 978-1-4766-6495-8; 978-1-4766-2774-8 (e-book).

In this well-written, 250-page text the author provides a valuable resource on HIV/AIDS. The cover of this second edition includes color graphics and images that imply wellness, health, and living for all ages. The text on the covers and spine is easy to read.

A contents section is useful and allows the reader to briefly scan the list of topics that follow throughout the text. Chapters include "Why Is This Book Needed?"; "The History of HIV and AIDS"; "HIV Prevention and Testing"; "HIV 101… The Basics"; "The Test Is Positive…Now What?"; "Your First Visit to the Doctor"; "Monitoring Your Health"; "Know Your HIV Medications"; "Opportunistic Infections"; "Associated Conditions"; "Treating the Whole Person"; "Substance Use and Abuse"; "Dental Care"; "Exercise and Nutrition"; and "Living with HIV." A bibliography and index round out the book.

In the introduction: "Why Is This Book Needed?," the author successfully conveys the need for this text considering the history, nature, and details of HIV and AIDS. Throughout the text there are numerous tables. Topics range from Where in the body Is HIV Located?, to Types of Tuberculosis, to What Do Your Pap Results Mean? The tables are well formatted and easy to read. Pictures are not included in this text. The topic of HIV and AIDS can involve a variety of medical terms and medications. The author describes such items in an easy-to-follow manner with clear definitions. The bibliography is comprehensive. In addition to referencing the resource, website addresses are provided. The author includes brief notes regarding "Where to Go to Learn More." Details include the pros and cons of the Internet, as well as the publication date of the materials. The index is comprehensive ranging from "abacavir" to "Zovirax."

This is a well-written and detailed text that is presented in a user-friendly manner. An informative resource with practical application, it will likely appeal to a wide variety of individuals. The author, an experienced health care clinician, has successfully presented a valuable resource on issues relating to living with HIV and AIDS.—**Paul M. Murphy III**

Allergies

792.   Sicherer, Scott H. **Food Allergies: A Complete Guide for Eating When Your Life Depends on It.** 2d ed. Baltimore, Md., Johns Hopkins University Press, 2017. 298p. index. $22.95pa. ISBN 13: 978-1-4214-2338-8; 978-1-4214-2339-5 (e-book).

Sicherer's update of his 2013 edition of this title presents a great deal of useful information for those dealing with allergies, including peanuts, milk, shellfish, and eggs, among other foods. From diagnosis to treatment (and prevention) and from allergy tests to the illnesses caused by the allergies, the text uses a simple question-and answer format to provide its guidance. Given that there are 72 sections listed in the table of contents, readers should be able to locate quickly the pages that are of most interest to them. A 12-page index also assists the effective navigation of the volume. One chapter is dedicated to one of the high-risk aspects of food allergies: anaphylaxis, which can be life-threatening. (That chapter alone has 129 questions and answers, plus a closing summary.) There is also a useful final chapter on "More Help and Information" which provides references to trustworthy websites, for both information and support, and a brief listing of further readings.

Any library should find readers for this book: parents or children wishing to learn more about the possible risks of their diet, high school or college students in health fields, and others. Given the reasonable price of the book, it should be available to a large population.—**Mark Schumacher**

Attention Deficit Hyperactivity Disorders

793.   Stolberg, Victor B. **ADHD Medications: History, Science, and Issues.** Santa Barbara, Calif., Greenwood Press/ABC-CLIO, 2017. 278p. index. (The Story of a Drug series). $60.00. ISBN 13: 978-1-61069-725-5; 978-1-61069-726-2 (e-book).

This book serves as a resource to expand meaningful discussions to matters that accompany Attention Deficit Hyperactivity Disorder (ADHD) and the use of ADHD medications. This book delivers an accurate depiction of the disorder—including inattention.

This excellent contribution assists those who might encounter negative social acceptance because of this disorder. The author clearly endorses early intervention to enhance positive performance in work and academic environments. The goal is to enhance quality of life and achieve positive relationships with peers, parents, teachers, and other authority figures. Otherwise, individuals with ADHD symptoms may experience feelings of anxiety, withdrawal, and depression.

This book addresses sensitive topics with dignity, compassion, and understanding of the social dimensions. Chapters and passages assist readers in exploring dilemmas associated with a diagnosis that persists into adolescence and adulthood. The primary focus is on medication effects, risks, misuse, and the possibility of overdose. Themes discusses the history, etiology, and symptoms of the major variants of this disorder. Furthermore, the content explains the benefits of treatment modalities, including ADHD medications and nonpharmacological supportive approaches. The book is reader friendly and offers a directory of resources, glossary, bibliography, and extensive index system. Information in the book is not meant to replace consultations with licensed health care professionals.

Every high school, community college, and university should consider adding this book to resource collections.—**Thomas E. Baker**

Autism

794.   **Autism and Pervasive Developmental Disorders Sourcebook.** 3d ed. Keith Jones, ed. Detroit, Omnigraphics, 2016. 490p. index. (Health Reference Series). $95.00. ISBN 13: 978-0-7808-1464-6; 978-0-7808-1463-9 (e-book).

An increasing number of children are being diagnosed with autism, Asperger syndrome, Rett syndrome, childhood disintegrative disorder, and pervasive developmental disorder. This updated third edition (see ARBA 2012, entry 1282) aims to provide families, caregivers, patients, and the general public basic information about autism spectrum disorder (ASD). A medical review team and advisory board vetted the information.

For ease of use, the book is broken into parts and chapters. Parts include: Overview of Autism Spectrum Disorder, Causes and Risk Factors Associated with Autism Spectrum Disorder, Identifying and Diagnosing Autism Spectrum Disorders, Conditions That May Accompany Autism Spectrum Disorders, Interventions and Treatments for Autism Spectrum Disorder, Education and Autism Spectrum Disorder, and Living with Autism Spectrum Disorder and Transitioning to Adulthood. A final section, Additional Help and Information, includes a glossary of ASD acronyms and terms and a directory of additional ASD resources. An index rounds out the work.

This sourcebook provides trustworthy, nuts-and-bolts information for the target audience. Recommended for public libraries.—**ARBA Staff Reviewer**

Brain Injuries

795.   Meehan, William Paul, III. **Concussions.** Santa Barbara, Calif., Greenwood Press/ ABC-CLIO, 2017. 224p. index. (Health & Medical Issues Today). $40.00. ISBN 13: 978-1-4408-3894-1; 978-1-4408-3895-8 (e-book).

This book addresses a topic that has received increased attention in recent years— sport-related concussions. Concussions are often hard to diagnose; often concussions go untreated. Sadly, concussions can lead to medical problems years after the injury occurs. This installment in the Health & Medical Issues today series is comprised of twenty-two chapters divided into three sections. The last section includes primary documents. The chapters discuss a variety of such topics as diagnosis and assessment treatment and athlete management, prevention, concussion history, and medical resources. The writing style is accessible and encourages readers to pursue the topic in further depth. A glossary, suggestions for further reading, and an extensive index round out the work. Recommended for public, school, and academic libraries.—**Thomas E. Baker**

Cancer

796.   **Cancer Survivorship Sourcebook.** 2d ed. Keith Jones, ed. Detroit, Omnigraphics, 2017. 574p. index. (Health Reference Series). $95.00. ISBN 13: 978-0-7808-1549-0; 978-0-7808-1550-6 (e-book).

There are more than 15.5 million cancer survivors in the United States; these numbers are expected to increase to more than 22 million by 2026. Statistical projections indicate that 67% of people diagnosed with cancer will live approximately five years and 17% may survive for as long as 20 years. Individuals who have cancer often experience depression, anxiety, and other related mental and physical challenges. Medical interventions mandate a protracted journey for survivors and their caregivers that can include acknowledging personal limitations and redefining lifestyles, careers, and even relationships. Survivors, their caregivers, and family friends need support and accurate information to evaluate treatment choices, but researching cancer, treatment advances, and clinical trials is a daunting, time-consuming, and emotionally laden task. This second edition (see ARBA 2008, entry 1254) offers suggestions for coping with the side effects and complications of cancer treatments. The section on challenges that surround the aftermath of various cancer treatment modalities is essential, compassionate, and supportive. This volume supports informed patient involvement and provides solid advice for survivors who strive to maintain dignity and normalcy while simultaneously finding a way to improve their quantity and quality of life. The text contains a glossary of terms, references for cancer patients, tests to diagnose and monitor cancer, a comprehensive index system, a reader-friendly format, and a concise writing style. Readers do not require prior knowledge to benefit from the sourcebook.

Recommended for high school, public, and university libraries.—**Thomas E. Baker**

797.   Steligo, Kathy. **The Breast Reconstruction Guidebook.** 4th ed. Baltimore, Md., Johns Hopkins University Press, 2017. 263p. index. $26.95pa. ISBN 13: 978-1-4214-2296-1.

This book offers clarity and compassion as it addresses the subject of breast reconstruction after a mastectomy. The book details everything from the decisions involved regarding the mastectomy surgery to the many options available with breast reconstruction, preparation for it, and recovery from it.

Short, well-organized chapters make information easy to locate and prevent it from overwhelming readers. The book makes excellent use of bullet points, tables, photographs, and illustrations and includes an extensive glossary and list of resources. Particular chapters include, among others: "How Mastectomy Affects Reconstruction," "Breast Implants," "Altering Your Opposite Breast," "Preparing for Surgery," and "Dealing with Problems" (e.g., pain, cosmetic issues, etc.). The book also addresses the many nonphysical issues which can be equally daunting, like dealing with partners or caregivers, fighting insurance companies, and returning to work. In this fourth edition, much of the information has been updated in accordance with advancements in reconstruction options and procedures such as fat grafting and tattooing.

The book's comprehensive, straightforward and sensitive approach makes it a valuable resource for health care practitioners and consumers alike. Recommended for public libraries.—**ARBA Staff Reviewer**

Eating Disorders

798.   **Eating Disorders: A Guide to Medical Care and Complications.** 3d ed. Philip S. Mehler and Arnold E. Andersen, eds. Baltimore, Md., Johns Hopkins University Press, 2017. 384p. index. $39.95pa. ISBN 13: 978-1-4214-2343-2.

Doctors Philip S. Mehler and Arnold E. Andersen and distinguished contributors offer insight into anorexia nervosa, bulimia, and many other eating disorders that are difficult to treat. This contribution merges the psychiatric and medical fields in a sincere effort to assist patients diagnosed with an eating disorder. The editors' overarching goal is to promote excellence in medical care, while attempting to minimize excessive medical terminology. This third edition delivers an accurate depiction of eating disorders and resulting complications. Revisions offer new and emerging research evidence. Individual chapters identify common questions and offer clinical cases with highlights pertinent to the subject. The authors elaborate on the signs and symptoms in individuals with eating disorders. The first chapter sets the foundation by discussing the diagnosis and treatment of the eating disorders spectrum in primary care medicine. The application of the case-study method offers illustrative examples for understanding the formulation of guidelines, diagnosis, and treatment strategies. Photographs, graphic illustrations, related readings, and a comprehensive index system assist in organizing 383 reader-friendly pages.

The book is primarily for clinicians. However, graduate students and upper-level discourses in correlated majors would benefit from the overlapping content. Recommended for university libraries.—**Thomas E. Baker**

799.   **Eating Disorders Information for Teens.** 4th ed. Keith Jones, ed. Detroit, Omnigraphics, 2017. 332p. index. $69.00. ISBN 13: 978-0-7808-1559-9; 978-0-7808-1560-5 (e-book).

This 4th edition (see ARBA 2014, entry 1217) addresses anorexia, bulimia, binge eating, and compulsive eating. These disorders affect millions in the United States, the majority of whom are between ages 12 and 15. Qualified, senior medical professionals consulted on this volume that approaches the subject of eating disorders in a sensitive manner. The book's material is easy to access, as the book uses bold fonts, bullet-point formatting, an age-appropriate writing style, and questions and answers. Users will also find additional information in textboxes. The material is based upon dependable resources so readers can rely on the information provided. Additional readings and an extensive index round out the work. Recommended for high school, public, and academic libraries.—**Thomas E. Baker**

Endocrine and Metabolic Disorders

800.   **Endocrine and Metabolic Disorders Sourcebook.** 3d ed. Keith Jones, ed. Detroit, Omnigraphics, 2017. 543p. index. (Health Reference Series). $95.00. ISBN 13: 978-0-7808-1543-8; 978-0-7808-1544-5 (e-book).

This volume from Omnigraphics' extensive Health Reference Series addresses the topic of endocrine and metabolic disorders. The book provides basic, comprehensive information designed to assist patients, caregivers, and others who are not versed in these medical conditions but may take a genuine, personal interest in them.

The volume is organized into eight parts, beginning with introductory material on endocrine functioning and metabolism and then moving through various disorders as they affect the pituitary gland (e.g., growth disorders), the thyroid and parathyroid gland (e.g., Graves disease), and the adrenal gland (e.g., Cushing Syndrome). Following parts address Pancreatic and Diabetic Disorders, Disorders of the Ovaries and Testes, and Other Disorders of Endocrine and Metabolic Functioning, such as Inborn Errors of Metabolism, Glycogen-Storage Diseases (GSDs), and more. Additional Help and Information includes a glossary of related terms and a listing of organizations (e.g., the Endocrine Society) and other resources.

Each part noted above is further divided into detailed chapters addressing the particulars of its subject. Part three, Thyroid and Parathyroid Gland Disorders, for example, contains 10 chapters focusing individually on separate conditions. Information for each condition is conveyed clearly and concisely, with much of it set up in an easy-to-follow Q&A format ("What is Graves Ophthalmopathy?", "How Common is Prolactinoma?" etc.). The book makes generous use of headers, subheaders, bullet points, tables, and other tools. Information is generous, but never overwhelming as this reference is definitely targeted to the layperson. Beyond basic subject material, chapters may include early signs, causes, risk factors, tests, prevention, associated conditions, treatment, and latest research.

This third edition presents the most up-to-date information in regards to endocrine and metabolic disorders relative to the rapid advancements in medical research and implementation happening as we write, such as the increased awareness of genetic counseling. The reference is not produced to replace professional medical counsel; however, it succeeds at providing intelligent, basic information about endocrine and metabolic disorders to a general audience.—**ARBA Staff Reviewer**

Respiratory Disorders

801.   **Respiratory Diseases Sourcebook.** Keith Jones, ed. Detroit, Omnigraphics, 2017. 698p. index. (Health Reference Series). $95.00. ISBN 13: 978-0-7808-1536-0; 978-0-7808-1537-7 (e-book).

A volume of the notable Health Reference Series published by Omnigraphics, this book is an invaluable reference regarding basic, comprehensive information about the wide spectrum of respiratory disorders. The reference is designed to assist general readers, patients, caregivers, and others who are not proficient in medical issues but may take a genuine, personal interest in them.

The volume is organized into eight parts, and opens with introductory material on Understanding and Preventing Respiratory Problems (e.g., how the respiratory system works, the effects of toxins and pollutants, etc.) and then moving through Infectious Respiratory Disorders (e.g., colds, pneumonia, tuberculosis, etc.), Inflammatory Respiratory Disorders (e.g., Asthma, COPD, etc.), Other Conditions That Affect Respiration (e.g., cystic fibrosis, lung cancer, etc.), Pediatric Respiratory Disorders, Diagnosing and Treating Respiratory Disorders and Living with Chronic Respiratory Problems. A closing section, Additional Help and Information, provides a glossary of specialized terms and a useful directory of organizations like The American Lung Association working to assist those suffering from respiratory disorders. This particular volume is notable for providing generous information on prevention and living with respiratory disorders.

Each part is further divided into detailed chapters addressing the particulars of its subject. For example, the 11 chapters in part two focus individually on separate diseases and their many related conditions. Topics within these chapters may include symptoms, causes, risk factors, tests, complications, associated conditions, treatments, latest research, and other information. Part six uses 18 chapters to convey the myriad medicines, tests, therapies, and more which aid with diagnoses and treatment. Chapters here may provide definitions, types of tests, what to expect during a test, what tests show, test risks, and other data.

All this information is conveyed clearly and concisely. Chapters employ headers (many in question format), subheaders, bullet points, lists, tables, and other tools for ease of navigation. Information is generous, but never overwhelming as this reference is definitely targeted to the layperson.

This fourth edition provides the most up-to-date information in regards to respiratory disorders relative to the rapid advancements in research, such as the effects of climate change, happening as we write this. The reference is not produced to replace professional medical counsel; however, it succeeds at providing intelligent, basic information about many facets of respiratory disorders to a general audience.—**ARBA Staff Reviewer**

Pharmacy and Pharmaceutical Sciences

Handbooks and Yearbooks

802. Boslaugh, Sarah E. **Drug Resistance.** Santa Barbara, Calif., Greenwood Press/ ABC-CLIO, 2017. 208p. index. (Health and Medical Issues Today). $40.00. ISBN 13: 978-1-4408-3924-5; 978-1-4408-3925-2 (e-book).

An estimated 700,000 people die each year around the world because they have an infection that has become immune to the drugs used to treat it. The Centers for Disease Control and the World Health Organization continue to address the worldwide drug resistance threat to public health. This outcome characterizes the fact that the present rate of discovery of new antibiotics is much slower than it was in the 1940s and 1950s—a period sometimes referred to as the Golden Age of Antibiotics Discovery.

The first chapter in *Drug Resistance* sets the foundation by offering readers an overview and historical background of drug resistance. Primary documents, an annotated timeline of drug discoveries (1632-2016), sources for further information, a convenient glossary, and a comprehensive index assist in organizing 208 reader-friendly pages. The author's writing style is clear and persuasive.

Recommended for community college and university libraries.—**Thomas E. Baker**

803. **Merck Index. https://www.rsc.org/merck-index.** [Website] West Point, Pa., Merck, 2017. Price negotiated by site. Date reviewed 2017.

The Merck Index Online, a project devised in conjunction with the United Kingdom's Royal Society of Chemistry, presents a searchable database of over 11,000 monographs related to chemical, drug, and biological information. The online edition is based on the

15th print edition of the extensive index, but subject to regular updates. The site offers two types of paid subscriptions: individuals can "Pay-Per-View" of selected monographs or institutions can inquire about other pricing options. The most significant content is available to subscribers; however, some information is free of charge. First time users may choose the Get Started with The Merck Index Online button in the middle of the homepage to access a video tutorial and information on how to register for the site to access the extensive, specialized material.

When conducting a search, there are a number of options available. Users can enter a name, Chemical Abstracts Service (CAS) Registry number, Molecular Weight, or Molecular Formula into the Quick Search bar. Users can also connect several parameters or search by chemical structure. A separate Search tab guides users to search via text or properties, and the Structure Search tab allows users to draw a chemical structure as the basis for a Substructure or Similarity Search. Users can alternatively Browse through an alphabetical directory of elements, compounds, and more, from the possibly complex Fagarine, Cacodylic Acid, Palitantin, Karaya Gum, or Nadoxolol to the humble Water. The Named Reaction tab alphabetically organizes over 500 selected reactions such as the Hammick Reaction, the Wacker Oxidation, and the Castro-Stephens Coupling. All site users are able to view a basic profile of the element, compound, reaction, etc. The profile for an element may generally include a monograph identification number, molecular formula, molecular weight, percent composition, or structure illustration. Paid subscribers may view an individual, full monograph at a cost of £5 (roughly $6.64 U.S.) each. For the reactions, all users can view a reaction scheme and brief description of the transformation, while subscribers can access other information such as key contributors and key references. The Reference Tables are also available only by subscription, although all users can view a listing of the supplemental information included here, such as a Glossary, a Chemical Terms Translator, a Company Register, Thermometric Equivalents, a Table of Minerals, the Periodic Chart of Elements, Latin Terms, and International Patent Country Codes. The free content on the site would certainly give potential users—various researchers, professionals, students, educators, and others—a good sense of the complete information, and thus they would be able to make a well-informed decision as to whether to subscribe. The "Pay-Per-View" Option is certainly a flexible method with which to explore more content. All things considered, the nature of the information and the relative ease of online access makes Merck Index Online a valuable reference.—**ARBA Staff Reviewer**

33 Technology

General Works

804. **Careers in Information Technology.** Michael Shally-Jensen, ed. Hackensack, N.J., Salem Press, 2017. 400p. index. $125.00. ISBN 13: 978-1-68217-148-6; 978-1-68217-149-3 (e-book).

Careers in Information Technology chapters commence with snapshots of information technology specialties that include career clusters, interests, occupation profiles, and future employment opportunities. Individual chapters offer informative overviews that include in-depth discussions regarding career preparation, work environment, earnings and advancement, and duties and responsibilities. Profiles outline working conditions, educational needs, and physical abilities. The academic content is on the cutting edge for maintaining reader interest through fascinating real-life experiences, insights, and employment trends. The transition, clarity, organization, and reader-friendly writing style facilitate reader comprehension and learning. Charts, tables, and employment projections from the Bureau of Labor Statistics enhance the work. Numerous visual tools, including Fun Facts and Famous First text boxes, stimulate reader interest. Chapters reflect on transferable skills and abilities that readers can apply to specific occupational categories. The concluding content offers readers an opportunity to assess career interests based on the Holland Code. The code suggests that people and work environments can be loosely classified into six different groups. Different personalities may find particular work environments that celebrate and embrace their uniqueness—the perfect match!

Careers in Information Technology offers high school and undergraduate audiences a well-balanced and thoughtful resource. Public libraries and community colleges will also benefit.—**Thomas E. Baker**

805. **Coding Your Passion.** New York, Rosen Publishing, 2017. 6v. index. $214.50/set ($34.75 individual title). ISBN 13: 978-1-4994-6628-7.

This series includes information using computer science in several different careers: digital gaming, digital music, financial technology, high-tech criminal justice, high-tech health and wellness, and online retail. The series features an impressive number of facts and primary sources in all sections of the books. Each book discusses multiple related careers, detailing what a person in the career does, what a person can do to prepare for the career, and the demand for people to work in that career. Words that may be new to the reader are defined within the text and are not bold, though a few specialty words are bulleted with their definitions. The books stress that good communication skills are needed for all of the career fields. This will help students see that reading, writing, speaking, and the ability to work together are important skills to learn in school. The book provides additional resources, a glossary, a bibliography, an index, and websites. Recommended.— **Janet Luch**

806. Condron, Melody. **Managing the Digital You: Where and How to Keep and Organize Your Digital Life.** Lanham, Md., Rowman & Littlefield, 2017. 150p. illus. index. $32.00; $30.00 (e-book). ISBN 13: 978-1-4422-7887-5; 978-1-4422-7888-2 (e-book).

Managing the Digital You is an excellent tool for coping with the volume of incoming data that we all deal with on a daily basis. Encompassing subjects of correspondence, financial and legal documents, legacy planning, multimedia, nondigital documents, password protection, photos, and social media archiving, this resource provides a clear path to avoiding electronic mayhem. Creating a system for digital management means simplification of life; files are organized for finding, photos will be in order, useless information deleted. After the preface, eight chapters categorize topics on how to succeed in cleaning up and sorting your digital chaos. Chapters 1 and 2 provide readers with a logical place to begin and an assessment of individual needs. Beyond introductory information, later chapters are unambiguous with titles such as "Legal, Financial, and Medical Documents" (chapter 3) or "Digital Photographs" (chapter 5). Text is supported with figures and tables throughout, all black and white. Visuals are not eye-catching but provide the visual documentation necessary. Summaries and bibliographic notes conclude each chapter. Two appendixes provide additional resources and a brief index offers entry to subjects such as backup, disaster preparedness, and file formats. Google, Microsoft Office, Photoshop, and Twitter are just some of the platforms discussed in relation to organization.

This title is one that most anyone should have on the shelf (or, yes, downloaded on your digital device!). Better yet, open it up, read a chapter, and get digitally organized! Highly recommended.—**Janis Minshull**

807. **Mobile Application Development, Usability, and Security.** Sougata Mukherjea, ed. Hershey, Pa., Information Science Reference/IGI Global, 2017. 320p. index. (Advances in Multimedia and Interactive Technologies (AMIT) Book Series). $180.00. ISBN 13: 978-1-52250-945-5; 978-1-52250-946-2 (e-book).

Mobile devices are universal in modern society—affecting both personal and professional lifestyles. Smartphones, tablets, and abundant mobile devices are driving new models of interacting with application users. *Mobile Application Development, Usability, and Security* provides a thorough overview on the different facets of mobile technology management and its integration into modern society, highlighting issues related to analytics, cloud computing, and different types of application development.

The development of mobile technology has experienced exponential growth in recent years, and this book helps prepare learners for careers in the expanding and evolving fields of mobile web and application development. Career graduates may find employment in all levels of government, including health care, education, business, marketing, and communications. Mobile designers create real-world applications and solutions using a variety of technologies and programming languages. Diverse topics, including user experience design, web security, online mobile marketing, user interface design, and native smartphone application development with the latest standard web technologies, represent important examinations.

The text is well-organized and well-written and makes effective use of graphs, charts, diagram, and figures. The book also includes a glossary, key terms and definitions, current references, and an index. *Mobile Application Development, Usability, and Security* is appropriate for college, university, and public libraries. Library acquisition decision-makers responsible for the selection and purchase of materials or resources will consider this book a welcome addition to research collections.—**Thomas E. Baker**

808. **XFR Collective. https://xfrcollective.wordpress.com/.** [Website] Free. Date reviewed: 2018.

The nonprofit XFR Collective partners with a variety of visual content producers in order to educate about the digital archiving process and encourage the preservation of content that may otherwise be lost. The website facilitates this goal via its collection of digital video sourced from a diverse community of activists, artists, and individual producers (mostly based around New York) that would generally not have content preservation resources. Site users can familiarize themselves with the digital transfer process and the goals of the collective via the Resources and Blog tabs on the homepage. Resources links to tutorials and other educational materials on archiving video. The Blog tab offers posts regarding XFR Collective community partnerships, goals, and more. One recent post notes that the collective is on hiatus from external work and the formation of new partnerships. As this hiatus is expected to end early in 2018, site users can presumably look forward to additional community partnerships and archived content. The Watch tab links to the XFR Collective page on the Internet Archive, displaying a list (may also be viewed as a gallery) of 113 videos reflecting a range of subjects, styles, and original formats. Information accompanying the videos may include creator, publication date, language, brief description, and identifying technical information. Users can also note number of views and leave reviews. Videos may be arranged by number of views, title, archive date, or creator. Though relatively small, the archive offers possibility for content producers, whether they aim to raise awareness of social justice issues (e.g., "The Day After Diallo") or preserve the work of a small theater company (e.g., "Marx Brothers on Horseback Salad").—**ARBA Staff Reviewer**

Computers

809. **Biteable. https://biteable.com/.** [Website] Free. Date reviewed: 2017.

Finding a way to help students make online videos easily and conveniently can be a challenge for teachers and librarians with limited time and resources. This free online resource offers the ability for students to create videos using fun cartoon-like characters without any need for voice narration or advanced knowledge of video editing skills. The site also allows for single sign-in with Google accounts, which enables students using G Suite accounts to get started quickly. Other features are step-by-step instructions regarding how to create an online video from a previously designed template or a blank presentation. Slides are easily edited and enhanced with fonts, music, and fun characters that will appeal to all ages, and publishing the movie is straightforward. School library media specialists can use this resource to easily create advocacy or promotional items such as new book announcements. There is a premium, paid version that removes the watermark from the end of the video as well as the ability to download videos, but the free version will meet the needs of most users. Highly recommended.—**Angela Wojtecki**

810.   **Encyclopedia of Cyber Warfare.** Paul J. Springer, ed. Santa Barbara, Calif., ABC-CLIO, 2017. 380p. index. $89.00. ISBN 13: 978-1-4408-4424-9; 978-1-4408-4425-6 (e-book).

In this encyclopedia, distinguished contributors provide insights into the cyber domain and related global threats. The well-organized book includes a list of A to Z entries, a guide to related topics, and primary documents. Additional readings, a chronology, and an extensive index system support readers. Entries are cross-referenced—a useful reading tool to enhance further investigation.

This reader-friendly book captures the essence of the remarkable world of computer networks and the advanced persistent threat (APT) and offers captivating reading for students, academics, government agencies, and curious readers. Public, private, and university libraries will consider this contribution an essential resource as will anyone working to secure cyber assets and prevent innovative forms of espionage, terror, or criminality.—**Thomas E. Baker**

811.   **FOLDOC. http://foldoc.org/.** [Website] Free. Date reviewed: 2017.

FOLDOC is a simple, easy-to-use, and downloadable resource for all computing vocabulary. Offering no bells or whistles, the site allows users to conduct a basic search for a wide range of computer terminology via the bar. Users can also select the Contents tab to access the full-text search function, or begin the browsing process. The site has several browsing capabilities. Users can browse entries by subject area (128 of them), browse by an alphabetical listing of entries, or browse a combined listing of both. FOLDOC currently contains over 15,000 terms, including acronyms and jargon (including numbers and symbols) for companies, individuals, software, languages, locations, applications, programming, networking, and much more. The definitions are as straightforward as the rest of the site, and generally note the category/subject area of the term and provide a brief statement which may include cross-referencing links if other FOLDOC terms are included in the definition. The entry may also include a sample of term usage, a listing of nearby terms, and a notation of the date the definition was last updated. Users can additionally submit a comment for each term to suggest an edit, etc.

Some of the most referenced subject categories within the site include "programming," "storage," "operating system," "networking," "language," and "hardware." Users will recognize common terms like ".com," "algorithm," "meme," "web browser," "screensaver," "Playstation," etc., alongside highly technical and perhaps less-established words and phrases such as "SAMeDL," "plesiochronus" and "wave a dead chicken." In fact, it may be worth pointing out that some definitions may themselves be highly technical, causing users to extend their research throughout the dictionary or other sources. Fortunately, FOLDOC can link to other search sites if a term is not found in its database or the definition is not sufficient to users. There is definitely a sense of inside humor running throughout the site (see "wave a dead chicken" above). Quite a few of the terms may be pejorative ("kangaroo code," "Stupids," etc.). The Random tab displays a different entry definition every time it is clicked for an element of fun.

Commercial advertisements run on the page, but do not interfere with the browsing experience of this valuable research tool that would appeal to everyone whether adept with computer technology or not.

Recommended to public, school, and academic libraries.—**ARBA Staff Reviewer**

812. Stolley, Karl. **How to Design and Write Web Pages Today.** 2d ed. Santa Barbara, Calif., Greenwood Press/ABC-CLIO, 2017. 372p. index. $40.00pa. ISBN 13: 978-1-4408-5742-3; 978-1-4408-4314-3 (e-book).

How to Design and Write Web Pages Today is divided into four main parts that guide readers through the logical order of creating online content. The first part asks designers to consider who potential users of a website are, and how they might view it—in other words, what sort of technology are they using and what limitations might they have. Purpose, context, and content are discussed, followed by responsive and standards-based design practices to increase accessibility across many different platforms. Tips on setting up and hosting websites are provided, as well as tips on tracking numerous versions of ever-changing designs. The second part tackles accessibility of content for the greatest number of people whether or not they have limitations, usability to make site use as intuitive as possible, and sustainability of Web design for long-term maintenance. The third part provides instruction on the actual design process, including HTML, CSS, and JavaScript coding. The last part addresses Web file organization for easy findability and maintenance, preprocessors to help with source code, dynamic interactive sites, and modifying websites for social media sharing. This book is best utilized by readers with at least a basic understanding of computer operations and terminology, and does a good job of breaking down processes and defining terms. Both novices and more experienced designers can benefit from the clear instruction and discussion in the text, and it is certainly beneficial to anyone interested in creating a well-designed site.—**Cynthia Goode**

813. Young Rewired State. Illustrated by Duncan Beedie. **Get Coding! Learn HTML, CSS, and JavaScript and Build a Website, App, and Game.** Somerville, Mass., Candlewick Press, 2017. 299p. illus. $12.99pa. ISBN 13: 978-0-7636-9276-6.

Young Rewired State is made up of tech-savvy gifted youths seeking to inspire other digital makers. This book covers three important coding languages—HTML, CSS, and JavaScript—and is well suited for the beginning self-starter. The text is organized by "missions" where users complete projects beginning with file folders and move on to more challenging app, game, and webpage creation, culminating in establishing a website. Chapters feature a Code Skills Checklist that highlights key points and summarizes new skills. Vocabulary is explained simply and allowances are made for both PC and MAC users. Young Rewired State provides a website (www.getcodingkids.com) to purchase the book or get more information on the missions. One additional application of the website could be for users to copy and paste the sample code to ensure less user error. This title is more like a textbook in that is not meant to be read cover to cover. Users will learn which programming language will suit their needs as well as some information about historic coders. Overall, this is a nice introduction to programming for upper middle schoolers. Recommended grades 7-12.—**Laura Dooley-Taylor**

Internet

814.   **Net Data Directory. http://netdatadirectory.org/.** [Website] Free. Date reviewed: 2018.

This straightforward website gathers and displays information about the Internet. It presents an alphabetical directory of organizations, committees, commissions, corporations, and other entities interested in issues about or components of the Internet, such as social media, broadband, civil rights, and cybersecurity. Users can scroll through the directory from the homepage, or can employ the Quick Start Guide from the link. Users can also conduct a basic search or can browse the directory by Geography (countries and regions) or a generous range of Topics, such as online dating, censorship, APIs, malware, mobile, phishing, net neutrality (particularly relevant), and many others. Entries will generally include a description of the entity, its URL, and a listing of associated topical or coverage tags. The description may also include links to particular portions of an entity's website. Selected directory entries include Internet Monitor, tracking global Internet content controls and activity; the Central Intelligence Agency, offering data on Internet hosts and users; Team Cymru, offering Internet security research and monitoring; Politiwoops, which tracks deleted tweets; and much, much more. The site also includes a Blog which spotlights current activity by directory entities. Net Data Directory would be an excellent resource for anyone conducting research on the Internet.—**ARBA Staff Reviewer**

34 Physical Sciences and Mathematics

Physical Sciences

General Works

Dictionaries and Encyclopedias

815. **Principles of Physical Science.** Donald R. Franceschetti, ed. Hackensack, N.J., Salem Press, 2017. 758p. illus. index. $165.00. ISBN 13: 978-1-68217-326-8; 978-1-68217-327-5 (e-book).

This volume is part of the Principles of series and purports to introduce the fundamentals of physical science to high school and undergraduate researchers. One hundred and twelve articles are listed from A to Z in dictionary style; however, there are no entries for topics starting with J, K, Q, U, and V. The articles cover a large range of subjects and their levels of complexity are highly variable. Each article includes the following sections: associated fields of study, summary, key terms, definitions and basic principles, background and history, "how it works," applications and products, impacts on industry, careers and course work, and social context and future prospects. Further readings and suggested websites accompany each article and a few black-and-white photographs are included. However, supporting charts, tables, and graphs for each article are scarce. The appendixes include a timeline of events in the history of science, a biographical dictionary of notable scientists, a bibliography, and an index. However, it is unclear why the timeline and biographical dictionary were included since they are both broad in nature and not specific to milestones or scientists in the physical sciences. The biographical dictionary is incomplete and does not contain entries for many key scientists in the physical sciences (e.g., Ampere, Aristotle, Avogadro, Bernoulli, Boyle, Dalton, Gauss, Hahn, Hertz, Lavoisier, Thomson, Volta, and Yang). A reader may also think that, logically, these two resources would complement each other; yet, the list of milestones includes key events but the corresponding scientists are not listed in the biographical dictionary. For example, Aristotle, who is credited on the timeline with the introduction of the scientific method, is not found in the biographical dictionary. Furthermore, the invention of the Voltaic pile is a key event on the timeline, but its inventor, Alessandro Volta, is not in the dictionary. Similarly, Sir Isaac Newton is identified as an important scientist in the dictionary but his laws of gravity and motion are not included on the historical timeline.—**Jennifer Brooks Huffman**

Chemistry

Dictionaries and Encyclopedias

816. **Hawley's Condensed Chemical Dictionary.** 16th ed. Larrañaga, Michael D., Richard J. Lewis, and Robert A. Lewis, eds. Hoboken, N.J., John Wiley & Sons, Ltd., 2016. 1568p. index. $150.00. ISBN 13: 978-1-119-19372-2.

This is the 16th edition of a work first published in 1919. The introduction explicates the many changes this work has undergone edition to edition. The most significant change to this version is the expansion of chemical and biological terms as a reflection of the growth in such fields as biology and biological engineering. Altogether, there are 1,472 new definitions, 5,236 revised or updated definitions, a new Chemical Abstract Number index, and updated trademarks. The Internet links to manufacturers and associations first included in the 14th edition have been largely removed from the 16th as this information is now more readily accessible on the World Wide Web.

The dictionary is designed as more than a place to find brief definitions, as it includes technical data and descriptive information. Users will find four distinct types of information: descriptions of chemicals, raw materials, processes, and equipment; expanded definitions of chemical entries, phenomena, and terminology; descriptions or identifications of a wide range of trademarked products used in the chemical industries; and definitions of biochemical materials, phenomena, and terminology. Also included are abbreviations, biographies of 403 notable chemists, information on the origin of some chemical terms, highlights in the history of chemistry, a list of manufacturers of trademarked products, tables, 14 black-and-white images, and *see* references. Entries vary. All include a CAS number, chemical structure, and definition, but some also have information on properties, use, hazards, method of purification, and derivation.

This book will have wide appeal to students, scholars, and the general public. Recommended for public and academic libraries.—**ARBA Staff Reviewer**

Handbooks and Yearbooks

817. **Classic Chemistry. https://web.lemoyne.edu/giunta/.** [Website] Free. Date reviewed: 2018.

This no-frills page provides access to a variety of academic papers, learning materials, and other resources for users interested in exploring the history of chemistry. Users can simply click on a series of links, each marked by a descriptive icon, which run horizontally across the page. Classic Papers presents an alphabetical list of subjects from which users can then browse. Alternatively, users can browse papers alphabetically by author. Papers cover topics under subjects such as Biochemistry, Combustion & Calcination, Gases, Kinetics, and Thermodynamics. Users may recognize works from Francis Bacon, Niels Bohr, Marie Curie, Benjamin Franklin, and others. Classic Calculations bring many of the concepts from Classic Chemistry papers to light through a series of quantitative exercises. Users can access them by name of the historical figure associated with the concept or by pedagogical topic. Exercises include a brief historical note, document reference, teaching notes, and solutions. Elements and Atoms gathers twenty foundational texts. Although noncomprehensive, the annotated papers provide good context for understanding the evolution of chemistry learning. The Calendar link aligns the current week with historical people, publications, and events in chemistry history, such as the January 1848 discovery of gold in California or the 1872 January birth of Morris Travers, codiscoverer of several elements. Users can examine the current corresponding week or select from any month of the year. A Glossary provides an extensive and generally cross-referenced listing of chemistry-related substances, descriptions, measurement units, and more. Internet Resources organizes and provides links to other scientific history websites by theme, e.g., collections of short biographies, exhibits and museums, groups and organizations, etc. While plain in structure and design, the site nonetheless is an important receptacle of historical scholarship in chemistry and would be a good resource for educators and students alike.—**ARBA Staff Reviewer**

818. **Gale Interactive: Chemistry.** [Website] Farmington Hills, Mich., Gale/Cengage Learning, 2017. Price negotiated by site. Date reviewed: 2017.

Students and faculty will welcome this database, which, under academic curation, brings alive the complexities of chemistry. The database, aimed at students in first- and second-year chemistry courses, aligns with a typical college course curriculum, making it an ideal companion to or substitute for traditional course materials. The ability to zoom, create, and manipulate using 3D technology boosts student understanding of such things as the periodic table, chemical reactions, and atomic structures, to name a few. Students can download material for learning on the go and faculty can use database features as part of a lecture or in place of a traditional lab. All of this technology is underpinned by the ability to search across concepts and to access supporting content. Moreover, the ability to self-test and work at an independent pace can increase student confidence. The database is an obviously strong tool for professors who use flipped instruction or for students who want to learn about a concept before a lecture.

This is a highly recommended purchase for academic libraries.—**ARBA Staff Reviewer**

Earth and Planetary Sciences

General Works

819. **The Dictionary of Physical Geography.** 4th ed. David S. G. Thomas, ed. Hoboken, N.J., Wiley-Blackwell, 2016. 632p. illus. maps. index. $150.00. ISBN 13: 978-1-118-78234-7.

This 4th edition comes approximately 15 years after publication of the 3d edition and includes 347 new or fully rewritten entries and 191 entirely new entries; there are 2,548 total entries. The editors removed 152 older entries, though these are still available via the book website (the URL is provided in the introduction). The additions and revisions reflect the changes in the discipline over the years and the inclusion of more international perspectives on the field. The entries are arranged in an A to Z format and vary in length. Many include references and/or provide suggestions for further reading. *See* references and cross-references facilitate navigation, and the entries are signed by the more than 100 professionals who contributed to the work. The dictionary makes generous use of images, and the companion website provides power points for all the figures from the book, as well as downloadable pdf files of all the tables. The book is intended for teachers, researchers, students, and professionals and is recommended for public and academic libraries.— **ARBA Staff Reviewer**

820.   **Encyclopedia of Marine Geosciences.** Jan Harff, Martin Meschede, Sven Petersen, and Jorm Thiede, eds. New York, Springer Publishing, 2016. 961p. index. (Encyclopedia of Earth Sciences Series). $499.00. ISBN 13: 978-94-007-6237-4.

This title in the Encyclopedia of Earth Sciences Series covers approximately 195 topics under the umbrella term marine geosciences, which incorporates marine geophysics, hydrography, climatology, marine biology, and ecology. To convey the current state of knowledge in marine geosciences, the encyclopedia includes entries on theoretical, applied, and technical aspects. Even at nearly one thousand pages, coverage is not totally inclusive. Coverage is nevertheless broad, from earthquakes and El Niño to mud volcanoes and mangrove coasts to tsunamis. Readers looking for classical marine geology topics can refer to other books in the series to find titles dedicated to coastal science, geochemistry, paleoclimatology, ancient environments, and sediments and sedimentary rocks.

The encyclopedia begins with a list of scholarly contributors and information on the editors and editorial board. There is also a preface and a list of each topic included. Entries vary in length depending on subject. Each entry includes a definition and bibliography and can include subsections, illustrations (black and white and color), figures, and cross-references. The book concludes with an author index and a subject index. The subject index serves as a good navigational tool in addition to the table of contents and guide words at the top of each page.

The writing and subject matter are advanced. For those libraries (academic and public) looking for a reliable and authoritative reference on marine geosciences, this is a highly recommended resource.—**ARBA Staff Reviewer**

Astronomy and Space Sciences

821.   **NASA Images and Video Library. https://images.nasa.gov.** [Website] Free. Date reviewed: 2018.

This site presents the large collection of photographs, audio recordings, and videos which serve as a multimedia document of the work of the National Aeronautics and Space Agency (NASA). Users will find stunning images of luminous star nurseries, roiling Jovian storms, and distant, sparkling galaxies alongside NASA's earthbound machines, operations, and more. The media does well to highlight particular NASA missions (e.g., the Mars Curiosity Rover, Apollo 11, etc.), and contains a number of truly iconic images. Users can conduct a basic search from the prominent bar, and filter by media (images, video or audio) and/or timespan. The homepage also displays a generous gallery of photographs reflecting either the Newest Uploads (currently, many photos of January 2018's Super Blood Moon Eclipse), or the Most Popular. Videos of note include the Cassini spacecraft's flyby of Saturn and the launch of the Endeavor Space Shuttle, while interesting audio selections encompass satellite beeps, interstellar plasma sounds, and eerie radio emissions, among other things. Information for each item may generally include file size and format,

NASA identification number, keywords, and date created. Narrative descriptions will vary in length, but some can provide extensive information about particular celestial objects, NASA missions, and the technology used to capture distant objects (time lapse, image compilation, etc.). There may also be links to affiliated websites. Users can download selected items and can share across a number of social media platforms. With continued technological advancements working in concert with our limitless drive to explore space, this collection will continue to grow as it continues to amaze and inspire. The site would appeal to students and educators working in astronomy, aeronautics, and related fields, in addition to armchair space explorers.—**ARBA Staff Reviewer**

822.   **NASA Software. https://software.nasa.gov/.** [Website] Free. Date reviewed: 2018.

This website is a catalog of over one thousand National Aeronautics and Space Agency (NASA) computer programs, some of which are available free of charge to general users (others may be restricted or licensed for specialized use only). Part of the space agency's Technology Transfer Program, the website works to disseminate NASA technology for use in a range of potential applications. Users can conduct a basic or advanced search from the bar, or browse through fifteen general categories, such as Propulsion, Data and Image Processing, System Testing, and Aeronautics. Each category is indicated by a colorful icon that users can click to access the particular portfolio of related programs. Within each category, the software program is listed alphabetically by program/code name and is accompanied by a brief description and release note (e.g., open source, general public release, U.S. Government purpose release). For example, the "Coastal Salinity and Temperature Monitoring" Web application, under general public release, could offer continuous environmental data to a wide range of users, while the "Booster Launch Operations Center Custom Software" would be proprietary to government employees and contractors. Selecting a particular program provides further descriptive information, including operating system, reference number, and contact information. At the bottom of the program page is a display of Recommended Software related to the chosen program. Users interested in the program can click a blue Request Now or Download Now button for further instructions. The homepage displays a Featured Software banner highlighting types of codes (e.g., Propulsion), Top Ten Software Codes, and more. There is also a link to Recent Releases and FAQs. Educators and students of a variety of disciplines, from engineering to environmental science would find this website interesting whether for actual programming capabilities or conceptual inspiration.—**ARBA Staff Reviewer**

823.   **UCS Satellite Database. https://www.ucsusa.org/nuclear-weapons/space-weapons/satellite-database#.WmopLE2Wzcs.** [Website] Free. Date reviewed: 2018.

The Union of Concerned Scientists created this database to track over 1,700 satellites currently orbiting the earth (updated as of August 2017). Users can learn a good amount of detail on the satellites, from altitude to basic activity data. The database is generally updated four times a year. From the homepage users can download the database in either text or Excel spreadsheet format, and can examine the satellite by official name only or by alternate name as well. The database notes over 20 categories of information, including country of origin, country of operation, operator, category of use (civil, military, etc.), purpose, class of orbit, period, launch mass in kilograms, location, launch date, expected lifetime, launch site, launch vehicle, identification numbers, comments, and source information. Aside from the database, the page contains auxiliary information on satellites which could be helpful to users, including an interactive map showing the countries that have employed satellite technology since 1966, Satellite Quick Facts, and a listing of sample questions which the data may answer. Resources include four pdfs covering changes to the database, a Quickguide to using the database, a broader user's manual, and an essay on common misperceptions (e.g., that the database can actually track satellites). Users can also examine an Interactive Visualization of satellites in orbit (as of 2015). Younger students will benefit from the site's straightforward presentation of the data in addition to the supplementary materials, while the range of technical data will broaden the site's appeal to more seasoned researchers.—**ARBA Staff Reviewer**

Climatology and Meteorology

824.   **Climate Change and American Policy: Key Documents, 1979-2015.** John R., Jr. Burch, ed. Jefferson, N.C., McFarland, 2016. 332p. index. $39.95pa. ISBN 13: 978-1-4766-6527-6; 978-1-4766-2685-7 (e-book).

With this work, editor John Burch, Jr., (Campbellsville University) has compiled significant documents highlighting the viewpoints, policies, and legislative actions of various individuals, organizations, and governments on the issue of climate change. Beginning with its formal recognition as a worldwide problem in the 1979 Declaration of the World Climate Conference, this compilation traces the development of the climate change issue over a 36-year time span. Presented chronologically, not only does the text include international landmark documents including the 1992 United Nations Framework Convention on Climate Change, the 1997 Kyoto Protocol, and the 2015 Paris Agreement, but it also includes other influential documents like congressional resolutions and statements of leading climate change scientists, governmental leaders, and professional organizations. The breadth of opinions, policies, and legislative documents provided and the analysis of their relationship with each other demonstrates how contentious the issue of climate change has remained over time. The significance of each document is described and a short analysis of the document's influence on the issue is provided. Finally, a list of suggested readings accompanies each document and an extensive bibliography and index are included.—**Jennifer Brooks Huffman**

825.   **Encyclopedia of Climate Change.** 2d ed. Steven I. Dutch, ed. Hackensack, N.J., Salem Press, 2017. 3v. illus. maps. index. $395.00/set. ISBN 13: 978-1-68217-141-7; 978-1-68217-145-5 (e-book).

Encyclopedia of Climate Change is an update to the previous Salem Press publication *Encyclopedia of Global Warming* (see ARBA 2010, entry 1352). The new edition follows the same formatting as the first, and most of the entries are revisions of the original. There are 551 signed essays, arranged alphabetically, on topics related to the scientific, social, geographical, and political aspects of climate change. Each essay is classified by both type and category, aiding those who need an overview of people, organizations, or laws. The three-volume set is especially suited to high school and undergraduate students, as well as to researchers from other disciplines needing a basic introduction to a climate change topic. There are a few completely new entries on important, timely topics including Atmospheric Rivers, Bakken Formation, Eyjafjallajokull, Fracking, the Mount Toba eruption, the 2015 El Nino, and the Seesaw theory, as well as overviews of the Obama administration's efforts on climate change and updated cases of the U.S. Supreme Court. Most of the entries have updated bibliographical references, including articles and websites from 2010-2016. The appendixes include a mediagraphy, timeline, glossary, organization websites, and an extensive and updated general bibliography. There is an index to the three volumes and a second table of contents arranged by category, to supplement the alphabetical listing. Purchase of the set includes online access; however, as the e-book is updated, continued online access requires purchasing the new edition. The set is similar in scope and arrangement to the *SAGE Encyclopedia of Global Warming and Climate Change* published in 2012. Since the two titles are on varied revision cycles, adding this new edition would provide an update on this rapidly changing, important, and popular topic.—**Theresa Muraski**

826.   **Environmental Sustainability and Climate Change Adaptation Strategies.** Wayne Ganpat and Wendy-Ann Isaac, eds. Hershey, Pa., IGI Global, 2017. 406p. illus. maps. index. (Advances in Environmental Engineering and Green Technologies). $200.00. ISBN 13: 978-1-52251-607-1; 978-1-52251-608-8 (e-book).

Our planet's changing climate poses many significant challenges, including intensified weather patterns resulting in longer droughts, more frequent storms, and precipitation events that lead to floods. These threats undoubtedly will have a more significant negative impact on developing nations with less infrastructure and capital. *Environmental Sustainability and Climate Change Adaptation Strategies* provides a useful overview of sustainable development, agricultural, and resource management adaptation strategies in the face of climate change threats. Primarily featuring authors from across the developing world, this reference work certainly includes perspectives of those facing the climate change's greatest challenges. Topics include adaptations in land use and farming techniques, aquaculture, livestock management, agricultural pest management, water quality, risk assessment, and predictive modeling for tropical cyclones. These final topics are most timely given the devastating power of storms on display in Texas, Florida, Puerto Rico, and across the Caribbean during the 2017 hurricane season, and their relevance will only increase as weather conditions continue to change to favor more frequent and intense storms in the future. Intended as a reference for academics, researchers, and students in addition to NGOs and working professionals, this work should be of interest to a wide range of users. Recommended for academic and research libraries.—**Eric Tans**

827.   **International Cloud Atlas. https://cloudatlas.wmo.int/home.html.** [Website] Free. Date reviewed: 2018.

A project of the World Meteorological Organization (WMO), this website establishes the WMO classification system for clouds and other weather-related sky phenomena like lightning, hail, or rainbows. New users may wish to view a brief introductory video or examine the slide show of site highlights (e.g., Find A Cloud, Electrometeors, etc.). Users can also search from the bar or choose from a selection of menu items. The Clouds tab clarifies WMO standards (e.g., height, altitude, vertical extent, etc.) within Definitions of Clouds, Descriptions of Clouds, and more. Users will find explanations of cloud types (e.g., stratus, cumulonimbus,etc.) alongside tables, illustrations, photographs, and other information. Other Meteors classifies, defines, and describes a range of hydrometeors (e.g., fog), lithometeors (e.g., haze), photometeors (e.g., rainbows), and electrometeors (e.g., lightning). The Observing Clouds tab provides details on scientific cloud observation, delineating earth and aircraft observation and the elements observers look at, such as total cloud cover, cloud amounts, cloud direction, and speed. Images links to a searchable image gallery of nearly five hundred color photographs of clouds and other meteors. Users are able to compare two images in a side-by-side examination of characteristics. Information includes global positioning (longitude, latitude), creator, photograph date, and a brief description. An A-Z Glossary, cross-referenced, defines terms such as Accretion, Downburst, Mesocyclone, and Wind Shear. There is also a good series of appendixes under the Other Information tab which include essays on such topics as the "History of Cloud Nomenclature" and the "Etymology of Latin Names of Clouds."—**ARBA Staff Reviewer**

828.   Johansen, Bruce E. **Climate Change: An Encyclopedia of Science, Society, and Solutions.** Santa Barbara, Calif., ABC-CLIO, 2017. 3v. $309.00/set. ISBN 13: 978-1-4408-4085-2; 978-1-4408-4086-9 (e-book).

Climate Change: An Encyclopedia of Science, Society, and Solutions is the fourth encyclopedia on climate change authored or edited by Bruce E. Johansen. This three-volume set is organized into topical areas, with each volume focusing on a broad subject: Land and Oceans, Weather and Global Warming, and Human Impact. The third volume also includes a selection of primary sources. Within each volume topics are grouped into two to five main subcategories, and then individual topics. Topics span famous people, weather events and their increasing severity, deforestation, pests such as pine bark beetles, allergies, warming temperatures, melting sea ice, and solutions to climate change like solar power, wind energy, academic protests, and political action. Most entries are short, running three to five pages in length, with some reaching seven to eight pages. Some include sidebars addressing complementary issues, and each entry has a further reading list. Johansen actively references other sources, and volume three has an 80-page bibliography varying from newspaper articles to government reports to scholarly books and journal articles. The author tends to overemphasize direct quotes and statistics to tell the story of climate change, in effect replacing his voice with others. Without a single voice this work lacks coherency, and when combined with emphasis on statistics or data, makes it hard for readers to remain engaged. Also, topics seem somewhat haphazard. For example, the discussion of the effects of climate change on indigenous peoples only includes four North American groups, ignoring other areas of the world. Under the broad heading, Agriculture and Food, there are entries on rice and wine grapes, but climate effects on other crops are not addressed. Due to these shortcomings, librarians are advised to consider other reference sources on this subject.—**Kevin McDonough**

829.   **National Weather Service. http://www.weather.gov/.** [Website] Free. Date reviewed: 2017.

This site from the National Oceanic & Atmospheric Administration (NOAA) is the essential weather resource. It presents a generous series of maps and subject tabs where users can find a wealth of information on all types of weather affecting the continental United States, Alaska, Hawaii, and territory islands. The site is easy to navigate with an abundance of tabs linking to regional weather information and specialized features. The homepage initially presents the general national outlook statement on all regions, then displays a large national map demarcated by counties which are colored according to any current and/or developing weather pattern. A key below details 27 categories of weather scenarios, such as Flood Warning, Winter Weather Advisory, Gale Warning, and Fire Weather Watch. Clicking links below the map allows users to follow the weather in the American territories of Samoa, Guam, Puerto Rico, and the Virgin Islands. Clicking on a county will redirect users to the National Weather Service page for that weather reporting station and its forecast. From the menu bar, users can select from a variety of tabs. The Forecast can be aimed at a number of individual categories such as Aviation, Marine, Hurricanes, Severe Weather, Sun/Moon, Long Range Forecasts and more. Past Weather will note Records, Astronomical Data, and 24 hour Temperature Readings. Clicking on the Safety tab links to a listing of topical pages addressing the extreme of tsunamis or tornadoes in addition to the common issues of fog, heat, or wind. Other tabs include Active Alerts, which also relates to various categories (river, flooding, drought, etc.) and can be searched by state. Forecast Maps offer an excellent selection of graphics illustrating a long list of weather variables, such as Temperature, Precipitation, Short or Medium Range Forecast, Wind Speed & Directions, and Sky Cover. Other maps, including Previous Days, Animated, and High-Resolution are also available here. Users can also access maps and information exclusive to Rivers, Lakes & Precipitation, or Air Quality, view composite Satellite Image maps (updated every 30 minutes), and much more. Additional resources are plentiful and include Information and Education tabs linking to many Publications, Brochures, a Glossary, the Daily Briefing, Statistics, Initiatives, and many other resources.

Well organized and extensive, the material on this site would appeal to students, professionals, and casual weather observers alike. Highly recommended for public, school, and academic libraries.—**ARBA Staff Reviewer**

830. **Notable Natural Disasters.** 2d ed. Robert S. Carmichael, ed. Hackensack, N.J., Salem Press, 2017. 3v. illus. index. $275.00/set. ISBN 13: 978-1-68217-332-9; 978-1-68217-333-6 (e-book).

This second edition improves upon shortcomings identified by C.A. Sproules and her review in *Choice* (November 2007, Volume 45, Issue 3). Glaring factual errors and omissions are corrected. Confusion as to why human events like explosions and factory fires are included in a book on natural disasters is explained in the introduction: "others [disasters] are a combination of spontaneous natural occurrences and elements of human activity like carelessness, failure of design or technology, inadequate planning, or lack of response." The problem, though, is that the instances of human influenced disasters are very few, drawing into question the selection criteria. Sproules also expressed concern about the 2007 edition because few contributors had science backgrounds. Approximately 30 percent of contributors in the second edition are not associated with universities and therefore their qualifications are unknown. Yet, a sample of university contributors indicates strong science backgrounds. Thus, Sproules' criticism is hard to verify. The layout and coverage of the second edition parallels the previous. Volume one provides an overview of significant natural events (fires, floods, droughts, etc.), while volumes two and three provide entries on 163 notable disasters. Most entries are 4-6 pages, with a few stretching to 10+. A short bibliography for further reading accompanies each entry. The most pressing concern remaining is the cost. At $275/set this is an expensive source when information on these disasters is readily available elsewhere. Most appropriate for public libraries.—**Kevin McDonough**

831.   **World Meteorological Organization. https://publi.wmo.int/en.** [Website] Free. Date reviewed: 2018.

The World Meteorological Organization (WMO) is a specialized agency of the United Nations that works to facilitate the international exchange of ideas and information related to global Weather, Climate, and Water issues. This website shows visitors the array of WMO Projects, Programmes, and Resources from which they can gather research, data, and ideas related to current and future meteorological concerns. Users can select the Weather, Climate, or Water icons near the top of the home page to find information exclusive to each subject, or can select from several tabs at the top of the home page for a broader approach. The Programmes tab presents a display of WMO and affiliated programs, which can be sorted alphabetically or by most recent. Information for each program (tagged for subject, location, etc.) may generally include Scope, Objectives, Structure, Components, and Background. There may also be video content and a list of related publications. Users can find information on the Aeronautical Meteorology Program, the Disaster Risk Reduction Program, The Global Observing System, and much more. Projects presents a tagged gallery of regional, national, multinational, and global projects affiliated with WMO work. Pins on the global map graphic show project locations and types. Information may describe project background, status, partners, funding, implementation location, or strategic priority, among other things. Notable projects include the Flash Flood Guidance System with Global Coverage, which has been implemented in over fifty countries, and the Polar Prediction Project which aims to improve the science of polar weather forecasting. Users can access official WMO publications under the Resources tab, which includes a library of expert reports, working papers, journals, statistical reports, and other information. The WMO Youth Website (www.youth.wmo.int) may appeal to educators and younger students with its materials addressing Environmental Challenges, Desertification, and other timely topics. And the Meteoterm link provides access to the WMO terminology database of basic scientific terms, the International Meteorological Vocabulary, and International Glossary of Hydrology. The WMO website would appeal to policy makers, environmentalists, activists, educators, and others invested in world climate and related issues.—**ARBA Staff Reviewer**

Geology

832.   **Encyclopedia of Deserts.** Michael A. Mares, ed. Norman, Okla., University of Oklahoma Press, 2017. 694p. illus. maps. index. $50.00pa. ISBN 13: 978-0-8061-5608-8.

In this encyclopedia of arid lands worldwide, users will find 665 major topics covered in alphabetic order under the editorship of Michael Mares, professor of zoology at the University of Oklahoma. The text, intended as a one-stop source for information, is written in an accessible manner that will appeal to upper-level high school students and undergraduates. Mares chose to make the essays more inclusive, rather than having a serious of short entries on discrete topics. According to the editor, there is a North American bias due to available research. Vertebrates also receive more coverage than invertebrates. The front matter includes a preface, list of contributors, and an introduction. The entries vary in length from about half a page to over ten pages. Each has a set of further readings and, when appropriate, *see* and *see also* references. All are signed by the author. Coverage is broad—flora, fauna, people, concepts, geology, etc. An index rounds out the work. The index uses bold face for topics that have major encyclopedia accounts, which further facilitates navigation. This book would work well for community college, academic, and public libraries. High school libraries looking for such a book would benefit as well.—**ARBA Staff Reviewer**

833.   **Glaciers and Landforms Photograph Collection. http://content.lib.washington. edu/epicweb/index.html.** [Website] Free. Date reviewed: 2018.

This digital collection embodies years of glacial and geological study in photographs taken mainly throughout the northwestern region of the United States (mostly Alaska). Users can conduct a basic or advanced search from the bar, or select the Browse Collection tab from the homepage. The homepage also displays the works of three Featured Photographers, and users who click on their names will access their photographs. The Browse Collection tab leads to a thumbnail gallery of over five thousand black-and-white images (there may be a few color images). Within the gallery, a search can be narrowed by photograph latitude or mountain range. Users will find expansive landscape panoramas alongside artful reproductions of geologic formation and activity in icefalls, volcanoes, glaciers, moraines, mud flows, craters, faults, peaks, landslides, crater lake icebergs, and more. Selected photos can be enlarged, rotated, or downloaded. Information accompanying each photograph generally includes title, photographer, photograph date, altitude, judicial district, and collection. This collection would be useful to students and educators within geological sciences but could also appeal to others who appreciate evocative photography of the natural world.—**ARBA Staff Reviewer**

834.   **Land Processes Distributed Active Archive Center. https://lpdaac.usgs.gov.** [Website] Free. Date reviewed: 2018.

A collaboration between NASA and the U.S. Geological Service, the Land Processes Distributed Active Archive Center (LP DAAC) holds an archive of land remote sensing data amassed from NASA's Earth Observing System Data and Information System (EOSDIS) for use in a variety of applications, such as volcanic activity monitoring and global surface temperature recordings. Users can select from one of six programs from the drop down menu under the Dataset Discovery tab. For each program, the website provides an overview page, general system operating information, and a description of applicable data products. For example, data generated from the ECOSTRESS program (running on the International Space Station) can be used in the Evaporative Stress Index (ESI), a major drought indicator. There are also links to the individual program's data product distribution and citation policies. Underneath the Tools tab, users will find assistance regarding Data Access (e.g., searches), Data Manipulation (e.g., formatting), Utilities (e.g., isolating specific data), and Web Services (e.g., data interaction). Users will also find a list of relevant acronyms on this page.—**ARBA Staff Reviewer**

835.   **Natural Wonders of the World.** New York, DK Smithsonian, 2017. 440p. illus. maps. index. $50.00. ISBN 13: 978-1-4654-6417-0.

This beautifully illustrated book presents 240 of the Earth's natural wonders using satellite terrain data and imagery to reveal perspectives not visible to the naked eye. The images work hand-in-hand with the text to explain the concepts that help readers understand the geology and, in some cases, the physics, chemistry, botany, and zoology behind mountains, rivers, glaciers, wetlands, deserts, forests, and more.

The book begins with a discussion of Earth's structure, tectonic plates, Earth's Past, and life on Earth. It next travels around the world geographically starting in North America and moving to Central and South America, Europe, Africa, Asia, Australia and New Zealand, and Antarctica. The last two chapters cover the oceans and extreme weather. These main sections are followed by a directory of 250 natural wonders not covered in the book. A glossary and an index round out the work.

This is a big book in terms of size (10 x 12) and content. Modestly priced, it is highly recommended for public and school libraries.—**ARBA Staff Reviewer**

836.   **USGS ShakeMap. https://earthquake.usgs.gov/data/shakemap/.** [Website] Free. Date reviewed: 2018.

ShakeMap from the U.S. Geological Survey (USGS) works with regional networks to gather and disseminate a large variety of data regarding ground motion and movement intensity. Data is presented in a number of ways and would appeal to a range of research needs in the scientific and public safety realms. Users can select from a number of links on the left side of the page, or scroll down for similar options. The Search ShakeMap Archives link allows both basic and advanced searches with the basic search requiring magnitude, data time, and geographic region parameters. Users can also access the Significant Earthquakes Archive page here, which provides a listing of USGS-defined major quakes marked by year, magnitude, surface location, and depth. Data available for individual earthquake events can be quite extensive and may include a variety of maps, reports, charts, and more, such as an Interactive Map showing epicenter, faults, and intensity, Regional Information, a Felt Report recording civilian reactions to an earthquake, Intensity Map, colored ShakeMap, Origin detail, Nearby Seismicity report, and Tsunami reports. The Atlas presents a global map which illustrates over six thousand significant seismic events over a fifty-year period or current real-time events tracked over a period of one day. Earthquake Scenarios are speculative maps which use hypothetical magnitude, location, and fault-rupture geometry to estimate impacts. Users can examine Scenario Catalogs, Related Scenarios & Exercises, and more. Other links include Earthquakes, which offers more maps, lists, and statistics regarding the latest and largest shakers. Users can find information on the Top 20 Largest quakes, fatality statistics, Special Earthquake Studies and more. Hazards contains Seismic Hazard Maps and an Interactive Fault Map covering the United States. Data & Products repackages much of the previously mentioned information in list form for ease of reference.—**ARBA Staff Reviewer**

Oceanography

837.   **Ecological Marine Unit Explorer. https://livingatlas.arcgis.com/emu/.** [Website] Free. Date reviewed: 2018.

The Ecological Marine Unit (EMU) Explorer is an interactive map that allows users to examine data on areas of ocean marked by distinct physiographic and ecological characteristics. Users simply click on any ocean area of the global map graphic to access data in tables and graphs which help to create an overall description of the individual EMU. Data generally includes measurements of temperature, salinity, dissolved oxygen, nitrate, phosphate, silicate, thickness, and depth, and will summarize particular EMU findings as normal, moderate, low, etc. Users can also see a graph visualization or "profile" of each individual measurement against ocean depth as well. A table compares depth and thickness readings across several different EMUs. The color-coded map clearly delineates particular EMUs and the zoom feature helps users identify the unique physiographic attributes of the selected ocean area. There is little contextual information to accompany the data (e.g., what do the readings mean?). Adding some could potentially expand the site audience. Nonetheless, the site would appeal to marine scientists, ocean advocacy groups, conservationists, educators and students of environmental studies, and others.—**ARBA Staff Reviewer**

838.   **Encyclopedia of Estuaries.** Michael J. Kennish, ed. New York, Springer Publishing, 2016. 760p. illus. index. (Encyclopedia of Earth Sciences Series). $549.00. ISBN 13: 978-94-017-8800-7; 978-94-017-8801-4 (e-book).

This encyclopedia contains approximately 260 entries on estuaries. Entries range in length from less than a page to more than 12 pages. They all include a definition and a bibliography. Some of the bibliographies are quite extensive, which will facilitate further research. All entries include the name and affiliation of the entry author. Entries are subdivided when necessary and can include such subsections as essential concepts, summary, history, and data applications. The content is further enhanced by the use of hundreds of color and black-and-white illustrations and tables. From algal blooms to delta plain to invasive species to microfauna to wetlands, users will find foundational information about the physical, chemical, and biological characteristics of estuaries. The book is easy to navigate as it lists individual topics in the table of contents, uses guide words, and provides subject and author indexes. The book content was guided by Michael Kennish, an estuarine scientist at Rutgers University, along with an editorial board. Estuaries play important ecological roles and have economic, recreational, and commercial value. This reliable and scholarly resource is highly recommended for academic and public libraries.—**ARBA Staff Reviewer**

839.   **ReefBase Directory. http://www.reefbase.org/main.aspx.** [Website] Free. Date reviewed: 2018.

The ReefBase Directory is an excellent resource for information on coral reefs. It maintains a large database tracking data for reefs all over the world, a digital library of reference material (articles, reports and more), over four thousand color photographs, and an online Geographic Information System allowing users to create custom maps. These features can be accessed from corresponding tabs located throughout the homepage. The Global Database covers a strong variety of particular data organized into four umbrella categories: Resources, Threats, Status, and Management. These categories are further delineated with Resources providing foundational information about reef locations, structure, and local biodiversity and Status providing a coral reef and affiliated reef fish health status report. The project considers data on Threats within natural (e.g., disease), human (e.g., coastal development), climate (e.g., storms), and bleaching subcategories. The Management area of the database notes a location's monitoring activity, protected areas, legislation, and more. It also provides recommendations for improving research and management. Users can search a particular coral reef location against each data parameter, examining a map, thumbnail photos (if available), and a listing of applicable records. The GIS & Maps tab allows users to create and save a personalized map with select data (e.g., Reefs at Risk, Coral Diseases, etc.) from the larger database in addition to select reef characteristics (type, geomorphology, depth). Users can zoom in on a particular reef location, note Marine Protected Areas, show impacts of natural disasters, and more. Key Topics offer several general summaries on the pressing issues concerning coral reefs today, such as Tsunami Impacts; Poverty and Reefs; Population, and Consumption & the Environment, with links to relevant site resources. The generous information on the site can be viewed freely; however, registered (free) users may upload and download the materials. The site would appeal to a wide range of researchers across a number of topics.—**ARBA Staff Reviewer**

35 Resource Sciences

Energy

Dictionaries and Encyclopedias

840. **Dictionary of Energy.** 2d ed. Cleveland Cutler and Christopher Morris, eds. San Diego, Calif., Elsevier Science, 2015. 700p. illus. $111.00. ISBN 13: 978-0-0809-6811-7; 978-0-0809-6812-4 (e-book).

This updated, second edition builds on the format and purpose of the first (Elsevier, 2005). The editors designed the first edition as an interdisciplinary, broad dictionary that covered all the disciplines and the multifaceted aspects of the concept of energy for use by students, researchers, and the general public. While acknowledging that subject specialists may be disappointed not to find definitions of discipline-specific terms, the editors explained that other resources filled this need; more important for the purposes of this dictionary was the need to provide a compilation of commonly agreed on terms and definitions to enhance understanding and communication, particularly in cases in which the same term can mean different things (e.g., elasticity and efficiency mean different things to economists and engineers).

The second edition increases the number of headwords and entries from 8,000/10,000 to 10,000/13,000. Each subject area has new entries, but the section on oil and gas accounts for the largest percentage of new entries, 175 more, largely due to newer extraction techniques, new fields, modern exploration technology, and industry terms. The effect of energy on the natural world, environmental and alternative energy sources and technology, and other developments account for a number of new entries as well. The second edition has expanded in other ways: there are more biographies, more quotations on energy (a third of which predate 1900), and more color images.

Prior to the prefaces, users will find a list of the subject areas covered in the dictionary and dozens of special essays on important energy terms. The subject areas are worth listing as they convey the scope of the dictionary: biographies, biological energetics, biomass, chemistry, climate change, coal, communication, consumption and efficiency, conversion, earth science, ecology, economics and business, electricity, environment, geothermal, global issues, health and safety, history, HVAC, hydrogen, hydropower, lighting, materials, measurements, mining, nuclear, oil and gas, organizations, photovoltaic, physics, policy, refrigeration, renewable/alternative fuels, social issues, solar, storage, sustainable development, thermodynamics, transportation, and wind. A subject area appears in italics after each headword in the dictionary. The special essays section serves the needs of readers who are most likely familiar with terms like cap and trade, solar, carbon footprint, climate change, and smog, but may want to read a succinct and authoritative explanation of the origins of the word or term. There are also essays on terms that are likely less familiar (Otto cycle, Ghawar, Hubbert curve, etc.). An introduction explains the layout of the dictionary, and there is a list of abbreviations commonly used in energy.

This is a comprehensive, authoritative, and easy-to-use dictionary that is highly recommended for public and academic libraries.—**ARBA Staff Reviewer**

Handbooks and Yearbooks

841.   **Project Sunroof. https://www.google.com/get/sunroof#p=0&spf=1518827384384.** [Website] Free. Date reviewed: 2018

This project employs Google mapping technology to articulate local and regional data regarding solar energy. With the primary focus set on educating consumers about the cost savings of using solar energy, the site could nonetheless meet a variety of other research needs. Users can learn basic information about solar energy (how it works in general and how it works for the home), access regional, community, or individual consumer data, and more. Straightforward information and bright graphics make the site easy to navigate. Users can scroll through the page to find information or select from several tabs in the upper right corner of the homepage. Entering an individual address in the bar, or selecting the Savings Estimator tab, displays the Google Map with pinned location and property analysis which notes the number of hours of usable sunlight per year, roof area (square feet) available for solar panels, and an estimated energy savings over twenty years. The map also marks roof areas affected by shade. Both the Explore Your Area or Data Explorer links let users enter a city or county to display an area profile with a map illustrating rooftop sunlight and including statistics on current solar installations and general solar viability. Additional information may include median household income and more. Users can also examine the methodology for determining area statistics. The Solar 101 and FAQ tabs link to basic, foundational information regarding consumer use of solar energy, its technology, economics, and other material.—**ARBA Staff Reviewer**

Environmental Science

Directories

842.   **Canadian Environmental Resource Guide 2017-2018.** 22d ed. Amenia, N.Y., Grey House Publishing, 2017. 696p. $439.00pa. ISBN 13: 978-1-68217-471-5; 978-1-68217-472-2 (e-book).

The *Canadian Environmental Resource Guide* contains not only directory information of organizations concerning environmental resources and services but also rankings, a chronicle of recent events, descriptions of environmental issues, and profiles of prominent researchers, maps, and charts. The guide is arranged into three main sections. The first, Environmental Update 2017, offers a chronology of events; profiles of Canadian environmentalists; charts, tables, and statistics covering "every aspect of Canada's environment"; a listing of trade shows, conferences, and seminars; and indicators showing how Canada compares with the rest of the world. The second section, Industry Resources, provides a directory of approximately seven hundred Canadian companies engaged in environmental activities and a product and services buyers guide; a directory of manufacturers of products that deal with environmental issues; and law firms across Canada with a specialization in environmental law. The third part, Environmental Government Listings, is a directory of Intergovernmental Offices and Councils, Environmental Trade Representatives Abroad, and Municipal Listings. The guide is indexed by subject, geographic, executive, and ISO; a list of abbreviations is included. Each directory item contains name, address, phone, fax, website, year founded, and products/services/areas of specialization. The *Canadian Environmental Resource Guide* is a very thorough and detailed source of information and is highly recommended to researchers looking for statistics and locating information resources including trade associations and manufacturers; also very helpful are the profiles of Canadian environmentalists including contact information for those who might want to conduct interviews for research papers or find a consultant. Academic and research libraries with extensive collections on environmental studies should own this book, especially those academic libraries supporting a curriculum in environmental studies.—**Lucy Heckman**

Handbooks and Yearbooks

843.   **Protected Areas of the U.S. https://maps.usgs.gov/padus/.** [Website] Free. Date reviewed: 2018.

This site contains a database map that displays information on over two hundred thousand individual parks and protected areas within the United States, including Alaska and Hawaii. These areas stretch across roughly three billion acres of public land and waterways within the United States, requiring the management of close to fifteen thousand public agencies and nongovernmental organizations. Users can examine the map under a selection of colored layers which illustrate Manager Name, Manager Type, Protected Areas by Manager, and Public Access. The map—its view expanding to include the outlying states, also uses a GAP Status Layer, referring to type of area management, such as biodiversity management, multiple use management, etc. The Now Viewing tab to the left of the map provides the color key for all available options of each category. Users can also use the Search bar to identify particular locations via address, landmark, or data set. Clicking on a particular point of the map (colored to reflect selected layers) accesses a listing of nearby parks/areas and/or managers. The listing includes manager name (e.g., U.S. Forest Service, Bureau of Land Management, etc.), designation (e.g., Wilderness Area, Study Area, Native American land, etc.), Acreage, Accessibility, GAP status, and more. Users will undoubtedly recognize the larger, more popular land areas like national parks or marine sanctuaries, but the database also includes areas of privately held land, vista points, Native American tribal lands, golf courses, preserves, reservoirs, military land, bike paths, easements, and much more.—**ARBA Staff Reviewer**

844.   Walker, Teri J. **Today's Environmental Issues: Democrats and Republicans.** Santa Barbara, Calif., ABC-CLIO, 2017. 382p. index. $97.00. ISBN 13: 978-1-4408-4709-7; 978-1-4408-4710-3 (e-book).

Environmental issues cross partisan politics, and this title attempts to identify similarities and differences of the two major American political parties on a variety of environmental issues of interest today—climate change, hydraulic fracturing (fracking), and genetically modified food, to name a few. The book is organized into thirty-one chapters, each an essay dealing with one environmental issue. The chapters open with an introduction of the issue, and then some general positions Republicans and Democrats have in regards to the issue, followed by a more in-depth overview of the issue. Details on the positions Democrats and Republicans have on the issue are next, with some references provided for further reading on the topic rounding out each chapter. Some chapters may also have a sidebar with brief information on individuals, policies, or court decisions connected to that chapter's issue. A glossary and selected bibliography round out the title. Scholars and students should find the information useful to their studies.—**Denise A. Garofalo**

Water

Handbooks and Yearbooks

845.   **Reclamation: Managing Water in the West. https://water.usbr.gov/.** [Website] Free. Date reviewed: 2018.

The pilot Reclamation Water Information System from the U.S. Bureau of Reclamation acts as a hub of water data collected from reclamation regions throughout the western United States. Users can select data regionally via the Map link or can conduct a text based search using the Query Tool. The map delineates water reclamation regions throughout the continental United States, but consolidates data for states west of and including Texas, Kansas, Oklahoma, Nebraska, and the Dakotas. Sites are marked on the map by colored symbols denoting type (Agrimet, Canal, Diversion, Reservoir, Stream or Weather). Selecting an area symbol provides its description such as latitude, longitude, site type, site identification number, and name. The map can be filtered to show only information for particular types of sites. The query link can generate specified data in several formats, such as an interactive plot. Users select a site(s), applicable parameters, and date range. Available information may include reservoir levels and inflows, stream or canal flow, water temperature, stream gauge height, reservoir evaporation, precipitation, and more. The Visualization Demos link provides a sample of how the data can be used.— **ARBA Staff Reviewer**

846.   **Technologies for the Treatment and Recovery of Nutrients from Industrial Wastewater.** Angeles Val del Río and José Luis Campos Gómez, eds. Hershey, Pa., Information Science Reference/IGI Global, 2017. 391p. index. (Advances in Environmental Engineering and Green Technologies (AEEGT) Book Series). $200.00. ISBN 13: 978-1-52251-037-6; 978-1-52251-038-3 (e-book).

Technologies for the Treatment and Recovery of Nutrients from Industrial Wastewater focuses on industrial nutrient recovery—a hot topic in wastewater treatment. Articles are written by scholars from Spain, Chile, Italy, Mexico, France, Denmark, Portugal, The Netherlands, Poland, and the Czech Republic on such topics as "Nutrients Pollution in Water Bodies: Related Legislation in Europe and the United States," "Fundamentals of the Biological Processes for Nitrogen Removal," and "Aerobic Granular Sludge: Treatment of Wastewaters Containing Toxic Compounds."

Written for an academic audience, the book is enhanced by generous use of headings and subheadings for ease of navigation. Tables, charts, and visual illustrations supplement explanations while key terms and definitions assist reader understanding of technical terms. The book concludes with a compilation of references and a professionally prepared master index. Recommended.—**Thomas E. Baker**

36 Transportation

General Works

847.   **DDOT Back in Time.** [Website] Free. Date reviewed: 2018.

This site contains a photo archive documenting the history of the District Department of Transportation (DDOT) in the U.S. capitol. Although the website is currently under construction, it houses numerous items which help tell the story of the modes and methods of transportation in the district, from bicycling and driving to street design and public transit. Users can access good foundational information from the About and History of DDOT tabs on the left side of the homepage. The Browse Collection tab links to 18 collections grouping archived items according to theme, such as DC Highways; Interstates & Freeways; Pedestrians, Bicycles & Footbridges; and Rivers & Bodies of Water. Users can alternatively Browse Items and find nearly 175 individual historic items (one singular item may include a number of individual photo files). Information available for each item generally includes title, subject, description, creator, date, format, tags, and more. Archive highlights capture road flooding during 1972's Hurricane Agnes, the 14th street bridge complex project, numerous street views, and other events. The Map feature currently allows users to search three items by location. As the archive develops, it will enhance this feature and eventually add newspaper articles, maps, documents, and more photographs.—**ARBA Staff Reviewer**

848.   Haajanen, Lennart W. **Illustrated Dictionary of Automobile Body Styles.** 2d ed. Jefferson, N.C., McFarland, 2017. 196p. illus. index. $39.95pa. ISBN 13: 978-0-7864-9918-2; 978-1-4766-2404-4 (e-book).

The second edition of The *Illustrated Dictionary of Automobile Body Styles* from McFarland (see ARBA 2004, entry 1567) is expanded by 20 pages and includes several new illustrations as well.

Author Haajanen dives through the etymology of words or phrases used to describe various styles of automobiles, sometimes going back to horse and buggy and carriage builder terms, and even includes "chariot" in his definitions. He then traces that word or design to see how it influenced naming things in the automotive age. Automakers frequently misapply terms when naming car styles and models. For example, manufacturers will call something a "brougham" or a "cabriolet" when it does not meet the traditional definition of those words. These exceptions and deviations are noted. The author includes terms from Britain, the United States, Italy, France, and Germany. So, for example, under the definition for the British "bonnet," Haajanen gives the word each of those languages uses for the same meaning; an arrow indicates which have an entry in this dictionary. In this case "hood" from the United States has an entry, but the others do not. Some slang is included such as "ragtop" for convertible, or "woodie" for wood paneled cars. The book also includes terms like "hot rod," which has nothing to do with manufacturer's name designations, but has to do with a style of automobile built by consumers.

The length of entries varies from a few lines to about four pages. One can obtain quite an education on the history of various styles from reading these entries. Over 150 line drawings are used throughout to give examples of the styles under discussion. Also noted is the important period that the word or phrase was used. The book includes a bibliography and a graphic appendix presenting the evolution of some body styles. Recommended.—**Robert M. Lindsey**

849.　**Marine Traffic. https://www.marinetraffic.com/.** [Website] Free. Date reviewed: 2018.

Marine Traffic is a free-to-use global tracking database recording current ocean vessel (nonmilitary) positions and related information through the use of AIS (Automatic Identification System) data. Users can navigate over the central map graphic on the homepage and observe real-time positions of all reporting vessels from the local pleasure craft to the large container ship. Vessels are represented by colored and sized icons signifying vessel type and direction of travel. The map reflects an overview of worldwide maritime traffic or, with the use of the zoom function, a close-up view of traffic in a particular ocean area. Premium data is available via paid subscription, but nonregistered users still have generous access to maritime data. Hovering over an icon on the map accesses information on the vessel, which may include flag, origin, destination, estimated time of arrival, past track, route forecast, speed, draught, photos, and more. Information for ports includes such things as latitude, longitude, local time, number of vessels in port, number of expected arrivals, and wind forecasts. Users can conduct a basic search or a number of advanced searches relating to specific category of marine item (e.g., vessel, port, etc.). Alternatively, users can search Vessels, Ports, or Photos from the bar above the map. The toolbar on the left side of the map allows users to select filters which, for example, allow the tracking of particular vessel types only, or layers for weather, ports, and time zones. At the bottom of the toolbar, users can note the number of vessels on the whole map (currently over 130,000) as well as the number of vessels in the local area.—**ARBA Staff Reviewer**

850.　**National Transportation Atlas Database. https://www.bts.gov/geospatial/ national-transportation-atlas-database.** [Website] Free. Date reviewed: 2018.

This geographic database from the U.S. Department of Transportation collects a wide range of information on U.S. transportation facilities, networks, and more. It gathers datasets from various agencies in one place and employs geospatial mapping to help visualize and articulate particular data themes with national, regional, and local significance. Selecting the Data tab from the left side of the page allows users to examine Data by Mode (rail, aviation, roads, transit, or marine) or Data by Category, which encompasses Performance, Safety, Freight, Energy & Environment, Infrastructure, Passenger Movement, Boundaries & Landmarks, and Characteristics. Selected modes or categories will display a satellite or map view of associated data terminals and a listing of affiliated datasets by title alongside a brief description (if available) and the number of attributes and locations tracked. The dataset page presents a listing of Dataset Attributes, Related Datasets, and Tags, and allows users to view in table format. Users can also select particular attributes to chart in several ways. Users can examine or download the data or save particular datasets under the My Favorites tab. Datasets cover railroad crossings, rail lines, airport schedules, runways, road noise, navigable waterways, dams, and much more. The Map tab on the homepage links to twenty-seven national maps illustrating a range of transportation data, including the Average Number of Ferry Passengers and Vehicles (2014), Enplanements at Top 50 U.S. Airports (2015), and Highway Crash Fatalities (2015). The Applications gallery provides nine examples of mapping visualizations, include the National Aviation Noise Application and the Hurricane Application, in addition to the ability to incorporate select data into personalized maps.—**ARBA Staff Reviewer**

Author/Title Index

Reference is to entry number.

Subject Index

Reference is to entry number.